IMPERIAL UNITS

 KU-534-053

ac	acre
bbl	barrel
cu ft	cubic foot
cu in.	cubic inch
cu yd	cubic yard
cwt	hundred weight
fbm	foot board measure
ft	foot or feet
gal	gallon(s)
in.	inch(es)
lb	pound
lf	linear foot (feet)
mi	mile(s)
mph	miles per hour
psi	pounds per square inch
sq ft	square foot (feet)
sq in.	square inch(es)
sq yd	square yard(s)
mf bm	thousand foot board measure
m gal	thousand gallons
yd	yard(s)

METRIC UNITS

C	Celsius
cm	centimeter
ha	hectare
kg	kilogram(s)
km	kilometer(s)
kN	kilonewton(s)
kPa	kilopascal(s)
L	liter(s)
m	meter(s)
m^2	square meter
m^3	cubic meter
mm	millimeter(s)
t	tonne

SURVEYING
with Construction Applications

Seventh Edition

Barry F. Kavanagh
Seneca College, Emeritus

Boston   Columbus   Indianapolis   New York   San Francisco
Upper Saddle River   Amsterdam   Cape Town   Dubai   London   Madrid
Milan   Munich   Paris   Montreal   Toronto   Delhi   Mexico City   Sao Paulo
Sydney   Hong Kong   Seoul   Singapore   Taipei   Tokyo

Vice President and Executive Editor:
Vernon R. Anthony
Acquisitions Editor: David Ploskonka
Editorial Assistant: Nancy Kesterson
Director of Marketing: David Gesell
Executive Marketing Manager:
Derril Trakalo

Senior Marketing Coordinator:
Alicia Wozniak
Production Manager: Fran Russello
Senior Art Director: Jayne Conte
AV Project Manager: Janet Portisch
Printer/Binder: Courier Companies, Inc.
Text Font: 10/12 Times

Credits and acknowledgments borrowed from other sources and reproduced, with permission, in this textbook appear on the appropriate page within text.

If you purchased this book within the United States or Canada you should be aware that it has been wrongfully imported without the approval of the Publisher or the Author.

Copyright © 2010, 2007, 2004, 2001, 1997 Pearson Education, Inc., publishing as Prentice Hall, One Lake Street, Upper Saddle River, New Jersey, 07458. All rights reserved. Manufactured in the United States of America. This publication is protected by Copyright, and permission should be obtained from the publisher prior to any prohibited reproduction, storage in a retrieval system, or transmission in any form or by any means, electronic, mechanical, photocopying, recording, or likewise. To obtain permission(s) to use material from this work, please submit a written request to Pearson Education, Inc., Permissions Department, One Lake Street, Upper Saddle River, New Jersey, 07458.

Many of the designations by manufacturers and seller to distinguish their products are claimed as trademarks. Where those designations appear in this book, and the publisher was aware of a trademark claim, the designations have been printed in initial caps or all caps.

Prentice Hall
is an imprint of

10 9 8 7 6 5 4 3 2 1
ISBN 13: 978-0-13-136937-5
ISBN 10:   0-13-136937-7

Preface

This edition has some changes in the order of chapters. Reflecting the additional complexities in electronic distance measurement, the order of presentation of surveying topics has been revised as follows: The leveling chapter has been moved forward to Chapter 2, allowing instructors to introduce the simpler instruments before the more complex total stations; distance measurement has been moved to Chapter 3; total stations have been combined with electronic theodolites in Chapter 4 (optical theodolites have been moved to Appendix G); and satellite positioning has been revised and moved up in the presentation order to Chapter 7.

Revision to the text and the addition of new material have been focused on the chapters describing topics where the technology and applications are still evolving. Revised text and new material are included in the following: Chapter 5, Total Stations—where the introduction has been re-written and the topics on combined total station/GPS instruments and ground-based lidar imaging have been revised and/or added; and Chapter 7—where the introductory topics were revised and the topics on wide area augmentation, CORS, OPUS, and real-time GPS networks were expanded.

End-of-chapter problems have been expanded and refreshed. The websites given in selected chapters and in Appendix B have been updated and verified.

The text continues to be divided into three parts:

- Part I "Surveying Principles," includes chapters on the basics of surveying, leveling, distance measurement (taping and electronic distance measurement), theodolites, total stations, traverse surveys and computations, satellite positioning, geomatics, and control surveys.
- Part II "Construction Applications," includes chapters on machine guidance and control, highway curves, highway construction, municipal street construction, pipeline and tunnel construction, culvert and bridge construction, building construction, and quantity and final surveys.
- Part III "Appendix," includes the following information: trigonometry and geometry review, surveying and mapping Internet websites, glossary, typical field projects, answers to selected text problems, steel tape corrections, early surveying, and a color photo gallery.

As with the earlier editions of this text, material here is presented in a clear and logical fashion, a style that reflects the many years of surveying field experience and classroom instruction accumulated by the author.

The following online supplements are available for instructors:

- Online Instructor's Manual, including problem solutions, typical tests, and typical class handouts.
- Online PowerPoint Slides, illustrating all text topics.

To access and download the above supplements, instructors need to request an instructor access code. Go to *http://www.pearsonhighered.com/ric*, where you can request an instructor access code. Within 48 hours after registering, you will receive a confirming e-mail. Once you have received your code, go to the site and log on for full instructions on downloading the materials you wish to use.

Comments and suggestions about this text are welcomed by the author at *barry.kavanagh@cogeco.ca*.

Barry F. Kavanagh

Acknowledgments

The author is grateful for the comments and suggestions received from those who adopted previous editions of this text and from the faculty of the Civil and Resources Engineering Technology School at Seneca College.

In addition, particular thanks are due to Frank Corso, Illinois Central College; Deogratias Eustace, University of Dayton; Dennis Hughes, CS Mott Community College; Hesham Mahgoub, South Dakota State University; George Murgel, Boise State University; Dan Perry, Utah Valley University; Walid H. Shayya, Morrisville State College; Dianne Slattery, Southern Illinois University, Edwardsville; Brian L. Smith, University of Virginia; Eileen Young, Bristol Community College; Daniel Reed, Point Park University for their assistance with the seventh edition text reviews.

The following surveying, engineering, and equipment manufacturers have provided generous assistance:

American Congress on Surveying and Mapping, Bethesda, Maryland

American Society for Photogrammetry and Remote Sensing, Bethesda, Maryland

Applanix, Richmond Hill, Ontario

Bird and Hale, Ltd., Toronto, Ontario

Canadian Institute of Geomatics, Ottawa, Ontario

CST/Berger, Watseka, Illinois

Environmental Systems Research Institute, Inc. (ESRI), Redlands, California

Geomagnetic Laboratory, Geological Survey of Canada, Ottawa

International Systemap Corp., Vancouver, British Columbia

Laser Atlanta, Norcross, Georgia

Leica Geosystems Inc., Norcross, Georgia

MicroSurvey International, Kelowna, British Columbia

National Geodetic Survey (NGS), Silver Spring, Maryland

OPTECH, Vaughn, Ontario

Pacific Crest Corporation, Santa Clara, California

Position Inc., Calgary, Alberta

Sokkia Corporation, Olathe, Kansas

Texas DOT, Austin, Texas

Topcon Positioning Systems, Pleasanton, California

Trimble, Sunnyvale, California

Tripod Data Systems, Corvallis, Oregon

U.S. Geological Survey, Denver, Colorado—John M. Quinn

U.S. Geological Survey, Sioux Falls, South Dakota—Ron Beck

Contents

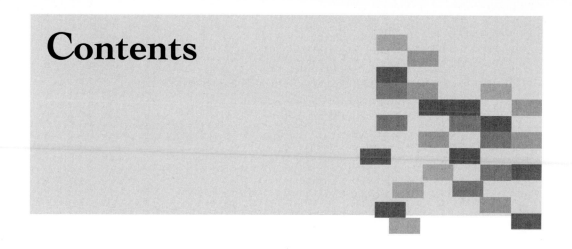

FIELD NOTE INDEX

Contents

PART I
Surveying Principles

Part I, which includes Chapters 1–9, introduces you to traditional and state-of-the-art techniques in data collection, layout, and presentation of field data. Chapter 1 covers surveying fundamentals. Elevation determination is covered in the chapters on leveling (Chapter 2), total stations (Chapter 5), and satellite positioning (Chapter 7). Distance measurement, using both conventional taping techniques and electronic distance measurement (EDM), is covered in Chapter 3. Data presentation is covered in Chapters 5 and 8. Angle measurements and geometric analysis of field measurements are covered in Chapters 4–6. Horizontal positioning is covered in Chapter 7, and control for both data-gathering and layout surveys is covered in Chapter 9.

Although most distance measurements are now done with EDM techniques, many applications still exist for steel taping on the short-distance measurements often found in construction layouts. Taping correction techniques can be found in Chapter 3 and Appendix F.

Chapter 1

Surveying Fundamentals

1.1 Surveying Defined

Surveying is the art and science of taking field measurements on or near the surface of the Earth. Survey field measurements include horizontal and slope distances, vertical distances, and horizontal and vertical angles. In addition to measuring distances and angles, surveyors can measure position as given by the northing, easting, and elevation of a survey station by using satellite-positioning and remote-sensing techniques. In addition to taking measurements in the field, the surveyor can derive related distances and directions through geometric and trigonometric analysis.

Once a survey station has been located by angle and distance, or by positioning techniques, the surveyor then attaches to that survey station (in handwritten or electronic field notes) a suitable identifier or attribute that describes the nature of the survey station. In Chapter 8, you will see that attribute data for a survey station can be expanded from a simple descriptive label to include a wide variety of related information that can be tagged specifically to that survey station.

Since the 1980s, the term **geomatics** has come into popular usage to describe the computerization and digitization of data collection, data processing, data analysis, and data output. Geomatics includes traditional surveying as its cornerstone, but it also reflects the now-broadened scope of measurement science and information technology. Figure 8.1 shows a computerized surveying data model. This illustration gives you a sense of the diversity of the integrated scientific activities now covered by the term *geomatics*.

The vast majority of engineering and construction projects are so limited in geographic size that the surface of the Earth is considered to be a plane for all X (easterly) and Y (northerly) dimensions. Z dimensions (height) are referred to a datum, usually mean sea level. Surveys that ignore the curvature of the Earth for horizontal dimensions are called **plane surveys**. Surveys that cover a large geographic area—for example, state or provincial boundary surveys—must have corrections made to the field measurements so that these measurements reflect the curved (ellipsoidal) shape of the Earth. These surveys are called **geodetic surveys**. The Z dimensions (**orthometric heights**) in geodetic surveys are also referenced to a datum—usually mean sea level.

In the past, geodetic surveys were very precise surveys of great magnitude, for example, national boundaries and control networks. Modern surveys (data gathering, control, and layout) utilizing satellite-positioning systems are geodetic surveys based on the ellipsoidal shape of the Earth and referenced to the geodetic reference system (GRS80) ellipsoid. Such survey measurements must be translated mathematically from ellipsoidal coordinates and ellipsoidal heights to plane grid coordinates and to orthometric heights (referenced to mean sea level) before being used in leveling and other local surveying projects.

Engineering or construction surveys that span long distances (e.g., highways, railroads) are treated as plane surveys, with corrections for the Earth's curvature being applied at regular intervals (e.g., at 1-mile intervals or at township boundaries). **Engineering surveying** is defined as those activities involved in the planning and execution of surveys for the location, design, construction, maintenance, and operation of civil and other engineered projects.* Such activities include the following:

1. Preparation of surveying and related mapping specifications.
2. Execution of photogrammetric and field surveys for the collection of required data, including topographic and hydrographic data.
3. Calculation, reduction, and plotting (manual and computer-aided) of survey data for use in engineering design.
4. Design and provision of horizontal and vertical control survey networks.
5. Provision of line and grade and other layout work for construction and mining activities.
6. Execution and certification of quality control measurements during construction.
7. Monitoring of ground and structural stability, including alignment observations, settlement levels, and related reports and certifications.
8. Measurement of material and other quantities for inventory, economic assessment, and cost accounting purposes.
9. Execution of as-built surveys and preparation of related maps, plans, and profiles upon completion of the project.
10. Analysis of errors and tolerances associated with the measurement, field layout, and mapping or other plots of survey measurements required in support of engineered projects.

Engineering surveying does not include surveys for the retracement of existing land ownership boundaries or the creation of new boundaries. These activities are reserved for licensed property surveyors—also known as land surveyors or cadastral surveyors.

---

*Definition adapted from the definition of *engineering surveying* as given by the American Society of Civil Engineers (ASCE) in their *Journal of Surveying Engineering* in 1987.

1.2   Surveying: General Background

Surveys are usually performed for one of two reasons. First, surveys are made to collect data, which can then be plotted to scale on a plan or map (these surveys are called **preliminary surveys** or **preengineering surveys**); second, field surveys are made to lay out dimensions taken from a design plan and thus define precisely, in the field, the location of the proposed construction works. The layouts of proposed property lines and corners as required in land division are called **layout surveys**; the layouts of proposed construction features are called **construction surveys**. Preliminary and construction surveys for the same area must have this one characteristic in common: Measurements for both surveys must be referenced to a common base for X, Y, and Z dimensions. The establishment of a base for horizontal and vertical measurements is known as a **control survey**.

1.3   Control Surveys

Control surveys establish reference points and reference lines for preliminary and construction surveys. Vertical reference points, called benchmarks, are established using leveling surveys (Chapter 2) or satellite-positioning surveys (Chapter 7). Horizontal control surveys (Chapter 9) use any of a variety of measuring and positioning techniques capable of providing appropriately precise results; such surveys can be tied into (1) state or provincial coordinate grids, (2) property lines, (3) roadway centerlines, and (4) arbitrarily placed baselines or grids. When using positioning satellites to establish or re-establish ground positions, the always-available satellite systems themselves can be considered as a control net—thus greatly reducing the need for numerous on-the-ground reference stations. At present, the only fully deployed satellite-positioning system is the United States' Global Positioning System (GPS); the Russian system, called GLONASS, is about halfway to full deployment; and others plan to have positioning systems deployed within the next five or ten years—for example, Europe's Galileo System, China's Compass System, and an Indian positioning system.

1.4   Preliminary Surveys

Preliminary surveys (also known as preengineering surveys, location surveys, or data-gathering surveys) are used to collect measurements that locate the position of natural features, such as trees, rivers, hills, valleys, and the like, and the position of built features, such as roads, structures, pipelines, and so forth. Measured tie-ins can be accomplished by any of the following techniques.

1.4.1   Rectangular Tie-Ins

The rectangular tie-in (also known as the right-angle offset tie) was once one of the most widely used field location techniques for preelectronic surveys. This technique, when used to locate point P in Figure 1.1(a) to baseline AB, requires distance AC (or BC), where C is on AB at 90° to point P, and it also requires measurement CP.

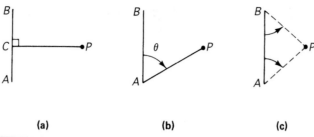

(a)　　　　　　**(b)**　　　　　　**(c)**

FIGURE 1.1　Location ties.

1.4.2　Polar Tie-Ins

Polar tie-ins (also known as the angle/distance technique) are now the most (refer also to Section 1.4.4) widely used location technique (Chapters 4 and 5). Here, point P is located from point A on baseline AB by measuring angle θ and distance AP [Figure 1.1(b)].

1.4.3　Intersection Tie-Ins

This technique is useful in specialized location surveys. Point P in Figure 1.1(c) is located to baseline AB either by measuring angles from A and B to P or by swinging out arc lengths AP and BP until they intersect. The angle intersection technique is useful for near-shore marine survey locations using theodolites or total stations set up on shore control points. The distance arc intersection technique is an effective method for replacing "lost" survey points from preestablished reference ties.

1.4.4　Positioning Tie-Ins

The second most widely used technique for locating topographic features utilizes direct positioning techniques common to ground-scanning techniques (Chapter 5), satellite-positioning techniques (Chapter 7), and remote-sensing techniques (Chapter 8).

1.5　Surveying Instruments

The instruments most commonly used in field surveying are (1) level and rod, (2) steel tapes, (3) theodolite, (4) total station, and (5) satellite-positioning receiver. The level and rod are used to determine differences in elevation and elevations in a wide variety of surveying, mapping, and engineering applications. Levels and rods are discussed in Chapter 2. Steel tapes are relatively precise measuring instruments and are used mostly for short measurements in both preliminary and layout surveys. Steel tapes and their use are discussed in detail in Chapter 3.

Theodolites (also called transits—short for transiting theodolites) are instruments designed for use in measuring horizontal and vertical angles and for establishing linear and curved alignments in the field. During the last 60 years, the theodolite has evolved through four distinct phases:

1. An open-faced, vernier-equipped (for angle determination) theodolite was commonly called a transit. The metallic horizontal and vertical circles were divided into half-degree (30′) or third-degree (20′) of arc. The accompanying 30′ or 20′ vernier scales allowed the surveyor to read the angle to the closest 1′ or 30″ of arc. A plumb bob was used to center the transit over the station mark. See Figures G.8 and G.9. Vernier transits are discussed in detail in Section G.3.

2. In the 1950s, the vernier transit gave way to the optical theodolite. This instrument came equipped with optical glass scales, permitting direct digital readouts or micrometer-assisted readouts. An optical plummet was used to center the instrument over the station mark. See Figures 4.4–4.7.

3. Electronic theodolites first appeared in the 1960s. These instruments used photoelectric sensors capable of sensing vertical and horizontal angles and displaying horizontal and vertical angles in degrees, minutes, and seconds. Optical plummets (and later, laser plummets) are used to center the instrument over the station mark (Figure 1.7). Optical and electronic theodolites are discussed in detail in Chapter 4.

4. The total station appeared in the 1980s. This instrument combines electronic distance measurement (EDM), which was developed in the 1950s, with an electronic theodolite. In addition to electronic distance- and angle-measuring capabilities, this instrument is equipped with a central processor, which enables the computation of horizontal and vertical positions. The central processor also monitors instrument status and helps the surveyor perform a wide variety of surveying applications. All data can be captured into electronic field books or into on-board storage as the data are received. See Figure 1.6. Total stations are described in detail in Chapters 4 and 5.

Satellite-positioning system receivers (Figures 7.2–7.6) capture signals transmitted by four or more positioning satellites to determine position coordinates (e.g., northing, easting, and elevation) of a survey station. Satellite positioning is discussed in Chapter 7.

Positions of ground points and surfaces can also be collected using various remote-sensing techniques (e.g., panchromatic, multispectral, lidar, and radar) utilizing ground stations as well as satellite and airborne platforms (Chapter 8).

1.6   Construction Surveys

Construction surveys provide the horizontal location and the height above sea level (also known as the provision of **line and grade**) for all component of a wide variety of construction projects—for example, highways, streets, pipelines, bridges, buildings, and site grading. Construction layout marks the horizontal location (line) as well as the vertical location or elevation (grade) for the proposed work. The builder can measure from the surveyor's markers to the exact location of each component of the facility to be constructed. Layout markers can be wood stakes, steel bars, nails with washers, spikes, chiseled marks in concrete, and so forth. Modern layout techniques also permit the contractor to position construction equipment for line and grade using machine guidance techniques involving lasers, total stations, and satellite-positioning receivers (Chapter 10, Sections 10.3–10.6). When commencing a construction survey, it is important that the surveyor use the same control survey points as those used for the preliminary survey on which the construction design was based.

1.7 Distance Measurement

Distances between two points can be **horizontal**, **slope**, or **vertical** and are recorded in feet or in meters (Figure 1.2).

Vertical distances can be measured with a tape, as in construction work. However, they are more usually measured with a surveyor's level and rod (Figures 1.3 and 1.4) or with a total station (Figure 1.6).

Horizontal and slope distances can be measured with a fiberglass or steel tape (Figure 1.5) or with an electronic distance-measuring device (Figure 1.6). When surveying, the horizontal distance is always required for plan-plotting purposes. A distance

FIGURE 1.2 Distance measurement.

Example:
Rod Reading (R.R.) @ C = 7.21 ft
Rod Reading (R.R.) @ D = 2.63 ft
Difference in Elev.   = 4.58 ft

FIGURE 1.3 Leveling technique.

Level Rod (Foot)

FIGURE 1.4   Level and rod. (Courtesy of SOKKIA Corp.)

FIGURE 1.5   Preparing to measure to a stake tack, using a plumb bob and steel tape.

Chap. 1   Surveying Fundamentals

Total Station

Data Collector

Radio

FIGURE 1.6 Sokkia total station.

measured with a steel tape on slope can be trigonometrically converted to its horizontal equivalent by using either the slope angle or the difference in elevation (vertical distance) between the two points.

1.8 Angle Measurement

Horizontal and vertical angles can be measured with a theodolite or total station. Theodolites are manufactured to read angles to the closest $1'$, $20''$, $10''$, $6''$, or $1''$. Figure 1.7 shows a $20''$ electronic theodolite. Slope angles can also be measured with a clinometer (Chapter 3); the angle measurement precision of that instrument is typically $10'$.

1.9 Position Measurement

The position of a natural or built entity can be determined by using a satellite-positioning system receiver, which is simultaneously tracking four or more positioning satellites. The position can be expressed in geographic or grid coordinates, along with ellipsoidal or orthometric elevations (in feet or meters).

Position can also be recorded using airborne and satellite imagery. Such imagery includes aerial photography, lidar imaging, radar imaging, and spectral scanning (Chapter 8).

Carrying Handle

Vertical Clamp

Vertical Tangent Screw

Optical Sight

Internal Switch Port

Battery Case

Optical Plummet

Plate Level

Power Switch

Horizontal Tangent Screw

Leveling Screw

Base Plate

(a)

VA (Vertical Angle) or % (Percentage of Grade) Display Symbol

G (GON) Display Symbol (Available)

HA (Clockwise Horizontal Angle) or HL (Counter-clockwise Horizontal Angle) Display Symbol

Battery Charge Level Indicator

HOLD (Horizontal Angle Hold) Display (Available)

Vertical Angle/Grade Display Key

Horizontal Angle Zero Reset Key

Horizontal Angle Selection Key
R: Clockwise
L: Counterclockwise

Horizontal Angle HOLD Key

(b)

FIGURE 1.7 Nikon NE-20S electronic digital theodolite. (a) Theodolite; (b) operation keys and display. (Courtesy of Nikon Instruments, Inc.)

1.10   Units of Measurement

Although the foot system of measurement has been in use in the United States from colonial days until the present, the metric system is in use in most other countries. In the United States, the Metric Conversion Act of 1975 made conversion to the metric system largely voluntary, but subsequent amendments and government actions have now made use of the metric system mandatory for all federal agencies as of September 1992. By January 1994, the metric system was required in the design of many federal facilities. Many states' departments of transportation have also commenced the switch to the metric system for field work and highway design. Although the enthusiasm for metric use in the United States by many surveyors seems to have waned in recent years, both metric units and English units are used in this text because both units are now in wide use.

The complete changeover to the metric system will take many years, perhaps several generations. The impact of all this on the American surveyor is that, from now on, most surveyors will have to be proficient in both the foot and the metric systems. Additional equipment costs in this dual system are limited mostly to measuring tapes and leveling rods.

System International (SI) units are a modernization (1960) of the long-used metric units. This modernization included a redefinition of the meter (international spelling: metre) and the addition of some new units (e.g., Newton; see Table 3.1).

Table 1.1 describes and contrasts metric and foot units. Degrees, minutes, and seconds are used almost exclusively in both metric and foot systems; however, in some European countries, the circle has also been graduated into 400 gon (also called grad). In that system, angles are expressed to four decimals (e.g., a right angle = 100.0000 gon).

1.11   Stationing

While surveying, measurements are often taken along a baseline and at right angles to that baseline. Distances along a baseline are referred to as **stations** or **chainages**, and distances at right angles to the baseline (offset distances) are simple dimensions. The beginning of the survey baseline—the zero end—is denoted as 0 + 00; a point 100 ft (m) from the zero end is denoted as 1 + 00; a point 156.73 ft (m) from the zero end is 1 + 56.73; and so on.

In the preceding discussion, the full stations are at 100-ft (m) intervals, and the half stations are at even 50-ft (m) intervals. Twenty-meter intervals are often used as the key partial station in the metric system for preliminary and construction surveys. With the ongoing changeover to metric units, most municipalities have kept the 100-unit station (i.e., 1 + 00 = 100 m), whereas highway agencies have adopted the 1,000-unit station (i.e., 1 + 000 = 1,000 m).

Figure 1.8 shows a school building tied in to the centerline (℄) of Regent St. The figure also shows the ℄ (used here as a baseline) distances as stations, and the offset distances as simple dimensions.

Table 1.1 MEASUREMENT DEFINITIONS AND EQUIVALENCIES

Linear Measurement	Foot Units

1 mi = 5,280 ft
     = 1,760 yd
     = 320 rods
     = 80 chains
1 ac = 43,560 sq. ft = 10 square chains
	1 ft = 12 in.
	1 yd = 3 ft
	1 rod = 16½ ft
	1 chain = 66 ft
	1 chain = 100 links

Linear Measurement		Metric (SI) Units
1 km	=	1,000 m
1 m	=	100 cm
1 cm	=	10 mm
1 dm	=	10 cm
1 ha	=	10,000 m^2
1 sq. km	=	1,000,000 m^2 100 ha

Foot to Metric Conversion	
1 ft = 0.3048 m (exactly) 1 km = 0.62137 mi 1 ha = 2.471 ac 1 sq. km = 247.1 ac	1 in. = 25.4 mm (exactly)*

Angular Measurements	
1 revolution = 360° 1 degree = 60′ (minutes) 1 minute = 60″ (seconds)	1 revolution = 400.0000 gon†

*Prior to 1959, the United States used the relationship 1 m = 39.37 in., which resulted in a U.S. survey foot of 0.3048006 m.

†Used in some European countries.

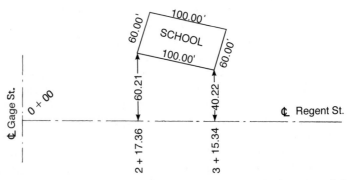

FIGURE 1.8 Baseline stations and offset distances, showing the location of the school on Regent St.

1.12 Types of Construction Projects

The first part of this text covers the surveying techniques common to most surveying endeavors. The second part of the text is devoted to construction surveying applications—an area that accounts for much surveying activity. Listed below are the types of construction projects that depend a great deal on the construction surveyor or engineering surveyor for the successful completion of the project:

1. Streets and highways
2. Drainage ditches
3. Intersections and interchanges
4. Sidewalks
5. High- and low-rise buildings
6. Bridges and culverts
7. Dams and weirs
8. River channelization
9. Sanitary landfills
10. Mining—tunnels, shafts
11. Gravel pits, quarries
12. Storm and sanitary sewers
13. Water and fuel pipelines
14. Piers and docks
15. Canals
16. Railroads
17. Airports
18. Reservoirs
19. Site grading, landscaping
20. Parks, formal walkways
21. Heavy equipment locations (millwright)
22. Electricity transmission lines.

1.13 Random and Systematic Errors

An **error** is the difference between a measured, or observed, value and the "true" value. No measurement can be performed perfectly (except for counting), so every measurement must contain some error. Errors can be minimized to an acceptable level by the use of skilled techniques and appropriately precise equipment. For the purposes of calculating errors, the "true" value of a dimension is determined statistically after repeated measurements have been taken.

Systematic errors are defined as those errors for which the magnitude and the algebraic sign can be determined. The fact that these errors can be determined allows the surveyor to eliminate them from the measurements and thus further improve accuracy. An example of a systematic error is the effect of temperature on a steel tape. If the temperature is quite warm, the steel expands, and thus the tape is longer than normal. For example, at 83°F, a 100-ft steel tape can expand to 100.01 ft, a systematic error of 0.01 ft. Knowing this error, the surveyor can simply subtract 0.01 ft each time the full tape is used at that temperature.

Random errors are associated with the skill and vigilance of the surveyor. Random errors (also known as accidental errors) are introduced into each measurement mainly because no human can perform perfectly. Random errors can be illustrated by the following example. Let's say that point B is to be located a distance of 109.55 ft from point A. If the tape is only 100.00 ft long, an intermediate point must first be set at 100.00 ft, and then 9.55 ft must be measured from the intermediate point. Random errors occur as the surveyor is marking out 100.00 ft. The actual mark may be off a bit; that is, the mark may actually be made at 99.99 or 99.98, and so on. When the final 9.55 ft are measured out, two more opportunities for error exist: The lead surveyor will have the same opportunity for error as existed at the 100.00 mark, and the rear surveyor may introduce a random error by inadvertently holding something other than 0.00 ft (e.g., 0.01) on the intermediate mark.

This example illustrates two important characteristics of random errors. First, the magnitude of the random error is unknown. Second, because the surveyor is estimating too high (or too far right) on one occasion and probably too low (or too far left) on the next occasion, random errors tend to cancel out over the long run.

A word of caution: Large random errors, possibly due to sloppy work, also tend to cancel out. Thus, sloppy work can give the appearance of accurate work—even when highly inaccurate.

1.14 Accuracy and Precision

Accuracy is the relationship between the value of a measurement and the "true" value of the dimension being measured; the greater the accuracy, the smaller the error. **Precision** describes the degree of refinement with which the measurement is made. For example, a distance measured four times with a steel tape by skilled personnel will be more precise than the same distance measured twice by unskilled personnel using a fiberglass tape. Figure 1.9 illustrates the difference between accuracy and precision by showing the results of target shooting using both a high-precision rifle and a low-precision shotgun.

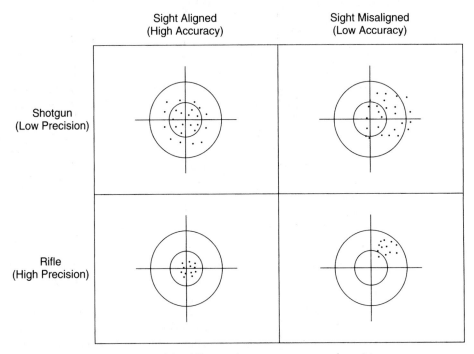

FIGURE 1.9 An illustration of the difference between accuracy and precision.

The **accuracy ratio** of a measurement or a series of measurements is the ratio of the error of closure to the distance measured. The error of closure is the difference between the measured location and its theoretically correct location. Because relevant systematic errors and mistakes can and should be eliminated from all survey measurements, the error of closure will normally be composed of random errors.

To illustrate, a distance is measured and found to be 196.33 ft. The distance was previously known to be 196.28 ft. The error is 0.05 ft in a distance of 196.28 ft:

$$\text{Accuracy ratio} = \frac{0.05}{196.28} = \frac{1}{3,926} \approx \frac{1}{3,900}$$

The accuracy ratio is expressed as a fraction whose numerator is 1 and whose denominator is rounded to the closest 100 units. Many engineering surveys are specified at 1/3,000 and 1/5,000 levels of accuracy; property surveys used to be specified at 1/5,000 and 1/7,500 levels of accuracy. With polar layouts now being used more often in total station surveys, the coordinated control stations needed for this type of layout must be established using techniques giving higher orders of accuracy (e.g., 1/10,000, 1/15,000, etc.). Sometimes the accuracy ratio, or error ratio, is expressed in parts per million (ppm). One ppm is simply the ratio of 1/1,000,000; 50 ppm is 50/1,000,000, or 1/20,000. See Tables 3.1 and 3.2 and Tables 9.2–9.5 for more current survey specifications and standards.

1.15 Mistakes

Mistakes are blunders made by survey personnel. Examples of mistakes are transposing figures (recording a value of 86 as 68), miscounting the number of full tape lengths in a long measurement, and measuring to or from the wrong point. You should be aware that mistakes will occur! Mistakes must be discovered and eliminated, preferably by the people who made them. *All survey measurements are suspect until they have been verified.* Verification may be as simple as repeating the measurement, or verification may result from geometric or trigonometric analysis of related measurements. As a rule, all measurements are immediately checked or repeated. This immediate repetition enables the surveyor to eliminate most mistakes and at the same time to improve the precision of the measurement.

1.16 Field Notes

One of the most important aspects of surveying is the taking of neat, legible, and complete field notes. The notes will be used to plot scale drawings of the area surveyed and also to provide a permanent record of the survey proceedings. Modern surveys, employing electronic *data collectors*, automatically store point-positioning angles, distances, and attributes, which will later be transferred to the computer. Surveyors have discovered that some handwritten field notes are also valuable for these modern surveys. (See also Section 5.5.)

An experienced surveyor's notes should be complete, without redundancies; be arranged to aid comprehension; and be neat and legible to ensure that the correct information is conveyed. Sketches are used to illustrate the survey and thus help remove possible ambiguities.

Handwritten field notes are placed in bound field books or in loose-leaf binders. Loose-leaf notes are preferred for small projects because they can be filed alphabetically by project name or in order by number. Bound books are advantageous on large projects, such as highway construction or other heavy construction operations, where the data can readily fill one or more field books.

1.16.1 Requirements for Bound Books

Bound field books should include the following information:

1. Name, address, and phone number should be in ink on the outside cover.
2. Pages are numbered throughout.
3. Space is reserved at the front of the field book for a title, an index, and a diary.
4. Each project must show the date, title, surveyors' names, and instrument numbers.

1.16.2 Requirements for Loose-Leaf Books

Loose-leaf field books should include the following information:

1. Name, address, and phone number should be in ink on the binder.
2. Each page must be titled and dated, and must be identified by project number, surveyors' names, and instrument numbers.

1.16.3 Requirements for All Field Notes

All field notes, whether bound into books or organized into loose-leaf binders, should follow this checklist:

1. Entries should be in pencil, written with 2H–4H lead (lead softer than 2H will cause unsightly smears on the notes).
2. All entries are neatly printed. Uppercase letters can be used throughout, or they can be reserved for emphasis.
3. All arithmetic computations must be checked and signed.
4. Although sketches are not scale drawings, they are drawn roughly to scale to help order the inclusion of details.
5. Sketched details are arranged on the page such that the north arrow is oriented toward the top of the page.
6. Sketches are not freehand; straightedges and curve templates are used for all line work.
7. Do not crowd information on the page. Crowded information is one of the chief causes of poor field notes.
8. Mistakes in the entry of measured data are to be carefully lined out, not erased.
9. Mistakes in entries other than measured data (e.g., descriptions, sums or products of measured data) may be erased and reentered neatly.
10. If notes are copied, they must be clearly labeled as such so that they are not thought to be field notes.

11. Lettering on sketches is to be read from the bottom of the page or from the right side; any other position is upside down.

12. Note keepers verify all given data by repeating the data aloud as they enter the data in their notes; the surveyor who originally gave the data to the note keeper listens and responds to the verification callout.

13. If the data on an entire page are to be voided, the word VOID, together with a diagonal line, is placed on the page. A reference page number is shown for the new location of the relevant data.

Review Questions

1.1 Describe four different procedures used to locate a physical feature in the field so that it can be plotted later in its correct position on a scaled plan.

1.2 Describe how a very precise measurement can be inaccurate.

1.3 How do plane surveys and geodetic surveys differ?

1.4 How is a total station different from an electronic theodolite?

1.5 How can you ensure that a survey measurement is free of mistakes?

1.6 Why do surveyors usually convert measured slope distances to their horizontal equivalents?

1.7 Describe the term *error*. How does this term differ from *mistake*?

1.8 What is the difference between a layout survey and a preliminary survey?

1.9 If a 100-ft steel tape were broken and then poorly repaired, resulting in a tape that was only 99.00-ft long, that tape would be
(a) inaccurate
(b) imprecise
(c) both inaccurate and imprecise

1.10 If the poorly repaired tape from Question 1.9 were used to measure between two field points, the measurement errors resulting from the poorly repaired tape would be classified as being:
(a) random
(b) systematic

Chapter 2

Leveling

2.1   General Background

Leveling is the procedure used when one is determining differences in elevation between points that are some distance from each other. An **elevation** is a vertical distance above or below a reference datum. In surveying, the reference datum that is universally employed is **mean sea level (MSL)**. In North America, nineteen years of observations at tidal stations in twenty-six locations on the Atlantic, Pacific, and Gulf of Mexico shore-lines were reduced and adjusted to provide the National Geodetic Vertical Datum (NGVD) of 1929. That datum has been further refined to reflect gravimetric and other anomalies in the 1988 general control re-adjustment called the North American Vertical Datum (NAVD88). Because of the inconsistencies found in widespread determinations of MSL, the NAVD88 datum has been tied to one representative tidal gage bench mark known as **Father Point**, which is located on the south shore of the mouth of the St. Lawrence River at Rimouski, Quebec. Although the NAVD does not precisely agree with MSL at some specific points on the Earth's surface, the term *mean sea level* is often used to describe the datum. MSL is assigned a vertical value (elevation) of 0.000 ft or 0.000 m. See Figure 2.1. (Some specifications for vertical control in the United States and Canada are shown in Tables 2.1–2.3.)

   A **vertical line** is a line from the surface of the Earth to the Earth's center. It is also referred to as a plumb line or a line of gravity.

   A **level line** is a line in a level surface. A level surface is a curved surface parallel to the mean surface of the Earth. A level surface is best visualized as being the surface of a large body of water at rest.

   A **horizontal line** is a straight line perpendicular to a vertical line.

FIGURE 2.1 Leveling concepts.

Table 2.1 NATIONAL OCEAN SURVEY, U.S. COAST, AND GEODETIC SURVEYS: CLASSIFICATION, STANDARDS OF ACCURACY, AND GENERAL SPECIFICATIONS FOR VERTICAL CONTROL

Classification	First Order Class I, Class II	Second Order Class I	Second Order Class II	Third Order
Principal uses Minimum standards; higher accuracies may be used for special	Basic framework of the National Network and of metropolitan area control Extensive engineering projects Regional crustal movement investigations Determining geopotential values	Secondary control of the National Network and of metropolitan area control Large engineering projects Local crustal movement and subsidence investigations Support for lower-order control	Control densification, usually adjusted to the National Network Local engineering projects Topographic mapping Studies of rapid subsidence Support for local surveys	Miscellaneous local control; may not be adjusted to the National Network Small engineering projects Small-scale topographic mapping Drainage studies and gradient establishment in mountainous areas
*Maximum closures** Section: forward and backward	3 mm $\sqrt{K}$ (*Class I*) 4 mm $\sqrt{K}$ (*Class II*)	6 mm $\sqrt{K}$	8 mm $\sqrt{K}$	12 mm $\sqrt{K}$
Loop or line	4 mm $\sqrt{K}$ (*Class I*) 5 mm $\sqrt{K}$ (*Class II*)	6 mm $\sqrt{K}$	8 mm $\sqrt{K}$	12 mm $\sqrt{K}$

*Check between forward and backward runnings where K is the distance in kilometers.

2.2 Theory of Differential Leveling

Differential leveling is used to determine differences in elevation between points (that are some distance from each other) by using a surveyors' level and a graduated measuring rod. The surveyors' level consists of a cross hair–equipped telescope and an attached spirit level, both of which are mounted on a sturdy tripod. The surveyor can sight through the leveled telescope to a rod graduated in feet or meters and determine a measurement reading at the point where the cross hair intersects the rod.

Table 2.2 CLASSIFICATION STANDARDS OF ACCURACY AND GENERAL SPECIFICATIONS FOR VERTICAL CONTROL—CANADA

Classification	Special Order	First Order	Second Order (First-Order Procedures Recommended)	Third Order	Fourth Order
Allowable discrepancy between forward and backward levelings	$\pm$ 3 mm $\sqrt{K}$ $\pm$ 0.012 ft $\sqrt{m}$	$\pm$ 4 mm $\sqrt{K}$ $\pm$ 0.017 ft $\sqrt{m}$	$\pm$ 8 mm $\sqrt{K}$ $\pm$ 0.035 ft $\sqrt{m}$	$\pm$ 24 mm $\sqrt{K}$ $\pm$ 0.10 ft $\sqrt{m}$	$\pm$ 120 mm $\sqrt{K}$ $\pm$ 0.5 ft $\sqrt{m}$
Instruments:					
Self-leveling high-speed compensator	Equivalent to 10″/2 mm level vial	Equivalent to 10″/2 mm level vial	Equivalent to 20″/2 mm level vial	Equivalent to sensitivity	Equivalent to sensitivity below
Level vial	10″/2 mm	10″/2 mm	20″/2 mm	40″ to 50″/2 mm	40″ to 50″/2 mm
Telescopic magnification	40×	40×	40×		

Source: Adapted from "Specifications and Recommendations for Control Surveys and Survey Markers" (Surveys and Mapping Branch, Department of Energy, Mines and Resources, Ottawa, Canada 1973).

In Figure 2.2, if the rod reading at A = 6.27 ft and the rod reading at B = 4.69 ft, the difference in elevation between A and B is 6.27 − 4.69 = 1.58 ft. If the elevation of A is 61.27 ft (above MSL), then the elevation of B is 61.27 + 1.58 = 62.85 ft. That is, 61.27 (elev. A) + 6.27 (rod reading at A) − 4.69 (rod reading at B) = 62.85 (elev. B).

In Figure 2.3, you can see a potential problem. Whereas elevations are referenced to level lines (surfaces), the line of sight through the telescope of a surveyors' level is, in fact, almost a horizontal line. All rod readings taken with a surveyors' level will contain an error *c* over a distance *d*. I have greatly exaggerated the curvature of the level lines shown in Figures 2.1–2.3 for illustrative purposes. In fact, the divergence between a level line and a horizontal line is quite small. For example, over a distance of 1,000 ft, the divergence is 0.024 ft, and for a distance of 300 ft, the divergence is only 0.002 ft (0.0008 m in 100 m).

2.3 Curvature and Refraction

The previous section introduced the concept of curvature error—that is, the divergence between a level line and a horizontal line over a specified distance. When considering the divergence between level and horizontal lines, you must also account for the fact that all sight lines are refracted downward by the Earth's atmosphere. Although the magnitude of the refraction error depends on atmospheric conditions, it is generally considered to be about

Table 2.3(a) CALTRANS ORDERS OF SURVEY ACCURACY—CHAPTER 5, SURVEY MANUAL (COURTESY OF CALIFORNIA DEPARTMENT OF TRANSPORTATION—CALTRANS 2006)

Caltrans Order (Note 1)	Standards			Monument Spacing and Survey Methods (Note 2)			Application—Typical Surveys	
	Classical		Positional	Monument Spacing (Minimum)	Typical Survey Method			
	Horizontal (Note 4)	Vertical (Note 4)			Horizontal	Vertical	Horizontal	Vertical
B (Note 3)	1:1,000,000 (Note 10)	Not Applicable	Per NGS Specifications	6 miles	GPS: Static	Not Applicable	High Precision Geodetic Network (HPGN)	Not Applicable
First (Note 3)	1:100,000	$e = 0.025\sqrt{E}$ (Note 5)	Per NGS Specifications	10,000 feet	GPS: Static Fast Static	Electronic/Digital Bar-Code Level	Basic (Corridor) Control – HPGN-D Project Control – Horizontal (preferred, when feasible)	Rarely used, Crustal Motion Surveys, etc.
Second	1:20,000	$e = 0.04\sqrt{E}$ (Note 5)	(Note 8)	1,600 feet	GPS: Static Fast Static TSSS: Net Traverse	Electronic/Digital Bar-Code Level or 3-Wire Leveling TSSS: Trig Leveling	Project Control – Horizontal (see First Order also)	Basic (Corridor) Control HPGN and HPGN-D Project Control
Third	1:10,000	$e = 0.04\sqrt{E}$ (Note 5) $e = 0.06\sqrt{E}$ (Note 5)	(Note 8)	As Required	GPS: Static Fast Static, Kinematic, RTK (Note 13) TSSS: Net Traverse Resection, Double Tie (Note 9)	Electronic/Digital Bar-Code Level Pendulum type Automatic Level	Supplemental Control > Engineering > • Construction • Interchange Major Structure Photo. Control – Horizontal Right of Way Surveys Construction Surveys (Note 6) Topographic Surveys (Note 6) Major Structure Points (Staked)	Project Control – Vertical Supplemental Control Photo. Control – Vertical Construction Surveys (Note 6) Topographic Surveys (Note 6) Major Structure Points (Staked)
G (General)	As required, see appropriate survey procedure section in this manual for accuracy standards/tolerances.			Not Applicable	GPS: Fast Static Kinematic RTK TSSS: Radial	GPS: Fast Static Kinematic, RTK (Note 12) TSSS: Trig Leveling, Single Wire, Direct Elevation Rod	Topographic Surveys (Data Points), Supplement Design Data Surveys, Construction Surveys (Staked Points), Environmental Surveys, GIS Data Surveys, Right of Way Flagging	

Notes

1. The standards, specifications, and procedures included in this Manual are based on Federal Geodetic Control Subcommittee (FGCS) standards and specifications. Except where otherwise noted, the FGCS requirements have been modified to meet Caltrans needs.
2. Refer to other Manual sections for detailed procedural specifications for specific survey methods and types of surveys.
3. "B" Order and First Order surveys are performed to FGCS standards and specifications or other requirements approved by National Geodetic Survey.
4. Distance accuracy standard.
5. Closure between established control; e = maximum misclosure in feet, E = distance in miles.
6. Survey setup points used for radial stake out.
7. For example a static GPS may be used to establish NAV88 at the project site from a distant NAVD National Spatial Reference System Control.
8. As required by the local survey needs.
9. Instead of including a point as a network point, certain survey points may be positioned by observations from two or more control points (i.e. double tied). If survey points are not included in a network, double ties must be performed to ensure that blunders are eliminated and the positions established are within stated accuracy standard. Double tie procedures should be only used when appropriate; possible examples are photo control points, land net and monumentation points, and major structure stake points.
10. The distance accuracy standard for Basic (Corridor) Control – HPGN-D surveys is 1:500,000.
11. Not to include vertical project control or vertical for major structure points.
12. Not to include pavement elevations.
13. Not to include major structures.

Table 2.3(b) CALTRANS ORDERS OF SURVEY ACCURACY—CHAPTER 5, SURVEY MANUAL (COURTESY OF CALIFORNIA DEPARTMENT OF TRANSPORTATION—CALTRANS 2006)

Caltrans Order (Note 1)	Standards				Survey Methods (Note 2) Typical Survey Method		Application - Typical Surveys	
	Horizontal	Monument Spacing (Minimum)	Vertical (Note 4)	Positional	Horizontal	Vertical	Horizontal	Vertical
B (Note 3)	0.03 feet 0.06 feet 0.15 feet	8.76 miles 17.5 miles 43.8 miles	Not Applicable	Per NGS Specifications	GPS: Static	Not Applicable	High Precision Geodetic Network (HPGN)	Not Applicable
First (Note 3)	0.03 feet 0.06 feet 0.15 feet	4626 feet 1.75 miles 4.38 miles	e = 0.025$\sqrt{E}$ (Note 5)	Per NGS Specifications	GPS: Static, Fast Static	Electronic/Digital Bar-Code Level	Basic (Corridor) Control – HPGN-D Project Control – Horizontal (preferred, when feasible)	Rarely used. Crustal Motion Surveys, etc.
Second	0.03 feet 0.06 feet 0.15 feet	919 feet 1837 feet 4593 feet	e = 0.04$\sqrt{E}$ (Note 5)	(Note 6)	GPS: Static, Fast Static, TSSS: Net Traverse	Electronic/Digital Bar-Code Level or 3-Wire Leveling TSSS: Trig Leveling	Project Control – Horizontal (see First Order also)	Basic (Corridor) Control HPGN and HPGN-D Project Control
Third	0.03 feet 0.06 feet 0.15 feet	459 feet 918 feet 2297 feet	e = 0.04$\sqrt{E}$ (Note 5) e = 0.06$\sqrt{E}$ (Note 5)	(Note 6)	GPS: Static, Fast Static, Kinematic, RTK TSSS: Net Traverse, Resection, Double Tie (Note 7)	Electronic/Digital Bar-Code Level Pendulum type Automatic Level	Supplemental Control > Engineering > • Construction • Interchange Major Structure Photo. Control – Horizontal Right of Way Surveys Construction Surveys (Note 5) Topographic Surveys (Note 5) Major Structure Points (Staked)	Project Control – Vertical Supplemental Control Photo Control – Vertical Construction Surveys (Note 5) Topographic Surveys (Note 5) Major Structure Points (Staked)
G (General)	As required, see appropriate survey procedure section in this manual for accuracy standards/tolerances			Not Applicable	GPS: Fast Static, Kinematic, RTK TSSS: Radial	GPS: Fast Static Kinematic, RTK TSSS: Trig Leveling, Single Wire Direct Elevation Rod	Topographic Surveys (Data Points). Supplement Design Data Surveys, Construction Surveys (Staked Points), Environmental Surveys, GIS Data Surveys, Right of Way Flagging	

Notes

1. The standards, specifications, and procedures included in this Manual are based on FGCS standards and specifications. Except where otherwise noted, the FGCS requirements have been modified to meet Caltrans needs.
2. Refer to other Manual sections for detailed procedural specifications for specific survey methods and types of surveys.
3. "B" Order and First Order surveys are performed to FGCS standards and specifications or other requirements approved by National Geodetic Survey.
4. Closure between established control; e = maximum misclosure in feet, E = distance in miles.
5. Survey setup points used for radial stake out.
6. As required by the local survey needs.
7. Instead of including a point as a network point, certain survey points may be positioned by observations from two or more specifications control points (i.e., double tied). If survey points are not included in a network, double ties must be performed to ensure that blunders are eliminated and the positions established are within stated accuracy standard. Double tie procedures should be only used when appropriate; possible examples are photo control points, land net and monumentation points, and major structure stake points.
8. Not to include vertical project control or vertical for major structure points.
9. Not to include pavement elevations.

$a' - b'$ = Difference in Elevation between A and B

FIGURE 2.2   Leveling process.

c is the amount by which a level line and a horizontal line diverge over distance *d*

FIGURE 2.3   Relationship between a horizontal line and a level line.

one-seventh of the curvature error. You can see in Figure 2.4 that the refraction error of AB compensates for part of the curvature error of AE, resulting in a net error due to curvature and refraction ($c + r$) of BE. From Figure 2.4, the curvature error can be computed as follows:

$$(R + c)^2 = R^2 + KA^2$$
$$R^2 + 2Rc + c^2 = R^2 + KA^2$$

Line of Sight

Horizontal   K   A   r

Level

d

B

E

c

c + r

Vertical

R

Vertical

R

R = Mean Radius of Earth = 3,959 mi or 6,370 km

0

FIGURE 2.4   Effects of curvature and refraction.

$$c(2R + c) = KA^2$$

$$c = \frac{KA^2}{2R + c^*} \approx \frac{KA^2}{2R} \qquad (2.1)$$

Consider $R = 6370$ km:

$$c = \frac{KA^2}{2 \times 6,370} = 0.0000785 \ KA^2 \ \text{km} = 0.0785 \ KA^2 \ \text{m}$$

Refraction (r) is affected by atmospheric pressure, temperature, and geographic location but, as noted earlier, it is usually considered to be about one-seventh of the curvature error (c). If $r = 0.14c$, then

$$c + r = 0.0675 \ K^2$$

where $K = KA$ (Figure 2.4) and is the length of sight in kilometers. The combined effects of curvature and refraction ($c + r$) can be determined from the following formulas:

$$(c + r)_\text{m} = 0.0675 K^2 \quad (c + r)_\text{m} \text{ in meters}, \quad K \text{ in kilometers} \qquad (2.2)$$

$$(c + r)_\text{ft} = 0.0574 K^2 \quad (c + r)_\text{ft} \text{ in feet}, \quad K \text{ in miles} \qquad (2.3)$$

$$(c + r)_\text{ft} = 0.0206 M^2 \quad (c + r)_\text{ft} \text{ in feet}, \quad M \text{ in thousands of feet} \qquad (2.4)$$

■ EXAMPLE 2.1

Calculate the error due to curvature and refraction for the following distances:

(a) 2,500 ft

(b) 400 ft

---

*In the term $(2R + c)$, c is so small when compared to R that it can be safely ignored.

Table 2.4 SELECTED VALUES FOR ($c + r$) AND DISTANCE

Distance (m)	30	60	100	120	150	300	1 km
$(c + r)_m$	0.0001	0.0002	0.0007	0.001	0.002	0.006	0.068
Distance (ft)	100	200	300	400	500	1,000	1 mi
$(c + r)_{ft}$	0.000	0.001	0.002	0.003	0.005	0.021	0.574

(c) 2.7 miles

(d) 1.8 km

Solution

(a) $(c + r) = 0.0206 \times 2.5^2 = 0.13$ ft

(b) $(c + r) = 0.0206 \times 0.4^2 = 0.003$ ft

(c) $(c + r) = 0.574 \times 2.7^2 = 4.18$ ft

(d) $(c + r) = 0.0675 \times 1.8^2 = 0.219$ m

You can see from the values in Table 2.4 that ($c + r$) errors are relatively insignificant for differential leveling. Even for precise leveling, where distances of rod readings are seldom in excess of 200 ft (60 m), it would seem that this error is of only marginal importance. We will see in Section 2.11 that the field technique of balancing the distances of rod readings (from the instrument) effectively cancels out this type of error.

2.4 Types of Surveying Levels

2.4.1 Automatic Level

The automatic level (Figures 1.4 and 2.5) employs a gravity-referenced prism or mirror compensator to orient the line of sight (line of collimation) automatically. The instrument is leveled quickly when a circular spirit level is used; when the bubble has been centered (or nearly so), the compensator takes over and maintains a horizontal line of sight, even if the telescope is slightly tilted. Automatic levels are extremely popular in present-day surveying operations and are available from most survey instrument manufacturers. They are quick to set up, easy to use, and can be obtained for use at almost any required precision.

A word of caution: All automatic levels employ a compensator referenced by gravity. This operation normally entails freely moving prisms or mirrors, some of which are hung by fine wires. If a wire or fulcrum breaks, the compensator will become inoperative, and all subsequent rod readings will be incorrect.

The operating status of the compensator can be verified by tapping the end of the telescope or by slightly turning one of the leveling screws (one manufacturer provides a push button), causing the telescopic line of sight to veer from horizontal. If the compensator is operative, the cross hair will appear to deflect momentarily before returning to its original rod reading. Constant checking of the compensator will avoid costly mistakes caused by broken components.

1. The magnet produces magnetic field NS

2. When a conductor, placed in the magnetic field moves...

3. ...The motion generates electromagnetic induction to produce eddy current in the conductor

4. The eddy current creates a force against the motion of the conductor

Pendulum

Magnet

Direction of Motion

Conductor

(b)

Sighting Collimator

Magnetic Dampening System

Objective Lens

Line of Sight

Rugged Compensator Suspension

Endless Tangent Drive

Compensator Optics

(a)

Leveling Base

Adjustable Lateral Friction Clutch

FIGURE 2.5 (a) Schematic of an engineer's automatic level. (b) Magnetic dampening system. (Courtesy of SOKKIA Corp.)

Most levels (most surveying instruments) now come equipped with a three-screw leveling base. Whereas the support for a four-screw leveling base (see Appendix G) is the center bearing, the three-screw instruments are supported entirely by the foot screws themselves. Thus, the adjustment of the foot screws of a three-screw instrument effectively raises or lowers the height of the instrument line of sight. Adjustment of the foot screws of a four-screw instrument does not affect the height of the instrument line of sight because the center bearing supports the instrument. The surveyor should thus be aware that adjustments made to a three-screw level in the midst of a setup operation will effectively change the elevation of the line of sight and could cause significant errors on very precise surveys (e.g., benchmark leveling or industrial surveying).

The bubble in the circular spirit level is centered by adjusting one or more of the three independent screws. Figure 2.6 shows the positions for a telescope equipped with a tube level when using three leveling foot screws. If you keep this configuration in mind when leveling the circular spirit level, the movement of the bubble can be predicted easily.

Levels used to establish or densify vertical control are designed and manufactured to give precise results. The magnifying power, setting accuracy of the tubular level or compensator, quality of optics, and so on, are all improved to provide precise rod readings. The least count on leveling rods is 0.01 ft or 0.001 m. Precise levels are usually equipped with optical micrometers so that readings can be determined one or two places beyond the rod's least count.

FIGURE 2.6   Telescope positions when leveling a three-screw instrument.

Many automatic levels utilize a concave base so that, when the level is attached to its domed-head tripod top, it can be roughly leveled by sliding the instrument over the tripod top. This rough leveling can be accomplished in a few seconds. If the bull's-eye bubble is nearly centered by this maneuver and the compensator is activated, the leveling screws may not be needed at all to level the instrument.

2.4.2 Digital Level

Figure 2.7 shows a digital level and bar-code rod. This level features digital electronic image-processor that uses a charge-coupled device (CCD) for determining heights and distances with the automatic recording of data for later transfer to a computer. The digital level is an automatic level (pendulum compensator) capable of normal optical leveling with a rod graduated in feet or meters. When used in electronic mode and with the rod face graduated in bar code, this level can, with the press of a button, capture and process the image of the bar-code rod for distances in the range of about 1.8 m to about 100 m. This simple one-button operation initiates storage of the rod reading and distance measurement and the computation of the point elevation. The processed image of the rod reading is compared, using the instrument's central processing unit (CPU), with the image of the

FIGURE 2.7   DNA03 digital level and bar-code rod. (Courtesy of Leica Geosystems)

whole rod, which is stored permanently in the level's memory module, thus determining height and distance values. Data can be stored in internal on-board memory or on easily transferable PC cards and then transferred to a computer via an RS232 connection or by transferring the PC card from the digital level to the computer. Most levels can operate effectively with only 30 cm of the rod visible. Work can proceed in the dark by illuminating the rod face with a small flashlight. The rod shown in Figure 2.7 is 4.05-m long (others are 5-m long); it is graduated in bar code on one side and in either feet or meters on the other side.

After the instrument has been leveled, the image of the bar code must be focused properly by the operator. Next, the operator presses the measure button to begin the image processing, which takes about 3 s. Although the heights and distances are automatically determined and recorded (if desired), the horizontal angles are read and recorded manually.

Preprogrammed functions include level loop survey, two-peg test, self-test, set time, and set units. Coding can be the same as that used with total stations (see Chapter 5), which means that the processed leveling data can be transferred directly to the computer database. The bar code can be read in the range of 1.8–100 m away from the instrument; the rod can be read optically as close as 0.5 m. If the rod is not plumb or is held upside down, an error message flashes on the screen. Other error messages include "Instrument not level," "Low battery," and "Memory almost full." Rechargeable batteries are said to last for more than 2,000 measurements. Distance accuracy is in the range of 1/1,000, whereas leveling accuracy (for the more precise digital levels) is stated as having a standard deviation for a 1-km double run of 0.3–1.0 mm for electronic measurement and 2.0 mm for optical measurement. Manufacturers report that use of the digital level increases productivity by about 50 percent, with the added bonus of the elimination of field-book entry mistakes. The more precise digital levels can be used in first- and second-order leveling, whereas the less precise digital levels can be used in third-order leveling and construction surveys.

2.4.3 Tilting Level

This, mostly obsolete, tilting level is roughly leveled by observing the bubble in the circular spirit level. Just before each important rod reading is to be taken, and while the telescope is pointing at the rod, the telescope is leveled precisely by manipulating a tilting screw, which effectively raises or lowers the eyepiece end of the telescope. The level is equipped with a tube level, which is leveled precisely by operating the tilting screw. The bubble is viewed through a separate eyepiece or, as you can see in Figure 2.8, through the telescope. The image of the bubble is longitudinally split in two and viewed with the aid of prisms. One-half of each end of the bubble can be observed [Figure 2.8(b)] and, after adjustment, the two half-ends are brought to coincidence and appear as a continuous curve. When coincidence has been achieved, the telescope has been leveled precisely. It has been estimated (by Leica Geosystems) that the accuracy of centering a level bubble with reference to the open tubular scale graduated at intervals of 2 mm is about one-fifth of a division, or 0.4 mm. With coincidence-type

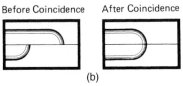

Before Coincidence   After Coincidence

(a)

(b)

FIGURE 2.8   (a) Leica engineering tilting level, GK 23 C. (b) Split bubble, before and after coincidence. (Courtesy of Leica Geosystems)

(split-bubble) levels, however, this accuracy increases to about one-fortieth of a division, or 0.05 mm. These levels are useful when a relatively high degree of precision is required; if tilting levels are used on ordinary work (e.g., earthwork), however, the time (expense) involved in setting the split bubble to coincidence for each rod reading can scarcely be justified. Automatic levels, digital levels, and total stations have mostly replaced these levels.

The level tube, used in many levels, is a sealed glass tube filled mostly with alcohol or a similar substance with a low freezing point. The upper (and sometimes lower) surface has been ground to form a circular arc. The degree of precision possessed by a surveyors' level is partly a function of the sensitivity of the level tube; the sensitivity of the level tube is directly related to the radius of curvature of the upper surface of the level tube. The larger the radius of curvature, the more sensitive the level tube. Sensitivity is usually expressed as the central angle subtending one division (usually 2 mm) marked on the surface of the level tube. The sensitivity of many engineers' levels is 30″; that is, for a 2-mm arc, the central angle is 30″ ($R = 13.75$ m, or 45 ft). See Figure 2.9. The sensitivity of levels used for precise work is usually 10″; that is, $R = 41.25$ m, or 135 ft.

Precise tilting levels, in addition to possessing more sensitive level tubes, have improved optics, including a greater magnification power. The relationship between the quality of the optical system and the sensitivity of the level tube can be simply stated: *for any observable movement of the bubble in the level tube, there should be an observable movement of the cross hair on the leveling rod.*

Example: For an Engineer's Level Having a Central Angle of 30″ Subtended by One 2-mm Division, Calculate the Radius of Curvature of the Upper Tube Surface.

Establish an Angle/Arc Ratio

$$\frac{30''}{360°} = \frac{0.002}{2\pi R} \; , R = \frac{360}{0.00833} \times \frac{0.002}{2\pi} \; , R = 13.75 \text{ m (or 45 ft.)}$$

FIGURE 2.9 Level tube showing the relationship between the central angle per division and the radius of curvature of the level tube upper surface. (Courtesy of Leica Geosystems)

2.5   Leveling Rods

Leveling rods are manufactured from wood, metal, or fiberglass and are graduated in feet or meters. The foot rod can be read directly to 0.01 ft, whereas the metric rod can usually be read directly only to 0.01 m, with millimeters being estimated. Metric rod readings are normally booked to the closest one-third or one-half of a centimeter (i.e., 0.000, 0.003, 0.005, 0.007, and 0.010). More precise values can be obtained by using an optical micrometer. One-piece rods are used for more precise work. The most precise work requires the face of the rod to be an invar strip held in place under temperature-compensating spring tension (invar is a metal that has a very low rate of thermal expansion).

Most leveling surveys utilize two- or three-piece rods graduated in either feet or meters. The sole of the rod is a metal plate that withstands the constant wear and tear of leveling. The zero mark is at the bottom of the metal plate. The rods are graduated in a wide variety of patterns, all of which respond readily to logical analysis. The surveyor should study an unfamiliar rod at close quarters prior to leveling to ensure that he or she understands the graduations thoroughly. (See Figure 2.10 for a variety of graduation markings.)

The rectangular sectioned rods are of either the folding (hinged) or the sliding variety. Newer fiberglass rods have oval or circular cross sections and fit telescopically

Level Rod Faces

Rod faces pictured are approximately one-half actual size.

No. 1	No. 2	No. 3	No. 4	No. 5
SK, Phila. & S.F.; Feet, 10ths, 100ths	Phila. & S.F.; Meters, decimeters, centimeters	Direct Elevation; Feet, 10ths, 100ths	Stadia; Feet, 10ths, ½ 10ths	Stadia; Meters, decimeters, centimeters

FIGURE 2.10 Traditional rectangular cross-section leveling rods showing various graduation markings. (Courtesy of SOKKIA Corp.)

together for heights of 3, 5, and 7 m, from a stored height of 1.5 m (equivalent foot rods are also available). Benchmark leveling utilizes folding (one-piece) rods or invar rods, both of which have built-in handles and rod levels. All other rods can be plumbed by using a rod level (Figure 2.11), or by waving the rod (Figure 2.12).

(a)

FIGURE 2.11 (a) Circular rod level. (Courtesy of Keuffel & Esser Co.) (b) Circular level, shown with a leveling rod.

(b)

FIGURE 2.12 (a) Waving the rod.

(*continued*)

FIGURE 2.12. (*continued*) (b) Waving the rod slightly to and from the instrument allows the instrument operator to take the most precise (lowest) reading.

2.6 Definitions for Differential Leveling

A **benchmark (BM)** is a permanent point of known elevation. BMs are established by using precise leveling techniques and instrumentation; more recently, precise GPS techniques have been used. BMs are bronze disks or plugs set usually into vertical wall faces. It is important that the BM be placed in a structure with substantial footings (at least below minimum frost depth penetration) that will resist vertical movement due to settling or upheaval. BM elevations and locations are published by federal, state or provincial, and municipal agencies and are available to surveyors for a nominal fee. See Figure 2.13 for an illustration of the use of a BM.

A **temporary benchmark (TBM)** is a semipermanent point of known elevation. TBMs can be flange bolts on fire hydrants, nails in the roots of trees, top corners of concrete culvert head walls, and so on. The elevations of TBMs are not normally published, but they are available in the field notes of various surveying agencies.

A **turning point (TP)** is a point temporarily used to transfer an elevation (Figure 2.14).

A **backsight (BS)** is a rod reading taken on a point of known elevation to establish the elevation of the instrument line of sight (Figures 2.13 and 2.14).

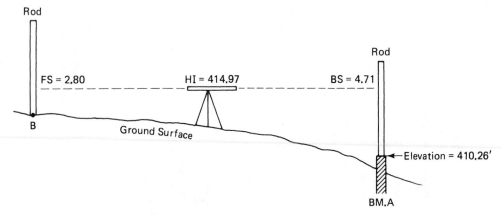

FIGURE 2.13   Leveling procedure: one setup.

The **height of instrument (HI)** is the elevation of the line of sight through the level (i.e., elevation of BM + BS = HI; Figures 2.13 and 2.14).

A **foresight (FS)** is a rod reading taken on a TP, BM, or TBM to determine its elevation [i.e., HI − FS = elevation of TP (or BM or TBM); Figures 2.13 and 2.14].

An **intermediate foresight (IS)** is a rod reading taken at any other point where the elevation is required (Figures 2.18 and 2.19), i.e., HI − IS = elevation.

Most engineering leveling projects are initiated to determine the elevations of intermediate points (as in profiles, cross sections, etc.). The addition of BSs to elevations to obtain heights of instrument and the subtraction of intermediate sights (ISs) and FSs from heights of instrument to obtain new elevations are known as note reductions.

2.7   Techniques of Leveling

In leveling (as opposed to theodolite work), the instrument can usually be set up in a relatively convenient location. If the level has to be set up on a hard surface, such as asphalt or concrete, the tripod legs are spread out to provide a more stable setup. When the level is to be set up on a soft surface (e.g., turf), the tripod is first set up so that the tripod top is nearly horizontal, and then the tripod legs are pushed firmly into the earth. The tripod legs are snugly tightened to the tripod top so that a leg, when raised, just falls back under the force of its own weight. Undertightening can cause an unsteady setup, just as overtightening can cause an unsteady setup due to torque strain. On hills, it is customary to place one leg uphill and two legs downhill; the instrument operator stands facing uphill while setting up the instrument. The tripod legs can be adjustable or straight-leg. The straight-leg tripod is recommended for leveling because it contributes to a more stable setup. After the tripod has been set roughly level, with the feet firmly pushed into the ground, the instrument can be leveled using the leveling screws.

Four-screw instruments (see Appendix G) are attached to the tripod via a threaded base and are leveled by rotating the telescope until it is directly over a pair of opposite leveling screws, and then by proceeding as described in Section G.2 and Figure G.7. Three-screw

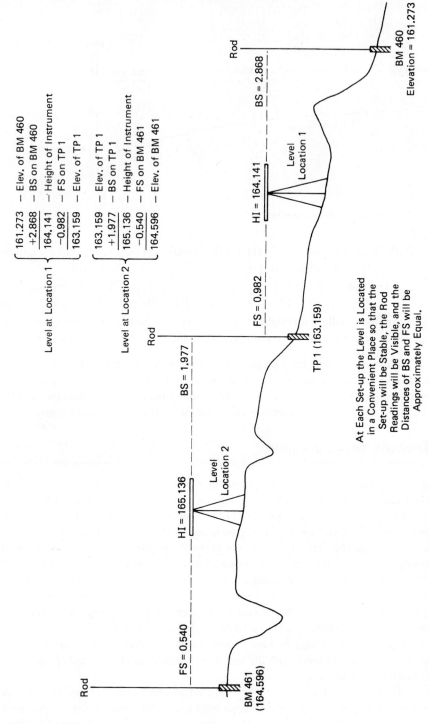

Level at Location 1 $\left\{\begin{array}{ll}161.273 & -\text{ Elev. of BM 460} \\ +2.868 & -\text{ BS on BM 460} \\ \hline 164.141 & -\text{ Height of Instrument} \\ -0.982 & -\text{ FS on TP 1} \\ \hline 163.159 & -\text{ Elev. of TP 1} \end{array}\right.$

Level at Location 2 $\left\{\begin{array}{ll}163.159 & -\text{ Elev. of TP 1} \\ +1.977 & -\text{ BS on TP 1} \\ \hline 165.136 & -\text{ Height of Instrument} \\ -0.540 & -\text{ FS on BM 461} \\ \hline 164.596 & -\text{ Elev. of BM 461} \end{array}\right.$

At Each Set-up the Level is Located
in a Convenient Place so that the
Set-up will be Stable, the Rod
Readings will be Visible, and the
Distances of BS and FS will be
Approximately Equal.

FIGURE 2.14 Leveling procedure: more than one setup.

instruments are attached to the tripod via a threaded bolt that projects up from the tripod top into the leveling base of the instrument. The three-screw instrument, which usually has a circular bull's-eye bubble level, is leveled as described in Section 2.4.1 and Figure 2.6. Unlike the four-screw instrument, the three-screw instrument can be manipulated by moving the screws one at a time, although experienced surveyors usually manipulate at least two at a time. After the bubble has been centered, the instrument can be revolved to check that the circular bubble remains centered.

Once the level has been set up, preparation for the rod readings can take place. The eyepiece lenses are focused by turning the eyepiece focusing ring until the cross hairs are as black and as sharp as possible (it helps to have the telescope pointing to a light-colored background for this operation). Next, the rod is brought into focus by turning the telescope focusing screw until the rod graduations are as clear as possible. If both these focusing operations have been carried out correctly, the cross hairs appear to be superimposed on the leveling rod. If either focusing operation (cross hair or rod focus) has not been carried out properly, the cross hair appears to move slightly up and down as the observer's head moves slightly up and down. The apparent movement of the cross hair can cause incorrect readings. If one or both focus adjustments have been made improperly, the resultant reading error is known as a **parallax** error.

Figure 2.13 shows one complete leveling cycle; actual leveling operations are no more complicated than that shown. Leveling operations typically involve numerous repetitions of this leveling cycle. Some operations require that additional (intermediate) rod readings be taken at each instrument setup.

$$\text{Existing elevation} + \text{BS} = \text{HI} \tag{2.5}$$

$$\text{HI} - \text{FS} = \text{new elevation} \tag{2.6}$$

These two equations describe the differential leveling process completely.

When leveling between BMs or TPs, the level is set approximately midway between the BS and FS locations to eliminate (or minimize) errors due to curvature and refraction (Section 2.3) and errors due to a faulty line of sight (Section 2.11). To ensure that the rod is plumb, the surveyor either uses a rod level (Figure 2.11) or gently "waves" the rod to and away from the instrument. The correct rod reading is the lowest reading observed. The surveyor must ensure that the rod does not sit up on the back edge of the base and thus effectively raises the zero mark on the rod off the BM (or TP). The instrument operator is sure that the rod has been waved properly if the readings first decrease to a minimum value and then increase (Figure 2.12).

The elevation of B in Figure 2.13 can be determined as follows:

Elevation BM.A	410.26 ft
BS rod reading at BM.A	+4.71 BS (ft)
Height (elevation) of instrument line of sight	414.97 HI (ft)
FS rod reading at TBM B	−2.80 FS (ft)
Elevation TBM B	412.17 ft

After the rod reading of 4.71 is taken at BM.A, the elevation of the line of sight of the instrument is known to be 414.97 (410.26 + 4.71). The elevation of TBM B can be determined by holding the rod at B, sighting the rod with the instrument, and reading the rod

(2.80 ft). The elevation of TBM B is therefore 414.97 − 2.80 = 412.17 ft. In addition to determining the elevation of TBM B, the elevations of any other points lower than the line of sight and visible from the level can be determined in a similar manner.

The situation depicted in Figure 2.14 shows the technique used when the point whose elevation is to be determined (BM 461) is too far from the point of known elevation (BM 460) for a single-setup solution. The elevation of an intermediate point (TP 1) is determined, thus allowing the surveyor to move the level to a location where BM 461 can be "seen." Real-life situations may require numerous setups and the determination of the elevation of many TPs before getting close enough to determine the elevation of the desired point. When the elevation of the desired point has been determined, the surveyor must then either continue the survey to a point (BM) of known elevation or return (loop) the survey to the point of commencement. The survey must be closed onto a point of known elevation so that the accuracy and acceptability of the survey can be determined. If the closure is not within allowable limits, the survey must be repeated.

The arithmetic can be verified by performing the **arithmetic check** (page check). All BSs are added, and all FSs are subtracted. When the sum of BS is added to the original elevation and then the sum of FS is subtracted from that total, the remainder should be the same as the final elevation calculated (Figure 2.15).

BENCHMARK VERIFICATION

BM460 to BM461

KANEN−天
Job SOMERVILLE−ROD, LEVEL #09 19°C, CLOUDY
Date   MAY 11, 2009   Page   62

STA	B.S. (+)	H.I.		F.S. (−)	ELEV.	DESCRIPTION
BM 460	2.868	164.141			161.273	BRONZE PLATE SET IN --- ETC.
T.P.1	1.977	165.136		0.982	163.159	NAIL IN ROOT OF MAPLE --- ETC.
BM 461				0.540	164.596	BRONZE PLATE SET IN --- ETC.
Σ	4.845			1.522		
ARITHMETIC CHECK:						
	161.273 + 4.845 − 1.522		=		164.596	

FIGURE 2.15 Leveling field notes and arithmetic check (data from Figure 2.14).

$$\text{Starting elevation} + \Sigma\text{BS} - \Sigma\text{FS} = \text{ending elevation}$$

In the 1800s and early 1900s, leveling procedures like the one described here were used to survey locations for railroads that traversed North America between the Atlantic Ocean and the Pacific Ocean.

2.8 Benchmark Leveling (Vertical Control Surveys)

BM leveling is the type of leveling employed when a system of BMs is to be established or when an existing system of BMs is to be extended or densified. Perhaps a BM is required in a new location, or perhaps an existing BM has been destroyed and a suitable replacement is required. BM leveling is typified by the relatively high level of precision specified, both for the instrumentation and for the technique itself.

The specifications shown in Tables 2.1 and 2.2 cover the techniques of precise leveling. Precise levels with coincidence tubular bubbles of a sensitivity of 10 s per 2-min division (or the equivalent for automatic levels) and with parallel-plate micrometers are used almost exclusively for this type of work. Invar-faced rods, together with a base plate (Figure 2.16), rod level, and supports, are used in pairs to minimize the time required for successive readings.

Tripods for this type of work are longer than usual, thus enabling the surveyor to keep the line of sight farther above the ground to minimize interference and errors due to refraction. Ideally the work is performed on a cloudy, windless day, although work can proceed on a sunny day if the instrument is protected from the sun and its possible differential thermal effects.

At the national level, BMs are established by federal agencies utilizing first-order methods and first-order instruments. The same high requirements are also specified for state and provincial grids, but as work proceeds from the whole to the part (i.e., down to municipal or regional grids), the rigid specifications are relaxed somewhat. For most engineering works, BMs established (from the municipal or regional grid) at third-order specifications. BMs established to control isolated construction projects may be at even lower orders of accuracy.

It is customary in BM leveling at all orders of accuracy to verify first that the elevation of the starting BM is correct. Two-way leveling to the closest adjacent BM satisfies this verification requirement. This check is particularly important when the survey loops back to close on the starting BM and no other verification is planned.

With the ongoing improvements in GPS techniques and in geoid modeling (Geoid99), first- and second-order vertical control surveys are now performed routinely using GPS surveys (see Chapter 7). The GPS approach to vertical control surveys is reported to be much more productive (up to ten times) than conventional precise spirit leveling.*

In addition to GPS, another alternative to spirit leveling for the establishment of BMs is the use of total stations. Instrument manufacturers now refer angle accuracies of theodolites and total stations to the Deutsches Institut für Normung (DIN; http://www.din.de) and

---

*Professional Surveyor Magazine Newsletter, December 12, 2002.

(a)

(b)

(c)

FIGURE 2.16 (a) Invar rod, also showing the footplate, which ensures a clearly defined rod position. (Courtesy of Leica Geosystems) (b) Philadelphia rod (*left*), which can be read directly by the instrument operator or the rod holder after the target has been set. (Courtesy of Keuffel & Esser Co.) Frisco rod (*right*) with two or three sliding sections having replaceable metal scales. (c) Metric rod; horizontal cross-hair reading on 1.143 m. (Courtesy of Leica Geosystems) to the International Organization of Standards (ISO; http://www.iso.ch). Both organizations use the same procedures to determine the standard deviation (*So*) of a horizontal direction. Angle accuracies are covered in DIN 18723, part 3, and in ISO 12857, part 2. These standards indicate that a surveyor can obtain results consistent with stated instrument accuracies by using two sets of observations (direct and reverse) on each prism. In addition, the surveyor should try to set the total station midway between the two prisms being measured and apply relevant atmospheric corrections and prism constant corrections.

2.9   Profile and Cross-Section Leveling

In engineering surveying, we often consider a route (road, sewer pipeline, channel, etc.) from three distinct perspectives. The **plan** view of route location is the same as if we were in an aircraft looking straight down. The **profile** of the route is a side view or elevation (Figure 2.17) in which the longitudinal surfaces are highlighted (e.g., road, top and bottom of pipelines). The **cross section** shows the end view of a section at a station (0 + 60 in Figure 2.17) and is at right angles to the centerline. These three views (plan, profile, and cross section) together completely define the route in *X*, *Y*, and *Z* coordinates.

Profile levels are taken along a path that holds interest for the designer. In roadwork, preliminary surveys often profile the proposed location of the centerline (₵) (Figure 2.18). The proposed ₵ is staked out at an even interval (50–100 ft, or 20–30 m). The level is set up in a convenient location so that the BM—and as many intermediate points as possible—can be sighted. Rod readings are taken at the even station locations and at any other point

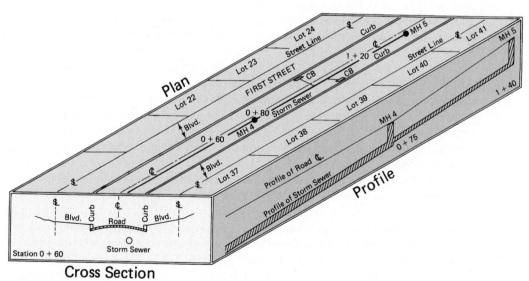

FIGURE 2.17   Relationship of plan, profile, and cross-section views.

FIGURE 2.18 Example of profile leveling; see Figure 2.19 for survey notes.

where the ground surface has a significant change in slope. When the rod is moved to a new location and it cannot be seen from the instrument, a TP is called for so that the instrument can be moved ahead and the remaining stations leveled.

The TP can be taken on a wood stake, the corner of a concrete step or concrete head wall, a lug on the flange of a hydrant, and so on. The TP should be a solid, well-defined point that can be precisely described and, it is hoped, found again at a future date. In the case of leveling across fields, it usually is not possible to find TP features of any permanence. In that case, stakes are driven in and then abandoned when the survey is finished. In the field notes shown in Figure 2.19, the survey was closed at an acceptable point: to BM 461. Had there been no BM at the end of the profile survey, the surveyor would have looped back and closed to the initial BM. The note on Figure 2.18 at the BM 461 elevation shows that the correct elevation of BM 461 is 164.591 m, which means that there was a survey error of 0.005 m over a distance of 200 m. Using the standards shown in Tables 2.1 and 2.2, we find this result qualifies for consideration at the third level of accuracy in both the United States and Canada.

The ISs in Figure 2.19 are shown in a separate column, and the elevations at the ISs show the same number of decimals as are shown in the rod readings. Rod readings on turf, ground, and the like are usually taken to the closest 0.1 ft or 0.01 m. Rod readings taken on concrete, steel, asphalt, and so on are usually taken to the closest 0.01 ft or 0.003 m. It is a waste of time and money to read the rod more precisely than conditions warrant. (Refer to Chapter 8 for details on plotting the profile.)

When the final route of the facility has been selected, additional surveying is required. Once again, the ℄ is staked (if necessary), and cross sections are taken at all even

SMITH—NOTES
BROWN—π
JONES—ROD

PROFILE OF PROPOSED
ROAD 0 + 00 to 2 + 00

Job 21°C — SUNNY LEVEL L—14
Date AUG 3, 2009 Page 72

STA.	B.S.	H.I.	I.S	F.S.	ELEV.	DESCRIPTION
BM 460	2.868	164.141			161.273	BRONZE PLATE SET IN ––– ETC.
0 + 00			2.06		162.08	₵
0 + 06			1.17		162.97	₵ –TOP OF BERM
0 + 20			1.63		162.51	₵
0 + 40			1.62		162.52	₵
0 + 60			1.41		162.73	₵
0 + 80			1.01		163.13	₵
T.P. 1	1.977	165.136		0.982	163.159	NAIL IN ROOT OF MAPLE ––– ETC.
1 + 00			1.73		163.41	₵
1 + 20			1.70		163.44	₵
1 + 30			1.89		163.25	₵ BOTTOM OF GULLY
1 + 40			1.67		163.47	₵
1 + 60			1.60		163.54	₵
1 + 80			1.31		163.83	₵
1 + 91			1.93		163.21	₵ BOTTOM OF GULLY
2 + 00			0.64		164.50	₵
BM 461				0.540	164.596	BRONZE PLATE SET IN ––– ETC.
						164.591 – PUBLISHED ELEV.
	Σ=4.845			Σ=1.522		E = 164.596
ARITHMETIC CHECK: 161.273 + 4.845 −1.522						164.591
				= 164.596		0.005
						ALLOWABLE ERROR (3ᴿᴰ ORDER)
						= 12 mm √K, = .012 √.2 = .0054 m
						ABOVE ERROR (.005) SATISFIES 3ᴿᴰ ORDER.

FIGURE 2.19 Profile field notes.

stations. In roadwork, rod readings are taken along a line perpendicular to the ₵ at each even station. The rod is held at each significant change in surface slope and at the limits of the job. In uniformly sloping land areas, the only rod readings required at each cross-sectioned station are often at the ₵ and the two street lines (for roadwork). Chapter 8 shows how the cross sections are plotted and then utilized to compute volumes of cut and fill.

Figure 2.20 illustrates the rod positions required to define the ground surface suitably at 2 + 60, at right angles to the ₵. Figure 2.21 shows the field notes for this typical cross section—in a format favored by municipal surveyors. Figure 2.22 shows the same field data entered in a cross-section note form favored by many highway agencies. Note that the HI (353.213) has been rounded to two decimals (353.21) in Figures 2.21 and 2.22 to facilitate reduction of the two-decimal rod readings. The rounded value is placed in brackets to distinguish it from the correct HI, from which the next FS will be subtracted (or from which any three-decimal intermediate rod readings are subtracted).

FIGURE 2.20 Cross-section surveying.

SMITH—NOTES   JONES—ROD
BROWN—$\bar{x}$ TYLER—TAPE

CROSS—SECTIONS FOR PROPOSED ......

LOCATION OF DUNCAN ROAD ......

Job _14°C_   CLOUDY   LEVEL #6

Date ..... **NOV 24, 2009** ..... Page 23

STA.	B.S.	H.I.	I.S.	F.S.	ELEV.	DESCRIPTION
BM #28	2.011	178.218			176.207	BRONZE PLATE SET IN SOUTH WALL 0.50m.
		(178.22)				ABOVE GROUND, CIVIC #2242, 23RD AVE.
2 + 60						
10m LT			0.81		177.41	S. $\text{\textsterling}$
2.7m LT			1.48		176.74	BOTTOM OF SWALE
¢			1.22		177.00	¢
8.2m RT			0.87		177.35	CHANGE IN SLOPE
10m RT			0.21		178.01	N. $\text{\textsterling}$
2 + 80						
10m LT			1.02		177.20	S. $\text{\textsterling}$
3.8m LT			1.64		176.58	BOTTOM OF SWALE
¢			1.51		176.71	¢
7.8m RT			1.10		177.12	CHANGE IN SLOPE
10m RT			0.43		177.79	N. $\text{\textsterling}$

FIGURE 2.21 Cross-section notes (municipal format).

CROSS-SECTIONS FOR PROPOSED ....
LOCATION OF DUNCAN HIGHWAY ....

SMITH—NOTES   JONES—ROD
BROWN—X   TYLER—TAPE
Job 14°C   CLOUDY   LEVEL 6 ....
Date .... NOV 24, 2009 .... Page 23

STA.	B.S.	H.I.	I.S	F.S.	ELEV.					
	2.011	178.218			176.207	BRONZE PLATE SET IN SOUTH WALL				
		(178.22)				0.50 ABOVE GROUND, CIVIC #2242, 23RD AVE.				
						LEFT		℄		RIGHT
2 + 60						10.0	2.7		8.2	10.0
						0.81	1.48	1.22	0.87	0.21
						177.41	176.74	177.00	177.35	178.01
2 + 80						10.0	3.8		7.8	10.0
						1.02	1.64	1.51	1.10	0.43
						177.20	176.58	176.71	177.12	177.79

FIGURE 2.22 Cross-section notes (highway format).

Road and highway construction often requires the location of granular (e.g., sand, gravel) deposits for use in the highway roadbed. These **borrow pits** (gravel pits) are surveyed to determine the volume of material "borrowed" and transported to the site. Before any excavation takes place, one or more reference baselines are established, and two BMs (at a minimum) are located in convenient locations. The reference lines are located in secure locations where neither the stripping and stockpiling of topsoil nor the actual excavation of the granular material will endanger the stake (Figure 2.23). Cross sections are taken over (and beyond) the area of proposed excavation. These original cross sections will be used as data against which interim and final survey measurements will be compared to determine total excavation. The volumes calculated from the cross sections (see Chapter 8) are often converted to tons (tonnes) for payment purposes. In many locations, weigh scales are located at the pit to aid in converting the volumes and as a check on the calculated quantities.

The original cross sections are taken over a grid at 50-ft (20-m) intervals. As the excavation proceeds, additional rod readings (in addition to 50-ft grid readings) for the top and bottom of the excavation are required. Permanent targets can be established to assist in

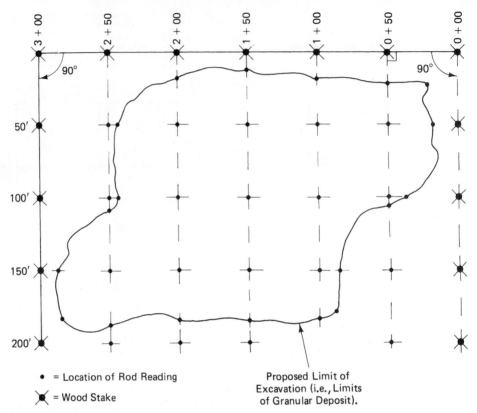

FIGURE 2.23 Baseline control for a borrow pit survey.

- • = Location of Rod Reading
- ✖ = Wood Stake

Proposed Limit of
Excavation (i.e., Limits
of Granular Deposit).

the visual alignment of the cross-section lines running perpendicular to the baseline at each 50-ft station. If permanent targets have not been erected, a surveyor on the baseline can keep the rod on line by using a prism or estimated right angles.

2.10 Reciprocal Leveling

Section 2.7 advised the surveyor to keep BS and FS distances roughly equal so that instrumental and natural errors cancel out. In some situations, such as river or valley crossings, it is not always possible to balance BS and FS distances. The reciprocal leveling technique is illustrated in Figure 2.24. The level is set up and readings are taken on TP 23 and TP 24. Precision can be improved by taking several readings on the far point (TP 24) and then averaging the results. The level is then moved to the far side of the river, and the process is repeated. The differences in elevation thus obtained are averaged to obtain the final result. The averaging process eliminates instrumental errors and natural errors, such as curvature. Errors due to refraction can be minimized by ensuring that the elapsed time for the process is kept to a minimum.

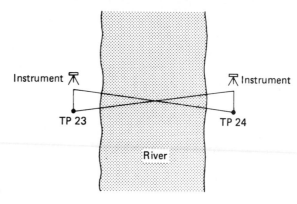

FIGURE 2.24   Reciprocal leveling.

2.11   Peg Test

The purpose of the peg test is to check that the line of sight through the level is horizontal (i.e., parallel to the axis of the bubble tube). The line-of-sight axis is defined by the location of the horizontal cross hair (Figure 2.25). Refer to Chapter 4 for a description of the horizontal cross-hair orientation adjustment.

To perform the peg test, the surveyor first places two stakes at a distance of 200–300 ft (60–90 m) apart. The level is set up midway (paced) between the two stakes, and rod readings are taken at both locations [Figure 2.26(a)]. If the line of sight through the level is not horizontal, the errors in rod readings (Δe_1) at both points A and B are identical because the level is halfway between the points. The errors are identical, so the calculated difference in elevation between points A and B (difference in rod readings) is the *true* difference in elevation.

The level is then moved to one of the points (A) and set up close (e.g., at the minimum focusing distance) to the rod, and then a normal sighting (a_2) is taken. Any rod reading error introduced using this very short sight is relatively insignificant. Once the rod reading at A has been determined and booked, the rod is held at B and a normal rod reading is obtained.

■   EXAMPLE 2.2

Refer to Figure 2.26.

First setup: Rod reading at A, a_1 = 1.075 m

Rod reading at B, b_1 = 1.247 m

True difference in elevations = 0.172 m

FIGURE 2.25   Optical axis and level tube axis.

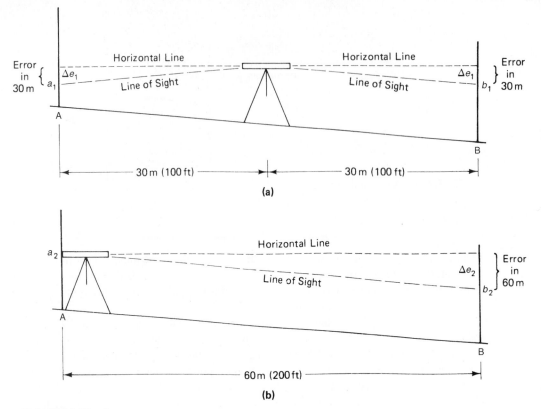

FIGURE 2.26 Peg test.

$$\text{Second setup: Rod reading at A, } a_2 = 1.783 \text{ m}$$
$$\text{Rod reading at B, } b_1 = \underline{1.946}^* \text{ m}$$
$$\text{Apparent difference in elevation} = 0.163 \text{ m}$$
$$\text{Error}(\Delta e_2) \text{ in 60 m} = 0.009 \text{ m}$$

This is an error of -0.00015 m/m. Therefore, the collimation correction (C factor) $= +0.00015$ m/m.

In Section 2.7, you were advised to keep the BS and FS distances equal; the peg test illustrates clearly the benefits to be gained from the use of this technique. If the BS and FS distances are kept roughly equal, errors due to a faulty line of sight simply do not have the opportunity to develop. The peg test can also be accomplished by using the techniques of reciprocal leveling (Section 2.10).

*Had there been no error in the instrument line of sight, the rod reading at b_2 would have been 1.955, i.e., 1.783 + 0.172.

■ **EXAMPLE 2.3**

If the level used in the peg test of Example 2.2 is used in the field with a BS distance of 80 m and an FS distance of 70 m, the net error in the rod readings would be 10 × 0.00015 = 0.0015 (0.002m). That is, for a relatively large differential between BS and FS distances and a large line-of-sight error (0.009 for 60 m), the effect on the survey is negligible for ordinary work.

2.12 Three-Wire Leveling

Leveling can be performed by utilizing the stadia cross hairs found on most levels and on all theodolites (Figure 2.27). Each BS and FS is recorded by reading the stadia hairs in addition to the horizontal cross hair. The stadia hairs (wires) are positioned an equal distance above and below the main cross hair and are spaced to give 1.00 ft (m) of interval for each 100 ft (m) of horizontal distance that the rod is away from the level. The three readings are averaged to obtain the desired value.

The recording of three readings at each sighting enables the surveyor to perform a relatively precise survey while utilizing ordinary levels. Readings to the closest thousandth of a foot (mm) are estimated and recorded. The leveling rod used for this type of work should be calibrated to ensure its integrity.

Figure 2.28 shows typical notes for BM leveling. A realistic survey would include a completed loop or a check into another BM of known elevation. If the collimation correction as calculated in Section 2.11 (10.00015 m/m) is applied to the survey shown in Figure 2.28, the correction to the elevation is as follows:

$$C = +0.00015 \times (62.9 - 61.5) = +0.0002 \text{ m}$$

Sum of FS corrected to 5.7196 + 0.0002 = 5.7198 m

The elevation of BM 201 in Figure 2.28 is calculated as follows:

$$
\begin{aligned}
\text{Elev. BM17} &= \quad 186.2830 \\
+ \Sigma\, \text{BS} &= + \quad 2.4143 \\
\hline
&\quad 188.6973 \\
- \Sigma\, \text{FS (corrected)} &= - \quad 5.7198 \\
\text{Elev. BM 201} &= \quad 182.9775 \text{ (corrected for collimation)}
\end{aligned}
$$

When levels are being used for precise purposes, it is customary to determine the collimation correction at least once each day.

FIGURE 2.27 Reticle cross hairs. 100 X Stadia Hair Interval = Distance

B.M. LEVELING—3 WIRE
B.M. 17 to B.M. 201
(RETURN RUN ON P.48)

JONES—NOTES
SMITH—$\bar{x}$
BROWN—ROD
GREEN—ROD

Job ROD 19, INST. L.33 8°C, CLOUDY
Date MAR 3, 2009 Page 47

STA.	B.S.	DIST.	F.S.	DIST.	ELEV.	DESCRIPTION
BM 17					186.2830	BRONZE PLATE SET IN WALL --- ETC.
	0.825		1.775			
	0.725	10.0	1.673	10.2	+0.7253	
	0.626	9.9	1.572	10.1	187.0083	
	2.176	19.9	5.020	20.3	−1.6733	
	+0.7253		−1.6733			
TP 1					185.3350	N. LUG TOP FLANGE FIRE HYD. N/S
						MAIN ST. OPP. CIVIC #181.
	0.698		1.750			
	0.571	12.7	1.620	13.0	+0.5710	
	0.444	12.7	1.490	13.0	185.9060	
	1.713	25.4	4.860	26.0	−1.6200	
	+0.5710		−1.6200			
TP 2					184.2860	N. LUG TOP FLANGE FIRE HYD. N/S
						MAIN ST. OPP. CIVIC #163.
	1.199		2.509			
	1.118	8.1	2.427	8.2	+1.1180	
	1.037	8.1	2.343	8.4	185.4040	
	3.354	16.2	7.279	16.6	−2.4263	
	+1.1180		−2.4263			
BM 201					182.9777	BRONZE PLATE SET IN ESTLY FACE
						OF RETAINING WALL --- ETC.
Σ	+2.4143	61.5m	−5.7196	62.9m		

ARITHMETIC CHECK: 186.283 + 2.4143 − 5.7196 = 182.9777 ✓

FIGURE 2.28 Survey notes for three-wire leveling.

2.13 Trigonometric Leveling

The difference in elevation between A and B in (Figure 2.29) can be determined if the vertical angle (a) and the slope distance (S) are measured. These measurements can be taken with total stations or with electronic distance measurement (EDM)/theodolite combinations.

$$V = S \sin \alpha \qquad (2.7)$$

$$\text{Elevation at } \bar{\wedge} + \text{ hi} \pm V - \text{rod reading (RR)} = \text{elevation at rod} \qquad (2.8)$$

The hi in this case is not the elevation of the line of sight (HI), as it is in differential leveling. Instead, hi here refers to the distance from point A up to the optical center of the theodolite or total station, measured with a steel tape or rod. Modern practice involving the use of total stations routinely gives the elevations of sighted points by processing the differences in elevation between the total station point and the sighted points—along with the horizontal distances to those points. See also Section 5.3.1, which discusses total station techniques of trigonometric leveling. Instruments with dual-axis compensators can produce very accurate results.

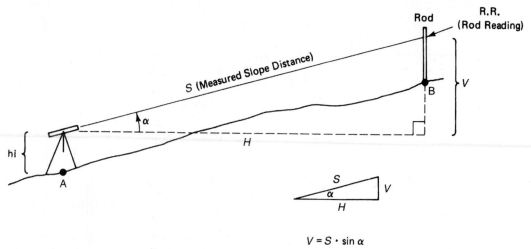

$$V = S \cdot \sin \alpha$$

FIGURE 2.29 Trigonometric leveling.

■ **EXAMPLE 2.4**

See Figure 2.30. Using Equation 2.7, we have

$$V = S \sin \alpha$$
$$= 82.18 \sin 30° 22'$$
$$= 41.54 \text{ ft}$$

Using Equation 2.8, we have

$$\text{Elev. at } \overline{\wedge} + \text{ hi } \pm V - \text{RR} = \text{elevation at rod}$$
$$361.29 + 4.72 - 41.54 - 4.00 = 320.47$$

The RR in Example 3.4 *could* have been 4.72, the value of the hi. If that reading had been visible, the surveyor would have sighted on it to eliminate +hi and –RR from the calculation; that is,

$$\text{Elev. at } \overline{\wedge} - V = \text{elevation at rod} \qquad (2.9)$$

In this example, the station (chainage) of the rod station can also be determined.

2.14 Level Loop Adjustments

In Section 2.7, we noted that level surveys had to be closed within acceptable tolerances or the survey would have to be repeated. The tolerances for various orders of surveys were shown in Tables 2.1 and 2.2.

If a level survey were performed to establish new BMs, it would be desirable to proportion any acceptable error throughout the length of the survey. Because the error tolerances shown in Tables 2.1 and 2.2 are based on the distances surveyed, adjustments to the level

FIGURE 2.30 Example of trigonometric leveling (see Example 2.4 in Section 2.13).

loop are based on the relevant distances, or on the number of instrument setups, which is a factor directly related to the distance surveyed.

■ **EXAMPLE 2.5**

A level circuit is shown in Figure 2.31. The survey, needed for local engineering projects, commenced at BM 20. The elevations of new BMs 201, 202, and 203 were determined. Then the level survey was looped back to BM 20, the point of commencement (the survey could have terminated at any established BM).

Solution

According to Table 2.1, the allowable error for a second-order, class II (local engineering projects) survey is $0.008 \sqrt{K}$; thus, $0.008 \sqrt{4.7} = 0.017$ m is the permissible error.

The error in the survey of this example was found to be -0.015 m over a total distance of 4.7 km—in this case, an acceptable error. It only remains for this acceptable error to be distributed over the length of the survey. The error is proportioned according to the fraction of cumulative distance over total distance, as shown in Table 2.5. More complex adjustments are normally performed by computer, using the adjustment method of least squares.

2.15   Suggestions for Rod Work

The following list provides some reminders when performing rod work:

1. The rod should be extended and clamped properly. Ensure that the bottom of the sole plate does not become encrusted with mud and the like, which could result in mistaken readings. If a rod target is being used, ensure that it is positioned properly and that it cannot slip.

FIGURE 2.31 Level loop. Total Distance Around Loop is 4.7 km.

Table 2.5 LEVEL LOOP ADJUSTMENTS

BM	Loop Distance, Cumulative (km)	Field Elevation (m)	Correction, Cumulative Distance × E = Total Distance (m)	Adjusted Elevation (m)
20		186.273 (fixed)		186.273
201	0.8	184.242	+ 0.8/4.7 × 0.015 = + 0.003 =	184.245
202	2.4	182.297	+ 2.4/4.7 × 0.015 = + 0.008 =	182.305
203	3.0	184.227	+ 3.0/4.7 × 0.015 = + 0.010 =	184.237
20	4.7	186.258	+ 4.7/4.7 × 0.015 = + 0.015 =	186.273
			$E = 186.273 - 186.258 = -0.015$ m	

2. The rod should be held plumb for all rod readings. Use a rod level, or wave the rod to and from the instrument so that the lowest (indicating a plumb rod) reading can be determined. This practice is particularly important for all BSs and FSs.

3. Ensure that all points used as TPs are describable, identifiable, and capable of having the elevation determined to the closest 0.01 ft or 0.001 m. The TP should be nearly equidistant from the two proposed instrument locations.

4. Ensure that the rod is held in precisely the same position for the BS as it was for the FS for all TPs.

5. If the rod is being held temporarily near, but not on, a required location, the face of the rod should be turned away from the instrument so that the instrument operator cannot take a mistaken reading. This type of mistaken reading usually occurs when the distance between the two surveyors is too far to allow for voice communication and sometimes even for good visual contact.

2.16 Suggestions for Instrument Work

The following list of reminders will be useful when performing instrument work:

1. Use a straight-leg (nonadjustable) tripod, if possible.

2. Tripod legs should be tightened so that when one leg is extended horizontally, it falls slowly back to the ground under its own weight.

3. The instrument can be carried comfortably resting on one shoulder. If tree branches or other obstructions (e.g., door frames) threaten the safety of the instrument, it should be cradled under one arm, with the instrument forward, where it can be seen. Heavier instruments and more sensitive instruments should be removed from the tripod and safely carried (by available handle or in its instrument case) to the next setup position.

4. When setting up the instrument, gently force the legs into the ground by applying weight on the tripod shoe spurs. On rigid surfaces (e.g., concrete), the tripod legs should be spread farther apart to increase stability.

5. When the tripod is to be set up on a side-hill, two legs should be placed downhill and the third leg placed uphill. The instrument can be set up roughly level by careful manipulation of the third, uphill leg.

6. The location of the level setup should be chosen after considering the ability to see the maximum number of rod locations, particularly BS and FS locations.

7. Prior to taking rod readings, the cross hair should be sharply focused; it helps to point the instrument toward a light-colored background (e.g., the sky).

8. When the surveyor observes apparent movement of the cross hairs on the rod (parallax), he or she should carefully check the cross-hair focus adjustment and the objective focus adjustment for consistent results.

9. The surveyor should read the rod consistently at either the top or the bottom of the cross hair.

10. Never move the level before a FS is taken; otherwise, all work done from that HI will have to be repeated.

11. Check to ensure that the level bubble remains centered or that the compensating device (in automatic levels) is operating.

12. Rod readings (and the line of sight) should be kept at least 18 in. (0.5 m) above the ground surface to help minimize refraction errors when performing a precise level survey.

2.17 Mistakes in Leveling

Mistakes in level loops can be detected by performing arithmetic checks and also by closing on the starting BM or on any other BM whose elevation is known. Mistakes in rod readings that do not form part of a level loop, such as in intermediate sights taken in profiles, cross sections, or construction grades, are a much more irksome problem. It is bad enough to discover that a level loop contains mistakes and must be repeated, but it is a far more serious problem to have to redesign a highway profile because a key elevation contains a mistake, or to have to break out a concrete bridge abutment (the day after the concrete was poured) because the grade stake elevation contains a mistake. Because intermediate rod readings cannot be checked (without releveling), it is essential that the opportunities for mistakes be minimized.

Common mistakes in leveling include the following: misreading the foot (meter) value, transposing figures, not holding the rod in the correct location, resting the hands on the tripod while reading the rod and causing the instrument to go off level, entering the rod readings incorrectly (i.e., switching BS and FS), giving the wrong station identification to a correct rod reading, and making mistakes in the note reduction arithmetic. Most mistakes in arithmetic can be eliminated by having the other crew members check the reductions and initial each page of notes checked. Mistakes in the leveling operation cannot be completely eliminated, but they can be minimized if the crew members are aware that mistakes can (and probably will) occur. All crew members should be constantly alert to the possible occurrence of mistakes, and all crew members should try to develop strict routines for doing their work so that mistakes, when they do eventually occur, will be all the more noticeable.

Problems

2.1 Compute the error due to curvature and refraction for the following distances:
   (a) 800 ft
   (b) 4,000 ft
   (c) 700 m
   (d) 1.5 miles
   (e) 2,500 m
   (f) 3 km

2.2 Determine the rod readings indicated on the foot and metric rod illustrations shown in Figure 2.32. The foot readings are to the closest 0.01 ft, and the metric readings are to the closest one-half or one-third centimeter.

(a) Foot Rod (b) Metric Rod   (c) Foot Rod   (d) Metric Rod

FIGURE 2.32 (a) Foot rod; (b) Metric rod; (c) Foot rod; (d) Metric rod; (Courtesy of Sokkia Co. Ltd.)

(*continued*)

(e) Foot Rod   (f) Metric Rod

FIGURE 2.32   *(continued)* (e) Foot rod; (f) Metric rod.

2.3 An offshore drilling rig is being towed out to sea. What is the maximum distance away that the navigation lights can still be seen by an observer standing at the shoreline? The observer's eye height is 5′8″, and the uppermost navigation light is 230 ft above the water.

2.4 Prepare a set of level notes for the survey in Figure 2.33. Show the arithmetic check.

2.5 Prepare a set of profile leveling notes for the survey in Figure 2.34. In addition to computing all elevations, show the arithmetic check and the resulting error in closure.

2.6 Complete the accompanying set of differential leveling notes, and perform the arithmetic check.

Station	BS (m)	HI (m)	FS (m)	Elevation (m)
BM 3	1.613			133.005
TP 1	1.425		1.927	
TP 2	1.307		1.710	
TP 3	1.340		1.273	
BM 3			0.780	

FIGURE 2.33

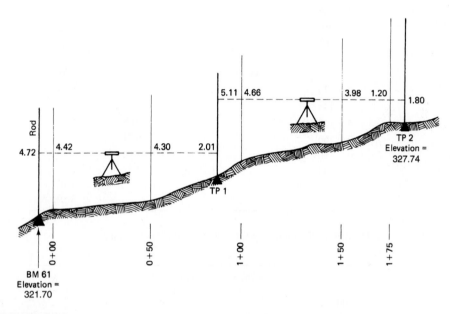

FIGURE 2.34

2.7 If the loop distance in Problem 2.6 is 700 m, at what order of survey do the results qualify? (Use Table 2.1 or Table 2.2.)

2.8 Reduce the accompanying set of differential leveling notes, and perform the arithmetic check.

Station	BS (ft)	HI (ft)	FS (ft)	Elevation (ft)
BM 100	2.71			141.44
TP 1	3.62		4.88	
TP 2	3.51		3.97	
TP 3	3.17		2.81	
TP 4	1.47		1.62	
BM 100			1.21	

2.9 If the distance leveled in Problem 2.8 is 1,000 ft, for what order of survey do the results qualify? (See Tables 2.1 and 2.2.)

2.10 Reduce the accompanying set of profile notes, and perform the arithmetic check.

Station	BS (m)	HI (m)	IS (m)	FS (m)	Elevation (m)
BM S.101	0.475				171.845
0 + 000			0.02		
0 + 020			0.41		
0 + 040			0.73		
0 + 060			0.70		
0 + 066.28			0.726		
0 + 080			1.38		
0 + 100			1.75		
0 + 120			2.47		
TP 1	0.666			2.993	
0 + 140			0.57		
0 + 143.78			0.634		
0 + 147.02			0.681		
0 + 160			0.71		
0 + 180			0.69		
0 + 200			1.37		
TP 2	0.033			1.705	
BM S. 102				2.891	

2.11 Reduce the following set of municipal cross-section notes.

Station	BS (ft)	HI (ft)	IS (ft)	FS (ft)	Elevation (ft)
BM 41	6.21				314.88
TP 13	4.10			0.89	
12 + 00					
50 ft left			3.9		
18.3 ft left			4.6		
₵			6.33		
20.1 ft right			7.9		
50 ft right			8.2		
13 + 00					
50 ft left			5.0		
19.6 ft left			5.7		
₵			7.54		
20.7 ft right			7.9		
50 ft right			8.4		
TP 14	7.39			1.12	
BM S.22				2.41	

2.12 Complete the accompanying set of highway cross-section notes.

Station	BS (ft)	HI (ft)	FS (ft)	Elevation (ft)	Left		₵	Right	
BM 107	7.71			232.66					
80 + 50					60'	28'		32'	60'
					9.7	8.0	5.7	4.3	4.0
81 + 00					60'	25'		30'	60'
					10.1	9.7	6.8	6.0	5.3
81 + 50					60'	27'		33'	60'
					11.7	11.0	9.2	8.3	8.0
TP 1			10.17						

2.13 A level is set up midway between two wood stakes that are about 300 ft apart. The rod reading on stake A is 8.72 ft and it is 5.61 ft on stake B. The level is then moved to point B and set up so that the eyepiece end of the telescope is just touching the rod as it is held plumb on the stake. A reading of 5.42 ft is taken on the rod at B by sighting backward through the telescope. The level is then sighted on the rod held on stake A, where a reading of 8.57 ft is noted.

  (a) What is the correct difference in elevation between the tops of stakes A and B?

  (b) If the level had been in perfect adjustment, what reading would have been observed at A from the second setup?

  (c) What is the line-of-sight error in 300'?

  (d) Describe how you would eliminate the line-of-sight error from the telescope.

2.14 A preengineering baseline was run down a very steep hill (Figure 2.35). Rather than measure horizontally downhill with the steel tape, the surveyor measured the vertical angle with a theodolite and the slope distance with an EDM. The vertical angle was $-21°26'$, turned to a prism on a plumbed range pole 4.88 ft above the ground. The slope distance from the theodolite to the prism was 148.61 ft. The theodolite's optical center was 4.669 above the upper baseline station at 110 + 71.25.

  (a) If the elevation of the upper station is 324.28, what is the elevation of the lower station?

  (b) What is the chainage of the lower station?

2.15 You must establish the elevation of point B from point A (elevation 187.298 m). Points A and B are on opposite sides of a 12-lane highway. Reciprocal leveling is used, with the following results:

Setup at A side of highway:

  Rod reading on A = 0.673 m

  Rod readings on B = 2.416 and 2.418 m

FIGURE 2.35

Setup at B side of highway:

    Rod reading on B = 2.992 m

    Rod readings on A = 1.254 and 1.250 m

(a) What is the elevation of point B?

(b) What is the leveling error?

2.16 Reduce the following set of differential leveling notes and perform the arithmetic check.

Station	BS (m)	HI (m)	FS (m)	Elevation (m)
BM 130	0.702			168.657
TP 1	0.970		1.111	
TP 2	0.559		0.679	
TP 3	1.744		2.780	
BM K110	1.973		1.668	
TP 4	1.927		1.788	
BM 132			0.888	

(a) Determine the order of accuracy. Refer to Table 2.1 or 2.2.

(b) Adjust the elevation of BM K110. The length of the level run was 780 m, with setups equally spaced. The elevation of BM 132 is known to be 167.629 m.

Chapter 3

Distance Measurement

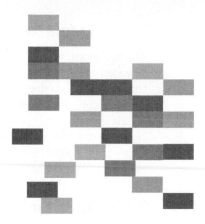

3.1 Methods of Linear Measurement

Historically, distances have been directly measured by applying an instrument of known length against the distance between two or more ground points. As noted in Appendix G, early (3000 B.C.) Egyptians used ropes for distance measurements, having knots tied at convenient points on the rope to aid in the measurement process. Much later, in the 1500s, Edmund Gunter (see next section) invented a 66-ft chain, comprised of 100 links. The Gunter's chain has significance for North American surveyors because it was that instrument that was originally used to lay out most of the continent's townships in the 1700s and 1800s. In the early 1900s, various types of reel-mounted tapes came into use; these tapes were made of cloth, copper wire-reinforced cloth, fiberglass, and steel; all precise measurements were made with steel tapes. In the second half of the twentieth century, EDM instruments came into wide use, especially as integrated components of total stations.

Examples of calculated measurements occur when the desired measurement (perhaps over water) is one side of a triangle whose other side(s) and angles have been measured, also, when the slope distance and slope angle have been measured between two points and the required horizontal distance is then calculated.

3.1.1 Pacing

Pacing is a useful method of approximate measure. Surveyors can determine the length of pace that, for them, can be comfortably repeated (for convenience, some surveyors use a 3-ft stride). Pacing is particularly useful when looking for survey markers in the field. The plan distance from a found marker to another marker can be paced off to aid in locating that marker. Another important use for pacing is for a rough check of all key points in construction layouts.

3.1.2 Odometer

Automobile odometer readings can be used to measure from one fence line to another when they intersect the road right-of-way. These readings are precise enough to differentiate rural fence lines and can thus assist in identifying platted property lines. This information is useful when collecting information to begin a survey. Odometers are also used on measuring wheels that are simply rolled along the ground on the desired route; this approximate technique is employed where low-order precision is acceptable. For example, surveyors from the assessor's office often check property frontages this way, and police officers sometimes use this technique when preparing sketches of automobile accident scenes.

3.1.3 Electronic Distance Measurement

Most EDM instruments function by sending a light wave along the path to be measured from the instrument station, and then the instrument measures the phase differences between the transmitted light wave and the light wave as it is reflected back to its source from a reflecting prism at the second point. Pulse laser EDMs operate by measuring the time for a laser pulse to be transmitted to a reflector and then returned to the EDM; with the velocity of light programmed into the EDM, the distance to the reflector and back is quickly determined.

3.1.4 Distances Derived from the Analysis of Position Coordinates

Spatial point positioning can be determined by using satellite-positioning techniques, and by using various scanning techniques (from satellite, aerial, and ground platforms). Once the spatial coordinates of ground points are known, it is a simple matter, using trigonometric relationships, to compute the horizontal distances (and directions) between them. Also, when the ground coordinates of a key survey point marker are known, the surveyor can use a satellite-positioning receiver to navigate to, and thus locate the marker on the ground (which may be buried).

3.1.5 Subtense Bar

A subtense bar is a tripod-mounted bar with targets set precisely 2 m apart. The targets are kept precisely 2 m apart by the use of invar wires under slight tension. The subtense bar is positioned over the point and then positioned perpendicular to the survey line. A theodolite (1-second capability) is used to measure the angle between the targets. The farther the subtense bar is from the theodolite, the smaller will be the angle subtending the 2-m bar. Because trigonometric functions (tangent) of small angles become less reliable as the angle decreases, the longer the distance, the smaller the angle, and the less precise will be the solution. This technique is accurate (1/5,000) at short distances, that is, less than 500 ft. This instrument was used to obtain distances over difficult terrain, for example, across freeways, water, or steep slopes. See Figure 3.1. Field use of this instrument has declined with the widespread use of EDM instruments. Subtense bars have recently been used in calibrating baselines in electronic coordinate determination: a technique of precise positioning using two or more electronic theodolites interfaced to a computer. This technique has been used, for example, to position robotic welding machines on automobile assembly lines.

Distance AB = Cot $\frac{\alpha}{2}$ m

FIGURE 3.1 Subtense bar.

3.2 Gunter's Chain

The measuring device in popular use during settlement of North America (eighteenth and nineteenth centuries) was the Gunter's chain; it was 66-ft long and subdivided into 100 links. It has more than historical interest to surveyors because many property descriptions still on file include dimensions in chains and links. This chain, named after its inventor (Edmund Gunter, 1581–1626), was uniquely suited for work in English units:

$$1 \text{ chain} = 100 \text{ links}$$
$$1 \text{ rod} = 25 \text{ links}$$
$$4 \text{ rods} = 1 \text{ chain}$$
$$80 \text{ chains} = 1 \text{ mile}$$
$$10 \text{ sq chains} = 1 \text{ acre } (10 \times 66^2 = 43{,}560 \text{ sq. ft})$$

Because Gunter's chains were used in many of the original surveys of North America, most of the continent's early legal plans and records contain dimensions in chains and links. Present-day surveyors occasionally must use these old plans and must make conversions to feet or meters.

■ EXAMPLE 3.1

An old plan shows a dimension of 5 chains, 32 links. Convert this value to (a) feet and (b) meters.

Solution

(a) $5.32 \times 66 = 351.12$ ft

(b) $5.32 \times 66 \times 0.3048 = 107.02$ m

3.3 Tapes

Woven tapes made of linen, Dacron, and the like can have fine copper strands interwoven to provide strength and to limit deformation due to long use and moisture. See Figure 3.2. Measurements taken near electric stations should be made with dry nonmetallic or fiberglass tapes. Fiberglass tapes have now come into widespread use.

	(a)		(b)

Graduated in 10ths and Metric

| 7 | 8 | 9 | 1|F | 1 |

| 0·2 | ▲ | 0·3 |

Printed on two sides—one side in 10ths and 100ths
of a foot; the second side in metric with increments
in meters, cm, and 2 mm.

Graduated in 8ths and Metric

| 8 | 9 | 1|0 | 1|1 | 1|F | 1 |

| 0·2 | ▲ | 0·3 |

Printed on two sides—one side in feet, inches, and
8ths; the second side in metric with increments in
meters, cm, and 2 mm.

(c)

FIGURE 3.2 Fiberglass tapes. (a) Closed case; (b) open reel; (c) tape graduations. (Courtesy of CST/Berger, Illinois)

All tapes come in various lengths, the 100-ft and 30-m tapes being the most popular, and are used for many types of measurements where high precision is not required. All woven tapes should be checked periodically (e.g., against a steel tape) to verify their precision.

Many tapes are now manufactured with foot units on one side and metric units on the reverse side. Foot-unit tapes are graduated in feet, 0.10 ft, and 0.05 ft or in feet, inches, and ¼ inches. Metric tapes are graduated in meters, centimeters (0.01 m), and ½ centimeters (0.005 m).

3.4   Steel Tapes

3.4.1   General Background

Not so many years ago, most precise measurements were made using steel tapes. Although EDM is now favored because of its high precision and the quickness of repeated measurements, even over rough ground and very long distances, there are some drawbacks when EDM is used for single distances, particularly in the short-distance situations that regularly crop up in engineering applications. The problems with EDM in short-distance situations are twofold: (1) the time involved in setting up the EDM and the prism, and (2) the unreliable accuracies in some short-distance situations. For example, if a single-check distance is required in a construction layout, and if the distance is short (especially distances less than one tape-length), it is much quicker to obtain the distance through taping. Also, because most EDMs now have stated accuracies in the range of $\pm$(5 mm + 5 ppm) to $\pm$(2 mm + 2 ppm), the 5-mm to 2-mm errors occur regardless of the length of distance measured. These errors have little impact on long distances but can severely impact the measurement of short distances. For example, at a distance of 10.000 m, an error of 0.005 m limits accuracy to 1:2,000. The opportunity for additional errors can occur when centering the EDM instrument over the point (e.g., an additional 0.001–0.002 m for well-adjusted laser plummets), and when centering the prism over the target point, either by using tribrach-mounted prisms or by using prism-pole assemblies. The errors here can range from 2 mm for well-adjusted optical/laser plummets to several millimeters for well-adjusted prism-pole circular bubble levels. When laser or optical plummets are poorly adjusted and/or when prism-pole levels are poorly adjusted, serious errors can occur in distance measurements—errors that do diminish in relative severity as the distances measured increase. For these reasons, the steel tape remains a valuable tool for the engineering surveyor.

Steel tapes (Figure 3.3) are manufactured in both foot and metric units and come in a variety of lengths, graduations, and unit weights. Commonly used foot-unit tapes are of 100-, 200-, and 300-ft lengths, with the 100-ft length being the most widely used. Commonly used metric-unit tapes are of 20-, 30-, 50-, and 100-m lengths. The 30-m length is the most widely used because it closely resembles the 100-ft length tape in field characteristics.

Generally, lightweight tapes are graduated throughout and are used on the reel; heavier tapes are designed for use off the reel (drag tapes) and do not have continuous small-interval markings. Drag tapes are popular in route surveys (highways, railways, etc.), whereas lightweight tapes are more popular in building and municipal works.

FIGURE 3.3   Steel tape and plumb bob.

Invar tapes are composed of 35 percent nickel and 65 percent steel. This alloy has a very low coefficient of thermal expansion, which made this tape useful for pre-EDM precise distance measurement. Steel tapes are occasionally referred to as chains, a throwback to early surveying practice.

3.4.2 Types of Readouts

Steel tapes are normally graduated in one of three ways; consider a distance of 38.82 ft (m):

1. The tape is graduated throughout in feet and hundredths (0.01) of a foot, or in meters and millimeters (see Figures 3.3 and 3.4). The distance (38.82 ft) is read directly from the steel tape.

2. The cut tape is marked throughout in feet, with the first and last foot graduated in tenths and hundredths of a foot [Figure 3.4(a)]. The metric cut tape is marked throughout in meters and decimeters, with the first and last decimeters graduated in millimeters. A measurement is made with the cut tape by one surveyor holding the even-foot mark (39 ft in this example). This arrangement allows the other surveyor to read a distance on the first foot (decimeter), which is graduated in hundredths of a foot (millimeters). For example, the distance from A to B in Figure 3.4(a) is determined by holding 39 ft at B and reading 0.18 ft at A. Distance AB = 38.82 ft (i.e., 39 ft cut 0.18). Because each measurement involves this type of mental subtraction, care and attention are required from the surveyor to avoid unwelcome blunders.

3. The add tape is also marked throughout in feet, with the last foot graduated in hundredths of a foot. An additional foot, graduated in hundredths, is included prior to the zero mark. For metric tapes, the last decimeter and the extra before-the-zero

(a)

(b)

(c)

FIGURE 3.4 Various steel tape markings (hundredth marks not shown). (a) Fully graduated tape; (b) cut tape; (c) add tape.

decimeter are graduated in millimeters. The distance AB in Figure 3.4(b) is determined by holding 38 ft at B and reading 0.82 ft at A. Distance AB is 38.82 ft (i.e., 38 ft add 0.82).

As noted, cut tapes have the disadvantage of creating opportunities for subtraction mistakes; the add tapes have the disadvantage of forcing the surveyor to adopt awkward measuring stances when measuring from the zero mark. The full meter add tape is the most difficult to use correctly because the surveyor must fully extend his or her left (right) arm (which is holding the end of the tape) to position the zero mark on the tape over the ground point. The problems associated with both add and cut tapes can be eliminated if, instead, the surveyor uses tapes graduated throughout. These tapes are available in both drag- and reel-type tapes.

3.5 Taping Accessories and Their Use

3.5.1 Plumb Bob

Plumb bobs are normally made of brass and weigh from 8 to 18 oz, with 10 and 12 oz being the most common. Plumb bobs are used in taping to transfer from tape to ground (or vice versa) when the tape is being held off the ground to maintain its horizontal alignment. Plumb bobs (and their strings) are also used routinely to provide theodolite or total station sightings. See Figures 3.5 and 3.9.

3.5.2 Hand Level

The hand level (Figure 3.6) can be used to keep the steel tape horizontal when measuring. The surveyor at the lower elevation holds the hand level, and a sight is taken back at the higher-elevation surveyor. For example, if the surveyor with the hand level is sighting with the instrument cross hair horizontally on his or her partner's waist, and if both are roughly the same height, then the surveyor with the hand level is lower by the distance from eye to waist. The low end of the tape is held that distance off the ground (using a plumb bob), the high end of the tape being held on the mark.

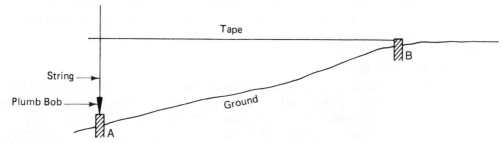

FIGURE 3.5 Use of a plumb bob.

(a)

Ground

(b)

FIGURE 3.6 (a) Hand level.
(Courtesy of CST/Berger, Illinois)
(b) Hand-level application.

Figure 3.7(a) shows an Abney hand level (clinometer). In addition to the level bubble and cross hair found on the standard hand level, the clinometer can take vertical angles (to the closest 10 minutes). The clinometer is used mainly to record vertical angles for slope distance reduction to horizontal or to determine the heights of objects. These two applications are illustrated in Examples 3.2 and 3.3.

■ EXAMPLE 3.2

For height determination, a value of 45° is placed on the scale. The surveyor moves back and forth until the point to be measured is sighted [e.g., the top of the building shown in Figure 3.7(b)]. The distance from the observer to the surveyor at the base of the building is measured with a fiberglass tape. The hand level can be set to zero to determine where the surveyor's eye height intersects the building wall. The partial height of the building (h_1) is equal to this measured distance (i.e., h_1/measured distance = tan 45° = 1). If the distance h_2 [eye height mark above the ground; Figure 3.7(b)] is now added to the measured distance, the height of the building (in this example) is found. In addition to determining the heights of buildings, this technique is particularly useful in determining the heights of electric power lines for highway construction clearances. In Figure 3.7(b), if the measured distance to the second surveyor at the building is 63.75 ft, and if the horizontal line of sight hits the building (the clinometer scale is set to zero for horizontal sights) at 5.55 ft (h_2), the height of the building is 63.75 + 5.55 = 69.30 ft.

■ EXAMPLE 3.3

The clinometer is useful when working on route surveys for which extended-length tapes (300 ft or 100 m) are being used. The long tape can be used in slope position under proper tension. (Because the tape will be touching the ground in many places, it will be mostly supported, and the tension required will not be too high.) The clinometer can be used to measure the slope angle for each tape measurement. These

Chap. 3   Distance Measurement

FIGURE 3.7   (a) Abney hand level; scale graduated in degrees with a vernier reading to 10 minutes. (Courtesy of CST/Berger, Illinois) (b) Abney hand-level application in height determination. (c) Abney hand-level typical application in taping.

slope angles and related slope distances can be used later to compute the appropriate horizontal distances. The angles, measured distances, and computed distances for a field survey are summarized in Figure 3.7(c).

3.5.3   Additional Taping Accessories

Range poles are 6-ft wooden or aluminum poles with steel points. The poles are usually painted red and white in alternate 1-ft sections. Range poles [Figure 3.8(a)] are used in taping and theodolite work to provide alignment sights. The clamp handle [Figure 3.8(b)]

(a)   (b)   (c)

FIGURE 3.8   Taping accessories. (a) Two-section range pole; (b) tape clamp handle; (c) tension handle.

helps grip the tape at any intermediate point without bending or distorting the tape. Tension handles [Figure 3.8(c)] are used in precise work to ensure that the appropriate tension is being applied. They are graduated to 30 lb, in $1/2$-lb graduations (50 N = 1.24 lb).

Chaining pins (marking arrows) come in sets of eleven. They are painted alternately red and white and are 14–18 in. long. Chaining pins are used to mark intermediate points on the ground; the pin is pushed into the ground at an angle of 45° to the ground and at 90° to the direction of the measurement (to keep the tape clear of the measuring process). In route surveying, the whole set of pins is used to mark out the centerline. The rear surveyor is responsible for checking the number of whole tape lengths by keeping an accurate count of the pins collected. Eleven pins are used to measure out 1,000 ft.

Tape repair kits are available so that broken tapes can be put back into service quickly. The repair kits come in three main varieties: (1) punch pliers and repair eyelets, (2) steel punch block and rivets, and (3) tape repair sleeves. The second technique (punch block) is the only method that gives lasting repair; although the technique is simple, great care must be exercised to ensure that the integrity of the tape is maintained.

Plumb bob targets are also used to provide alignment sights (Figure 3.9). The plumb bob string is threaded through the upper and lower notches so that the target centerline is superimposed on the plumb bob string. The target, which can be adjusted up and down the string for optimal sightings, is preferred to the range pole because of its portability—it fits in the surveyor's pocket.

FIGURE 3.9 Plumb bob cord target used to provide an instrument sighting.

3.6 Taping Techniques

Taping is normally performed with the tape held horizontally. If the distance to be measured is across smooth, level land, the tape can simply be laid on the ground and the end mark lined up against the initial survey marker; the tape is properly aligned and tensioned, and then the zero mark on the tape can be marked on the ground. If the distance between two marked points is to be measured, the tape is read as already described in Section 3.4.2.

If the distance to be measured is across sloping or uneven land, at least one end of the tape must be raised up from the ground to keep the tape horizontal. The raised end of the tape is referenced back to the ground mark with the aid of a plumb bob (Figure 3.10). Normally the only time that both ends of the tape are plumbed is when the ground—or other obstruction—rises between the marks being measured (Figure 3.11).

3.6.1 Measuring Procedures

The measurement begins with the head surveyor carrying the zero end of the tape forward toward the final point. He or she continues walking until the tape has been unwound and the rear surveyor calls, "Tape," thus alerting the head surveyor to stop walking and to

FIGURE 3.10 Horizontal taping; plumb bob used at one end.

FIGURE 3.11 Horizontal taping; plumb bob used at both ends.

prepare for measuring. If a drag tape is being used, the tape is removed from the reel and a leather thong is attached to the reel end of the tape (the zero end is already equipped with a leather thong). If the tape is not designed to come off the reel, the winding handle is folded to the lock position so that the reel can be used to help hold the tape. The rear surveyor can keep the head surveyor on line by sighting a range pole or other target that has been erected at the final mark. In precise work, these intermediate marks can be aligned by theodolite.

The rear surveyor holds the appropriate graduation against the mark from which the measurement is being taken. The head surveyor, after ensuring that the tape is straight, slowly increases tension to the proper amount and then marks the ground with a chaining pin or other marker. Once the mark has been made, both surveyors repeat the measuring procedure to check the measurement. If necessary, corrections are made and the check procedure is repeated.

If the ground is not horizontal (determined by estimation or by use of a hand level), one or both surveyors must use a plumb bob. While plumbing, the tape is often held at waist height, although any height between the shoulders and the ground is common. Holding the tape above the shoulders creates more chance for error because the surveyor must move his or her eyes up and down to include both the ground mark and the tape

Chap. 3   Distance Measurement

graduation in his or her field of view. When the surveyor's eyes are on the tape, the plumb bob may move off the mark, and when his or her eyes are on the ground mark, the plumb bob string may move off the correct tape graduation.

The plumb bob string is usually held on the tape with the left thumb (for right-handed people); take care not to cover the graduation mark completely because, as the tension is increased, it is not unusual for the surveyor to take up some of the tension with the left thumb, causing the thumb to slide along the tape. If the graduations have been covered completely with the left thumb, the surveyor is not aware that the thumb (and thus the string) has moved, resulting in an erroneous measurement. When plumbing, hold the tape close to the body to provide good leverage for applying or holding tension, and to transfer accurately from tape to ground, and vice versa. If the rear surveyor is using a plumb bob, he or she shouts out "Mark," or some other word indicating that at that instant in time, the plumb bob is right over the mark. If the head surveyor is also using a plumb bob, he or she must wait until both plumb bobs are simultaneously over their respective marks.

You will discover that plumbing and marking are difficult aspects of taping. You may find it difficult to hold the plumb bob steady over the point and at the same time apply the appropriate tension. To help steady the plumb bob, hold it only a short distance above the mark and continually touch down to the point. This momentary touching down dampens the plumb bob oscillations and generally steadies the plumb bob. Do not allow the plumb bob point to rest on the ground or other surface because you could obtain an erroneous measurement.

3.6.2 Breaking Tape

A slope is sometimes too steep to permit an entire tape length to be held horizontal. When this occurs, shorter measurements are taken, each with the tape held horizontal; these shorter measurements are then totaled to provide the overall dimension. This technique, called breaking tape, must be done with greater care because the extra marking and measuring operations provide that many more opportunities for the occurrence of random errors—errors associated with marking and plumbing. There are two common methods of breaking tape. First, the head surveyor takes the zero end forward one tape length and then walks back to a point where he or she can hold the tape horizontal with the rear surveyor; if working downhill, the tape can be held at shoulder height. With a plumb bob, the ground can be marked at an even foot or meter graduation (say, 80 ft or 25 m). The rear surveyor then comes forward and holds that same graduation on the ground mark while the head surveyor moves forward to the next pre-selected tape graduation, which is also to be held at shoulder height (say, 30 ft or 10 m). This procedure is repeated until the head surveyor can hold the zero graduation and thus complete one full tape length. In the second method of breaking tape, the head surveyor can proceed forward only until his or her shoulders are horizontal with the rear surveyor's knees or feet and can then mark the zero end on the ground. The rear surveyor, who is probably holding an even foot or meter right on the mark, calls out that value, which is then recorded. This process is repeated until the whole distance has been measured and all the intermediate measurements are totaled for the final answer. See Figure 3.12, which shows the distance AB, comprising the increments AL, LM, and MB.

FIGURE 3.12 Breaking tape.

3.6.3   Taping Summary

The rear surveyor follows these steps when taping:

1. Aligns the head surveyor by sighting to a range pole or other target, which is placed at the forward station.
2. Holds the tape on the mark, either directly or with the aid of a plumb bob. He or she calls out "Mark," or some other word to signal that the tape graduation—or the plumb bob point marking the tape graduation—is momentarily on the mark.
3. Calls out the station and tape reading for each measurement and listens for verification from the head surveyor.
4. Keeps a count of all full tape lengths included in each overall measurement.
5. Maintains the equipment (e.g., wipes the tape clean at the conclusion of the day's work or as conditions warrant).

The head surveyor follows these steps during taping:

1. Carries the tape forward, ensuring that the tape is free of loops, which can lead to kinks and tape breakage.
2. Prepares the ground surface for the mark (e.g., clears away grass, leaves, etc.).
3. Applies proper tension after first ensuring that the tape is straight.
4. Places marks (e.g., chaining pins, wood stakes, iron bars, nails, rivets, cut crosses).
5. Takes and records measurements of distances and other factors (e.g., temperature).
6. Supervises the taping work.

3.7   Taping Corrections

3.7.1   General Background

As noted in Section 1.12, no measurements can be perfectly performed; thus, all measurements (except for counting) must contain some errors. Surveyors must use measuring techniques that minimize random errors to acceptable levels and they must make corrections to systematic errors that can affect the accuracy of the survey. Typical taping errors are summarized below:

Systematic Taping Errors[*]	Random Taping Errors[†]
1. Slope	1. Slope
2. Erroneous length	2. Temperature
3. Temperature	3. Tension and sag
4. Tension and sag	4. Alignment
	5. Marking and plumbing
[*]See Section 3.8.	[†]See Section 3.9.

3.7.2   Standard Conditions for the Use of Steel Tapes

Tape manufacturers, noting that steel tapes behave differently in various temperature, tension, and support situations, specify the accuracy of their tapes under the following standard conditions:

Foot System	Metric System
1. Temperature = 68°F	1. Temperature = 20°C
2. Tape fully supported throughout	2. Tape fully supported throughout
3. Tape under a tension of 10 lb	3. Tape under a tension of 50 N (Newtons)
	(a 1 lb force = 4.448 N, so 50 N = 11.24 lbs)

Field conditions usually dictate that some or all of the above standard conditions cannot be met. The temperature is seldom exactly 68°F (20°C), and because many measurements are taken on a slope, the condition of full support is also not regularly fulfilled when one end of the tape is held off the ground, to keep it horizontal, and plumbed.

3.8   Systematic Taping Errors and Corrections

The previous section outlined the standard conditions for a steel tape to give precise results. The standard conditions referred to a specific temperature and tension and to a condition of full support. In addition, the surveyor must be concerned with horizontal versus slope distances and with ensuring that the actual taping techniques are sufficiently precise to provide the desired accuracy. Systematic errors in taping are slope, erroneous length, temperature, tension, and sag. The effects of slope and tension/sag on field measurements are discussed in the next section; the techniques for computing corrections for errors in erroneous length, temperature, tension, and sag are discussed in Appendix F.

3.8.1   Slope Corrections

Survey distances can be measured either horizontally or on a slope. Survey measurements are usually shown on a plan; if they are taken on a slope, they must then be converted to horizontal distances (plan distances) before they can be plotted. To convert slope distances to their horizontal equivalents, the surveyor must know the slope angle (θ), the zenith angle ($90 - \theta$), or the vertical distance (V):

$$\frac{H \text{ (horizontal)}}{S \text{ (slope)}} = \cos \theta \qquad (3.1)$$

Equation 3.1 can also be written as follows:

$$\frac{H}{S} = \sin (90 - \theta) \quad \text{or} \quad H = S \sin (90 - \theta)$$

where θ is the angle of inclination and ($90 - \theta$) is the zenith angle.

$$H = \sqrt{S^2 - V^2} \qquad (3.2)$$

where V is the difference in elevation. See Example 3.4, part (c).

Slope can also be defined as gradient, or rate of grade. The gradient is expressed as a ratio of the vertical distance over the horizontal distance; this ratio, when multiplied by 100, gives a percentage gradient. For example, if the ground rises 2 ft (m) in 100 ft (m), it is said to have a 2-percent gradient (i.e., $2/100 \times 100 = 2$). If the ground rises 2 ft (m) in 115 ft (m), it is said to have a 1.74-percent gradient (i.e., $2/115 \times 100 = 1.739$).

If the elevation of a point on a gradient is known (Figure 3.13), the elevation of any other point on that gradient can be calculated as follows:

$$\text{Difference in elevation} = 150 \times \left(\frac{2.5}{100}\right) = -3.75$$
$$\text{Elevation at } 1 + 50 = 564.22 - 3.75 = 560.47 \text{ ft}$$

If the elevations of two points, as well as the distance between them (Figure 3.14), are known, the gradient between can be calculated as follows:

$$\text{Elevation difference} = 5.40$$
$$\text{Distance} = 337.25$$
$$\text{Gradient} = \frac{5.40}{337.25} \times 100 = +1.60\%$$

Station	Elevation
0 + 00	564.22 ft
(Gradient = −2.5%)	
1 + 50	Required

FIGURE 3.13 Computation of the elevation of station 1 + 50.

Station	Elevation
1 + 00	471.37
4 + 37.25	476.77

FIGURE 3.14 Gradient computation.

FIGURE 3.15 Horizontal distance computation.

■ **EXAMPLE 3.4** *Slope Corrections*

(a) Given the slope distance (S) and slope angle θ, use Equation 3.1 and Figure 3.15 to find the horizontal distance (H):

$$\frac{H}{S} = \cos\theta$$

$$H = S\cos\theta$$
$$= 141.216 \cos 1°20'$$
$$= 41.178 \text{ m}$$

(b) Given the slope distance (S) and the gradient (slope), find the horizontal distance. See Figures 3.16 and 3.17. First, find the vertical angle (θ).

$$\frac{1.50}{100} = \tan\theta$$
$$\theta = 0.85937°$$

Second, use Equation 3.1 to determine the horizontal distance (H).

$$\frac{H}{113.281} = \cos 0.85937°$$
$$H = 113.268 \text{ m}$$

FIGURE 3.16 Slope angle determination.

FIGURE 3.17 Horizontal distance computation.

FIGURE 3.18 Horizontal distance computation (metric).

FIGURE 3.19 Horizontal distance computation (foot units).

(c) Metric units: Given the slope distance (S) and difference in elevation (V), use Equation 3.2 and Figure 3.18 to find the horizontal distance (H).

$$H = \sqrt{S^2 - V^2}$$
$$= \sqrt{(253.101^2 - 3.721^2)}$$
$$= 253.074 \text{ m}$$

Foot units: Given the slope distance (S) and the difference in elevation (V), use Equation 3.2 and Figure 3.19 to find the horizontal distance (H).

$$H = \sqrt{(99.82^2 - 1.6^2)}$$
$$= 99.807 \text{ ft}$$
$$= 99.8 \text{ ft}$$

3.8.2 Tension/Sag

The error in measurement due to sag can sometimes be eliminated by increasing the applied tension. Tension that eliminates sag errors is known as **normal tension**. Normal tension ranges from about 19 lb (light 100-ft tapes) to 31 lb (heavy 100-ft tapes).

$$P_n = \frac{0.204 \, W \sqrt{AE}}{\sqrt{P_n - P_s}} \tag{3.3}$$

This formula gives a value for P_n that eliminates the error caused by sag. The formula is solved by making successive approximations for P_n until the equation is satisfied. This formula is not used often because of the difficulties in determining the individual tape characteristics. See Table F.1 for the units employed in the tension and sag correction formulas found in Appendix F.

■ **EXAMPLE 3.5** *Experiment to Determine Normal Tension*

Normal tension can be determined experimentally for individual tapes, as shown in the following procedure:

1. Lay the tape flat on a horizontal surface; an indoor corridor is ideal.
2. Select (or mark) a well-defined point on the surface at which the 100-ft mark is held.
3. Attach a tension handle at the zero end of the tape. Apply standard tension—say, 10 lb—and mark the surface at 0.00 ft.
4. Repeat the process, switching personnel duties and ensuring that the two marks are, in fact, exactly 100.00 ft apart.

5. Raise the tape off the surface to a comfortable height (waist). While the surveyor at the 100-ft end holds a plumb bob over the point, the surveyor at the zero end slowly increases tension until his or her plumb bob is also over the mark. The tension read from the tension handle will be normal tension for that tape. The readings are repeated several times, and the average results are used for subsequent field work.

The most popular steel tapes (100 ft) now in use require a normal tension of about 24 lb. For most 30-m steel tapes now in use (lightweight), a normal tension of 90 N (20 lb) is appropriate. For structural and bridge surveys, very lightweight 200-ft tapes are available and can be used with a comfortable normal tension—in some cases, about 28 lb.

3.9 Random Taping Errors

Random errors occur because surveyors cannot measure perfectly. A factor of estimation is always present in all measuring activities (except counting). In the previous section, various systematic errors were discussed; in each of the areas discussed, there was also the opportunity for random errors to occur. For example, the temperature problems all require the determination of temperature. If the temperature used is the estimated air temperature, a random error could be associated with the estimation. The temperature of the tape can also be significantly different from that of the air. In the case of sag and tension, random errors can exist when one is estimating applied tension or even estimating between graduations on a spring balance. The higher the precision requirements, the greater must be the care taken in all aspects of the survey.

In addition to the above-mentioned random errors are perhaps more significant random errors associated with alignment, plumbing, marking, and estimating horizontal positions. Alignment errors occur when the tape is inadvertently aligned off the true path (Figure 3.20). Usually a rear surveyor can keep the head surveyor on line by sighting a range pole marking the terminal point. It would take an alignment error of about $1^1/_2$ ft to produce an error of 0.01 ft in 100 ft. Because it is not difficult to keep the tape aligned by eye to within a few tenths of a foot (0.2–0.3 ft), alignment is not normally a major concern. Note that, although most random errors are compensating, alignment errors are cumulative (misalignment can randomly occur on the left or on the right, but in both cases, the result of the misalignment is to make the measurement too long). Alignment errors can be nearly eliminated on precise surveys by using a theodolite to align all intermediate points.

Marking and plumbing errors are often the most significant of all random taping errors. Even experienced surveyors must exercise great care to place a plumbed mark

FIGURE 3.20 Alignment errors.

accurately within 0.02 ft of true value—in a distance of 100 ft. Horizontal measurements, taken with the tape fully supported on the ground, can be determined more accurately than measurements that are taken on a slope and require the use of plumb bobs. Also rugged terrain conditions that require many breaks in the taping process will cause marking and plumbing errors to multiply significantly.

Errors are also introduced when surveyors estimate a horizontal tape position for a plumbed measurement. The effect of this error is identical to that of the alignment error previously discussed, although the magnitude of these errors is often larger than alignment errors. Skilled surveyors can usually estimate a horizontal position to within 1 ft (0.3 m) over a distance of 100 ft (30 m). Even experienced surveyors can be seriously in error, however, when measuring across side-hills, where one's perspective with respect to the horizon can be distorted. Using a hand level can largely eliminate these errors.

3.10 Techniques for "Ordinary" Taping Precision

"Ordinary" taping has been referred to as taping at the level of 1/5,000 accuracy. The techniques used for "ordinary" taping, once mastered, can easily be maintained. It is possible to achieve an accuracy level of 1/5,000 with little more effort than is required to attain the 1/3,000 level. Because the bulk of all taping measurements is at either the 1/3,000 or the 1/5,000 level, experienced surveyors often use 1/5,000 techniques even for 1/3,000 level work. This practice permits good measuring work habits to be reinforced continually without appreciably increasing surveying costs. Because of the wide variety of field conditions that can be encountered, absolute specifications cannot be prescribed. The specifications in Table 3.1 can be considered typical for "ordinary" 1/5,000 taping.

To determine the total random error in one tape length, take the square root of the sum of the squares of the individual maximum anticipated errors, as shown in the following example:

Feet	Meters
0.005^2	0.0014^2
0.006^2	0.0018^2
0.005^2	0.0015^2
0.001^2	0.0004^2
0.015^2	0.0046^2
0.005^2	0.0015^2
0.000337	0.000031

Error = $\sqrt{(0.000337)}$ = 0.018 ft   or   Error = $\sqrt{(0.000031)}$ = 0.0056 m

Accuracy = 0.018/100 = 1/5,400   or   Accuracy = 0.0056/30 = 1/5,400

Table 3.1 SPECIFICATIONS FOR 1/5,000 ACCURACY

	Maximum Effect on One Tape Length	
Source of Error	100 ft	30 m
Temperature estimated to closest 7°F (4°C)	±0.005 ft	±0.0014 m
Care is taken to apply at least normal tension (lightweight tapes), and tension is known to within 5 lb (20 N)	±0.006 ft	±0.0018 m
Slope errors are no larger than 1 ft/100 ft (0.30 m/30 m)	±0.005 ft	±0.0015 m
Alignment errors are no larger than 0.5 ft/100 ft (0.15 m/30 m)	±0.001 ft	±0.0004 m
Plumbing and marking errors are at a maximum of 0.015 ft/100 ft (0.0046 m/30 m)	±0.015 ft	±0.0046 m
Length of tape is known to within ±0.005 ft (0.0015 m)	±0.005 ft	±0.0015 m

3.11 Mistakes in Taping

If errors can be associated with inexactness, mistakes must be thought of as being blunders. Whereas errors can be analyzed and to some degree predicted, mistakes are unpredictable. Just one undetected mistake can nullify the results of an entire survey; thus, it is essential to perform the work so that you minimize the opportunity for mistakes to occur and also allow for verification of the results.

Setting up and then rigorously following a standard method of performing the measurement minimizes the opportunities for the occurrence of mistakes. The more standardized and routine the measurement manipulations, the more likely it is that the surveyor will spot a mistake. The immediate double-checking of all measurements reduces the opportunities for mistakes to go undetected and at the same time increases the precision of the measurement. In addition to checking all measurements immediately, the surveyor is constantly looking for independent methods of verifying the survey results.

Gross mistakes can often be detected by comparing the survey results with distances scaled (or read) from existing plans. The simple check technique of pacing can be a valuable tool for rough verification of measured distances—especially construction layout distances. The possibilities for verification are limited only by the surveyor's diligence and imagination.

Common mistakes encountered in taping are the following:

1. Measuring to or from the wrong marker.
2. Reading the tape incorrectly or transposing figures (e.g., reading or recording 56 instead of 65).
3. Losing proper count of the number of full tape lengths involved in a measurement.
4. Recording the values incorrectly in the notes. Sometimes the note keeper hears the rear surveyor's callout correctly, but then transposes the figures when he or she enters it into the notes. This mistake can be eliminated if the note keeper calls out each value as it is recorded. The rear surveyor listens for these callouts to ensure that the numbers called out are the same as the data originally given.

5. Calling out figures ambiguously. The rear surveyor can call out 20.27 as "twenty (pause) two seven." This might be interpreted as 22.7. To avoid mistakes, this number should be called out as "twenty, decimal (or point), two, seven."

6. Not identifying correctly the zero point of the tape when a cloth or fiberglass tape is used. This mistake can be avoided if the surveyor checks unfamiliar tapes before use. The tape itself can be used to verify the zero mark.

7. Making arithmetic mistakes in sums of dimensions and in error corrections (e.g., temperature). These mistakes can be identified and corrected if each member of the crew is responsible for checking (and initialing) all computations.

3.12 Field Notes for Taping

Section 1.15 introduced field notes and stressed the importance of neatness, legibility, completeness, and clarity of presentation. Sample field notes will be included in this text for all typical surveying operations. Figures 3.21 and 3.22 represent typical field notes from taping surveys.

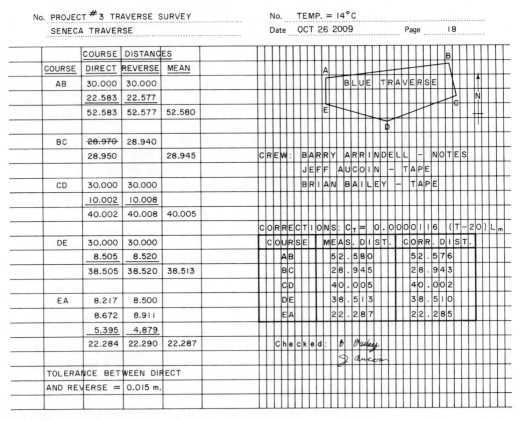

FIGURE 3.21 Taping field notes for a closed traverse.

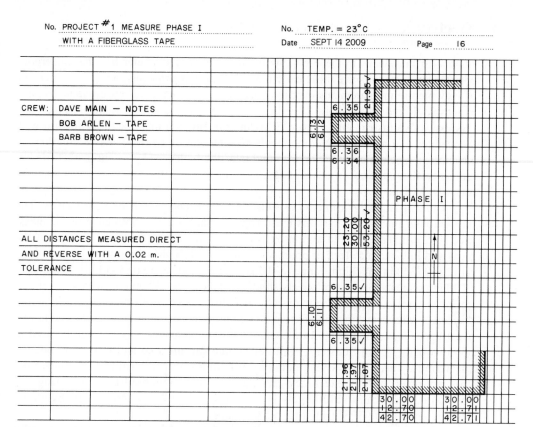

FIGURE 3.22 Taping field notes for building dimensions.

Figure 3.21 shows the taping notes for a traverse survey. The sides of the traverse have been measured forward and back, with the results being averaged (mean) if the discrepancy is within acceptable limits (0.015 in this example). Observe that the notes are clear and complete and generally satisfy the requirements listed in Section 1.15.

Figure 3.22 shows taping notes for a building dimension survey. In this example, the measurements are entered right on the sketch of the building. If the sketch has lines that are too short to show the appropriate measured distance, those distances can be entered neatly in an uncrowded portion of the sketch, with arrows joining the measurements to the correct lines on the sketch. In this example, the required building walls have been measured, with the results entered on the sketch. Each wall is remeasured, and if the result is identical to the first measurement, a check mark is placed beside that measurement; if the result varies, the new measurement is also entered beside the original. If the two measurements do not agree within the specified tolerance (0.02 m), the wall is measured again until the tolerance has been met. Compare the page of field notes in Figure 3.22 to the requirements listed in Section 1.15.

3.13 Electronic Distance Measurement

EDM, first introduced in the 1950s by the founders of Geodimeter Inc., has undergone continual refinement since those early days. The early instruments, which were capable of very precise measurements over long distances, were large, heavy, complicated, and expensive. Rapid advances in related technologies have provided lighter, simpler, and less expensive instruments. These EDM instruments are manufactured for use with theodolites and as modular components of total station instruments. Technological advances in electronics continue at a rapid rate—as evidenced by recent market surveys indicating that most new models of electronic instruments have been on the market for less than 2 years.

Current EDM instruments use infrared light, laser light, or microwaves. The once-popular microwave systems use a receiver/transmitter at both ends of the measured line, whereas infrared and laser systems utilize a transmitter at one end of the measured line and a reflecting prism at the other end. EDM instruments come in long range (10–20 km), medium range (3–10 km), and short range (0.5–3 km). Some laser EDM instruments measure relatively shorter distances (100–2,000 m) without a reflecting prism, reflecting the light directly off the feature (e.g., building wall) being measured. Microwave instruments were often used in hydrographic surveys and have a usual upper measuring range of 50 km. Although microwave systems can be used in poorer weather conditions (fog, rain, etc.) than can infrared and laser systems, the uncertainties caused by varying humidity conditions over the length of the measured line may result in lower accuracy expectations. Hydrographic EDM measuring and positioning techniques have largely been supplanted, in a few short years, by global positioning system (GPS) techniques (see Chapter 7).

EDM devices can be mounted on the standards or the telescope of most theodolites; they can also be mounted directly in a tribrach. When used with an electronic theodolite, the combined instruments can provide both the horizontal and the vertical position of one point relative to another. The slope distance provided by an add-on EDM device can be reduced to its horizontal and vertical equivalents by utilizing the slope angle provided by the theodolite. In total station instruments, this reduction is accomplished automatically.

3.14 Electronic Angle Measurement

The electronic digital theodolite, first introduced in the late 1960s by Carl Zeiss Inc., set the stage for modern field data collection and processing. (See Figure 4.7, which shows electronic angle measurement using a rotary encoder and photoelectric converters.) When the electronic theodolite is used with a built-in EDM device (e.g., Trimble 3300 series; Figure 3.23) or an add-on and interfaced EDM device (e.g., Wild T-1000; Figure 3.24), the surveyor has a very powerful instrument. Add to that instrument an onboard microprocessor that automatically monitors the instrument's operating status and manages built-in surveying programs, and a data collector (built-in or interfaced) that stores and processes

FIGURE 3.23 Trimble total station. The Trimble 3303 total stations incorporate DR technology (no prism required) and include the choice of the integrated Zeiss Elta control unit, detachable Geodimeter control unit or handheld TSCe data collector, and a wide range of software options. (Courtesy of Trimble Geomatics & Engineering Division, Dayton, Ohio)

FIGURE 3.24 Wild T-1000 electronic theodolite, shown with DI 1000 Distomat EDM and the GRE 3 data collector. (Courtesy of Leica Geosystems)

measurements and attribute data, and you have what is known as a total station. (Total stations are described in more detail in Chapters 4 and 5.)

3.15 Principles of EDM

Figure 3.25 shows a wave of wavelength λ. The wave is traveling along the x-axis with a velocity of 299,792.458 km/s (in vacuum). The frequency of the wave is the time taken for one complete wavelength:

$$\lambda = \frac{c}{f} \tag{3.4}$$

where λ = wavelength in meters
  c = velocity in km/s
  f = frequency in hertz (one cycle per second)

Figure 3.26 shows the modulated electromagnetic wave leaving the EDM device and being reflected (light waves) or retransmitted (microwaves) back to the EDM device. You can see that the double distance (2L) is equal to a whole number of wavelengths (nλ), plus the partial wavelength (φ) occurring at the EDM instrument:

$$L = \frac{(n\lambda + \phi)}{2} \text{ meters} \tag{3.5}$$

The partial wavelength (φ) is determined in the instrument by noting the phase delay required to match the transmitted and reflected or retransmitted waves precisely. Some instruments can count the number of full wavelengths (nλ) or, instead, the instrument can send out a series (three or four) of modulated waves at different frequencies. (The frequency is typically reduced each time by a factor of 10 and, of course, the wavelength is increased

FIGURE 3.25 Light wave.

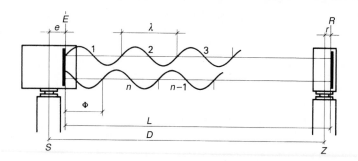

S Station
Z Target
E Reference plane within the distance
   meter for phase comparison
   between transmitted and received
   wave
R Reference plane for the reflection
   of the wave transmitted by the
   distance meter
a Addition constant
e Distance meter component of
   addition constant
r Reflector component of addition
   constant
λ Modulation wavelength
Φ Fraction to be measured of a whole
   wavelength of modulation ($\triangle \lambda$)

The addition constant *a* applies to
a measuring equipment consisting of a
distance meter and reflector. The
components *e* and *r* are only auxiliary
quantities.

FIGURE 3.26 Principles of
EDM measurement. (Courtesy
of Leica Geosystems)

each time also by a factor of 10.) By substituting the resulting values of λ and φ into
Equation 3.5, the value of *n* can be found. The instruments are designed to carry out this procedure in a matter of seconds and then to display the value of *L* in digital form.

The velocity of light (including infrared) through the atmosphere can be affected by
(1) temperature, (2) atmospheric pressure, and (3) water-vapor content. In practice, the
corrections for temperature and pressure can be performed manually by consulting
nomographs similar to that shown in Figure 3.27, or the corrections can be performed

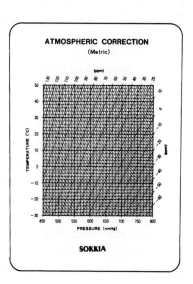

FIGURE 3.27 Atmospheric correction
graph. (Courtesy of SOKKIA Corp.)

Table 3.2 ATMOSPHERIC ERRORS

Parameter	Error	Error (Parts per Million)	
		Light Wave	Microwave
Temperature (t)	$+1°C$	-1.0	-1.25
Pressure (p)	$+1$ mm Hg	$+0.4$	$+0.4$
Partial water-vapor pressure (e)	1 mm Hg	-0.05	$+7$ at 20°C
			$+17$ at 45°C

automatically on some EDM devices by the onboard processor/calculator after the values for temperature and pressure have been entered.

For short distances using light-wave EDM, atmospheric corrections have a relatively small significance. For long distances using light-wave instruments and especially microwave instruments, atmospheric corrections can become quite important. Table 3.2 shows the comparative effects of the atmosphere on both light waves and microwaves.

At this point, it is also worth noting that several studies of general EDM use show that more than 90 percent of all distance determinations involve distances of 1,000 m or less and that more than 95 percent of all layout measurements involve distances of 400 m or less. The values in Table 3.2 seem to indicate that, for the type of measurements normally encountered in the construction and civil engineering fields, instrumental errors and centering errors hold much more significance than do atmosphere-related errors.

3.16 EDM Characteristics

Following are the typical characteristics of recent models of add-on EDM devices. Generally, the more expensive instruments have longer distance ranges and higher precision.

Distance range: 800 m–1 km (single prism with average atmospheric conditions).
Short-range EDM can be extended to 1,300 m using 3 prisms.
Long-range EDM can be extended to 15 km using 11 prisms (Leica Geosystems).
Accuracy range:
$\pm(5$ mm $+5$ ppm) for short-range EDM.
$\pm(2$ mm $+1$ ppm) for long-range EDM.
Measuring time: 1.5 s for short-range EDM to 3.5 s for long-range EDM.
(Both accuracy and time are considerably reduced for tracking mode measurements.)
Slope reduction: manual or automatic on some models.
Average of repeated measurements: available on some models.
Battery capability: 1,400–4,200 measurements, depending on the size and condition of the battery and the temperature.

Temperature range: –20°C to +50°C. (*Note*: In the northern United States and Canada, temperatures can easily drop below –20°C during the winter months.)

Nonprism measurements: available on some models; distances from 100 to 1,200 m (see Section 2.21).

3.17 Prisms

Prisms are used with electro-optical EDM (light, laser, and infrared) to reflect the transmitted signals (Figure 3.28). A single reflector is a cube corner prism that has the characteristic of reflecting light rays back precisely in the same direction as they are received. This retro-direct capability means that the prism can be somewhat misaligned with respect to the EDM instrument and still be effective. Cutting the corners off a solid glass cube forms a cube corner prism; the quality of the prism is determined by the flatness of the surfaces and the perpendicularity of the 90° surfaces. Prisms can be tribrach-mounted on a tripod, centered by optical or laser plummet, or attached to a prism pole held vertical on a point with the aid of a bull's-eye level. Prisms must be tribrach-mounted, however, if a higher level of accuracy is required.

In control surveys, tribrach-mounted prisms can be detached from their tribrachs and then interchanged with a theodolite/total station similarly mounted at the other end of the line being measured. This interchangeability of prism and theodolite/total station (also targets) speeds up the work because the tribrach mounted on the tripod is centered and leveled only once. Equipment that can be interchanged and mounted on tribrachs already set up is known as **forced-centering** equipment.

Prisms mounted on adjustable-length prism poles are portable and thus are particularly suited for stakeout and topographic surveys. Figure 3.29 shows the prism being steadied by the use of a bipod—instead of a single prism pole. It is particularly important that prisms mounted on poles or tribrachs be permitted to tilt up and down so that they can be perpendicular to short-distance signals that are being sent from much higher or lower positions.

FIGURE 3.28 Various target and reflector systems in tribrach mounts. (Courtesy of Topcon Positioning Systems, Inc.)

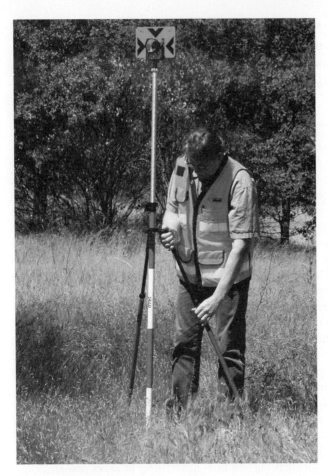

FIGURE 3.29 Steadying the EDM reflector by using a bipod. (Courtesy of SECO Manufacturing, Redding, CA. Photo by Eli Williem)

3.18 EDM Instrument Accuracies

EDM accuracies are stated in terms of a constant instrumental error and a measuring error proportional to the distance being measured. Typically, accuracy is claimed as ±(5 mm + 5 ppm) or ±(0.02 ft + 5 ppm). The 5 mm (0.02 ft) is the instrument error that is independent of the length of the measurement, whereas the 5 ppm (5 mm/km) denotes the distance-related error.

Most instruments now on the market have claimed accuracies in the range of ±(2 mm + 1 ppm) to ±(10 mm + 10 ppm). The proportional part error (ppm) is insignificant for most work, and the constant part of the error assumes less significance as the distances being measured lengthen. At 10 m, an error of 5 mm represents an accuracy of 1:2,000; at 100 m, an error of 5 mm represents an accuracy of 1/20,000. At 1,000 m, the same instrumental error represents an accuracy of 1/200,000.

When dealing with accuracy, note that both the EDM and the prism reflectors must be corrected for their off-center characteristics. The measurement being recorded goes from the electrical center of the EDM device to the back of the prism (allowing for

A ●————————————————————————— B ●————————————— C ●

FIGURE 3.30 Method of determining the instrument-reflector constant.

refraction through glass) and then back to the electrical center of the EDM device. The EDM device manufacturer at the factory compensates for the difference between the electrical center of the EDM device and the plumb line through the tribrach center. The prism constant (–30 to –40 mm) is eliminated either by the EDM device manufacturer at the factory or in the field.

The EDM/prism constant value can be field-checked in the following manner. A long line (>1 km) is laid out with end stations and an intermediate station (Figure 3.30). The overall distance AC is measured, along with partial lengths AB and BC. The constant value will be present in all measurements; therefore,

$$AC - AB - BC = \text{instrument/prism constant} \qquad (3.6)$$

the constant can also be determined by measuring a known baseline, if one can be conveniently accessed.

3.19 EDM Without Reflecting Prisms

Some EDM instruments (Figure 3.31) can measure distances without using reflecting prisms—the measuring surface itself is used as a reflector. Both phase-shift technology (Section 3.15) and time-of-flight technology (TOF), also known as pulsed lasers, can be used for reflectorless measurement. When the reflecting surface is uneven or not at right angles to the measuring beam, varying amounts of the light pulses are not returned to the instrument. When using longer-range pulsed-laser techniques, as many as 20,000 pulses per second are employed to ensure that sufficient data are received. The pulsing of this somewhat strong laser emission still results in a safety designation of Class I—the safest designation. The use of Class II, III, and IV lasers requires eye protection (see also Section 5.10). Another consideration is that various surfaces have different reflective properties; for example, a bright white surface at a right angle to the measuring beam may reflect almost 100 percent of the light, but most natural surfaces reflect light at a rate of only 18 percent (Table 3.3).

EDM instruments can be used conventionally with the reflecting prisms for distances up to 4 km; when used without prisms, the range drops to 100 up to 2,000 m, depending on the equipment, light conditions (cloudy days and night darkness provide better measuring distances), angle of reflection from the surface, and reflective properties of the measuring surface. With prisms, the available accuracy is about ±(1–3 mm + 1 ppm); without prisms, the available accuracy ranges from ±(3 mm + 3 ppm) up to about ±10 mm. Targets with light-colored and flat surfaces perpendicular to the measuring beam (e.g., building walls) provide the best ranges and accuracies. Because of the different reflective capabilities of various surfaces, comparison of different survey equipment must be made based on standard surfaces; the Kodak Gray Card has been chosen as such a standard. This card is gray on one side and white on the other. The white side reflects 90 percent of white light and gray side reflects 18 percent of white

(a)   (b)

FIGURE 3.31 Distance measurement without reflectors. (a) Wild T1010 electronic theodolite, together with an interfaced DIOR 3002S prismless EDM (angle accuracy is 3″). (b) Illustrations of two possible uses for this technique. Upper: tunnel cross sections. Lower: profiling a difficult-access feature. (Courtesy of Leica Geosystems)

Table 3.3 TRIMBLE DR RANGE TO VARIOUS TARGET SURFACES

Surface	Dr300+	Dr Standard
Kodak White Card, 90%	>800m (2,625 ft)	>240m (787 ft)
Kodak Gray Card, 18%	>300m (984 ft)	>120m (393 ft)
Concrete	>400m (1,312 ft)	>100m (328 ft)
Wood	>400m (1,312 ft)	>200m (656 ft)
Light rock	>300m (984 ft)	>150m (492 ft)
Dark rock	>200m (656 ft)	>80m (262 ft)

Source: From *Direct Reflex EDM Technology for the Surveyor and Civil Engineer*, R. Hoglund and P. Large, 2005, Trimble Survey, Westminister, Colorado, USA.

light. An EDM range to a Kodak Gray Card (18 percent reflective) is considered a good indicator of typical surveying capabilities.

EDM instruments also provide quick results (0.8 s in rapid mode and 0.3 s in tracking mode), which means that applications for moving targets are possible. Applications are expected for near-shore hydrographic surveying and in many areas of heavy construction. This technique is already being used, with an interfaced data collector, to measure cross sections automatically in mining applications—with plotted cross sections and excavated volumes automatically generated by digital plotter and computer. Other applications include cross-sectioning above-ground excavated works and material stockpiles; measuring to dangerous or difficult access points, for example, bridge components, cooling towers, and dam faces; and automatically measuring liquid surfaces, for example, municipal water reservoirs and catchment ponds. These new techniques may have some potential in indus-trial surveying, where production line rates require this type of monitoring.

EDM instruments can be used with an attached visible laser, which helps to identify positively the feature being measured; that is, the visible laser beam is set on the desired feature so that the surveyor can be sure that the correct surface, not some feature just beside or behind it, is being measured. Some instruments require the surveyor to measure to possibly conflicting objects (e.g., utility wires that may cross the line of sight closer to the instrument). In this situation, the surveyor first measures to the possibly conflicting wires and then directs the total station software only to show measurements beyond that range. Because the meas-urement is so fast, care must be taken not to measure mistakenly to an object that may tem-porarily intersect the measuring signal, for example, a truck or other traffic. See Section 5.10 for additional information on reflectorless distance measurement. Table 3.3 (the result of Trimble's research) shows ranges for reflectorless measurements using both TOF or pulsed-laser (DR300+) technology and phase-shift techniques (DR standard).

Problems

3.1 Answer the following statements T (true) or F (false):

(a) EDM tracking mode is a more precise technique, than is EDM regular mode

(b) A sag error is introduced when not enough tension is applied to a steel tape laid directly on a road surface

(c) A steel tape measurement was entered in the field book as being 100.00 ft. Because the temperature at the time of measurement was 53°F, resulting in the tape shrinking to only 99.99 ft, 0.01 ft must be added to the recorded distance to have the corrected value

(d) A 3.63-percent slope is one that rises 10.08 ft (m) in 277.77 ft (m)

(e) An EDM, with a specified accuracy of ±(0.02 ft + 5 ppm) was used to layout a 20.00-ft bridge component; this procedure would be more precise than would be the proper use of a fully supported steel tape used at 68°F

(f) Random taping errors can occur when the plumbed tape is not held exactly horizon-tal each time the tape is used. Because the surveyor may hold the tape too high on some occasions and too low other times, these random errors will cancel out and not affect the accuracy of the survey

(g) Invar steel is used to make steel tapes that are less susceptible to temperature variations

(h) The average time to complete an EDM distance measurement is 15 s

(i) A Kodak Gray Card reflects only 50 percent of white light

3.2 Describe the relative advantages and disadvantages of measuring with steel tapes and with EDMs.

3.3 Give two examples of possible uses for each of the following field measurement techniques: (a) pacing, (b) odometer, (c) EDM, (d) subtense bar, (e) fiberglass tape, (f) steel tape.

3.4 The following measurements were taken from an early topographic survey where the measurements were made with a Gunter's chain. Convert each of these measurements to both feet and meters: (a) 18 chains, 61 links; (b) 80.01 chains; (c) 9 chains, 37 links; (d) 5 chains, 11 links.

3.5 You must determine the ground clearance of an overhead electrical cable. Surveyor B is positioned directly under the cable (surveyor B's position can be checked by his sighting past the string of a plumb bob, held in his outstretched hand, to the cable); surveyor A sets her clinometer to 45° and then backs away from surveyor B until the overhead electrical cable is on the cross hair of the leveled clinometer. At this point, surveyors A and B determine the distance between them to be 43.6 ft. Surveyor A then sets the clinometer to 0° and sights surveyor B; this horizontal line of sight cuts surveyor B at a distance of 3.8 ft above the ground. Determine the ground clearance of the electrical cable.

3.6 A 100-ft cut steel tape was used to check the layout of a building wall. The rear surveyor held 71 ft while the head surveyor cut 0.68 ft. What is the distance measured?

3.7 A 100-ft add steel tape was used to measure a partial baseline distance. The rear surveyor held 50 ft, while the head surveyor held 0.27 ft. What is the distance measured?

3.8 The slope distance between two points is 17.277 m, and the slope angle is $1°42'$. Compute the horizontal distance.

3.9 The slope distance between two points is 98.17 ft, and the difference in elevation between them is 8.45 ft. Compute the horizontal distance.

3.10 A distance of 133.860 m was measured along a 2-percent slope. Compute the horizontal distance.

3.11 To verify the constant of a particular prism, a straight line ABC is laid out. The EDM instrument is first set up at A, with the following measurements recorded:

$$AC = 488.255 \text{ m}, \quad AB = 198.690 \text{ m}$$

The EDM instrument is then set up at B, where distance BC is recorded as 289.595 m. Determine the prism constant.

3.12 The EDM slope distance between two points is 2,183.71 ft, and the vertical angle is $+2°45'30''$ (the vertical angles were read at both ends of the line and then averaged). If the elevation of the instrument station is 285.69 ft and the heights of the instrument, EDM, target, and reflector are all equal to 5.08 ft, compute the elevation of the target station and the horizontal distance to that station.

3.13 A line AB is measured at both ends as follows:

Instrument at A, slope distance = 1458.777 m, zenith angle = $92°40'40''$

Instrument at B, slope distance = 1458.757 m, zenith angle = $87°20'00''$

The heights of the instrument, reflector, and target are equal for each observation.

(a) Compute the horizontal distance AB.

(b) If the elevation at A is 211.841 m, what is the elevation at B?

3.14 A coaxial EDM instrument at station K (elevation = 232.47 ft) is used to sight stations L, M, and N, with the heights of the instrument, target, and reflector equal for each sighting. The results are as follows:

Instrument at STA. L, zenith angle = 86°30′, EDM distance = 3,000.00 ft

Instrument at STA. M, zenith angle = 91°30′, EDM distance = 3,000.00 ft

Instrument at STA. N, zenith angle = 90°00′, EDM distance = 2,000.00 ft

Compute the elevations of L, M, and N

Chapter 4

Introduction to
Total Stations
and Theodolites

4.1 General Background

We noted in Section 1.8 that the units of angular measurement employed in North American practice are degrees, minutes, and seconds. For the most part, angles in surveying are measured with a theodolite or total station, although angles can be measured with clinometers, sextants (hydrographic surveys), or compasses.

4.2 Reference Directions for Vertical Angles

Vertical angles, which are used in slope distance corrections (Section 3.8) or in height determination (Section 2.13), are referenced to (1) the horizon by plus (up) or minus (down) angles, (2) the zenith, or (3) the nadir (Figure 4.1). **Zenith** and **nadir** are terms describing points on a celestial sphere (i.e., a sphere of infinitely large radius with its center at the center of the Earth). The zenith is directly above the observer and the nadir is directly below the observer; the zenith, nadir, and observer are all on the same vertical line.

4.3 Meridians

A line on the mean surface of the Earth joining the north and south poles is called a **meridian**. All lines of longitude are meridians. The term *meridian* can be defined more precisely by noting that it is the line formed by the intersection with the Earth's surface of a plane that includes the Earth's axis of rotation. The meridian, as described, is known as the **geographic meridian**.

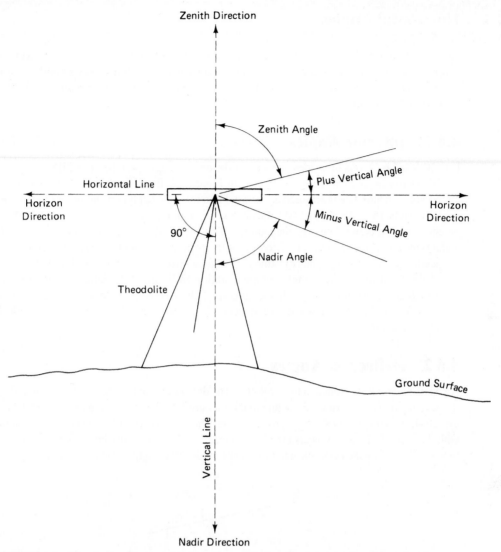

FIGURE 4.1   The three reference directions for vertical angles: horizontal, zenith, and nadir.

Magnetic meridians are meridians that are parallel to the directions taken by freely moving magnetized needles, as in a compass. Whereas geographic meridians are fixed, magnetic meridians vary with time and location. **Grid meridians** are lines that are parallel to a grid reference meridian (central meridian) and are described in detail in Chapter 9.

We saw in Section 4.2 that vertical angles were referenced to a horizontal line (plus or minus) or to a vertical line (from either the zenith or nadir direction); in contrast, we now see that all horizontal directions can be referenced to meridians.

4.4   Horizontal Angles

Horizontal angles are usually measured with a theodolite or total station whose precision can range from 1″ to 20″ of arc. Angles can be measured between lines forming a closed traverse, between lines forming an open traverse, or between a line and a point to aid in the location of that point.

4.4.1   Interior Angles

For all closed polygons of n sides, the sum of the interior angles will be $(n - 2)180°$; the sum of the exterior angles will be $(n + 2)180°$. In Figure 4.2, the interior angles of a five-sided closed polygon have been measured as shown. For a five-sided polygon, the sum of the interior angles must be $(5 - 2)180° = 540°$; the angles shown in Figure 4.2 do, in fact, total 540°. In practical field problems, however, the total is usually marginally more or less than $(n - 2)180°$, and it is then up to the surveyors to determine if the error of angular closure is within tolerances as specified for that survey. The adjustment of angular errors is discussed in Chapter 6.

Note that the exterior angles at each station in Figure 4.2 could have been measured instead of the interior angles as shown. (The exterior angle at A of 272°55″ is shown.) Generally, exterior angles are measured only occasionally to serve as a check on the interior angle.

4.4.2   Deflection Angles

An open traverse is illustrated in Figure 4.3(a). The **deflection angles** shown are measured from the prolongation of the back survey line to the forward line. The angles are measured either to the left (L) or to the right (R) of the projected line. The direction (L or R) must be shown, along with the numerical value. It is also possible to measure the change in direction [Figure 4.3(b)] by directly sighting the back line and turning the angle left or right to the forward line.

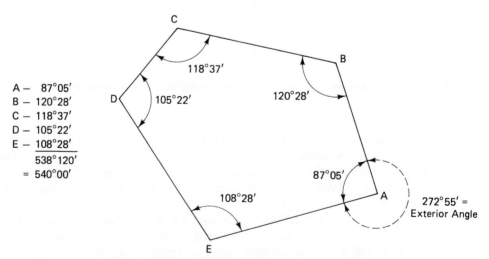

A —   87°05′
B — 120°28′
C — 118°37′
D — 105°22′
E — 108°28′
_____
538°120′
= 540°00′

FIGURE 4.2   Closed traverse showing the interior angles.

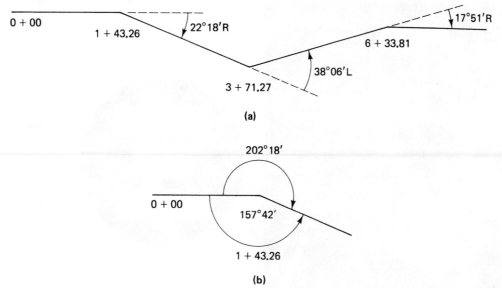

FIGURE 4.3 (a) Open traverse showing deflection angles. (b) Same traverse showing angle right (202°18′) and angle left (157°42′).

4.5 Theodolites

Theodolites are survey instruments designed to measure horizontal and vertical angles precisely. In addition to measuring horizontal and vertical angles, theodolites can also be used to mark out straight and curved lines in the field. Theodolites (also called transits) have gone through three distinct evolutionary stages during the twentieth century:

1. The open-face, vernier-equipped engineers' transit (American transit; Figure G.8).
2. The enclosed, optical readout theodolites with direct digital readouts, or micrometer-equipped readouts (for more precise readings; Figure 4.4).
3. The enclosed electronic theodolite with direct readouts (Figure 1.7).

Most recent manufactured theodolites are electronic, but many of the earlier optical instruments and even a few vernier instruments still survive in the field (and in the classroom)—no doubt a tribute to the excellent craftsmanship of the instrument makers. In past editions of this text, the instruments were introduced chronologically, but in this edition, the vernier transits and optical theodolites are introduced last (in Appendix G) in recognition of their fading importance.

The electronic theodolite will probably be the last in the line of transits/theodolites. Because of the versatility and lower costs of electronic components, future field instruments will be more like the total station (Chapter 5), which combines all the features of a theodolite with the additional capabilities of measuring horizontal and vertical distances (electronically), and storing all measurements, with relevant attribute data, for future transfer to the computer. By 2005, some total stations even included a global-positioning system (GPS) receiver

Vertical Scale

Micrometer Scale

Horizontal Scale

H 245° 50′
3′ 18″
_____
245° 53′ 18″

(a)   (b)

FIGURE 4.4 (a) Twenty-second micrometer theodolite, the Sokkia TM 20. (b) Horizontal and vertical scales with micrometer scale.

(Figure 5.28) to permit precise horizontal and vertical positioning. The sections in this chapter that deal with theodolite setup, instrument adjustments, and general use, such as prolonging a straight line, bucking-in, and prolonging a line past an obstacle, are equally applicable to total stations; total station operations are described more fully in Chapter 5.

4.6 Electronic Theodolites

Electronic theodolites operate similarly to optical theodolites (Section G.4); one major difference is that these instruments usually have only one motion (upper) and accordingly have only one horizontal clamp and slow-motion screw. Angle readouts can be to 1″, with precision ranging from 0.5″ to 20″. The surveyor should check the specifications of new instruments to determine their precision, rather than simply accept the lowest readout as relevant (some instruments with 1″ readouts may be capable of only 5″ precision).

Digital readouts eliminate the uncertainty associated with the reading and interpolation of scale and micrometer settings. Electronic theodolites have zero-set buttons for quick instrument orientation after the backsight has been taken (any angular value can be set for the backsight). Horizontal angles can be turned left or right, and repeat-angle averaging is available on some models. Figures 1.7 and 4.5 are typical of the more recently introduced theodolites. The display windows for horizontal and vertical angles are located at both the front and rear of many instruments for easy access.

Figure 1.7 shows the operation keys and display area typical of many of these instruments. After turning on some instruments, the operator must activate the vertical circle

Carrying Handle

Optical Sight

Objective

Vertical Clamp
and Tangent Screw

Horizontal Clamp
and Tangent Screw

Leveling Screw

Base Plate

Optical
Plummet

Circular Bubble

(a)

ROTARY ENCODER SYSTEM FOR ELECTRONIC THEODOLITES AND TRANSITS

Photoelectric converter A

Photoelectric converter B

Slit A ⎡ A phase difference of 1/4th pitch or
Slit B ⎣ 90° exists between slits A and B

Collimator lens

Stator   Rotor

Light Source (Light emitting diode)

Topcon electronic theodolites (ETL-1 and DT-05/05A) and electronic transit (DT-30) measure horizontal and vertical angles with an incremental encoder detection system that reads to 1, 5, 10, or 30″. Alternate dark and light patterns etched on the circles are detected by a light source and received by a photo detector, converting the beam into an electrical signal.

The signal is converted to a pulse signal corresponding to the angle turned and the pulse signal is passed on to the microprocessor, which displays an angle on the LCD.

FIGURE 4.5 Topcon DT-05 electronic digital theodolite. (a) Theodolite. (b) Encoder system for angle readouts. (Courtesy of Topcon Positioning Systems, Inc.)

by turning the telescope slowly through the horizon; newer instruments don't require this referencing action. The vertical circle can be set with zero at the zenith or at the horizon; the factory setting of zenith can be changed by setting the appropriate dip switch as described in the instrument's manual. The status of the battery charge can be monitored on the display panel, giving the operator ample warning of the need to replace and/or recharge the battery.

4.6.1 Angle Measurement

Most surveying measurements are performed at least twice; this repetition improves precision and helps eliminate mistakes. Angles are usually measured at least twice: once with the telescope in its normal position and once with the telescope inverted. After the theodolite has been set over a station, the angle measurement begins by sighting the left hand (usually) target and clamping the instrument's horizontal motion. The target is then sighted precisely by using the fine adjustment, or slow-motion screw. The horizontal angle is set to zero by pressing the zero-set button. Then the horizontal clamp is loosened and the right-hand target sighted. The clamp is tightened and the telescope fine-adjusted onto the target. The hold button is pressed and the angle is read and booked (pressing the hold button ensures that the original angle stays on the instrument display until the surveyor is ready to measure the angle a second time).

To prepare to double the angle (i.e., measure the same angle a second time), loosen the clamp and transit the telescope. The left-hand point is now resighted, as described above. To turn the double angle, simply press (release) the hold button, release the clamp, and resight the right-hand target a second time. After fine-adjusting on the target, the double angle is read and booked. To obtain the mean angle, divide the double angle by 2. See Figure 4.6 for typical field notes.

4.6.2 Typical Specifications for Electronic Theodolites

The typical specifications for electronic theodolites are listed below:

> Magnification: $26\times$ to $30\times$
> Field of view: $1.5°$
> Shortest viewing distance: 1.0 m
> Angle readout, direct: $1''$ to $20''$; accuracy: $1''$ to $20''$*
> Angle measurement, electronic and incremental: see Figure 4.5(b)
> Level sensitivity:
> > Plate bubble vial—$40''/2$ mm
> > Circular bubble vial—$10\times/2$ mm

---

*Accuracies are now specified by most surveying instrument manufacturers by reference to DIN 18723. DIN (Deutsches Institut für Normung) is known in English-speaking countries as the German Institute for Standards. These accuracies are tied directly to surveying practice. For example, to achieve a claimed accuracy (stated in terms of 1 standard deviation) of ±5 seconds, the surveyor must turn the angle four times (two on face 1 and two with the telescope inverted on face 2). This practice assumes that collimation errors, centering errors, and the like have been eliminated before measuring the angles. DIN specifications can be purchased at http://www2.din.de/index.php?lang=en.

FIGURE 4.6 Field notes for angles by repetition (closed traverse).

Electronic theodolites are quickly replacing optical theodolites (which replaced the vernier transit). They are simpler to use and less expensive to purchase and repair, and their use of electronic components seems to indicate a continuing drop in both purchase and repair costs. Some of these instruments have various built-in functions that enable the operator to perform other theodolite operations, such as determining remote object elevation and distance between remote points (see Chapter 5). The instrumentation technology is evolving so rapidly that most new instruments now on the market have been in production for only a year or two, and this statement has been valid since the early 1990s.

4.7 Total Station

Total stations combine all the aspects of advanced electronic theodolites with coaxial EDM. Horizontal and vertical angles are read in the range of 1″ to 10″, depending on the model, and distance accuracies are in the range of $\pm$(5 mm + 5 to 10 ppm) to $\pm$(2 mm + 1 ppm). In addition, total stations are equipped with microprocessors to monitor instrument status, control advanced functions, and facilitate a wide variety of onboard software applications programs. Specific total station applications are discussed in detail in Chapter 5.

One topic in this chapter (Section 4.10) deals with the tests for errors and adjustments (if necessary) for theodolite/total stations; it should be noted here that such adjustments for total stations can usually be accomplished in much less time using onboard software.

4.8   Theodolite/Total Station Setup

Follow this procedure to set up a theodolite or total station:

1. Place the instrument over the point, with the tripod plate as level as possible and with two tripod legs on the downhill side, if applicable.
2. Stand back a pace or two and see if the instrument appears to be over the station. If it does not appear centered, adjust the location, and check again from a pace or two away.
3. Move to a position 90° opposed to the original inspection location and repeat step 2. (*Note:* This simple act of "eyeing-in" the instrument from two directions, 90° opposed, takes only seconds but could save a great deal of time in the long run.)
4. Check to see that the station point can now be seen through the optical plummet (or that the laser plummet spot is reasonably close to the setup mark) and then firmly push in the tripod legs by pressing down on the tripod shoe spurs. If the point is now not visible in the optical plumb sight, leave one leg in the ground, lift the other two legs, and rotate the instrument, all the while looking through the optical plumb sight. When the point is sighted, carefully lower the two legs to the ground, keeping the station point in view.
5. While looking through the optical plummet (or at the laser spot), manipulate the leveling screws until the cross hair (bull's-eye) of the optical plummet or the laser spot is directly on the station mark.
6. Level the theodolite circular bubble by adjusting the tripod legs up or down. This step is accomplished by noting which leg, when slid up or down, would move the circular bubble into the bull's-eye. Upon adjusting that leg, either the bubble will move into the circle (the instrument is nearly level) or it will slide around until it is exactly opposite another tripod leg. That leg is then adjusted up or down until the bubble moves into the circle. If the bubble does not move into the circle, adjust the leg until the bubble is directly opposite another leg and repeat the process. If this manipulation has been done correctly, the bubble will be centered after the second leg has been adjusted; it is seldom necessary to adjust the legs more than three times. (Comfort can be taken from the fact that these manipulations take less time to perform than they do to read about!)
7. Perform a check through the optical plummet or note the location of the laser spot to confirm that it is still quite close to being over the station mark.
8. Turn one (or more) leveling screw(s) to ensure that the circular bubble is now centered exactly (if necessary).
9. Loosen the tripod clamp bolt a bit and slide the instrument on the flat tripod top (if necessary) until the optical plummet or laser spot is centered exactly on the

station mark. Retighten the tripod clamp bolt and reset the circular bubble, if necessary. When sliding the instrument on the tripod top, do not twist the instrument, but move it in a rectangular fashion. This precaution ensures that the instrument will not go seriously off level if the tripod top itself is not close to being level.

10. The instrument can now be leveled precisely by centering the tubular bubble. Set the tubular bubble so that it is aligned in the same direction as two of the foot screws. Turn these two screws (together or independently) until the bubble is centered. Then turn the instrument 90°; at this point, the tubular bubble will be aligned with the third leveling screw. Next, turn that third screw to center the bubble. The instrument now should be level, although it is always checked by turning the instrument through 180° and noting the new bubble location. See Section 4.13.2 for adjustment procedures. On instruments with dual-axis compensation, final leveling can be achieved by viewing the electronic display [Figure 5.24(b)] and then turning the appropriate leveling screws. This latter technique is faster because the instrument does not have to be rotated repeatedly.

4.9 Geometry of the Theodolite and Total Station

The vertical axis of the theodolite goes up through the center of the spindles and is oriented over a specific point on the Earth's surface. The circle assembly and alidade revolve about this axis. The horizontal axis of the telescope is perpendicular to the vertical axis, and the telescope and vertical circle revolve about it. The line of sight (line of collimation) is a line joining the intersection of the reticule cross hairs and the center of the objective lens. The line of sight is perpendicular to the horizontal axis and should be truly horizontal when the telescope level bubble (if there is one) is centered and when the vertical circle is set at 90° or 270° (or 0° for vernier transits). See Figure 4.7.

4.10 Adjustment of the Theodolite and Total Station

Figure 4.7 shows the geometric features of theodolites and total stations. The most important relationships are as follows:

1. The axis of the plate bubble should be in a plane perpendicular to the vertical axis.
2. The vertical cross hair should be perpendicular to the horizontal axis (tilting axis).
3. The line of sight should be perpendicular to the horizontal axis.
4. The horizontal axis should be perpendicular to the vertical axis (standards adjustment).

In addition, the following secondary feature must be considered:

5. The vertical circle should read 90° (or 270°) when the telescope is level.

These features are discussed in the following paragraphs. See Appendix G for additional adjustments applicable to the engineers' transit.

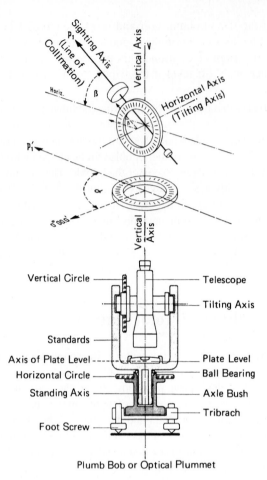

Vertical Axis

Sighting Axis
(Line of Collimation)

P₁

β

Horiz.

Horizontal Axis
(Tilting Axis)

V

P′₁

α

0.000°

Vertical Axis

Vertical Circle ———————————— Telescope

———————————— Tilting Axis

Standards ——————

Axis of Plate Level - - - - - - ———————— Plate Level

Horizontal Circle ———————————— Ball Bearing

Standing Axis ——————————— Axle Bush

———————— Tribrach

Foot Screw ——————

Plumb Bob or Optical Plummet

FIGURE 4.7 Geometry of the theodolite and total station. (Courtesy of Leica Geosystems)

4.10.1 Plate Bubbles

We have noted that, after a bubble has been centered by leveling in two positions, 90° opposed, its adjustment is checked by rotating the instrument through 180°. If the bubble does not remain centered, it can be set properly by bringing the bubble halfway back using the foot screws. For example, if you are checking a tubular bubble accuracy position and it is out by four division marks, the bubble can now be set properly by turning the foot screws until the bubble is only two division marks off center. The bubble should remain in this off-center position as the telescope is rotated, indicating that the instrument is, in fact, level. Although the instrument can now be safely used, it is customary to remove the error by adjusting the bubble tube.

The bubble tube can now be adjusted by turning the capstan screws at one end of the bubble tube until the bubble becomes precisely centered. The entire leveling and adjusting procedure is repeated until the bubble remains centered as the instrument is rotated and checked in all positions. All capstan screw adjustments are best done in small increments. That is, if the end of the bubble tube is to be lowered, first loosen the lower capstan screw a slight turn (say, one-eighth), and then tighten (snug) the top capstan screw to close the gap. This incremental adjustment is continued until the bubble is centered precisely.

4.10.2 Vertical Cross Hair

If the vertical cross hair is perpendicular to the horizontal axis, all parts of the vertical cross hair can be used for line and angle sightings. This adjustment can be checked by first sighting a well-defined distant point and then clamping the horizontal movements. The telescope (Figures 4.8 and 4.9) is now moved up and down so that the point sighted appears to move on the vertical cross hair. If the point appears to move off the vertical cross hair, an error exists and the cross-hair reticule must be rotated slightly until the sighted point appears to stay on the vertical cross hair as it is being revolved. The reticule can be adjusted slightly by loosening two adjacent capstan screws, rotating the reticule, and then retightening the same two capstan screws.

This same cross-hair orientation adjustment is performed on the level, but in the case of the level, the horizontal cross hair is of prime importance. The horizontal cross hair is checked by first sighting a distant point on the horizontal cross hair with the vertical clamp set. Then move the telescope left and right, checking to see that the sighted point remains on the horizontal cross hair. The adjustment for any maladjustment of the reticule is performed as described previously.

Diagram of a Telescope Optical System

FIGURE 4.8   Diagram of a telescope optical system. (Courtesy of SOKKIA Corp.)

FIGURE 4.9   Theodolite telescope. (Courtesy of SOKKIA Corp.)

4.10.3 Line-of-Sight Collimation Corrections

4.10.3.1 Vertical Cross Hair.
The vertical line of sight should be perpendicular to the horizontal axis so that a vertical plane is formed by the complete revolution of the telescope on its axis. The technique for this testing and adjustment is very similar to the surveying technique of double centering (described in Section 4.12). The testing and adjustment procedure is described in the following steps:

TEST

1. Set up the instrument at point A [Figure 4.10(a)].
2. Take a backsight on any well-defined point B (a well-defined point on the horizon is best).
3. Transit (plunge) the telescope and set a point C_1 on the opposite side of the theodolite 300–400 ft away, at roughly the same elevation as the instrument station.
4. After loosening the upper or lower horizontal plate clamp (if the instrument has two clamps), and with the telescope still inverted from step 3, sight point B again.
5. After sighting on point B, transit the telescope and sight in the direction of the previously set point C_1. It is highly probable that the line of sight will not fall precisely on point C_1, so set a new point—point C_2—adjacent to point C_1.
6. With a steel tape, measure between point C_1 and point C_2 and set point C midway between them. Point C will be the correct point—the point established precisely on the projection of line BA. These six steps describe double centering (a surveying technique of producing a straight line—see Section 4.12).

ADJUSTMENT

7. Because the distance C_1C or CC_2 is double the sighting error, the line-of-sight correction is accomplished by first setting point E midway between C and C_2 (or one-quarter of the way from C_1 to C_2).
8. After sighting the vertical cross hair on point E, the vertical cross-hair correction adjustment is performed by adjusting the left and right capstan screws (Figure 4.9) until the vertical cross hair is positioned directly on point C. The capstan screws are adjusted by first loosening one screw a small turn and then immediately tightening the opposite capstan screw to take up the slack. This procedure is repeated until the vertical cross hair is positioned precisely on point C.

Note: On instruments with dual-axis compensation, the components of the standing axis tilt are measured, thus enabling the instrument to correct angles automatically for the standing axis tilt.

4.10.3.2 Horizontal Cross Hair.
The horizontal cross hair must be adjusted so that it lies on the optical axis of the telescope. To test this relationship, set up the instrument at point A [Figure 4.10(b)], and place two stakes B and C in a straight line, B about 25 ft away and C about 300 ft away. With the vertical motion clamped, take a reading first on C(K) and then on B(J). Transit (plunge) the telescope and set the horizontal cross hair on the previous rod reading (J) at B and then take a reading at point C. If the theodolite is in perfect

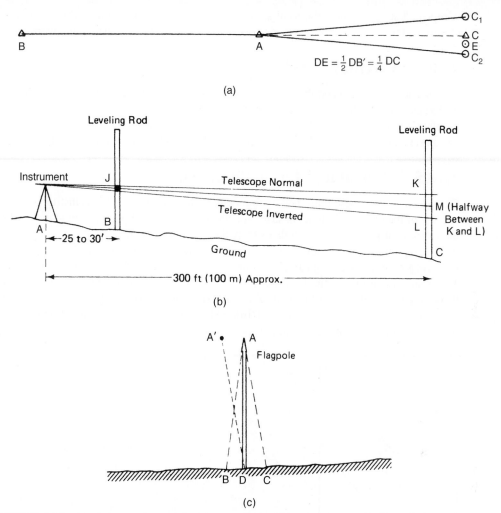

$$DE = \tfrac{1}{2} DB' = \tfrac{1}{4} DC$$

(a)

(b)

(c)

FIGURE 4.10 Instrument adjustments. (a) Line of sight perpendicular to horizontal axis. (b) Horizontal cross-hair adjustment. (c) Standards adjustment.

adjustment, the two rod readings at C will be the same; if the cross hair is out of adjustment, the rod reading at C will be at some reading L instead of K. To adjust the cross hair, adjust the cross-hair reticule up or down by first loosening and then tightening the appropriate opposing capstan screws until the cross hair lines up with the average of the two readings (M).

Note: Total station software can address both these errors in the following manner. After making sure the instrument is leveled precisely and after sighting a distant backsight, transit the telescope forward to sight a point on a rod (face 1); the horizontal and vertical angles are recorded. When sighting the point on the rod again in face 2 (the telescope is inverted for the backsight), the horizontal and vertical angles are noted again. The horizontal angle should be different from the face 1 reading by exactly 180°—any discrepancy is double the horizontal collimation error. Similarly, if the two vertical angles (faces 1 and 2) do not equal 360°, the discrepancy is twice the vertical collimation error. If this procedure is repeated several times, the total station software can estimate the collimation errors closely and proceed to remove these errors in future single-face measurement work.

4.10.4 Circular Level

Optical and electronic theodolites and total stations use a circular level for rough leveling as well as plate level(s) for fine leveling. (See Chapter 5 for electronic leveling techniques.) After the plate level has been set and adjusted, as described in Section 4.13.2, the circular bubble can be adjusted (centered) by turning one or more of the three adjusting screws around the bubble.

4.10.5 Optical and Laser Plummets

The optical axis of these plummets is aligned with the vertical axis of the instrument if the reticule of the optical plummet or laser dot stays superimposed on the ground mark when the instrument is revolved through 180°. If the reticule or laser dot does not stay on the mark, the plummet can be adjusted in the following manner. The reticule or laser dot is put over the ground mark by adjusting the plummet screws [Figure 4.11(a)]. If the plummet is not in adjustment, the reticule (laser dot) appears to be in a new location (X) after the theodolite is turned about 180°; point P is marked halfway between the two locations. The plummet-adjusting screws [Figure 4.11(b)] are turned until the reticule image or laser dot is over P, indicating that the plummet is now in adjustment.

(a)

(b)

FIGURE 4.11 Optical plummet adjustment. (a) Point P is marked halfway between the original position (·) and the 180° position (X). (b) Plummet adjusting screws are turned until X becomes superimposed on P. (Courtesy of Nikon Instruments, Inc.)

4.11 Laying Off Angles

4.11.1 Case 1

The angle is to be laid out no more precisely than the least count of the theodolite or total station. Assume that you must complete a route survey where a deflection angle (31°12′ R) has been determined from aerial photos to position the ℄ (centerline) clear of natural obstructions [Figure 4.12(a)]. The surveyor sets the instrument at the PI (point of intersection of the tangents), and then sights the back line with the telescope reversed and the horizontal circle set to zero. Next, the surveyor transits (plunges) the telescope, turns off the required deflection angle, and sets a point on line. The deflection angle is 31°12′ R and a point is set at a′. The surveyor then loosens the lower motion (repeating instruments), sights again at the back line, transits the telescope, and turns off the required value (31°12′ × 2 = 62°24′). It is very likely that this line of sight will not precisely match the first sighting at a′; if the line does not cross a′, a new mark a″ is made and the instrument operator gives a sighting on the correct point a, which is midway between a′ and a″.

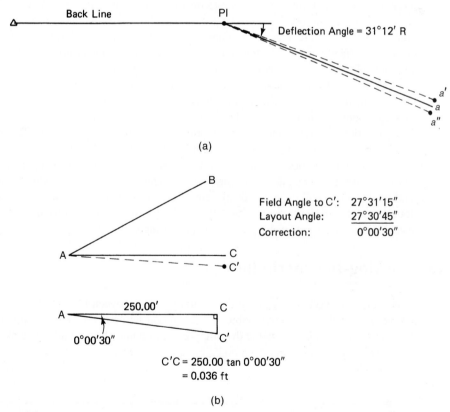

(a)

Field Angle to C′: 27°31′15″
Layout Angle: 27°30′45″
Correction: 0°00′30″

C′C = 250.00 tan 0°00′30″
    = 0.036 ft

(b)

FIGURE 4.12 Laying off an angle. (a) Case 1, angle laid out to the least count of the instrument. (b) Case 2, angle to be laid out more precisely than the least count permitted by the instrument.

4.11.2 Case 2

The angle is to be laid out more precisely than the least count of the instrument permits. Assume that an angle of 27°30′45″ is required in a heavy construction layout, and that a 01-minute theodolite is being used. In Figure 4.12(b), the theodolite is set up at A zeroed on B with an angle of 27°31′ turned to set point C′. The angle is then repeated to point C′ a suitable number of times so that an accurate value of that angle can be determined. Let's assume that the scale reading after four repetitions is 110°05′, giving a mean angle value of 27°31′15″ for angle BAC′. If the layout distance of AC is 250.00 ft, point C can be located precisely by measuring from C′ a distance C′C:

$$C'C = 250.00 \tan 0°00'30''$$
$$= 0.036 \text{ ft}$$

After point C has been located, its position can be verified by repeating angles to it from point B [Figure 4.12(b)].

4.12 Prolonging a Straight Line (Double Centering)

Prolonging a straight line (also known as **double centering**) is a common survey procedure used every time a straight line must be prolonged. The best example of this requirement is in route surveying, where straight lines are routinely prolonged over long distances and often over very difficult terrain. The technique of reversion (the same technique as used in repeating, or doubling, angles) is used to ensure that the straight line is prolonged properly.

In Figure 4.13, the straight line BA is to be prolonged to C [see also Figure 4.10(a)]. With the instrument at A, a sight is made carefully on station B. The telescope is transited, and a temporary point is set at C_1. The theodolite is revolved back to station B (the telescope is in a position reversed to the original sighting), and a new sighting is made. The telescope is transited, and a temporary mark is made at C_2, adjacent to C. (*Note:* Over short distances, well-adjusted theodolites will show no appreciable displacement between points C_1 and C_2. However, over the longer distances normally encountered in this type of work, all theodolites and total stations will display a displacement between direct and reversed sightings. (The longer the forward sighting, the greater the displacement.) The correct location of station C is established midway between C_1 and C_2 by measuring with a steel tape.

4.13 Bucking-In (Interlining)

It is sometimes necessary to establish a straight line between two points that themselves are not intervisible (i.e., a theodolite or total station set up at one point cannot, because of an intervening hill, be sighted at the other required point). It is usually possible to find an intermediate position from which both points can be seen.

FIGURE 4.13 Double centering to prolong a straight line.

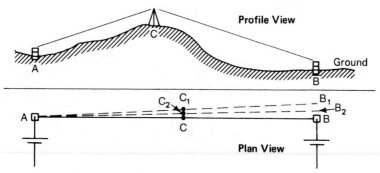

FIGURE 4.14 Bucking-in, or interlining.

In Figure 4.14, points A and B are not intervisible, but point C is in an area from which both A and B can be seen. The bucking-in procedure is as follows. The instrument is set up in the area of C (at C_1) and as close to line AB as is possible to estimate. The instrument is roughly leveled and a sight is taken on point A; then the telescope is transited and a sight is taken toward B. The line of sight will, of course, not be on B but on point B_1 some distance away. Noting roughly the distance B_1B and the position of the instrument between A and B (e.g., halfway, one-third, or one-quarter of the distance AB), the surveyor estimates proportionately how far the instrument is to be moved to be on the line AB. The instrument is once again roughly leveled (position C_2), and the sighting procedure is repeated.

This trial-and-error technique is repeated until, after sighting A, the transited line of sight falls on point B or close enough to point B so that it can be set precisely by shifting the theodolite on the leveling head shifting plate. When the line has been established, a point is set at or near point C so that the position can be saved for future use.

The entire procedure of bucking-in can be accomplished in a surprisingly short period of time. All but the final instrument setups are only roughly leveled, and at no time does the instrument have to be set up over a point.

4.14 Intersection of Two Straight Lines

The intersection of two straight lines is also a very common survey operation. In municipal surveying, street surveys usually begin (0 + 00) at the intersection of the centerlines ℄ of two streets, and the station and angle of the intersections of all subsequent streets' ℄ are routinely determined. Figure 4.15(a) illustrates the need for intersecting points on a municipal survey, and Figure 4.15(b) illustrates how the intersection point is located. In Figure 4.15(b), with the instrument set on a Main Street station and a sight taken also on the Main Street ℄ (the longer the sight, the more precise the sighting), two points (2–4 ft apart) are established on the Main Street ℄, one point on either side of where the surveyor estimates that the 2nd Avenue ℄ will intersect. The instrument is then moved to a 2nd Avenue station, and a sight is taken some distance away, on the far side of the Main Street ℄. The surveyor can stretch a plumb bob string over the two points (A and B) established on the Main Street ℄, and the instrument operator can note where on the string the 2nd Avenue ℄ intersects. If the two points (A and B) are reasonably close

FIGURE 4.15 Intersection of two straight lines. (a) Example of the intersection of the centerlines of streets. (b) Intersecting technique.

together (2–3 ft), the surveyor can use the plumb bob itself to take a line from the instrument operator on the plumb bob string; otherwise, the instrument operator can take a line with a pencil or any other suitable sighting target. The intersection point is then suitably marked (e.g., nail and flagging on asphalt, wood stake with tack on ground), and then the angle of intersection and the station (chainage) of the point can be determined. After marking and referencing the intersection point, the surveyors remove the temporary markers A and B.

4.15 Prolonging a Measured Line by Triangulation over an Obstacle

In route surveying, obstacles such as rivers or chasms must be traversed. Whereas double centering can conveniently prolong the alignment, the station (chainage) may be deduced from the construction of a geometric figure. In Figure 4.16(a), the distance from 1 + 121.271 to the station established on the far side of the river can be determined by solving the constructed triangle (triangulation). The ideal (geometrically strongest—see Section 9.8) triangle is one with angles close to 60° (equilateral), although angles as small as 20° may be acceptable. Rugged terrain and heavy tree cover adjacent to the river often result in a less than optimal geometric figure. The baseline and a minimum of two angles are measured so that the missing distance can be calculated. The third angle (on the far side of the river) should also be measured to check for mistakes and to reduce errors.

FIGURE 4.16 (a) Prolonging a measured line over an obstacle by triangulation. (b) Prolonging a line past an obstacle by triangulation.

See Figure 4.16(b) for another illustration of triangulation. In Figure 4.16(b), the line must be prolonged past an obstacle: a large tree. In this case, a triangle is constructed with the three angles and two distances measured, as shown. As we noted earlier, the closer the constructed triangle is to equilateral, the stronger is the calculated distance (BD). Also, the optimal equilateral figure cannot always be constructed due to topographic constraints, and angles as small as 20° are acceptable for many surveys.

4.16 Prolonging a Line Past an Obstacle

In property surveying, obstacles such as trees often block the path of the survey. In route surveying, it is customary for the surveyor to cut down the offending trees (later construction will require them to be removed in any case), but in property surveying, the property owner would be quite upset to find valuable trees destroyed just so the surveyor could establish a boundary line. Thus, the surveyor must find an alternative method of providing distances and/or locations for blocked survey lines.

Figure 4.17(a) illustrates the technique of right-angle offset. Boundary line AF cannot be run because of the wooded area. The survey continues normally to point B, just clear of the wooded area. At B, a right angle is turned (and doubled), and point C is located a sufficient distance away from B to provide a clear parallel line to the boundary line. The instrument is set at C and sighted at B (great care must be exercised because of the short sighting distance); an angle of 90° is turned to locate point D. Point E is located on the boundary line using a right angle and the offset distance used for BC. The survey can then continue to F. If distance CD is measured, then the required boundary distance (AF) is AB + CD + EF. If intermediate points are required on the boundary line between B and E (e.g., fencing layout), a right angle can be turned from a convenient location on CD, and the offset distance (BC) is used to measure back to the boundary line. Use of this technique minimizes the destruction of trees and other obstructions.

In Figure 4.17(b), trees are scattered over the area, preventing the establishment of a right-angle offset line. In this case, a random line (open traverse) is run (by deflection angles) through the scattered trees. The distance AF is the sum of AB, EF, and

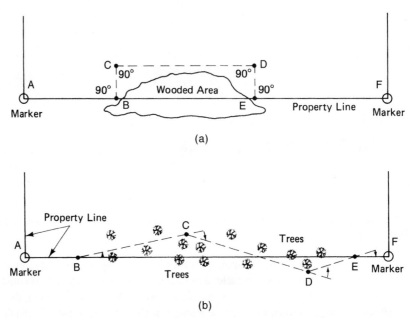

FIGURE 4.17 Prolonging a line past an obstacle. (a) Right-angle offset method. (b) Random-line method.

the resultant of BE. (See Chapter 6 for appropriate computation techniques for these types of missing-course problems.)

The technique of right-angle offsets has a larger potential for error because of the weaknesses associated with several short sightings; at the same time, however, this technique gives a simple and direct method for establishing intermediate points on the boundary line. By contrast, the random-line and triangulation methods provide for stronger geometric solutions to the missing property line distances, but they also require less direct and much more cumbersome calculations for the placement of intermediate line points (e.g., fence layout).

Review Questions

4.1 How does an electronic theodolite differ from a total station?

4.2 Describe, in point form, how to set up a theodolite or total station over a station point.

4.3 Describe, in point form, how you can use a theodolite or a total station to prolong a straight line XY to a new point Z. (Assume the instrument is set up over point Y and is level.)

4.4 How can you check to see that the plate bubbles of a theodolite or total station are adjusted correctly?

4.5 How can you determine the exact point of intersection of the centerlines of two cross streets?

4.6 What are some techniques of establishing a property line when trees block the instrument's line of sight?

4.7 Why do route surveyors prefer to use deflection angles instead of angles turned to the right or left when they are producing the survey line forward?

4.8 Describe how the introduction of electronic theodolites changed the field of surveying.

Chapter 5

Total Station Operations

5.1 General Background

The electronic digital theodolite, first introduced in the late 1960s by Carl Zeiss Inc., helped set the stage for modern field data collection and processing. (See Figure 4.5 for a typical electronic theodolite.) When the electronic theodolite is used with a built-in EDM or an add-on and interfaced EDM, the surveyor has a very powerful instrument. Add to that instrument an onboard microprocessor that automatically monitors the instrument's operating status and manages built-in surveying programs and a data collector (built-in or interfaced) that stores and processes measurements and attribute data, and you have what is known as a total station (Figures 5.1–5.4).

5.2 Total Station Capabilities

5.2.1 General Background

Total stations can measure and record horizontal and vertical angles together with slope distances. The microprocessors in the total stations can perform several different mathematical operations, for example, averaging multiple angle measurements; averaging multiple distance measurements; determining horizontal and vertical distances; determining X (easting), Y (northing), and Z coordinates; and determining remote object elevations (i.e., heights of sighted features) and distances between remote points. Some total stations also have the onboard capability of measuring atmospheric conditions and then applying corrections to field measurements. Some total stations are equipped to store collected data in onboard data cards (Figures 5.1 and 5.2), whereas other total stations come

(a)

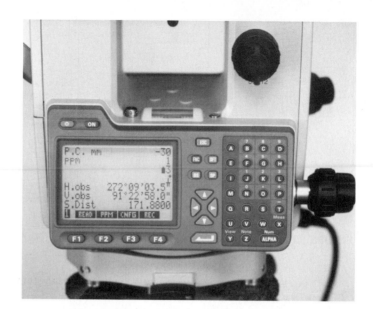

(b)

■ Graphic "Bull's-Eye" Level

A graphically displayed "bull's-eye" lets you quickly and efficiently level the instrument.

(c)

FIGURE 5.1 (a) Sokkia SET 1000 total station having angle display of 0.5″ (1″ accuracy) and a distance range of 2,400 m using one prism. The instrument comes with a complete complement of surveying programs, dual-axis compensation, and the ability to measure (to 120 m) to reflective sheet targets—a feature suited to industrial surveying measurements. (b) Keyboard and LCD display. (c) Graphics bull's-eye level allows you to level the instrument while observing the graphics display. (Courtesy of SOKKIA Corp.)

(continued)

Simultaneous Detection of Inclination in Two Directions and Automatic Compensation
The built-in dual-axis tilt sensor constantly monitors the inclination of the vertical axis in two directions. It calculates the compensation value and automatically corrects the horizontal and vertical angles. (The compensation range is +3′.)

(d)

FIGURE 5.1 (*continued*) (d) Dual-axis compensation illustration. (Courtesy of SOKKIA Corp.)

equipped with data collectors, also known as field controllers, that are connected by cable (or wirelessly) to the instrument (Figures 5.3 and 5.4).

Figure 5.1 shows a typical total station, one of a series of instruments that have angle accuracies from 0.5″ to 5″, and distance ranges (to one prism) from 1,600 to 3,000 m. We noted in Chapter 2 that modern levels employ compensation devices to correct the line of sight automatically to its horizontal position; total stations come equipped with single-axis or dual-axis compensation [Figure 5.1(d)]. With total stations, dual-axis compensation measures and corrects for left/right (lateral) tilt and forward/back (longitudinal) tilt. Tilt errors affect the accuracies of vertical angle measurements. Vertical angle errors can be minimized by averaging the readings of two-face measurements; with dual-axis compensation, however, the instrument's processor can determine tilt errors and remove their effects from the measurements, thus much improving the surveyor's efficiency. Dual-axis compensation also permits the inclusion of electronic instrument leveling [Figures 5.1(c) and 5.24(b)], a technique that is much faster than the repetitive leveling of plate bubbles in the two positions (180° opposed) required by instruments without dual-axis compensation.

Modern instruments have a wide variety of built-in instrument monitoring, data collection, and layout programs and rapid battery charging that can charge the battery in 70 min. Data are stored onboard in internal memory (about 1,300 points) and/or on memory cards (about 2,000 points per card). Data can be transferred directly to the computer from the total station via an RS232 cable, or data can be transferred from the data-storage cards first to a card reader-writer and from there to the computer. Newer total stations have the capability of downloading and uploading data wirelessly, via the Internet, using the latest in cell-phone technology. Instrument manufacturers will probably soon equip their field instruments with USB ports so that the recently introduced, low-cost, 1- to 2-GB USB storage devices can be employed to provide almost unlimited data storage.

Figure 5.2 shows another typical total station with card driver for application program cards (upper drive) and for data-storage cards (lower drive). The data-storage cards

Upper Card Drive
Holds Program Cards

Lower Card Drive
Holds Data Memory
Cards

(a)

(b)

FIGURE 5.2 (a) Nikon DTM 750 total station featuring onboard storage on PCMCIA computer cards; applications software on PCMCIA cards (upper drive): guidelight for layout work (to 100 m); dual-axis tilt sensor; EDM range of 2,700 m (8,900 ft) to one prism; angle precision of 1″ to 5″; distance precision of ±(2 + 2 ppm) mm. The operating system is MS-DOS compatible. (b) Menu schematic for the Nikon DTM 750. (Courtesy of Nikon Instruments Inc.)

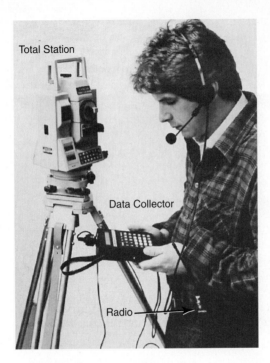

Total Station

Data Collector

Radio

FIGURE 5.3 Sokkia total station with cable-connected electronic field book. Also shown is a two-way radio (2-mi range) with push-to-talk headset.

(a)

(b)

FIGURE 5.4 (a) Topcon GTS 300 total station. The 300 series instruments have angle accuracies from 1″ to 10″ and single prism distances from 1,200 m (3,900 ft) to 2,400 m (7,900 ft) at 2 mm + 2 ppm accuracy. (b) Topcon FS2 data collector for use with GTS 300 series total stations. (Courtesy of Topcon Positioning Systems Inc.)

can be removed when they are full and read into a computer using standard PCMCIA card drives—now standard on most notebook computers. The operating system for this and some other total stations is MS-DOS compatible, which permits the addition of user-defined applications software.

All the data collectors (built-in and handheld) described here are capable of doing much more than just collecting data. The capabilities vary a great deal from one model to another. The computational characteristics of the main total stations themselves also vary widely. Some total stations (without the attached data collector) can compute remote elevations and distances between remote points, whereas others require the interfaced data collector to perform these functions.

Many recently introduced data collectors are really handheld computers, ranging in price from $600 to $2,000. Costs have moderated recently because the surveying field has seen an influx of various less expensive handheld or pocket PCs (e.g., from Compaq and Panasonic) for which total station data-collection software has been written. Some data collectors have graphics touch screens (stylus or finger) that permits the surveyor to input or edit data rapidly. For example, some collectors allow the surveyor to select (by touching) the line-work function that enables displayed points to be joined into lines—without the need for special line-work coding (see Section 5.5). If the total station is used alone, the capability of performing all survey computations—including traverse closures and adjustments—is highly desirable. If the total station is used in topographic surveys as a part of a system (field data collection, data processing, and digital plotting), however, the extended computational capacity of some data collectors (e.g., traverse closure computations) becomes less important. If the total station is used as part of a topographic surveying system (field data collection–data processing–digital plotting), the data collector need collect only the basic information, that is, slope distance, horizontal angle, and vertical angle, giving coordinates, and the sighted points' attribute data, such as point number, point description, and any required secondary tagged data. Computations and adjustments to the field data are then performed by one of the many coordinate geometry (COGO) programs now available for surveyors and engineers. However, more sophisticated data collectors are needed in many applications, for example, machine guidance, construction layouts, GIS surveys, and real-time GPS surveys (see Chapter 7).

Most early total stations (and some current models) use the absolute method for reading angles. These instruments are essentially optical coincidence instruments with photoelectronic sensors that scan and read the circles, which are divided into preassigned values, from 0° to 360° (or 0–400 grad or gon). Other models employ a rotary encoder technique of angle measurement (Figure 4.5). These instruments have two (one stationary and one rotating) glass circles divided into many graduations (5,000–20,000). Light is projected through the circles and is converted to electronic signals, which the instrument's processor converts to the angle measurement between the fixed and rotating circles. Accuracies can be improved by averaging the results of the measurements on opposite sides of the circles. Some manufacturers determine the errors in the finished instrument and then install a processor program to remove such errors during field use, thus giving one-face measurements the accuracy of two-face measurements. Both systems enable the surveyor to assign 0° (or any other value) conveniently to an instrument setting after the instrument has been sighted-in and clamped.

Total stations have onboard microprocessors that monitor the instrument status (e.g., level and plumb orientation, battery status, return signal strength) and make corrections to measured data for the first of these conditions when warranted. In addition, the microprocessor controls the acquisition of angles and distances and then computes horizontal distances, vertical distances, coordinates, and the like. Many total stations are designed so that the data stored in the data collector can be downloaded quickly to a computer. The manufacturer usually supplies the download program; a second program is required to translate the raw data into a format that is compatible with the surveyor's COGO (i.e., processing) programs.

Most total stations also enable the topographic surveyor to capture the slope distance and the horizontal and vertical angles to a point simply by pressing one button. The point number (most total stations have automatic point-number incrementation) and point description for that point can then be entered and recorded. In addition, the wise surveyor prepares field notes showing the overall detail and the individual point locations. These field notes help the surveyor to keep track of the completeness of the work, and they are invaluable during data editing and preparation of the plot file.

5.2.2   Total Station Instrument Errors

Section 4.10 explained the basic tests for checking theodolite and total station errors. One advantage of total stations over electronic theodolites is that the total station has built-in programs designed to monitor the operation of the instrument and to recalibrate as needed. One error, the line-of-sight error (see Section 4.10.3), can be removed by using two-face measurements (double centering), or simply by using the instrument's onboard calibration program. This line-of-sight error affects the horizontal angle readings more seriously as the vertical angle increases. The tilting axis error [Figure 5.1(d)], which has no impact on perfectly horizontal sightings, also affects the horizontal angle reading more seriously as the vertical angle increases. The effect of the error can also be removed from measurements by utilizing the total station's built-in calibration procedures or by using two-face measurements. The automatic target recognition (ATR) collimation error reflects the angular divergence between the line of sight and the digital camera axis. This ATR is calibrated using onboard software (see Section 5.7.1).

5.3   Total Station Field Techniques

Total stations and/or their attached data collectors have been programmed to perform a wide variety of surveying functions. All total station programs require that the instrument station and at least one reference station be identified so that all subsequent tied-in stations can be defined by their X (easting), Y (northing), and Z (elevation) coordinates. The instrument station's coordinates and elevation, together with the azimuth to the backsight (BS) reference station (or its coordinates), can be entered in the field or uploaded prior to going out to the field. After setup and before the instrument has been oriented for surveying as described above, the hi (height of instrument above the instrument station) and prism heights must be measured and recorded. When using a total station equipped with automatic target acquisition, or ATR (see Section 5.7.1), the instrument can sometimes be (e.g., in a high-volume topographic survey) set up higher than usual to avoid close-to-the-ground potential obstacles (e.g., parked cars); in this type of survey, the operator doesn't have to sight through the telescope to locate the prism. If necessary, the lock-on procedure can be speeded up by the operator manually spinning the electronic tangent screws—both horizontal and vertical. The ATR-equipped total station will signal when lock-on has occurred and the operator can then initiate the automatic measuring process.

Typical total station programs include point location, missing line measurement, resection, azimuth determination, remote object elevation, offset measurements, layout or setting out positions, and area computations. All these topics are discussed in the following sections.

5.3.1   Point Location

5.3.1.1   General Background.
After the instrument has been properly oriented, the coordinates (northing, easting, and elevation) of any sighted point can be determined, displayed, and recorded in the following format: N. E. Z. or E. N. Z.; the order you choose reflects the format needs of the software program chosen to process the field data. At this time, the sighted point is numbered and coded for attribute data (point description)—all of which is recorded with the location data. This program is used extensively in topographic surveys. See Figure 5.5.

5.3.1.2   Trigonometric Leveling.
Chapter 2 explained how elevations were determined using automatic and digital levels, and Sections 2.8 and 2.13 briefly introduced the concept of trigonometric leveling. Field practice has shown that total station

Known: • N, E, and Z coordinates of the instrument station ($\overline{\wedge}$).
• N, E, and Z coordinates of reference control point, or at least the azimuth of the line joining the instrument station and the control point. The above station/control point information can be uploaded from the computer prior to going into the field or manually entered in the field.

Measured: • Angles, or azimuths, from the control point and distances to the new point from the instrument station.

Computed: • N, E, and Z coordinates of new points.
• Azimuth of the line (and its distance) joining the instrument station to the new point.

FIGURE 5.5   Point location program inputs and solutions.

observations can produce elevations at a level of accuracy suitable for the majority of topographic and engineering applications. For elevation work, the total station should be equipped with dual-axis compensation to ensure that angle errors remain tolerable, and for more precise work, the total station should have the ability to measure to $1''$ of arc.

In addition to the uncertainties caused by errors in the zenith angle, the surveyor should be mindful of the errors associated with telescope collimation; other instrument and prism imperfections; measurement of the height of the instrument (hi); measurement of the height of the prism (HR); curvature, refraction, and other natural effects; and errors associated with the use of a handheld prism pole. Also to improve precision, multiple readings can be averaged, readings can be taken from both face 1 and face 2 of the instrument, and reciprocal readings can be taken from either end of the line, with the results averaged. If the accuracy of a total station is unknown or suspect and if the effects of the measuring conditions are unknown, the surveyor should compare his or her trigonometric leveling results with differential leveling results (using the same control points) under similar measuring conditions.

Table 5.1 shows the effect of angle uncertainty on various distances. The basis for the tabulated results is the cosine function of ($90° \pm$ the angle uncertainty) times the distance. Analyze the errors shown in Table 5.1 with respect to the closure requirements shown in Tables 2.1 and 2.2.

5.3.2 Missing Line Measurement

This program enables the surveyor to determine the horizontal and slope distances between any two sighted points, as well as the directions of the lines joining those sighted points (Figure 5.6). Onboard programs first determine the N, E, and Z coordinates of the sighted points and then compute (inverse) the adjoining distances and directions.

5.3.3 Resection

This technique permits the surveyor to set up the total station at any convenient position (sometimes referred to as a **free station**) and then to determine the coordinates and elevation of that instrument position by sighting previously coordinated reference stations (Figure 5.7).

Table 5.1 ELEVATION ERRORS CAUSED BY ZENITH ANGLE UNCERTAINTY

Distance (ft/m)	Zenith Angle Uncertainty				
	$1''$	$5''$	$10''$	$20''$	$60''$
100	0.0005	0.0024	0.005	0.0097	0.029
200	0.0010	0.0048	0.010	0.0194	0.058
300	0.0015	0.0072	0.015	0.029	0.087
400	0.0019	0.0097	0.019	0.039	0.116
500	0.0024	0.0121	0.024	0.049	0.145
800	0.0039	0.0194	0.039	0.078	0.233
1,000	0.0048	0.0242	0.0485	0.097	0.291

Known:	• N, E, and Z coordinates of the instrument station ($\overline{\curlywedge}$). • N, E, and Z coordinates of a reference control point, or at least the azimuth of the line joining the instrument station and the control point.
Measured:	• Angles, or azimuths, from the control point and distances to the new points from the instrument station.
Computed:	• N, E, and Z (elevation) coordinates of new points. • Azimuths and horizontal, slope and vertical distances between the sighted points. • Slopes of the lines joining any sighted points.

FIGURE 5.6   Missing line measurement program inputs and solutions. (Graphics courtesy of SOKKIA Corp.)

Known:	• N, E, and Z coordinates of control point 1. • N, E, and Z coordinates of control point 2. • N, E, and Z coordinates of additional sighted control stations (up to a total of ten control points). These can be entered manually or uploaded from the computer— depending on the instrument's capabilities.
Measured:	• Angles between the sighted control points. • Distances are also required from the instrument station to the control points, if only two control points are sighted. • The more measurements (angles and distances) to different control stations, the better the resection solution.
Computed:	• N, E, and Z (elevation) coordinates of the instrument station ($\overline{\curlywedge}$).

FIGURE 5.7   Resection program inputs and solutions. (Graphics courtesy of SOKKIA Corp.)

When sighting only two points of known position, it is necessary to measure and record both the distances and the angle between the reference points. When sighting several points (three or more) of known position, it is necessary only to measure the angles between the points. It is important to stress that most surveyors take more readings than are minimally necessary to obtain a solution; these redundant measurements give the surveyor increased precision and a check on the accuracy of the results. Once the instrument station's coordinates have been determined, the instrument can now be oriented, and the surveyor can continue to survey using any of the other techniques described in this section.

5.3.4   Azimuth

When the coordinates of the instrument station and a BS reference station have been entered into the instrument processor, the azimuth of a line joining any sighted points can

Known: • N, E, and Z coordinates of the instrument station (π).
• N, E, and Z coordinates of a reference control point, or at least the azimuth of the line joining the instrument station and the control point.

Measured: • Angles from the control point and distances to the new points from the instrument station.

Computed: • Azimuth of the lines joining the new points to the instrument station.
• Slopes of the lines joining any sighted points.
• Elevations of any sighted points.
• Coordinates of sighted points.

FIGURE 5.8 Azimuth program inputs and solutions.

be readily displayed and recorded (Figure 5.8). When using a motorized total station equipped with ATR, the automatic angle measurement program permits you to repeat angles automatically to as many as ten previously sighted stations (including on faces 1 and 2). Just specify the required accuracy (standard deviation) and the sets of angles to be measured (up to twenty angles sets at each point), and the motorized instrument performs the necessary operations automatically.

5.3.5 Remote Object Elevation

The surveyor can determine the heights of inaccessible points (e.g., electrical conductors, bridge components) by simply sighting the pole-mounted prism while it is held directly under the object. When the object itself is then sighted, the object height can be promptly displayed (the prism height must first be entered into the total station). See Figure 5.9.

Known: • N, E, and Z coordinates of the instrument station (π).
• N, E, and Z coordinates of a reference control point, or at least the azimuth of the line joining the instrument station and the control point.

Measured: • Horizontal angle, or azimuth, from the reference control point (optional) and distance from the instrument station to the prism held directly below (or above) the target point.
• Vertical angles to the prism and to the target point hi and height of the prism.

Computed: • Distance from the ground to the target point (and its coordinates if required).

FIGURE 5.9 Remote object elevation program inputs and solutions. (Graphics courtesy of SOKKIA Corp.)

5.3.6 Distance Offset Measurements

When an object is hidden from the total station, a measurement can be taken to the prism held out in view of the total station. The offset distance is measured from the prism (Figure 5.10). The angle (usually 90°) or direction to the hidden object, along with the measured distance, is entered into the total station, enabling it to compute the position of the hidden object.

5.3.7 Angle Offset Measurements

When the center of a solid object (e.g., a concrete column, tree) is to be located, its position can be ascertained by turning angles from each side to the centerpoint (Figure 5.11). The software then computes the center location of the measured solid object.

Known:	• N, E, and Z coordinates of the instrument station ($\bar{\wedge}$). • N, E, and Z coordinates (or the azimuth) for the reference control point.
Measured:	• Distance from the instrument station to the offset point. • Distance (*l*) from the offset point (at a right angle to the instrument line of sight) to the measuring point.
Computed:	• N, E, and Z (elevation) coordinates of the hidden measuring point. • Azimuths and distance from the instrument station to the hidden measuring point.

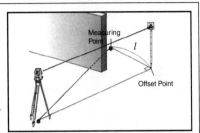

FIGURE 5.10 Offset measurements (distance) program solutions and inputs. (Graphics courtesy of SOKKIA Corp.)

Known:	• N, E, and Z coordinates of the instrument station ($\bar{\wedge}$). • N, E, and Z coordinates (or the azimuth) of the reference control point.
Measured:	• Angles from the prism being held on either side of the measuring point, to the target centerpoint. (The prism must be held such that both readings are the same distance from the instrument station—if both sides are measured).
Computed:	• N, E, and Z coordinates of the hidden measuring points. • Azimuths and distance from the instrument station to the hidden measuring point. • When the measuring point is to the center of a tree, some programs will use this application to determine tree's diameter and then to estimate the tree's height (knowing the height allows the CAD software to insert the correctly sized tree symbol on the digital drawing).

FIGURE 5.11 Offset measurements (angles) program inputs and solutions. (Graphics courtesy of SOKKIA Corp.)

5.3.8   Layout or Setting-Out Positions

After the station numbers, coordinates, and elevations of the layout points have been uploaded into the total station, the layout/setting-out software enables the surveyor to locate any layout point by simply entering that point's number when prompted by the layout software. The instrument's display shows the left/right, forward/back, and up/down movements needed to place the prism in each of the desired position locations (Figure 5.12). This capability is a great aid in property and construction layouts.

5.3.9   Area Computation

While this program has been selected, the processor computes the area enclosed by a series of measured points. The processor first determines the coordinates of each station as described earlier and then, using those coordinates, computes the area in a manner similar to that described in Section 6.12. See Figure 5.13.

Known: • N, E, and Z coordinates of the instrument
             station ($\overline{\wedge}$).
           • N, E, and Z coordinates of a reference control
             point, or at least the azimuth of the line joining
             the instrument station and the control point.
           • N, E, and Z coordinates of the
             proposed layout points (entered manually
             or previously uploaded from the computer).

Measured: • Indicated angles (on the instrument display),
             or azimuths, from the control point and
             distances to each layout point.
           • The angles may be turned manually or
             automatically if a servomotor-driven
             instrument is being used.
           • The distances (horizontal and vertical)
             are continually remeasured as the prism is
             eventually moved to the required layout position.

FIGURE 5.12   Laying out or setting out program inputs and solutions. (Graphics courtesy of SOKKIA Corp.)

Known: • N, E, and Z coordinates of the instrument station ($\overline{\wedge}$).
           • N, E, and Z coordinates of a reference control
             point, or at least the azimuth of the line joining
             the instrument station and the control point.

Measured: • Angles, or azimuths, from the control point and
             distances to the new points from the instrument station.

Computed: • N, E, and Z coordinates of the area boundary points.
           • Area enclosed by the coordinated points.

FIGURE 5.13   Area computation program inputs and solutions. (Graphics courtesy of SOKKIA Corp.)

5.3.10 Summary of Typical Total Station Characteristics

The following lists summarize the characteristics of a typical total station.

PARAMETER INPUT

1. Angle units: degrees or gon
2. Distance units: feet or meters
3. Pressure units: inches HG or millimeters HG*
4. Temperature units: °F or °C*
5. Prism constant (usually −0.03 m). This constant is normally entered at the factory. When measuring to reflective paper, this prism constant must be corrected.
6. Offset distance (used when the prism cannot be held at the center of the object)
7. Face 1 or face 2 selection (telescope erect or telescope inverted)
8. Automatic point number incrementation (yes or no)
9. Height of instrument (hi)
10. Height of reflector (HR)
11. Point numbers and code numbers for occupied and sighted stations
12. Date and time settings (for total stations with onboard clocks)

CAPABILITIES (COMMON TO MANY TOTAL STATIONS)

1. Telescope magnification power of 26× to 33× (most common is 30×)
2. Capable of orienting the horizontal circle to zero (or any other value) after sighting a BS
3. Electronic leveling
4. Out-of-level warning
5. Dual-axis compensation
6. ATR
7. Typical distance accuracy of $\pm(3 \text{ mm} + 2 \text{ ppm})$
8. Typical angle accuracy (and display) ranges from 1″ to 10″
9. Prismless measurement (70–2,000 m measurement range). This range depends on both the instrument's capabilities and on the reflective properties of the target's measuring surface.
10. Guide lights to permit prism-holder's self-alignment
11. Horizontal and vertical collimation corrections—stored onboard and automatically applied
12. Vertical circle indexing and other error corrections—stored onboard and automatically applied

---

*Some newer instruments have built-in sensors that detect atmospheric effects and automatically correct readings for these natural errors.

13. Central processor monitors and/or controls:
    - Battery status, signal attenuation, horizontal and vertical axes status, collimation factors
    - Computes coordinates: northing, easting, and elevation, or easting, northing, and elevation
    - Traverse closure adjustments and traverse areas
    - Topography reductions
    - Remote object elevation (i.e., object heights)
    - Distances between remote points (missing line measurement)
    - Inversing (determining distance and direction between two points if their N, E, and Z coordinates are known)
    - Resection
    - Layout (setting out; e.g., 3D and 2D highway layout programs)
    - Records search and review
    - Programmable features—that is, load external programs
    - Transfer of data to the computer (downloading)
    - Transfer of computer files to the data collector (uploading) for layout and reference purposes
14. Robotic capabilities (700–1,200 m range for control):
    - Servomotors—one to six speeds
    - ATR
    - Target tracking/searching
15. Digital imaging (e.g., Topcon GPT 7000i)

5.4 Field Procedures for Total Stations in Topographic Surveys

Total stations can be used in any type of preliminary survey, control survey, or layout survey. They are particularly well suited for topographic surveys, in which the surveyor can capture the northings, eastings, and elevations of a large number of points—700–1,000 points per day. This significant increase in productivity means that in some medium-density areas, ground surveys are once again competitive in cost with aerial surveys. Although the increase in efficiency in the field survey is notable, an even more significant increase in efficiency can occur when the total station is part of a computerized surveying system—data collection, data processing (reductions and adjustments), and plotting (Figure 7.1).

One of the notable advantages of using electronic surveying techniques is that data are recorded in electronic field books; this cuts down considerably on the time required to record data and to transfer such data to the computer, and on the opportunities of making transcription mistakes. Does this mean that manual field notes are a thing of the past? The answer is no. Even in electronic surveys, there is a need for neat, comprehensive field notes. At the very least, such notes will contain the project title, field personnel, equipment description, date, weather conditions, instrument setup station identification, and BS station(s) identification. In addition, for topographic surveys, many surveyors include in the manual notes a sketch showing the area's selected (in some cases, all) details—individual details such as trees, catch basins, and poles, and stringed detail such as the water's edge, curbs, walks, and building outlines. As the survey proceeds, the surveyor places all or selected point identification numbers directly on the sketch feature, thus clearly showing the type of detail being recorded. Later, after the data have been transferred to the computer, and as the graphics features are being edited, manual field notes are invaluable in clearing up problems associated with any incorrect or ambiguous labeling and numbering of survey points. It seems that surveyors who use modern data collectors with touch-screen graphics capability have a reduced need for manual field notes as they can update the graphics on their displays as the survey proceeds.

5.4.1 Initial Data Entry

Most data collectors are designed to prompt for, or accept, some or all of the following initial configuration and operation data:

- Project description
- Date and crew
- Temperature
- Pressure (some data collectors require a ppm correction input, which is read from a temperature/pressure graph; Figure 3.27)
- Prism constant (–0.03 m is a typical value: check the instrument's specifications)
- Curvature and refraction settings (see Chapter 2)
- Sea-level corrections (see Chapter 9)
- Number of measurement repetitions—angle or distance (the average value is computed)
- Choice of face 1 and face 2 positions (telescope erect or telescope inverted)
- Choice of automatic point-number increments (yes/no), and the value of the first point number in a series of measurements
- Choice of Imperial units or SI units for all data

Many of these prompts can be bypassed, causing the microprocessor to use previously selected, or default, values in its computations. After the initial data have been entered, and the operation mode has been selected, most data collectors prompt the operator for all station and measurement entries.

5.4.2 Survey Station Descriptors

Each survey station, or shot location (point), must be described with respect to surveying activity (e.g., BS, intermediate sight, foresight), station identification, and descriptive attribute data. In many cases, total stations prompt for the data entry [e.g., occupied station, BS reference station(s)] and then automatically assign appropriate labels, which will then show up on the survey printout. Point description data can be entered as alphabet or numeric codes (Figure 5.14). This descriptive data will also show up on the printout and can (if desired) be tagged to show up on the plotted drawing. Some data collectors can be equipped with bar-code readers that permit instantaneous entry of descriptive data when they are used with prepared code sheets.

Point Identification Codes
(shown is part of Seneca dictionary)

Survey Points

01	BM	Bench Mark
02	CM	Concrete Monument
03	SIB	Standard Iron Bar
04	IB	Iron Bar
05	RIB	Round Iron Bar
06	IP	Iron Pipe
07	WS	Wooden Stake
08	MTR	Coordinate Monument
09	CC	Cut Cross
10	N&W	Nail and Washer
11	ROA	Roadway
12	SL	Street Line
13	EL	Easement Line
14	ROW	Right of Way
15	CL	Centerline

Topography

16	EW	Edge Walk
17	ESHLD	Edge Shoulder
18	C&G	Curb and Gutter
19	EWAT	Edge of Water
20	EP	Edge of Pavement
21	RD	CL Road
22	TS	Top of Slope
23	BS	Bottom of Slope
24	CSW	Concrete Sidewalk
25	ASW	Asphalt Sidewalk
26	RW	Retaining Wall
27	DECT	Deciduous Tree
28	CONT	Coniferous Tree
29	HDGE	Hedge
30	GDR	Guide Rail
31	DW	Driveway
32	CLF	Chain Link Fence
33	PWF	Post and Wire Fence
34	WDF	Wooden Fence

Code Sheet for Field Use

1 BM	2 CM	3 SIB	4 IB	5 RIB
6 IP	7 WS	8 MTR	9 CC	10 N W
11 ROA	12 SL	13 EL	14 ROW	15 CL
16 EW	17 ESHL	18 C G	19 EWAT	20 EP
21 RD	22 TS	23 BS	24 CSW	25 ASW
26 RW	27 DECT	28 CONT	29 HDGE	30 GDR
31 DW	32 CLF	33 PWF	34 WDF	35 SIGN
36 MB	37 STM	38 HDW	39 CULV	40 SWLE
41 PSTA	42 SAN	43 BRTH	44 CB	45 DCB
46 HYD	47 V	48 V CH	49 M CH	50 ARV
51 WKEY	52 HP	53 UTV	54 LS	55 TP
56 PED	57 TMH	58 TB	59 BCM	60 GUY
61 TLG	62 BLDG	63 GAR	64 FDN	65 RWYX
66 RAIL	67 GASV	68 GSMH	69 G	70 GMRK
71 TL	72 PKMR	73 TSS	74 SCT	75 BR
76 ABUT	77 PIER	78 FTG	79 EDB	80 POR
81 SLS	82 WTT	83 STR	84 BUS	85 PLY
86 TEN	0	0	0	0
0	0	0	0	0
0	0	0	0	0

(a)   (b)

FIGURE 5.14 (a) Alphanumeric codes for sighted point descriptions. (b) Code sheet for field use.

Some data collectors are designed to work with all (or most) total stations on the market. Figure 5.15 shows two such data collectors. Each of these data collectors has its own unique routine and coding requirements. As this technology continues to evolve and continues to take over many surveying functions, more standardized procedures will likely develop. Newer data collectors (and computer programs) permit the surveyor to enter not only the point code, but also various levels of attribute data for each coded point. For example, a tie-in to a utility pole can also tag the pole number, the use (e.g., electricity, telephone), the material (e.g., wood, concrete, steel), connecting poles, year of installation, and so on. This type of expanded attribute data is typical of the data collected for a municipal geographic information system (GIS; Chapter 8).

FIGURE 5.15 Trimble's TSCe data collector for use with robotic total stations and GPS receivers. When used with TDS Survey Pro Robotics software, this collector features real-time maps, 3D design stakeout, and interactive DTM with real-time cut-and-fill computations. When used with TDS Survey Pro GPS software, this collector can be used for general GPS work, as well as for RTK measurements at centimeter-level accuracy. (Portions © 2001 Trimble Navigation Limited. All Rights Reserved)

Figure 5.15 shows a Trimble TSCe collector/control unit. This data collector can be used with both robotic total stations and GPS receivers. When used with TDS SurveyPro robotics software, this collector/controller features real-time maps, 3D design stakeout, and interactive digital terrain modeling (DTM) with real-time cut-and-fill computations. When used with TDS SurveyPro GPS software, this collector/controller can be used for general GPS work as well as for real-time kinematic (RTK) measurements at centimeter-level accuracy.

All total station/GPS manufacturers produce data collectors and software to execute topographic and layout surveys. Independent companies are also in the market. MicroSurvey Software Inc. has a touch-screen data collector, using total station/GPS software called FieldGenius, that works with most surveying hardware and sells for less than $2,000 (including a collector). Another example is Penmap PC, marketed by Strata Software, using a GPS receiver and collecting data in a large-format, touch-screen tablet PC (Figure 7.22).

5.4.3 AASHTO's Survey Data Management System

The American Association of State Highway and Transportation Officials (AASHTO) developed the Survey Data Management System (SDMS) in 1991 to aid in the nationwide standardization of field coding and computer processing procedures used in highway surveys. The field data can be captured automatically in the data collector, as in the case of total stations, or the data can be entered manually into the data collector for a wide variety of theodolite and level surveys. AASHTO's software is compatible with most recently designed total stations and some third-party data collectors, and data processing can be accomplished using most MS-DOS-based computers. For additional information on these coding standards, contact AASHTO at 444 N. Capitol St., N.W., Suite 225, Washington, DC 20001 (202-624-5800).

5.4.4 Occupied Point (Instrument Station) Entries

The following information is entered into the instrument to describe the setup station:

- Height of instrument above the station (measured value is entered)
- Station number, for example, 111 (see the example in Figure 5.16)
- Station identification code [see the code sheet in Figure 5.14(b)]
- Coordinates of occupied station—the coordinates can be assumed, state plane, or Universal Transverse Mercator (UTM)
- Coordinates of BS station, or reference azimuth to BS station

Note: With some data collectors, the coordinates of the above stations may instead be uploaded from computer files. Once the surveyor identifies by point number specific points as being instrument station and BS reference station(s), the coordinates of those stations then become active in the processor.

5.4.5 Sighted Point Entries

The following information is entered into the instrument to describe the sighted points:

- Height of prism/reflector (HR)—measured value is entered
- Station number—for example, 114 (BS); see Figure 5.16
- Station identification code (Figure 5.14)

FIGURE 5.16 Sketch showing intermediate shoreline ties to a control traverse.

5.4.6   Procedures for the Example Shown in Figure 5.16

1. Set the total station at station 111 and enter the initial data and instrument station data, as shown in Sections 5.4.1 and 5.4.4.

2. Measure the height of the instrument and the height of the reflector, or adjust the height of the reflector to equal the height of the instrument.

3. Sight at station 114; zero the horizontal circle (any other value can be set instead of zero, if desired). Most total stations have a zero-set button.

4. Enter code (e.g., BS), or respond to the data collector prompt.

5. Measure and enter the height of the prism/reflector (HR). If the height of the reflector has been adjusted to equal the height of the instrument, the value of 1.000 is often entered for both values because these hi and HR values usually cancel each other in computations (an advantage of limited value in this electronic age).

6. Press the appropriate measure buttons, for example, slope distance, horizontal angle, vertical angle (an advantage of limited value in this electronic age).

7. Press the record button after each measurement; most instruments measure and record slope, horizontal, and vertical data after the pressing of just one button (when they are in the automatic mode).

8. After the station measurements have been recorded, the data collector program prompts for the station point number (e.g., 114) and the station identification code (e.g., 02 from Figure 5.14, which identifies "concrete monument").

9. If appropriate, as in traverse surveys, the next sight is to the FS station; repeat steps 5–8, using relevant data.

10. While at station 111, any number of intermediate sights (IS) can be taken to define the topographic features being surveyed. Most instruments have the option of speeding up the work by employing "automatic point number incrementation." For example, if the topographic readings are to begin with point number 1000, the surveyor will be prompted to accept the next number in sequence (1001, 1002, 1003, etc.) at each new reading; if the prism is later being held at a previously numbered point (e.g., control point 107), the prompted value can easily be temporarily overridden with 107 being entered.

    In topographic work, the prism/reflector is usually mounted on an adjustable-length prism pole, with the height of the prism (HR) being set at a convenient height, for example, high enough to permit readings over parked vehicles in an urban environment. The prism pole can be steadied by using a bipod (as shown in Figure 3.29), to improve the accuracy for more precise sightings.

    Some software permits the surveyor to identify, by attribute name or an additional code number, points that will be connected (stringed) on the resultant plan (e.g., shoreline points in this example). This connect (on and off) feature permits the field surveyor to prepare the plan (for graphics terminal or digital plotter) while performing the actual field survey. Also, the surveyor can later connect the points while in edit mode on the computer, depending on the software in use; clear field notes are essential for this activity. Data collectors with touch-screen graphics can have points joined by screen touches—without any need for special stringed coding.

11. When all the topographic detail in the area of the occupied station (111) has been collected, the total station can be moved* to the next traverse station (e.g., 112 in this example), and the data collection can proceed in the same manner as that already described, that is, BS @ STA.111, FS @ STA.113, and take all relevant IS readings.

5.4.7 Data Download and Processing

In the example shown in Figure 5.16, the collected data now must be downloaded to a computer. The download computer program is normally supplied by the total station manufacturer, and the actual transfer can be cabled through an RS232 or USB interface cable. Once the data are in the computer, the data must be sorted into a format that is compatible with the computer program that will process the data; this translation program is usually written or purchased separately by the surveyor.

Many modern total stations have data stored onboard, which eliminates the handheld data collectors. Some instruments store data on a module that can be transferred to a computer-connected reading device. Some manufacturers use PCMCIA cards, which can be read directly into a computer through a PCMCIA reader (Figure 5.2). Other total stations, including the geodimeter (Figure 5.25), can be downloaded by connecting the instrument (or its keyboard) directly to the computer; as noted earlier, some total stations can download wirelessly using modern cell-phone technology.

If the topographic data have been tied to a closed traverse, the traverse closure is calculated, and then all adjusted values for northings, eastings, and elevations (Y, X, Z, respectively) are computed. Some total stations have sophisticated data collectors (which are actually small computers) that can perform preliminary analysis, adjustments, and coordinate computations, whereas others require the computer program to perform these functions.

Once the field data have been stored in coordinate files (modern total stations are capable of downloading the field data already processed into coordinate files), the data required for plotting by digital plotters can be assembled, and the survey can be plotted quickly at any desired scale. The survey can also be plotted at an interactive graphics terminal for graphics editing with the aid of one of the many available computer-aided design (CAD) programs.

5.5 Field-Generated Graphics

Modern data collectors, with touch-screen capabilities, enable the surveyor to continually update the associated field graphics (e.g., joining line points to properly depict features). Having the graphics built in the field is an excellent preparation for related computer graphics, once the field data are downloaded. Older total stations required the surveyor to use coded entries to achieve the same result.

To illustrate the use of coded graphics, consider the following two examples. Earlier versions of Microsoft Software Inc. had a typical "description to graphics" feature that enables the surveyor to join field shots, such as curb-line shots (Figure 5.17) by adding a

---

*When the total station is to be moved to another setup station, the instrument is always removed from the tripod and carried separately by its handle or in its case.

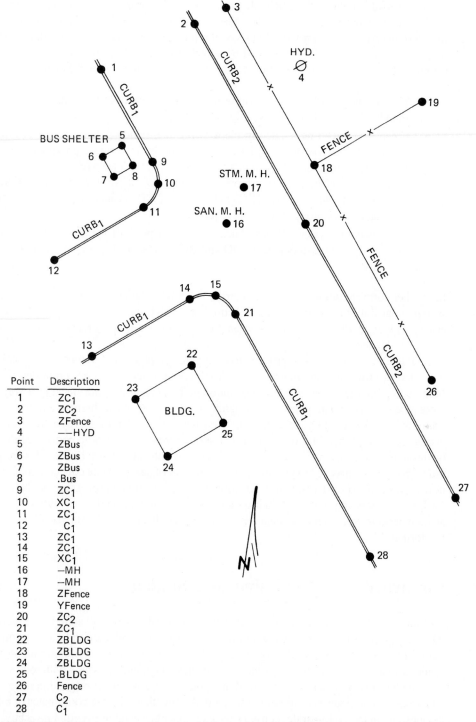

Point	Description
1	ZC_1
2	ZC_2
3	ZFence
4	−−HYD
5	ZBus
6	ZBus
7	ZBus
8	.Bus
9	ZC_1
10	XC_1
11	ZC_1
12	C_1
13	ZC_1
14	ZC_1
15	XC_1
16	−MH
17	−MH
18	ZFence
19	YFence
20	ZC_2
21	ZC_1
22	ZBLDG
23	ZBLDG
24	ZBLDG
25	.BLDG
26	Fence
27	C_2
28	C_1

FIGURE 5.17 Field notes for total station graphics descriptors—MicroSurvey Software Inc. codes.

"Z" prefix to all but the last "CURB" descriptor. When the program first encounters the "Z" prefix, it begins joining points with the same descriptors; when the program encounters the first curb descriptor without the "Z" prefix, the joining of points is terminated. Rounding (e.g., curved curbs) can be introduced by substituting an "X" prefix for the "Z" prefix (Figure 5.17). Other typical MicroSurvey graphics prefixes include the following:

- "Y" joins the last identical descriptor by drawing a line at a right angle to the established line (see the fence line in Figure 5.17).
- "-" causes a dot to be created in the drawing file, which is later transferred to the plan. The dot on the plan can itself be replaced by inserting a previously created symbol block, for example, a tree, a manhole, a hydrant (see MH in Figure 5.17). If a second dash follows the first prefix dash, the ground elevation will not be transferred to the graphics file (see HYD in Figure 5.17). This capability is useful because some feature elevations may not be required.
- "." instructs the system to close back on the first point of the string of descriptors with the same characters (see BLDG and BUS shelter in Figure 5.17 and POND in Figure 5.19).

In another software solution for coded stringing, Sokkia, give the software code itself a stringing capability (e.g., fence1, curb1, curb2, ℄) which the surveyor can easily turn on and off (Figure 5.18). Such coded entries produced the computer graphics after the data were downloaded.

It is safe to say that most projects requiring that graphics be developed from total station surveys utilize a combination of touch-screen point manipulation, point description field coding, and postsurvey point description editing. Note that the success of some of these modern surveys still depends to a significant degree on old-fashioned, reliable survey field notes. It is becoming clear that the "drafting" of the plan of survey is increasingly becoming the responsibility of the surveyor, either through direct field coding techniques or through postsurvey data processing. All recently introduced surveying software programs enable the surveyor to produce a complete plan of survey. Data collector software is now capable of exporting files in DXF format for AutoCad postprocessing or shape files for further processing in ESRI GIS programs. Also, alignments and cross sections are created on desktop computers and then exported to data collectors in the standard Land XML file format.

5.6   Construction Layout Using Total Stations

We saw in the previous section that total stations are particularly well suited for collecting data in topographic surveys; we also noted that both the collected data and computed values (e.g., point coordinates) could be readily downloaded to a computer along with point attribute data. The significant increases in efficiency made possible with total station topographic surveys can also be realized in layout surveys when the original point coordinates exist in computer memory or computer disks, together with the coordinates of all the key design points. To illustrate, consider the example of a road construction project.

Point	Description
1	$CURB_1$
2	$CURB_2$
3	FL1
4	HYD
5	BLD_1
6	BLD_1
7	BLD_1
8	BLD_1 CLOSE
9	$CURB_1$ PC
10	$CURB_1$
11	$CURB_1$ PT
12	$CURB_1$
13	$CURB_1$ ST
14	$CURB_1$ PC
15	$CURB_1$
16	SAN
17	STM
18	FL_1
19	FL_2 JP
20	$CURB_2$
21	$CURB_1$ PT
22	BLD_2
23	BLD_2
24	BLD_2
25	BLD_2 CLOSE
26	FL_1
27	$CURB_2$
28	$CURB_1$

FIGURE 5.18   Field notes for total station graphics descriptors—SOKKIA codes.

First, the topographic detail is collected using total stations set up at various control points (preliminary survey). The detail is then transferred to the computer (and adjusted, if necessary), and converted into Y, X, and Z coordinates. Various COGO and road design programs can then be used to design the proposed road. When the proposed horizontal, cross-section, and profile alignments have been established, the proposed coordinates (Y, X, and Z) for all key horizontal and vertical (elevation) features can be computed and stored in computer files. The points coordinated include top-of-curb and centerline (℄) positions at regular stations, as well as all changes in direction or slope. Catch basins, traffic islands, and the like are also included, as are all curved or irregular road components.

The computer files now include coordinates of all control stations, all topographic detail, and (finally) all design component points. Control point and layout point coordinates (Y, X, and Z) can then be uploaded into the total station. The layout is accomplished by setting the instrument to layout mode, then setting up at an identified control point, and properly orienting the sighted instrument toward another identified control point. Second, while still in layout mode, and after the first layout point number is entered into the instrument, the required layout angle or azimuth and layout distance are displayed. To set the selected layout point from the instrument station, the layout angle (or azimuth) is then turned (automatically by motorized total stations) and the distance is set by following the display instructions (backward/forward, left/right, up/down) to locate the desired layout point. When the total station is set to tracking mode, the surveyor can first set the prism close to target by rapid trial-and-error measurements.

Figure 5.19 illustrates a computer printout for a road construction project. The total station is set at control monument CX-80 with a reference BS on RAP (reference azimuth point) 2 (point 957 on the printout). The surveyor has a choice of (1) setting the actual azimuth (213°57′01″, line 957) on the BS and then turning the horizontal circle to the printed azimuths of the desired layout points or (2) setting 0° for the BS and then turning the clockwise angle listed for each desired layout point. As a safeguard, after sighting the reference BS, the surveyor usually sights a second or third control monument (see the top twelve points on the printout) to check the azimuth or angle setting. The computer printout also lists the point coordinates and baseline offsets for each layout point.

Figure 5.20 shows a portion of the construction drawing that accompanies the computer printout shown in Figure 5.19. The drawing (usually drawn by digital plotter from computer files) is an aid to the surveyor in the field for laying out the works correctly. All the layout points listed on the printout are also shown on the drawing, together with curve data and other explanatory notes. Modern total stations offer an even more efficient technique. Instead of having the layout data only on a printout similar to that shown in Figure 5.20, as noted earlier, the coordinates for all layout points can be uploaded into the total station microprocessor. The surveyor in the field can then identify the occupied control point and the reference BS point(s), thus orienting the total station.

The desired layout point number is then entered, with the required layout angle and distance being inversed from the stored coordinates, and displayed. The layout can proceed by setting the correct azimuth. Then, by trial and error, the prism is moved to the layout distance (the total station is set to tracking mode for all but the final measurements). With some total stations, the prism is simply tracked with the remaining left/right ($\pm$) distance being displayed alongside the remaining near/far ($\pm$) distance. When the correct location

Chap. 5   Total Station Operations

THE MUNICIPALITY OF METROPOLITAN TORONTO - DEPARTMENT OF ROADS AND TRAFFIC

W.R. ALLEN ROAD FROM SHEPPARD AVENUE TO STANSTEAD DRIVE

ENGINEERING STAKEOUT

FROM STATION   269+80.00   TO STATION   271+30.00

BASE LINE

INSTRUMENT ON CONST CONTROL MON CX-80

AZIMUTH 213-57- 1

SIGHTING   RAP #2 - ANTENNA C.F.B.

POINT NO.	STATION	DESCRIPTION	OFFSET FROM BASELINE		AZIMUTH DEG-MIN-SEC	DISTANCE	CLOCKWISE TURN ANGLE	ELEVATION	COORDINATES NORTH	EAST
876	269+89.355	CONST CONTROL MON CX-76	22.862	LEFT	170-49-16	80.430	316-52-15	0.0	4845374.460	307710.370
885	271+29.785	CONST CONTROL MON CX-85	22.857	LEFT	350-49- 8	60.000	136-52- 7	0.0	4845513.091	307687.967
877	269+95.164	CONST CONTROL MON CX-77	22.861	RIGHT	139-19-24	87.513	285-22-24	0.0	4845387.490	307754.580
878	269+97.098	CONST CONTROL MON CX-78	38.095	RIGHT	130-50-11	94.861	276-53-11	0.0	4845391.830	307769.310
879	270+27.530	CONST CONTROL MON CX-79	38.081	RIGHT	115-33-22	74.155	261-36-21	0.0	4845421.870	307764.440
881	270+69.932	CONST CONTROL MON CX-81	22.862	RIGHT	80-38- 4	45.719	226-41- 3	0.0	4845461.300	307742.650
958	290+51.899	RAP #3 - RADIO TOWER	294.749	LEFT	344-19-40	1990.850	130-22-40	0.0	4847370.697	307159.747
884	271+29.932	CONST CONTROL MON CX-84	22.862	RIGHT	28- 3-30	75.551	174- 6-29	0.0	4845520.531	307733.077
959	0+00.000	RAP #4 - CN TOWER	0.0		152-46-14	********	298-49-14	0.0	4833410.793	313894.638
933	270+16.535	CONST CONTROL MON CX-133	61.272	RIGHT	113- 9- 1	99.566	259-12- 0	0.0	4845414.717	307789.088
956	271+72.134	RAP #1 - BILLBOARD FRAME	471.682	RIGHT	69- 7-32	505.019	215-10-31	0.0	4845633.810	308169.411
960	269+67.759	CONTROL MON MTR77-6119	9.329	RIGHT	153-18-33	106.983	299-21-32	196.768	4845358.277	307745.594
957	268+98.575	RAP #2 - ANTENNA C.F.B.	183.253	LEFT	213-57- 1	234.606	0- 0- 0	0.0	4845259.249	307566.519
483	269+83.555	BC CORNER ROUND	25.637	LEFT	172-39-51	86.275	318-42-51	0.0	4845368.291	307708.556
753	269+83.622	CATCH BASIN GUTTER	25.142	LEFT	172-20-12	86.193	318-23-11	0.0	4845368.437	307709.034
485	269+84.988	PI CORNER ROUND	13.500	LEFT	164-31-15	85.312	310-34-15	0.0	4845371.643	307720.309
486	269+88.075	MP CORNER ROUND	16.973	LEFT	166-41-56	81.922	312-44-55	0.0	4845374.136	307716.388
446	269+88.654	PI CORNER ROUND	13.500	RIGHT	146-40-47	88.906	292-43-46	0.0	4845379.569	307746.378
2103	269+90.000	C/L OF CONSTRUCTION	0.0		154-49-55	82.995	300-52-54	196.352	4845378.744	307732.836
444	269+90.625	BC CORNER ROUND	28.986	RIGHT	137-35-48	94.626	283-38-47	0.0	4845383.986	307761.351
754	269+91.351	CATCH BASIN GUTTER	34.690	RIGHT	134-33- 3	97.281	280-36- 2	0.0	4845385.613	307766.866
461	269+91.604	BC CORNER ROUND	36.674	RIGHT	133-31-51	98.267	279-34-50	0.0	4845386.179	307768.784
434	269+92.355	BULLNOSE TOP OF CURB	1.500	RIGHT	153-21-22	81.172	299-24-21	196.425	4845381.308	307733.941
437	269+93.105	BC BULLNOSE TOP OF CURB	2.250	RIGHT	152-41-18	80.687	298-44-17	196.395	4845382.168	307734.562
435	269+93.105	CP BULLNOSE TOP ISLAND	1.500	RIGHT	153-11-45	80.456	299-14-44	196.410	4845382.048	307733.821
436	269+93.105	EC BULLNOSE TOP OF CURB	0.750	RIGHT	153-42-23	80.233	299-45-22	196.425	4845381.929	307733.081
447	269+93.947	MP CORNER ROUND	18.162	RIGHT	142-24-37	86.221	288-27-36	0.0	4845385.538	307750.135
482	269+97.210	CENTER PT CORNER ROUND	27.250	LEFT	174-16-54	72.708	320-19-53	0.0	4845381.513	307704.785
484	269+97.210	EC CORNER ROUND-TOP CURB	13.500	LEFT	163-28-17	73.176	309-31-16	196.290	4845383.707	307718.358
755	269+98.000	CATCH BASIN TOP OF CURB	13.500	LEFT	163-23-29	72.392	309-26-28	196.270	4845384.488	307718.232
2107	270+00.000	TOP OF CURB	13.500	LEFT	163-10-51	70.410	309-13-51	196.036	4845386.462	307717.913
2106	270+00.000	C/L OF CONSTRUCTION	0.0		152-40-57	73.433	298-43-56	196.156	4845388.616	307731.240
443	270+04.265	CENTER PT CORNER ROUND	27.250	RIGHT	133-24-39	82.485	279-27-38	0.0	4845397.175	307757.460
445	270+04.265	EC CORNER ROUND-TOP CURB	13.500	RIGHT	141-47-32	74.932	287-50-31	196.050	4845394.981	307743.887
756	270+05.265	CATCH BASIN TOP OF CURB	13.500	RIGHT	141-25- 0	74.059	287-28- 0	196.110	4845395.968	307743.727
2111	270+10.000	TOP OF CURB	13.500	RIGHT	139-30-47	69.973	285-33-46	195.854	4845400.642	307742.971
2110	270+10.000	TOP OF CURB	13.500	LEFT	161-55-21	60.513	307-58-20	195.854	4845396.334	307716.317
2109	270+10.000	C/L OF CONSTRUCTION	0.0		149-53-42	64.006	295-56-41	195.974	4845398.488	307729.644
2113	270+20.000	TOP OF CURB	13.500	LEFT	160-10-24	50.657	306-13-23	195.686	4845406.206	307714.722

CITY OF TORONTO
MANAGEMENT SERVICES DEPARMENT DATA PROCESSING CENTRE

FIGURE 5.19 Computer printout of layout data for a road construction project. (Courtesy of Department of Roads and Traffic, City of Toronto)

has been reached, both displays show 0.000 m (0.00 ft). When a motorized total station is used (see Section 5.7.2), the instrument itself turns the appropriate angle after the layout point number has been entered.

If the instrument is set up at an unknown position (free station), its coordinates can be determined by sighting control stations whose coordinates have been previously uploaded into the total station microprocessor. This technique, known as resection, is available on all modern total stations (see Section 5.3.3). Sightings on two control points can locate the instrument station, although additional sightings (up to a total of four) are recommended to provide a stronger solution and an indication of the accuracy level achieved.

Some theodolites and total stations come equipped with a guide light, which can help move the prism-holder on-line very quickly (see Figures 5.21 and 5.22). The TC 800 is a total station that can be turned on and used immediately (no initialization procedure). It comes equipped with internal storage for 2,000 points and an electronic guide light, which is very useful in layout surveys because prism-holders can quickly place themselves on-line by noting the colored lights sent from the total station. The flashing lights (yellow

Sec. 5.6   Construction Layout Using Total Stations   **143**

LIVERPOOL JOHN MOORES UNIVERSITY
LEARNING SERVICES

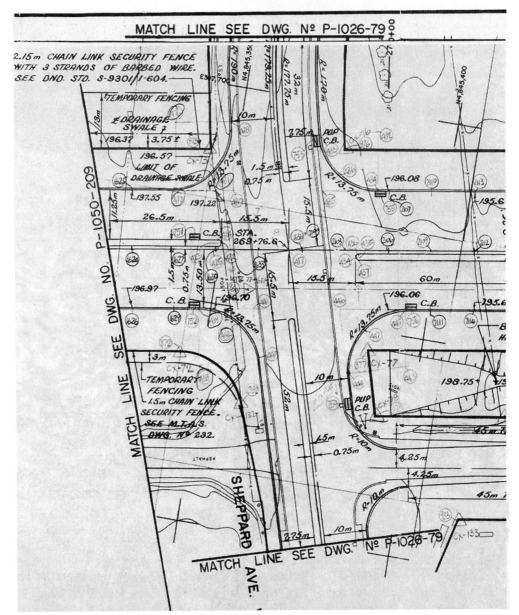

FIGURE 5.20 Portion of a construction plan showing layout points. (Courtesy of Department of Roads and Traffic, City of Toronto)

on the left and red on the right, as viewed by the prism-holder), which are 12-m wide at a distance of 100 m, enable the prism-holder to place the prism on-line, with final adjustments as given by the instrument operator. With ATR (see Section 5.7.1), the sighting-in process is completed automatically.

FIGURE 5.21 Leica TC 800 total station with electronic guide light. (Courtesy of Leica Geosystems Inc.)

FIGURE 5.22 Electronic guide light. (Courtesy of Leica Geosystems Inc.)

5.7 Motorized Total Stations

One significant improvement to the total station has been the addition of servomotors to drive both the horizontal and the vertical motions of these instruments. Motorized instruments have been designed to search automatically for prism targets and then lock onto them precisely, to turn angles automatically to designated points using the uploaded coordinates of those points, and to repeat angles by automatically double-centering. These instruments, when combined with a remote controller held by the prism surveyor, enable the survey to proceed with a reduced need for field personnel.

5.7.1 Automatic Target Recognition

Some instruments are designed with ATR, which utilizes an infrared light bundle or laser beam that is sent coaxially through the telescope to a prism, or from the prism assembly to the total station. The return signal is received by an internal charge-coupled device (CCD) camera. First, the telescope must be pointed roughly at the target prism, either manually or under software control. Then the motorized instrument places the cross hairs almost on the prism center (within 2″ of arc). Any residual offset error is measured automatically and applied to the horizontal and vertical angles. The ATR module is a digital camera that notes the offset of the reflected (or transmitted) laser beam, permitting the instrument then to move automatically until the cross hairs have been set on the point electronically. After the point has thus been precisely sighted, the instrument can then read and record the angle and distance. Reports indicate that the time required for this process (which eliminates manual sighting and focusing) is only one-third to one-half the time required to obtain the same results using conventional total station sighting techniques. ATR comes with a lock-on mode, where the instrument, once sighted on the prism, continues to follow the prism as it is moved from station to station. (ATR is also referred to as autolock and autotracking.) To ensure that the prism is always pointed at the instrument, a 360° prism (see Figures 5.21 and 5.23) assists the surveyor in keeping the

FIGURE 5.23 Leica 360° prism—used with remote-controlled total stations and with automatic target recognition (ATR) total stations. ATR eliminates fine pointing and focusing. The 360° feature means that the prism is always facing the instrument. (Courtesy of Leica Geosystems Inc.)

lock-on for a period of time. If lock-on is lost because of intervening obstacles, it is reestablished after manually and roughly pointing at the prism. ATR recognizes targets up to 2,200 m away, functions in darkness, requires no focusing or fine pointing, works with all types of prisms, and maintains a lock on 360° prisms moving up to speeds of 11 mph, or 5 mps (at a distance of 100 m).

5.7.2 Remote-Controlled Surveying

Geodimeter, the company that first introduced EDM equipment in the early 1950s, introduced in the late 1980s a survey system in which the total station (Geodimeter series 4000; Figure 5.24) was equipped with motors to control both horizontal and vertical movements. This total station can be used as a conventional instrument, but when it is interfaced with a controller located with the prism, the surveyor at the prism station, by means of radio telemetry, can remotely control the station instrument. Some instruments introduced more recently use laser fan emissions to establish the instrument/remote controller or prism assembly/instrument geometric connections.

When the remote control button on the total station is activated, control of the station instrument is transferred to the remote controller. See Figure 5.25. The remote controller consists of the pole (with circular bubble), the prism, a data collector (up to 10,000 points), and telemetry equipment for communicating with the station instrument. A typical operation requires that the station unit be placed over a control station or over a free station whose coordinates can be determined using resection techniques (see Section 5.3.3) and that a BS be taken to another control point, thus fixing the location and orientation of the total station. The operation then begins with both units being activated at the remote controller. The remote controller sighting telescope is aimed at the station unit, and the sensed vertical angle is sent via telemetry to the station unit. The station unit then sets its telescope automatically at the correct angle in the vertical plane and begins a horizontal search for the remote controller prism. The search area can be limited to a specific sector (e.g., 70°), thus reducing search time. The limiting range of this station instrument/remote controller connection is said to be about 700 m. When the measurements (angle and distance) have been completed, the point number and attribute data codes can be entered into the data collector attached to the prism pole.

When used for setting out, the desired point number is entered at the remote controller keyboard. The total station instrument then automatically turns the required angle, which it computes from previously uploaded coordinates held in storage (both the total station and the remote controller have the points in storage). The remote controller operator can position the prism roughly on-line by noting the Track-Light®, which shows as red or green (for this instrument), depending on whether the operator is left or right, respectively, of the line, and as white when the operator is on the line (see also the electronic guide light shown in Figures 5.21 and 5.22).

Distance and angle readouts are then observed by the operator to position the prism pole precisely at the layout point location. Because the unit can fast-track (0.4 s) precise measurements and because it is also capable of averaging multiple measurement readings, very precise results can be obtained when using the prism pole by slightly "waving" the pole left and right and back and forth in a deliberate pattern. All but the BS reference are obtained using infrared and telemetry, so the system can be used effectively after dark, thus

(a)

(b)

FIGURE 5.24 (a) Geodimeter 4400 base station. A total station equipped with servomotors controlling both the horizontal and vertical circle movements. Can be used alone as a conventional total station or as a robotic base station controlled by the remote-positioning unit (RPU) operator. (b) Geodimeter keyboard showing in-process electronic leveling. Upper cursor can also be centered by finally adjusting the third leveling screw.

permitting nighttime layouts for next-day construction and for surveys in high-volume traffic areas that can be accomplished efficiently only in low-volume time periods.

Figure 5.26 shows a remotely controlled total station manufactured by Leica Geosystems Incorporated. This system utilizes ATR and the electronic guide light to search

FIGURE 5.25 Remote-positioning unit (RPU)—a combination of prism, data collector, and radio communicator (with the base station) that permits the operator to engage in one-person surveys.

FIGURE 5.26 Leica TPS System 1000, used for roadway stakeout. The surveyor is controlling the remote-controlled total station (TCA 1100) at the prism pole using the RCS 1000 controller together with a radio modem. The assistant is placing the steel bar marker at the previous set-out point. (Courtesy of Leica Geosystems Inc.)

for and then position the prism on the correct layout line—where the operator then notes the angle and distance readouts to determine the precise layout location. Figure 5.27 shows a motorized total station (Trimble 5600 total station). It has many features, including a four-speed servo; Autolock, a coaxial prism sensor that locks quickly and precisely on the target

(b)

(a)   (c)

FIGURE 5.27 (a) Trimble 5600 robotic total station. (b) Trimble ACU controller, featuring wireless communications and a choice of software for all robotic total station applications as well as all GPS applications. (c) Remote pole unit containing an ACU controller, 360° prism, and radio. (Courtesy of Trimble)

prism and then follows it as it moves; robotic operation (one-person operation) utilizing radio control from the remote roving station instrument [Figure 5.27(c)]; direct reflex (DR) EDM, which permits measurements to features without the use of reflecting prisms up to 600–1,200 m away (depending on the model), aided by a laser marking device; Tracklight®, a multicolored beam that provides a fast technique of positioning the prism-holder in setting-out activities; and a full complement of computational, point acquisition, and setting-out software.

5.7.3 Emerging Robotic Total Station Technology

In 2007, Trimble introduced the *VX Spatial Station*, a robotic total station to which 3D spatial scanning and live video on the controller screen have been added (Figure 5.28). This combination permits the surveyor to identify and capture data points by tapping the images on the controller's touch screen using total station measurements or scanning measurements, and greatly reduces the need for conventional field survey notes. This instrument combines millimeter-accuracy total station measurements to points conventional distances from the instrument, with "sub-meter" accuracy scanning measurements

(a)

(b)

(c)

FIGURE 5.28 (a) ILRIS–3DMCER scanner; (b) bridge photo; and (c) 3-D lidar image of same bridge captured by the lidar scanner. (Courtesy of Optech Incorporated, Toronto) for points up to about 150 m away from the instrument. Trimble uses its extraction software, *Realworks*, to determine feature positions and descriptions. With its 2D and 3D capabilities, this instrument could also find relevance in working to establish 3D works files for machine guidance and control projects. It is expected that other manufactures in the surveying field will soon join in these exciting new developments, thus fostering ever more developments in this technology.

5.8   Summary of Modern Total Station Characteristics and Capabilities

Modern total stations have some or all of the capabilities listed below:

- Some instruments require that horizontal and vertical circles be revolved through 360° to initialize angle-measuring operations, whereas some newer instruments require no such initialization for angle-measuring readiness.
- They can be equipped with servomotors to drive the horizontal and vertical motions (the basis for robotic operation).
- A robotic instrument can be controlled at a distance of 700–1,200 m from the prism pole.
- Telescope magnification for most total stations is at 26× or 30×.
- The minimum focus distance is in the range of 0.5–1.7 m.
- Distance measurement to a single prism is in the range of 2–5 km (10 km for a triple prism).
- A coaxial visible laser has a reflectorless measuring range of 250–2,000 m.
- Angle accuracies are in the range of 1″ to 10″. Accuracy is defined as the standard deviation, direct and reverse in DIN specification 18723.
- Distance accuracies, using reflectors, are as follows: normal, $\pm(2 \text{ mm} + 2 \text{ ppm})$; tracking, $\pm(5 \text{ mm} + 2 \text{ ppm})$; reflectorless, $\pm(3\text{–}10 \text{ mm}, + 2 \text{ ppm})$; longer-range reflectorless, $\pm(5 \text{ mm} + 2 \text{ ppm}.)$
- Eye-safe lasers are class 1 and class 2 (class 2 requires some caution).
- Reflectorless ranges are up to 2,000 m to a 90-percent (reflection) Kodak Gray Card, and up to 300 m to a 18-percent (reflection) Kodak Gray Card.
- Auto focusing.
- Automatic environment sensing (temperature and pressure) with ppm corrections applied to measured distances, or manual entry for measured corrections.
- Wireless Blue Tooth communications, or cable connections.
- Standard data collectors (onboard or attached), or collectors with full graphics (four to eight lines of text) with touch-screen command capabilities for quick editing and line-work creation, in addition to keyboard commands.
- Onboard calibration programs for line-of-sight errors, tilting axis errors, compensator index errors, vertical index errors, and automatic target lock-on calibration. Corrections for sensed errors can be applied automatically to all measurements.

- Endless drives for horizontal and vertical motions (nonmotorized total stations).
- Laser plummets.
- Guide lights for prism placements, with a range of 5–150 m, used in layout surveys.
- ATR, also known as autolock and autotracking, with an upper range of 2,000 m for standard prisms, and about half that value for 360° prisms.
- Single-axis or dual-axis compensation.

The capabilities of total stations are constantly being improved. Thus, this list is not meant to be comprehensive.

5.9 Instruments Combining Total Station Capabilities and GPS Receiver Capabilities

Leica Geosystems Inc. was the first in early 2005 to market a total station equipped with an integrated dual-channel GPS receiver (Figure 5.29). All TPS 1200 total stations can be upgraded to achieve total station/GPS receiver capability. The GPS receiver, together with a communications device, are mounted directly on top of the total station yoke so that they are on the vertical axis of the total station and thus correctly positioned over the station point. The total station keyboard can be used to control all total station and GPS receiver operations. RTK accuracies are said to be ±(10 mm + 1 ppm) horizontal and ±(20 mm + 1 ppm) vertical. The GPS receiver can identify the instrument's first uncoordinated position (free station) to high accuracy when working differentially with a GPS base station (located within 50 km). Once the instrument station has been coordinated, a second station can be similarly established, and the total station can then be oriented while you are backsighting the first established station. All necessary GPS software is included in the total station processor. (Also see Chapter 7.) Early comparative trials indicate that, for some applications, this new technology can be 30–40 percent faster than traditional total station surveying. Because nearby ground control points may not have to be occupied, the surveyor saves the time it takes to set up precisely over a point and to bring control into the project area from control stations that are too far away to be of immediate use. If the instrument is set up in a convenient uncoordinated location where you can see the maximum number of potential survey points, you need only to turn on the GPS receiver and then level and orient the total station to a BS reference. By the time the surveyor is ready to begin the survey and assuming a GPS reference base station is within 50 km, the GPS receiver is functioning in RTK mode. The survey can commence with the points requiring positioning being determined using total station techniques and/or by using the GPS receiver after it has been transferred from the total station and placed on a rover antenna pole for roving positioning. The GPS data, collected at the total station, are stored along with all the data collected using total station techniques on compact memory flash cards. Data can be transferred to internet-connected cell phones using wireless (e.g., Bluetooth) technology before being transmitted to the project computer for downloading. This new technology, which represents a new era in surveying, will change the way we look at traditional traverses and control surveying in general, as well as topographic surveys and layout surveys.

FIGURE 5.29 Leica SmartStation total station with integrated GPS. (Courtesy of Leica Geosystems Inc.)

5.10 Portable/Handheld Total Stations

Several instrument manufacturers produce lower-precision reflectorless total stations that can be handheld, like a camcorder, or pole/tripod-mounted, like typical surveying instruments. These instruments have three integral components:

1. The pulse laser [Food and Drug Administration (FDA) Class 1*] distance meter measures reflectorlessly and/or to reflective papers and prisms. When used reflectorlessly, the distance range of 300–1,200 m varies with different manufacturers and model

---

*FDA Class 1 lasers are considered safe for the eyes. Class 2 lasers should be used with caution and should not be operated at eye level. Class 3A, 3B, and 4 lasers should be used only with appropriate eye protection.

types; the type of sighted surface (masonry, solid trees, bushes, etc.) determines the distance range because some surfaces are much more reflective than others. Masonry and concrete surfaces reflect light well, while trees, bushes, sod, etc. reflect light to lesser degrees (see Table 3.3). When used with prisms, the distance range increases to 5–8 km. Some instruments can be limited to an expected distance-range envelope. This measuring restriction instructs the instrument not to measure and record distances outside the envelope. This feature permits the surveyor to sight more distant points through nearby clutter such as intervening electrical wires, branches, and other foliage. Distance accuracies are in the range of 1–10 cm, and ±(5 cm + 20 ppm) is typical. Power is supplied by two to six AA batteries or two C-cell batteries; battery type depends on the model. See Figure 5.30.

2. Angle encoders and built-in inclinometers determine the horizontal and vertical angles, much like the total stations described earlier in this chapter, and can produce accuracies up to greater than 1′ of arc. The angle accuracy range of instruments on the market in 2005 is 0.01° to 0.2°. Obviously, mounted instruments produce better accuracies than do handheld units.

FIGURE 5.30 The reflectorless total station is equipped with integrating distance measurement, angle encoding, and data collection. (Courtesy of Riegl USA Inc., Orlando, Florida)

3. Data collection can be provided by many of the collectors on the market. These handheld total stations can be used in a wide variety of mapping and GIS surveys or they can be used in GPS surveys. For example, GPS surveys can be extended into areas under tree canopy or structural obstructions (where GPS signals are blocked), with the positional data collected directly into the GPS data collector.

Review Questions

5.1 What are the advantages of using a total station rather than an electronic theodolite and steel tape?

5.2 When would you use a steel tape rather than a total station to measure a distance?

5.3 What impact did the creation of electronic angle measurement have on surveying procedures?

5.4 With the ability to record field measurements and point descriptions in an instrument controller or electronic field book, why are manual field notes still important?

5.5 Explain the importance of electronic surveying in the extended field of surveying and data processing, now often referred to as the science of geomatics.

5.6 Using a programmed total station, how would you tie in (locate) a water valve "hidden" behind a building corner?

5.7 Some total station settings can be entered once and then are seldom changed, while other settings must be changed each time the instrument is set up. Prepare two lists of instrument settings, one for each instance.

5.8 After a total station has been set up over a control station, describe what actions and entries must then be completed before you can begin a topographic survey.

5.9 On a busy construction site, most control stations are blocked from a proposed area of layout. Describe how to create a convenient free station control point using resection techniques.

5.10 Describe a technique for identifying survey sightings on a curb line so that a series of curb-line shots are joined graphically when they are transferred to the computer (or data collector graphics).

5.11 Describe a total station technique for laying out precoordinated construction points.

5.12 What are the advantages of motorized total stations?

5.13 What are the advantages of using automatic target recognition?

5.14 Describe how you would extend vertical control from local benchmarks to cover a large construction site using a total station (see Section 3.8).

Chapter 6

Traverse Surveys
and Computations

6.1   General Background

A traverse is a form of control survey used in a wide variety of engineering and property surveys. Essentially, **traverses** are a series of established stations tied together by angle and distance. Angles are measured by theodolites or total stations; the distances can be measured by electronic distance measurement (EDM) instruments, sometimes by steel tapes. Traverses can be open, as in route surveys, or closed, as in closed geometric figures (Figures 6.1 and 6.2).

Traverse computations are used to do the following: balance field angles, compute latitudes and departures, compute traverse error, distribute the errors by balancing the latitudes and departures, adjust original distances and directions, compute coordinates of the traverse stations, and compute the area enclosed by a closed traverse. In modern practice, these computations are routinely performed on computers and/or on some total stations— or their electronic field books/data collectors (see Chapter 5). In this chapter, we will perform traverse computations manually (using calculators) to demonstrate and reinforce the mathematical concepts underlying each stage of these computations.

In engineering work, traverses are used as control surveys (1) to locate topographic detail for the preparation of topographic plans and engineering design plan and profiles, (2) to lay out (locate) engineering works, and (3) for the processing and ordering of earthwork and other engineering quantities. Traverses can also help provide horizontal control for aerial surveys in the preparation of photogrammetric mapping (see Chapter 8).

6.1.1   Open Traverse

An open traverse (Figure 6.1) is particularly useful as a control for preliminary and construction surveys for highways, roads, pipelines, electricity transmission lines, and the like. These surveys may be from a few hundred feet (meters) to many miles (kilometers) in

FIGURE 6.1 Open traverse.

FIGURE 6.2 Closed traverse (loop).

length. The distances are normally measured by using EDM (sometimes steel tapes). Each time the survey line changes direction, a deflection angle is measured with a theodolite or total station. **Deflection angles** are measured from the prolongation of the back line to the forward line (Figure 6.1); the angles are measured either to the right or to the left (L or R), and the direction (L or R) is shown in the field notes, along with the numerical values. Angles are measured at least twice (see Sections 4.6.1, G.3.8, and G.4 for measuring angles by repetition) to eliminate mistakes and to improve accuracy. The distances are shown in the form of stations (chainages), which are cumulative measurements referenced to the initial point of the survey, 0 + 00. See Figure 6.3 for typical field notes for a route survey.

Open traverses may extend for long distances without the opportunity for checking the accuracy of the ongoing work. Thus, all survey measurements are repeated carefully at the time of the work, and every opportunity for checking for position and direction is utilized (adjacent property surveys and intersecting road and railroad rights-of-way are checked when practical.) Global positioning system (GPS) surveying techniques are also used to determine and verify traverse station positioning.

STATION	DIRECT	DOUBLE	MEAN	L/R
0 + 00	90° 11'	180° 20'	90° 10'	SEE SKETCH.
	DEFLECTION ANGLES			
3+71.26	9° 31'	19° 02'	9° 31'	R
7+60.20	24° 51'	49° 44'	24° 52'	L
10+42.63	11° 32'	23° 04'	11° 32'	R

CHAINAGES				
	DIRECT	REVERSE	MEAN	CHAINAGES
				0 + 00.00
	371.24	371.28	371.26	3 + 71.26
	388.93	388.60		
		388.95	388.94	7 + 60.20
	282.43	282.43	282.43	10 + 42.63
	565.44	565.49	565.46	16 + 08.09
			1608.09	

FIGURE 6.3 Field notes for open traverse. (*Note:* The terms *chainages* and *stations* are interchangeable.)

Many states and provinces have provided densely placed control monuments as an extension to their coordinate grid systems. It is now possible to tie in the initial and terminal survey stations of a route survey to coordinate control monuments. Because the Y and X (and Z) coordinates of these monuments have been precisely determined, the route survey changes from an open traverse to a closed traverse and is then subject to geometric verification and analysis (see Sections 6.6 through 6.12). Of course, it is now also possible, using appropriate satellite-positioning techniques, to directly determine the easting, northing, and elevation of all survey stations.

6.1.2 Closed Traverse

A closed traverse is one that either begins and ends at the same point or begins and ends at points whose positions have been previously determined (as described above). In both cases, the angles can be closed geometrically, and the position closure can be determined mathematically. A closed traverse that begins and ends at the same point is called a loop traverse (Figure 6.2). In this case, the distances are measured from one station to the next and verified, using a steel tape or EDM instrument. The interior angle is measured at each

DISTANCES

COURSE	FORWARD	REVERSE	MEAN
AB	100.00	100.00	
	64.94	64.96	
	164.94	164.96	164.95
BC	88.41	88.41	88.41
CD	100.00	100.00	
	21.70	21.68	
	121.70	121.68	121.69
DE	100.00	100.00	
	15.88	15.90	
	115.88	115.90	115.89
EA	68.42	~~68.57~~	
	68.42	68.42	68.42

ANGLES

STATION	DIRECT	DOUBLE	MEAN	
A	101° 28'	202° 56'	101° 28'	
B	102° 11'	204° 23'	102° 11'	30"
C	104° 42'	209° 24'	104° 42'	
D	113° 05'	226° 11'	113° 05'	30"
E	118° 34'	237° 08'	118° 34'	
			538°120'	60"
			= 540°	01'

L. CROCKER — NOTES, TAPE
K. SINGH — INSTRUMENT
D. JANCIE — TAPE

FIGURE 6.4 Field notes for closed traverse.

station, and each angle is measured at least twice. Figure 6.4 illustrates typical field notes for a loop traverse survey. In this type of survey, distances are booked simply as dimensions, not as stations or chainages.

6.2 Balancing Field Angles

For a closed polygon of n sides, the sum of the interior angles is $(n - 2)180°$. In Figure 6.2, the interior angles of a five-sided polygon have been measured as shown in the field notes in Figure 6.4. For a five-sided closed figure, the sum of the interior angles must be $(5 - 2)180° = 540°$. You can see in Figure 6.4 that the interior angles add to 540°01'—an excess of 1'.

Before mathematical analysis can begin—that is, before the bearings or azimuths can be computed—the field angles must be adjusted so that their sum exactly equals the correct geometric total. The angles can be balanced by distributing the error evenly to each angle, or one or more angles can be arbitrarily adjusted to force the closure. The total allowable error of angular closure is quite small (see Chapter 9); if the field results exceed the allowable error, the survey must be repeated.

Table 6.1 TWO METHODS OF ADJUSTING FIELD ANGLES

Station	Field Angle	Arbitrarily Balanced	Equally Balanced
A	101°28′	101°28′	101°27′48″
B	102°11′30″	102°11′	102°11′18″
C	104°42′	104°42′	104°41′48″
D	113°05′30″	113°05′	113°05′18″
E	118°34′	118°34′	118°33′48″
	=538°120′60″	=538°120′	=538°117′180″
	=540°01′00″	=540°00′	=540°00′00″

       The angles for the traverse in Figure 6.4 are shown in Table 6.1. Also shown are the results of equally balanced angles and arbitrarily balanced angles. The angles can be arbitrarily balanced if the required precision will not be affected or if one or two setups are suspect (e.g., due to unstable ground, or very short sightings).

6.3   Meridians

A line on the surface of the earth joining the north and south poles is called a geographic, astronomic, or "true" meridian. Figure 6.5 illustrates that **geographic meridian** is another term for a line of longitude. The figure also illustrates that all geographic meridians converge at the poles. **Grid meridians** are lines that are parallel to a grid reference meridian (a central

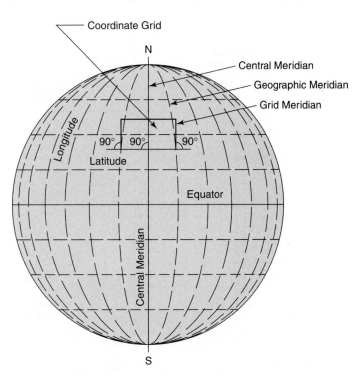

FIGURE 6.5 Relationship between geographic and grid meridians.

meridian—Figure 6.5). Rectangular coordinate grids are discussed further in Chapter 9. **Magnetic meridians** are lines parallel to the directions taken by freely moving magnetized needles, as in a compass. Whereas geographic and grid meridians are fixed, magnetic meridians can vary with time and location.

Geographic meridians can be established by tying into an existing survey line whose geographic direction is known or whose direction can be established by observations on the sun or on Polaris (the North Star) or through GPS surveys. Grid meridians can be established by tying into an existing survey line whose grid direction is known or whose direction can be established by tying into coordinate grid monuments whose rectangular coordinates are known. On small or isolated surveys of only limited importance, meridians are sometimes assumed (e.g., one of the survey lines is simply designated as being "due north"), and the whole survey is referenced to that assumed direction.

Meridians are important to the surveyor because they are used as reference directions for surveys. All survey lines can be related to each other and to the real world by angles measured from meridians. These angles are called bearings and azimuths.

6.4   Bearings

A **bearing** is the direction of a line given by the acute angle between that line and a meridian. The bearing angle, which can be measured clockwise or counterclockwise from the north or south end of a meridian, is always accompanied by the letters that describe the quadrant in which the line is located (NE, SE, SW, and NW). Figure 6.6 illustrates the

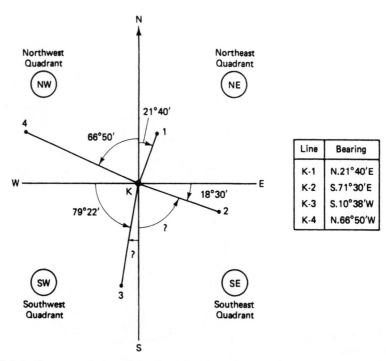

FIGURE 6.6   Bearings calculated from given data (answers in box).

Line	Bearing
K1	N.21°40′E
1K	S.21°40′W

FIGURE 6.7 Illustration of reversed bearings.

concepts of bearings. The given angles for lines K1 and K4 are acute angles measured from the meridian and, as such, are bearing angles. The given angles for lines K2 and K3 are both measured from the E/W axis and therefore are not bearing angles; here, the given angles must be subtracted from 90° to determine the bearing angle.

All lines have two directions: forward and reverse. Figure 6.7 shows that to reverse a bearing, the letters are simply switched, for example, N to S and E to W. To illustrate, consider walking with a compass along a line in a northeasterly direction. If you were to stop and return along the same line, the compass would indicate that you would then be walking in a southwesterly direction. In Figure 6.7, when the meridian is drawn through point K, the line K1 is being considered, and the bearing is NE. If the meridian is drawn through point 1, however, the line 1K is being considered, and the bearing is SW. In computations, the direction of a line therefore depends on which end of the line the meridian is placed. When computing the bearings of adjacent sides (as in a closed traverse), the surveyor must routinely reverse bearings as the computations proceed around the traverse (Figure 6.8).

Figure 6.8 shows a five-sided traverse with geometrically closed angles and a given bearing for side AE of S 7°21′ E. The problem here is to compute the bearings of the remaining sides. To begin, the surveyor must decide whether to solve the problem going clockwise or counterclockwise. In this example, the surveyor decided to work clockwise, and the bearing of side AB is computed first using the angle at A. Had the surveyor decided to work the computations counterclockwise, the first computation would be for the bearing of side ED, using the angle at E.

The bearing of side AB can be computed by first drawing the two sides AB and AE, together with a meridian through point A. The known data are then placed on the sketch, and a question mark is placed in the location of the required bearing angle. Step 1 in Figure 6.8 shows the bearing angle of 7°21′ and the interior angle at A of 101°28′. A question mark is placed in the position of the required bearing angle for side AB. If the sketch has been drawn and labeled properly, the procedure for the solution will become apparent. Here, it is apparent that the required bearing angle (AB) + the interior angle (A) + the bearing angle (AE) = 180°; that is, the bearing of AB = N 71°11′ E.

FIGURE 6.8 Bearing computations.

To compute the bearing of the next side, BC, the surveyor should draw the lines BA and BC, together with a meridian through point B. Once again, the known data are placed on the sketch, and a question mark is placed in the position of the required bearing angle for side BC. In step 1, the bearing of AB was computed as N 71°11′ E. When this information is to be shown on the sketch for step 2, it is obvious that something must be done to make these data comply with the new location of the meridian—that is, the bearing must be reversed. With the meridian through point B, the line being considered is BA (not AB) and the bearing becomes S 71°11′ W. It is apparent from the sketch and data shown in step 2 that the required bearing angle (BC) = the interior angle (B) − the bearing angle (AB), a value of S 31°00′ E.

The remaining bearings are computed in steps 3–5. Step 5 involves the computation of the bearing for side EA. This last step provides the surveyor with a check on all the computations; that is, if the computed bearing turns out to be the same as the starting bearing (7°21′), the work is correct. If the computed bearing does not agree with the starting value, the work must be checked and the mistake found and corrected. If the work has been done with neat, well-labeled sketches similar to that shown in Figure 6.8, any mistake(s) will be found quickly and corrected.

6.5 Azimuths

An **azimuth** is the direction of a line given by an angle measured clockwise from the north end of a meridian. In some astronomic, geodetic, and state plane grid projects, azimuths are measured clockwise from the south end of the meridian, but in this text, azimuths are referenced from north only. Azimuths can range in magnitude from 0° to 360°. Values in excess of 360°, which are sometimes encountered in computations, are valid but are usually reduced by 360° before final listing.

Figure 6.9 illustrates the concepts of azimuths. The given angle for K1 is a clockwise angle measured from the north end of the meridian and, as such, is the azimuth of K1. The given angle for K2 is measured clockwise from the easterly axis, which itself is already measured 90° from the north end of the meridian. The azimuth of K2 is therefore 90° + 18°46′ = 108°46′.

The given angle for K3 is measured clockwise from the south end of the meridian, which itself is 180° from the north end; the required azimuth of K3 is therefore 180° + 38°07′ = 218°07′. The given angle for K4 is measured counterclockwise from the north end of the meridian; the required azimuth is therefore 360° (359°60′) − 25°25′ = 334°35′.

We noted in the previous section that each line has two directions: forward and reverse. In Figure 6.10, when the reference meridian is at point K, the line K1 is being considered, and its azimuth is 10°20′. When the reference meridian is at point 1, however, the line 1K is being considered, and the original azimuth must be reversed by 180°; its azimuth is now 190°20′.

To summarize, bearings are reversed by simply switching the direction letters, for example, N to S and E to W; azimuths are reversed by numerically changing the value by 180°.

Figure 6.11 shows a five-sided traverse with geometrically closed angles and a given azimuth for side AE of 172°39′. Note that this azimuth of 172°39′ for AE is identical in

FIGURE 6.9 Azimuths calculated from given data (answers in box).

Line	Azimuth
K1	10°20′
K2	108°46′
K3	218°07′
K4	334°35′

direction to the bearing of S 7°21′ E for AE in Figure 6.8. In fact, the problems illustrated in Figures 6.8 and 6.11 are identical, except that the directions are given in bearings in Figure 6.8 and in azimuths in Figure 6.11.

If we wish to compute the azimuths proceeding in a clockwise manner, we must first compute the azimuth of side AB. To compute the azimuth of AB, the two sides AB and AE are drawn, together with a meridian drawn through point A. The known data are then placed on the sketch along with a question mark in the position of the required azimuth. In step 1, it is apparent that the required azimuth (AB) = [the given azimuth (AE) − the interior angle (A)], a value of 71°11′.

The azimuth of the next side, BC, can be computed by first drawing the lines BC and BA, together with a meridian through point B. Once again, the known data are placed on the sketch, and a question mark is placed in the position of the required azimuth angle for side BC.

In step 1, the azimuth of AB was computed to be 71°11′; when this result is transferred to the sketch for step 2, it is obvious that it must be altered to comply with the new location of the meridian at point B. That is, with the meridian at B, the line BA is being considered, and the azimuth of line AB must be changed by 180°, resulting in a value of 251°11′; this "back azimuth" computation is shown in the boxes in the sketches for steps 2–5 in Figure 6.11.

The remaining azimuths are computed in steps 3–5. Step 5 provides the azimuth for side EA. This last step gives the surveyor a check on all the computations because the final azimuth (when reversed by 180°) should agree with the azimuth originally given for that line (AE). If the check does not work, all the computations must be reworked to find the mistake(s).

Line	Azimuth
K1	10°20′
1K	190°20′

FIGURE 6.10 Illustration of reversed azimuths.

Scrutinizing the five steps in Figure 6.11 reveals that the same procedure is involved in all the steps; that is, *in each case, when working clockwise, the desired azimuth is determined by subtracting the interior angle from the back azimuth of the previous course. This relationship is true every time the computations proceed in a clockwise direction.* If this problem had been solved by proceeding in a counterclockwise direction—that is, the azimuth of ED is computed first—you would have noted that, *in each case, when working counterclockwise, the desired azimuth was computed by adding the interior angle to the back azimuth of the previous course.*

The counterclockwise solution for azimuth computation is shown in Figure 6.12. Note that the computation follows a very systematic routine; it is so systematic that sketches are not required for each stage of the computation. A sketch is required at the beginning of the computation to give the overall sense of the problem and to ensure that the given azimuth is properly recognized as a forward or a back azimuth. (The terms *back azimuth* and *forward azimuth* are usually found only in computations; their directions depend entirely on the choice of clockwise or counterclockwise for the direction of the computation stages.)

Normally, surveying problems are worked out by using either bearings or azimuths for the directions of survey lines. The surveyor must be prepared to convert readily from one system to the other. Figure 6.13 illustrates and defines the relationships of bearings and azimuths in all four quadrants.

FIGURE 6.11 Azimuth computations.

AZ.AE =	172°39′	Forward Azimuth
+ 180°		
AZ.EA =	352°39′	Back Azimuth
+ E	118°34′	Interior Angle
AZ.ED =	470°73′	Forward Azimuth
↓OR	− 360°	↓
*AZ.ED =	111°13′	Forward Azimuth
+ 180°00′		
AZ.DE =	291°13′	Back Azimuth
+ D	113°05′	Interior Angle
AZ.DC =	404°18′	Forward Azimuth
↓OR	− 360°	↓
*AZ.DC =	44°18′	Forward Azimuth
+ 180°		
AZ.CD =	224°18′	Back Azimuth
+ C	104°42′	Interior Angle
*AZ.CB =	329°00′	Forward Azimuth
− 180°		
AZ.BC =	149°00′	Back Azimuth
+ B	102°11′	Interior Angle
*AZ.BA =	251°11′	Forward Azimuth
− 180°		
AZ.AB =	71°11′	Back Azimuth
+ A	101°28′	Interior Angle
*AZ.AE =	172°39′	CHECK Forward Azimuth

*Computed Counterclockwise
Forward Azimuth

Technique for Counterclockwise Solution:
Back Azimuth of Previous Course + Interior Angle = Forward Azimuth

FIGURE 6.12 Azimuth computations, counterclockwise solution.

6.6 Latitudes and Departures

In Chapter 1, we spoke of the need for the surveyor to check the survey measurements to ensure that the required accuracies were achieved and to ensure that mistakes were eliminated. Checking can consist of repeating the measurements in the field, and/or checking can be accomplished using mathematical techniques. One such mathematical technique involves the computation and analysis of latitudes and departures.

In Section 1.4, we noted that a point can be located by polar ties (direction and distance) or by rectangular ties (two distances at 90°). In Figure 6.14(a), point B is located by polar ties from point A by direction (N 71°11′ E) and distance (164.95′). In Figure 6.14(b), point B is located by rectangular ties from point A by distance north ($\Delta N = 53.20′$) and distance east ($\Delta E = 156.13′$).

- By definition, **latitude** is the north/south rectangular component of a line (ΔN). To differentiate direction, north is considered positive (+), and south is considered negative (−).
- **Departure** is the east/west rectangular component of a line (ΔE). To differentiate direction, east is considered positive (+), and west is considered negative (−).

When working with azimuths, the plus/minus designation of the latitude and departure is given directly by the appropriate trigonometric function:

$$\text{Latitude [N]} = \text{distance [S] cos bearing} \qquad (6.1)$$

or

$$\text{Latitude [N]} = \text{distance [S] cos azimuth} \qquad (6.2)$$

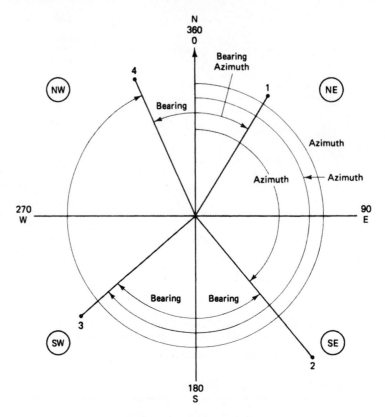

1. NE quadrant: bearing = azimuth
2. SE quadrant: bearing = 180° − azimuth
3. SW quadrant: bearing = azimuth − 180°
4. NW quadrant: bearing = 360° − azimuth

FIGURE 6.13 Relationships between bearings and azimuths.

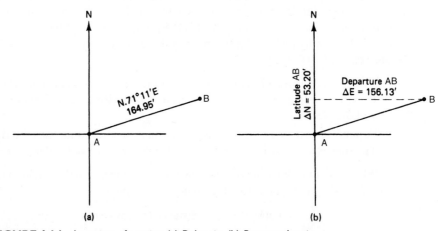

FIGURE 6.14 Location of a point. (a) Polar tie. (b) Rectangular tie.

FIGURE 6.15 Closure of latitudes and departures (clockwise solution).

$$\text{Departure } [E] = \text{distance } [S] \sin \text{bearing} \qquad (6.3)$$

or
$$\text{Departure } [E] = \text{distance } [S] \sin \text{azimuth} \qquad (6.4)$$

Latitudes (lats) and departures (deps) can be used to compute the precision of a traverse survey by noting the plus/minus closure of both latitudes and departures. If the survey has been perfectly measured (angles and distances), the plus latitudes will equal the minus latitudes, and the plus departures will equal the minus departures.

In Figure 6.15, the survey has been analyzed in a clockwise manner (all algebraic signs and letter pairs are simply reversed for a counterclockwise approach). Latitudes DE, EA, and AB are all positive and should precisely equal (if the survey measurements were perfect) the latitudes of BC and CD, which are negative. Departures AB and BC are positive and ideally should equal the departures CD, DE, and EA, which are negative.

The following sections in this chapter involve traverse computations that use trigonometric functions of direction angles—either bearings or azimuths—to compute latitudes and departures. When bearings are used, the algebraic signs of the lats and deps are assigned according to the N/S and E/W directions of the bearings. When azimuths are used, the algebraic signs of the lats and deps are given directly by the calculator or computer, according to the trigonometric conventions illustrated in Figure 6.16.

■ **EXAMPLE 6.1** *Computation of Latitudes and Departures to Determine the Error of Closure and the Precision Ratio of a Traverse Survey*

The survey data shown in Figure 6.2 are used for this illustrative example. Following are all the steps required to adjust the field data and perform the necessary computations.

FIGURE 6.16 Algebraic signs of latitudes and departures by trigonometric functions where α is the azimuth.

Solution

Step 1. *Balance the angles.* See Table 6.1; the arbitrarily balanced angles are used here.

Step 2. *Compute the bearings or azimuths.* See Figure 6.8 for bearings and Figure 6.11 or Figure 6.12 for azimuths.

Step 3. *Compute the latitudes and departures.* Table 6.2 shows a typical format for a closed traverse computation. Columns are included for both bearings and azimuths, although only one of those direction angles is needed for computations. Table 6.2 also shows that the latitudes fail to close by $+0.13'$ and that the departures fail to close by $-0.11'$.

Step 4. *Compute the linear error of closure.* See Figure 6.17 and Table 6.2. The linear error of closure is the net accumulation of the random errors associated with the traverse measurements. In Figure 6.17, the total error is showing up

Table 6.2 CLOSED TRAVERSE COMPUTATIONS

Course	Distance	Bearing	Azimuth	Latitude	Departure
AB	164.95′	N 71°11′ E	71°11′	+53.20	+156.13
BC	88.41′	S 31°00′ E	149°00′	−75.78	+45.53
CD	121.69′	S 44°18′ W	224°18′	−87.09	−84.99
DE	115.89′	N 68°47′ W	291°13′	+41.94	−108.03
EA	68.42′	N 7°21′ W	352°39′	+67.86	−8.75
	$P = 559.36'$			$\Sigma_{\text{lat}} = +0.13$	$\Sigma_{\text{dep}} = -0.11$

$$E = \sqrt{\Sigma_{\text{lat}}^2 + \Sigma_{\text{dep}}^2} \qquad E = \sqrt{0.13^2 + 0.11^2} \qquad E = 0.17'$$

where E is the linear error of closure

Traverse Computation Begins at A, and Terminates at A′

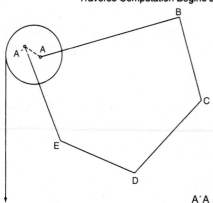

Closure Error = AA′
Closure Correction = A′A

$$A'A = \sqrt{c_{lat}^2 + c_{dep}^2} = 0.17$$

Bearing of A′A Can Be Computed from the Relationship:

$$\text{Tan Bearing} = \frac{c_{dep}}{c_{lat}} = \frac{0.11}{-0.13}$$

Bearing Angle = 40.23636°
Bearing A′A = S.40°14′11″E

Σ_{lat} = error in latitudes
Σ_{dep} = error in departures
C_{lat} = required correction in latitudes
C_{dep} = required correction in departures

FIGURE 6.17 Closure error and closure correction.

at A simply because the computation started at A. If the computation had started at any other station, the identical error of closure would have shown up at that station:

$$\text{Precision ratio} = \frac{E}{P}$$

where P = the perimeter of the traverse.

$$\text{Precision ratio} = \frac{0.17}{559.36} = \frac{1}{3,290} = \frac{1}{3,300}$$

Line A′A in Figure 6.17 is a graphical representation of the linear error of closure. The length of A′A is the square root of the sums of the squares of the C_{lat} and the C_{dep}:

$$A'A = \sqrt{C_{lat}^2 + C_{dep}^2} = \sqrt{0.13^2 + 0.11^2} = 0.17$$

C_{lat} and C_{dep} are equal to and opposite in sign to Σ lat and Σ dep and reflect the consistent direction (in this example) with the clockwise approach to this problem. Sometimes it is advantageous to know the bearing of the linear error of closure. Figure 6.17 shows that C_{dep}/C_{lat} = tan bearing angle:

$$\text{Brg A}'\text{A} = \text{S}\,40°14'11''\,\text{E}$$

Step 5. *Compute the precision ratio of the survey.* Table 6.2 shows that the precision ratio is the linear error of closure (E) divided by traverse perimeter (P). The resultant fraction (E/P) is always expressed with a numerator of 1 and with the denominator rounded to the closest 100 units.

$$\text{Precision ratio} \left(\frac{E}{P}\right) = \frac{0.17}{559.36} = \frac{1}{3,290} = \frac{1}{3,300}.$$

The concept of an accuracy ratio was introduced in Section 1.12. Most states and provinces have these ratios legislated for minimally acceptable surveys for property boundaries (see also Chapter 9). These values vary from one area to another, but they are usually in the range of 1/5,000 to 1/7,500. In some cases, higher ratios (e.g., 1/10,000) are stipulated for high-cost downtown urban areas.

Engineering and construction surveys are performed at levels of 1/3,000 to 1/10,000, depending on the importance of the work and the materials being used. For example, a ditched highway could well be surveyed at 1/3,000, whereas overhead rails for a monorail transit system may require accuracies in the range of 1/7,500 to 1/10,000. Control surveys for both engineering and legal projects must be executed at higher levels of accuracy than are necessary for the actual location of the engineering or legal markers that are to be surveyed from those control surveys.

6.6.1 Summary of Initial Traverse Computations

The initial steps for computing the traverse are:

1. Balance the angles.
2. Compute the bearings and/or the azimuths.
3. Compute the latitudes and the departures.
4. Compute the linear error of closure.
5. Compute the precision ratio of the survey.

If the precision ratio is satisfactory, further treatment of the traverse data (e.g., coordinate and area computations) is possible. If the precision ratio is unsatisfactory (e.g., a precision ratio of only 1/2,500 when 1/3,000 was specified), complete the following steps:

1. Double-check all computations.
2. Double-check all field-book entries.

3. Compute the bearing of the linear error of closure, and check to see if it is similar to one of the course bearings ($\pm 5°$).*

4. Remeasure the sides of the traverse, beginning with a course having a bearing similar to the bearing of the linear error of closure (if there is one).

5. When a mistake (or error) is found, try the corrected value in the traverse computation to determine the new precision ratio.

The search for mistakes and errors is normally confined only to the distance measurements. The angle measurements are initially checked by doubling the angles (Sections 4.6.1 and G.4), and the angular geometric closure is checked at the conclusion of the survey for compliance with the survey specifications, that is, within a given tolerance of $(n - 2)180°$ (see Section 6.2).

6.7 Traverse Precision and Accuracy

The presumed accuracy of a survey, as given by the precision ratio, can be misleading. The opportunity exists for significant errors to cancel each other out, which results in "high precision" closures from relatively imprecise field techniques. Many new surveying students are introduced to taped traverses when they are asked to survey a traverse at the 1/3,000 or 1/5,000 levels of precision. Whereas most new student crews will struggle to achieve 1/3,000, there always seems to be one crew (using the same equipment and techniques) that reports back with a substantially higher precision ratio, say, 1/8,000. In this case, it is safe to assume that the higher precision ratio obtained by the one crew is probably due to compensating errors rather than to superior skill.

For example, in a square-shaped traverse, systematic taping errors (e.g., long or short tape; see Section F.1) will be completely balanced and beyond mathematical detection. In fact, if a traverse has any two courses that are close to being parallel, identical systematic or random errors made on those courses will likely cancel out: The bearings will be reversed, and the nearly parallel latitudes and departures will have opposite algebraic signs.

To be sure that the computed precision ratio truly reflects the field work, the surveyor must perform the traverse survey according to specifications that will produce the desired results. For example, if a taped survey is to result in an accuracy of 1/5,000, then the field distance-measuring techniques should resemble those specified in Table 3.1. Also, the angle-measuring techniques should be consistent with the distance-measuring techniques. Figure 6.18 illustrates the relationship between angular and linear measurements; the survey specifications should be designed so that the maximum allowable error in angle

---

*If a large error (or mistake) has been made on the measurement of one course, it will significantly affect the bearing of the linear error of closure. Thus, if a check on the field work is necessary, the surveyor first computes the bearing of the linear error of closure and checks that bearing against the course bearings. If a similarity exists ($\pm 5°$), that course is the first course remeasured in the field.

Point Y is to Be Set Out from Fixed Points X and Z

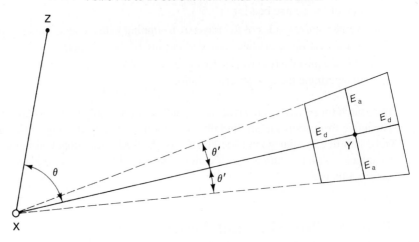

For the Line XY

E_d is the Possible Error in Distance Measurement and E_a is the Position Error Resulting from a Possible Angle Error of θ' in an Angle of θ.

FIGURE 6.18 Relationship between errors in linear and angular measurements.

(E_a) should be roughly equivalent to the maximum allowable error in distance (E_d). If the linear accuracy is restricted to 1/5,000, the angular error (θ) should be consistent:

$$1/5,000 = \tan \theta$$
$$\theta = 0°00'41''$$

See Table 6.3 for additional linear and angular error relationships. For a five-sided closed traverse with a specification for precision of 1/3,000, the maximum angular error of closure is $01' \sqrt{5} = 02'$ (to the closest minute), and for a specified precision of 1/5,000, the maximum error of closure of the field angles is $30'' \sqrt{5} = 01'$ (to the closest 30'').

Table 6.3 LINEAR AND ANGULAR ERROR RELATIONSHIPS[*]

Linear Accuracy Ratio	Maximum Angular Error (E)	Least Count of Angle Scale
1/1,000	0°03'26''	01'
1/3,000	0°01'09''	01'
1/5,000	0°00'41''	30''
1/7,500	0°00'28''	20''
1/10,000	0°00'21''	20''
1/20,000	0°00'10''	10''

[*]The overall allowable angular error in a closed traverse of n angles is $E_a \sqrt{n}$. Random errors accumulate as the square root of the number of observations.

6.8 Compass Rule Adjustment

The compass rule is used in many survey computations. The compass rule distributes the errors in latitude and departure for each traverse course in the same proportion as the course distance is to the traverse perimeter; that is, generally:

$$C_{lat} \, AB/\Sigma_{lat} = \frac{AB}{P} \quad \text{or} \quad C_{lat} \, AB = \Sigma_{lat} \times \frac{AB}{P} \tag{6.5}$$

where $C_{lat} \, AB$ = correction in latitude AB
Σ_{lat} = error of closure in latitude
AB = distance AB
P = perimeter of traverse

and

$$C_{dep} \frac{AB}{\Sigma_{dep}} = \frac{AB}{P} \quad \text{or} \quad C_{dep} \, AB = \Sigma_{dep} \times \frac{AB}{P} \tag{6.6}$$

where $C_{dep} \, AB$ = correction in departure AB
Σ_{dep} = error of closure in departure
AB = distance AB
P = perimeter of traverse

Refer to Example 6.1. Table 6.2 has been expanded in Table 6.4 to provide space for traverse adjustments. The magnitudes of the individual corrections are shown next:

$$C_{lat} \, AB = 0.13 \times \frac{164.95}{559.36} = 0.04 \qquad C_{dep} \, AB = 0.11 \times \frac{164.95}{559.36} = 0.03$$

$$C_{lat} \, BC = 0.13 \times \frac{88.41}{559.36} = 0.02 \qquad C_{dep} \, BC = 0.11 \times \frac{88.41}{559.36} = 0.02$$

$$C_{lat} \, CD = 0.13 \times \frac{121.69}{559.36} = 0.03 \qquad C_{dep} \, CD = 0.11 \times \frac{121.69}{559} = 0.03$$

$$C_{lat} \, DE = 0.13 \times \frac{115.89}{559.36} = 0.03 \qquad C_{dep} \, DE = 0.11 \times \frac{115.89}{559.36} = 0.02$$

$$C_{lat} \, EA = 0.13 \times \frac{68.42}{559.36} = \underline{0.01} \qquad C_{dep} \, EA = 0.11 \times \frac{68.42}{559.36} = \underline{0.01}$$

$$\text{Check: } C_{lat} = 0.13 \qquad\qquad \text{Check: } C_{dep} = 0.11$$

When these computations are performed on a handheld calculator, the constants 0.13/559.36 and 0.11/559.36 can be entered into storage for easy retrieval and thus quick computations.

The next step is to determine the algebraic sign to be used with the corrections. Quite simply, the corrections are opposite in sign to the errors. Therefore, for this example, the latitude corrections are all negative, and the departure corrections are all positive. The corrections are now added algebraically to arrive at the balanced values. For example, in Table 6.4, the correction for latitude BC is -0.02, which is to be "added" to latitude BC, -75.78. Because the correction is the same sign as the latitude, the two values are added to get the

Table 6.4 EXAMPLE 6.1: COMPASS RULE ADJUSTMENTS

Course	Distance	Bearing	Latitude	Departure	C_{lat}	C_{dep}	Latitudes (Balanced)	Departures (Balanced)
AB	164.95'	N 71°11' E	+53.20	+156.13	−0.04	+0.03	+53.16	+156.16
BC	88.41'	S 31°00' E	−75.78	+45.53	−0.02	+0.02	−75.80	+45.55
CD	121.69'	S 44°18' W	−87.09	−84.99	−0.03	+0.03	−87.12	−84.96
DE	115.89'	N 68°47' W	+41.94	−108.03	−0.03	+0.02	+41.91	−108.01
EA	68.42'	N 7°21' W	+67.86	−8.75	−0.01	+0.01	+67.85	−8.74
	$P = 559.36'$		$\Sigma_{lat} = +0.13$	$\Sigma_{dep} = -0.11$	$C_{lat} = -0.13$	$C_{dep} = +0.11$	0.00	0.00

answer. In the case of course AB, the latitude correction (−0.04) and the latitude (+53.20) have opposite signs, indicating that the difference between the two values is the desired value (i.e., subtract to get the answer).

The work can be checked by totaling the balanced latitudes and balanced departures to see if their respective sums are zero. The balanced latitude or balanced departure totals sometimes fail to equal zero by one last-place unit (0.01 in this example). This discrepancy is probably caused by rounding off and is normally of no consequence; the discrepancy is removed by arbitrarily changing one of the values to force the total to zero.

Note that when the error (in latitude or departure) to be distributed is quite small, the corrections can be assigned arbitrarily to appropriate courses. For example, if the error in latitude (or departure) is only 0.03 ft in a five-sided traverse, it is appropriate to apply corrections of 0.01 ft to the latitude of each of the three longest courses. Similarly, when the error in latitude for a five-sided traverse is +0.06, it is appropriate to apply a correction of −0.02 to the longest course latitude and a correction of −0.01 to each of the remaining four latitudes, the same solution provided by the compass rule.

Although the computations shown here are not tedious, you will be pleased to know that the computation of latitudes and departures and all the adjustments (usually using the least squares methods) to those computations are routinely performed on computers using different computer programs based on coordinate geometry (COGO). Some total station instruments also have these computational capabilities onboard. Balancing traverse errors by the use of the somewhat intuitive technique of balancing latitudes and departures provides for acceptable results for the vast majority of engineering surveys.

6.9 Effects of Traverse Adjustments on Measured Angles and Distances

Once the latitudes and departures have been adjusted, the original polar coordinates (distance and direction) are no longer valid. In most cases, the adjustment required for polar coordinates is too small to warrant consideration. If the data are to be used for construction layout purposes, however, the corrected distances and directions should be used.

By way of example, consider the traverse data summarized in Table 6.4. We can use the corrected lats and deps to compute distances and bearings (azimuths) consistent with those corrected lats and deps. Figures 6.14 and 6.17 illustrate the trigonometric

Table 6.5 ADJUSTMENT OF ORIGINAL DISTANCES AND BEARINGS

Course	Balanced Latitude	Balanced Departure	Adjusted Distance	Adjusted Bearing	Original Distance	Original Bearing
AB	+53.16	+156.16	164.969'	N 71°12'01" E	164.95'	N 71°11' E
BC	−75.80	+45.55	88.43'	S 31°00'10" E	88.41'	S 31°00' E
CD	−87.12	−84.96	121.69'	S 44°16'51" W	121.69'	S 44°18' W
DE	+41.91	−108.01	115.86'	N 68°47'34" W	115.89'	N 68°47' W
EA	+67.85	−8.74	68.41'	N 7°20'24" W	68.42'	N 7°21' W
	0.00	0.00	$P = 559.35'$		$P = 559.36'$	

relationships among bearings, course distances, lats, and deps. It is clear that the distance $= \sqrt{\text{lat}^2 + \text{dep}^2}$ and that the tangent of the course bearing (azimuth) = dep/lat. In Example 6.1,

$$\text{Adjusted distance AB} = \sqrt{53.16^2 + 156.16^2} = 164.96'$$

$$\text{Tan of adjusted bearing AB} = \frac{156.16}{53.16}$$

$$\text{Adjusted bearing AB} = \text{N } 71°12'01''\text{E}$$

The remaining corrected distances and bearings can be found in Table 6.5.

6.10 Omitted Measurement Computations

The techniques developed in the computation of latitudes and departures can be used to solve for missing course information on a closed traverse. These techniques can also be utilized to solve any surveying problem that can be arranged in the form of a closed traverse. The case of one missing course is illustrated in Example 6.2 and in Section 14.7. Such a case requires the solution of a problem in which the bearing (azimuth) and distance for one course in a closed traverse are missing. Other variations of this problem include the case where the distance of one course and the bearing of another course are unknown. These cases can be solved by using missing course techniques (as outlined below), together with the sine law and/or cosine law (see Appendix A), which may be required for intermediate steps or cutoff lines.

■ **EXAMPLE 6.2**

In Figure 6.19, data for three of the four sides of the closed traverse are shown. In the field, the distances for AB, BC, and CD were measured. The interior angles at B and C were also measured. The bearing (azimuth) of AB was available from a previous survey. The bearings of BC and CD were computed from the given bearing and the measured angles at B and C.

Solution

Required are the distance DA and the bearing (azimuth) of DA. The problem is set up in the same manner as a closed traverse; see Table 6.6. When the latitudes and departures of AB, BC, and CD are computed and summed, the results indicate that

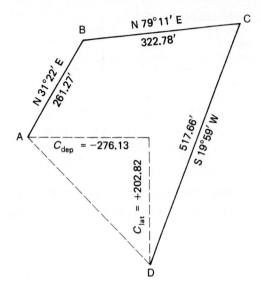

FIGURE 6.19 Example 6.2, missing course computation.

Table 6.6 EXAMPLE 6.2: MISSING COURSE

Course	Distance	Bearing	Latitude	Departure
AB	261.27	N 31°22′ E	+223.09	+135.99
BC	322.78	N 79°11′ E	+60.58	+317.05
CD	517.66	S 19°59′ W	−486.49	−176.91
			$\Sigma_{lat} = -202.82$	$\Sigma_{dep} = +276.13$
DA			$C_{lat} = +202.82$	$C_{dep} = -276.13$

the traverse failed to close by a line having a latitude of −202.82 and a departure of +276.13—that is, line AD, in Figure 6.19. To be consistent with direction (clockwise in this example), we can say that the missing course is line DA with a latitude of +202.82 and a departure of −276.13 (i.e., C_{lat} and C_{dep}, Figure 6.19).

$$\text{Distance DA} = \sqrt{\text{lat DA}^2 + \text{dep DA}^2}$$
$$= \sqrt{202.82^2 + 276.13^2}$$
$$= 342.61'$$

$$\text{Tan brg. DA} = \frac{\text{dep AD}}{\text{lat AD}}$$
$$= \frac{-276.13}{+202.82}$$
$$= -1.3614535$$

$$\text{Brg. DA} = \text{N } 53°42' \text{ W (to the closest minute)}$$

Note that this technique does not permit a check on the precision ratio of the field work. Because DA is the closure course, its computed value will also contain all the accumulated errors in the field work (see Example 6.1, step 4).

6.11 Rectangular Coordinates of Traverse Stations

6.11.1 Coordinates Computed from Balanced Latitudes and Departures

Rectangular coordinates define the position of a point with respect to two perpendicular axes. Analytic geometry uses the concepts of a *y*-axis (north–south) and an *x*-axis (east–west), concepts that are obviously quite useful in surveying applications. In Universal Transverse Mercator (UTM) grid systems, the equator is used as the *x*-axis, and the *y*-axis is a central meridian through the middle of the 6° zone in which the grid is located (see Chapter 9). For surveys of a limited nature, where a coordinate grid has not been established, the coordinate axes can be assumed. If the axes are to be assumed, values are chosen so that the coordinates of all stations will be positive (i.e., all stations will be in the northeast quadrant).

The traverse tabulated in Table 6.4 will be used for illustrative purposes. Values for the coordinates of station A are assumed to be 1000.00 north and 1000.00 east. The coordinates of the other traverse stations can be calculated by applying the balanced latitudes and departures to the previously calculated coordinates. In Figure 6.20, the balanced latitude and departure of course AB are applied to the assumed coordinates of station A to

FIGURE 6.20 Station coordinates using balanced latitudes and departures.

Table 6.7 COMPUTATION OF COORDINATES USING BALANCED LATITUDES AND DEPARTURES

Course	Balanced Latitude	Balanced Departure	Station	Northing	Easting
			A	1,000.00	1,000.00
AB	+53.16	+156.16		+53.16	+156.16
			B	1,053.16	1,156.16
BC	−75.80	+45.55		−75.80	+45.55
			C	977.36	1,201.71
CD	−87.12	−84.96		−87.12	−84.96
			D	890.24	1,116.75
DE	+41.91	−108.01		+41.91	−108.01
			E	932.15	1,008.74
EA	+67.85	−8.74		+67.85	−8.74
			A	1,000.00	1,000.00
				Check	Check

determine the coordinates of station B, and so on. These simple computations are shown in Table 6.7. A check on the computation is possible by using the last latitude and departure (EA) to recalculate the coordinates of station A.

If a scale drawing of the traverse is required, it can be accomplished by methods of rectangular coordinates (where each station is located independently of the other stations by scaling the appropriate north and east distances from the axes) or the traverse can be drawn by the direction and distance method of polar coordinates (i.e., by scaling the interior angle between courses and by scaling the course distances; the stations are located in counterclockwise or clockwise sequence). In the rectangular coordinate system, plotting errors are isolated at each station, but in the polar coordinate layout method, all angle and distance scale errors are accumulated and show up only when the last distance and angle are scaled to relocate the starting point theoretically. The resultant plotting error is similar in type to the linear error of traverse closure (AA') illustrated in Figure 6.17.

The use of coordinates to define the positions of boundary markers has been steadily increasing over the years. The storage of property-corner coordinates in large-memory civic computers permits lawyers, municipal authorities, and others to retrieve instantly current land registration assessment and other municipal information, for example, information concerning census and the level of municipal services. Although such use is important, the truly impressive impact of coordinate use results from the coordination of topographic detail (digitization) so that plans can be prepared by computer-assisted plotters (see Chapter 8), and from the coordination of all legal and engineering details. Not only are the plans produced by computer-assisted plotters, but the survey layout is also accomplished by sets of computer-generated coordinates (rectangular and polar) fed either manually or automatically through total stations (see Chapter 5). Complex construction layouts can then be accomplished quickly by a few surveyors from one or two centrally located control points, with a higher level of precision and a lower incidence of mistakes and work-related injuries.

6.11.2 Adjusted Coordinates Computed from Raw-Data Coordinates

Section 6.8 demonstrated the adjustment of traverse errors by the adjustment of the individual ΔY's (northings) and ΔX's (eastings) for each traverse course using the compass rule. This traditional technique has been favored for many years. Because of the wide use of the computer in surveying solutions, however, coordinates are now often first computed from raw (unadjusted) bearing/distance data and then adjusted using the compass rule or the least squares technique. Because we are now working with coordinates and not individual ΔY's and ΔX's, the distance factor to be used in the compass rule must be cumulative. This technique will be illustrated using the same field data from Example 6.1. Corrections (C) to raw-data coordinates are shown in Tables 6.8 and 6.9.

Table 6.8 COMPUTATION OF RAW-DATA COORDINATES

Station/Course	Bearing	Distance	ΔY	ΔX	Coordinates (Raw-Data) Northing	Coordinates (Raw-Data) Easting
A					1,000.00	1,000.00
AB	N 71°11' E	164.95	+53.20	+156.13		
B					1,053.20	1,156.13
BC	S 31°00' E	88.41	−75.78	+45.53		
C					977.42	1,201.66
CD	S 44°18' W	121.69	−87.09	−84.99		
D					890.33	1,116.67
DE	N 68°47' W	115.89	+41.94	−108.03		
E					932.27	1,008.64
EA	N 7°21' W	68.42	+67.86	−8.75		
A					1,000.13	999.89
			$\Sigma\Delta Y = +0.13$	$\Sigma\Delta X = -0.11$		

Table 6.9 COMPUTATION OF ADJUSTED COORDINATES

Station	Coordinates (Raw-Data) Northing	Coordinates (Raw-Data) Easting	$C\Delta Y$	$C\Delta X$	Coordinates (Adjusted) Northing	Coordinates (Adjusted) Easting
A	1,000.00	1,000.00			1,000.00	1,000.00
B	1,053.20	1,156.13	−0.04	+0.03	1,053.16	1,156.16
C	977.42	1,201.66	−0.06	+0.05	977.36	1,201.71
D	890.33	1,116.67	−0.09	+0.07	890.24	1,116.74
E	932.27	1,008.64	−0.11	+0.10	932.16	1,008.74
A	1,000.13	999.89	−0.13	+0.11	1,000.00	1,000.00

$C\Delta Y$ = correction in northing (latitude) and $C\Delta X$ = correction in easting (departure). Correction C is opposite in sign to errors ΣY and ΣX.

Station B

$$C\Delta Y \text{ is } (AB/P) \, \Sigma\Delta Y = (164.95/559.36) \, 0.13 = -0.04$$
$$C\Delta X \text{ is } (AB/P) \, \Sigma\Delta X = (164.95/559.36) \, 0.11 = +0.03$$

Station C

$$C\Delta Y \text{ is } [(AB + BC)/P] \, \Sigma\Delta Y = (253.36/559.36) \, 0.13 = -0.06$$
$$C\Delta X \text{ is } [(AB + BC)/P] \, \Sigma\Delta X = (253.36/559.36) \, 0.11 = +0.05$$

Station D

$$C\Delta Y \text{ is } [(AB + BC \ 1 \ CD)/P] \, \Sigma\Delta Y = (375.05/559.36) \, 0.13 = -0.09$$
$$C\Delta X \text{ is } [(AB + BC \ 1 \ CD)/P] \, \Sigma\Delta Y = (375.05/559.36) \, 0.11 = +0.07$$

Station E

$$C\Delta Y \text{ is } [(AB + BC + CD + DE)/P] \, \Sigma\Delta Y = (490.94/559.36) \, 0.13 = -0.11$$
$$C\Delta X \text{ is } [(AB + BC + CD + DE)/P] \, \Sigma\Delta X = (490.94/559.36) \, 0.11 = +0.10$$

Station A

$$C\Delta Y \text{ is } [(AB + BC + CD + DE + EA)/P] \, \Sigma\Delta Y = (559.36/559.36) \, 0.13 = -0.13$$
$$C\Delta X \text{ is } [(AB + BC + CD + DE + EA)/P] \, \Sigma\Delta X = (559.36/559.36) \, 0.11 = +0.11$$

6.12 Area of a Closed Traverse by the Coordinate Method

When the coordinates of the stations of a closed traverse are known, it is a simple matter then to compute the area within the traverse, either by computer or by handheld calculator. Figure 6.21(a) shows a closed traverse 1, 2, 3, 4 with the appropriate X and Y coordinate distances. Figure 6.21(b) illustrates the technique used to compute the traverse area.

In Figure 6.21(b), you can see that the desired area of the traverse is, in effect, area 2 minus area 1. Area 2 is the sum of the areas of trapezoids $4'433'$ and $3'322'$. Area 1 is the sum of trapezoids $4'411'$ and $1'122'$:

$$\text{Area 2} = \frac{1}{2}(X_4 + X_3)(Y_4 - Y_3) + \frac{1}{2}(X_3 + X_2)(Y_3 - Y_2)$$

$$\text{Area 1} = \frac{1}{2}(X_4 + X_1)(Y_4 - Y_1) + \frac{1}{2}(X_1 + X_2)(Y_1 - Y_2)$$

$$2A = [(X_4 + X_3)(Y_4 - Y_3) + (X_3 + X_2)(Y_3 - Y_2)]$$
$$- [(X_4 + X_1)(Y_4 - Y_1) + (X_1 + X_2)(Y_1 - Y_2)]$$

Expand this expression, and collect the remaining terms:

$$2A = X_1(Y_2 - Y_4) + X_2(Y_3 - Y_1) + X_3(Y_4 - Y_2) + X_4(Y_1 - Y_3) \qquad (6.7)$$

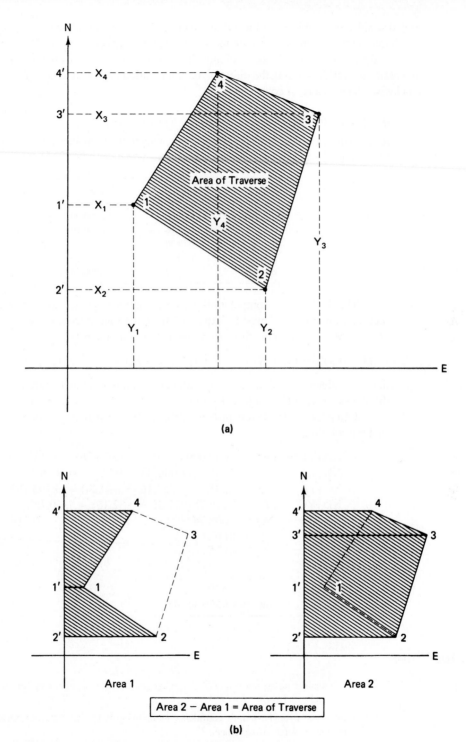

FIGURE 6.21 Area by rectangular coordinates.

Stated simply, the double area of a closed traverse is the algebraic sum of each X coordinate multiplied by the difference between the Y values of the adjacent stations. This double area is divided by 2 to determine the final area. The final area can be positive or negative, the algebraic sign reflecting only the direction of computation approach (clockwise or counterclockwise). The area is, of course, positive.

■ **EXAMPLE 6.3** *Area Computation by Coordinates*

Refer to the traverse example (Example 6.1) in Section 6.6. As illustrated in Figure 6.20, the station coordinates are summarized below:

Station	Northing	Easting
A	1,000.00	1,000.00
B	1,053.16	1,156.16
C	977.36	1,201.71
D	890.24	1,116.75
E	932.15	1,008.74

The double area computation uses the relationships developed earlier in this section. Equation (6.7) must be expanded from the four-sided traverse shown in the illustrative example to the five-sided traverse of Example 6.1:

$$2A = X_1(Y_5 - Y_2) + X_2(Y_1 - Y_3) + X_3(Y_2 - Y_4) + X_4(Y_3 - Y_5) + X_5(Y_4 - Y_1)$$

that is, for the double area, each X coordinate is multiplied by the difference between the Y coordinates of the adjacent stations.

Using the station letters instead of the general case numbers shown above, we find the solution:

$$XA(YE - YB) = 1,000.000(932.15 - 1,053.16) = -121,010$$
$$XB(YA - YC) = 1,156.16(1,000.00 - 977.36) = +26,175$$
$$XC(YB - YD) = 1,201.71(1,053.16 - 890.24) = +195,783$$
$$XD(YC - YE) = 1,116.75(977.36 - 932.15) = +50,488$$
$$XE(YD - YA) = 1,008.74(890.24 - 1,000.00) = -110,719$$
$$2A = 40,677 \text{ sq. ft}$$
$$A = 20,338 \text{ sq. ft}$$
$$A = \frac{20,338}{43,560} = 0.47 \text{ ac}$$
$$(1 \text{ ac} = 43,560 \text{ sq. ft})$$

Questions

6.1 When measuring distances and angles, what are four ways of checking for mistakes and improving precision?

6.2 Why do surveyors have more confidence in the integrity of closed traverse measurements over open traverse measurements?

6.3 The trigonometric functions (sin, cos, tan) of angle 371°23′30″ are identical to the trigonometric functions of 11°23′30″. True or false?

6.4 Plotted property surveys usually show the direction of property lines as bearings (and not azimuths). True or false?

6.5 When computing bearings or azimuths of a closed polygon figure (having been given the direction of one course and all the balanced angles), can you check to see that your direction computations are free of mistakes?

Problems

6.1 A closed, five-sided traverse has the following interior angles: A = 113°44′, B = 99°41′, C = 91°12′, D = 120°52′, E = ? Find the angle at E.

6.2 A five-sided, closed traverse has the following interior angles:

$$A = 70°10′30″$$
$$B = 142°43′00″$$
$$C = 83°49′30″$$
$$D = 117°27′30″$$
$$E = 125°47′00″$$

Determine the angular error, and balance the angles by applying equal corrections to each angle.

6.3 Convert the following azimuths to bearings:
  (a) 187°29′   (b) 141°54′   (c) 345°16′30″
  (d) 56°09′   (e) 253°18′   (f) 124°51′

6.4 Convert the following bearings to azimuths:
  (a) N 12°51′ W   (b) N 66°14′ E   (c) S 35°04′ E
  (d) S 3°12′ W   (e) N 33°13′ W   (f) S 0°06′ E

6.5 Convert each of the azimuths given in Problem 6.3 to reverse (back) azimuths.

6.6 Convert each of the bearings given in Problem 6.4 to reverse (back) bearings.

6.7 An open traverse that runs from A to H has the following deflection angles: B = 1°03′R; C = 2°58′ R; D = 7°24′ L; E = 6°31′ L; F = 1°31′ R; G = 8°09′ L. If the bearing of AB is N 21°21′ E, compute the bearings of the remaining sides.

6.8 Closed traverse ABCD has the following bearings: AB = N 63°14′ E, BC = S 66°06′ E, CD = S 2°41′ W, DA = N 69°37′ W. Compute the interior angles, and show a geometric check for your work.

Use the sketch in Figure 6.22 and the following interior angles for Problems 6.9–6.11.

Angles

A = 101°28′
B = 102°11′
C = 104°42′
D = 113°05′
E = 118°34′
538°120′ = 540°00′

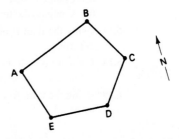

FIGURE 6.22 Sketch for Problems 6.9–6.11.

6.9 If bearing AB is N 54°00′ E, compute the bearings of the remaining sides. Provide two solutions, one working clockwise and one working counterclockwise.

6.10 If the azimuth of AB is 62°30′, compute the azimuths of the remaining sides. Provide two solutions, one working clockwise and one working counterclockwise.

6.11 If the azimuth of AB is 55°55′, compute the azimuths of the remaining sides. Provide two solutions, one working clockwise and one working counterclockwise.

6.12 See Figure 6.23. The four-sided, closed traverse has the following angles and distances:

A = 51°23′   AB = 713.93 ft
B = 105°39′   BC = 606.06 ft
C = 78°11′   CD = 391.27 ft
D = 124°47′   DA = 781.18 ft

The bearing of AB is N 67°17′ E.   **FIGURE 6.23**   Sketch for Problem 6.12.
(a) Perform a check for angular closure.
(b) Compute both bearings and azimuths for all sides.
(c) Compute the latitudes and departures.
(d) Compute the linear error of closure and the precision ratio.

6.13 Using the data from Problem 6.12, and the compass rule, balance the latitudes and departures. Compute corrected distances and directions.

6.14 Using the data from Problem 6.13, compute the coordinates of stations B, C, and D. Assume that the coordinates of station A are 1,000.00 ft N and 1,000.00 ft E.

6.15 Using the data from Problem 6.14, compute the area (in acres) enclosed by the traverse.

6.16 See Figure 6.24. The five-sided, closed traverse has the following angles and distances:

A = 38°30′   AB = 371.006 m
B = 100°38′   BC = 110.222 m
C = 149°50   CD = 139.872 m
D = 85°59′   DE = 103.119 m
E = 165°03′   EA = 319.860 m

Side AB has an azimuth of 306°31′.   **FIGURE 6.24**   Sketch for Problem 6.16.
(a) Perform a check for angular closure.
(b) Compute both bearings and azimuths for all sides.
(c) Compute the latitudes and departures.
(d) Compute the linear error of closure and the precision ratio.

6.17 Using the data from Problem 6.16 and the compass rule, balance the latitudes and departures.

6.18 Using the data from Problem 6.17, compute the coordinates of stations C, D, E, and A. Assume that the coordinates of station B are 1,000.000 m N and 1,000.000 m E.

6.19 Using the data from Problem 6.18, compute the area (in hectares) enclosed by the traverse.

6.20 See Figure 6.25. The two frontage corners (A and D) of a large tract of land are joined by the following open traverse:

Course	Distance (ft)	Bearing
AB	80.32	N 70°10′07″ E
BC	953.83	N 74°29′00″ E
CD	818.49	N 70°22′45″ E

FIGURE 6.25 Sketch for Problem 6.20.

Compute the distance and bearing of the property frontage AD.

6.21 Given the following data for a closed property traverse, compute the missing data (i.e., distance CD and bearing DE).

Course	Distance (m)	Bearing
AB	537.144	N 37°10′49″ E
BC	1,109.301	N 79°29′49″ E
CD	?	S 18°56′31″ W
DE	953.829	?
EA	483.669	N 26°58′31″ W

6.22 A six-sided traverse has the following station coordinates:

A: 559.319 N, 207.453 E; B: 738.562 N, 666.737 E; C: 541.742 N, 688.350 E;

D: 379.861 N, 839.008 E; E: 296.099 N, 604.048 E; F: 218.330 N, 323.936 E

Compute the distance and bearing of each side.

6.23 Using the data from Problem 6.22, compute the area (hectares) enclosed by the traverse.

6.24 A total station was set up at control station K, which is within the limits of a five-sided property (see Figure 6.26). The coordinates of station K are 2,000.000 N, 2,000.000 E. Azimuth angles and polar distances to the five property corners are as follows:

Direction	Azimuth	Horizontal Distance (m)
KA	286°51′30″	34.482
KB	37°35′28″	31.892
KC	90°27′56″	38.286
KD	166°26′49″	30.916
KE	247°28′43″	32.585

FIGURE 6.26 Sketch for Problem 6.24.

Compute the coordinates of the property corners A, B, C, D, and E.

6.25 Using the data from Problem 6.24, compute the area (hectares) of the property.

6.26 Using the data from Problem 6.24, compute the bearings (to the closest second) and distances (to three decimals) of the five sides of the property.

Chapter 7

Satellite Positioning

7.1   General Background

After Russia launched (1957) the first artificial satellite, Sputnik, scientists at Johns Hopkins University Applied Physics Laboratory (APL) began tracking the satellite signals noting Doppler shift data. (The Doppler effect is the shift in frequency and wavelength noted by an observer when the source of the waves moves relative to the observer.) After acquiring data for several days, scientists were able to define Sputnik's orbit, and from this predictability of orbit, scientists saw that the technology could be developed to determine various receivers' positions on Earth (see resection techniques in Section 6.2.3); thus began positioning and navigation by satellite tracking. The U.S. Navy took an interest in this development because it was keen to use such navigation capabilities for their Polaris submarines while they were at sea. The U.S. Navy Navigation Satellite System, called Transit, was started in 1959 and completed in 1964. In 1967, the U.S Government made this navigation system available to commercial ships and aircraft of all nations. By 1996, the Transit Satellite System was retired, giving way to the United States' more modern Navigation Satellite Timing and Ranging (NAVSTAR) Satellite System, which presently (2009) has about thirty-two operational satellites; the system was declared to be in full operation capability (FOC) as of April 27, 1995.

Satellite positioning is presently provided by two operating satellite constellations. The oldest, and the only complete system at present (2009), is the NAVSTAR global positioning system (GPS)—generally referred to as the GPS. The Russian system, GLONASS, is partially completed and the new European Union (EU) thirty-satellite system, *Galileo*, may be completed by 2012; see http://europa.eu.int/comm/dgs/energy_transport/galileo/index_enhtm for current information on Galileo's deployment. Also at the proposal stage is China's Compass Satellite System (also known as Beidou), which will consist of thirty satellites and will complement China's geostationary satellite system, expected to increase in numbers from three to five satellites. Some authorities are beginning to call all these existing and proposed satellite systems the **Global Navigation Satellite System (GNSS)**. In addition to the four precise positioning systems described above, there are other augmentation and enhancement satellites (see Section 8.6.2), both in place and planned, that are designed for specific purposes. For example, Japan has authorized (launches beginning in 2008) the creation of a three-satellite system known as **Quasi-Zenith Satellite System (QZSS)**. This system does not have stand-alone high accuracy, but can be used with GNSS satellites to provide survey-level positioning. As the name suggests, these satellites are not directly overhead, but each orbits for 12 hr each day at elevations above 70°. These high-orbiting (42,164 km) satellites allow for better positioning in urban canyons where lower-orbiting satellite signals can be blocked by building walls. India plans to launch a similar high-orbiting satellite system, the Indian Radionavigation Satellite System (IRNSS), composed of seven satellites expected to be operational in the near future.

7.1.1 Operating Systems

By the mid-1980s, the U.S. Department of Defense (DoD) second-generation guidance system NAVSTAR GPS had evolved to many of its present capabilities. In December 1993, the U.S. Government officially declared that the system had reached its initial operational capability (IOC) with twenty-six satellites (twenty-three Block II satellites) then potentially available for tracking. Additional Block II satellites continue to be launched (a satellite's life span is thought to be about 7 years). Current GPS satellite status and the constellation configuration can be accessed via the Internet at http://www.navcen.uscg.gov/navinfo/gps/ActiveNanu.aspx (Table 7.1). Table 7.2 shows a satellite status reports for the Russian GLONASS system (http://www.glonass-ianc.rsa.ru—click on the British flag). Some GPS receivers can track both GPS and GLONASS satellite signals (as well as future satellites), thus providing the potential for improved positioning. Tables 7.1 and 7.2 show that, on the specific date queried, the GPS constellation had thirty-two satellites in orbit, of which thirty-one were operational (healthy), and that the GLONASS constellation had twenty orbiting satellites, of which nineteen were operational.

As noted earlier, prior to NAVSTAR, precise positioning was often determined by using low-altitude satellites or inertial guidance systems. The first-generation satellite-positioning system Transit consisted of six satellites in polar orbit at an altitude of only 1,100 km. Precise surveys, with positioning from 0.2 to 0.3 m, could be accomplished using translocation techniques; that is, one receiver occupied a position of known coordinates while another occupied an unknown position. Data received at the known position were used to model signal transmission and determine orbital errors, thus permitting more precise results. The positioning analysis techniques used in the Transit system utilized a ground receiver capable of noting the change in satellite frequency transmission as the satellite first approached and then receded from the observer. The change in frequency was affected by the velocity of the satellite itself.

The change in frequency of transmissions from the approaching and then receding satellite, known as the Doppler effect, is proportional to the change of distance between the satellite and the receiver over a given time interval. When the satellite's orbit is precisely known and the position of the satellite in that orbit is also precisely known through ephemeris data and universal time (UT), the position of the receiving station can be computed.

Table 7.1 UNITED STATES NAVAL OBSERVATORY (USNO) GPS CONSTELLATION STATUS

Information in this file is retained for approximately seven days or until completion of the event; be aware that the information provided below may change.

A. Block II/IIA/IIR/IIR-M Individual Satellite Status

23	32	Launched 26 NOV 1990; usable 26 FEB 2008; operating on Rb std
24	24	Launched 04 JUL 1991; usable 30 AUG 1991; operating on Cs std
25	25	Launched 23 FEB 1992; usable 24 MAR 1992; operating on Rb std
26	26	Launched 07 JUL 1992; usable 23 JUL 1992; operating on Rb std
27	27	Launched 09 SEP 1992; usable 30 SEP 1992; operating on Cs std
30	30	Launched 12 SEP 1996; usable 01 OCT 1996; operating on Cs std
33	03	Launched 28 MAR 1996; usable 09 APR 1996; operating on Cs std
34	04	Launched 26 OCT 1993; usable 22 NOV 1993; operating on Rb std
35	05	Launched 30 AUG 1993; usable 28 SEP 1993; operating on Rb std
		Scheduled unusable 17 Feb 1400 UT to 18 Feb 0200 UT for maintenance (NANU 2009005)
36	06	Launched 10 MAR 1994; usable 28 MAR 1994; operating on Rb std
37	01	Launched 13 MAY 1993;
		Discontinued Transmition of L-Band; PRN01 available (NANU 2009001)
38	08	Launched 06 NOV 1997; usable 18 DEC 1997; operating on Cs std
39	09	Launched 26 JUN 1993; usable 21 JUL 1993; operating on Rb std
40	10	Launched 16 JUL 1996; usable 15 AUG 1996; operating on Cs std
41	14	Launched 10 NOV 2000; usable 10 DEC 2000; operating on Rb std
43	13	Launched 23 JUL 1997; usable 31 JAN 1998; operating on Rb std
44	28	Launched 16 JUL 2000; usable 17 AUG 2000; operating on Rb std
45	21	Launched 31 MAR 2003; usable 12 APR 2003; operating on Rb std
46	11	Launched 07 OCT 1999; usable 03 JAN 2000; operating on Rb std
47	22	Launched 21 DEC 2003; usable 12 JAN 2004; operating on Rb std
48	07	Launched 15 MAR 2008; usable 24 MAR 2008; operating on Rb std
51	20	Launched 11 MAY 2000; usable 01 JUN 2000; operating on Rb std
52	31	Launched 25 SEP 2006; usable 12 OCT 2006; operating on Rb std
53	17	Launched 26 SEP 2005; usable 16 DEC 2005; operating on Rb std
54	18	Launched 30 JAN 2001; usable 15 FEB 2001; operating on Rb std
55	15	Launched 17 OCT 2007; usable 31 OCT 2007; operating on Rb std
56	16	Launched 29 JAN 2003; usable 18 FEB 2003; operating on Rb std
57	29	Launched 20 DEC 2007; usable 02 JAN 2008; operating on Rb std
58	12	Launched 17 NOV 2006; usable 13 DEC 2006; operating on Rb std
59	19	Launched 20 MAR 2004; usable 05 APR 2004; operating on Rb std
		Unusable 11 Feb 2234 UT to 12 Feb 0503 UT due to repositioning maintenance (NANUs 2009003, 2009004/12 FEB)
60	23	Launched 23 JUN 2004; usable 09 JUL 2004; operating on Rb std
61	02	Launched 06 NOV 2004; usable 22 NOV 2004; operating on Rb std

ftp://tycho.usno.navy.mil/pub/gps/gpstd.txt
Monday, February 16, 2009 2:45:22 PM

Table 7.2 RUSSIAN SPACE AGENCY

GLONASS constellation status, 16.02.2009r.

Total satellites in constellation	20 SC
Operational	19 SC
In commissioning phase	–
In maintenance	1 SC
In decommissioning phase	–

GLONASS Constellation Status at 16.02.2009 based on both the almanac analysis and navigation messages received at 19:00 16.02.09 (UTC) in IAC PNT TsNllmash

Orb. pl.	Orb. slot	RF chnl	# GC	Launched	Operation begins	Operation ends	Life-time (months)	In almanac	In ephemeris (UTC)	Comments
	2	01	728	25.12.08	20.01.09		1.7	+	+18:55 16.02.09	In operation
	3	05	727	25.12.08	17.01.09		1.7	+	+18:55 16.02.09	In operation
	4	06	795	10.12.03	29.01.04		62.3	+	+18:55 16.02.09	In operation
I	6	01	701	10.12.03	08.12.04	12.01.09	62.3	–	–11:54 16.02.09	Maintenance
	7	05	712	26.12.04	07.10.05		49.7	+	+13:55 16.02.09	In operation
	8	06	729	25.12.08	12.02.09		1.7	+	+16:04 16.02.09	In operation
	9	–2	722	25.12.07	25.01.08		13.8	+	+14:17 16.02.09	In operation (L1 only)
	10	04	717	25.12.06	03.04.07		25.8	+	+16:05 16.02.09	In operation
	11	00	723	25.12.07	22.01.08		13.8	+	+18:17 16.02.09	In operation
II	13	–2	721	25.12.07	08.02.08		13.8	+	+18:55 16.02.09	In operation
	14	04	715	25.12.06	03.04.07		25.8	+	+18:55 16.02.09	In operation
	15	00	716	25.12.06	12.10.07		25.8	+	+11:30 16.02.09	In operation
	17	–1	718	26.10.07	04.12.07		15.7	+	+15:22 16.02.09	In operation
	18	–3	724	25.09.08	26.10.08		4.7	+	+16:39 16.02.09	In operation
	19	03	720	26.10.07	25.11.07		15.7	+	+17:40 16.02.09	In operation
	20	02	719	26.10.07	27.11.07		15.7	+	+18:25 16.02.09	In operation
III	21	–1	725	25.09.08	05.11.08		4.7	+	+18:55 16.02.09	In operation
	22	–3	726	25.09.08	13.11.08		4.7	+	+18:55 16.02.09	In operation
	23	03	714	25.12.05	31.08.06		37.8	+	+13:41 16.02.09	In operation
	24	02	713	25.12.05	31.08.06		37.8	+	+14:56 16.02.09	In operation

© Information-analytical centre, 2006. E-mail: glonass-ianc@mcc.rsa.ru
http://www.glonass-ianc.rsa.ru/pls/htmldb/f?p=202:20:14637162736231801312::NO
Monday, February 16, 2009 2:49:29 PM

7.1.2 Inertial Measuring Systems

Another, quite different positioning system utilizes inertial measurement units (IMUs) and requires a vehicle (truck, airplane, or helicopter), or a surveyor on foot or in an all-terrain vehicle, to occupy a point of known coordinates (northing, easting, and elevation) and remain stationary for a zero velocity update. As the IMU moves, its location is constantly updated by the use of three computer-controlled accelerometers, each aligned to the north–south, east–west, or vertical axis. The accelerometer platform is oriented north–south, east–west, and

FIGURE 7.1 Six degree of freedom inertial measuring unit (IMU—SAGEM 33 BM). (Courtesy of SAGEM SA, Paris—La Defense, France) (arranged by Applanix Corp.)

plumb by means of three computer-controlled gyroscopes, each of which is aligned to one of three axes (Figure 7.1). Analysis of acceleration data gives rectangular (latitude and longitude) displacement factors for horizontal movement, in addition to vertical displacement. When an IMU is used in conjunction with real-time kinematic (RTK) GPS, several benefits occur (see Section 7.11.4). First, the roving surveyor, using both IMU and GPS receivers, determines position readily, even if the GPS signals are blocked by tree canopy or other obstructions. After the obstruction has been bypassed, the rover can continue to receive both IMU and GPS signals, with the IMU readily updating its position from the newly acquired GPS signals. This technique permits positioning to continue and even permits (theoretically) indoor surveying. Second, the combination of IMU and GPS can be used to control data collection for airborne imagery, including **lidar** (**l**ight **d**etection **a**nd **r**anging) images (see Section 8.7.1.1). The presence of IMU data along with the GPS positioning data makes the processing of all collected data possible in a very short period of time. The points within the lidar point cloud are individually referenced with respect to their three-dimensional geospatial positions. Applanix Corporation, a recent Trimble acquisition, is the present leader in this field. The corporation manufactures IMU/GPS positioning devices for use in a backpack, or on motorized vehicles, aircraft, or marine vessels. See Figure 7.2 for an illustration of this technology.

7.2   U.S. Global Positioning System

Satellite positioning is based on accurate ephemeris data for the real-time location of each satellite and on very precisely kept time. It uses satellite signals, accurate time, and sophisticated algorithms to generate distances to ground receivers and thus provide resectioned positions anywhere on Earth. Satellite signals can also provide navigation data, such as the speed and direction of a mobile receiver, directions to an identified (via coordinates) location, and estimated arrival times.

Satellite orbits have been designed so that ground positioning can usually be determined at any location on Earth at any time of the day or night. A minimum of four satellites must be

FIGURE 7.2 Combined IMU and RTK unit (see Section 8.11.4) carried in a backpack. This unit continues to determine position even when GPS signals are blocked by tree canopy or other obstructions. (Courtesy of Applanix Corp., Richmond Hill, Ontario)

tracked to solve the positioning intersection equations dealing with position (x, y, and z coordinates, which later can be translated to easting, northing, and elevation) and with clock differences between the satellites and ground receivers. In reality, five or more satellites are tracked, if possible, to introduce additional redundancies and to strengthen the geometry of the satellite array. Additional satellites (more than the required minimum) can provide more accurate positioning and can also reduce the receiver occupation time at each survey station.

The U.S. GPS consists of twenty-four operational satellites (plus six or more spares) deployed in six orbital planes 20,200 km above the Earth, with orbit times of 12 hr. Spacing is such that at least six satellites are always visible anywhere on Earth. In addition to the satellites arrayed in space, the U.S. GPS includes five tracking stations (and three ground antennas) evenly spaced around the Earth. Stations are located at Colorado Springs, Colorado (the master control station), and on the islands of Ascension, Diego Garcia, Kwajalein, and Hawaii. All satellites' signals are observed at each station, with all the clock and ephemeris data being transmitted to the control station at Colorado Springs. The system is kept at peak efficiency because corrective data are transmitted back to the satellites from Colorado Springs (and a few other ground stations) every few hours. More recently, satellites have also been given the ability to communicate with each other.

The U.S. GPS, originally designed for military guidance and positioning, has attracted a wide variety of civilian users in the positioning and navigation applications fields. Already additional applications have been developed in commercial aviation navigation, boating and shipping navigation, trucking and railcar positioning, emergency routing, automobile dashboard electronic charts, and orienteering navigation (see Section 7.12). Also, manufacturers are now installing GPS chips in cell phones to help satisfy the 911 service requirement for precise caller locations.

7.3   Receivers

GPS receivers range in ability (and cost) from survey-level (millimeter) receivers capable of use in surveys requiring high accuracy and costing more than $20,000, to mapping and geographic information system (GIS) receivers (submeter accuracy) costing about $3,000 each, to marine navigation receivers (accuracy 1–5 m) costing about $1,000, and finally to orienteering (hiking) and low-precision mapping/GIS receivers costing only a few hundred dollars (Figures 7.3–7.5).

FIGURE 7.3 Leica SYS 300. System includes the following: SR 9400 GPS single-frequency receiver, with AT 201 antenna, and CR333 controller, which collects data and provides software for real-time GPS. It can provide the following accuracies: 10–20 mm +2 ppm using differential carrier techniques; and 0.30–0.50 m using differential code measurements. (Courtesy of Leica Geosystems, Inc.)

FIGURE 7.4 Trimble navigation total station GPS. Real-time positioning for a wide variety of applications. Features include GPS antenna and electronic field book at the adjustable pole; and receiver, radio, and radio antenna in the backpack. The receiver has been equipped with GPS processing software and the electronic field book has been equipped with the applications software (e.g., layout), thus permitting real-time data capture or layout. (Courtesy of Trimble Navigation, Sunnyvale, CA)

The major differences in the receivers are the number of channels available (the number of satellites that can be tracked at one time) and the condition whether or not the receiver, can observe both L1 and L2 frequencies and measure both code and carrier phases. Generally speaking, the higher-cost dual-frequency receivers require much shorter observation times for positioning measurements than do the less expensive single-frequency receivers and can be used for real-time positioning. Some low-end general-purpose GPS receivers track only one channel at a time (sequencing from satellite to satellite as tracking progresses). An improved low-end general-purpose receiver tracks on two channels, but it still must sequence the tracking to other satellites to achieve positioning. Some low-end surveying receivers can continuously observe on five channels (sequencing not required), while higher-end surveying receivers can observe on twelve channels. Some receivers can control photogrammetric camera operation. The more expensive receivers can datalog every second and can be used in all GPS survey modes with shorter observation times, whereas less expensive receivers may datalog every 15 s and can be restricted to a certain type of survey and will require longer observation times and perhaps longer processing times as well. At the time of this writing, new software and hardware are still being developed that will increase capabilities while reducing costs.

FIGURE 7.5 Garmin e-Map hand-held GPS receiver (accuracy: 15 m), used in navigation and GIS-type data location. It can be used with a DGPS radio beacon receiver to improve accuracy to within a few meters or less.

The cost for three precise surveying receivers, together with appropriate software, may range upward to $50,000, but lower costs are expected as production increases and technology improves. By contrast, two lower-order receivers can be used in differential positioning to determine position to within a few decimeters, a precision that could be acceptable for selected mapping and GIS databases. The total cost (including software) of this system can be less than $10,000. As noted in Section 7.6, surveys can be performed while using only one receiver if access to radio-transmitted corrections from a permanent receiver/beacon is available, which is the case with the U.S. Coast Guard's (USCG) differential global positioning system (DGPS) and the national differential global positioning system (NDGPS); see Section 7.6.2.

7.4 Satellite Constellations

GPS satellites (Figure 7.6) are manufactured by Rockwell International, weigh about 1,900 pounds, span 17 ft (with solar panels deployed), and orbit the Earth at 10,900 nautical miles (20,000 km) in a period of 12 hr (actually 11 hr, 58 min). The satellites' constellation

FIGURE 7.6 GPS satellite (Courtesy of Leica Geosystems, Inc.)

FIGURE 7.7 GPS satellites in orbit around the Earth.

(Figure 7.7) consists of twenty-four satellites (plus spares) placed in six orbital planes. This configuration ensures that at least four satellites (the minimum number needed for precise measurements) are always potentially visible anywhere on Earth.

Russia has also created a satellite constellation, called GLONASS, which was originally planned to consist of twenty-four satellites, placed in three orbital planes at 19,100 km with an orbit period of 11 hr, 15 min. As with GPS, GLONASS satellites continuously broadcast their own precise positions along with less precise positions for all other same-constellation satellites.

Tables 7.1 and 7.2 show the status for both GPS and GLONASS satellites, respectively. Daily updates of satellite status are available on the Internet at the addresses shown in the tables. Note that on February 16, 2009, there were thirty-one operating satellites in the GPS constellation and nineteen operating satellites in the GLONASS constellation. From time to time, operating satellites are set "unhealthy" (i.e., temporarily taken out of service) in order to make adjustments and re-calibrations; knowing the "health" of the visible satellites on any given day is critical to mission planning.

Some GPS receivers are now capable of tracking both GPS and GLONASS satellite signals. Using both constellations has two advantages. Additional satellites results in the potential for shorter observation times and increased accuracy. The increased number of satellites available to a receiver can also reduce interruptions due to poor satellite geometry or by local obstructions caused by buildings, tree canopy, and the like.

A new satellite-positioning constellation called Galileo is being implemented by the EU. It will be comprised of twenty-seven operational satellites plus three spares. Satellite construction contracts were awarded beginning in 2004 and the constellation is expected to be operational by 2012 or earlier. Galileo satellites will broadcast on four frequencies:

- E1: 1,587–1,591 MHz; OS, SOL, and CS (see below)
- E2: 1,559–1,563 MHz; PRS
- E5: 1,164–1,188 MHz; OS, SOL, and CS
- E6: 1,260–1,300 MHz; PRS and CS

The services provided by the Galileo system include open services (OS)—free of charge; public regulated service (PRS) (e.g., police, emergency, national security); open and safety-of-life (SOL) services; commercial services (CS), which are available for a fee; and international search and rescue (SAR).

Galileo's satellites will be in circular orbits 23,617 km above the Earth and the system will be under civilian control. Galileo is designed primarily for transportation (rail, auto, and air) and is Europe's contribution to the GNSS. Galileo will be managed by the Galileo Joint Undertaking, located in Brussels, Belgium. See their website at http://europa.eu.int/comm/dgs/energy_transport/galileo/index_en.htm.

In addition to providing positioning data, GNSS provides real-time navigation data for land, marine, and air navigation. Present-day accuracies are now sufficient for most applications, and the Federal Aviation Administration (FAA) is expected to provide certification for precision aircraft flight approaches about the same time as this text is published in 2010.

7.5 GPS Satellite Signals

GPS satellites transmit at two L-band frequencies with the following characteristics.

1. The L1 frequency is set at 1,575.42 MHz, and because $\lambda = c/f$ (where λ is the wavelength, c is the speed of light, and f is the frequency; see Equation 3.8), the wavelength of L1 is determined as follows:

$$\lambda = \frac{300,000,000 \text{ m/s}}{1,575,420,000 \text{ Hz}} = 0.190 \text{ m, or about 19 cm.}$$

The L1-band carries the following codes: C/A code (civil), P code (military), Y code (anti-spoofing code), and the navigation message that includes clock corrections and orbital data.

2. The L2 frequency is set at 1,227.60 MHz, and using Equation 3.8, the wavelength is determined to 0.244 m or about 24 cm. The L2 band carries the P and Y codes only.

The civil or coarse acquisition (C/A) code is available to the public, whereas the P code was designed for military use exclusively. Only the P code was originally modulated on the L2 band. The DoD once implemented selective availability (SA), which was designed to degrade signal accuracy (in times of national emergency), resulting in errors in the range of 100 m, and occurred on both L1 and L2. SA has been permanently deactivated as of May 2000. This policy change improved GPS accuracies in basic point positioning by a fivefold factor (e.g., down from 100 m to about 10–20 m). Another method designed to deny accuracy to the user is called anti-spoofing (AS). AS occurs when the P code is encrypted to prevent tinkering by hostile forces. At present, AS, along with most natural and other errors associated with the GPS measurements, can be eliminated by using differential positioning techniques.

The more types of data collected, the faster and more accurate the solutions. For example, some GPS suppliers have computer programs designed to deal with some or all of the following collected data: C/A code pseudorange on L1; both L1 and L2 P code pseudoranges; both L1 and L2 carrier phases; both L1 and L2 Doppler observations; and a measurement of the cross-correlation of the encrypted P code (Y code) on the L1 and L2 frequencies. These data are used to produce real-time or postprocessing solutions.

The United States announced in early 1999 its intention to modernize the GPS system and to add two additional civilian signals on the next generation of satellites. The second civilian signal (L2C) was added in 2005 (PRN17) and 2006 (PRN31 and PRN12) to the Block IIR-M satellites (Table 7.1). A third civilian signal, called L5, will be included on the new Block IIF satellites, scheduled for to begin launching in 2009. This new civilian signal will transmit on a frequency of 1,176.45 MHz. Once the modernized constellation is complete, the addition of these two new civil signals will make positioning faster and more accurate under many measuring conditions and will make the GPS system comparable with the proposed Galileo system for civilian applications. Eventually, expanding Block II satellites in the constellation consisting of more advanced Block III satellites will gradually replace the present GPS system. Some believe that the completed constellation of L2C and L5 capable satellites, as well as the proposed Block III satellite constellation (which may include the fourth civil signal called L1C), is still many years away.

One key dimension in positioning is the parameter of time. Time is kept onboard the satellites by so-called atomic clocks with a precision of 1 ns (0.000000001 s). The ground receivers are equipped with less precise quartz clocks. Uncertainties caused by these less precise clocks are resolved when observing the signals from four satellites instead of the basic three-satellite configuration required for x, y, and z positioning. Some predict that future increases in spatial positioning accuracy will result from improvements in satellite onboard clocks planned for future satellite constellations.

7.6   GPS Position Measurements

Position measurements generally fall into one of two categories: code measurement and carrier phase measurement. Civilian code measurement is presently restricted to the C/A code, which can provide accuracies only in the range of 10–15 m when used in point positioning, and accuracies in the submeter to 5 m range when used in various differential positioning techniques. P code measurements can apparently provide the military with much better accuracies. Point positioning is the technique that employs one GPS receiver to track satellite code signals so that it can directly determine the coordinates of the receiver station.

7.6.1   Relative Positioning

Relative positioning is a technique that employs two GPS receivers to track satellite code signals and/or satellite carrier phases to determine the baseline vector (X, Y, and Z) between the two receiver stations. The two receivers must collect data from the same satellites simultaneously (same epoch), and their observations are then combined to produce results that are superior to those achieved with just a single-point positioning. Using this technique, we observe that computed (postprocessed) baseline accuracies can be in the submeter range for C/A code measurements and in the millimeter range for carrier-phase measurements.

7.6.2   GPS Augmentation Services: Differential GPS

The theory behind differential positioning is based on the use of two or more GPS receivers to track the same satellites simultaneously. Unlike relative positioning, at least one of the GPS receivers must be set up at a station of known coordinates. This base station receives satellites' signals so it can compare its computed position with its known position and derive a difference value. Because this difference reflects all the measurement errors (except for multipath) for nearby receivers, this "difference" can be included in the nearby roving GPS receivers' computations to remove the common errors in their measurements. Differential corrections in positioning computations can be incorporated in several ways:

- Postprocessing computations, using data manually collected from the base station and rovers.
- A commercial service (e.g., OmiSTAR—http://www.omniSTAR.com) that collects GPS data at several sites and weights them to produce an "optimized" set of corrections that are then uplinked to geostationary satellites, which, in turn, broadcast the corrections to subscribers who pay an annual fee for this service. This service provides real-time measurements because the corrections are automatically applied to data collected by the subscribers' GPS roving receivers.
- A radio-equipped GPS receiver at one or more base stations (stations whose coordinates have already been precisely determined) that can compute errors and broadcast corrections to any number of radio-equipped roving receivers in the area, or a radio-equipped GPS receiver that can transmit GPS signals to a central server so

that the server station can then compute difference corrections (see Section 7.6.5) and transmit them to roving receivers. These techniques are extremely useful for RTK measurements.

- Postprocessing computations using code range and carrier-phase data available from the National Geodetic Survey's (NGS) continuously operating reference system (CORS)—a nationwide network of stations (including links to the Canadian Active Control System). This service can be accessed at http://www.ngs.noaa.gov/CORS (see also Section 7.8).

- Real-time mapping-level measurements can also be made by accessing DGPS/NDGPS radio corrections that are broadcast from permanent GPS receiver locations established by the USCG and other cooperating agencies (see Sections 7.6.2.1 and 7.6.2.2). The roving receiver must be equipped with an ancillary or built-in radio beacon receiver.

Some GPS receivers are now manufactured with built-in radio receivers for use with each of the above real-time techniques. Roving receivers equipped with appropriate software can then determine the coordinates of the stations in real time.

The types of surveying applications where code pseudorange measurements or carrier measurements are made at a base station and then used to correct measurements made at another survey station are called differential positioning. Although the code measurement accuracies (submeter to 10 m) may not be sufficient for traditional control and layout surveys, they are ideal for many navigation needs and for many GIS and mapping surveys.

7.6.2.1 U.S. Coast Guard's DGPS System.
The USCG Maritime Differential GPS Service has created a DGPS, consisting of more than eighty remote broadcast sites and two control centers. It was originally designed to provide navigation data in coastal areas, the Great Lakes, and major river sites. This system received FOC in 1999. The system includes continuously operating GPS receivers, at locations of known coordinates, that determine pseudorange values and corrections and then radiotransmit the differential corrections to working navigators and surveyors at distances ranging from 100 to 400 km. The system uses international standards for its broadcasts, published by the Radio Technical Commission for Maritime (RTCM) services. Effectively the surveyor or navigator, using the DGPS broadcasts along with his/her own receiver, has the advantages normally found when using two receivers. Because the corrections for many of the errors (orbital and atmospheric) are very similar for nearby GPS receivers, once the pseudoranges have been corrected the accuracies thus become much improved.

Information on DGPS and on individual broadcast sites can be obtained on the Internet at the USCG Navigation Center website: http://www.navcen.uscg.gov/. Figure 7.8 shows typical data available for site 839, Youngstown, New York. Effective April 2004, the USCG, together with the Canadian Coast Guard, implemented a seamless positioning service in the vicinity of their common border.

7.6.2.2 National DGPS.
The success of the USCG's DGPS prompted the U.S. Department of Transportation (DoT), in 1997, to design a terrestrial expansion over the land surfaces of the conterminous or continental United States (CONUS), and major transportation routes in Alaska and in Hawaii. The USCG was given the task of being the lead

```
┌─────────────────────────────────────────────────────────────────┐
│              DGPS SITE STATUS AND OPERATING PARAMETERS            │
│                    STATUS AS OF 08/02/05                          │
│                                                                   │
│  Site Name:                    YOUNGSTOWN, NY                     │
│  Status:                       Operational                        │
│  RBn Antenna Location:         43° 13.8' N;78° 58.2' W            │
│  REFSTA Ant Location (A):      43° 13.8748' N;78° 58.20992' W     │
│  REFSTA Ant Location (B):      43° 13.87466' N;78° 58.18778' W    │
│  REFSTA RTCM SC-104 ID (A):    118                                │
│  REFSTA RTCM SC-104 ID (B):    119                                │
│  REFSTA FIRMWARE VERSION:      RD00-1C19                          │
│  Broadcast Site ID:            839                                │
│  Transmission Frequency:       322 KHZ                            │
│  Transmission Rate:            100 BPS                            │
│  Signal Strength:              75uV/m at 150 SM                   │
│  Outages:                                                         │
│  No Current Outages.                                              │
│                                                                   │
│  USERS SHOULD NOTIFY THE NIS WATCHSTANDER AT (555)313-5900 OF ANY │
│  OBSERVED OUTAGES, PROBLEMS, OR REQUESTS. ALL CURRENT OUTAGE      │
│  INFORMATION WILL BE LISTED FOLLOWING EACH SITE.                  │
│                                                                   │
│  THE COAST GUARD DGPS SERVICE IS AVAILABLE FOR POSITIONING AND    │
│  NAVIGATION USERS MAY EXPERIENCE SERVICE INTERRUPTIONS WITHOUT    │
│  ADVANCE NOTICE. COAST GUARD DGPS BROADCASTS SHOULD NOT BE        │
│  USED UNDER ANY CIRCUMSTANCES WHERE A SUDDEN SYSTEM FAILURE       │
│  OR INACCURACY COULD CONSTITUTE A SAFETY HAZARD.                  │
│                                                                   │
│  NOTE: Differential corrections are based on the NAD 83 position  │
│  of the reference station (REFSTA) antenna. Positions             │
│  obtained using DGPS should be referenced to NAD 83               │
│  coordinate system only. All sites are broadcasting               │
│  RTCM Type 9-3 correction messages.                               │
└─────────────────────────────────────────────────────────────────┘
```

FIGURE 7.8 Status report for DGPS station. See http://www.navcen.uscg.mil/ADO/ dgpslateststausbysite.asp; select DGPS, and then select status for specified scrolled sites. (Courtesy of the U.S. Coast Guard)

agency in this venture which essentially consisted of expanding the maritime DGPS across all land areas. By 2007, about thirty-seven NDGPS station were operating. In January 2007, work on NDGPS was halted pending congressional review of future project funding, but then a decision was made to continue funding for the immediate future. See the website at http://www.navcen.uscg.gov for updates.

7.6.2.3 Wide Area Augmentation System.

Wide Area Augmentation System (WAAS) was designed and built by the FAA and uses twenty-five ground stations in the CONUS, with additional stations in Alaska, Canada, and Mexico either operating or planned. The northing, easting, and elevation coordinates of these ground stations have been precisely determined. Signals from available GPS satellites are collected and analyzed by all stations in the network to determine errors (orbit, clock, atmosphere, etc.). The differential corrections are then forwarded to one of the two master stations (one located on each U.S. coast).

The master stations create differential correction messages that are relayed to one of two geostationary satellites located near the equator. The WAAS geostationary satellites then rebroadcast the differential correction messages on the same frequency as that used by GPS to receivers located on the ground, at sea, or in the air. This positional service is free and all modern GPS receivers have the built-in capability of receiving WAAS corrections.

Accuracy specifications call for a position accuracy of 7.6 m (horizontal and vertical) more than 95 percent of the time, and current field trials consistently produce results in the 1.5-m range for horizontal position and 1.5 m in the vertical position. But WAAS has not yet (as of 2009) met all the criteria for certification in precision aircraft flight approaches.

Satellite Pacific Ocean Region (POR) serves the Pacific Ocean region and western North America; satellite Atlantic Ocean Region-West (AOR-W) serves the Atlantic Ocean area and eastern North America as well as South America. It is planned eventually to cover Europe with satellite Atlantic Ocean Region-East (AOR-E) and satellite Indian Ocean Region (IOR), as well as the European Space Agency (ESA) satellite aircraft-based augmentation system (ARTEMIS), which uses both GPS and GLONASS signals. International coverage will be expanded beyond the WAAS area of interest by the creation and development of Europe's Euro Geostationary Navigational Overlay Service (EGNOS) and Japan's Multi-Functional Satellite Augmentation System (MSAS).

7.6.3 GPS Code Measurements

As previously noted, the U.S. military can utilize both the P and the C/A codes. The C/A code is used by the military to access the P code quickly. Until the L2C signal becomes operative on more satellites, the civilian user must be content with using only the C/A code. Both codes are digital codes comprised of zeros and ones [Figure 7.9(a)], and each satellite transmits codes unique to that satellite. Although both codes are carefully structured, because the codes sound like random electronic "noise," they have been given the name pseudo random noise (PRN). The PRN code number (Table 7.1) indicates which of the thirty-seven 7-day segments of the P code PRN signal is presently being used by each satellite (it takes the P code PRN signal 267 days to transmit). Each 1-week segment of the P code is unique to each satellite and is reassigned each week (Table 7.1). Receivers have replicas of all satellite codes in the onboard memory, which they use to identify the satellite and then to measure the time difference between the signals from the satellite to the receiver. Time is measured as the receiver moves the replica code (retrieved from memory) until a match between the transmitted code and the replica code is achieved [Figure 7.9(b)]. Errors caused by the slowing effects of the atmosphere on the transmission of satellite radio waves can be corrected by simultaneously performing position measurements utilizing two different wavelengths, such as L1 and L2.

The distance, called pseudorange, is determined by multiplying the time factor by the speed of light:

$$\rho = t(300,000,000)$$

where ρ (lowercase Greek letter rho) = the pseudorange in meters
t = travel time of the satellite signal in seconds
300,000,000 = velocity of light in meters per second (actually 299,792,458 m/s)

FIGURE 7.9   (a) C/A codes and P codes. (b) Time determination.

When the pseudorange (ρ) is corrected for clock errors, atmospheric delay errors, multi-path errors, and the like, it is then called the range and is abbreviated by the uppercase Greek letter rho, P; that is, P = ρ + error corrections.

Figure 7.10 shows the geometry involved in point positioning. Computing three pseudoranges (P_{AR}, P_{BR}, P_{CR}) is enough to solve the intersection of three developed spheres, although this computation gives two points of intersection. One point (a superfluous point) will be obviously irrelevant; that is, it probably will not even fall on the surface of the Earth. The fourth pseudorange (ρ_{DR}) is required to remove the fourth unknown, the receiver clock error.

7.6.4   GPS Carrier-Phase Measurement

GPS codes, which are modulations of the carrier frequencies, are comparatively lengthy. Compare the C/A code at 293 m and the P code at 29.3 m (Figure 7.9) with the wave-lengths of L1 and L2 of 0.19 m and 0.24 m, respectively. It follows that carrier-phase measurements have the potential for much higher accuracies than do code measurements.

We first encountered phase measurements in Chapter 3, when we observed how elec-tronic distance measurement (EDM) equipment measured distances (Figure 3.18). Essentially, EDM distances are determined by measuring the phase delay required to

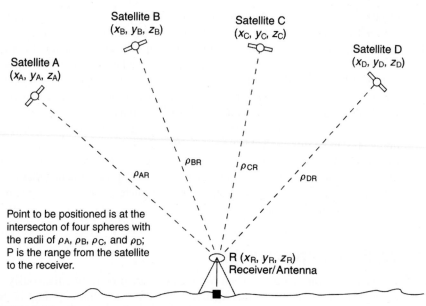

Satellite A
(x_A, y_A, z_A)

Satellite B
(x_B, y_B, z_B)

Satellite C
(x_C, y_C, z_C)

Satellite D
(x_D, y_D, z_D)

ρ_{BR}

ρ_{CR}

ρ_{AR}

ρ_{DR}

Point to be positioned is at the
intersecton of four spheres with
the radii of ρ_A, ρ_B, ρ_C, and ρ_D;
P is the range from the satellite
to the receiver.

R (x_R, y_R, z_R)
Receiver/Antenna

FIGURE 7.10 Geometry of point positioning.

match up the transmitted carrier wave signal with the return signal (two-way signaling). Equation 3.10 (repeated below) calculates this distance:

$$L = \frac{n\lambda + \varphi}{2}$$

where φ is the partial wavelength determined by measuring the phase delay (through comparison with an onboard reference), n is the number of complete wavelengths (from the EDM to the prism and back to the EDM instrument), and λ is the wavelength. The integer number of wavelengths is determined as the EDM instrument successively sends out (and receives back) signals at different frequencies, thus permitting the creation of equations allowing for the computation of the unknown n.

Because GPS ranging involves only one-way signaling, other techniques must be used to determine the number of full wavelengths. GPS receivers can measure the phase delay (through comparison with onboard carrier replicas) and count the full wavelengths after lockon to the satellite has occurred, but more complex treatment is required to determine N, the initial cycle ambiguity. That is, N is the number of full wavelengths sent by the satellite prior to lock-on. Because a carrier signal is comprised of a continuous transmission of sine-like waves with no distinguishing features, the wave count cannot be accomplished directly.

$$P = \varphi + N\lambda + \text{ errors}$$

where P = satellite–receiver range
φ = measured carrier phase
λ = wavelength
N = initial ambiguity (the number of full wavelengths at lock-on)

Once the cycle ambiguity between a receiver and a satellite has been resolved, it does not have to be addressed further unless a loss of lock occurs between the receiver and the satellite. When loss of lock occurs, the ambiguity must be resolved again. Loss of lock results in a loss of the integer number of cycles and is called a cycle slip. The surveyor is alerted to loss of lock when the receiver commences a beeping sequence. As an example, loss of lock can occur when a roving receiver passes under a bridge, a tree canopy, or any other obstruction that blocks all or some of the satellite signals.

Cycle ambiguity can be determined through the process of differencing. GPS measurements can be differenced between two satellites, between two receivers, and between two epochs. An **epoch** is short observation interval in a longer series of observations. After the initial epoch has been observed, later epochs will reflect the fact that the constellation has moved relative to the ground station and, as such, presents a new geometrical pattern and thus new intersection solutions.

7.6.5 Differencing

Relative positioning occurs when two receivers are used to simultaneously observe satellite signals and to compute the vectors (known as a baseline) joining the two receivers. Relative positioning can provide better accuracies because of the correlation possible between measurements simultaneously made over time by two or more different satellite receivers. Differencing is the technique of simultaneous baseline measurements and falls into the categories of single difference, double difference, and triple difference.

- *Single difference*: When two receivers simultaneously observe the same satellite, it is possible to correct for most of the effects of satellite clock errors, orbit errors, and atmospheric delay. See Figure 7.11(a).

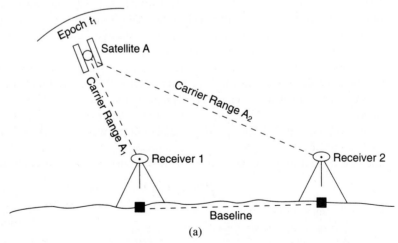

(a)

FIGURE 7.11 Differencing. (a) Single difference: two receivers observing the same satellite simultaneously (i.e., difference between receivers).

(*continued*)

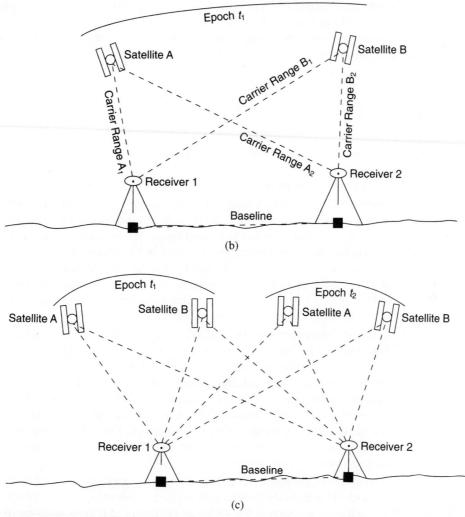

FIGURE 7.11 (*continued*) (b) Double difference: two receivers observing the same satellites simultaneously (i.e., difference between receivers and between satellites). (c) Triple difference: the difference between two double differences (i.e., the difference among receivers, satellites, and epochs).

- *Double difference*: When one receiver observes two (or more) satellites, the measurements can be freed of receiver clock error and also atmospheric delay errors. Further, when using both differences (between the satellites and between the receivers), a double difference occurs. Clock errors, atmospheric delay errors, and orbit errors can all be eliminated. See Figure 7.11(b).

- *Triple difference*: The difference between two double differences is the triple difference. That is, the double differences are compared over two (or more) successive epochs. This procedure is also effective in detecting and correcting cycle slips and for computing first-step approximate solutions that are used in double-difference techniques. See Figure 7.11(c).

Cycle ambiguities can also be resolved by utilizing algorithms dealing with double differences, and triple differences by using both code and carrier-phase measurements. The references, in Section 7.16, provide more information on the theory of signal observations and ambiguity resolution.

7.7   Errors

The chief sources of error in GPS are described below:

1. Clock errors of the receivers.
2. Ionosphere refraction (occurring 50–1,000 km above Earth) and troposphere refraction (occurring from the Earth's surface to 80 km above Earth). Signals are slowed as they travel through these Earth-centered layers. The errors worsen as satellite signals are received near the horizon. These errors can be reduced by scheduling nighttime observations, by gathering sufficient redundant data and using reduced baseline lengths (1–5 km), or by collecting data on both frequencies over long distances (20 km or more). Most surveying agencies do not record observations from satellites below 10° to 15° of elevation above the horizon.
3. Multipath interference, which is similar to the ghosting effect seen on early TVs. Some signals are received directly and others are received after they have been reflected from adjacent features such as tall buildings, steel fences, etc. Recent improvements in antenna design have significantly reduced these errors. In data collection surveys, roving receivers must be positioned according to the presence of topographic features so the surveyor cannot avoid tall structures, chain link fences, and the like, but when considering the placement of base station receivers for RTK surveys, the surveyor should make every effort to avoid all features that may contribute to multipath errors.
4. A weak geometric figure that results from poorly located, four-satellite signal intersections. This consideration is called the dilution of precision (DOP). See also *strength of figure*, Section 9.8. DOP can be optimized if many satellites (beyond the minimum of four) are tracked; the additional data strengthen the position solution. Most survey-level receivers are now capable of tracking five to twelve satellites simultaneously.

    The geometric effect of satellite vector measurement errors together with receiver clock errors is called the general DOP (GDOP). Elevation solutions require a strong GDOP, and these solutions are strengthened when satellite elevations in excess of 70° are available for the observed satellite orbits. Observations used to be discontinued if the GDOP was above 7; now, some receiver manufacturers suggest that a GDOP of 8 is acceptable.
5. Errors associated with the satellite orbital data.
6. Setup errors. Centering errors can be reduced if the equipment is checked to ensure that the optical plummet is true, and hi measuring errors can be reduced by utilizing

equipment that provides a built-in (or accessory) measuring capability to precisely measure the antenna reference height (ARH) (directly or indirectly) or by using fixed-length tripods and bipods.

7. Selective availability (SA)—a denial of accuracy that was turned off in May, 2000. Many of the effects of the above errors, including denial of accuracy by the DoD (if it were to be re-introduced), can be surmounted by using differential positioning surveying techniques. Most of the discussion in this text is oriented to relatively short baselines; for long lines (>150 km), more sophisticated processing is required to deal with natural and human-made errors.

7.8 Continuously Operating Reference Station

The CORS system is a differential measurement system developed by the NGS that has now become nationwide (Figure 7.12). By 2007 the network included about 1,200 sites, growing at about fifteen sites each month. The goal is to expand the network until all points within the CONUS will be within 200 km of at least one operational CORS site. The GPS satellite signals observed at each site are used to compute the base station position, which is then compared with the correct position coordinates (which have been previously and precisely determined). The *difference* (thus differential) between the correct position and the computed position is then made available over the Internet for use in the postprocessing of the field observations collected by the roving receivers of a wide variety of government and private surveyors.

The CORS network includes stations set up by the NGS, the USCG, the U.S. Army Corps of Engineers (USACE), and, more recently, stations set up by other federal and local

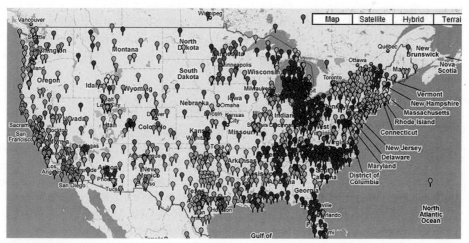

FIGURE 7.12 CORS coverage as of July 2008. This map and more specific site data are available (and continually updated) at http://www.ngs.noaa.gov/CORS. (Courtesy of the National Geodetic Survey—NGS)

agencies. CORS stations must be able to determine North American datum of 1983 (NAD83) positions for the site that are accurate to 2 cm in horizontal coordinates and 4 cm in vertical coordinates, with 95-percent confidence using just 15 min of data.

The coordinates at each site are computed from 24-hr data sets collected over a period of 10–15 days. These highly accurate coordinates are then transformed into the NAD83 horizontal datum for use by local surveyors. Each CORS continuously tracks GPS satellite signals and creates files of both carrier measurements and code range measurements, which are available to the public via the Internet, to assist in positioning surveys. NGS converts all receiver data and individual site meteorological data to receiver independent exchange (RINEX) format, version 2. The files can be accessed via the Internet at http://www.ngs.noaa.gov. Once in the website, the new user should select "Products and Services" and then "GPS Continuously Operating Reference Station (CORS)". The user is instructed to download and read the "readme" files and the "frequently asked questions" file on the first visit. The NGS stores data from all sites for 31 days, and then the data are normally transferred to CD-ROMs, which are available for a fee. The data are often collected at a 30-s epoch rate, although some sites collect data at 1-, 5-, 10-, and 15-s epoch rates. The local surveyor, armed with data sets in his or her locality at the time of an ongoing survey and having entered these data into his or her GPS program, has the equivalent of an additional dual-frequency GPS receiver. A surveyor with just one receiver can proceed as if two receivers were being used in the differential positioning mode.

Data from the CORS stations form the foundation of the National Spatial Reference System (NSRS). At the time of this writing, positions are given in both NAD83 coordinates (used in the United States for surveying and civil applications) and International Terrestrial Reference Framework (ITRF—ITRF05) position coordinates. Future CORS receivers will be capable of receiving signals from GLONASS and Galileo satellites in addition to GPS satellites. Some future CORS sites will be established at additional U.S. tide gauge stations to help track sea-level fluctuations. Also, selected CORS sites will be identified as Foundation CORS and will be under government control and selected for use in tying the NSRS to the ITRF; they will be the first to receive instrumentation modernizations and ties to gravity-tracking stations (extracted from the NGS 10-year work plan issued for discussion in 2007).

7.8.1 Online Positioning User Service

This online positioning user service (OPUS) enables surveyors, working in the static mode with just one dual-frequency receiver, to receive precise differentially corrected positioning data for the survey station. The surveyor sends the receiver data files as collected, or in RINEX format, to NGS via the web. The process is almost automatic with the user following these steps: select antenna type from list, enter the ARH, enter the date, enter the approximate location, and transfer the receiver's GPS data to OPUS either in receiver format or in RINEX format. The OPUS program then selects three neighboring CORS sites, each of which will participate in a single-baseline solution with the user's station using double-differencing techniques to provide coordinates in ITRF 2000 (ITRF00) and NAD83 (NSRS2007—released in February 2007) reference frames (ITRF05 will be available soon). Grid Coordinates can be output in Universal Transversal Mercator (UTM), State Plane

Coordinates (SPC), or U.S. National Grid (USNG) values (northing and easting). Elevations are given as both ellipsoidal heights and as orthometric heights.

Two hours (minimum) of data are required and processing is based on three close reference stations (CORS). Clients can select reference stations from a scrollable list if that is their wish. The client must also provide the ARH above the positioning mark and the antenna type, which they select from a list of calibrated antennas. The output coordinates can be selected for ITRF, NAD83, UTM, and SPC. The solution is sent via e-mail within 3 min. See http://www.ngs.noaa.gov/OPUS/ for further information.

In January 2007, NGS declared its new processing tool operational, OPUS-RS (Rapid Static). This processing tool needs only 15 min of GPS dual-frequency observations (as opposed to 2 hr of regular OPUS observations) to provide precise positioning. NGS officials predict that the present 15,000 OPUS solutions per month will increase tenfold with these much shorter occupation times. Accuracy, at the 92-percent level, is claimed as 5 cm north and east and 10 cm for ellipsoidal height.

7.9 Canadian Active Control System

The Geodetic Survey Division (GSD) of Geomatics Canada has combined with the Geological Survey of Canada to establish a network of active control points (ACPs) in the Canadian Active Control System. The system includes ten unattended dual-frequency tracking stations (ACPs) that continuously measure and record carrier-phase and pseudor-ange measurements for all satellites in view at a 30-s sampling interval. A master ACP in Ottawa coordinates and controls the system. The data are archived in RINEX format and available online 4 hr after the end of the day. Precise ephemeris data, computed with input from 24 globally distributed core GPS tracking stations of the International GPS Service for Geodynamics (IGS), are available online within 2–5 days after the observations; precise clock corrections are also available in the 2- to 5-day time frame. The Canadian Active Control System is complemented by the Canadian Base Network, which provides 200-km coverage in Canada's southern latitudes for high-accuracy control (centimeter accuracy). These control stations are used to evaluate and to complement a wide variety of control stations established by various government agencies over the years. These products, which are available for a subscription fee, enable a surveyor to position any point in the country with a precision ranging from a centimeter to a few meters. Code observation positioning at the meter level, without the use of a base station, is possible using precise satellite corrections. Real-time service at the meter level is also available. The data can be accessed on the web at http://www.geod.nrcan.gc.ca.

7.10 Survey Planning

Planning is important for GPS surveys so that almanac data can be analyzed to obtain optimal time sets when a geometrically strong array of operating satellites is available above 15° of elevation (above the horizon) and to identify topographic obstructions that may hinder signal reception. Planning software can graphically display GDOP (geometric dilution of precision) at each time of the day (GDOP of 7 or below is usually considered suitable for positioning—a value of 5 or lower is ideal). See Figures 7.13–7.16 for a variety of computer

FIGURE 7.13 GPS planning software. Graphical depiction of satellite availability, elevation, and GDOP as almanac data are processed by software for a specific day and location. (Courtesy of Leica Geosystems, Inc.)

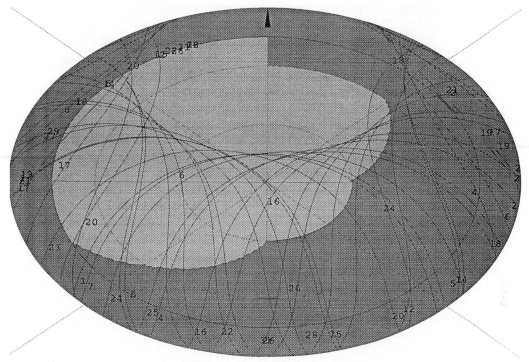

FIGURE 7.14 GPS planning software. Computer "Sky Plot" display showing satellite orbits and obstructions (darker shading) for a particular station. (Courtesy of Leica Geosystems, Inc.)

screen plots that the surveyor can use to help the mission-planning process and select not only the optimal days for the survey, but also the hours of the day that result in the best data. Continual checks on the operating status of the GPS and GLONNAS constellations (Tables 7.1 and 7.2) will keep the surveyor aware of instances where satellites are temporarily set "unhealthy" (outage or maintenance) to effect necessary adjustments and recalibrations.

7.10.1 Static Surveys

For static surveys (see Section 7.11.2 for a definition), survey planning includes a visit to the field in order to inspect existing stations and to place monuments for new stations. A compass and clinometer (Figure 3.7) are handy in sketching the location and elevation of potential obstructions at each station on a visibility (obstruction) diagram (Figure 7.17). These obstructions are entered into the software for later display. The coordinates (latitude and longitude) of stations should be scaled from a topographic map. Scaled coordinates can help some receivers to lock onto the satellites more quickly.

Computer graphics displays include the number of satellites available (Figure 7.13); satellite orbits and obstructions, showing orbits of satellites as viewed at a specific station on a specific day (Figure 7.14); a visibility plot of all satellites over 1 day (Figure 7.15); and a polar plot of all visible satellites—at a moment in time (Figure 7.16). Figure 7.14 shows that for the location shown (latitude and longitude) most satellite orbits are in the

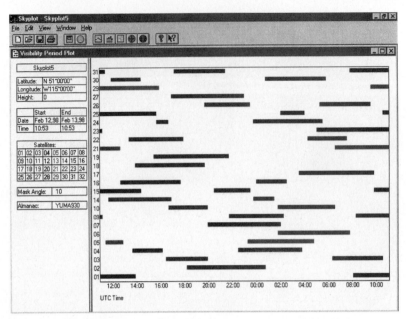

FIGURE 7.15 Visibility plot—from Skyplot series (color-coded in original format). (Courtesy of Position, Inc., Calgary, Alberta)

FIGURE 7.16 Skyplot showing the available satellites at one geographic point at a specific day and time. (Courtesy of Leica Geosystems, Inc.)

GPS Station Obstruction Diagram

Magnetic Declination 18° 54' E.

Declination applied to this figure?   Yes (✓)
                                        No ( )

Height above marker that horizon was mapped
from: 1.5 m

Station Name _____	Date March 3, 2009
Station Number 1079	Operator RJB
Latitude 46° 36' 30" N.	Longitude 122° 18' 00" W.

FIGURE 7.17 Station visibility diagram.

southerly sky; accordingly survey stations at that location should be located south of high obstructions, where possible, to minimize topographic interference. Almanac data, used in survey planning, can be updated on a regular basis through satellite observations, and, as well, most software suppliers provide almanac updates via their computer bulletin boards.

Static surveys work best with receivers (at least two) of the same type; that is, they should have the same number of channels, the same type of antennas, and the same signal processing techniques. Also, the sampling rate must be set; faster rates require more storage, but can be helpful in detecting cycle slips, particularly on longer baselines (>50 km). The time (hours) of observation must be determined, given the available GDOP and the need for accuracy as well as the start/stop times for each session. All this information is entered into the software, with the results uploaded into the receivers.

7.10.2   Kinematic Surveys

Much of the discussion above, for planning static surveys, also applies to kinematic surveys (see Section 7.11.3 for definitions). For kinematic surveys, the route also must be planned for each roving receiver so that best use is made of control points, crews, and equipment. The type of receiver chosen will depend to some degree on the accuracy required. For topographic or GIS surveys, low-order (submeter) survey roving receivers (e.g., Figures 7.3 and 7.4) may be a good choice. For construction layout in real time, high-end roving receivers capable of centimeter accuracy (e.g., Figure 7.5) may be selected. The base station receiver must be compatible with the survey mission and the roving receivers; one base station can support any number of roving receivers. The technique to be used for initial ambiguity resolution must be determined; that is, will it be antenna swap, or known station occupation, or on-the-fly (OTF)? The stations at which this resolution is to take place must also be specified.

If the survey is designed to locate topographic and built features, then the codes for the features should be defined or accessed from a symbols library, just the same as for total station surveys (see Chapter 5). If required, additional asset data (attribute data) should be tied to each symbol; hopefully the GPS software will permit the entry of several layers of asset data. For example, if the feature to be located is a pole, the pole symbol can be backed up with pole use (illumination, electric wire, telephone, etc.); the type of pole can be booked (concrete, wood, metal, etc.); and the year of installation can be entered (municipal computers can automatically generate work orders for any facility's maintenance based on the original date of installation). Planning ensures that when the roving surveyor is at the feature point, all possible prompts are displayed to completely capture the data for each waypoint. The success of any kinematic survey depends a great deal on the thoroughness of the pre-survey reconnoiter and on the preparation of the job file and on using the GPS software.

7.11   GPS Field Procedures

7.11.1   Tripod and Pole-Mounted Antenna Considerations

GPS antennas can be mounted directly to tripods via optical plummet-equipped tribrachs. All static survey occupations and base station occupations for all other types of GPS surveys require the use of a tripod. Care must be taken to center the antenna precisely and to measure the ARH precisely. Earlier antennas had a direction mark (often an N or arrow, or a series of numbered notches along the outside perimeter of the antenna), which enabled the surveyor to align the roving antenna in the same direction (usually north) as the base station antenna. Having the antennas similarly oriented helps to eliminate any bias in the antennas. The measured ARH (corrected or uncorrected) is entered into the receiver, and when "lock" has been established to the satellites, a message is displayed on the receiver display, and observations begin. If the ARH cannot be measured directly, then slant heights are measured. Some agencies measure in two or three slant locations and average the results. <u>The vertical height can be</u> computed using the Pythagorean theorem: hi = $\sqrt{\text{slant height}^2 - \text{antenna radius}^2}$ (Figure 7.18).

GPS receiver antennas can also be mounted on adjustable-length poles (similar to prism poles) or bipods. These poles and bipods may have built-in power supply conduits, a built-in circular bubble, and the ability to display the ARH. When using poles, the GPS receiver program automatically prompts the surveyor to accept the last-used ARH; if there has been no change in the antenna height, the surveyor simply accepts the prompted value. As with most surveys, field notes are important, both as backup and as confirmation of entered data. The ARH at each station is booked along with equipment numbers, session times, crew, file (job) number, and any other pertinent data (Figure 7.18).

7.11.2 Static Surveys

7.11.2.1 Traditional Static.
In this technique of GPS positioning, two, or more, receivers collect data from the same satellites during the same epochs. Accuracy can be improved by using the differential techniques of relative positioning whereby one base receiver antenna (single or dual frequency) is placed over a point of known coordinates (X, Y, and Z) on a tripod, while other antennas are placed, also on tripods, over permanent stations that are to be positioned. Observation times are 2 hr or more, depending on the receiver, the accuracy requirements, the length of the baseline, the satellites' geometric configuration, and atmospheric conditions. This technique is used for long lines in geodetic control, control densification, and photogrammetric control for aerial surveys and precise engineering surveys; it is also used as a fallback technique when the available geometric array of satellites is not compatible with other GPS techniques (see the sections describing GPS measurement methods). The preplanning of station locations takes into consideration potential obstructions presented by trees and buildings, which must be considered and minimized. Some recommend that, for best results, dual-frequency receivers be used, the GDOP be less than eight and that a minimum of five satellites be tracked.

7.11.2.2 Rapid Static.
This technique, which was developed in the early 1990s, can be employed where dual-frequency receivers are used over short (up to 15 km) baselines. As with static surveys, this technique requires one receiver antenna to be positioned (on a tripod) at a known base station while the roving surveyor moves from station to station with the antenna pole-mounted. With good geometry, initial phase ambiguities can be resolved within a minute (3–5 min for single-frequency receivers). With this technique, there is no need to maintain lock on the satellites while moving rover receivers. The roving receivers can even be turned off to preserve their batteries. Accuracies of a few millimeters are possible using this technique. Observation times of 5–20 min are typical, depending on the length of the baseline.

7.11.3 Kinematic Surveys

This is an efficient way to survey detail points for engineering and topographic surveys.

Project Name _____

Project Number _____

Receiver Model/No. _____

Receiver Software Version _____

Data Logger Type/No. _____

Antenna Model/No. _____

Cable Length _____

Ground Plane Extensions Yes ( ) No ( )

Station Name _____

Station Number _____

4-Character ID _____

Date   _____

Obs. Session _____

Operator   _____

Data Collection

Collection Rate _____

Start Day/Time _____

End Day/Time _____

Receiver Position

Latitude _____

Longitude _____

Height   _____

Obstruction or possible interference sources _____

_____

General weather conditions _____

_____

Detailed meteorological observations recorded: Yes ( ) No ( )

Antenna Height Measurement

Show on sketch measurements taken to derive the antenna height. If slant measurements are taken, make measurement on two opposite sides of the antenna. Make measurements before and after observing session.

Vertical measurements ( )

Slant measurements ( ): radius _____ m

	BEFORE		AFTER	
	_____ m	_____ in.	_____ m	_____ in.
	_____ m	_____ in.	_____ m	_____ in.
Mean	_____			
Corrected to vertical if slant measurement	_____			
Vertical offset to phase center	_____			
Other offset (indicate on sketch)	_____			
TOTAL HEIGHT	_____			

Verified by: _____

FIGURE 7.18 GPS Field Log. (Courtesy of Geomatics, Canada)

This technique begins with both the base unit and the roving unit occupying a 10-km (or shorter) baseline (two known positions) until ambiguities are resolved. Alternatively, short baselines with one known position can be used where the distance between the stations is short enough to permit antenna swapping. Here, the base station and a nearby (within reach of the antenna cable) undefined station are occupied for a short period of time (say, 2 min) in the static mode, after which the antennas are swapped (while still receiving the satellite signals but now in the rove mode) for a further few minutes of readings in the static mode (techniques may vary with different manufacturers). Receivers having wireless technology (e.g., Bluetooth wireless technology) need not have the baselines restricted by the length of antenna cable. After the antennas have been returned to their original tripods and after an additional short period of observations in the static mode, the roving receiver in rove mode then moves (on a pole, backpack, truck, boat, etc.) to position all required detail points—keeping a lock on the satellite signals. If the lock is lost, the receiver is held stationary for a few seconds until the ambiguities are once again resolved so that the survey can continue. The base station stays in the static mode unless it is time to interchange the base and a rover station. A third technique, called OTF ambiguity resolution, occurs as the base station remains fixed at a position of known coordinates and the rover receiver is able to determine the integer number of cycles using software designed for that purpose, even as the receiver is on the move.

All kinematic positioning techniques compute a relative differential position at preset time intervals instead of at operator-selected points. Lock must be maintained to a minimum of four satellites, or it must be reestablished (usually by OTF) when lost. This technique is used for road profiling, ship positioning in sounding surveys, and aircraft positioning in aerial surveys. Continuous surveying can be interrupted to take observations (a few epochs) at any required waypoints.

7.11.4 Real-Time Kinematic

The real-time combination of GPS receivers, mobile data communications, onboard data processing, and onboard applications software contributes to an exciting new era in surveying. As with the motorized total stations described in Section 5.7, real-time positioning offers the potential of one-person capability in positioning, mapping, and quantity surveys (the base station receiver can be unattended). Layout surveys need two RTK surveyors, one to operate the receiver and one to mark the stations in the field.

RTK surveys require that a GPS receiver be set up at a station of known coordinates (base station) and receive satellite signals to determine the station's coordinates; the new coordinates are compared with the previously determined correct coordinates of the base station and a difference is computed. This difference is the sum of the satellite errors (except for multipath) on that date and time. The differences are then transmitted by radio or cell phone to any number of roving receivers that are simultaneously tracking the same satellites; the roving GPS receivers can then can use the transmitted data to remove most errors from their readings and thus determine accurate position coordinates in real time. Multibase RTK radio-equipped base receivers, which transmit on different radio channels, require that the roving surveyor switch through the roving receiver's channels to receive all transmissions. The epoch collection rate is usually set to 1 s. Messages to the rover are updated every 0.5–2 s, and the baseline processing can be done in 0.5–1 s. Figure 7.19

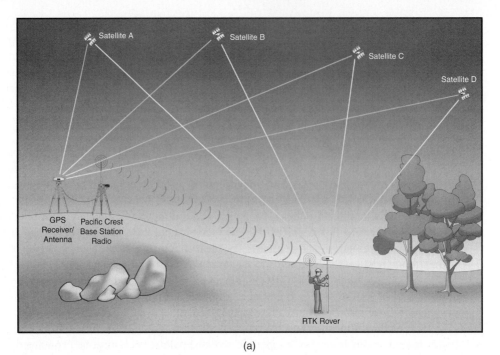

FIGURE 7.19 (a) A base station GPS receiver and base station radio, as well as roving GPS receiver equipped with a radio receiver that allows for real-time positioning.

(continued)

shows a typical radio and amplifier used in code and carrier differential surveys. Radio reception requires a line of sight to the base station.

By 2001, cell phones were also introduced at the base station for field rover communications. The use of cell phones (in areas of cellular coverage) can overcome the interference on radio channels that sometimes frustrates and delays surveyors. Since then, rapid improvements have occurred in both cellular coverage and mobile phone technology. Third-generation (G3) mobile phone technology has created the prospect of transferring much more than voice communications and small data-packets; this evolving technology will enable the surveyor to transfer much larger data files from one phone to another, and also will enable the surveyor to access computer files via the Internet, both with data uploads and downloads. This new wireless technology will greatly impact both the collection of field data and the layout of surveying and engineering works.

RTK positioning can commence without the rover first occupying a known baseline. The base station transmits code and carrier-phase data to the roving receiver, which can use these data to help resolve ambiguities and to solve for coordinate differences between the reference and the roving receivers. The distance and line-of-sight range of the radio transmission (earlier radios) from the base to the rover can be extended by booster radios to a distance of about 10 km. Longer ranges require commercially licensed radios, as do even shorter ranges in some countries. The RTK technique can utilize either single-frequency or dual-frequency receivers. The more expensive dual-frequency receiver has better potential for surveys in areas where satellite visibility may be reduced by topographic obstructions.

FIGURE 7.19 (*continued*) (b) Base station radio. (Courtesy of Pacific Crest Corporation, Santa Clara, California)

(b)

Loss of signal lock can be regained with single-frequency receivers by reoccupying a point of known position, and with dual-frequency receivers either by remaining stationary for a few minutes or by using OTF resolution, while proceeding to the next survey position. When the second and third civilian frequencies are provided for GPS users in the near future, solutions will be greatly enhanced.

The GPS roving receiver includes the antenna and data collector mounted on an adjustable-length pole, with the receiver, radio, and radio antenna mounted in the back-pack. More recent models have all equipment mounted on the pole; the pole kit weighs only 8.5 pounds.

7.11.5 Real-Time Networks

RTK is the positioning technique that has seen the greatest technological advances and greatest surveyor acceptance over the past few years. Private companies, municipalities, and even states are now installing (or planning to install) RTK base station networks to service their constituent private and public surveyors. With the large number of CORS stations now established, the need for additional RTK base stations has been reduced because the existing CORS can also be used in RTK operations. Multibase RTK networks can greatly expand the area in which a wide variety of surveyors can operate. It is reported that multibase RTK base stations, using cellular communications, can cover a much larger area (up to four times) than can radio-equipped RTK base stations.

In 2004, Trimble Inc. introduced a variation on the multibase network concept called virtual reference station (VRS) technology. This real-time network (RTN) requires a minimum of three base stations up to 60 km apart (the maximum practical spacing for postprocessing in CORS), with communications to rovers and to a processing center via cell phones. This process requires that the rover surveyor dial into the system and provide his or her approximate location. The network processor determines measurements similar to what would have been received had a base station been at the rover's position and transmits those measurements to the rover receiver. The accuracies and initialization times in this system (using 30-km baselines) are said to be comparable with results obtained in very short (1–2 km) baseline situations. Accuracies of 1 cm in northing and easting and 2 cm in elevation are expected.

RTN found immediate popularity. Since 2004 there has been much work in establishing RTNs across North America, parts of Asia, and Europe. Trimble's main competitors (Topcon, Leica, and Sokkia) have all joined in the expansion of RTNs using their own hardware and software in network design. Once the network of base stations has been established, GPS signals, continuously received at each base station, can be transmitted via the Internet to a central Internet server. Server software can model measurement errors and then provide appropriate corrections to any number of roving receivers via Internet protocol-equipped cell phones working within allowable distances of the base stations. A roving GPS surveyor now has the same capabilities as roving GPS surveyors working with their own dedicated base stations.

Some RTNs have been established by state DOT agencies for their own use, but they also make the service freely available to the public. Other RTNs have been established by entrepreneurs who license (monthly or annual) use of their network to working surveyors.

It is expected that all these continuously operating base station receivers will be added to the CORS network thus greatly expanding that system.

7.12 GPS Applications

Although GPS was originally devised to assist in military navigation, guidance, and positioning, civil applications continue to evolve at a rapid rate. From its earliest days, GPS was welcomed by the surveying community and recognized as an important tool in precise positioning. Prior to GPS, published surveying accuracy standards, then tied to terrestrial techniques (e.g., triangulation, trilateration, and precise traversing), had an upper accuracy limit of 1:100,000. With GPS, accuracy standards have risen as follows: AA (global), 1:100,000,000; A (national—primary network), 1:10,000,000; and B (national—secondary network), 1:1,000,000. In addition to continental control, GPS has now become a widely used technique for establishing and verifying state/provincial and municipal horizontal control, as well as for horizontal control for large-scale engineering and mapping projects.

7.12.1 General Techniques

In the field, the surveyor first sets the receiver over the point and then measures, records (in the field log), and enters the ARH into the receiver. The session programming is verified, and the mode of operation is selected. Satellite lock and position computation are then verified. As the observations proceed, the process is monitored. When the session is complete, the roving receiver is moved to the next waypoint.

Newer data collectors, designed for RTK surveys, make the surveyor's job much simpler (Figure 7.20). Some of these data collectors come with interactive graphics screens

(a)   (b)

FIGURE 7.20 (a) Penmap GPS-RTK. This cm-level GPS system features a Pentium tablet PC as the data collector/controller. (b) Its touch-screen capabilities speed up all the data collection/controller operations. (Courtesy of Penmap, Strata Software, Bradford, West Yorkshire, UK) (which the surveyor taps with a stylus to select operations or to issue commands) and provide features that enable the surveyor to initialize the base station and rovers, set up the radio communications, set up the antenna heights and descriptions, load only that part of the geoid (e.g., GEOID03) that is needed, select a working grid, display how many satellites are visible, display skyplot and PDOP/GDOP, indicate when fixed lock occurs, display horizontal and vertical root-mean-square errors, and perform other operations. The survey controller (data collector) has application programs for topography; radial and linear stakeout; cut and fill; and intersections by bearing–bearing, bearing–distance, and distance–distance. In addition, the controller performs inverse, sea level, curvature and refraction, and datum transformations. See Figure 7.21 for typical operations capability with data collectors that are used for both total station surveys and GPS surveys.

7.12.2   Topographic Surveys

When GPS is used for topographic surveys, detail is located by short occupation times and described with the input of appropriate coding. Input may be accomplished by keying in, screen-tapping, using bar-code readers, or keying in prepared library codes. Line work may require no special coding (see Z codes, Section 5.12) because features (curbs, fences, etc.) can be joined by their specific codes (curb2, fence3, etc.), or by tapping the display screen to activate the appropriate stringing feature. Some software will display the accuracy of each observation for horizontal and vertical position, giving the surveyor the opportunity to take additional observations if the displayed accuracy does not yet meet job specifications. In addition to positioning random detail, this GPS technique permits the collection of data on specified profile, cross-section, and boundary locations—utilizing the navigation functions; contours may be readily plotted from the collected data. GPS is also useful when beginning the survey in locating boundary and control markers that may be covered by snow or other ground cover; if the marker's coordinates are in the receiver, the navigation mode can take the surveyor directly to its location. Data captured using these techniques can be added to a mapping or GIS database or directly plotted to scale using a digital plotter (see Chapter 8). Although it is widely reported that GPS topographic surveys can be completed more quickly than total station topographic surveys, they do suffer from one major impediment: A GPS receiver must have line of sight to four (preferably five) satellites to determine position. When topographic features are located under tree canopy or hidden by other obstructions, a GPS receiver cannot be used directly determine position. In this case offset tools are required, such as hand-held or portable total stations.

7.12.3   Layout Surveys

For layout work, the coordinates of all relevant control points and layout points are uploaded from computer files before going out to the field. After the base station receiver has been set up over a control point and the roving receiver appropriately referenced by first occupying a control station for a backsight, the layout can begin. As each layout point number is keyed into the collector, the azimuth, distance, and elevation to the required position are displayed on the screen. The surveyor, guided by these directions, eventually moves to the desired point, which is then staked. One base receiver can support any number of rover receivers, permitting the instantaneous layout of large-project boundaries,

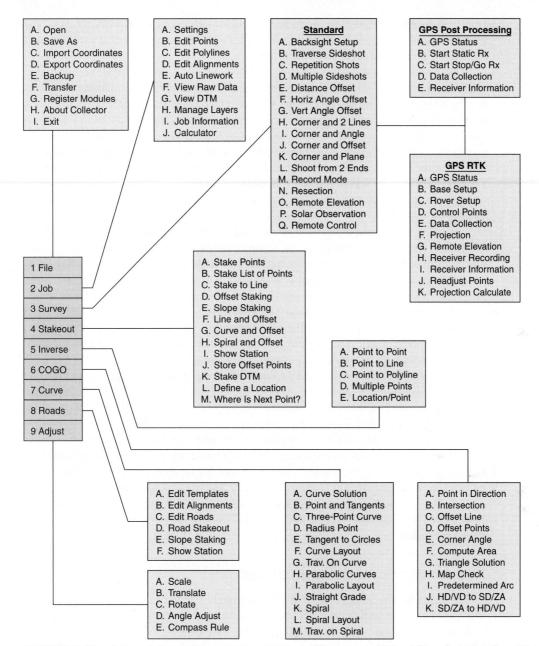

FIGURE 7.21 Adapted data collector menu structure. (Courtesy of Tripod Data Systems, Corvallis, Oregon)

pipelines, roads, and building locations by several surveyors, each working only on a specific type of facility or by all roving surveyors working on all proposed facilities—but on selected geographic sections of the project.

As with topographic applications, the precision of the proposed location is displayed on the receiver as the antenna pole is held on the grade stake or other marker to confirm that layout specifications have been met; if the displayed precision is below specifications, the surveyor simply waits at the location until the processing of data from additional epochs provides the surveyor with the necessary precision. On road layouts, both line and grade can be given directly to the builder (by marking grade stakes), and progress in cut and fill can be monitored. Slope stakes can be located without any need for intervisibility. The next logical stage was to mount GPS antennas directly on various construction excavating equipment to directly provide line and grade control (see Machine Control, in Chapter 10).

As with the accuracy/precision display previously mentioned, not only are cut and fill, grades, and the like displayed at each step along the way, but also a permanent record is kept on all of these data in case a review is required. Accuracy can also be confirmed by re-occupying selected layout stations and noting and recording the displayed measurements, an inexpensive, yet effective, method of quality control.

When used for material inventory measurements, GPS techniques are particularly useful in open-pit mining, where original, in-progress, and final surveys can easily performed for quantity and payment purposes. Also, material stockpiles can be surveyed quickly and volumes computed using appropriate onboard software.

For both GPS topographic and layout work, there is no way to get around the fact that existing and proposed stations must be occupied by the antenna. If some of these specific locations are such that satellite visibility is impossible, perhaps because obstructions are blocking the satellites' signals (even when using receivers capable of tracking multiple constellations), then ancillary surveying techniques must be used.

Some examples of such equipment include a backpacked IMU/GPS equipped GPS receiver (Figure 7.2), a total station with a built-in GPS receiver (Figure 5.29), and handheld and portable total stations (Figures 7.22 and 7.23). In cases where millimeter accuracy is needed in vertical dimensions (e.g., some structural layouts), one GPS manufacturer has incorporated a stand-alone precise fan laser level into the GPS receiver–controller instrumentation package.

7.12.4   Additional Applications

GPS is ideal for the precise type of measurements needed in deformation studies—whether they are for geological events (e.g., plate slippage) or for structure stability studies such as for bridges and dams monitoring. In both cases, measurements from permanently established remote sites can be transmitted to more central control offices for immediate analysis.

In addition to the static survey control as described above, GPS can also be utilized in dynamic applications of aerial surveying and hydrographic surveying where onboard GPS receivers can be used to supplement existing ground or shore control or where they can now be used in conjunction with inertial guidance equipment [Inertial Navigation System (INS)] for control purposes, without the need for external (shore or ground) GPS

FIGURE 7.22 MapStar Compass Module II, which has reflectorless EDM capabilities and azimuth determination (accuracy of ±0.6°). (Courtesy of Laser Technology Inc., Englewood, Centennial, Colorado)

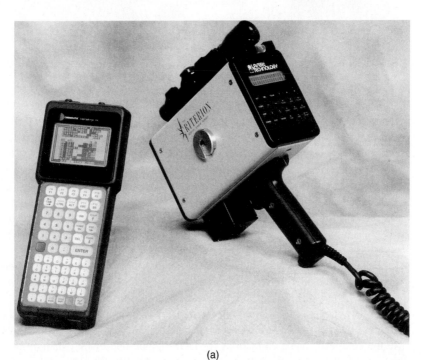

(a)

FIGURE 7.23 (a) Criterion hand-held survey laser (300), with data collector; angles by fluxgate compass; distance without a prism to 1,500 ft (to 40,000 ft with a prism). This instrument is used to collect data with an accuracy of ±0.3° and ±0.3 ft for mapping and GIS databases. It provides a good extension to canopy-obstructed GPS survey points. (Courtesy of Laser Technology Inc., Englewood, Colorado).

(continued)

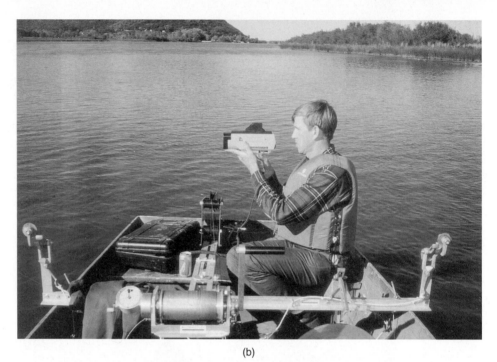

(b)

FIGURE 7.23 (*continued*)   (b) Prosurvey 1000 hand-held survey laser; used to record distances and angles to survey stations. Shown here being used to determine river width in a hydorgraphic survey. (Courtesy of Laser Atlanta, Norcross, Georgia)

receivers. Navigation has always been one of the chief uses made of GPS. Civilian use in this area has become very popular. Commercial and pleasure boating now have an accurate and relatively inexpensive navigation device. With the cessation of SA, the precision of low-cost receivers has improved to the <10-m range and that can be further improved to the submeter level using differential (e.g., DGPS radio beacon) techniques. Using low-cost GPS receivers, sailors can now navigate to the correct harbor, and can even navigate to the correct mooring within that harbor. Also, GPS, together with onboard inertial systems (INS), is rapidly becoming the norm for aircraft navigation during airborne remote-sensing missions.

GPS navigation has now become a familiar tool for backpackers, where the inexpensive GPS receiver (often less than $300) has become a superior adjunct to the compass (Figure 7.6). Using GPS, the backpacker can determine geographic position at selected points (waypoints) such as trail intersections, river crossings, campsites, and other points of interest. Inexpensive software (for less than $100) can be used to transfer collected waypoints to the computer, make corrections for DGPS input, and display data on previously loaded maps and plans. Also, the software can be utilized to identify waypoints on a displayed map, which can be coordinated and then downloaded to a GPS receiver so that the backpacker can go to the field and navigate to the selected waypoints. Many backpackers continue to use a compass while navigating from waypoint to waypoint to maneuver under tree canopy, for example, where GPS signals are blocked, and to conserve GPS receiver battery life.

7.13 Vertical Positioning

Until recently, most surveyors have been able to ignore the implications of geodesy for normal engineering plane surveys. The distances encountered are so relatively short that global implications are negligible. However, the elevation coordinate (h) given by GPS solutions refers to the height from the surface of the reference ellipsoid (GRS80; Figure 7.24) to the ground station, whereas the surveyor needs the orthometric height (H). The ellipsoid is referenced to a spatial Cartesian coordinate system (Figure 7.25) called the ITRF—ITRF00 is the latest model—in which the center (0, 0, 0) is the center of the mass of the Earth and the X axis is a line drawn from the origin through the equatorial plane to the Greenwich meridian. The Y axis is in the equatorial plane perpendicular to the X axis, and the Z axis is drawn from the origin perpendicular to the equatorial plane, as shown in Figure 7.26.

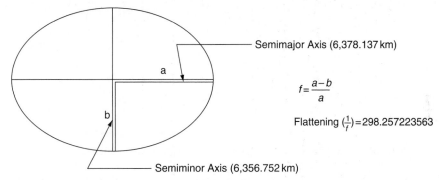

Semimajor Axis (6,378.137 km)

$$f = \frac{a-b}{a}$$

Flattening $(\frac{1}{f}) = 298.257223563$

Semiminor Axis (6,356.752 km)

FIGURE 7.24 Ellipse parameters of the GRS80 Ellipsoid

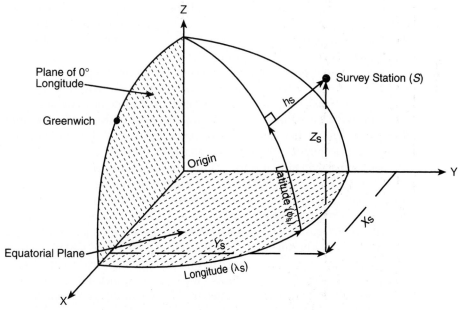

FIGURE 7.25 Cartesian (X, Y, Z) and geodetic ($\varphi_s, \lambda_s, h_s$) coordinates.

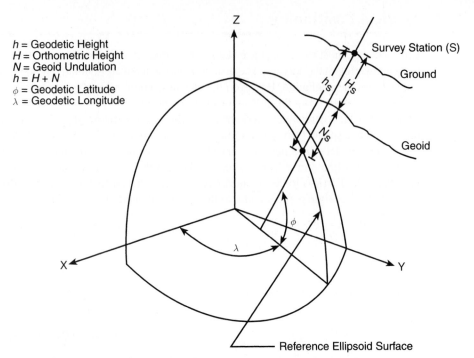

h = Geodetic Height
H = Orthometric Height
N = Geoid Undulation
h = H + N
ϕ = Geodetic Latitude
λ = Geodetic Longitude

FIGURE 7.26 Relationship of geodetic height (*h*) and orthometric height (*H*).

Essentially, GPS observations permit the computation of *Y*, *X*, and *Z* Cartesian coordinates of a geocentric ellipsoid. These Cartesian coordinates can then be transformed to geodetic coordinates: latitude (φ), longitude (λ), and ellipsoidal height (*h*). The geodetic coordinates, together with geoid corrections, can be transformed to UTM, state plane, or other grids (see Figure 7.25 and Section 7.13.1) to provide working coordinates (northing, easting, and elevation) for the field surveyor.

The ellipsoid presently used most often to portray the Earth is the WGS84 (as described by World Geodetic System), which is generally agreed to represent the Earth more accurately than previous versions. (Ongoing satellite observations permitted scientists to improve their estimates about the size and mass of the Earth.) An earlier reference ellipsoid (GRS80)—the Geodetic Reference System of the International Union of Geodesy and Geophysics (IUGG)—was adopted in 1979 by that group as the model then best representing the Earth. It is the ellipsoid on which the horizontal datum, the NAD83, is based (Figure 7.24). In this system, the geographic coordinates are given by the ellipsoidal latitude (φ), longitude (λ), and height (*h*) above the ellipsoidal surface to the ground station. The GEOID03 model (see Section 7.13.1) is based on known relationships between NAD83 and the ITRF spatial reference frames, together with GPS height measurements on the North American vertical datum of 1988 (NAVD88) benchmarks.

Traditionally, surveyors are used to working with spirit levels and reference orthometric heights (*H*) to the average surface of the Earth, as depicted by mean sea level (MSL). The surface of MSL can be approximated by the equipotential surface of the Earth's gravity field, called the **geoid**. The density of adjacent landmasses at any particular survey station influences the geoid, which has an irregular surface. Thus, its surface does not follow the

Chap. 7   Satellite Positioning

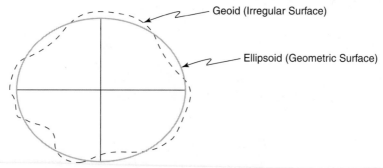

FIGURE 7.27 GRS80 ellipsoid and the geoid.

surface of the ellipsoid; sometimes it is below the ellipsoid surface and other times above it. Wherever the mass of the Earth's crust changes, the geoid's gravitational potential also changes, resulting in a non-uniform and unpredictable geoid surface. Because the geoid does not lend itself to mathematical expression, as does the ellipsoid, geoid undulation (the difference between the geoid surface and the ellipsoid surface) must be measured at specific sites to determine the local geoid undulation value (see Figures 7.27 and 7.28).

7.13.1 Geoid Modeling

Geoid undulations can be determined both by gravimetric surveys and by the inclusion of points of known elevation in GPS surveys. When the average undulation of an area has been determined, the residual undulations over the surveyed area must still be determined. While residual undulations are usually less than 0.020 m over areas of 50 sq. km, the Earth's undulation itself ranges from +75 m at New Guinea to −104 m at the south tip of India.

After all the known geoid separations have been plotted, the geoid undulations (N) at any given survey station can be interpolated; the orthometric height (H) can be determined from the relationship $H = h - N$, where h is the ellipsoid height (N is positive when the geoid is above the ellipsoid and negative when below the ellipsoid)—see Figures 7.26–7.28. Geoid modeling data can be obtained from government agencies, and in many cases, GPS receiver suppliers provide these data as part of their onboard software.

Because of the uncertainties still inherent in geoid modeling, it is generally thought that accuracies in elevation are only about half the accuracies achievable in horizontal positioning. That is, if a horizontal accuracy is defined to be ±(5 mm + 1 ppm), the vertical accuracy is probably close to ±(10 mm + 2 ppm). However, the accuracy of geoid models is improving with each new version. As more and more GPS observations on NAVD88 benchmarks (GPSBMs) are included in the net, we move ever closer to the goal of a geoid accurate to 1 cm. GPS observations can directly deliver ellipsoidal heights, but beginning in 1996, GPS manufacturers made it possible to field surveyors to determine orthometric heights quickly from GPS observations by incorporating geoid models directly into their receivers.

7.13.1.1 CGG2000 GEOID (Canada). Natural Resources, Canada (NRCan) has developed an improved geoid model, the Canadian Gravimetric Geoid model (CGG2000), which is a refinement of previous models (GSD95 and GSD91). It takes into account about 700,000 surface gravity observations in Canada, with the addition of about 1,477,000

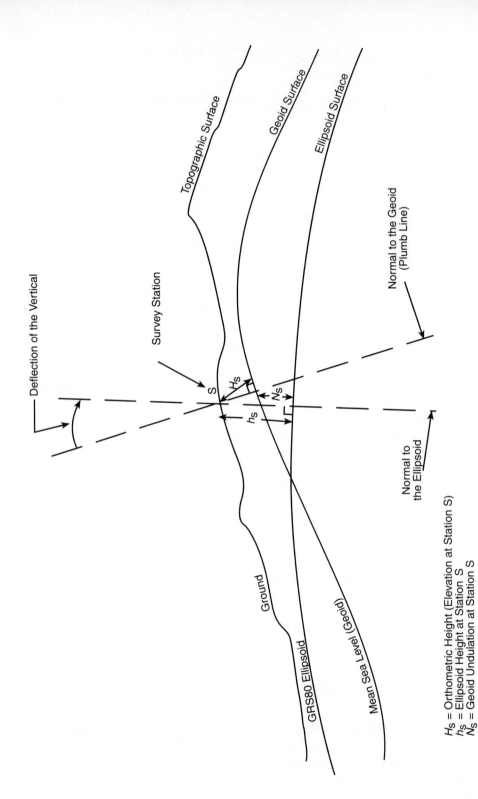

H_S = Orthometric Height (Elevation at Station S)
h_S = Ellipsoid Height at Station S
N_S = Geoid Undulation at Station S

(N Is Positive When Geoid Is Above the Ellipsoid)

$$h_S = H_S + N_S$$

FIGURE 7.28   The three surfaces of geodesy (undulations greatly exaggerated).

observations taken in the United States, and 117,100 observations taken in Denmark. Although the model covers most of North America, it was designed for use in Canada. Geoid data (the GPS.H package includes the new geoid model and GPS.Hv2.1, which is the latest software) are available at the ministry's website at http://www.geod.nrcan.gc.ca (under "Products and Services").

7.13.1.2 GEOID03 (United States).

GEOID03 (a refinement of GEOID99, GEOID96, GEOID93, and GEOID90) is a geoid-elevation estimation model of the CONUS, referenced to the GRS80 ellipsoid. Thus, it enables mainland surveyors to convert ellipsoidal heights (NAD 83/GRS80) reliably to the more useful orthometric heights (NAVD88) at the centimeter level. GEOID03 was created from 14,185 points, including 579 in Canada and used updated GPSBMs that were not available for the previous geoid model (GEOID99). GEOID03 files are among the many services to be found at the NGS's Geodetic tool kit website at http://www.ngs.noaa.gov/TOOLS/.

7.14 Conclusion

Table 7.3 summarizes the GPS positioning techniques described in this chapter. GPS techniques hold such promise that most future horizontal and vertical control could be coordinated using these techniques. It is also likely that many engineering, mapping, and GIS surveying applications will be developed using emerging advances in real-time GPS data collection. In the future, the collection of GPS data will be enhanced as more and more North American local and federal agencies install continuously operating receivers and transmitters, which provide positioning solutions for a wide variety of private and government agencies involved in surveying, mapping, planning, GIS-related surveying, and navigation.

7.15 GPS Glossary

Absolute Positioning The direct determination of a station's coordinates by receiving positioning signals from a minimum of four GPS satellites. Also known as point positioning.

Active Control Station (ACS) See CORS.

Ambiguity Uncertainty as to the integer number of carrier cycles between the GPS receiver and a satellite.

Compass A proposed Chinese satellite-positioning system.

Continuously Operating Reference Station (CORS) An established GPS receiver station that collects positioning signals continually and compares computed position coordinates with already established coordinates for that station. The difference in position will reflect the errors caused by the atmosphere, etc., and the transmitted differences can be used (real time or postprocessing) by single-receiver surveyors working nearby at a specific time. The correction data can be transmitted via radio, cell phone or by contacting the NGS website. CORS-transmitted data can

Table 7.3 GPS MEASUREMENTS SUMMARY*

Two Basic Modes:

Code-based measurements: Satellite-to-receiver pseudorange is measured and then corrected to provide the range; four satellite ranges are required to determine position—by removing the uncertainties in X, Y, Z, and receiver clocks. Military can access both the P code and the C/A code; civilians can access only the C/A code.

Carrier-based measurements: The carrier waves themselves are used to compute the satellite(s)-to-receiver range; similar to EDM. Most carrier receivers utilize both code measurements and carrier measurements to compute positions.

Two Basic Techniques:

Point positioning: Code measurements are used to directly compute the position of the receiver. Only one receiver required.

Relative positioning: Code and/or carrier measurements are used to compute the baseline vector (ΔX, ΔY, and ΔZ) from a point of known position to a point of unknown position, thus enabling the computation of the coordinates of the new position.

Relative positioning: Two receivers required—simultaneously taking measurements on the same satellites.

Static: Accuracy: 5 mm + 1 ppm. Observation times: 1 hr to many hours. Use in control surveys: Standard method when lines longer than 20 km. Uses dual- or single-frequency receivers.

Rapid static: Accuracy: 5–10 mm + 1 ppm. Observation times: 5–15 min. Initialization time of 1 min for dual-frequency receivers and about 3–5 min for single-frequency receivers. Receiver must have specialized rapid static observation capability. The roving receiver does not have to maintain lock on satellites (useful feature in areas with many obstructions). Used for control surveys, including photogrammetric control for lines 10 km or less. The receiver program determines the total length of the sessions, and the receiver screen displays "time remaining" at each station session.

Re-occupation (also known as pseudostatic and pseudo-kinematic). Accuracy: 5–10 mm + 1 ppm. Observation times about 10 min, but each point must be re-occupied again after at least 1 hr, for another 10 min. No initialization time required. Useful when GDOP is poor. No need to maintain satellite lock. Same rover receivers must re-occupy the points they initially occupied. Moving the base station for the second occupation sessions may improve accuracy. Voice communications are needed to ensure simultaneous observations between base receiver and rover(s).

Kinematic: Accuracy: 10 mm + 2 ppm. Observation times: 1–4 epochs (1–2 min on control points); the faster the rover speed, the quicker must be the observation (shorter epochs). Sampling rate is usually between 0.5 and 5 s. Initialization by occupying two known points, 2–5 min, or by antenna swap, 5–15 min. Lock must be maintained on four satellites (five satellites are better in case one of them moves close to the horizon). Good technique for open areas (especially hydrographic surveys) and where large amounts of data are required quickly.

Stop and go: Accuracy: 10–20 mm + 2 ppm. Observation times: a few seconds to a minute. Lock must be maintained to four satellites and if loss of lock occurs, it must be reinitialized [i.e., occupy known point, rapid static techniques, or on-the-fly (OTF) resolution; OTF requires dual-frequency receivers]. This technique is one of the more effective ways of locating topographic and built features, as for engineering surveys.

DGPS: The U.S. Coast Guard's system of providing differential code measurement surveys. Accuracy-submeter to 10 m. Roving receivers are equipped with radio receivers capable of receiving base station broadcasts of pseudorange corrections, using radio technical commission for maritime services (RTCM) standards. For use by individual surveyors working within range of the transmitters (100–400 km). Positions can be determined in real time. Surveyors using just one receiver have the equivalent of two receivers.

Real-time differential surveys: Also known as RTK. Accuracies: 1–2 cm. Requires a base receiver occupying a known station, which then radiotransmits error corrections to any number of roving receivers thus permitting them to perform data gathering and layout surveys in real time. All required software is onboard the roving receivers. Dual-frequency receivers permit OTF re-initialization after loss of lock. Baselines are restricted to about 10 km. Five satellites are required. This, or similar techniques, is without doubt the future for many engineering surveys.

CORS: Nationwide differential positioning system. By 2007 this system of approximately 1,200 CORS (growing at a rate of about fifteen new stations each month) enables surveyors working with one GPS receiver to obtain the same high accuracy results as if working with two. The CORS receiver is a highly accurate dual-frequency receiver. Surveyors can access station data for the appropriate location, date, and time via the Internet; data are then input to the software to combine with the surveyor's own data to produce accurate (postprocessed) positioning. Canada's nationwide system, active control system (ACS), provides base station data for a fee.

---

*Observation times and accuracies are affected by the quality and capability of the GPS receivers, by signal errors, and by the geometric strength of the visible satellite array (GDOP). Vertical accuracies are about half the horizontal accuracies.

be used by single-receiver surveyors or navigators to permit higher-precision differential positioning through postprocessing computations.

Cycle Slip   A temporary loss of lock on satellite carrier signals causing a miscount in carrier cycles; lock must be reestablished to continue positioning solutions.

Differential Positioning   Obtaining satellite measurements at a known base station in order to correct simultaneous same-satellite measurements made at rover receiving stations. Corrections can be postprocessed, or corrections can be real time (RTK) as when they are broadcast directly to the roving receiver.

Epoch   An observational event in time that forms part of a series of GPS observations.

Galileo   A partially completed EU positioning satellite system which will consist of thirty satellites and may be completed by 2012.

General Dilution of Precision (GDOP)   A value that indicates the relative uncertainty in position, using GPS observations, caused by errors in time (GPS receivers) and satellite vector measurements. A minimum of four widely spaced satellites at high elevations usually produce accurate results (i.e., lower GDOP values).

Geodetic Height (h)   The distance from the ellipsoid surface to the ground surface.

Geoid Surface   A surface that is approximately represented by mean sea level (MSL), and is the equipotential surface of the Earth's gravity field.

Geoid Undulation (N)   The difference between the geoid surface and the ellipsoid surface. N is negative if the geoid surface is below the ellipsoid surface. Also known as *geoid height*.

Global Positioning System (GPS)   A ground positioning (Y, X, and Z) technique based on the reception and analysis of NAVSTAR satellite signals.

GLONASS   A partially completed Russian satellite positioning system, which presently (2009) has nineteen operating satellites.

Ionosphere   That section of the Earth's atmosphere that is about 50–1,000 km above the Earth's surface.

Ionosphere Refraction   The reduction in the velocity of signals (GPS) as they pass through the ionosphere.

NAVSTAR   A set of orbiting satellites used in navigation and positioning, also known as GPS.

Orthometric Height (H)   The distance from the geoid surface to the ground surface. Also known as *elevation*.

Pseudorange   The uncorrected distance from a GPS satellite to a GPS ground receiver determined by comparing the code transmitted from the satellite with the replica code residing in the GPS receiver. When corrections are made for clock and other errors, the pseudorange becomes the range.

Real-Time Positioning (RTK)   RTK requires a base station to measure the satellites' signals, process the baseline corrections, and then broadcast the corrections (differences) to any number of roving receivers that are simultaneously tracking the same satellites.

Relative Positioning   The determination of position through the combined computations of two or more receivers simultaneously tracking the same satellites, resulting in the determination of the baseline vector (X, Y, Z) joining two receivers.

Troposphere   That part of the Earth's atmosphere which stretches from the surface to about 80 km upward (including the stratosphere as its upper portion).

7.16   Recommended Readings

7.16.1   Books and Articles

El-Rabbany, Achmed, *Introduction to GPS: The Global Positioning System* (Norwood, MA: Artech House Publishers, 2002).

Geomatics Canada, *GPS Positioning Guide* (Ottowa, Canada: Natural Resources Canada, 1993).

Hofman-Wellenhof et al., *GPS Theory and Practice*, Fourth Edition (New York: Springer-Verlag Wien, 1997).

Leick, Alfred, *GPS Satellite Surveying*, Second Edition (New York: John Wiley & Sons, 1995).

Reilly, James P., *The GPS Observer* (ongoing columns), *Point of Beginning* (POB).

Spofford, Paul, and Neil Weston, *CORS—The National Geodetic Survey's Continuously Operating Reference Station Project. ACSM Bulletin*, March/April 1998.

Trimble Navigation Co., *GPS, A Guide to the Next Utility* (Information on these and other Trimble publications is available at the Trimble website shown on the following page, 1989).

Van Sickle, Jan, *GPS for Land Surveyors* (New York: Ann Arbor Press Inc., 1996).

Wells, David, et al., *Guide to GPS Positioning* (Fredericton, New Brunswick: Canadian GPS Associates, 1986).

7.16.2   Magazines for General Information (Including Archived Articles)

ACSM Bulletin, American Congress on Surveying and Mapping,   *http://www.survmap.org/* or *http://www.ascm.net*

American Surveyor,   *http://amerisurv.com*

GPS World,   *http://www.gpsworld.com/*

Point of Beginning (POB),   *http://www.pobonline.com/*

Professional Surveyor,   *http://www.profsurv.com*

7.16.3   Websites

Websites for general information, reference and web links, and GPS receiver manufacturers (see the list of additional Internet references in Appendix B)

Canada-Wide real-Time DGPS Service,   *http://www.cdgps.com*
DGPS   *http://www.navcen.uscg.gov/* (U.S. Coast Guard Navigation Center)
Galileo,   *http://europa.eu.int/comm/dgs/energy_transport/galileo/index_en.htm*
GLONASS,   *http://www.glonass.iane.rsa.ru* (click on the British flag)

Land Surveying and Geomatics, Maynard H. Riley, PLS, Illinois,
    http://surveying.mentabolism.org/
Land Surveyors' Reference Page, Stan Thompson, PLS, Huntington Technology
    Group, *http://www.lsrp.com/*
Leica, *http://www.leica.com/*
On-line positioning service (OPUS), *http://www.ngs.noaa.gov/OPUS/*
NOAA, What is Geodesy?
    http://www.nos.noaa.gov/education/kits/geodesy/geo01_intro.html
Natural Resources Canada, *http://www.nrcan.gc.ca/*
National Geodetic Survey (NGS), *http://www.ngs.noaa.gov/*
Sokkia, *http://www.sokkia.com/*
Topcon, *http://www.topconpositioning.com/home.html*
Trimble, *http://www.trimble.com/*

Also see the list of Internet references in Appendix B.

Review Questions

7.1 Why is it necessary to observe a minimum of four positioning satellites to solve for position?

7.2 How does the United States' GPS constellation compare with the GLONASS constellation and with the proposed Galileo constellation?

7.3 How does differential positioning work?

7.4 What is the difference between range and pseudorange?

7.5 What are the chief sources of error in GPS measurements? How can you minimize or eliminate each of these errors?

7.6 What are the factors that must be analyzed in GPS planning?

7.7 Describe RTK techniques used for a layout survey.

7.8 What effect has GPS had on national control surveys?

7.9 Explain why station visibility diagrams are used in survey planning.

7.10 Explain the difference between orthometric heights and ellipsoid heights.

7.11 Explain the CORS system.

Chapter 8

An Introduction to Geomatics

8.1　Geomatics Defined

Geomatics is a term used to describe the science and technology of dealing with Earth measurement data. It includes field data collection, processing, and presentation. It has applications in all disciplines and professions that use Earth-related spatial data. Some examples of these disciplines and professions include planning, geography, geodesy, infrastructure engineering, agriculture, natural resources, environment, land division and registration, project engineering, and mapping.

8.2　Branches of Geomatics

Figure 8.1 is a model of the science of geomatics and shows how all the branches and specializations are tied together by their common interest in Earth measurement data and in their common dependence on computer science and information technology (IT). This computerized technology has changed the way field data are collected and processed. To appreciate the full impact of this new technology, you must view the overall operation, that is, from field to computer, computer processing, and data portrayal in the form of maps and plans. Data collection techniques include field surveying, satellite positioning, and remotely sensed imagery obtained through aerial photography/imaging and satellite imagery. It also includes the acquisition of database material scanned from older maps and plans and data collected by related agencies, for example, census data such as TIGER. Data processing is handled through various computer programs designed to process the measurements and their attribute data, such as coordinate geometry (COGO), field data processing, and the processing of remotely sensed data from aerial photos (photogrammetry, including soft-copy photogrammetry) and satellite imagery analysis.

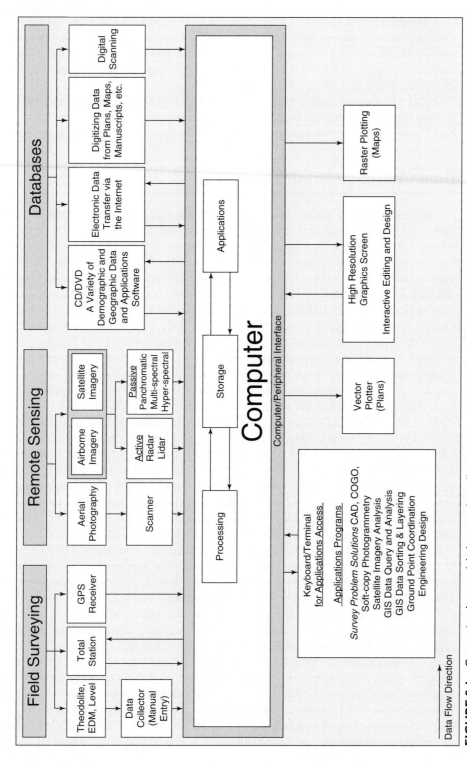

FIGURE 8.1 Geomatics data model, showing the collection, processing, analysis, design, and plotting of geodata.

Processed data can then be used in computer programs for engineering design, relational database management, and geographic information systems (GISs). Data presentation is handled through the use of mapping and other illustrative computer programs; the presentations are displayed on computer screens (where interactive editing can occur) and are output from digital vector and raster plotting devices.

Once the positions and attributes of geographic entities have been digitized and stored in computer memory, they are available to a wide variety of users. Through the use of modern IT, geomatics brings together professionals in all related disciplines and professions.

8.3   Data Collection Branch

Advances in computer science have had a tremendous impact on all aspects of modern technology, and the effects on the collection and processing of data in both field surveying and remotely sensed imagery have been significant. Chapters 1–5 described ground-based techniques for data collection. Survey data once laboriously collected with tapes, theodolites/transits, and levels can now be collected quickly and efficiently using total stations (Chapter 5) and GPS receivers (Chapter 7)—both featuring onboard (or attached) data collection. These latter techniques can provide the high-accuracy results usually required in control surveys (see Chapter 9) and engineering surveys. When high accuracy is not a prime requirement, as in some GIS surveys (see Section 8.9) and many mapping surveys, data can be collected efficiently from airborne and satellite platforms (see Sections 8.6 and 8.7). The broad picture encompassing all aspects of data collection, as well as the storage, processing, analysis, planning and design, and presentation of the data, is now referred to as the field of geomatics.

The upper portion of the schematic in Figure 8.1 shows the various ways in which data can be collected and transferred to the computer. In addition to total station techniques, field surveys can be performed using conventional surveying instruments (theodolites, EDMs, and levels), with the field data entered into a data collector instead of conventional field books. This manual entry of field data lacks the speed associated with interfaced equipment, but after the data have been entered, all the advantages of electronic techniques are available to the surveyor. The raw field data, collected and stored by the total station, are transferred to the computer through a standard RS232 interface connection; via a memory card; and/or, more recently, via USB connection or even via wireless cellular connections. When the collected terrain data have been downloaded into a computer, COGO programs and/or imagery analysis programs can be used to determine the positions (northing, easting, and elevation values) of all survey points. Also at this stage, additional data points (e.g., inaccessible ground points) can be computed and added to the data file.

Existing maps and plans have a wealth of lower-precision data that may be relevant for an area survey database. If such maps and plans are available, the data can be digitized on a digitizing table or by digital scanners and added to the Y, X, and Z coordinates files. Ideally, such files would show the level of precision at which these data were collected—to distinguish these data from data that may have been precisely collected. One of the more important features of the digitizer is its ability to digitize maps and plans drawn at various scales and store the distances and elevations in the computer at their ground (or grid) values.

The stereo analysis of aerial photos (see Section 8.6) is a very effective method of generating topographic ground data, particularly in high-density areas, where the costs for conventional surveys would be high. Many municipalities routinely fly all major roads at regular intervals (e.g., every 5 years in developing areas) and create plans and profiles that can be used for design and construction (see Part II). With the advent of computerized (soft-copy) photogrammetric procedures, stereo-analyzers can coordinate all horizontal and vertical features from aerial images and transfer these Y (north), X (east), and Z (height) coordinates to computer storage.

You will see in Section 8.7 that satellite imagery is received from U.S. (e.g., EOS and Landsat), French, European, Japanese, Canadian, Chinese, and South American satellites, and that it can be processed by a digital image analysis system that classifies terrain into categories of soil and rock types and vegetative cover. These and other data can be digitized (georeferenced) and added to the spatial database.

8.3.1   General Background

Data collection surveys, including topographic surveys, are used to determine the positions of built and natural features (e.g., roads, buildings, trees, and shorelines). These built and natural features can then be plotted to scale on a map or plan. In addition, topographic surveys include the determination of ground elevations, which can later be plotted in the form of contours, cross sections, profiles, or simply spot elevations. In engineering and construction work, topographic surveys are often called preliminary or preengineering surveys. Large-area topographic surveys are usually performed using aerial photography/imaging, with the resultant distances and elevations being derived from the photographs through the use of photogrammetric principles. The survey plan is normally drawn on a digital plotter.

For small-area topographic surveys, various types of ground survey techniques can be employed. Ground surveys can be accomplished by using (1) theodolite and tape, (2) total station, and (3) global positioning system (GPS) (see Chapter 7). Surveys executed using theodolite/tape and level/rod are usually plotted using conventional scale/protractor techniques. On the other hand, if the survey has been executed using a total station or GPS receiver, the survey drawing is plotted on a digital plotter. When total stations are used for topographic surveys, the horizontal (X and Y) and the vertical location (elevation) can be captured easily with just one sighting, with point descriptions and other attribute data entered into electronic storage for later transfer to the computer. (Electronic surveying techniques were discussed in detail in Chapter 5.)

8.3.1.1   Precision Required for Topographic Surveys.   If we consider plotting requirements only, the survey detail need only be located at a precision level consistent with standard plotting precision. Many municipal plans (including plan and profile) are drawn at 1 in. = 50 ft or 1 in. = 40 ft (1:500 metric). If we assume that points can be plotted to the closest 1/50 in. (0.5 mm), then location ties need only be to the closest 1 ft or 0.8 ft (0.25 m). For smaller scale plans, the location precision can be relaxed even further.

In addition to providing plotting data, topographic surveys provide the designer with field dimensions that must be considered for related engineering design. For example, when you are designing an extension to an existing storm sewer, the topographic survey must include the location and elevations of all connecting pipe inverts (see Chapter 13). These values are determined more precisely (0.01 ft or 0.005 m) because of design requirements.

The following points should be considered with respect to levels of precision:

1. Some detail, for example, building corners, railway tracks, bridge beam seats, and pipe and culvert inverts, can be precisely defined and located.
2. Some detail cannot be defined or located precisely. Examples include stream banks, edges of gravel roads, limits of wooded areas, rock outcrops, and tops and bottoms of slopes.
3. Some detail can be located with only moderate precision with normal techniques. Examples are large single trees, manhole covers, and walkways.

When a topographic survey requires all three of the above levels of precision, the items in level 1 are located at a precision dictated by the design requirements; the items in levels 2 and 3 are usually located at the precision of level 3 (e.g., 0.1 ft or 0.01 m). Because most natural features are themselves not precisely defined, topographic surveys in areas having only natural features (e.g., stream or watercourse surveys, site development surveys, or large-scale mapping surveys) can be accomplished by using relatively imprecise survey methods (see aerial surveying in Section 8.6).

8.3.1.2 Traditional Rectangular Surveying Methods.
We focus here on the rectangular techniques, first introduced in Section 1.4, employing preelectronic field techniques. The rectangular technique discussed here utilizes right-angle offsets for detail location, and cross sections (level and rod) for elevations and profiles. Polar techniques (e.g., the use of total stations) are also used for both horizontal positioning and elevations.

Ground surveys are based on survey lines or stations that are part of, or tied in to, the survey control. Horizontal survey control can consist of boundary lines, or offsets to boundary lines, such as centerlines (℄s); coordinate grid monuments; route survey traverses; or arbitrarily placed baselines or control monuments. Vertical survey control is based on benchmarks that already exist in the survey area or benchmarks that are established through differential leveling from other areas.

Surveyors are conscious of the need for accurate and well-referenced survey control. If the control is inaccurate, the survey and any resultant design will also be inaccurate. If the control is not well referenced, it will be costly (perhaps impossible) to relocate the control points precisely in the field once they are lost. In addition to providing control for the original survey, the same survey control must be used if additional survey work is required to complete the preengineering project and, of course, the original survey control must be used for subsequent construction layout surveys that may result from designs based on the original surveys. It is not unusual to have one or more years pass between the preliminary survey and the related construction layout.

8.3.1.3 Tie-Ins at Right Angles to Baselines.
Some ground-based topographic surveys (excluding mapping surveys but including many preengineering surveys) utilize the right-angle offset technique to locate detail. This technique not only provides the location of plan detail but also provides location for area elevations taken by cross sections.

Plan detail is located by measuring the distance perpendicularly from the baseline to the object and, in addition, measuring along the baseline to the point of perpendicularity.

FIGURE 8.2 Double right-angle prism. (Courtesy of Keuffel & Esser Co.)

The baseline is laid out in the field with stakes (nails in pavement) placed at appropriate intervals, usually 100 ft, or 20–30 m. A sketch is entered in the field book before the measuring commences. If the terrain is smooth, a tape can be laid on the ground between the station marks. This technique permits the surveyor to move along the tape (toward the forward station), noting and booking the stations of the sketched detail on both sides of the baseline. The right angle for each location tie can be established by using a pentaprism (Figure 8.2), or a right angle can be established approximately in the following manner. The surveyor stands on the baseline facing the detail to be tied in. He then points one arm down the baseline in one direction and the other arm down the baseline in the opposite direction; after checking both arms (pointed index fingers) for proper alignment, the surveyor closes his eyes while he swings his arms together in front of him, pointing (presumably) at the detail. If he is not pointing at the detail, the surveyor moves slightly along the baseline and repeats the procedure until the detail has been correctly sighted in. The station is then read off the tape and booked in the field notes. This approximate method is used a great deal in route surveys and municipal surveys. This swung-arm technique provides good results over short offset distances (50 ft, or 15 m). For longer offset distances or for very important detail, a pentaprism or even a theodolite can be used to determine the station.

Once all the stations have been booked for the interval (100 ft, or 20–30 m), only the offsets left and right of the baseline are left to be measured. If the steel tape has been left lying on the ground during the determination of the stations, it is usually left in place to mark the baseline while the offsets are measured from it with another tape (e.g., a fiberglass).

Figure 8.3(a) illustrates topographic field notes that have been booked when a single baseline was used, and Figure 8.3(b) illustrates such notes when a split baseline was used. In Figure 8.3(a), the offsets are shown on the dimension lines, and the stations are shown opposite the dimension line or as close as possible to the actual tie point on the baseline. In Figure 8.3(b), the baseline has been "split"; that is, two lines are drawn representing the baseline, leaving a space of zero dimensions between them for the inclusion of stations. The split-baseline technique is particularly valuable in densely detailed areas where single-baseline notes would become crowded and difficult to decipher. The earliest topographic surveyors in North America used the split-baseline method of note keeping (Figure 8.4).

FIGURE 8.3 Topographic field notes. (a) Single baseline. (b) Split baseline.

Chap. 8   An Introduction to Geomatics

FIGURE 8.4 Original topographic field notes, 1907 (distances shown are in chains).

8.3.1.4   Cross Sections and Profiles.   **Cross sections** form series of elevations taken at right angles to a baseline at specific stations, whereas **profiles** are a series of elevations taken along a baseline at some specified repetitive station interval. The elevations thus determined can be plotted on maps and plans either as spot elevations or as contours, or they can be plotted as end areas for construction quantity estimating.

As in offset ties, the baseline interval is usually 100 ft (20–30 m), although in rapidly changing terrain, the interval is usually smaller (e.g., 50 ft or 10–15 m). In addition to the regular intervals, cross sections are taken at each abrupt change in the terrain (top and bottom of slopes, etc.).

Figure 8.5 illustrates how the rod readings are used to define the ground surface. In Figure 8.5(a), the uniform slope permits a minimum number of rod readings. In Figure 8.5(b), the varied slope requires several more (than the minimum) rod readings to define the ground surface adequately. Figure 8.5(c) illustrates how cross sections are taken before and after construction. Chapter 17 covers the calculation of the end area (lined section) at each station and then the volumes of cut and fill.

The profile consists of a series of elevations along the baseline. If cross sections have been taken, the necessary data for plotting a profile will also have been taken. If cross sections are not planned for an area for which a profile is required, the profile elevations can be determined by simply taking rod readings along the line at regular intervals and at all points where the ground slope changes (see Figure 2.19).

Typical field notes for profile leveling are shown in Figure 2.20. Cross sections are booked in two different formats. Figure 2.21 showed cross sections booked in standard level note format. All the rod readings for one station (that can be "seen" from the HI) are booked together. In Figure 2.22, the same data were entered in a format popular with highways agencies. The latter format is more compact and thus takes up less space in the field book; the former format takes up more space in the field book, but it allows for a description for each rod reading, an important consideration for municipal surveyors.

In cases where the terrain is very rugged, thus making the level and rod work very time consuming (many instrument setups), the surveys should be performed using total stations. Chapter 5 describes total station instruments. With polar techniques, these instruments can measure distances and differences in elevation very quickly. The roving surveyor holds a reflecting prism mounted on a range pole instead of holding a rod. Many of these instruments have the distance and elevation data recorded automatically for future computer processing, while others require that the data be entered manually into the data recorder.

8.4   Design and Plotting

Historically, map and plan preparation depended on measurements taken directly in the field, whereas modern data collection practice has been expanded to include both previously referenced and remotely sensed data. The concept of maps and plans has also been expanded to include electronic images (electronic charts are used a great deal in navigation and marine surveying). Maps and plans (hard-copy and electronic) are generally prepared for one of two reasons: (1) when measured data are displayed to scale on a map or plan, the ground data are presented as an inventory or record of the features surveyed, and (2) when the presented data are used to facilitate the design of infrastructure projects, private

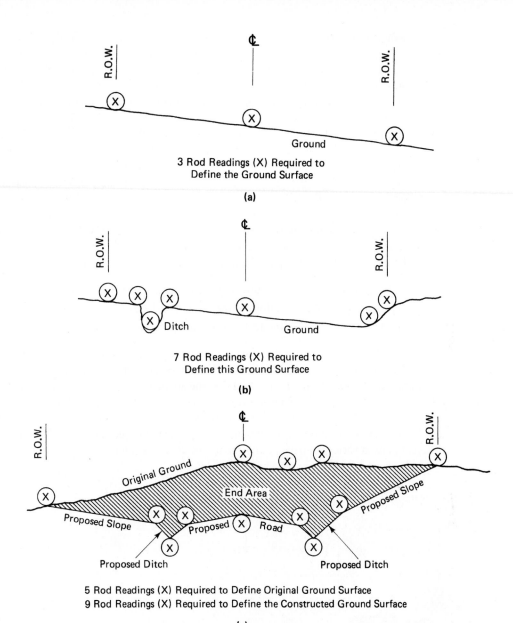

FIGURE 8.5 Cross sections used to define ground surface. (a) Uniform slope; (b) varied slope; (c) ground surface before and after construction.

projects, or land division, the design plan or map is used as a design and layout tool. If the data are to be digitally plotted, a plot file may be created that contains point plot commands (including symbols) and join commands for straight and curved lines. Labels and other attribute data are also included.

Design programs are available for all engineering and construction endeavors. These software programs can work with the stored coordinates to provide different possible designs, which can then be analyzed quickly with respect to cost and other factors. Some design programs incorporate interactive graphics, which permit a plot of the survey to be shown to scale on a high-resolution graphics screen. On this screen, points and lines can be moved, created, edited, and so forth, with the final positions coordinated right on the screen and the new coordinates captured and added to the coordinates files. Once the coordinates of all field data have been determined, the design software can then compute the coordinates of all key points in the new facility (e.g., roads, site developments, etc.). The surveyor can take this design information back to the field and perform a construction layout survey (see Part II) showing the contractor how much cut and fill, for example, is required to bring the land to the proposed elevations and locations. Also, the design data can now be transferred directly (sometimes wirelessly) to construction machine controllers for machine guidance and control functions.

Three types of basic geospatial data are collected and coordinated:

- The horizontal position of natural and constructed features or entities.
- The vertical position (elevation) of the ground surface or built features.
- Attribute data describing the features or entities being surveyed.

Survey drafting is a term that covers a wide range of scale graphics, including both manual and automatic plotting. If the data have been collected electronically, computer programs can digitize the data, thus enabling the surveyor to process and selectively plot areas of interest. Figure 8.6 shows a digital workstation, which includes the computer, printer, and digitizing table. Figure 8.7 shows a digital screen plot, which can be edited, and Figure 8.8 shows a digital plotter that can produce the plot at any scale using eight different pens; a variety of pens permit the use of different colors (or line widths).

FIGURE 8.6 Geomap workstation. (Courtesy of Leica Geosystems Inc.)

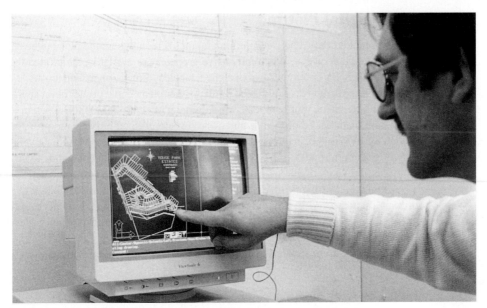

FIGURE 8.7 Land division design and editing on a desktop computer.

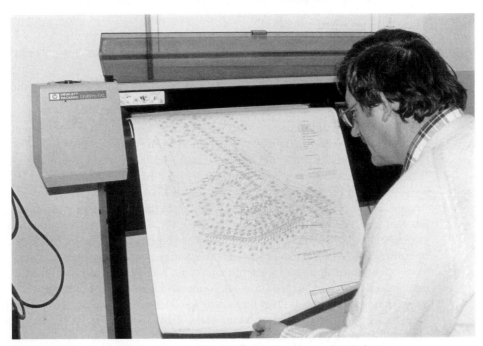

FIGURE 8.8 Land division plot on a Hewlett-Packard eight-pen digital plotter.

8.4.1 Digital Plotting

Data can be plotted onto a high-resolution graphics screen, where the plot can be checked for completeness and accuracy. When interactive graphics are available, the plotted features can be deleted, enhanced, corrected, cross-hatched, labeled, dimensioned, and so on. At this stage, a hard copy of the screen display can be printed either on a simple printer or on an ink-jet color printer. Plot files can be plotted directly on a digital plotter similar to that shown in Figure 8.8. The resultant plan can be plotted to any desired scale, limited only by the paper size. Some plotters have only one or two pens, although plotters are available with four to eight pens; a variety of pens permit colored plotting or plotting using various line weights. Plans, and plan and profiles, drawn on digital plotters are becoming more common on construction sites.

Automatic plotting (with a digital plotter) can be used when the field data have been coordinated and stored in computer memory. Coordinated field data are by-products of data collection by total stations; air photo stereo analysis; satellite imagery; and digitized, or scanned, data from existing plans and maps (Figure 8.1).

A plot file can be created that includes the following typical commands:

- Title
- Scale
- Limits (e.g., can be defined by the southwesterly coordinates, northerly range, and easterly range)
- Plot all points?
- Connect specific points (through feature coding or CAD commands)
- Pen number (various pens can have different line weights or colors; two to four pens are common)
- Symbol (symbols are predesigned and stored by identification number in a symbol library)
- Height of characters (the heights of labels, letters and numbers, coordinates, and symbols can be defined)

The actual plotting can be performed simply by keying in the plot command required by the specific software and then by keying in the name of the plot file to be plotted. Also, the coordinated field point files can be transferred to an interactive graphics terminal (Figure 8.7), with the survey plot being created and edited graphically right on the high-resolution graphics screen. Some surveying software programs have this graphics capability, whereas others permit coordinate files to be transferred easily to an independent graphics program (e.g., Autocad) for editing and plotting. Once the plot has been completed on the graphics screen (and all the point coordinates have been stored in the computer), the plot can be transferred to a digital plotter for final presentation.

Maps, which are usually drawn at a small scale, portray an inventory of all the topographic detail included in the survey specifications; on the other hand, plans, which are usually drawn at a much larger scale, not only show the existing terrain conditions but can also contain proposed locations for newly designed construction works. Table 8.1 shows typical scales for maps and plans, and Table 8.2 shows standard drawing sizes for both the foot and the metric systems.

The size of the drafting paper required can be determined by knowing the scale to be used and the area or length of the survey. Standard paper sizes are shown in Table 8.2.

Table 8.1 SUMMARY OF MAP SCALES AND CONTOUR INTERVALS

	Metric Scale		Foot/Inch Scale Equivalents	Contour Interval for Average Terrain*	Typical Uses
Large scale	1:10		$1'' = 1'$		Detail
	1:50		$1/4'' = 1'$, $1'' = 5'$		Detail
	1:100		$1/8'' = 1'$, $1'' = 10'$, $1'' = 8'$		Detail, profiles
	1:200		$1'' = 20'$		Profiles
	1:500		$1'' = 40'$, $1'' = 50'$	0.5 m, 1 ft	Municipal design plans
	1:1,000		$1'' = 80'$, $1'' = 100'$	1 m, 2 ft	Municipal services and site engineering
Intermediate Scale	1:2,000		$1'' = 200'$	2 m, 5 ft	Engineering studies and
	1:5,000		$1'' = 400'$	5 m, 10 ft	planning (e.g., drainage
	1:10,000		$1'' = 800'$	10 m, 20 ft	areas, route planning)
Small scale	1:20,000 1:25,000	1:25,000	$21/2'' = 1$ mi		
	1:50,000	1:63,360	$1'' = 1$ mi		Topographic maps, Geological maps, United States
	1:100,000	1:126,720	$1/2'' = 1$ mi		Geological maps, Canada and the United States
	1:200,000				
	1:250,000	1:250,000	$1/4'' = 1$ mi		Special-purpose maps and atlases (e.g., climate, minerals)
	1:500,000	1:625,000	$1/10'' = 1$ mi		
	1:1,000,000		$1/16'' = 1$ mi		

*The contour interval chosen must reflect the scale of the plan or map, but, additionally, the terrain (flat or steeply inclined) and the intended use of the plan are factors in choosing the appropriate contour interval.

The title block is often a standard size and has a format similar to that shown in Figure 8.9. The title block is usually placed in the lower right corner of the plan, but its location ultimately depends on the filing system used. Many consulting firms and engineering departments attempt to limit the variety of their drawing sizes so that plan filing can be standardized. Some vertical-hold filing cabinets are designed so that title blocks in the upper right corner can be seen more easily. Revisions to the plan are usually referenced immediately above the title block and show the date and a brief description of the revision.

8.4.2 Manual Plotting

Manual plotting begins by first plotting the survey control (e.g., ℄, traverse line, coordinate grid) on the drawing. The control is plotted so that the data plot will be centered suitably on the available paper. Sometimes the data outline is first plotted roughly on tracing paper so

Table 8.2 STANDARD DRAWING SIZES

	International Standards Organization (ISO)					ACSM[*] Recommendations (Metric)	
	Inch Drawing Sizes		Metric Drawing Sizes (Millimeters)				
Drawing Size	Border Size	Overall Paper Size	Drawing Size	Border Size	Overall Paper Size	Drawing Size	Paper Size
						—	150×200
A	8.00×10.50	8.50×11.00	A4	195×282	210×297	A4	200×300
B	10.50×16.50	11.00×17.00	A3	277×400	297×420	A3	300×400
C	16.00×21.00	17.00×22.00	A2	400×574	420×594	A2	400×600
D	21.00×33.00	22.00×34.00	A1	574×821	594×841	A1	600×800
E	33.00×43.00	34.00×44.00	A0	$811 \times 1,159$	$841 \times 1,189$	A0	$800 \times 1,200$

Ratio $1:\sqrt{2}$ Area of A0 size = 1 m^2

Metric Drawing Paper

*American Congress on Surveying and Mapping Metric Workshop, March 14, 1975. Paper sizes rounded off for simplicity still have cut-in-half characteristic.

that the plan's dimension requirements can be oriented properly on the available drafting paper. It is customary to orient the data plot so that north is toward the top of the plan; a north arrow is included on all property survey plans and many engineering drawings. The north direction on maps is indicated clearly by lines of longitude or by N–S, E–W grid lines. The plan portion of the plan and profile usually does not have a north indication; instead, local practice dictates the direction of increasing chainage (e.g., chainage increasing left to right for west to east and south to north directions). After the control has been plotted and checked, the surveyor can plot the ground features using either rectangular (X, Y coordinates) or polar (r, θ coordinates) methods.

Rectangular plots (X, Y coordinates) can be laid out with a T-square and set square (right-angle triangle), although the parallel rule has now largely replaced the T-square. When either the parallel rule or the T-square is used, the paper is first set properly on the drawing board and then held in place with masking tape. Once the paper is square and secure, the parallel rule, together with a set square and scale, can be used to lay out and measure rectangular dimensions.

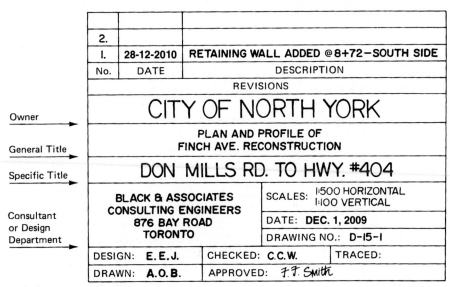

2.		
1.	28-12-2010	RETAINING WALL ADDED @8+72−SOUTH SIDE
No.	DATE	DESCRIPTION

REVISIONS

CITY OF NORTH YORK

PLAN AND PROFILE OF
FINCH AVE. RECONSTRUCTION

DON MILLS RD. TO HWY. #404

BLACK & ASSOCIATES CONSULTING ENGINEERS 876 BAY ROAD TORONTO	SCALES: 1:500 HORIZONTAL 1:100 VERTICAL
	DATE: DEC. 1, 2009
	DRAWING NO.: D-15-1

DESIGN: E.E.J.	CHECKED: C.C.W.	TRACED:
DRAWN: A.O.B.	APPROVED: J.J. Smith	

Owner → (Owner)
General Title →
Specific Title →
Consultant or Design Department →

FIGURE 8.9 Typical title block.

Polar plots are drawn with a protractor and scale. The protractor can be a plastic, graduated circle or half-circle with various size diameters (the larger the diameter, the more precise the protractor). A paper, full-circle protractor can also be used under or on the drafting paper. Finally, a flexible-arm drafting machine, complete with right angle–mounted graduated scales, can plot the data using polar techniques. See Figures 8.10 and 8.11 for standard map and plan symbols.

8.4.3 Computerized Surveying Computations and Drawing Preparation

Survey data can be transferred to the computer either as discrete plot points (northing, easting, and elevation) or as already joined graphic entities. If the data have been referenced to a control traverse for horizontal control, various software programs can quickly determine the acceptability of the traverse closure. Feature coding can produce graphics labels, or they can be created right in the CAD programs. Computer-generated models of surface elevations are called digital elevation models (DEMs) or digital terrain models (DTMs). Some agencies use these two terms interchangeably, while others regard a DTM as a DEM that includes the location of break lines. **Break lines** are joined coordinated points that define changes in slope, such as valley lines, ridge lines, the tops and bottoms of slopes, ditch lines, the tops and bottoms of curbs and walls, etc. They are necessary for the generation of realistic surface contours.

Computer programs are also available to help create designs in digital terrain modeling (together with contour production), land division and road layout, highway layout, etc. The designer can quickly assemble a database of coordinated points reflecting both the existing surveyed ground points and the proposed key points created through the various design programs. Some surveying software includes drawing capabilities, whereas others

Primary highway, hard surface . . . .

Secondary highway, hard surface . . . .

Light-duty road, hard or improved surface . . . .

Unimproved road . . . .

Road under construction, alignment known . . . .

Proposed road . . . .

Dual highway, dividing strip 25 feet or less . . . .

Dual highway, dividing strip exceeding 25 feet . . . .

Trail . . . .

Railroad: single track and multiple track . . . .

Railroads in juxtaposition . . . .

Narrow gage: single track and multiple track . . . .

Railroad in street and carline . . . .

Bridge: road and railroad . . . .

Drawbridge: road and railroad . . . .

Footbridge . . . .

Tunnel: road and railroad . . . .

Overpass and underpass . . . .

Small masonry or concrete dam . . . .

Dam with lock . . . .

Dam with road . . . .

Canal with lock . . . .

Buildings (dwelling, place of employment, etc.) . . . .

School, church, and cemetery . . . .

Buildings (barn, warehouse, etc.) . . . .

Power transmission line with located metal tower . . . . . .

Telephone line, pipeline, etc. (labeled as to type) . . . . . .

Wells other than water (labeled as to type) . . . . o Oil . . . . . o Gas

Tanks: oil, water, etc. (labeled only if water) . . . . ⊘ Water

Located or landmark object; windmill . . . . o

Open pit, mine, or quarry; prospect . . . . × x

Shaft and tunnel entrance . . . . Y

Horizontal and vertical control station:

   Tablet, spirit level elevation . . . . BM △ 5653

   Other recoverable mark, spirit level elevation . . . . △ 5455

Horizontal control station: tablet, vertical angle elevation VABM △ 95/9

   Any recoverable mark, vertical angle or checked elevation △3775

Vertical control station: tablet, spirit level elevation . . . . . BM × 957

   Other recoverable mark, spirit level elevation . . . . × 954

Spot elevation . . . . × 7369   × 7369

Water elevation 670   670

Boundaries: National . . . .

   State . . . .

   County, parish, municipio . . . .

   Civil township, precinct, town, barrio . . . .

   Incorporated city, village, town, hamlet . . . .

   Reservation, National or State . . . .

   Small park, cemetery, airport, etc. . . . .

   Land grant . . . .

Township or range line, United States land survey . . . . .

Township or range line, approximate location . . . .

Section line, United States land survey . . . .

Section line, approximate location . . . .

Township line, not United States land survey . . . .

Section line, not United States land survey . . . .

Found corner: section and closing . . . .

Boundary monument: land grant and other . . . . □

Fence or field line . . . .

Index contour . . . .   Intermediate contour . . .

Supplementary contour   Depression contours . . .

Fill . . . .   Cut . . . .

Levee . . . .   Levee with road . . . .

Mine dump . . . .   Wash . . . .

Tailings . . . .   Tailings pond . . . .

Shifting sand or dunes . . .   Intricate surface . . . . . .

Sand area . . . .   Gravel beach . . . .

Perennial streams . . . . .   Intermittent streams . . .

Elevated aqueduct . . . . .   Aqueduct tunnel . . . . . .

Water well and spring . . .   Glacier . . . .

Small rapids . . . .   Small falls . . . .

Large rapids . . . .   Large falls . . . .

Intermittent lake . . . . . .   Dry lake bed . . . .

Foreshore flat . . . .   Rock or coral reef . . . . .

Sounding, depth curve .   10   Piling or dolphin . . . . .

Exposed wreck . . . .   Sunken wreck . . . .

Rock, bare or awash; dangerous to navigation . . . .

Marsh (swamp) . . . .   Submerged marsh . . . .

Wooded marsh . . . .   Mangrove . . . .

Woods or brushwood . . .   Orchard . . . .

Vineyard . . . .   Scrub . . . .

Land subject to
controlled inundation   . . . .   Urban area . . . .

FIGURE 8.10 Topographic map symbols. (Courtesy of U.S. Department of Interior, Geological Survey)

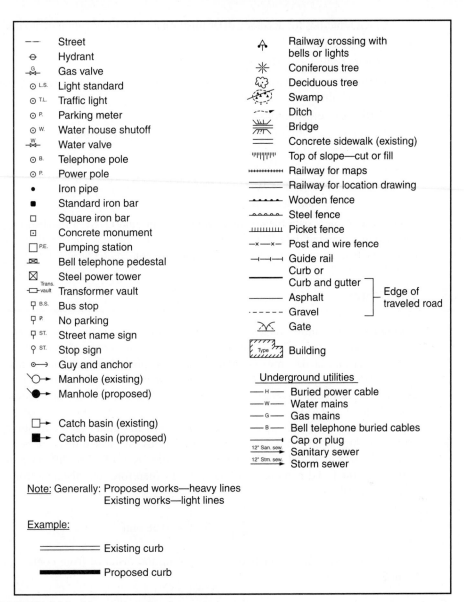

FIGURE 8.11 Municipal works plan symbols.

create DXF or DWG files designed for transfer to CAD programs; Autocad (ACAD) is the most widely used CAD program. Surveying, design, and drawing programs have some or all of the following capabilities:

- Survey data import
- Project definition with respect to map projection, horizontal and vertical datums, and ellipsoid and coordinate system

- COGO routines for accuracy determination and for the creation of auxiliary points
- Graphics creation
- Feature coding and labeling
- Digital terrain modeling and contouring, including break-line identification and contour smoothing
- Earthwork computations
- Design of land division, road (and other alignment) design, horizontal and vertical curves, site grading, etc.
- Creation of plot files
- File exports in DXF, DWG, and XML; compatibility with GIS through ESRI (e.g., Arcinfo) files and shape files

Engineering project data files include an original ground DTM, a finished project DTM, and design alignment data. The creation of these files enables construction companies to utilize machine guidance and control techniques to construct a facility (see Chapter 10).

8.5   Contours

Contours are lines drawn on a plan that connect points having the same elevation. Contour lines represent an even value (Table 8.1), with the selected contour interval kept consistent with the terrain, scale, and intended use of the plan. It is commonly accepted that elevations can be determined to half the contour interval; this convention permits, for example, a 10-ft contour interval on a plan where it is required to know elevations to the closest 5 ft.

Scaling between two adjacent points of known elevation enables the surveyor to plot a contour. Any scale can be used. In Figure 8.12(a), the scaled distance between points 1 and 2 is 0.75 unit, and the difference in elevation is 5.4 ft. The difference in elevation between point 1 and contour line 565 is 2.7 ft; therefore, the distance from point 1 to contour line 565 is

$$\frac{2.7}{5.4} \times 0.75 = 0.38 \text{ unit}$$

This computation can be verified by computing the distance from contour line 565 to point 2:

$$\frac{2.7}{5.4} \times 0.75 = 0.38 \text{ unit}$$

$$0.38 + 0.38 \approx 0.75 \text{ Check}$$

The scaled distance between points 3 and 4 is 0.86 unit, and their difference in elevation is 5.2 ft. The difference in elevation between point 3 and contour line 565 is 1.7 ft; therefore, the distance from point 3 to contour line 565 is

$$\frac{1.7}{5.2} \times 0.86 = 0.28 \text{ unit}$$

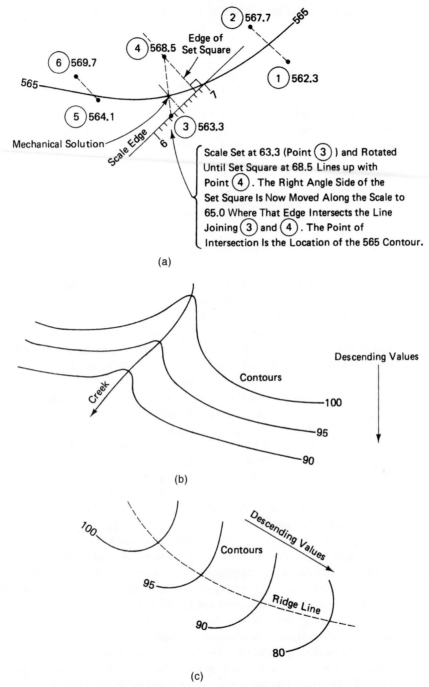

FIGURE 8.12 Contours. (a) Plotting contours by interpolation; (b) valley line; (c) ridge line.

This computation can be verified by computing the distance from contour line 565 to point 4:

$$\frac{3.5}{5.2} \times 0.86 = 0.58 \text{ unit}$$
$$0.58 + 0.28 \approx 0.86 \text{ Check}$$

The scaled distance between points 5 and 6 is 0.49 unit, and the difference in elevation is 5.6 ft. The difference in elevation between point 5 and contour line 565 is 0.9 ft; therefore, the distance from point 5 to contour line 565 is

$$\frac{0.9}{5.6} \times 0.49 = 0.08 \text{ unit}$$

and from line 565 to point 6 the distance is

$$\frac{4.7}{6.6} \times 0.49 = 0.41 \text{ unit}$$

In addition to the foregoing arithmetic solution, contours can be interpolated by using mechanical techniques. It is possible to scale off units on a barely taut elastic band and then stretch the elastic so that the marked-off units fit the interval being analyzed. The problem can also be solved by rotating a scale, while a set square is used to line up the appropriate divisions with the field points. In Figure 8.12(a), a scale is set up at 63.3 on point 3 and then rotated until the 68.5 mark lines up with point 4, a set square being used on the scale. The set square is then slid along the scale until it lines up with 65.0; the intersection of the set square edge (90° to the scale) with the straight line joining points 3 and 4 yields the solution (i.e., the location of elevation at 565 ft). This latter technique is faster than the arithmetic technique.

Surveyors plot contours by analyzing adjacent field points, so it is essential that the ground slope be uniform between those points. An experienced survey crew ensures that enough rod readings are taken to define the ground surface suitably. The survey crew can further define the terrain if care is taken in identifying and tying in valley lines, ridge lines, and other break lines. Figure 8.12(b) shows how contour lines bend uphill as they cross a valley; the steeper the valley, the more the line diverges uphill. Figure 8.12(c) shows how contour lines bend downhill as they cross ridge lines. Figure 8.13 shows the plot of control, elevations, and valley and ridge lines. Figure 8.14 shows contours interpolated from the data in Figure 8.13. Figure 8.15 shows a plan with a derived profile line (AB).

If the contours are to be plotted using computer software, as is usually the case, additional information is required to permit the computer/plotter to produce contours that truly represent the surveyed ground surface. In addition to defining ridge and valley lines, as noted earlier, it is necessary for the surveyor to identify the break lines—lines that join points that define significant changes in slope, such as toe of slope, top and bottom of ditches and swales, ₵s, and the like. When the point numbers defining break lines are appropriately tagged—as required by the individual software—truly representative contours will be produced on the graphics screen and by the digital plotter.

Contours are now almost exclusively produced using any of the current software programs. Most programs generate a triangulated irregular network (TIN); the sides of the triangles are analyzed so that contour crossings can be interpolated. The field surveyor

FIGURE 8.13 Plot of survey control, ridge and valley lines, and spot elevations.

must also note and mark break lines that define significant changes in topography (e.g., top and bottom of hills, channels, depressions, creeks, etc.) so that the software program can generate contours that accurately reflect actual field conditions.

Figure 8.16 shows the steps in a typical contour production process. Two basic methods are used: the uniform grid approach and the more popular TIN approach (used here). First the TIN is created from the plotted points and defined break lines [Figure 8.16(a)], and then the raw contours [Figure 8.16(b)] are computer-generated from that data. To make the contours pleasing to the eye, as well as representative of the ground surface, some form of ground-true smoothing techniques must be used to soften the sharp angles that occur when contours are generated from TINs (as opposed to the less angular lines resulting in contours derived from a uniform grid approach) [Figure 8.16(c)]. For more on this topic, refer to A. H. J. Christensen, "Contour Smoothing by an Eclectic Procedure," *Photogrammetric Engineering and Remote Sensing (RE & RS)*, April 2001: 516.

8.5.1 Summary of Contour Characteristics

The following list provides a summary of contours:

1. Closely spaced contours indicate steep slopes.
2. Widely spaced contours indicate moderate slopes (spacing here is a relative relationship).

FIGURE 8.14 Contours plotted by interpolating between spot elevations, with additional plotting information given when the locations of ridge and valley lines are known.

CONTOUR LINES

These are drawn through points having the same elevation. They show the height of ground above sea level (M.S.L.) in either feet or metres and can be drawn at any desired interval.

Close contour lines indicate a steep slope

When far apart they show a gentle slope

.158

Spot heights are heights between contour lines and are shown thus .158

FIGURE 8.15 Contour plan with derived profile (line AB). (Courtesy of Department of Energy, Mines, and Resources, Canada)

FIGURE 8.16 Contouring. (a) Break lines and TIN. (b) Raw contours. (c) Contour smoothing with the eclectic procedure. (Reproduced with permission, the American Society for Photogrammetry and Remote Sensing. A. H. J. Christensen, "Contour Smoothing by an Eclectic Procedure." *Photogrammetric Engineering and Remote Sensing [RE&RS]*. April 2001:516)

3. Contours must be labeled to give the elevation value. Either each line is labeled or every fifth line is drawn darker (wider) and labeled.

4. Contours are not shown going through buildings.

5. Contours crossing a built horizontal surface (roads, railroads) are straight parallel lines as they cross the facility.

6. Because contours join points of equal elevation, contour lines cannot cross. (Caves present an exception.)

7. Contour lines cannot begin or end on the plan.

8. Depressions and hills look the same; one must note the contour value to distinguish the terrain (some agencies use hachures or shading to identify depressions).

9. Contours deflect uphill at valley lines and downhill at ridge lines. Contour line crossings are perpendicular: U-shaped for ridge crossings, V-shaped for valley crossings.

10. Contour lines must close on themselves, either on the plan or in locations off the plan.

11. The ground slope between contour lines is uniform. If the ground slope is not uniform between the points, additional readings (by total station or level) are taken at the time of the survey.

12. Important points can be further defined by including a spot elevation (height elevation).

13. Contour lines tend to parallel each other on uniform slopes.

By now, you have probably determined that the manual plotting of contours involves a great deal of time-consuming scaling operations. Fortunately, all the advantages of computer-based digital plotting are also available for the production of contour plans. In addition to contours, some software programs (using 3D data files) provide a 3D perspective plot, which can portray the topography as viewed from any azimuth position and from various altitudes. See Figure 8.17 for a perspective view of a proposed road.

FIGURE 8.17 QuickSurf TGRID showing smoothed, rolling terrain coupled with road definition. (Courtesy of MicroSurvey Software, Inc.)

8.6   Aerial Photography

8.6.1   General Background

Airborne imagery introduces the reader to the topics of aerial photography (this section) and the more recent (2000) topic of airborne digital imagery (next section). Aerial photography has a history dating back to the mid-1800s, when balloons and even kites were used as camera platforms from which photos could be taken. About 50 years later, in 1908, photographs were taken from early aircraft. During World Wars I and II, the use of aerial photography mushroomed in the support of military reconnaissance. From the 1930s to the present, aerial photography became an accepted technique for collecting mapping and other ground data in North America. Most airborne imagery is still collected using aerial photographs, although it has been predicted that much of data capture and analysis will be accomplished using digital imagery techniques (see Section 8.7).

Under the proper conditions, cost savings for survey projects using aerial surveys rather than ground surveys can be enormous. Consequently, it is critical that the surveyor can identify the situations in which the use of aerial imagery is most appropriate. The first part of this section discusses the basic principles required to use aerial photographs intelligently, the terminology involved, the limitations of its use, and specific applications to various projects.

Photogrammetry is the science of making measurements from aerial photographs. Measurements of horizontal distances and elevations form the backbone of this science. These capabilities result in the compilation of **planimetric maps** or **orthophoto maps** showing the scaled horizontal locations of both natural and cultural features and in **topographic maps** showing spot elevations and contour lines.

Both black and white panchromatic and color film are used in aerial photography. Color film has three emulsions: blue, green, and red light sensitive. In color infrared (IR), the three emulsion layers are sensitive to green, red, and the photographic portion of near-IR—which are processed, in false color, to appear as blue, green, and red, respectively.

8.6.2   Aerial Camera Systems

The introduction of digital cameras has revolutionized photography. Digital and film-based cameras both use optical lenses. Whereas film-based cameras use photographic film to record an image, digital cameras record image data with electronic sensors: charge-coupled devices (CCDs) or complementary metal-oxide-semiconductor (CMOS) devices. One chief advantage to digital cameras is that the image data can be stored, transmitted, and analyzed electronically. Cameras onboard satellites can capture photographic data and then have these data, along with other sensed data, transmitted back to Earth for additional electronic processing.

Although airborne digital imagery is already making a significant impact in the remote-sensing field, we will begin by discussing film-based photography, a technology that still accounts for much of aerial imaging. The 9 in. by 9 in. format used for most film-based photographic cameras captures a wealth of topographic detail, and the photos, or the film itself, can be scanned efficiently (Figure 8.18), thus preparing the image data for electronic processing.

The camera used for most analog aerial photography is shown in Figure 8.19; it uses a fixed focal length, large-format negative, usually 9 in. (230 mm) by 9 in. (230 mm). The drive

FIGURE 8.18 DSW300 scanner with Sun Ultra 60® host computer. This high-precision photogrammetric photo and film scanner has four elements: (a) movable *xy* cross carriage stage with flat film platen; (b) fixed array charge-coupled device (CCD) camera and image optics; (c) xenon light source and color scanning software; and (d) computer hardware, including storage. (Courtesy of Leica Geosystems Inc.)

mechanism is housed in the camera body, as shown in Figure 8.19. It is motor-driven, and the time between exposures to achieve the required overlap is set based on the photographic scale and the ground speed of the aircraft. The film is thus advanced from the feed spool to the take-up spool at automatic intervals. The focal plane is equipped with a vacuum device to hold the film flat at the instant of exposure. The camera also has four fiducial marks built in so that each exposure can be oriented properly to the camera calibration. Most cameras also record the frame number, time of exposure, and height of the aircraft on each exposure. Some include the image of a level bubble.

The camera mount permits flexible movement of the camera for leveling purposes. Using the level bubble mounted on the top of the camera body as the indicator, the operator should make every attempt to have the camera as level as possible at the instant of exposure. This requires constant attention by the operator because the aircraft is subject to pitching and rolling, resulting in a tilt when the photographs are taken. The viewfinder is mounted vertically to show the area being photographed at any time.

Two points, N_F and N_R, are shown on the optical axis in Figure 8.19. These are the front and rear nodal points of the lens system, respectively. When light rays strike the front

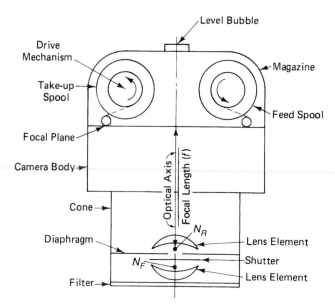

FIGURE 8.19 Components of aerial survey camera (large format).

nodal point (N_F), they are refracted by the lens so that they emerge from the rear nodal point (N_R) parallel with their original direction. The focal length (f) of the lens is the distance between the rear nodal point and the focal plane along the optical axis, as shown in Figure 8.19. The value of the focal length is accurately determined through calibration for each camera. The most common focal length for aerial cameras is 6 in. (152 mm).

Because atmospheric haze contains an excessive amount of blue light, a filter is used in front of the lens to absorb some of the blue light, thus reducing the haze on the actual photograph. A yellow, orange, or red filter is used, depending on atmospheric conditions and the flying height of the aircraft above mean ground level.

The shutter of a modern aerial camera is capable of speeds ranging from 1/50 s to 1/2,000 s. The range is commonly between 1/100 s and 1/1,000 s. A fast shutter speed minimizes blurring of the photograph, known as image motion, which is caused by the ground speed of the aircraft.

8.6.3 Photographic Scale

The scale of a photograph is the ratio between a distance measured on the photograph and the ground distance between the same two points. The features, both natural and cultural, shown on a photograph are similar to those on a planimetric map. There is one important difference. The planimetric map has been rectified through ground control so that the horizontal scale is consistent among any points on the map. The air photo contains scale variations unless the camera was perfectly level at the instant of exposure and the terrain being photographed was also level. Because the aircraft is subject to tip, tilt, and changes in altitude due to updrafts and downdrafts, the chances of the focal plane being level at the instant of exposure are minimal. In addition, the terrain is seldom flat. As illustrated in Figure 8.20, any change in elevation causes scale variations. The basic problem is transferring an uneven surface like the ground to the flat focal plane of the camera.

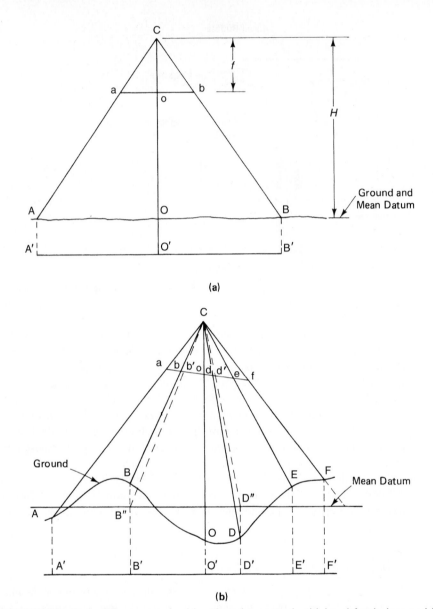

(a)

(b)

FIGURE 8.20 Scale differences caused by tilt and topography. (a) Level focal plane and level ground. (b) Tilted focal plane and hilly topography.

In Figure 8.20(a), points A, O, and B are at the same elevation and the focal plane is level. Therefore, all scales are true on the photograph because the distance AO = A′O′ and OB = O′B′. A, O, and B are points on a level reference datum that is comparable to the surface of a planimetric map. Therefore, under these unusual circumstances, the scale of the photograph is uniform because the ratio ao:AO is the same as the ratio ob:OB.

Figure 8.20(b) illustrates a more realistic situation. The focal plane is tilted and the topographic relief is variable. Points A, B, O, D, E, and F are at different elevations. You can see that, although A′B′ equals B′O′, the ratio ab:bo is far from equal. Therefore, the photographic scale for points between a and b is significantly different than that for points between b and o. The same variations in scale can also be seen for the points between d and e and between e and f.

The overall average scale of the photograph is based partially on the elevations of the mean datum shown in Figure 8.20(b). The mean datum elevation is intended to be the average ground elevation. Examining the most accurate contour maps of the area available permits the selection of the apparent average elevation. Distances between points on the photograph that are situated at the elevations of the mean datum will be at the intended scale. Distances between points having elevations above or below the mean datum will be at a different photograph scale, depending on the magnitude of the local relief.

The scale of a vertical photograph can be calculated from the focal length of the camera and the flying height above the mean datum. Note that the flying height and the altitude are different elevations having the following relationship:

$$\text{altitude} = \text{flying height} + \text{mean datum}$$

By similar triangles, as shown in Figure 8.20(a), we have the following relationship:

$$\frac{ao}{AO} = \frac{Co}{CO} = \frac{f}{H}$$

where AO/ao = scale ratio between the ground and the photograph
$\quad f$ = focal length
$\quad H$ = flying height above mean datum

Therefore, the scale ratio is

$$SR = \frac{H}{f} \tag{8.1}$$

For example, if $H = 1{,}500$ m and $f = 150$ mm, then

$$SR = \frac{1{,}500}{0.150} = 10{,}000$$

Therefore, the average scale of the photograph is 1:10,000. In the foot system, the scale would be stated as 1 in. = 10,000/12, or 1 in. = 833 ft. The conversion factor of 12 is required to convert both sides of the equation to the same unit.

8.6.4 Flying Heights and Altitude

When planning an air photo acquisition mission, the flying height and altitude must be determined, particularly if the surveyor is acquiring supplementary aerial photography using a small-format camera. The flying height is determined using the same relationships discussed in Section 8.6.3 and illustrated in Figure 8.20. Using the relationship in Equation 8.1, we have $H = SR \times f$.

■ **EXAMPLE 8.1**

If the desired scale ratio (SR) is 1:10,000 and the focal length of the lens (f) is 150 mm, find H.

Solution
Use Equation 8.1:

$$H = 10,000 \times 0.150 = 1,500 \text{ m}$$

■ **EXAMPLE 8.2**

If the desired scale ratio (SR) is 1:5,000 and the focal length of the lens is 50 mm, find H.

Solution
Use Equation 8.1:

$$H = 5,000 \times 0.050 = 250 \text{ m}$$

The flying heights calculated in Examples 8.1 and 8.2 are the vertical distances that the aircraft must fly above the mean datum, illustrated in Figure 8.20. Therefore, the altitude at which the plane must fly is calculated by adding the elevation of the mean datum to the flying height. If the elevation of the mean datum were 330 ft (100 m), the altitudes for Examples 8.1 and 8.2 would be 1,600 m (5,250 ft) and 350 m (1,150 ft), respectively. These values are the readings for the aircraft altimeter throughout the flight to achieve the desired average photographic scale.

If the scale of existing photographs is unknown, it can be determined by comparing a distance measured on the photograph with the corresponding distance measured on the ground or on a map of known scale. The points used for this comparison must be easily identifiable on both the photograph and the map. Examples include road intersections, building corners, and river or stream intersections. The photographic scale is found using the following relationship:

$$\frac{\text{photo scale}}{\text{map scale}} = \frac{\text{photo distance}}{\text{map distance}}$$

Because this relationship is based on ratios, the scales on the left side must be expressed in the same units. The same applies to the measured distances on the right side of the equation. For example, if the distance between two identifiable points on the photograph is 5.75 in. (14.38 cm), on the map, it is 1.42 in. (3.55 cm), and the map scale is 1:50,000, then the photo scale is

$$\frac{\text{photo scale}}{1:50,000} = \frac{5.75 \text{ in.}}{1.42 \text{ in.}}$$

$$\text{photo scale} = \frac{5.75}{50,000 \times 1.42}$$

$$= 1:12,348$$

If the scale is required in inches and feet, it is calculated by dividing 12,348 by 12 (number of inches per foot), which yields 1,029. Therefore, the photo scale is 1 in. = 1,029 ft between these points only. The scale will be different in areas that have different ground elevations.

8.6.5 Relief (Radial) Displacement

Relief displacement occurs when the point being photographed is not at the elevation of the mean datum. As previously explained and as illustrated in Figure 8.20(a), when all ground points are at the same elevation, no relief displacement occurs. However, the displacement of point b on the focal plane (photograph) in Figure 8.20(b) is illustrated. Because point B is above the mean datum, it appears at point b on the photograph rather than at point b′, which would be the location on the photograph for point B′, and point B′ on the mean datum.

Fiducial marks are placed precisely on the camera back plate so that they reproduce in exactly the same position on each air photo negative. These marks are located either in the corners, as illustrated in Figure 8.21, or in the middle of each side, as illustrated in Figure 8.22. Their primary function is the location of the principal point, which is located at the intersection of straight lines drawn between each set of opposite fiducial marks (as illustrated in Figure 8.22).

Relief displacement depends on the position of the point on the photograph and the elevation of the ground point above or below the mean datum. Note the following in Figure 8.20(b):

- The displacement at the center (or principal point), represented by O on the photograph, is zero.
- The farther that the ground point is located from the principal point, the greater the relief displacement. The displacement dd′ is less than bb′, even though the ground point D is farther below the mean datum than point B is above it.
- The greater the elevation of the ground point above or below the mean datum, the greater is the displacement. If the ground elevation of point B were increased so that it was farther above the mean datum, the displacement bb′ would increase correspondingly.

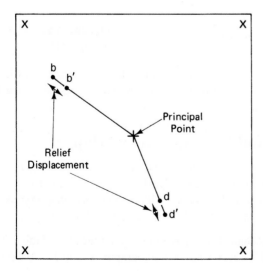

FIGURE 8.21 Direction of relief displacement [compare with Figure 8.20(b)]; X denotes fiducial marks.

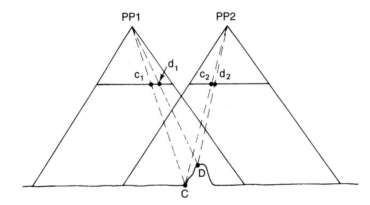

FIGURE 8.22 X parallax along the flight line.

Relief displacement is radial to the principal point of the photograph, as illustrated in Figure 8.21. The direction of the relief distortion on the photograph is shown for photo points b and d in Figure 8.20(b).

8.6.6 Flight Lines and Photograph Overlap

It is important for you to understand the techniques by which aerial photographs are taken. Once the photograph scale, flying height, and altitude have been calculated, the details of implementing the mission are carefully planned. Although the planning process is beyond the scope of this text, the most significant factors include the following:

- A suitable aircraft and technical personnel must be arranged, including their availability if the time period for acquiring the photography is critical to the project. The costs of having the aircraft and personnel available, known as mobilization, are extremely high.

- The study area must be outlined carefully and the means of navigating the aircraft along each flight line, using either ground features or magnetic bearings, must be determined. More recently, GPS is used in aircraft to maintain proper flight line alignment.
- The photographs must be taken under cloudless skies. The presence of high clouds above the aircraft altitude is unacceptable because of the shadows cast on the ground by the clouds. Therefore, the aircraft personnel are often required to wait for suitable weather conditions. This downtime can be very expensive. Most aerial photographs are taken between 10 a.m. and 2 p.m. to minimize the effect of long shadows, which obscure terrain features. Consequently, the weather has to be suitable at the right time.

To achieve photogrammetric mapping and to examine the terrain for air photo interpretation purposes, it is essential that each point on the ground appear in two adjacent photographs along a flight line so that all points can be viewed stereoscopically. Figure 8.23 illustrates the relative locations of flight lines and photograph overlaps, both along the flight line and between adjacent flight lines. An area over which it has been decided to acquire air photo coverage is called a block. The block is outlined on the most accurate available topographic map. The locations of the flight lines required to cover the area properly are then plotted. The flight lines A and B in Figure 8.23(a) are two examples. The aircraft proceeds along flight line A, and air photos are taken at time intervals calculated to provide 60 percent forward overlap between adjacent photographs. As illustrated in Figure 8.23(a), the format of each photograph is square. Therefore, the hatched area represents the forward overlap between air photos 2 and 3, flight line A. The minimum overlap to ensure that all ground points show on two adjacent photographs is 50 percent. However, at least 60 percent forward overlap is standard because the aircraft is subject to altitude variations, tip, and tilt as the flight proceeds. The extra 10 percent forward overlap allows for these variables. The air photo coverage of flight line B overlaps that of A by 25 percent, as illustrated in Figure 8.23(a). This overlap not only ensures that no gaps of unphotographed ground exist, but also extends control between flight lines for photogrammetric methods. (This technique is often called sidelap.)

The flight line in profile view is illustrated in Figure 8.23(b). The single-hatched areas represent the forward overlap between air photos 1 and 2 and photos 2 and 3. Because of the forward overlap of 60 percent, the ground points in the double-hatched area will appear on each of the three photographs, thus permitting full photogrammetric treatment.

Considering the number of air photos required to cover a block or study area is very important. Keep in mind that each air photo has to be cataloged and stored, or scanned into a digital file. Most important, these photographs have to be used individually and collectively and/or examined for photogrammetric mapping and/or air photo interpretation purposes. All other factors being equal, such as focal length and format size, the photographic scale is the controlling factor regarding the number of air photos required. The approximate number of air photos required to cover a given area stereoscopically (every ground point shows on at least two adjacent photos along the flight line) can be easily calculated. The basic relationships required for this computation are set out next for a forward overlap of 60 percent and a side overlap of 25 percent. For a photographic scale of 1:10,000, the area covered by one photograph, accounting for loss of effective area through overlaps, is

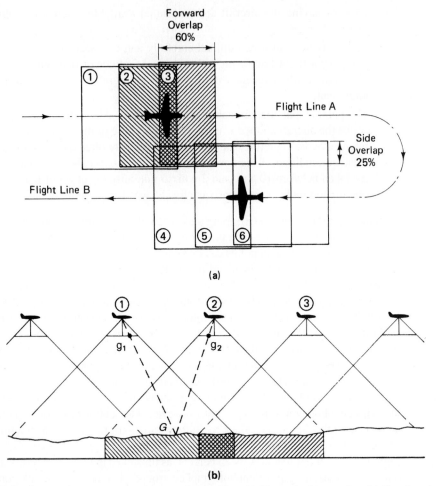

FIGURE 8.23 Flight lines and photographic overlap. (a) Photographic overlap. (b) Overlap along flight line.

0.4 sq. mi, or 1 sq. km. Therefore, the number of air photos required to cover a 200-sq.-mi (500 sq. km) area is 200/0.4 = 500, or 500/1 = 500.

It is important to realize that the approximate number of photographs varies as the square of the photographic scale. For example, if the scale were 1:5,000 versus 1:10,000 in Figure 8.22, the aircraft would be flying at one-half the altitude. Consequently, the ground area covered by each air photo would be reduced by half in *both* directions. Thus, twice the number of air photos would be required along each flight line, and the number of flight lines required to cover the same area would be doubled. The following list items illustrate the effect on the total number of air photos required, based on the coverage required for a 200-sq.-mi (500 sq. km) area:

1. For a scale of 1:5,000, the number of photographs is $500 \times (10,000/5,000)^2 = 2,000$.

2. For a scale of 1:2,000, the number of photographs is $500 \times (10,000/2,000)^2 = 12,500$.

3. For a scale of 1:20,000, the number of photographs is $500 \times (10,000/20,000)^2 = 125$.

Thus, you can see that the proper selection of scale for the mapping or air photo interpretation purposes intended is critical. The scale requirements for photogrammetric mapping depend on the accuracies of the analytical equipment to be used in producing the planimetric maps. For general air photo interpretation purposes, including survey boundary line evidence (cut lines, land-use changes), photographic scales of between 1:10,000 and 1:20,000 are optimal.

8.6.7 Ground Control for Mapping

As stated previously, the aerial photograph is not perfectly level at the instant of exposure and the ground surface is seldom flat. As a result, ground control points are required to manipulate the air photos physically or mathematically before mapping can be done. Recent advances in GPS and inertial measurement systems (IMS) permit the collection of aerial and airborne imaging to be georeferenced without the need for time-consuming extensive horizontal control surveys.

Ground control is required for each data point positioning. The accuracy with which the measurements are made varies depending on the following final product requirements:

- Measurements of distances and elevations, such as building dimensions, highway or road locations, and cross-sectional information for quantity payments for cut and fill in construction projects.
- Preparation of planimetric and topographic maps, usually including contour lines at a fixed interval
- Construction of controlled mosaics
- Construction of orthophotos and rectified photographs

8.6.8 Photogrammetric Stereoscopic Plotting Techniques

Stereoplotters have traditionally been used for image rectification, that is, to extract planimetric and elevation data from stereo-paired aerial photographs for the preparation of topographic maps. The photogrammetric process includes the following steps:

1. Establish ground control for aerial photos.
2. Obtain aerial photographs.
3. Orient adjacent photos so that ground control matches.
4. Use aerotriangulation to reduce the number of ground points needed.
5. Generate DEM/DTM.
6. Produce the orthophoto.
7. Collect data using photogrammetric techniques.

Steps 3–7 are accomplished using stereoplotting equipment and techniques. Essentially, stereoplotters incorporate two adjustable projectors that are used to duplicate the attitude of the camera at the time the film was exposed. Camera tilt and differences in flying height and flying speed can be noted and rectified. A floating mark can be made to rest on the ground surface when viewing is stereoscopic, thus enabling the skilled operator to trace planimetric detail and to deduce both elevations and contours.

In the past 50 years, aerial photo stereoplotting has undergone four distinct evolutions. The original stereoplotter (e.g., Kelsh Plotter) was a heavy and delicate mechanical device. Then came the analog stereoplotter and after it the analytical stereoplotter—an efficient technique that utilizes computer-driven mathematical models of the terrain. The latest technique (developed in the 1990s) is **soft-copy (digital) stereoplotting**. Each new generation of stereoplotting reflects revolutionary improvements in the mechanical, optical, and computer components of the system. Common features of the first three techniques were the size, complexity, high capital costs, and high operating costs of the equipment—and the degree of skill required by the operator. Soft-copy photogrammetry utilizes (1) high-resolution scanners to digitize the analog aerial photos and (2) sophisticated algorithms to process the digital images on workstations and on personal computers with the Windows NT operating system.

8.7 Airborne and Satellite Imagery

Remote sensing is a term used to describe geodata collection and interpretive analysis for both airborne and satellite imagery. Satellite platforms collect geodata using various digital sensors, for example, multispectral scanners, lidar, and radar. Multispectral scanning techniques—in addition to the traditional aerial photography techniques—are now also available on airborne platforms.

Both airborne digital imagery and satellite imagery have some advantages over airborne film-based photography:

- Large data-capture areas can be processed more quickly using computer-based analyses.
- Satellite imagery can be recaptured every few days or weeks, permitting the tracking of rapidly changing conditions (e.g., disaster response for forest fires, flooding).
- Feature identification can be much more effective when combining multispectral scanners with panchromatic imagery. For example, with the analysis of spectral reflectance variations, even tree foliage differentiation is possible. In near-IR, for instance, coniferous trees are distinctly darker in tone than are deciduous trees.
- Ongoing measurements track slowly changing conditions (e.g., crop diseases, etc.).
- With the relatively low cost of imaging, the consumer need purchase only that level of image processing needed for a specific project.
- Data in digital format is ready for computer processing.
- With the use of radar, which has the ability to penetrate cloud cover, remotely sensed data can be collected under an expanded variety of weather conditions, night and day, and even in the polar regions during periods of darkness.
- With the use of lidar measurements, DEMs can be created from ground-surface measurements relatively inexpensively day or night from aircraft or from satellites.
- Imaging results are a good source for the data needed to build GIS layers.

As with all measurement techniques, however, multispectral scanned imagery is susceptible to errors and other problems requiring analysis, as the following list demonstrates:

- Although individual ground features typically reflect light from unique portions of the spectrum, reflectance can vary for the same type of features.
- Sensors are sensitive only to specified wavelengths, and there is a limit to the number of sensors that can be deployed on a satellite or on an aircraft.
- The sun's energy, the source of reflected and emitted signals, can vary over time and location.
- Atmospheric scattering and absorption of the sun's radiation can vary unpredictably over time and location.
- Depending on the resolution of the images, some detail may be missed or mistakenly identified.
- Although vast amounts of data can be collected very quickly, processing the data takes considerable time. For example, the space shuttle *Endeavor's* 10-day radar topography of the Earth mission in 2000 collected about 1 trillion images; it took more than 2 years to process the data into map form.
- Scale, or resolution, may be a limiting factor on some projects.
- The effect of ground moisture on longer wavelengths, microwaves in particular, makes some analyses complex.

Because aerial imaging is usually at a much larger scale than is satellite imaging, aerial images are presently more suitable for projects requiring maximum detail and precision, that is, engineering works. However, the functional planning of corridor works such as highways, railways, canals, electrical transmission lines, etc. has been greatly assisted with the advances in satellite imagery.

Remotely sensed data do not necessarily have their absolute geographic positions recorded at the time of data acquisition (lidar positioning can be an exception). Each point (pixel or picture element) within an image is located with respect to other pixels within a single image, but the image must be geocorrected before it can be inserted accurately into a GIS or a design document. In addition to the geocorrections needed to establish spatial location (GPS and inertial measurement techniques are now used for much of this work), the identification of remotely sensed image features must be verified using ground-truth techniques, that is, analyzing aerial photos, on-site reconnaissance with visual confirmations, map analysis (e.g., soils maps), etc. Ground-truth techniques are not only required to verify or classify surface features but also to calibrate sensors. A major advantage of remote-sensing information is the ability to provide a basis for repeated and inexpensive updates on GIS information. "A chief use of remote sensing is the classification of the myriad of features in a scene—usually presented as an image—into meaningful categories or classes. The image then becomes a thematic map (the theme is selectable, e.g., land use, geology, vegetation types, rainfall)."*

---

*From NASA's home page: http://www.nasa.gov/. Accessed June 2002.

8.7.1 Techniques of Remote Sensing

Two main categories of remote sensing exist: active and passive. Active remote-sensing instruments (e.g., radar and lidar) transmit their own electromagnetic waves and then develop images of the Earth's surface as the electromagnetic pulses (known as backscatter) are reflected back from the target surface. Passive remote-sensing instruments develop images of the ground surface as they detect the natural energy that is either reflected (if the sun is the signal source) or emitted from the observed target area.

8.7.1.1 Lidar Mapping.
Light detection and ranging (**lidar**) is a laser mapping technique that has recently become popular in both topographic and hydrographic surveying. Over land, laser pulses can be transmitted and then returned from ground surfaces. The time required to send and then receive the laser pulses is used to create a DEM of the Earth's surface. Processing software can separate rooftops from ground surfaces, and treetops and other vegetation from the bare ground surface beneath the trees. Although the laser pulses cannot penetrate very heavily foliaged trees, they can penetrate tree cover and other lower-growth vegetation at a much more efficient rate than does either aerial photography or digital imaging because of the huge number of measurements—thousands of terrain measurements every second. Bare-Earth DEMs are particularly useful for design and estimating purposes.

One of the important advantages to using this technique is the rapid processing time. One supplier claims that 1,000 sq. km of hilly, forested terrain can be surveyed by laser in less than 12 hr and that the DEM data are available within 24 hr of the flight. That is, data processing doesn't take much longer than does data collection. Because each laser pulse is georeferenced individually, there is no need for the orthorectification steps, which are necessary in aerial photo processing. Additional advantages of lidar mapping include the following:

- Laser mapping can be done during the day or at night when there are fewer clouds and calmer air.
- Vertical accuracies of 15 cm (or better) can be achieved.
- No shadow or parallax problems occur, as they do with aerial photos.
- Laser data are digital and are thus ready for digital processing.
- It is less expensive than other techniques of aerial imaging for the creation of DEMs.

Lidar can be mounted in a helicopter or fixed-wing aircraft, and the lower the altitude the better the resulting ground resolution. Typically, lidar can be combined with a digital imaging (panchromatic and multispectral) sensor; an inertial measurement unit (IMU) to provide data to correct pitch, yaw, and roll; and GPS receivers to provide precise positioning. When the data-gathering package also includes a digital camera to collect panchromatic imagery and appropriate processing software, it is possible to produce high-quality orthorectified aerial imagery so that each pixel can be assigned x, y, and z values.

Ground lidar operates in the near-IR portion of the spectrum, which produces wavelengths that tend to be absorbed by water; asphalt surfaces, such as roofing and highways; and rain and fog. These surfaces produce "holes" in the coverage, which can be recognized as such and then edited during data processing. Even rolling traffic on a highway at the time of data capture can be removed through editing.

The growing numbers of applications for lidar include:

- Highway design and redesign.
- Flood plain mapping.
- Forest inventory, including canopy coverage, tree density and heights, and timber output.
- Line-of-sight modeling using lidar-generated 3D building renderings, which are used in telecommunications and airport facilities design.
- Shallow-water hydrographic soundings.

In the past few years, airborne laser bathymetry (ALB) has become operational in the field of shallow-water hydrographic surveying. Most systems employ two spectral bands, one to detect the water surface (1064-nm IR band) and the other to detect the bottom (532-nm blue/green band). The depth of the water is determined from the time difference of laser returns reflected from the surface and from the waterbed.

8.7.2 Electromagnetic Spectrum

The fundamental unit of electromagnetic radiation is the photon. The photon, which has energy but no mass, moves at the speed of light. The wave theory of light holds that light travels in wavelike patterns, with its energy characterized by its wavelength or frequency. The speed of light is generally considered to be 300,000 km/s, or 186,000 mi/s. From Chapter 3, we have the following equation (Equation 3.4) for the speed of light:

$$c = f\lambda$$

where c = the velocity of light in meters/second
$\quad f$ = the frequency of the light energy in hertz**
$\quad \lambda$ = the wavelength, in meters, as measured between successive wave crests (see Figures 3.25 and 3.26)

Figure 8.24 shows the electromagnetic spectrum, with wavelengths ranging in size from the very small (cosmic, gamma, and X-rays) to the very large (radio and television) waves. In most remote-sensing applications, radiation is described by its wavelength, although applications using microwave (radar) sensing have traditionally used frequency instead to describe these much longer wavelength signals.

Visible light is that very small part of the electromagnetic spectrum ranging from about 0.4 to 0.7 μm (μm is the symbol for micrometer or micron, a unit that is one millionth of a meter; Table 8.3). IR radiation ranges from about 0.7 to 100 μm, and that range can be further subdivided into reflected IR (ranging from about 0.7 to about 3.0 μm) and the thermal region (ranging from about 3.0 to about 100 μm). The other commonly used region of the spectrum is that of microwaves (e.g., radar), which range from about 1 mm to 1 m.

**Hertz (Hz) is a frequency of one cycle per second; kilohertz (KHz) is 10^3 Hz; megahertz (MHz) is 10^6 Hz; and gigahertz (GHz) is 10^9 Hz. Frequency is the number of cycles of a wave passing a fixed point in a given time period.

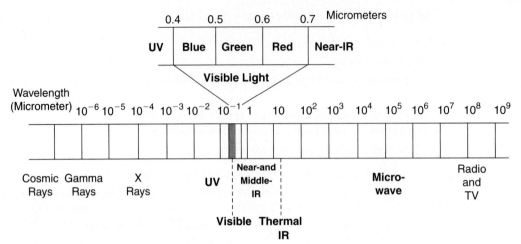

FIGURE 8.24 Electromagnetic spectrum.

Table 8.3 VISIBLE SPECTRUM

Color	Bandwidth (μm)
Violet	0.4−0.446
Blue	0.446−0.500
Green	0.500−0.578
Yellow	0.578−0.592
Orange	0.593−0.620
Red	0.620−0.7

Radiation, having different wavelengths, travels through the atmosphere with varying degrees of success. Radiation is scattered unpredictably by particles in the atmosphere, and atmospheric constituents such as water vapor, carbon dioxide, and ozone absorb radiation. Radiation scattering and absorption rates vary with the radiation wavelengths and the atmospheric particle size. Only radiation in the visible, IR, and microwave sections of the spectrum travel through the atmosphere relatively free of blockage. These atmospheric transmission anomalies, known as atmospheric windows, are utilized for most common remote-sensing activities (Figure 8.25).

Radiation that is not absorbed or scattered in the atmosphere (incident energy) reaches the surface of the Earth, where three types of interaction can occur (Figure 8.26).

- Transmitted energy passes through an object surface with a change in velocity.
- Absorbed energy is transferred through surface features by way of electron or molecular reactions.
- Reflected energy is reflected back to a sensor, with the incident angle equal to the angle of reflection (those wavelengths that are reflected determine the color of the surface).

Incident energy = transmitted energy + absorbed energy + reflected energy

FIGURE 8.25 Electromagnetic spectrum showing atmospheric transmission windows in the visible, near, middle, and thermal infrared and microwave regions. Notice the excellent atmospheric transmission capabilities in the entire range of the microwave. (Courtesy of NASA)

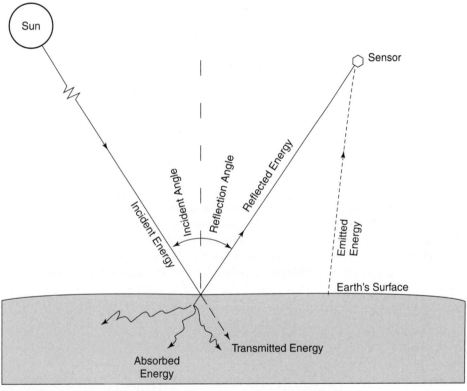

FIGURE 8.26 Interaction of electromagnetic radiation with the Earth.

For example, chlorophyll—a constituent of plants' leaves—absorbs radiation in the red and blue wavelengths but reflects the green wavelengths. Thus, at the height of the growing season, when chlorophyll is strongly present, leaves appear greener. Water absorbs the longer wavelengths in the visible and near-IR portions of the spectrum and reflects the shorter wavelengths in the blue/green part of the spectrum, which results in the often seen blue/green hues of water.

In addition, energy emitted from an object can be detected in the thermal IR section of the spectrum and recorded. Emitted energy can be the result of the previous absorption of energy—a process that creates heat. Remote-sensing instruments can be designed to detect reflected and/or emitted energy (Figure H.8).

8.7.3 Reflected Energy

Different types of feature surfaces reflect radiation differently. Smooth surfaces act like mirrors and reflect most light in a single direction, a process called specular reflection. At the other extreme, rough surfaces reflect radiation equally in all directions, a process called diffuse reflection. Between these two extremes are an infinite number of reflection possibilities, which are often a characteristic of a specific material or surface condition (Figure 8.27).

8.7.4 Selection of Radiation Sensors

Satellite sensors are designed to meet various conditions, such as the following:

- Using those parts of the electromagnetic spectrum that are less affected by scatter and absorption.
- Sensing data from different sources (active or passive sensing).
- Selecting the spectral ranges of energy that react most favorably with specified target surfaces.

Because various types of ground cover, rocks and soils, water, and built features react differently with radiation from different parts of the spectrum, it is common to install sensors (e.g., multispectral scanners) on spacecraft that can detect radiation from several appropriate wavelength ranges.

Most remote-sensing instruments use scanners to evaluate small portions of the Earth at instants in time. At each instant, the sensor quantizes the Earth's surface into pixels (picture elements) or bands. Pixel resolution can range from 0.4 m (QuickBird satellite) to greater than 1 km, depending on the instrumentation and altitude of the sensing platform. As in aerial photography, spectral scanning utilizes lenses and, like aerial photography, stereo-paired images can be captured and DEMs can be created; stereo (3D) viewing is a great aid in visual imaging.

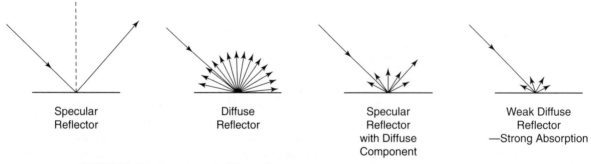

| Specular Reflector | Diffuse Reflector | Specular Reflector with Diffuse Component | Weak Diffuse Reflector —Strong Absorption |

FIGURE 8.27 Specular and diffuse reflection.

There are two main types of scanners: across-track scanners and along-track scanners. Across-track scanners, also called whisk-broom scanners, scan lines perpendicular to the forward motion of the spacecraft using rotating mirrors. As the spacecraft moves across the Earth, a series of scanned lines are collected, producing a 2D image of the Earth. Each onboard sensor in the vehicle collects reflected or emitted energy in a specific range of wavelengths; these electrical signals are converted to digital data and stored until they are transmitted (satellite) or returned (aerial) to Earth. Along-track scanners, also called push-broom scanners, utilize the forward motion of the spacecraft itself to record successive scan lines. Instead of rotating mirrors, these scanners are equipped with linear array CCDs that build the image as the satellite moves forward.

Once the data have been captured and downloaded to Earth, much more work has to be done to convert the data into a usable format. These processes, which include image enhancement and image classification, are beyond the scope of this text.

8.7.5   An Introduction to Image Analysis

Analysis of remotely sensed images is a highly specialized field. Because environmental characteristics include most of the physical sciences, the image interpreter should have an understanding of the basic concepts of geography, climatology, geomorphology, geology, soil science, ecology, hydrology, and civil engineering. For this reason, multi-disciplinary teams of scientists, geographers, and engineers, all trained in image interpretation, are frequently used to help develop the software utilized in this largely automated process.

Just as photogrammetry/air photo interpretation helps the analyst to identify objects in an aerial photograph, digital image analysis helps the analyst to identify objects depicted in satellite and airborne images. With the blossoming of computerized image analyses that employ automated digital image processing, the relative numbers of trained analysts needed to process data have declined sharply. Satellite imagery has always been processed in digital format, and aerial photos (films) can be scanned easily to convert from analog to digital format. As with aerial photography, satellite images must have ground control and must be corrected for geometric distortion and relief displacement, and also for distortions caused by the atmosphere, radiometric errors, and the Earth's rotation. Satellite imagery can be purchased with some or many of these distortions removed. The price of the imagery is directly related to the degree of processing requested.

Unlike aerial photography images, different satellite images of the same spatial area—taken by two or more different sensors—can be fused together to produce a new image with distinct characteristics and thus provide even more data. A digital image target may be a point, line, or area (polygon) feature that is distinguishable from other surrounding features. Digital images are comprised of many pixels, each of which has been assigned a digital number (DN). The DN represents the brightness level for that specific pixel—for example, in eight-bit (2^8) imagery, the 256 brightness levels range from 0 (black) to 255 (white).

Each satellite has the capability of capturing images and then transmitting the images, in digital format, to ground receiving stations that are located around the globe. Modern remote-sensing satellites are equipped with sensors collecting data from selected bands of the electromagnetic spectrum. For example, Landsat 7's sensors collect data from eight bands (channels)—seven bands of reflected energy and one band of emitted energy.

FIGURE 8.28 Spectral reflectance curves of four different targets. (Adapted from NASA's *Landsat 7 Image Assessment System Handbook*, 2000; courtesy NASA)

Because radiation from various portions of the electromagnetic spectrum reacts in a unique fashion with different materials found on the surface of the Earth, it is possible to develop a signature of the reflected and emitted signal responses and to identify the object or class of objects from those signatures.

When the energy reflections from the ground surface (collected by the various onboard sensors) are plotted, the resultant unique curves, called spectral signatures, are used to help identify various surface materials. Figure 8.28 shows four signatures of different ground surfaces, with the reflection as a function of wavelength used for plotting purposes. The curves were plotted from data received from the eight sensors on board Landsat 7. When the results are plotted as a percentage reflectance for two or more bands (Figure 8.29), in multidimensional space, the ability to identify the surface materials precisely increases markedly. This spectral separation permits the effective analysis of

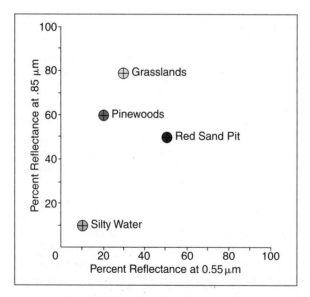

FIGURE 8.29 Spectral separability using just two bands. (Adapted from NASA's *Landsat 7 Image Assessment Handbook*, 2000; courtesy NASA)

Table 8.4 APPLICATIONS OF REMOTELY SENSED IMAGES

Field	Applications
Forestry/agriculture	Inventory of crop and timber acreage, estimating crop yields, crop disease tracking, determination of soil conditions, assessment of fire damage, precision farming, and global food analysis.
Land use/mapping	Classification of land use, mapping and map updating, categorization of land use capability, monitoring urban growth, local and regional planning, functional planning for transportation corridors, mapping land/water boundaries, and flood plain management.
Geology	Mapping of major geologic units, revising geologic maps, recognition of rock types, mapping recent volcanic surface deposits, mapping land forms, mineral and gas/oil exploration, and estimating slope failures.
Natural resources	Natural resources exploration and management.
Water resources	Mapping of floods and flood plains, determining extent of areal snow and ice, measurement of glacial features, measurement of sediment and turbidity patterns, delineation of irrigated fields, inventory of lakes, and estimating snow-melt runoff.
Coastal resources	Mapping shoreline changes; mapping shoals and shallow areas; and tracing oil spills, pollutants, and erosion.
Environment	Monitoring effect of human activity (lake eutrophication, defoliation), measuring the effects of natural disasters, monitoring surface mining and reclamation, assessing drought impact, siting for solid-waste disposal, siting for power plants and other industries, regulatory compliance studies, and development impact analysis.

satellite imagery, most of which can be performed through computer applications. Image analysis can be applied productively to a broad range of scientific inquiry (Table 8.4).

8.7.6 Classification and Feature Extraction

Satellite imagery contains a wealth of information, all of which may not be relevant for specific project purposes. A decision must be made about which feature classifications are most relevant. Once the types of features to be classified have been determined, a code library giving a unique code for each included feature is constructed. The pixel identification can then be represented by a unique code (e.g., R for residential) rather than a DN giving the gray-scale designation. For example, a typical GIS project may require the following features to be classified:

- Pervious/impervious surfaces (needed for rainfall runoff calculations)
- Water
- Wetland
- Pavement
- Bare ground
- Residential areas
- Commercial areas
- Industrial areas
- Grass
- Tree stands
- Transportation corridors

LIVERPOOL
JOHN MOORES UNIVERSITY
AVRIL ROBARTS LRC
TITHEBARN STREET
LIVERPOOL L2 2ER
TEL. 0151 231 4022

Feature extraction (image interpretation) can be accomplished using manual methods or automated methods. Automated methods employ computer algorithms to classify images in relation to surface features, and four techniques are presently in use:

- Unsupervised—this technique relies on color and tone as well as statistical clustering to identify features.
- Supervised—this technique requires comparative examples of imaging for each ground feature category.
- Hybrid—this technique is a combination of the first two (unsupervised and supervised).
- Classification and regression tree (CART) analysis—CART analysis uses binary partitioning software to analyze and arrive eventually at a best estimate about the ground feature identification.

8.7.7 Ground-Truthing, or Accuracy Assessment

How do we know if the sophisticated image analysis techniques in use are giving us accurate identifications? We have to establish a level of reliability to give credibility to the interpretation process. With aerial photo interpretation, we begin with a somewhat intuitive visual model of the ground feature; with satellite imagery, we begin with pixels identified by their gray-scale DN—characteristics that are not intuitive. What we need is a process whereby we can determine the accuracy and reliability of interpretation results. In addition to providing reliability, such a process enables the operator to correct errors and to compare the successes of the various types of feature extraction that may have been used in the project. This process is also invaluable in the calibration of imaging sensors.

Ground-truthing, or accuracy assessment, can be accomplished by comparing the automated feature extraction identifications with feature identifications given by other methods for a given sample size. Alternative interpretation or extraction techniques may include air photo interpretation, analyses of existing thematic maps of the same area, and field work involving same-area ground sampling.

It is not practical to check the accuracy of each pixel identification, so a representative sample is chosen for accuracy assessment. The sample is representative with respect to both the size and locale of the sampled geographic area. Factors to be considered when defining the sample include the following:

- Is the land privately owned and/or restricted to access?
- How will the data be collected?
- How much money can you afford to dedicate to this process?
- Which geographic areas should be sampled: areas that consist of homogeneous features together with areas consisting of a wide mix of features, even overlapping features?
- How can the randomness of the sample points be ensured, given practical constraints (e.g., restricted access to specified ground areas, lack of current air photos and thematic maps, etc.)?
- If verification data are to be taken from existing maps and plans, what impact will their dates of data collection have on the analysis (i.e., the more current the data, the better the correlation)?

Reference Data (Sampling Data)

Diagonal	Water	Agricultural	Urban	Row Totals
Water	17 Correct	5	1	23
Agricultural	10	22 Correct	10	42
Urban	2	5	28 Correct	35
Column Total	29	32	39	100

Interpreted Data

FIGURE 8.30 Error matrix example.

The answers to many of the questions above come only with experience. Much of this type of work is based on trial-and-error decisions. For example, when the results of small samples compare favorably with the results of large samples, it may be assumed that, given similar conditions, such small samples may be appropriate in subsequent investigations. On the other hand, if large samples give significantly different (better) results than do small sample sizes, one may assume that such small sample sizes should not be used again under similar circumstances.

Figure 8.30 shows an error matrix consisting of ground point identifications that have been extracted using automated techniques and ground point identifications determined using other techniques (including field sampling). With the example shown here, seventeen of twenty-three sampling sites for water were verified, twenty-two of forty-two sampling sites for agricultural were verified, and twenty-eight of thirty-five sampling points for urban were verified. These verified points, shown along the diagonal, total sixty-seven from a total of 100. Thus, the verified accuracy was 67 percent in this example.

Is 67 percent accuracy acceptable? The answer depends on the intended use of the data and, once again, experience is a determining factor. It may be decided that this method of data collection (e.g., satellite imagery) is inappropriate (i.e., not accurate enough or too expensive) for the intended purposes of the project.

8.8 Remote-Sensing Satellites

8.8.1 Landsat 7 Satellite

Landsat 7 was launched April 15, 1999, from Vandenburg Air Force Base on a Delta-11 launch vehicle. The spacecraft weighs 4,800 lbs, measures about 14 ft long by 9 ft in diameter, and flies at an altitude of 705 km. Landsat 7 employs an extended thematic mapper (ETM+ is

Table 8.5 BANDWIDTH CHARACTERISTICS FOR LANDSAT 7

TM and ETM+ Spectral Bandwidths (μm)

Sensor	Band 1	Band 2	Band 3	Band 4	Band 5	Band 6	Band 7	Band 8
TM	0.45–0.52	0.52–0.60	0.63–0.69	0.76–0.90	1.55–1.75	10.4–12.5	2.08–2.35	N/A
ETM+	0.45–0.52	0.53–0.61	0.63–0.69	0.78–0.90	1.55–1.75	10.4–12.5	2.09–2.35	0.52–0.90
	Blue	Green	Red	Near-IR	Shortwave IR	Thermal IR	Shortwave IR	Panchromatic
Resolution (pixel size)	30 m	30 m	30 m	30 m	30 m	60 m	30 m	15 m

Band	Use
1	Soil/vegetation discrimination; bathymetry/coastal mapping; cultural/urban feature identification.
2	Green vegetation mapping; cultural/urban feature identification.
3	Vegetated versus nonvegetated and plant species discrimination.
4	Identification of plant/vegetation types, health and biomass content, water body delineation, soil moisture.
5	Sensitive to moisture in soil and vegetation; discriminating snow and cloud-covered areas.
6	Vegetation stress and soil moisture discrimination related to thermal radiation; thermal mapping (urban, water).
7	Discrimination of mineral and rock types; sensitive to vegetation moisture content.
8	Panchromatic: mapping, planning, design.

Source: Landsat 7 is operated under the direction of NOAA. Data can be obtained from USGS—EROS Data Center, Sioux Falls, SD 57198. Courtesy of NOAA.

a scan mirror spectrometer) and an eight-band multispectral scanner capable of providing high-resolution image information of the Earth's surface as it collects seven bands or channels of reflected energy and one band of emitted energy. The multispectral scanner's panchromatic band (0.52–0.90 μm) has a resolution of 15 m (Table 8.5). The Landsat program was designed to monitor small-scale processes seasonally on a global scale, for example, cycles of vegetation growth, deforestation, agricultural land use, erosion, etc.

Another NASA satellite, the experimental TERRA (EO-1), launched December 18, 1999, employs a push-broom spectrometer/radiometer—the Advanced Land Imager (ALI)—with many more spectral ranges (hyperspectral scanning) and flies the same orbits with the same altitude as does Landsat 7. It is designed to sample similar surface features at roughly the same time (only minutes apart) for comparative analyses. TERRA's panchromatic band (0.48–0.68 μm) has a resolution of 10 m. This experimental satellite is designed to obtain much more data at reduced costs and will influence the design of the present stage (2000–2015) of U.S. exploration satellites.

Whether by spectral analysis, radar imaging, or lidar (light detection and ranging), a huge amount of surface data can be collected and analyzed. Airborne imagery is flown at relatively low altitudes, giving the potential for high ground resolution. When these techniques are employed on satellite platforms, we receive huge amounts of data that can be collected again at regular intervals, thus adding a temporal (time) dimension to the measurement process. In all cases of satellite imagery, the data output is in digital form and ready for computer processing to elicit the required information. Although satellite imagery cannot give us the same resolutions as airborne imagery, we presently have QuickBird resolution at the level of 0.4 m, and predictions state that the next generation of satellite imagery will be in the one-third of a meter (or less) range for ground resolution. Satellite imagery has been used for many years to assess crop inventories, flood damages, and other large-scale geographic projects.

8.9 Geographic Information System

8.9.1 General Background

GIS is a tool used by engineers, planners, geographers, and other social scientists, so it is not surprising that there seems to be as many definitions for GIS as there are fields in which GIS is employed. My choice for a definition comes from the University of Edinborough's GIS faculty: "GIS is a computerized system for capturing, storing, checking, integrating, manipulating, analyzing, and displaying data related to positions on the Earth's surface."

Since the earliest days of mapping, topographic features have routinely been portrayed on scaled maps and plans. These maps and plans provided an inventory of selected or general features that were found in a given geographic area. With the emergence of large databases, which were collected primarily for mapping, attention was given to new techniques for analyzing and querying the computer-stored data. The introduction of topological techniques permitted the data to be connected in a relational sense, in addition to their spatial connections. Thus, it became possible not only to determine where a point (e.g., hydrant), a line (e.g., road), or an area (park, neighborhood, etc.) was located, but also to analyze those features with respect to the adjacency of other spatial features, connectivity (network analysis), and direction of vectors. Adjacency, connectivity, and direction opened the database to a wider variety of analyzing and querying techniques. For example, it is possible in a GIS real-estate application to display, in municipal map form, all the industrially zoned parcels of land with rail-spur possibilities, within 1.5 mi of freeway access, in the range of 1.2–3.1 acres in size. Relational characteristics also permit the database to be used for routing of, for example, emergency vehicles and vacationers.

GIS data can be assembled from existing databases; digitized or scanned from existing maps and plans; or collected using conventional surveying techniques, including GPS surveying techniques. One GPS method that has recently become very popular for GIS data collection is that of differential GPS (see Section 7.6). This technique utilizes a less expensive GPS receiver and radio signal corrections from a base station receiver to provide submeter accuracies that are acceptable for mapping and GIS database inventories. See Figure 8.31 for typical differential GPS equipment.

The ability to store a wide variety of data on feature-unique layers in computer memory permits the simple production of special-feature maps. For example, maps can be produced that show only the registered parcel outlines of an area, or only drainage and contour information, or any other feature-specific data. In fact, any selected layer or combination of selected layers can be depicted on a computer screen or on a hard-copy map (produced on a digital plotter) at any desired scale (Figure 8.32). In a GIS, spatial entities have two key characteristics: location and attributes. Location can be given by coordinates, street addresses, etc., and attributes describe some characteristic(s) of the feature being analyzed.

LIVERPOOL JOHN MOORES UNIVERSITY
LEARNING SERVICES

(a)   (b)

FIGURE 8.31   (a) Trimble's 5700 GPS receiver with the pole-mounted antenna and data collector shown being used to capture municipal asset data location for a GIS database. (b) Trimble's 5700 GPS receiver shown connected to a computer directly downloading to Trimble's Geomatics Office software. (Portions © 2001 Trimble Navigation Limited. All Rights Reserved)

GIS has now blossomed into a huge and diverse field of activity. Most activity can be identified as being in one of two broad fields: (1) geographic, feature-specific activities such as mapping, engineering, routing, environment, resources, and agriculture; and (2) cultural/social activities such as marketing research, census, demographics, and socioeconomic studies.

The switch from hard-copy maps to computerized GIS has provided many benefits. For example, now we can perform the following:

- Store and easily update large amounts of data.
- Sort and store spatial features, called entities, into thematic layers. Data are stored in layers so that complex spatial data can be manipulated and analyzed efficiently by layer rather than trying to deal with the entire database at the same time.

Coordinate Grid System

Elevation Data

Parcel Boundaries (LIS)

Hydrology/Wetlands

Transportation (GIS-T)

Soils/Geology

Land Use and Planning

Government Boundaries

Municipal Services (AM/FM)

Buildings and Other Structures

Ground Cover

MAP

Composite, Showing
a Combination of
Selected Layers

FIGURE 8.32 Illustration of thematic layers.

- Zoom into sections of the displayed data to generate additional graphics that may be hidden at default scales. We can also query items of interest to obtain tables of attribute information that may have been tagged to coordinated points of interest.
- Analyze both entities and their attribute data using sophisticated computer programs.
- Prepare maps showing only selected thematic layers of interest (and thus reduce clutter). We can update maps quickly as new data are assembled.
- Use the stored data to prepare maps for different themes and scales, for a wide range of purposes.
- Import stored data (both spatial and nonspatial) electronically from different agencies (via CDs, DVDs, and the Internet) and thus save the costs of collecting the data.
- Build and augment a database by combining digital data from all the data-gathering techniques illustrated in Figure 8.1—field surveying, remote sensing, map digitization, scanning, and Internet transfer/CD/DVD imports.
- Create new maps by modeling or re-interpreting existing data.

Some ask, How do GIS and CAD compare? Both systems are computer-based, but CAD is often associated with higher-precision engineering design and surveying applications, and GIS is more often associated with mapping and planning—activities requiring lower levels of precision. CAD is similar to mapping because it is essentially an inventory of entered data and computed data that can provide answers to the question, Where is it located? GIS has the ability to model data and to provide answers to the spatial and temporal questions: What occurred? What if . . . ? etc. Topology gives GIS the ability to determine spatial relationships such as adjacency and connectivity between physical features or entities. Typical subsets of geographic feature-specific GIS include land information systems (LISs), which deal exclusively with parcel title description and registration; automated mapping and facility management (AM/FM), which models the location of all utility/plant facilities; and transportation design and management (GIS-T).

8.9.2 Components of a GIS

GIS can be divided into four major activities:

- Data collection and input.
- Data storage and retrieval.
- Data analysis.
- Data output and display.

GIS may be further described by listing its typical components:

- The computer, which is the heart of GIS, along with the GIS software, typically uses Windows or Unix operating systems.
- Data collection can be divided into the geomatics components shown in Figure 7.1: field surveying, remote sensing, digitization of existing maps and plans, digital data transfer via the Internet or CD/DVD.
- Computer storage: hard drives, optical disks, etc.
- Software designed to download, edit, sort, and analyze data—e.g., database software, relational database software, GIS software, geometric and drawing software (COGO, CAD, etc.), soft-copy photogrammetry, and satellite imagery analysis software.
- Software designed to process and present data in the form of graphics and maps and plans.
- Hardware components, including the computer, surveying and remote-sensing equipment, CD and DVD, digitizers, scanners, interactive graphics terminals, and plotters and printers.

The growth in GIS is assured because it has been estimated that as much as 80 percent of all information used by local governments is geographically referenced. GIS is a tool that encourages planners, designers, and other decision makers to study and analyze spatial data along with an enormous amount of attribute data (cultural, social, geographic, economic, resources, environmental, infrastructure, etc.)—data that can be tagged to specific georeferenced spatial entities.

8.9.3   Sources for GIS Data

The most expensive part of any GIS is data collection. Obviously, if you can obtain suitable data collected from other sources, the efficiency of the process increases. When importing data from other sources, it is imperative that the accuracy level of the collected data be certified as appropriate for its intended use. For example, if you are building a database for use in high-accuracy design applications, it would not be suitable to import data digitized from U.S. Geological Survey (USGS) 1:100,000 topographic maps (as is much of the U.S. Census TIGER data), where accuracy can be restricted to ± 170 ft. However, for small-scale projects (e.g., planning, resources/environmental studies), the nationwide TIGER file has become one of the prime sources of easily available data in the United States. Government data sources (e.g., USGS, TIGER, etc.) provide free data (except for the cost of reproduction) to the general public.

Traditional sources for data collection include the following:

• Field surveying.
• Remotely sensed images—rectified and digitized aerial photographs (orthophotos) and processed aerial and satellite imagery.
• Existing topographic maps, plans, and photos—via digitizing and/or scanning.
• Census data.
• Electronic transfer of previously digitized data from government agencies or commercial firms.

8.9.4   Georeferencing

Like the map makers of the past, GIS specialists must find some way to relate geospatial data to the surface of the Earth. If all or most geographic data users employ the same (or well-recognized) Earth-reference techniques, data may be economically shared among agencies using different computer systems. Now, the most widely accepted shape of the Earth has been geometrically modeled as an ellipsoid of revolution with a semimajor axis of 6,378,135 m called the GRS-80 ellipsoid (see Section 9.1 and Figure 7.24). Once the shape of the Earth has been modeled and a geodetic datum defined, some method must be used to show the Earth's curved surface on plane-surface map sheets with minimal distortion. Several map projections have been developed for this purpose. In North America, the projections used most are the Lambert projection, the Transverse Mercator projection (used in the United States), and the Universal Transverse Mercator projection (used in Canada). Along with a specific projection, it is possible to define a coordinate grid that can be used to minimize distortion as we move from a spherical surface to a plane surface. (See Chapter 9 for more on this topic.) Measurements on the grid can be in feet, U.S. feet, or meters (Table 1.1).

8.9.4.1   Coordinate Grids.   U.S. states have adopted either the Lambert conical projection or the Transverse Mercator cylindrical projection and have created coordinate grid systems (false northing and easting) defined for each state. The State Plane Coordinate System 1983 (SPCS83), which superseded the SPCS27, has been applied to all

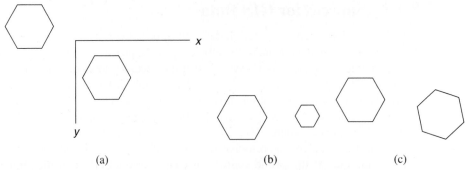

(a)   (b)   (c)

FIGURE 8.33   Transformation techniques. (a) Translation. (b) Scale. (c) Rotation.

states, and the Universal Transverse Mercator grid has been applied to Canada. Software programs readily convert coordinates based on one projection to any other commonly used projection. (Coordinate grids are discussed in Chapter 9.)

8.9.4.2   Transformation.   When data are being imported from various sources, it is likely that different Earth-reference models may have been used. If a GIS is tied to a specific coordinate grid and specific orientation, new data may have to be transformed to fit the working model. Transformations can be made in grid reference, scale, and orientation, and GIS programs are designed to translate from one grid reference to another, to convert from one scale to another, and to rotate to achieve appropriate orientation (Figure 8.33).

8.9.4.3   Geocoding.   Spatial data describe spatial location (e.g., geographic coordinates, map coordinates, street addresses, postal codes, etc.) of an entity, whereas attribute data (often shown in related tables) describe the different aspects of the entity being collected. Examples of attribute data include the population of towns, ground cover (including crop types), number of occupants in a dwelling, etc. The linking of entity and attribute data to a specific geographic location is known as **geocoding**. GIS programs should be able to recognize the defining characteristics of imported data in the geocodes from the metadata information supplied and then make the necessary conversions so that the imported data are tied to the same reference datum as are the working data.

8.10   Database Management

A GIS is concerned with large amounts of both spatial and nonspatial (attribute) data. Data must be organized so that information about entities and their attributes may be accessed by rapid computerized search-and-retrieval techniques. When data concerned with a specific category are organized in such a fashion, that data collection is known as a database. Data collections can range in complexity from simple unstructured lists and tables to ordered lists and tables (e.g., alphabetical, numerical, etc.); to indexes (see the index at the back of this text); and finally to sets of more complex, categorized tables.

The computerized tabular data structure used by many GIS programs is called a relational database. A relational database is a set theory–based data structure comprised of ordered sets of attribute data (entered in rows) known as tuples, and grouped in 2D tables called relations. When searching the columns of one or more databases for specific information, a key (called a primary key) or some other unique identifier must be used. A primary key is an unambiguous descriptor(s) such as a place name, the coordinates of a point, a postal code address, etc. The data in one table are related to similar data in another table by a GIS technique of relational join. Any number of tables can be related if they all share a common column.

For example, with a postal code address or even state plane coordinates, a wide variety of descriptive tables can be accessed that contain information relevant to that specific location. One table may contain parcel data, including current and former ownership, assessment, etc., while other tables may contain municipal services available at that location, rainfall/snowfall statistics, pedestrian and vehicular traffic counts at different periods of the day, etc.

Queries of a relational database are governed by a standard query language (SQL), developed by IBM in the 1970s, to access data in a logically structured manner. Traditional SQL continues to be modified by software designers (with assistance from the Open GIS Consortium—see the next section) for specific applications in GIS. Modifications include spatial operators and tools such as adjacency, overlap, buffering, area, etc. (See Section 8.17 at the end of this chapter for more information on this topic.)

8.11 Metadata

Metadata are "data about data." Metadata describe the content, quality, condition, and other characteristics of data. In 1994, the Federal Geographic Data Committee (FGDC) of the National Spatial Data Infrastructure (NSDI) approved standards for "Coordinating Geographic Data Acquisition and Access" (a pamphlet that was updated in 1998), and in 2000 FGDC published another pamphlet called "Content Standard for Geospatial Metadata Workbook"—available online at http://www.fgdc.gov/publications/documents/metadata/_workbook_0501_bmk.pdf.

As we noted earlier in this chapter, the cost of obtaining data is one of the chief expenses in developing a database. Many agencies and commercial firms cannot afford to create all the data that may be needed for various GIS analyses. Thus, the need for standards in the collection, dissemination, and cataloging of data sets (a data set is a collection of related data) is readily apparent.

FGDC lists the different aspects of data described by metadata:

- Identification: What is the name of the data set? Who developed the data set? What geographic area does it cover? What themes of information does it include? How current are the data? Are there restrictions on accessing or using the data?

- Data quality: Are the data reliable? Is information available that allows the user to decide if the data are suitable for the intended purpose? What is the positional and attribute accuracy? Are the data complete? What data were used to create the data set, and what processes were applied to these sources?

- Spatial data organization: What spatial data model was used to code the spatial data? How many spatial objects are there? Are methods other than coordinates, such as street addresses, used to encode locations?
- Spatial reference: Are coordinate locations encoded using longitude and latitude? Is a map projection or grid system such as the State Plane Coordinate System used? What horizontal and vertical datums are used? What parameters should be used to convert the data to another coordinate grid system?
- Entity and attribute information: What geographic information (roads, houses, elevation, temperature, etc.) is included? How is this information encoded? Were codes used? What do the codes mean?
- Distribution: From whom can you obtain the data? What formats are available? What media are available? Are the data available online? How much does acquisition of the data cost?
- Metadata reference: When were the metadata compiled? Who compiled the metadata?

8.12 Spatial Entities or Features

Spatial data have two characteristics: location and descriptive attributes. In GIS, entities are modeled as points, lines, or areas (polygons). When a polygon is given the dimension of height, an additional model, surface, is created (e.g., contoured drawing, rainfall runoff, etc.). Each entity can have various attributes assigned to it that describe something about that entity. Attributes can be kept in relational tables, as in the vector model, or attached to the layer grid cells themselves, as in the raster model. Spatial data describe the geographic location of a feature or entity, and its location with respect to other area features is also given either by rectangular coordinates (vector model) or by grid cells (raster model) described by grid column and row. Other locators, such as postal codes, route mileage posts, etc., can also be used.

Point is the simplest spatial entity because it has zero dimension. In vector representation [Figure 8.34(a)], a point is described by a set of x/y or east/north coordinates. In raster representation [Figure 8.34(b)], a point is described by a single grid cell. Points have attributes that describe the entity—e.g., a utility pole entity may have an attribute such as a traffic signal or traffic sign or electrical distribution, etc. In Figure 8.34, for example, the entity being described by the code number 6 could be industrially zoned property.

Line (arc) is a spatial entity having one dimension that joins two points; a string is comprised of a sequence of connected lines or arc segments. The line or arc can be defined by an ordered series of coordinated points (vector representation) or by a series of grid cells (raster representation). Lines or arcs have attributes that describe those particular entities. For example, a line entity may represent a ℄ section of a municipal pipeline, and attributes for that entity could include use, pipe type, slope, diameter, inverts, date of installation, date of last maintenance, etc. In vector models, these attribute data are stored in a table in a relational database.

Polygon is a spatial entity having two dimensions that is described by an enclosed area defined by an arc or a series of arcs closing back to the starting point. Polygons have attributes that describe the whole area, such as tree cover, land zoning, etc. In the case of

(a)

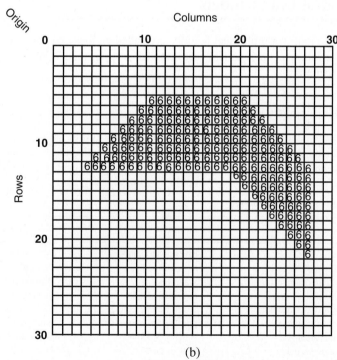

(b)

FIGURE 8.34 Data models used in GIS. (a) Vector model. (b) Raster model. 6 is a numeric attribute code that describes a function or description of the ground area being modeled. For example, 6 can be land-zoned for industrial development.

vector models, the polygon has a single number representing the attribute of the enclosed area. In the case of raster models, the code number representing the attribute for an area is displayed in each grid cell within that enclosed area. See Figure 8.34.

8.13 Typical Data Representation

The representation of data depends on the defined scale or the resolution. Table 8.6 shows typical representations for a point, a line or string, and a polygon. Consider the following when defining how data will be represented:

1. On larger-scale maps, large rivers, expressways, etc. are shown as having width and then classified as being polygons (when section end lines are drawn).
2. Before entities can be modeled as points, lines, polygons, or surfaces, the scale must be taken into consideration. For example, on small-scale maps, towns may show up as dots (points); on larger-scale maps, towns probably show up as polygons or areas.
3. Scale also affects the way entities are shown on a map. On small-scale maps, meandering rivers are shown with fewer and smoother bends, and small crop fields may not show up at all.

8.14 Spatial Data Models

In GIS, real-world physical features are called entities and are modeled using one or both of the following techniques: vector model or raster model. We discuss both in the following sections.

8.14.1 Vector Model

Surveying and engineering students are already familiar with the concept of vectors, where collected data are described and defined by their discrete Cartesian coordinates (x, y) or (easting, northing). The origin $(0, 0)$ of a rectangular grid is at the lower left corner of the

Table 8.6 DATA TYPES

Point	Line or String	Polygon (Area)
Well	River or shoreline	Pond or lake
Utility pole or tower	Distribution line	Transmission station
Hydrant or valve	Water line	Water line grid
Bus shelter	Sidewalk or road	Parking lot
Storm-water manhole	Storm water pipeline	Catchment/runoff area
Property monument	Lot line/fence line	Land parcel
Land parcel	Neighborhood	Town, city, or political boundary
Deciduous tree	Row of trees	Tree stand
Roads ℄ intersection	Road ℄	Section of road right-of-way (ROW)
Farm house	Irrigation channel	Crop field
Refreshment booth	Path	Park

grid. Points are identified by their coordinates; lines, or a series of lines, are identified by the coordinates of their endpoints. Areas or polygons are described by a series of lines (arcs) that loop back to the coordinated point of beginning. See Figure 8.34(a). Points are described as having zero dimension, lines have one dimension, and areas or polygons have two dimensions.

In addition to treating points, lines, and polygons, vector GIS also recognizes line/polygon intersections and the topological aspects of network analysis (connectivity and adjacency). These capabilities give GIS its unique capabilities of querying and routing.

Attribute data, which describe or classify entities, are located in a database (tables) linked to the coordinated vector model. Attributes can be numbers, characters, images, or even CAD drawings. Data captured using field data techniques usually come with acceptably accurate coordinates. When data are captured by digitizing (using a digitizing table or digitizing tablet) from existing maps and plans, some additional factors must be considered. First, the scale of the map or plan being digitized is a limiting factor in the accuracy of the resulting coordinates. Second, when irregular features are captured by sampling with the digitizing cursor or puck, some errors are introduced, depending on the sampling interval. For example, it is generally agreed that feature sample points should be digitized at each beginning and end point and at each change in direction, but how often do you sample curving lines? If the curved lines are geometrically defined (e.g., circular, spiral), a few sampling points may be sufficient, but if the curve is irregular, the sampling rate depends on the relative importance of the feature and perhaps the scale of any proposed output graphics.

8.14.2 Raster Model

Raster modeling was a logical consequence of the collection of data through remote-sensing and scanning techniques. Here, topographic images are represented by pixels (picture elements) that together form the structure of a multicelled grid. A raster is a GIS data structure comprised of a matrix of rectangular (usually square) grid cells. Each cell represents a specific area on the ground. The resolution of the raster is defined by the ground area represented by the raster grid cell. A cell can represent a 10 sq. ft (m^2), 100 sq. ft (m^2), or even 1,000 sq. ft (m^2) ground area—all depending on the resolution or scale of the grid cell. The higher the resolution of the grid, the more cells are required to portray a given area of the ground surface; the larger the ground area represented by a grid cell, the less precise is the cell's ability to define position. Thus, in the raster model, the considerations of scale are vital at the beginning of a project; the resolution of the raster is often a function of the scale of the map from which the spatial data may have been scanned or digitized [Figure 8.34(b)]. When you are first using GIS programs, it is extremely important to identify the resolution of the raster grid with which you are working because some GIS programs display cursor coordinates to two or three decimal places that change as the cursor is moved over the screen, even when the grid resolution is only 10–20 (or more) ft or m.

Raster grid cells are identified as being in rows and columns, with the location of any raster cell given by the column and row numbers. The zero row and column (the origin) is often located at the upper left of the raster grid (the location of the origin is defined differently by various software agencies). Features that are defined by their raster cell are thus not only geographically located but are also located relative to all other features in the raster. Because raster grid cells represent areas (not points) on the Earth, they cannot be used for precise measurements. Each cell contains an attribute value (often a number) that describes the entity being represented by that layer-specific cell. In multispectral imagery, the cell is identified by its gray-scale number, for example, a number in the range of 0–255 for eight-bit imagery.

Pixel is a term also employed in the field of remote sensing. Like grid cells in GIS, pixels portray an area subdivided into very small, (usually) square cells. Pixels are the result of capturing data through the digitization of aerial/satellite imagery. The distribution of the colors and tones in an image is established by assigning DN values to each pixel. Much of this can now be accomplished using automated soft-copy (digital) photogrammetry techniques and digital image analysis. Image resolution is stated by defining the ground area represented by one pixel. The concept of dots per inch (dpi) is also used in some applications, where each dot is a pixel. If an image has a dpi of 100, each dot or pixel has a grid cell side length of 1/100 of an inch.

Pixels are identified by unique numerical codes called DNs. Each cell has one DN only; much GIS software now uses eight-bit (2^8) data, which allow for 256 numbers, from 0 to 255. Early in the GIS design, different attributes were assigned to specific feature layers. As the GIS construction proceeds, each cell in each layer can also be given a unique code number or letter identifying the predominant (or average) attribute for that cell. For example, a grid cell code of 16 could be defined as representing areas zoned residential for housing.

8.15 GIS Data Structures

GIS software programs usually support both raster and vector models, and some programs readily convert from one to the other. The type of model selected is usually determined by the source of the data and the intended use of the data. For example, the vector model is used when there is access to coordinated data consistent with surveying field work, and the raster model is used when the data flow from scanned map data or remotely sensed imagery. When the project objectives concern large-scale engineering design or analysis, almost certainly a vector model GIS will be employed. If the objective concerns small-scale land zoning, planning analysis, or some types of cultural or social studies, a raster model GIS may be the best choice. An additional consideration deals with the nature of the data. For example, features that vary continuously, such as elevation or temperature, lend themselves to raster depiction, whereas discrete features, such as roads and pipelines, lend themselves to vector depiction.

Both vector and raster models permit the storing of thematic data on separate layers (Figure 8.32). Typical thematic layers include the following:

- Spatial reference system (e.g., coordinate grid system, etc.). The control data on this layer are used to correlate the placement of spatial data on all related layers.
- Elevation data (including contours).
- Parcel (property) boundaries.
- Hydrology (runoff and catchment areas, drainage, streams and rivers).
- Wetlands.
- Transportation.
- Soil types.

- Geology.
- Land use and zoning.
- Government boundaries.
- Municipal services.
- Buildings and other structures.
- Ground cover (including crop types and tree stands).

Individual layers, or any combination of layers, can be overlaid and analyzed or plotted together using digital plotters. Although vector models provide for a higher level of accuracy than do raster models, GIS vector analyses require a much higher level of processing and computer storage.

If large-scale graphics are an important consideration, we repeat that, in raster plots, lines may have a stepped appearance that detracts from the overall presentation. The lower the resolution of the grid cell, the more pronounced is the appearance of stepping. When performing overlay analysis, raster data are more efficient because all the cells from each layer match up; with network analysis, vector depiction is preferred because here we are dealing with attributes of discrete linear features (e.g., a road's speed limit, the number of stop signs, etc.).

8.15.1 Model Data Conversion

At times, data in vector format must be converted to raster format, and vice versa. To understand the working of the various software programs designed to perform those functions, it helps to analyze different data models representing the same planimetric features. Figure 8.35 shows features as depicted on a topographic map, along with both vector and raster models, of a simplified area. Figure 8.35(a) is a mapping representation of collected field data. The stream looks more natural here because it has been cartographically smoothed for the sake of appearance. In Figure 8.35(b), the data are shown in vectors. Although perhaps more geometrically correct, the stream is less pleasing to the eye. Here, the lines joining coordinated ground points define part of a stream chain, with each segment directionally defined.

To convert the vector model to raster format, we must overlay a raster of specified resolution with the vector model. The more grid cells, the higher the resolution—and the more realistic the portrayal of the area features. You can see that, in Figure 8.35(c), the length of the sides of each grid cell is half the length of the grid cells in Figure 8.35(d), resulting in four times as many cells. If GIS users were to define very high resolution raster grids in an attempt to improve the model's accuracy, appearance, etc., they may soon run into problems resulting from exponential increases in the quantity of data, with serious implications for computer memory requirements and program analyses runtimes. Another factor that weighs heavily here is the level of the accuracy of the original data and the way the GIS is used.

Vectors represent discrete coordinated locations, and raster grids represent grid cells with areas of some defined size, so precise conversions are not possible. As model data are being converted, some choices will have to be made. For example, each grid cell can have only one attribute, so what happens when more than one feature on a vector model is at least partially captured in a raster grid cell? Which of the possible feature attributes are designated for that specific grid cell?

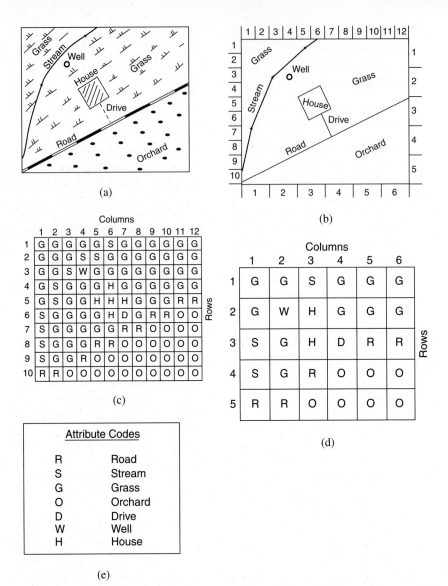

(a)

(b)

Columns
	1	2	3	4	5	6	7	8	9	10	11	12
1	G	G	G	G	G	S	G	G	G	G	G	G
2	G	G	G	S	S	G	G	G	G	G	G	G
3	G	G	S	W	G	G	G	G	G	G	G	G
4	G	S	G	G	G	H	G	G	G	G	G	G
5	G	S	G	G	H	H	H	G	G	G	R	R
6	S	G	G	G	G	H	D	G	R	R	O	O
7	S	G	G	G	G	G	R	R	O	O	O	O
8	S	G	G	G	R	R	O	O	O	O	O	O
9	S	G	G	R	O	O	O	O	O	O	O	O
10	R	R	O	O	O	O	O	O	O	O	O	O

Rows

(c)

Columns
	1	2	3	4	5	6
1	G	G	S	G	G	G
2	G	W	H	G	G	G
3	S	G	H	D	R	R
4	S	G	R	O	O	O
5	R	R	O	O	O	O

Rows

(d)

Attribute Codes	
R	Road
S	Stream
G	Grass
O	Orchard
D	Drive
W	Well
H	House

(e)

FIGURE 8.35 Different methods of displaying spatial data. (a) Topographic map. (b) Vector plot, with raster grids superimposed on edges. (c) Raster plot (120 grid cells). (d) Raster plot (30 grid cells). (e) Attribute codes.

In Figure 8.35, there are seven identified attributes: grass, stream, drive, road, orchard, well, and house. Many grid cells have at least two possible attributes. Which is more important—stream or grass? If we pick grass, the stream feature will not show up at all. The same is true for the well, the road, and the drive. If we want to portray these features, we have to find some consistent technique for ranking the importance of these

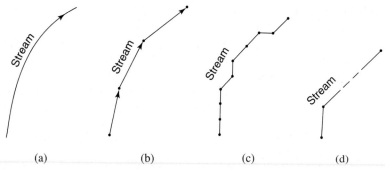

FIGURE 8.36 Stream feature depictions, using four models. (a) Topographic map plot: smoothed plot of data capture. (b) Vector model plot: coordinated tie-points are plotted. (c) Moderate resolution: raster model plot. (d) Coarse resolution: raster model plot. Raster plots are the result of joining the stream feature grid cell's midpoints. Illustrations (a)–(d) are derived from illustrations (a)–(d) of Figure 8.35.

features in the raster display. What happens when same-cell features are equally important? Generally, there are four methods of assigning cell attributes:

1. *Presence or absence*: First, we have to determine whether or not a specific feature is present within the area of the cell; a simple Boolean operator can be used in the software to effect this yes/no operation. This technique permits a quick search for specific features.
2. *Centerpoint*: Which feature is closest to the cell centerpoint?
3. *Dominant feature*: Which feature, if any, is more dominant within the cell (i.e., occupies more than 50 percent of the grid cell)?
4. *Precedence*: The rank of a feature within a cell is considered; that is, which of the captured features are more important? In Figure 8.35, the road, stream, drive, house, and well are more important features than the surrounding grass and orchard. The first five features are more dominant in the cells and closer to many of the cell's centers.

To convert from raster to vector, we must identify and join the cell centerpoints, which results in the stepped appearances displayed in Figure 8.36(c) and (d). As noted earlier, the lower the resolution, the more stepped is the appearance and the less realistic is the portrayal of that specific feature. As line-smoothing techniques are used to improve the stepped display appearance in raster models, errors are introduced that may be quite significant. Figure 8.36(a) and (b) shows the stream in topographic and vector modeling—a much smoother presentation. If the stream depictions shown in Figure 8.36(c) and (d) were smoothed, the result would not realistically reflect the poorer resolutions of the data plots.

8.16 Topology

Topology describes the relationships among geographic entities (polygons, lines, and points). The relationships may be spatial in nature (proximity, adjacency, connectivity) or the relationships may be based on entity attributes (e.g., tree species planted or harvested within a certain time period). Topology gives GIS its ability to analyze geospatial data. Topological structure is comprised of arcs and nodes. Arcs are one or more line segments that begin and end at a node. Nodes are the points of intersection of arcs, or the terminal points of arcs. Polygons are closed figures consisting of a series of three or more connected chains.

Topology does not define geometric relationships, only relational relationships. The example often used for this distinction is the use of rubber-sheeting techniques that join surfaces originally tied to different projections or coordinate grids, where surfaces are stretched to fit with other surfaces. This stretching process may affect distances and angles between entities but will not affect the relational (adjacency, networking, etc.) characteristics of the features.

Topology gives a vector GIS its ability to permit querying of a database and thus differentiates GIS from simple CAD systems, which merely show spatial location of entities and their attributes, not their relationships with each other. Topological relationships include the following:

- *Connectivity*: used to determine where (e.g., at which node) chains are connected and to give a sense of direction among connected chains by specifying "to nodes" and "from nodes."
- *Adjacency*: used to determine what spatial features (points, lines, and areas) are adjacent to chains and polygons. The descriptions "left" and "right" can be applied once direction has been established by defining "to" nodes and "from" nodes.
- *Containment*: used to determine which spatial features (points, lines, and smaller polygons) are enclosed within a specified polygon.

Entities such as polygons, chains, and nodes can have a wide variety of relational characteristics. For example, a polygon defining the location of a stand of spruce trees can overlap or be adjacent to a polygon defining a stand of pine trees (Figure 8.37). This simple two-attribute data set can be queried to identify six possibilities: those areas (polygons) that contain pine trees, spruce trees, only pine trees, only spruce trees, coniferous (spruce and pine) trees, or just that area of overlap containing both pine and spruce trees. Figure 8.37 also shows the Boolean operators that can be used to effect the same type of analysis. Also, if the appropriate data have been collected and input, the database can be further queried to ascertain attribute data, such as the age of various parts of each tree stand, tree diameters, and a potential selected harvest (e.g., board feet of lumber).

8.17   Remote Sensing Internet Websites and Further Reading

8.17.1   Satellite Websites

ENVISAT   *http://envisat.esa.int/*
Ikonus, IRS, Landsat 7   *http://www.intecamericas.com/satprices.htm*
IRS   *http://www.isro.org/programmes.htm*
JERS, Remote Sensing Technology Center of Japan   *http://www.restec.or.jp/ restec_e.html*

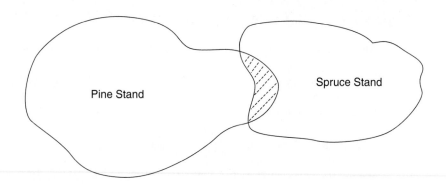

Choices

1. Pine
2. Spruce
3. Pine, Without Spruce
4. Spruce, Without Pine
5. Coniferous (Spruce and Pine)
6. Only Spruce and Pine Together

Boolean Operators

1.	Union		Pine and Spruce
2.	Minus		Pine but Not Spruce
3.	Intersect		Only Spruce and Pine Together
4.	Difference		Only Pine and Only Spruce (No Mixture)

FIGURE 8.37 Polygon analysis.

Landsat 7   *http://geo.arc.nasa.gov/sge/landsat/landsat.html*
OrbView   *http://www.orbital.com/www.orbimage.com*
QuickBird   *http://www.digitalglobe.com/*
Radarsat   *http://www.rsi.ca/*
Space Imaging   *http://spaceimaging.com*
SPOT   *http://www.spotimage.fr/html/_167_.php*
Terra (EO-1)   *http://asterweb.jpl.nasa.gov/*

8.17.2   Airborne Imagery Websites

Lidar links   *http://www.3dillc.com/rem-lidar.html*
Optech [airborne laser terrain mapper (ALTM)]   *http://www.optech.on.ca*
Scanning Hydrographic Operational Airborne Lidar Survey (**SHOALS**) system,
   U.S. Army Corps of Engineers (USACE)   *http://shoals.sam.usace.army.mil/*

8.17.3 General Reference Websites

American Society for Photogrammetry and Remote Sensing (ASPRS)   *http://www.asprs.org*

Australian Surveying and Land Information Group   *http://www.auslig.gov.au/acres/facts.htm*

European Space Agency   *http://www.esa.int/esacp/index.html*

Landsat 7   *http://landsat.usgs.gov*

NASA, EROS Data Center   *http://edcwww.cr.usgs.gov*

Natural Resources, Canada   *http://www.nrcan_rncan.gc.ca/inter/index_e.php*

Natural Resources Canada Tutorial   *http://www.ccrs.nrcan.gc.ca/ccrs/learn/learn_e.html*

Remote Sensing Tutorial (NASA)   *http://rst.gsfc.nasa.gov*

8.17.4 Further Reading

American Society for Photogrammetry and Remote Sensing, *Digital Photogrammetry: An Addendum to the Manual of Photogrammetry* (Bethesda, MD: ASPRS, 1996).

Anderson, Floyd M., and Lewis, Anthony J. (eds.), *Principles and Applications of Imaging Radar, Manual of Remote Sensing*, Third Edition, Volume 2 (New York: Wiley, 1998).

Jensen, John R., *Remote Sensing of the Environment*, An Earth Resource Perspective, Prentice Hall Series in Geographic Information Science (Upper Saddle River, NJ: Prentice Hall, 2000).

Lillesand, Thomas M., and Kiefer, Ralph W., *Remote Sensing and Image Interpretation*, Fourth Edition (New York: John Wiley and Sons, 2000).

Wolf, Paul R., and Dewitt, Bob A. *Elements of Photogrammetry*, Third Edition (New York: McGraw Hill, 2000).

Review Questions

8.1 What are the chief differences between maps based on satellite imagery and maps based on airborne imagery?

8.2 What are the advantages inherent in the use of hyperspectral sensors over multispectral sensors?

8.3 Describe all the types of data collection that can be used to plan the location of a highway/utility corridor spanning several counties.

8.4 How does the use of lidar imaging enhance digital imaging?

8.5 Why is radar imaging preferred over passive sensors for Arctic and Antarctic data collection?

8.6 Compare and contrast the two techniques of remote sensing—aerial and satellite imageries—by listing the possible uses for which each technique is appropriate. Use the comparative examples shown in Figures H.5–H.8 as a basis for your response.

8.7 Why can't aerial photographs be used for scaled measurements?

8.8 What is the chief advantage of using digital cameras over film-based cameras?

8.9 What effects does aircraft altitude have on aerial imagery?

8.10 Why are overlaps and sidelaps designed into aerial photography acquisition?

Problems

A topographic survey was performed on a tract of land, leveling techniques were used to obtain elevations, and total station techniques were used to locate the topographic detail. Figure 8.38 shows the traverse (A to G) used for survey control and the grid baseline (0 + 00 @ A) used to control the leveling survey. Offset distances are at 90° to the baseline. All the necessary information is provided, including:

(a) Bearings and lengths of the traverse sides.
(b) Grid elevations.
(c) Angle and distance ties for the topographic detail.
(d) Northings and eastings of the stations.

Distances used can be in either foot units or metric units. See Figure 8.38 and Tables 8.7–8.10.

8.1 Establish the grid, plot the elevations (the decimal point is the plot point), and interpolate the data to establish contours at 1-m (ft) intervals. Scale at 1:500 for metric units or 1 in. = 10 ft for foot units. Use pencil.

8.2 Compute the interior angles of the traverse and check for geometric closure [i.e., $(n-2)180°$].

8.3 Plot the traverse using the interior angles and the given distances or using the coordinates. Scale as in Problem 7.1.

8.4 Plot the detail using the plotted traverse as control. Scale as in Problem 7.1.

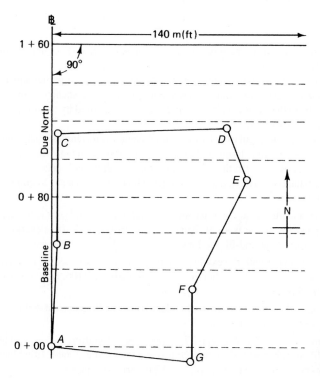

FIGURE 8.38 Grid traverse and control.

Table 8.7 SURVEYING GRID ELEVATIONS

STA.	℄	20 m (ft) E	40 m (ft) E	60 m (ft) E	80 m (ft) E	100 m (ft) E	120 m (ft) E	140 m (ft) E
1 + 60	68.97	69.51	70.05	70.53	70.32			
1 + 40	69.34	69.82	71.12	71.00	71.26	71.99		
1 + 20	69.29	70.75	69.98	71.24	72.07	72.53	72.61	
1 + 00	69.05	71.02	70.51	69.91	72.02	73.85	74.00	75.18
0 + 80	69.09	71.90	74.13	71.81	69.87	71.21	74.37	74.69
0 + 60	69.12	70.82	72.79	72.81	71.33	70.97	72.51	73.40
0 + 40	68.90	69.66	70.75	72.00	72.05	69.80	71.33	72.42
0 + 20	68.02	68.98	69.53	70.09	71.11	70.48	69.93	71.51
0 + 00 @STA.A	67.15	68.11	68.55	69.55	69.92	71.02		

Table 8.8 BALANCED TRAVERSE DATA

Course	Bearing	Distance, m(ft)
AB	N 3°30′ E	56.05
BC	N 0°30′ W	61.92
CD	N 88°40′ E	100.02
DE	S 23°30′ E	31.78
EF	S 28°53′ W	69.11
FG	South	39.73
GA	N 83°37′ W	82.67

Table 8.9 STATION COORDINATES

	Northing	Easting
A	1,000.00	1,000.00
B	1,055.94	1,003.42
C	1,117.86	1,002.88
D	1,120.19	1,102.87
E	1,091.05	1,115.54
F	1,030.54	1,082.16
G	990.81	1,082.16

8.5 Determine the area enclosed by the traverse in sq. ft or m² using one or more of the following methods.

 (a) Use grid paper as an overlay or underlay. Count the squares and partial squares enclosed by the traverse. Determine the area represented by one square at the chosen scale and, from that relationship, determine the area enclosed by the traverse.

 (b) Use a planimeter to determine the area.

 (c) Divide the traverse into regularly shaped figures (squares, rectangles, trapezoids, triangles) using a scale to determine the figure dimensions. Calculate the areas of the individual figures, and sum them to produce the overall traverse area.

 (d) Use the given balanced traverse data and the technique of coordinates to compute the traverse area.

A highway is to be constructed so that it passes through points A and E of the traverse. The proposed highway ℄ grade is +2.30 percent rising from A to E (℄ elevation at A = 68.95). The proposed cut-and-fill sections are shown in Figure 8.39(a) and (b).

8.6 Draw profile A–E, showing both the existing ground and the proposed ℄ of the highway. Use the following scales. Metric: horizontal, 1:500; vertical, 1:100. Foot: horizontal, 1 in. = 10 ft or 15 ft; vertical, 1 in. = 2 ft or 3 ft.

8.7 Plot the highway ℄ and 16-m (ft) width on the plan. Show the limits of cut and fill on the plan. Use the sections shown in Figure 8.39.

8.8 Combine Problems 7.1, 7.3, 7.4, 7.6, and 7.7 on one sheet of drafting paper. Arrange the plan and profile together with the balanced traverse data and a suitable title block. All line work is to be in ink. Use C (Imperial) or A2 (metric) size paper.

Table 8.10 SURVEY NOTES

	Horizontal Angle	Distance, m(ft)	Description
STA.	π STA. B (SIGHT C, 0°00′)		
1	8°15′	45.5	S. limit of treed area
2	17°00′	57.5	S. limit of treed area
3	33°30′	66.0	S. limit of treed area
4	37°20′	93.5	S. limit of treed area
5	45°35′	93.0	S. limit of treed area
6	49°30′	114.0	S. limit of treed area
	π @ STA. A (SIGHT B, 0°00′)		
7	50°10′	73.5	₵ gravel road (8 m ± width)
8	50°10′	86.0	₵ gravel road (8 m ± width)
9	51°30′	97.5	₵ gravel road (8 m ± width)
10	53°50′	94.5	N. limit of treed area
11	53°50′	109.0	N. limit of treed area
12	55°00′	58.0	₵ gravel road
13	66°15′	32.0	N. limit of treed area
14	86°30′	19.0	N. limit of treed area
	π @ STA. D (SIGHT E, 0°00′)		
15	0°00′	69.5	₵ gravel road
16	7°30′	90.0	N. limit of treed area
17	64°45′	38.8	N.E. corner of building
18	13°30′	75.0	N. limit of treed area
19	88°00′	39.4	N.W. corner of building
20	46°00′	85.0	N. limit of treed area

FIGURE 8.39 Proposed cross sections (Problems 8.6–8.8). (a) Cut section. (b) Fill section.

8.9 Calculate the flying heights and altitudes, given the following information:
  (a) Photographic scale = 1:20,000, lens focal length = 153 mm, elevation of mean datum = 180 m.
  (b) Photographic scale 1 in. = 20,000 ft, lens focal length = 6.022 in., elevation of mean datum = 520 ft.

8.10 Calculate the photo scales, given the following data:

    (a) Distance between points A and B on a topographic map. Scale 1:50,000 = 4.75 cm, distance between same points on air photo = 23.07 cm.

    (b) Distance between points C and D on topographic map. Scale 1:100,000 = 1.85 in., distance between same points on air photo = 6.20 in.

8.11 Calculate the approximate numbers of photographs required for stereoscopic coverage (60 percent forward overlap and 25 percent side overlap) for each of the following conditions:

    (a) Photographic scale = 1:30,000; ground area to be covered is 30 km by 45 km.

    (b) Photographic scale 1:15,000; ground area to be covered is 15 mi by 33 mi.

    (c) Photographic scale is 1 in. = 500 ft; ground area to be covered is 10 mi by 47 mi.

8.12 Calculate the dimensions of the area covered on the ground in a single stereo model having a 60 percent forward overlap, if the scale of the photograph (9 in. by 9 in. format) is:

    (a) 1: 10,000

    (b) 1 in. = 400 ft

8.13 Calculate how far the camera would move during the exposure time for each of the following conditions:

    (a) Ground speed of aircraft = 350 km/hr; exposure time = 1/100 s.

    (b) Ground speed of aircraft = 350 km/hr; exposure time = 1/1,000 s.

    (c) Ground speed of aircraft = 200 mi/hr; exposure time = 1/500 s.

Chapter 9

Horizontal Control Surveys

9.1 General Background

The highest order of control surveys was once thought to be national or continental in scope. With the advent of the global positioning system (GPS; see Chapter 7), control surveys are now based on frameworks that cover the entire surface of the Earth, and they must take into account its ellipsoidal shape. Surveys that take into account the ellipsoidal shape of the Earth are called **geodetic surveys**.

The early control net of the United States was tied into the control nets of both Canada and Mexico, giving a consistent continental net. The first major adjustment in control data was made in 1927, which resulted in the North American Datum (NAD27). Since that time, a great deal more has been learned about the shape and mass of the Earth; these new and expanded data come to us from releveling surveys, precise traverses, very long baseline interferometry (VLBI), satellite laser ranging (SLR) surveys, Earth movement studies, GPS observations, gravity surveys, etc. The data thus accumulated have been utilized to update and expand existing control data. The new geodetic data have also provided scientists with the means to define more precisely the actual geometric shape of the Earth.

The reference solid previously used for this purpose (the Clarke spheroid of 1866) was modified to reflect the knowledge of the Earth's dimensions at that time. Thus, a world geodetic system, first proposed in 1972 (WGS '72) and later endorsed in 1979 by the International Association of Geodesy (IAG), included proposals for an Earth-mass-centered ellipsoid (GRS80 ellipsoid) that would represent more closely the planet on which we live. The ellipsoid was chosen over the spheroid as a representative solid model because of the slight bulging of the Earth near the equator. The bulge is caused by the Earth spinning on its polar axis. See Table 9.1 for the parameters of four models. See also Figure 7.26.

Table 9.1 TYPICAL REFERENCE SYSTEMS

Reference System	a (Semimajor) (m)	b (Semiminor) (m)	$1/f$ (Flattening)
NAD83 (GRS80)	6,378,137.0	6,356,752.3	298.257222101
WGS84	6,378,137.0	6,356,752.3	298.257223563
ITRS	6,378,136.49	6,356,751.75	298.25645
NAD27 (Clarke, 1866)	6,378,206.4	6,356,583.8	294.978698214

GRS80 was used to define the North American Datum of 1983 (NAD83), which covers the North American continent, including Greenland and parts of Central America. All individual control nets were included in a weighted simultaneous computation. A good tie to the global system was given by satellite positioning. The geographic coordinates of points in this system are latitude (ϕ) and longitude (λ). Although this system is widely used in geodetic surveying and mapping, it is too cumbersome for use in everyday surveying. For example, the latitude and longitude angles must be expressed to three or four decimals of a second (01.0000″) to give positions to the closest 0.01 ft. At latitude 44°, 1″ of latitude equals 101 ft and 1″ of longitude equals 73 ft. Conventional field surveying (as opposed to control surveying) is usually referenced to a plane grid (see Section 9.2).

In most cases, the accuracies between NAD83 first-order stations were better than 1:200,000, which would have been unquestioned in the pre-GPS era. However, the increased use of very precise GPS surveys and the tremendous potential for new applications for this technology created a demand for high-precision upgrades, using GPS techniques, to the control net.

9.1.1 Modern Considerations

A cooperative network upgrading program under the guidance of the National Geodetic Survey (NGS), including both federal and state agencies, began in 1986 in Tennessee and was completed in Indiana in 1997. This high-accuracy reference network (HARN)—sometimes called the high-precision geodetic network (HPGN)—resulted in about 16,000 horizontal control survey stations being upgraded to AA-, A-, or B-order status. Horizontal AA-order stations have a relative accuracy of 3 mm ± 1:100,000,000 relative to other AA-order stations; horizontal A-order stations have a relative accuracy of 5 mm ± 1:10,000,000 relative to other A- and AA-order stations; horizontal B-order stations have a relative accuracy of 8 mm ± 1:1,000,000 relative to other AA-, A-, and B-order stations. Of the 16,000 survey stations, the NGS has committed to the maintenance of about 1,400 AA- and A-order stations, which form the federal base network (FBN); individual states maintain the remainder of the survey stations, the B-order stations, which form the cooperative base network (CBN).

See Table 9.2 for accuracy standards for the new HARN, using GPS techniques and traditional (pre-GPS) terrestrial techniques. The Federal Geodetic Control Subcommittee (FGCS) has published guidelines for the GPS field techniques (see Chapter 7) needed to achieve the various orders of surveys shown in Table 9.2. For example, AA-, A-, and B-order surveys require the use of receivers having both L1 and L2 frequencies, whereas the C-order results can be achieved using only a single-frequency (L1) receiver. Orders AA

Table 9.2 POSITIONING ACCURACY STANDARDS (95 PERCENT CONFIDENT LEVEL; MINIMUM GEOMETRIC ACCURACY STANDARD)

Survey Categories	Order	Base Error e (cm)	p (ppm)	Line-Length Dependent Error a (1:a)
HARN				
Federal base network (FBN)				
Global-regional geodynamics	**AA**	0.3	0.01	1:100,000,000
National Geodetic Reference System, primary network	**A**	0.5	0.1	1:10,000,000
Cooperative base network (CBN)				
National Geodetic Reference System, secondary networks	**B**	0.8	1	1:1,000,000
Terrestrial-based				
National Geodetic Reference System	**C**			
	1	1.0	10	1:100,000
	2-I	2.0	20	1:50,000
	2-II	3.0	50	1:20,000
	3	5.0	100	1:10,000

Source: From Geometric Geodetic Accuracy Standards Using GPS Relative Positioning Techniques. [Federal Geodetic Control Subcommittee (FGCS) 1988]. Publications are available through the National Geodetic Survey (NGS), (301) 443–8631.

and A require five receivers observing simultaneously, order B requires four receivers observing simultaneously, and order C requires three receivers observing simultaneously.

Work was also completed on an improved vertical control net with revised values for about 600,000 benchmarks in the United States and Canada. This work was largely completed in 1988, resulting in a new North American Datum (NAVD88). The original adjustment of continental vertical values was performed in 1927.

The surface of the Earth has been approximated by the surface of an ellipsoid, that is, the surface developed by rotating an ellipse on its minor axis. An ellipse (defined by its major axis and flattening), that most closely conformed to the geoid of the area of interest, which was usually continental in scope, was originally chosen. The reference ellipsoid chosen by the United States of America and Canada was one recommended by the IAG called the Geodetic Reference System 1980 (GRS80). See Table 9.1 for reference ellipsoid parameters; see Figures 7.25–7.29 for more on this topic.

The origin of a three-dimensional coordinate system was defined to be the center of the mass of the Earth (geocentric), which is located in the equatorial plane. The z-axis of the ellipsoid was defined as running from the origin through the mean location of the North Pole, more precisely, the international reference pole as defined by the International Earth Rotation Service (IERS); z-coordinates are measured upward (positive) or downward (negative) from the equatorial plane (see Figures 9.1 and 7.26). The x-axis runs from the origin to a point of 0° longitude (Greenwich meridian) in the equatorial plane. The x-coordinates are measured from the y–z plane, parallel to the x-axis. They are positive from the 0 meridian 90° east and west; for the remaining 180°, they are negative. The y-axis forms a right-handed coordinate

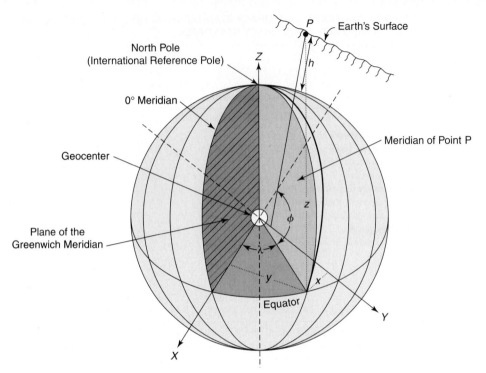

FIGURE 9.1 Ellipsoidal and geographic reference systems.

frame (easterly from the x-axis) 90° to the x and z axes. The y-coordinates are measured perpendicular to the plane through the 0 meridian and are positive in the eastern hemisphere and negative in the western hemisphere. The semimajor axis (a) runs from the origin to the equator, and the semiminor axis (b) runs from the origin to the Earth's North Pole. Another defining parameter used to define ellipsoids is the flattening (f), which is defined to be $f = (a - b)/a$, or $f = 1 - b/a$ (see Figure 7.25 and Table 9.1).

Figure 9.1 shows the relationships between the ellipsoidal coordinates x, y, and z and the geodetic (or geographic) coordinates of latitude (φ), longitude (λ), and ellipsoidal height (h). Note that the x, y, and z dimensions are measured parallel to the X, Y, and Z axes, respectively, and that h is measured vertically up from the ellipsoidal surface to a point on the surface of the Earth. For use in surveying, the ellipsoidal coordinates/geodetic coordinates are transformed into plane grid coordinates such as those used for the state plane grid or the Universal Transverse Mercator (UTM) grid. The ellipsoidal height (h) is also transformed into an orthometric height (elevation) by determining the geoid separation at a specified geographic location, as described in Section 7.13.

The axes of this coordinate system have not remained static for several reasons; for example, the Earth's rotation varies, and the vectors between the positions of points on the surface of the Earth do not remain constant because of plate tectonics. It is now customary to publish the x, y, and z coordinates along with velocities of change (plus or minus), in meters/year, for all three directions (vx, vy, and vz) for each station. For this reason, the axes are defined with respect to positions on the Earth's surface at a particular epoch. The NAD83, adopted in 1986, was first determined through measurements using VLBI and satellite ranging.

These ongoing geodetic measurements together with continuous GPS observations (e.g., CORS) have discovered discrepancies, resulting in several upgrades to the parameters of NAD83. The IERS continues to monitor the positioning of the coordinates of their global network of geodetic observation stations, which now include GPS observations. This network is known as the International Terrestrial Reference Frame, with the latest reference epoch, at the time of this writing, set at the year 2000 (ITRF2000 or ITRF00).

For most purposes, the latest versions of NAD83 and WGS84 are considered identical. Because of the increases in accuracy occasioned by improvements in measurement technology, the NGS is commencing an adjustment to their National Spatial Reference System (NSRS) of all GPS HARN stations (CORS stations' coordinates will be held fixed). This adjustment, when combined with the newest geoid model, expected by 2009, should result in horizontal and vertical coordinate accuracies in the 1- to 2-cm range, including orthometric heights. The adjustments will affect all HARN stations in the FBN, specifically its AA- and A-order stations, and all B-order stations in the CBN. This adjustment (begun in 2005 and expected to be finished by 2007 or earlier) and both NAD83 (NSRS) and ITRF00 [or the latest ITRF (e.g., ITRF200x)] positional coordinates will be produced and published. The ITRF reference ellipsoid is very similar to GRS80 and WGS84, with slight changes in the a and b parameters and more significant changes in the flattening values (see Table 9.1). NGS reports that NAD83 is not being abandoned because many states have legislation specifying that datum. See the latest NGS news on this topic at http://www.ngs.noaa.gov/NationalReadjustment/.

9.1.2 Traditional Considerations

First-order horizontal control accuracy using terrestrial (preelectronics) techniques were originally established using **triangulation**. This technique involved (1) a precisely measured baseline as a starting side for a series of triangles or chains of triangles; (2) the determination of each angle in the triangle using a precise theodolite, which permitted the computation of the lengths of each side; and (3) a check on the work made possible by precisely measuring a side of a subsequent triangle (the spacing of check lines depended on the desired accuracy level). See Figure 9.2.

Triangulation was originally favored because the basic measurement of angles (and only a few sides) could be taken more quickly and precisely than could the measurement of all the distances (the surveying solution technique of measuring only the sides of a triangle is called **trilateration**). The advent of EDM instruments in the 1960s changed the approach to terrestrial control surveys. It became possible to measure the length of a triangle side precisely in about the same length of time as was required for angle determination.

Figure 9.2 shows two control survey configurations. Figure 9.2(a) depicts a simple chain of single triangles. In triangulation (angles only), this configuration suffers from the weakness that essentially only one route can be followed to solve for side KL. Figure 9.2(b) shows a chain of double triangles, or quadrilaterals. This configuration is preferred for triangulation because side KL can be solved using different routes (many more redundant measurements). Modern terrestrial control survey practice favors a combination of triangulation and trilateration (i.e., measure both the angles and the distances), which ensures many redundant measurements even for the simple chain of triangles shown in Figure 9.2(a).

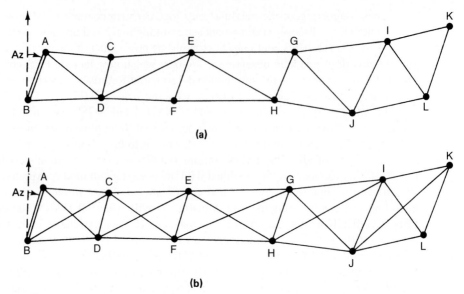

FIGURE 9.2 Control survey configurations. AB is the measured baseline, with known (or measured) azimuth. (a) Chain of single triangles. (b) Chain of double triangles (quadrilaterals).

Whereas triangulation control surveys were originally used for basic state or provincial controls, precise traverses and GPS surveys are now used to densify the basic control net. The advent of reliable and precise EDM instruments has elevated the traverse to a valuable role, both in strengthening a triangulation net and in providing a stand-alone control figure itself. To provide reliability, traverses must close on themselves or on previously coordinated points. Table 9.3 summarizes characteristics and specifications for traverses. Tables 3.1 and 3.2 summarized characteristics and specifications for vertical control for the United States and Canada.

Table 9.3   TRAVERSE SPECIFICATIONS—UNITED STATES

| Classification | First Order | Second Order | | Third Order | |
		Class I	Class II	Class I	Class II
Recommended spacing of principal stations	Network stations 10–15 km; other surveys seldom less than 3 km	Principal stations seldom less than 4 km except in metropolitan area surveys, where the limitation is 0.3 km	Principal stations seldom less than 2 km except in metropolitan area surveys, where the limitation is 0.2 km	Seldom less than 0.1 km in tertiary surveys in metropolitan area surveys; as required for other surveys	
Position closure After azimuth adjustment	0.04 m $\sqrt{K}$ or 1:100,000	0.08 m $\sqrt{K}$ or 1:50,000	0.2 m $\sqrt{K}$ or 1:20,000	0.4 m $\sqrt{K}$ or 1:10,000	0.8 m $\sqrt{K}$ or 1:5,000

Source: Federal Geodetic Control Committee, United States, 1974.

More recently, with the introduction of the programmed total station, the process called resection is used much more often. **Resection** permits the surveyor to set up the total station at any convenient location and then, by sighting (measuring just angles or both angles and distances) to two or more coordinated control stations, the coordinates of the setup station can then be computed. See Section 5.3.3.

In traditional (pre-GPS) surveying, the surveyor had to use high-precision techniques to obtain high accuracy for conventional field control surveys. Several types of high-precision equipment, used to measure angles and vertical and horizontal slope distances, are illustrated in Figures 9.3–9.5. Specifications for horizontal high-precision techniques stipulate the least angular count of the theodolite or total station, the number of observations, the rejection of observations exceeding specified limits from the mean, the spacing of major stations, and the angular and positional closures.

Higher-order specifications are seldom required for engineering or mapping surveys. An extensive interstate highway control survey could be one example where higher-order specifications are used in engineering work. Control for large-scale projects (e.g., interchanges, large housing projects) that are to be laid out using polar ties (angle/distance) by total stations may require accuracies in the range of 1/10,000 to 1/20,000, depending on the project, and would fall between second- and third-order accuracy specifications (Table 9.2). Control stations established using GPS techniques have the inherent potential for higher orders of accuracy. The lowest requirements are reserved for small engineering or mapping projects that are limited in scope—for example, traffic studies, drainage studies, borrow pit volume surveys, etc.

(a)

(b)

FIGURE 9.3 (a) Kern DKM 3 precise theodolite; angles read directly to 0.5″; used in first-order surveys. (b) Kern DKM 3 scale reading (vertical angle = 82°53′01.8″). (Courtesy of Leica Geosystems Inc.)

FIGURE 9.4 Precise level. Precise optical levels have accuracies in the range of 1.5–1.0 mm for 1-km two-way leveling—depending on the instrument model and the type of leveling rod used. See also Figure 2.7. (Courtesy of Trimble)

FIGURE 9.5 Kern Mekometer ME 3000, a high-precision EDM [SE = ±(0.2 mm ± 1 ppm)] with a triple-prism distance range of 2.5 km. Used wherever first-order results are required, for example, deformation studies, network surveys, plant engineering, and baseline calibration. (Courtesy of Leica Geosystems Inc.)

The American Congress on Surveying and Mapping (ACSM) and the American Land Title Association (ALTA) collaborated to produce new classifications for cadastral surveys based on present and proposed land use. These 1992 classifications (subject to state regulations) are shown in Table 9.4. Recognizing the impact of GPS techniques on all branches of surveying, in 2005 the National Society of Professional Surveys (NSPS) and ALTA published positional tolerances for surveys—effective January 1, 2006; the six-page standards document can be accessed at http://www.acsm.net/ALTA.doc (see Table 9.5 for an extract from these standards showing the allowable *relative positioning* accuracy standard).

To enable the surveyor to perform reasonably precise surveys and still use plane geometry and trigonometry for related computations, several forms of plane coordinate grids have been introduced. These grids will be described in the next section.

Table 9.4 AMERICAN CONGRESS ON SURVEYING AND MAPPING MINIMUM ANGLE, DISTANCE, AND CLOSURE REQUIREMENTS FOR SURVEY MEASUREMENTS THAT CONTROL LAND BOUNDARIES FOR ALTA-ACSM LAND TITLE SURVEYS (1)

Direct Reading of Instrument (2)	Instrument Reading, Estimated (3)	Number of Observations per Station (4)	Spread from Mean of D&R Not to Exceed (5)	Angle Closure Where N = No. of Stations Not to Exceed . . .	Linear Closure (6)	Distance Measurement (7)	Minimum Length of Measurements (8), (9), (10)
20″<1′> $\boxed{10″}$	5″<0.1′>N.A	2 D&R	5″<0.1′> $\boxed{5″}$	$10″\sqrt{N}$	1:15,000	EDM or double-tape with steel tape	(8) 81 m, (9) 153 m, (10) 20 m

Note (1): All requirements of each class must be satisfied to qualify for that particular class of survey. The use of a more precise instrument does not change the other requirements, such as number of angles turned, etc.

Note (2): Instrument must have a direct reading of at least the amount specified (not an estimated reading), i.e.,: 20″ = micrometer reading theodolite, <1′> = scale reading theodolite, $\boxed{10″}$ = electronic reading theodolite.

Note (3): Instrument must have the capability of allowing an estimated reading below the direct reading to the specified reading.

Note (4): D&R means the direct and reverse positions of the instrument telescope; that is, urban surveys require that two angles in the direct and two angles in the reverse position be measured and meaned.

Note (5): Any angle measured that exceeds the specified amount from the mean must be rejected, and the set of angles must be remeasured.

Note (6): Ratio of closure after angles are balanced and closure is calculated.

Note (7): All distance measurements must be made with a property calibrated EDM or steel tape, applying atmospheric, temperature, sag, tension, slope, scale factor, and sea-level corrections as necessary.

Note (8): EDM having an error of 5 mm, independent of distance measured (manufacturer's specifications).

Note (9): EDM having an error of 10 mm, independent of distance measured (manufacturer's specifications).

Note (10): Calibrated steel tape.

Table 9.5 2005 MINIMUM STANDARD DETAIL REQUIREMENTS FOR ALTA/ACSM LAND TITLE SURVEYS AS ADOPTED BY AMERICAN LAND TITLE ASSOCIATION AND NATIONAL SOCIETY OF PROFESSIONAL SURVEYORS (A MEMBER ORGANIZATION OF THE AMERICAN CONGRESS ON SURVEYING AND MAPPING)

Computation of Relative Positional Accuracy*

Relative Positional Accuracy may be tested by:

(1) comparing the relative location of points in a survey as measured by an independent survey of higher accuracy or

(2) the results of a minimally constrained, correctly weighted least square adjustment of the survey.

Allowable Relative Positional Accuracy for Measurements Controlling Land Boundaries on ALTA/ACSM Land Title Surveys

$\boxed{0.07 \text{ ft (or 20 mm)} + 50 \text{ ppm}}$

*Extracted from six-page document available at http://www.acsm.net/ ALTA2005.doc. Revised standards were put into effect on Jan 1, 2006.

9.2 Plane Coordinate Grids

9.2.1 General Background

The Earth is ellipsoidal in shape, and if you try to portray a section of the Earth on a flat map or plan, a certain amount of distortion is unavoidable. Also, some allowances must be made when you wish to create plane grids and use plane geometry and trigonometry to define the Earth's curved surface. Over the years, various grids and projections have been employed. The United States uses the state plane coordinate grid system (SPCS), which utilizes both a Transverse Mercator (TM) cylindrical projection and the Lambert conformal conic projection.

As already noted, geodetic control surveys are based on the best estimates of the actual shape of the Earth. For many years, geodesists used the Clarke 1866 spheroid as a base for their work, including the development of the first NAD27. The NGS created the state plane coordinate system (SPCS27) based on the NAD27 datum. In this system, map projections are used that best suit the geographic needs of individual states (Table 9.6): The Lambert conformal conical projection is used in states with larger east/west dimensions (Figures 9.6 and 9.7), and the TM cylindrical projection (Figure 9.8) is used in states with larger north/south dimensions. To minimize the distortion that always occurs when a spherical surface is converted to a plane surface, the Lambert projection grid is limited to a relatively narrow strip of about 158 mi in a north/south direction, and the TM projection grid is limited to about 158 mi in an east/west direction. At the maximum distance of 158 mi, or 254 km, a maximum scale factor of 1:10,000 exists at the zone boundaries. Also, as already noted, modernization in both instrumentation and technology permitted the establishment of a more representative datum based on the GRS80, which was used to define the new

Table 9.6 STATE PLANE COORDINATE SYSTEMS

Transverse Mercator System		Lambert System		Both Systems
Alabama	Mississippi	Arkansas	North Dakota	Alaska
Arizona	Missouri	California	Ohio	Florida
Delaware	Nevada	Colorado	Oklahoma	New York
Georgia	New Hampshire	Connecticut	Oregon	
Hawaii	New Jersey	Iowa	Pennsylvania	
Idaho	New Mexico	Kansas	Puerto Rico	
Illinois	Rhode Island	Kentucky	South Carolina	
Indiana	Vermont	Louisiana	South Dakota	
Maine	Wyoming	Maryland	Tennessee	
		Massachusetts	Texas	
		Michigan	Utah	
		Minnesota	Virginia	
		Montana	Virgin Islands	
		Nebraska	Washington	
		North Carolina	West Virginia	
			Wisconsin	

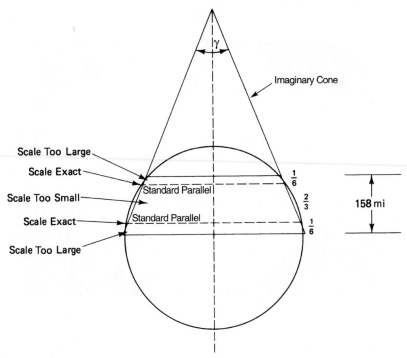

FIGURE 9.6 Lambert secant projection.

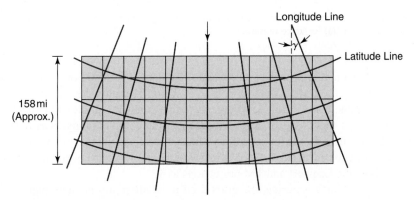

FIGURE 9.7 Lines of latitude (parallels) and lines of longitude (meridians) on the Lambert projection grid.

NAD83 datum. A new state plane coordinate system of 1983 (SPCS83) was developed based on the NAD83 datum.

Surveyors using both the old and new versions of SPCS can compute positions using tables and computer programs made available from NGS. SPCS83, which enables the surveyor to work in a more precisely defined datum than did SPCS27, uses similar

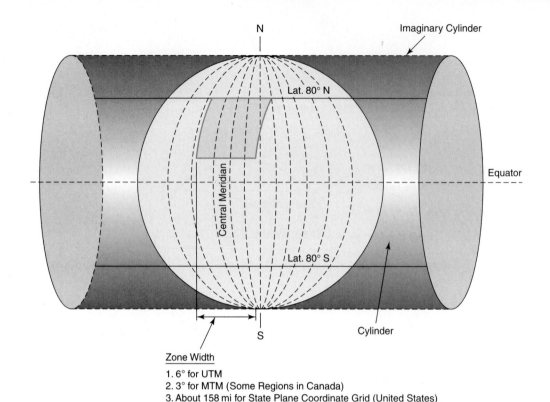

FIGURE 9.8 Transverse Mercator projection cylinder *tangent* to the Earth's surface at the central meridian (CM) [see Figure 9.12(a) for zone number].

Within the figure:

N

Imaginary Cylinder

Lat. 80° N

Central Meridian

Equator

Lat. 80° S

S

Cylinder

Zone Width
1. 6° for UTM
2. 3° for MTM (Some Regions in Canada)
3. About 158 mi for State Plane Coordinate Grid (United States)

mathematical approaches with some new nomenclature. For example, in SPCS27, the Lambert coordinates were expressed as *X* and *Y*, with values given in feet (U.S. survey foot; Table 1.1), and the convergence angle (mapping angle) was displayed as θ; alternately, in the TM grid, the convergence angle (in seconds) was designated by $\Delta\lambda''$. SPCS83 uses metric values for coordinates (designated as eastings and northings) as well as foot units (U.S. survey foot or international foot). The convergence angle is now shown in both the Lambert and TM projections as γ.

In North America, the grids used most often are the state plane coordinate grids. These grids are used in each U.S. state; the UTM grid is used in much of Canada. The Federal Communications Commission recently mandated that all cell phones be able to provide the spatial location of all 911 callers. By 2002, half the telephone carriers had opted for network-assisted GPS (NA-GPS) for 911 caller location. The other carriers proposed to implement caller location using the enhanced observed time difference of arrival (E-OTD); this technique utilizes the cellular network itself to pinpoint the caller location.

With such major initiatives in the use of GPS to help provide caller location, some believe that to provide seamless service, proprietary map databases should be referenced to a common grid, that is, a U.S. National Grid (USNG) for spatial addressing (see Section 9.5.3).

One such grid being considered is the military grid reference system (MGRS), which is based on the UTM grid. In addition to the need for a national grid for emergency (911) purposes, the Federal Geographic Data Committee (FGDC) recognizes the benefits of such a national grid for the many applications now developed for the GIS field. The ability to share data from one proprietary software program to another depends on a common grid, such as that proposed in the USNG. See http://www.fgdc.gov/standards/documents/proposals/usngprop.html.

In addition to supplying tables for computations in SPCS83, the NGS provides both interactive computations on the Internet and PC software available for downloading at http://www.ngs.noaa.gov [see also Section 8.8.1, which describes the NGS online user positioning system (OPUS)]. Many surveyors prefer computer-based computations to working with cumbersome tables. A manual that describes SPCS83 in detail, NOAA Manual NOS NGS 5: *State Plane Coordinate System of 1983*, is available from NGS.* This manual contains an introduction to SPCS; a map index showing all state plane coordinate zone numbers (zones are tied to state counties), which are required for converting state plane coordinates to geodetic positions; a table showing the SPCS legislative status of all states (1988); a discussion of the $(t - T)$ convergence second term correction, which is needed for precise surveys of considerable extent (Figure 9.18); and the methodology required to convert NAD83 latitude/longitude to SPCS83 northing/easting, plus the reverse process. This manual also contains the four equations needed to convert from latitude/longitude to northing/easting (i.e., for northing, easting, convergence, and the grid scale factor) and the four equations to convert from northing/easting to latitude/longitude (latitude, longitude, convergence factor, and grid scale factor). Refer to the NGS manual for these conversion equation techniques. NGS uses the term *conversion* to describe this process and reserves the term *transformation* to describe the process of converting coordinates from one datum or grid to another, for example, from NAD27 to NAD83, or from SPCS27 to SPCS83 to UTM, etc.

The NGS also has a range of software programs designed to assist the surveyor in several areas of geodetic inquiry. You can find the NGS toolkit at http://www.ngs.noaa.gov/TOOLS/. This site has online calculations capability for many of the geodetic activities listed below (to download PC software programs, go to http://www.ngs.noaa.gov/ and click on the PC software icon):

- DEFLEC99—computes deflections of the vertical at the surface of the Earth for the continental United States, Alaska, Puerto Rico, Virgin Islands, and Hawaii.
- G99SSS—computes the gravimetric height values for the continental United States.
- GEOID99—computes geoid height values for the continental United States.
- HTDP—time-dependent horizontal positioning software that allows users to predict horizontal displacements and/or velocities at locations throughout the United States.
- NADCON—transforms geographic coordinates between the NAD27, Old Hawaiian, Puerto Rico, or Alaska Island data and NAD83 values.
- State plane coordinate GPPCGP—converts NAD27 state plane coordinates to NAD27 geographic coordinates (latitudes and longitudes), and vice versa.

---

*To obtain NGS publications, contact NOAA, National Geodetic Survey, N/NGS12, 1315 East–West Highway, Station 9202, Silver Springs, MD 20910–3282. Publications can also be ordered by phoning (301) 713–3242.

- SPCS83—converts NAD83 state plane coordinates to NAD83 geographic positions, and vice versa.
- Surface gravity prediction—predicts surface gravity at a specified geographic position and topographic height.
- Tidal information and orthometric elevations of a specific survey control mark—can be viewed graphically; these data can be referenced to NAVD88, NGVD29, and mean lower low water (MLLW) data.
- VERTCON—computes the modeled difference in orthometric height between the North American Vertical Datum of 1988 (NAVD88) and the National Geodetic Vertical Datum of 1929 (NGVD29) for any given location specified by latitude and longitude.

In Canada, software programs designed to assist the surveyor in various geodetic applications are available on the Internet from the Canadian Geodetic Survey at http://www.geod.nrcan.gc.ca. The following list is a selection of available services, including online applications and programs that can be downloaded:

- Precise GPS satellite ephemerides.
- GPS satellite clock corrections.
- GPS constellation information.
- GPS calendar.
- National gravity program.
- UTM to and from geographic coordinate conversion (UTM is in 6° zones with a scale factor of 0.9996).
- TM to and from geographic coordinate conversion (TM is in 3° zones with a scale factor of 0.9999, similar to U.S. state plane grids).
- GPS height transformation (based on GSD99; see Section 8.13).

■ **EXAMPLE 9.1** *Use of the NGS Toolkit to Convert Coordinates*

(a) Convert geodetic positions to state plane coordinates.

(b) Convert state plane coordinates to geodetic positions.

Solution

(a) When user selects http://www.ngs.noaa.gov//TOOLS/spc.html and selects latitude/longitude > SPC, he or she is asked to choose NAD83 or NAD27, and to enter the geodetic coordinates and the zone number (the zone number is not really required here because the program automatically generates the zone number directly from the geodetic coordinates of latitude and longitude). The longitude degree entry must always be three digits, 079 in this example:

O NAD 83
O NAD 27
Latitude **N 42°14′23.0000″**

Longitude **W 079°20′35.0000″**

Zone [   ] (This can be left blank.)

The program response is:

INPUT =	Latitude N421423.0000	Longitude W0792035.0000	Datum NAD 83	Zone 3103

North (Y) Meters	East (X) Meters	Area	Convergence DD MM SS.ss	Scale
248,999.059	287,296.971	NY W	−0 30 38.62	0.99998586

(b) When the user selects http://www.ngs.noaa.gov/TOOLS/spc.html and then selects SPC > latitude/longitude, he or she must select either NAD83 or NAD27, and must enter the state plane coordinates and the SPCS zone number:

O NAD 83

O NAD 27

Northing = **248,999.059**

Easting = **287,296.971**

Zone = **3,103**

The program response is:

INPUT =	North (Meters) 248,999.059	East (Meters) 287,296.971	Datum NAD 83	Zone 3103

Latitude DD MM SS.sssss	Longitude DD MM SS.sssss	Area	Convergence	Scale Factor
42 14 23.00000	079 20 35.00001	NY W	−0°30 38.62	0.9999859

■ **EXAMPLE 9.2** *Use of the Canadian Geodetic Survey Online Sample Programs*
The programs can be downloaded free. Use the same geographic position as in Section 9.2.2:

(a) Convert geographic position to Universal Transverse Mercator.

(b) Convert Universal Transverse Mercator to geographic position.

Solution

(a) Go to http://www.geod.nrcan.gc.ca and select *English—Online Applications—GSRUG* and then select *Geographic to UTM*. Enter the geographic coordinates of the point you want to compute. For this example, enter the following:

Latitude: **42°14′23.0000″ N**
Longitude: **079°20′35.0000″ W**
Ellipsoid: **GRS80 (NAD83, WGS84)**
Zone width: **6° UTM**

The desired ellipsoid and zone width, 6° or 3°, are selected by highlighting the appropriate entry while scrolling through the list. The program response is as follows:

Input Geographic Coordinates
Latitude: 42°14′23.0000″ N
Longitude: 079°20′35.0000″ W
Ellipsoid: NAD83 (WGS84)
Zone width: 6° UTM

Output: UTM Coordinates:
UTM Zone: 17
Northing: 4,677,721.911 m North
Easting: 636,709.822 m

(b) Go to http://www.geod.nrcan.gc.ca and select *English—Online Applications—GSRUG* and then select *UTM to Geographic*. Enter the UTM coordinates of the point you want to compute. For this example, enter the following:

Zone: **17**
Northing: **4,677,721.911 m North**
Easting: **636,709.822 m**
Ellipsoid: **GRS80 (NAD83, WGS84)**
Zone width: **6° UTM**

The program's response is:

Input Geographic Coordinates
UTM Zone 17
Northing: 4,677,721.911 m North
Easting: 636,709.822 m
Ellipsoid: NAD83 (WGS84)
Zone width: 6° UTM

Output Geographic Coordinates
Latitude: 42°14′23.000015″ N
Longitude: 79°20′34.999989″ W

9.3 Lambert Projection Grid

The Lambert projection is a conical conformal projection. The imaginary cone is placed around the Earth so that the apex of the cone is on the Earth's axis of rotation above the North Pole for northern hemisphere projections, and below the South Pole for southern hemisphere projections. The location of the apex depends on the area of the ellipsoid that is being projected. Figures 9.6 and 9.7 confirm that, although the east–west direction is relatively distortion-free, the north–south coverage must be restrained (e.g., to 158 mi) to maintain the integrity of the projection; therefore, the Lambert projection is used for states having a greater east–west dimension, such as Pennsylvania and Tennessee. Table 9.6 lists all the states and the type of projection each uses; New York, Florida, and Alaska utilize both the TM and the Lambert projections. The NGS publication *State Plane Coordinate Grid System of 1983* gives a more detailed listing of each state's projection data.

9.4 Transverse Mercator Grid

The TM projection is created by placing an imaginary cylinder around the Earth, with the cylinder's circumference tangent to the Earth along a meridian (central meridian; Figure 9.8). When the cylinder is flattened, a plane is developed that can be used for grid purposes. At the central meridian, the scale is exact [Figures 9.8 and 9.9(a)], and the scale becomes progressively more distorted as the distance east and west of the central meridian increases. This projection is used in states with a more predominant north/south dimension, such as Illinois and New Hampshire. The distortion (which is always present when a spherical surface is projected onto a plane) can be minimized in two ways. First, the distortion can be minimized by keeping the zone width relatively narrow (158 mi in SPCS); second, the distortion can be lessened by reducing the radius of the projection cylinder (secant projection) so that, instead of being tangent to the Earth's surface, the cylinder cuts through the Earth's surface at an optimal distance on either side of the central meridian [Figures 9.9(b) and 9.10]. Thus, the scale factor at the central meridian is less than unity (0.9999); it is unity at the line of intersection at the Earth's surface and greater than unity between the lines of intersection and the zone limit meridians. Figure 9.11 shows a cross section of an SPCS TM zone. For both the Lambert and TM grids, the scale factor of 0.9999 (this value is much improved for some states in the SPCS83) at the central meridian gives surveyors the ability to work within a specification of 1:10,000 while neglecting the impact of scale distortion.

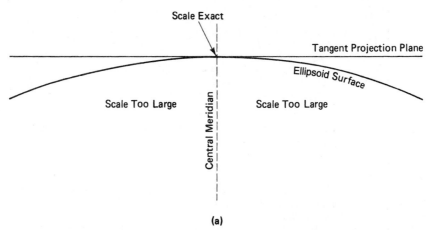

(a)

FIGURE 9.9 (a) Section view of the projection plane and Earth's surface (*tangent projection*).

(*continued*)

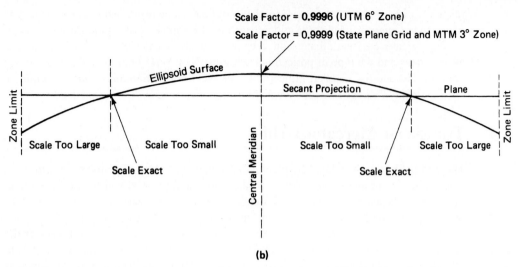

Scale Factor = **0.9996** (UTM 6° Zone)

Scale Factor = **0.9999** (State Plane Grid and MTM 3° Zone)

FIGURE 9.9 (*continued*)　(b) Section view of the projection plane and the Earth's surface (*secant projection*).

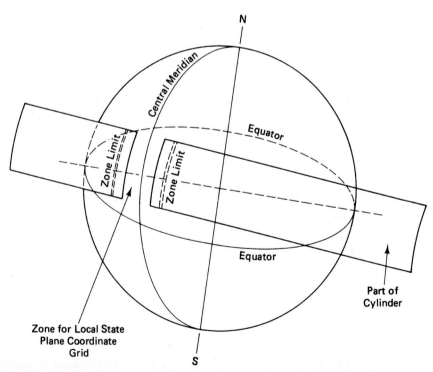

FIGURE 9.10　Transverse Mercator projection. *Secant* cylinder for state plane coordinate grids.

FIGURE 9.11 Section of the projection plane and the Earth's surface for state plane grids (*secant projection*).

9.5 UTM Grid

9.5.1 General Background

The UTM grid is much as described above except that the zones are wider—set at a width 6° of longitude. This grid is used worldwide for both military and mapping purposes. UTM coordinates are now published (in addition to SPCS and geodetic coordinates) for all NAD83 control stations. With a wider zone width than the SPCS zones, the UTM has a scale factor at the central meridian of only 0.9996. Surveyors working at specifications better than 1:2,500 must apply scale factors in their computations.

UTM zones are numbered beginning at longitude 180° W from 1 to 60. Figure 9.12(a) shows that U.S. territories range from zone 1 to zone 20 and that Canada's territory ranges from zone 7 to zone 22. The central meridian of each zone is assigned a false easting of 500,000 m, and the northerly is based on a value of 0 m at the equator.

CHARACTERISTICS OF THE UTM GRID SYSTEM

1. Zone is 6° wide (zone overlap of 0°30′; Table 9.7).
2. Latitude of the origin is the equator, 0°.
3. Easting value of each central meridian = 500,000.000 m.
4. Northing value of the equator = 0.000 m (10,000,000.000 m in the southern hemisphere).

FIGURE 9.12 (a) Universal Transverse Mercator grid zone numbering system.

(*continued*)

5. Scale factor at the central meridian is 0.9996 (i.e., 1/2,500).
6. Zone numbering commences with one in the zone 180° W to 174° W and increases eastward to zone 60 at the zone 174° E to 180° E [Figure 9.12(a)].
7. Projection limits of latitude 80° S to 80° N.

See Figure 9.13 for a cross section of a 6° zone (UTM).

9.5.2 Modified Transverse Mercator Grid System

Some regions and agencies outside the United States have adopted a modified TM (MTM) system. The modified projection is based on 3° wide zones instead of 6° wide zones. By narrowing the zone width, the scale factor at the central meridian is improved from 0.9996 (1/2,500) to 0.9999 (1/10,000), the same as for the SPCS grids. The improved scale factor permits surveyors to work at moderate levels of accuracy without having to account for projection corrections. The zone width of 3° (about 152 mi wide at latitude 43°) compares very closely with the 158-mi-wide zones used in the United States for TM and Lambert projections in the state plane coordinate system.

FIGURE 9.12 (*continued*) (b) Basic plan of the 100,000-m square identification of the United States National Grid (USNG).

(*continued*)

CHARACTERISTICS OF THE 3° ZONE

1. Zone is 3° wide.
2. Latitude of origin is the equator, 0°.
3. Easting value of the central meridian, for example, 1,000,000.000 ft or 304,800.000 m, is set by the agency.
4. Northing value of the equator is 0.000 ft or m.
5. Scale factor at the central meridian is 0.9999 (i.e., 1/10,000).

Keep in mind that narrow grid zones (1:10,000) permit the surveyor to ignore only corrections for scale and that other corrections to field measurements, such as for elevation, temperature, sag, etc., and the balancing of errors are still routinely required. See Figures 9.13 and 9.14 for cross sections of the UTM and MTM projection planes.

FIGURE 9.12 (*continued*)   (c) Organization of the USNG 100,000-m grid squares.

Table 9.7 UTM ZONE WIDTH

North Latitude	Width (km)
42°00′	497.11827
43°00′	489.25961
44°00′	481.25105
45°00′	473.09497
46°00′	464.79382
47°00′	456.35005
48°00′	447.76621
49°00′	439.04485
50°00′	430.18862

Source: Ontario Geographical Referencing Grid, Ministry of Natural Resources, Ontario, Canada.

FIGURE 9.13 Cross section of a 6° zone (UTM).

9.5.3 The United States National Grid

As noted in previous sections, points on the surface of the Earth can be identified by several types of coordinate systems, for example, the geographic coordinates of latitude and longitude, state plane coordinates, UTM coordinates, and MTM coordinates. Points on the Earth's surface in the United States can be identified (georeferenced) by using the USNG; the USNG is an expansion of the long-established MGRS, which is used in many countries. The need for a simpler georeferencing system became apparent with the advent of 911 emergency procedures. A GPS-equipped cell phone (or handheld GPS receiver) can display location information in different coordinate systems such as latitude and longitude, UTM coordinates, USNG coordinates, etc. Many think that the USNG is easier for the general population to comprehend and that it could be a good choice when a standard grid is selected for nationwide use.

FIGURE 9.14 Section of the projection plane for the modified Transverse Mercator (3°) grid and the Earth's surface (secant projection).

Based on the framework of the worldwide UTM coordinate system, USNG is an alphanumeric reference grid that includes three levels of identity. It covers the Earth's surface from 80° south to 84° north of the equator. The first level of location precision is denoted by the UTM zone number and the latitude band letter, and is known as the *grid zone designation* (GZD). It usually covers an area of 6° in an east/west direction and 8° in a north/south direction. UTM zones, each covering 6° of longitude, are numbered eastward from the 180° meridian [Figure 9.12(a)]. For example, the state of Florida is in zone 17. In North America, the zones in the conterminous United States run from zone 10 (meridian 126° W) eastward to zone 20 (meridian 60° W), and the zones in Canada run from zone 7 (meridian 144° W) eastward to zone 22 (meridian 48° W).

Latitude bands, for the most part, cover 8° of latitude (the exception is band X, which covers from 72° north to 84° north) and are identified by letters. In the northern hemisphere, latitude band coverage is as follows:

LATITUDE BAND	COVERAGE
N	0° N to 8° N
P	8° N to 16° N
Q	16° N to 24° N
R	24° N to 32° N
S	32° N to 40° N
T	40° N to 48° N
U	48° N to 56° N
V	56° N to 64° N
W	64° N to 72° N
X	72° N to 84° N

Note that the letters O, Y, and Z are not used for designating a latitude band. In the conterminous United States, latitude band letters run northerly from letter R (latitude 24° N) in the southern United States to letter U (latitude 56° N) for the northern states. The latitude bands covering Canada run from the letter T (latitude 40° N) in southern Ontario and Quebec up to letter W (latitude 72° N) for the rest of the country. Refer to Figure 9.12(a) to see that the GZD for the state of Florida is 17R.

The second level of location precision is a 100,000-m^2 designation. This designation is given by two unique letters that repeat every three UTM zones (east/west) and every 2,000,000 m north of the equator; thus, there is little opportunity for mistaken identification. These 100,000-m^2 identifiers are defined in the document *United States National Grid*, Standards Working Group, Federal Geographic Data Committee, December 2001, available at http://www.fgdc.gov/standards/status/usng.html. See Figure 9.12(b) and 9.12(c). Note that the northerly progression of letters in the first column (180° meridian) begins at AA at the equator and progresses northerly for twenty bands (2,000,000 m) to AV (letters I, O, X, W, Y, and Z are not used). They commence again at AA and continue on northerly. Also note that in the easterly progression of letters, at the equator, the letters progress easterly from AA (at 180° meridian) through twenty-four squares to AZ (letters I and O are not used). In each zone, the most westerly and easterly columns of "squares" become progressively narrower than 100,000 m as the meridians converge northerly. Just as with the UTM, the false northing is 0.00 m at the equator, and the false eastings are set at 500,000 m at the central meridian of each zone.

The third level of location precision is given by coordinates unique to a specific 100,000-m^2 grid. The coordinates are an even number of digits ranging from 2 to 10. The coordinates are written in a string, with no space between easting and northing values (easting is always listed first). These grid coordinates follow the GZD and the 100,000-m^2 identification letters in the string identification. For example, the *United States National Grid* (page 8) shows the following coordinates:

- 18SUJ20 locates a point with 10-km precision (18 S is the GZD and UJ is the 100,000-m^2 identification, 18 is the UTM zone extending from longitude 78° W to 72° W, and band S extends from 32° N to 40° N).
- 18SUJ2306 locates a point with 1-km precision. (The first half of the grid numbers is the grid easting and the second half is the grid northing—i.e., 23 km east, 06 km north.)
- 18SUJ234064 locates a point with 100-m precision.
- 18SUJ23480647 locates a point with 10-m precision.
- 18SUJ2348306479 locates a point with 1-m precision (23,483 m east and 6,479 m north, measured from the southwest corner of square UJ, in the S band and in UTM zone 18).

The NGS toolkit contains interactive software to convert UTM and latitude/longitude to USNG, and vice versa; see http://www.ngs.noaa.gov/Tools/usng.html.

9.6   Use of Grid Coordinates

9.6.1   Grid/Ground Distance Relationships: Elevation and Scale Factors

When local surveys (traverse or trilateration) are tied into coordinate grids, corrections must be provided so that

1. Grid and ground distances can be reconciled by applying elevation and scale factors.
2. Grid and geodetic directions can be reconciled by applying convergence corrections.

9.6.1.1   Elevation Factor.   Figures 9.14 and 9.15 show the relationship among ground distances, sea-level distances, and grid distances. A distance measured on the

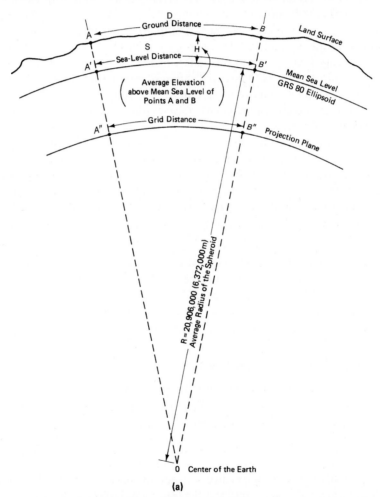

(a)

FIGURE 9.15   (a) General case: relationship of ground distances to sea-level distances and grid distances.

(continued)

Elevation Factor

$$\frac{S}{D} = \frac{R}{R + h}$$

$$S = D\left(\frac{R}{R + h}\right)$$

$$h = N + H$$

$$S = D\left(\frac{R}{R + N + H}\right)$$

Where S = Geodetic Distance
D = Horizontal Distance
H = Mean Elevation
N = Mean Geoid Height
R = Mean Radius of Earth
(6,372,000 m, or
20,906,000 ft)

(b)

FIGURE 9.15 (*continued*)   (b) Impact of geoid separation on elevation factor determination. Used only on very precise surveys.

Earth's surface must first be reduced for equivalency at sea level, and then it must be further reduced (in Figure 9.14) for equivalency on the projection plane. The first reduction involves multiplication by an **elevation factor** (sea-level factor); the second reduction (adjustment) involves multiplication by the **scale factor**.

The elevation (sea-level) factor can be determined by establishing a ratio, as is illustrated in Figures 9.15(a) and 9.16:

$$\text{Elevation factor} = \frac{\text{sea-level distance}}{\text{ground distance}} = \frac{R}{R + H} \tag{9.1}$$

where R is the average radius of the Earth (average radius of sea-level surface = 20,906,000 ft or 6,372,000 m) and H is the elevation above mean sea level. For example, at 500 ft, the elevation factor would be

$$\frac{20,906,000}{20,906,500} = 0.999976$$

and a ground distance of 800.00 ft at an average elevation of 500 ft would become 800 × 0.999976 = 799.98 at sea level.

Note: Figure 9.15(b) shows the case (encountered in very precise surveys) where the geoid separation (N) must also be considered. Geoid separation (also known as geoid height and geoid undulation) is the height difference between the sea-level surface and the

(a)

For example: 1,000.00 × 0.9995530 = 999.553 m

(b)

FIGURE 9.16 Conversion of a ground distance to a grid distance using the elevation factor and the scale factor. (a) SPCS83 grid. (b) Universal Transverse Mercator (UTM) grid, 6° zone.

ellipsoid surface. NOAA Manual NOS NGS5, *State Plane Coordinate System of 1983*, notes, for example, that a geoid height of -30 m (in the conterminous United States, the ellipsoid is above the geoid) systematically affects reduced distances by -4.8 ppm (1:208,000), which is certainly not a factor in any but the most precise surveys. See also Section 8.13.

9.6.1.2 Scale Factor.

For state plane projections, the computer solution gives scale factors for positions of latitude difference (Lambert projection) or for distances east or west of the central meridian (TM projections). By way of illustration, scale factors for the TM projections may also be computed by the following equation:

$$M_p = M_0 (1 + x^2/2R^2) \tag{9.2}$$

where M_p = the scale factor at the survey station
$\quad\quad M_0$ = the scale factor at the central meridian (CM)
$\quad\quad\quad x$ = the east/west distance of the survey station from the central meridian
$\quad\quad\quad R$ = the average radius of the spheroid.
$x^2/2R^2$ can be expressed in feet, meters, miles, or kilometers.

For example, survey stations 12,000 ft from a central meridian, and having a scale factor of 0.9999, have the scale factor determined as follows:

$$M_p = 0.9999 \left(1 + \frac{12,000^2}{2 \times 20,906,000^2} \right) = 0.9999002$$

9.6.1.3 Combined Factor.

When the elevation factor is multiplied by the scale factor, the result is known as the combined factor. This relationship is expressed in the following equation:

$$\text{Ground distance} \times \text{combined factor} = \text{grid distance} \tag{9.3}$$

Equation 9.3 can also be expressed as follows:

$$\frac{\text{grid distance}}{\text{combined factor}} = \text{ground distance}$$

In practice, it is seldom necessary to use Equations 9.1 and 9.2 because computer programs are now routinely used for computations in all state plane grids and the UTM grid. Computations were previously based on data from tables and graphs (Figure 9.17 and Tables 9.8 and 9.9).

■ **EXAMPLE 9.3**
Using Table 9.8 (MTM projection), determine the combined scale and elevation factor (combined factor) of a point 125,000 ft from the central meridian (scale factor = 0.9999) and at an elevation of 600 ft above mean sea level.

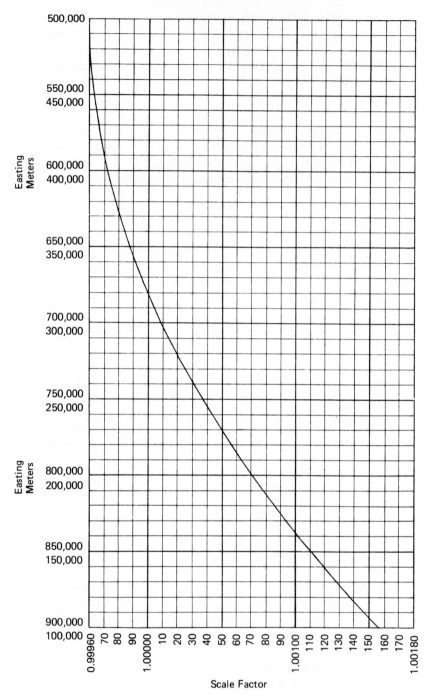

FIGURE 9.17 Universal Transverse Mercator scale factors. (Courtesy of U.S. Department of the Army TM5-241-4/1)

Table 9.8 3° MTM COMBINED GRID FACTOR BASED ON CENTRAL SCALE FACTOR OF 0.9999 FOR THE MODIFIED TRANSVERSE MERCATOR PROJECTION*

Elevation (ft)	Distance from Central Meridian (Thousands of Feet)												
	0	50	100	150	200	250	300	350	400	450	500	550	600
0	0.999900	0.999903	0.999911	0.999926	0.999946	0.999971	1.000003	1.000040	1.000083	1.000131	1.000186	1.000245	1.000311
250	0.999888	0.999891	0.999899	0.999914	0.999934	0.999959	0.999991	1.000028	1.000071	1.000119	1.000174	1.000234	1.000299
500	0.999876	0.999879	0.999888	0.999902	0.999922	0.999947	0.999979	1.000016	1.000059	1.000107	1.000162	1.000222	1.000287
750	0.999864	0.999867	0.999876	0.999890	0.999910	0.999936	0.999967	1.000004	1.000047	1.000095	1.000150	1.000210	1.000275
1,000	0.999852	0.999855	0.999864	0.999878	0.999898	0.999924	0.999955	0.999992	1.000035	1.000083	1.000138	1.000198	1.000263
1,250	0.999840	0.999843	0.999852	0.999864	0.999886	0.999912	0.999943	0.999980	1.000023	1.000072	1.000126	1.000186	1.000251
1,500	0.999828	0.999831	0.999840	0.999854	0.999874	0.999900	0.999931	0.999968	1.000011	1.000060	1.000114	1.000174	1.000239
1,750	0.999816	0.999819	0.999828	0.999842	0.999862	0.999888	0.999919	0.999956	0.999999	1.000048	1.000102	1.000162	1.000227
2,000	0.999804	0.999807	0.999816	0.999830	0.999850	0.999876	0.999907	0.999944	0.999987	1.000036	1.000090	1.000150	1.000216
2,250	0.999792	0.999795	0.999804	0.999818	0.999838	0.999864	0.999895	0.999932	0.999975	1.000024	1.000078	1.000138	1.000204
2,500	0.999781	0.999784	0.999792	0.999806	0.999626	0.999852	0.999883	0.999920	0.999963	1.000012	1.000066	1.000126	1.000192
2,750	0.999796	0.999771	0.999780	0.999794	0.999814	0.999840	0.999871	0.999908	0.999951	1.000000	1.000054	1.000114	1.000180

*Ground distance × combined factor = grid distance.

Source: Adapted from the "Horizontal Control Survey Precis," Ministry of Transportation and Communications, Ottawa, Canada, 1974.

Table 9.9 COMBINED SCALE AND ELEVATION FACTORS: UTM

Distance from CM (km)	Elevation Above Mean Sea Level (m)										
	0	100	200	300	400	500	600	700	800	900	1,000
0	0.999600	0.999584	0.999569	0.999553	0.999537	0.999522	0.999506	0.999490	0.999475	0.999459	0.999443
10	0.999601	0.999586	0.999570	0.999554	0.999539	0.999523	0.999507	0.999492	0.999476	0.999460	0.999445
20	0.999605	0.999589	0.999574	0.999558	0.999542	0.999527	0.999511	0.999495	0.999480	0.999464	0.999448
30	0.999611	0.999595	0.999580	0.999564	0.999548	0.999533	0.999517	0.999501	0.999486	0.999470	0.999454
40	0.999620	0.999604	0.999588	0.999573	0.999557	0.999541	0.999526	0.999510	0.999494	0.999479	0.999463
50	0.999631	0.999615	0.999599	0.999584	0.999568	0.999552	0.999537	0.999521	0.999505	0.999490	0.999474
60	0.999644	0.999629	0.999613	0.999597	0.999582	0.999566	0.999550	0.999535	0.999519	0.999503	0.999488
70	0.999660	0.999645	0.999629	0.999613	0.999598	0.999582	0.999566	0.999551	0.999535	0.999519	0.999504
80	0.999679	0.999663	0.999647	0.999632	0.999616	0.999600	0.999585	0.999569	0.999553	0.999538	0.999522
90	0.999700	0.999684	0.999668	0.999653	0.999637	0.999621	0.999606	0.999590	0.999574	0.999559	0.999543
100	0.999723	0.999707	0.999692	0.999676	0.999660	0.999645	0.999629	0.999613	0.999598	0.999582	0.999566
110	0.999749	0.999733	0.999717	0.999702	0.999686	0.999670	0.999655	0.999639	0.999623	0.999608	0.999592
120	0.999777	0.999761	0.999746	0.999730	0.999714	0.999699	0.999683	0.999667	0.999652	0.999636	0.999620
130	0.999808	0.999792	0.999777	0.999761	0.999745	0.999730	0.999714	0.999698	0.999683	0.999667	0.999651
140	0.999841	0.999825	0.999810	0.999794	0.999778	0.999763	0.999747	0.999731	0.999716	0.999700	0.999684
150	0.999877	0.999861	0.999845	0.999830	0.999814	0.999798	0.999783	0.999767	0.999751	0.999736	0.999720
160	0.999915	0.999899	0.999884	0.999868	0.999852	0.999837	0.999821	0.999805	0.999790	0.999774	0.999758
170	0.999955	0.999940	0.999924	0.999908	0.999893	0.999877	0.999861	0.999846	0.999830	0.999814	0.999799
180	0.999999	0.999983	0.999967	0.999952	0.999936	0.999920	0.999905	0.999889	0.999873	0.999858	0.999842
190	1.000044	0.999983	1.000013	0.999997	0.999981	0.999966	0.999950	0.999934	0.999919	0.999903	0.999887
200	1.000092	1.000028	1.000061	1.000045	1.000029	1.000014	0.999998	0.999982	0.999967	0.999951	0.999935
210	1.000142	1.000076	1.000111	1.000095	1.000080	1.000064	1.000048	1.000033	1.000017	1.000001	0.999986
220	1.000195	1.000127	1.000164	1.000148	1.000133	1.000117	1.000101	1.000086	1.000070	1.000054	1.000039
230	1.000251	1.000180	1.000219	1.000204	1.000188	1.000172	1.000157	1.000141	1.000125	1.000110	1.000094
240	1.000309	1.000235	1.000277	1.000262	1.000246	1.000230	1.000215	1.000199	1.000183	1.000168	1.000152
250	1.000369	1.000293	1.000338	1.000322	1.000306	1.000290	1.000275	1.000259	1.000243	1.000228	1.000212

Solution

Elevation	Distance from Central Meridian (Thousands of Feet)		125 (Interpolated)
	100	150	
500	0.999888	0.999902	0.999895
750	0.999876	0.999890	0.999883
			0.000012

To determine the combined factor for a point 125,000 ft from the central meridian and at an elevation of 600 ft, a solution involving double interpolation must be used. We must interpolate between the combined values for 500 ft and for 750 ft elevation, and between combined values for 100,000 ft and for 150,000 ft from the central meridian. First, the combined value for 125,000 ft from the central meridian can be interpolated simply by averaging the values for 100,000 and 150,000. Second, the value for 600 ft can be determined as follows (from Table 9.8, for 600 ft):

$$\frac{100}{250} \times 12 = 5$$

$$\text{Combined factor} = 0.999895$$
$$-0.000005$$
$$= 0.999890$$

For important survey lines, grid factors can be determined for both ends and then averaged. For lines longer than 5 mi, intermediate computations are required to maintain high precision.

9.6.2 Grid/Geodetic Azimuth Relationships

9.6.2.1 Convergence. In plane grids, the difference between grid north and geodetic north is called convergence (also called the mapping angle). In the SPCS27 TM grid, convergence was denoted by $\Delta\alpha''$; in the Lambert grid, it was denoted as θ. In SPCS83, convergence (in both projections) is denoted by γ (gamma). On a plane grid, grid north and geodetic north coincide only at the central meridian. As you work farther east or west of the central meridian, convergence becomes more pronounced.

Using SPCS83 symbols, approximate methods can be determined as follows:

$$\gamma'' = \Delta\lambda'' \sin \varphi P \tag{9.4a}$$

where $\Delta\lambda''$ = the difference in longitude, in seconds, between the central meridian and point P
φP = the latitude of point P

When long sights (>5 mi) are taken, a second term (present in the interactive Internet programs used in Examples 9.1 and 9.2 and in all precise computations) is required to maintain directional accuracy. See also Section 9.6.2.2.

When the direction of a line from P_1 to P_2 is being considered, the expression becomes

$$\gamma'' = \Delta\lambda'' \left(\frac{\sin(\varphi P_1 + \varphi P_2)}{2} \right) \tag{9.4b}$$

If the distance from the central meridian is known, the expression can be written as follows:

$$\gamma'' = 32.370 \, dk \tan\varphi \tag{9.5}$$

or

$$\gamma'' = 52.09 \, d \tan\varphi \tag{9.6}$$

where γ = convergence angle, in seconds
  d = departure distance from the central meridian, in miles (dk is the same distance, in kilometers)
  φ = average latitude of the line.

9.6.2.2 Corrections to Convergence.
When high precision and/or long distances are involved, there is a second-term correction required for convergence. This term δ refers to $t - T$ (the grid azimuth − the projected geodetic azimuth) and results from the fact that the projection of the geodetic azimuth δ onto the grid is not the grid azimuth but the projected geodetic azimuth, symbolized as T. Figure 9.18 (which comes from Section 2.5 of the *State Plane Coordinate System of 1983*) shows the relationships between geodetic and grid azimuths.

9.7 Illustrative Examples

These approximate methods are included only to broaden your comprehension in this area. For current precise solution techniques, see NOAA Manual NOS NGS 5, *State Plane Coordinate System of 1983*, or the geodetic toolkit discussed in Section 9.2.

■ EXAMPLE 9.4
You are given the Transverse Mercator coordinate grid of two horizontal control monuments and their elevations (see Figure 9.19 for additional given data). Compute the ground distance and geodetic direction between them.

Station	Elevation	Northing	Easting
Monument 870	595 ft	15,912,789.795 ft	1,039,448.609 ft
Monument 854	590 ft	15,913,044.956 ft	1,040,367.657 ft

Scale factor at CM = 0.9999.

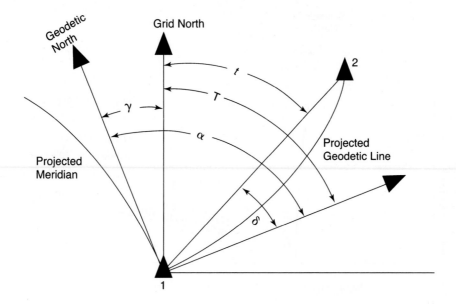

$$t = \alpha - \gamma + \delta$$

α = Geodetic Azimuth Reckoned from North

T = Projected Geodetic Azimuth

t = Grid Azimuth Reckoned from North

γ = Convergence Angle (Mapping Angle)

$\delta = t - T$ = Second Term Correction = Arc-to-Chord Correction

FIGURE 9.18 Relationships among geodetic and grid azimuths. (From the NOAA Manual NOS NGS 5, *State Plane Coordinate System of 1983*, Section 2.5)

Solution

By subtraction of coordinate distances, $\Delta N = 255.161$ ft, $\Delta E = 919.048$ ft. The solution is obtained as follows:

1. Grid distance 870 to 854:

$$\text{Distance} = \sqrt{255.161^2 + 919.048^2} = 953.811 \text{ ft}$$

2. Grid bearing:

$$\text{tan bearing} = \frac{\Delta E}{\Delta N} = \frac{919.048}{255.161} = 3.6018357$$

$$\text{grid bearing} = 74.48\ 342°$$

$$= \text{N } 74° \ 29'00'' \text{ E}$$

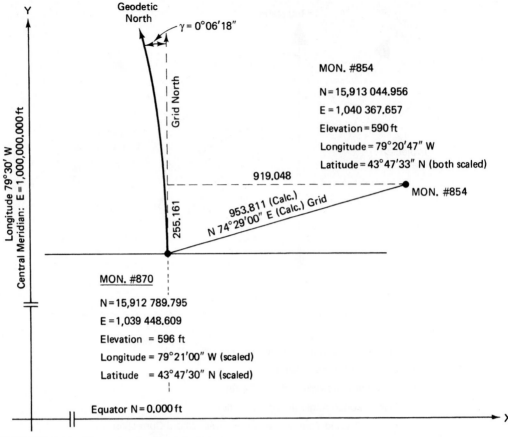

Y

Geodetic North

γ = 0°06′18″

Grid North

Longitude 79°30′ W
Central Meridian: E = 1,000,000.000 ft

MON. #854

N = 15,913 044.956

E = 1,040 367.657

Elevation = 590 ft

Longitude = 79°20′47″ W

Latitude = 43°47′33″ N (both scaled)

919.048

MON. #854

255.161

953.811 (Calc.)

N 74°29′00″ E (Calc.) Grid

MON. #870

N = 15,912 789.795

E = 1,039 448.609

Elevation = 596 ft

Longitude = 79°21′00″ W (scaled)

Latitude = 43°47′30″ N (scaled)

Equator N = 0.000 ft

X

FIGURE 9.19   Illustration for Example 9.4.

3. Convergence: use method (a) or (b). Average latitude = 43°47′31″; average longitude = 79°20′54″ (see Figure 9.19).

(a) We can use Equation 9.6:

$$\gamma'' = 52.09d \tan \varphi$$

$$= 52.09 \times \frac{(40,367.657 + 39,448.609)}{2 \times 5,280} \tan 43°47'31''$$

$$= 377.45''$$

$$\gamma = 0°06'17.5''$$

(b) We can use Equation 9.4:

$$\gamma'' = \Delta\lambda'' \sin \varphi P$$

$$= (79°30'' - 79°20'54'') \sin 43°47'31''$$

$$= 546'' \times \sin 43°47'31''$$

$$= 377.85''$$

$$\gamma = 0°06'17.9''$$

FIGURE 9.20   Illustration for Example 9.4.

The slight difference here (0.4″) between methods (a) and (b) reflects this approximate approach. Use a convergence of 6°18′.

Convergence, in this case, neglects the second-term correction and is computed only to the closest second of arc. (*Note:* The average latitude need not have been computed because the latitude range, 03″, in this case was insignificant.)

Refer to Figure 9.20:

$$\text{Grid bearing} = \text{N } 74°29'00'' \text{ E}$$

$$+ \text{ convergence} = 0°06'18''$$

$$\text{geodetic bearing} = \text{N } 74°35'18'' \text{ E}$$

4. Scale factor:

$$\text{Scale factor at CM, } M_0 = 0.9999$$

$$\text{Distance}(x) \text{ from CM} = \frac{40{,}368 + 39{,}449}{2} = 39{,}908 \text{ ft}$$

From Equation 9.2, we can calculate the scale factor at midpoint 870 to 854:

$$M_p = M_0 \left(1 + \frac{x^2}{2R^2} \right)$$

$$= 0.9999 \left(1 + \frac{39{,}908^2}{2 \times 20{,}906{,}000^2} \right)$$

$$= 9999018$$

5. We use Equation 9.1 for the elevation factor:

$$\text{Elevation factor} = \frac{\text{sea-level distance}}{\text{ground distance}} = \frac{R}{R + H}$$

$$= \frac{20{,}906{,}000}{20{,}906{,}000\,+\,593} = 0.999716$$

593 ft is the midpoint (average) elevation.

6. Combined factor: Use method (a), which is a computation involving Equation 9.5, or method (b).

    (a) Combined factor = scale factor $\times$ elevation factor

$$= 0.9999018 \times 0.9999716$$

$$= 0.9998734$$

    (b) The combined factor can also be determined through double interpolation of Table 9.8. The following values are taken from Table 9.8. The required elevation is 593 ft at 39,900 ft from the CM.

	Distance from Central Meridian (Thousands of Feet)		
Elevation, ft	0	50	39.9 (Interpolated)
500	0.999876	0.999879	0.999878
593			
750	0.999864	0.999867	0.999866

After first interpolating the values at 0 and 50 for 39,900 ft from the CM, it is a simple matter to interpolate for the elevation of 593 ft:

$$0.999878 - (0.000012) \times \frac{93}{250} = 0.999873$$

Thus, the combined factor at 39,900 ft from the CM at an elevation of 593 ft is 0.999873.

7. For ground distance, we can use the relationship given previously in Equation 9.3:

$$\text{Ground distance} \times \text{combined factor} = \text{grid distance}$$

or

$$\text{Ground distance} = \frac{\text{grid distance}}{\text{combined factor}}$$

In this example,

$$\text{Ground distance (870 to 854)} = \frac{953.811}{0.9998734} = 953.93 \text{ ft}$$

■ **EXAMPLE 9.5**

You are given the coordinates (on the UTM 6° coordinate grid, based on the Clarke 1866 ellipsoid) of two horizontal control monuments (Mon. 113 and Mon. 115) and their elevations. Compute the ground distance and geodetic direction between them [Figure 9.21(a)].

(a)

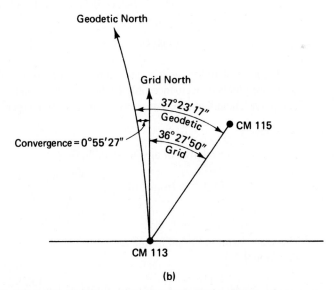

(b)

FIGURE 9.21 Illustration for Example 9.5. (a) Grid. (b) Application of convergence.

Station	Elevation	Northing	Easting
113	181.926 m	4,849,872.066 m	632,885.760
115	178.444 m	4,849,988.216 m	632,971.593

Zone 17 UTM; CM at 81° longitude west [Figure 9.12(a)]
Scale factor at CM = 0.9996
ϕ (lat.) = 43°47′33″ [scaled from topographic map for midpoint of line joining Mon. 113 and Mon. 115, or as shown in Example 9.2(b).]
λ (long.) = 79°20′52″

Solution
Analysis of the coordinates of Stations 113 and 115 gives the coordinate distances of ΔN = 116.150 m, ΔE = 85.833 m.

1. Grid distance from Mon. 113 to Mon. 115:

$$\text{Distance} = \sqrt{116.150^2 + 85.833^2} = 144.423 \text{ m}$$

2. Grid bearing:

$$\tan \text{bearing} = \frac{\Delta E}{\Delta N} = \frac{85.833}{116.150}$$

$$\text{Bearing} = 36.463811°$$

$$\text{Grid bearing} = \text{N } 36°27″50″ \text{ E}$$

3. From Equation 9.4, we can calculate the convergence:

$$\gamma'' = \Delta\lambda'' \sin \varphi \, P$$
$$= (81° - 79°20′52″) \sin 43°47′33″$$
$$= 4116″$$
$$\gamma = 1°08′36″$$

See Figure 9.21(b) for application of convergence. As we saw in Example 9.4, this technique yields convergence only to the closest second of arc. For more precise techniques, including second-term correction for convergence, see the NGS toolkit.

4. Scale factor:

$$\text{Scale factor at CM} = 0.9996$$

$$\text{Distance from CM} = \frac{132,885.760 + 132,971.593}{2}$$

$$= 132,928.677 \text{ m, or } 132.929 \text{ km}$$

The scale factor at midpoint line from Mon. 113 to Mon. 115 is computed from Equation 9.2:

$$M_p = M_0 \left(\frac{1 + x^2}{2R^2} \right) \quad M_p = 0.9996 \left(1 + \frac{132.929^2}{2 \times 6372^2} \right) = 0.999818$$

The average radius of the sea-level surface = 20,906,000 ft, or 6,372,000 m.

5. The elevation factor is calculated using Equation 9.1:

$$\text{Elevation factor} = \frac{\text{sea-level distance}}{\text{ground distance}} = \frac{R}{R + H}$$

$$= \frac{6,372}{6,372.00 + 0.180} = 0.999972$$

0.180 is the midpoint elevation divided by 1,000.

6. Combined factor:

    (a) Combined factor = elevation factor $\times$ scale factor

$$= 0.999972 \times 0.999818 = 0.999790$$

or

    (b) Use Table 9.9:

	Distance from CM (km)		
Elevation	130	140	132.9 (Interpolated)
100	0.999792	0.999825	0.999802
200	0.999777	0.999810	0.999787

The last computation is the interpolation for the elevation value of 180 m; that is:

$$0.999802 - \left(\frac{80}{100} \times 0.000015 \right) = 0.999790$$

7. Ground distance:

$$\text{Ground distance} = \frac{\text{grid distance}}{\text{combined factor}}$$

In this example,

$$\text{Ground distance from Mon. 113 to Mon. 115} = \frac{144.423}{0.999790} = 144.453 \text{ m}$$

9.8 Horizontal Control Techniques

Typically, the highest-order control is established by federal agencies, the secondary control is established by state or provincial agencies, and the lower-order control is established by municipal agencies or large-scale engineering works' surveyors. Sometimes the federal agency establishes all three orders of control when requested to do so by the state, province, or municipality.

In triangulation surveys, a great deal of attention was paid to the geometric strength of figure of each control configuration. Generally, an equilateral triangle is considered strong, whereas triangles with small (less than 10°) angles are considered relatively weak. Trigonometric functions vary in precision as the angle varies in magnitude. The sines of small angles (near 0°), the cosines of large angles (near 90°), and the tangents of both small (0°)

and large (90°) angles are all relatively imprecise. That is, there are relatively large changes in the values of the trigonometric functions that result from relatively small changes in angular values. For example, the angular error of 5″ in the sine of 10° is 1/7,300, whereas the angular error of 5″ in the sine of 20° is 1/15,000, and the angular error of 5″ in the sine of 80° is 1/234,000 (see Example 9.6).

You can see that if sine or cosine functions are used in triangulation to calculate the triangle side distances, care must be exercised to ensure that the trigonometric function itself is *not* contributing to the solution errors more significantly than the specified surveying error limits. When all angles and distances are measured for each triangle, the redundant measurements ensure an accurate solution, and the configuration strength of figure becomes somewhat less important. Given the opportunity, however, most surveyors still prefer to use well-balanced triangles and to avoid using the sine and tangent of small angles and the cosine and tangent of large angles to compute control distances. This concept of strength of figure helps to explain why GPS measurements are more precise when the observed satellites are spread across the visible sky instead of being bunched together in one portion of the sky.

■ **EXAMPLE 9.6** *Effect of the Angle Magnitude on the Accuracy of Computed Distances*

(a) Consider the right-angle triangle in Figure 9.22, with a hypotenuse 1,000.00 ft long. Use various values for θ to investigate the effect of 05″ angular errors.

FIGURE 9.22

1. $\theta = 10°$ $X = 173.64818$ ft
 $\theta = 10°00'05''$ $X = 173.67205$ ft
 Difference = 0.02387 in 173.65 ft, an accuracy of 1/7,300.

2. $\theta = 20°$ $X = 342.02014$ ft
 $\theta = 20°00'05''$ $X = 342.04292$ ft
 Difference = 0.022782 in 342.02 ft, an accuracy of 1/15,000.

3. $\theta = 80°$ $X = 984.80775$ ft
 $\theta = 80°00'05''$ $X = 984.81196$ ft
 Difference = 0.00421 in 984.81 ft, an accuracy of 1/234,000.

(b) Consider the right triangle in Figure 9.23, with the adjacent side 1,000.00 ft long. Use various values for θ to investigate the effect of 05″ angular errors.

FIGURE 9.23

1. $\theta = 10°$ $X = 176.32698$ ft
   $\theta = 10°00'05''$ $X = 176.35198$ ft
   Difference = 0.025 accuracy of 1/7,100.

2. $\theta = 45°$ $X = 1,000.00$ ft
   $\theta = 45°00'05''$ $X = 1,000.0485$ ft
   Difference = 0.0485, an accuracy of 1/20,600.

3. $\theta = 80°$ $X = 5,671.2818$ ft
   $\theta = 80°00'05''$ $X = 5,672.0858$ ft
   Difference = 0.804, an accuracy of 1/7,100.

4. In part (b)3, if the angle can be determined to the closest second, the accuracy would be as follows:
   $\theta = 80°$ $X = 5,671.2818$ ft
   $\theta = 80°00'01''$ $X = 5,671.4426$ ft
   Difference = 0.1608, an accuracy of 1/35,270.

Example 9.6 illustrates that the surveyor should avoid using weak (relatively small) angles in distance computations. If weak angles must be used, they should be measured more precisely than would normally be required. Also illustrated in the example is the need for the surveyor to analyze the proposed control survey configuration beforehand to determine optimal field techniques and attendant precisions.

9.9   Project Control

9.9.1   General Background

Project control begins with either a boundary survey (e.g., for large housing projects) or an all-inclusive peripheral survey (e.g., for construction sites). If possible, the boundary or site peripheral survey is tied into state or provincial grid control monuments or is located precisely using appropriate GPS techniques so that references can be made to the state or provincial coordinate grid system. The peripheral survey is densified with judiciously placed control stations over the entire site. The survey data for all control points are entered into the computer for accuracy verification, error adjustment, and finally for coordinate determination of all control points. All key layout points (e.g., lot corners, radius points, ¢ stations, curve points, construction points) are also coordinated using coordinate geometry computer programs. Printout sheets are used by the surveyor to lay out (using total stations) the proposed facility from coordinated control stations. The computer results give the surveyor the azimuth and distance from one, two, or perhaps three different control points to one layout point. Positioning a layout point from more than one control station provides the opportunity for an exceptional check on the accuracy of the work. When GPS is used, the surveyor first uploads the relevant stations' coordinates into the receiver-controller before going to the field so that the GPS receiver can lead the surveyor directly to the required point.

To ensure that the layout points have been accurately located (e.g., with an accuracy level of between 1/5,000 and 1/10,000), the control points themselves must be located to an even higher level of accuracy (i.e., typically better than 1/15,000). These accuracies can be achieved using GPS techniques for positions, and total stations for distances and angles. As we noted earlier, the surveyor must use "quality" geometrics, in addition to quality instrumentation, in designing the shape of the control net. A series of interconnected equilateral triangles provides the strongest control net.

When positioning control points, keep in mind the following:

1. Good visibility to other control points and an optimal number of layout points is important.

2. The visibility factor is considered not only for existing ground conditions but also for potential visibility lines during all stages of construction.

3. At least two reference ties (three is preferred) are required for each control point so that it can be reestablished if it is destroyed. Consideration must be given to the availability of features suitable for referencing (i.e., features into which nails can be driven or cut-crosses chiseled, etc.). Ideally, the three ties are each 120° apart.

4. Control points should be placed in locations that will not be affected by primary or secondary construction activity. In addition to keeping clear of the actual construction site positions, the surveyor must anticipate temporary disruptions to the terrain resulting from access roads, materials stockpiling, and so on. If possible, control points are safely located adjacent to features that will *not* be moved (e.g., electrical or communications towers; concrete walls; large, valuable trees).

5. Control points must be established on solid ground (or rock). Swampy areas or loose fill areas must be avoided.

Once the control point locations have been tentatively chosen, they are plotted so that the quality of the control net geometrics can be considered. At this stage, it may be necessary to return the field and locate additional control points to strengthen weak geometric figures. When the locations have been finalized on paper, each station is given a unique identification code number, and then the control points are set in the field. Field notes, showing reference ties to each point, are carefully taken and then field. Now the actual measurements of the distances and angles of the control net are taken. When all the field data have been collected, the closures and adjustments are computed. The coordinates of any layout points are then computed, with polar ties being generated for each layout point, from two or possibly three control stations.

Figure 9.24(a) shows a single layout point being positioned by angle only from three control sights. The three control sights can simply be referenced to the farthest of the control points themselves (e.g., angles A, B, and C). If a reference azimuth point (RAP) has been identified and coordinated in the locality, it would be preferred because it is no doubt farther away and thus capable of providing more precise sightings (e.g., angles 1, 2, and 3). RAPs are typically communications towers, church spires, or other identifiable points that can be seen from widely scattered control stations. Coordinates of RAPs are computed by turning angles to the RAP from project control monuments or preferably from state or provincial control grid monuments. Figure 9.24(b) shows a bridge layout involving

FIGURE 9.24   Examples of coordinate control for polar layout. (a) Single-point layout, located by three angles.

(continued)

azimuth and distance ties for abutment and pier locations. Note that, although the perfect case of equilateral triangles is not always present, the figures are quite strong, with redundant measurements providing accuracy verification.

Figure 9.25 illustrates a method of recording angle directions and distances to control stations with a list of derived azimuths. Station 17 can be found quickly by the surveyor from the distance and alignment ties to the hydrant, the cut-cross on the curb, and the nail in the pole. (Had station 17 been destroyed, it could have been reestablished from these and other reference ties.) The row marked "check" in Figure 9.25 indicates that the surveyor has "closed the horizon" by continuing to revolve the theodolite or total station back to the initial target point (100 in this example) and then reading the horizontal circle. An angle difference of more than 5″ between the initial reading and the check reading usually means that the series of angles in that column must be repeated.

After the design of a facility has been coordinated, polar layout coordinates can be generated for points to be laid out from selected stations. The surveyor can copy the computer data directly into the field book (Figure 9.26) for use later in the field. On large projects (expressways, dams, etc.), it is common practice to print bound volumes that

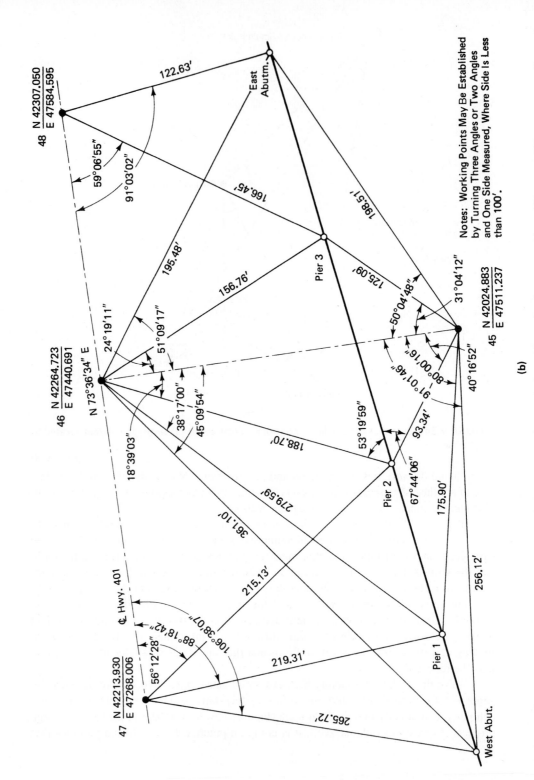

FIGURE 9.24 *(continued)* (b) Bridge layout, located by angle and distance. (Adapted from the *Construction Manual*, Ministry of Transportation, Ontario)

Notes: Working Points May Be Established by Turning Three Angles or Two Angles and One Side Measured, Where Side Is Less than 100'.

FAIRVIEW SUBDIVISION

CONTROL NET

Date APR 17, 2010 Page 52

CLEAR 23°C

INST. @ STA. 17				
DIRECTION 17–100 KNOWN +119° 39' 06"				

RICHARDSON-NOTES
DAWES-x(WILD T-2 #08)
BALOG-PRISM,

POINT	DIRECT	REVERSE	DIRECT	REVERSE	DISTANCE DIRECTION
100°	0°00'07"	180°00'17"	90°05'02"	270°04'55"	
REDUCED	0°00'00"	180°00'00"	90°00'00"	270°00'00"	0°00'00"
18.	41°45'44"	221°45'47"	131°50'28"	311°50'22"	142.188m.
REDUCED	41°45'37"	221°45'30"	" 45'26"	" 45'27"	41°45'30"
HYD.	113°47'41"	293°48'08"			2.906m
REDUCED	113°47'34"	" 47'51"			113°47'42"
13.	232°50'25"	52°50'30"	332°55'13"	142°55'11"	250.113m.
REDUCED	232°50'18"	" 50'13"	" 50'11"	" 50'16"	232°50'14"
11.	268°27'56"	88°28'02"	358°32'41"	178°32'37"	179.375m.
REDUCED	268°27'49"	" 27'45"	" 27'39"	" 27'42"	268°27'44"
8.	334°36'22"	154°36'27"	64°41'15"	244°41'07"	138.125m.
REDUCED	334°36'15"	" 36'10"	" 36'13"	" 36'12"	334°36'12"
CHECK	0°00'08"	180°00'15"	90°05'05"	270°04'52"	

LINE	AZIMUTH
STA.17 – 100	119° 39' 06" (Given)
STA.17 – STA.18	161° 24' 36"
STA.17 – HYD.	233° 26' 48"
STA.17 – STA.13	352° 29' 20"
STA.17 – STA.11	28° 06' 50"
STA.17 – STA. 8	94° 15' 18"

DISTANCE BY WILD DI4
SEE PAGE #51

FIGURE 9.25 Field notes for control point directions and distances.

include polar coordinate data for all control stations and all layout points. Modern total station and GPS practices also permit the direct uploading of the coordinates of control points and layout points to be used in layout surveys (see Chapter 5).

Figure 9.27 shows a primary control net established to provide control for a construction site. The primary control stations are tied in to a national, state, or provincial coordinate grid by a series of precise traverses or triangular networks. Points on baselines (secondary points) can be tied in to the primary control net by polar ties, intersection, or resection. The actual layout points of the structure (columns, walls, footings, etc.) are established from these secondary points. International standard ISO 4463 (from the International Organization for Standardization) points out that the accuracy of key building or structural layout points should not be influenced by possible discrepancies in the state or provincial coordinate grid. For that reason, the primary project control net is analyzed and adjusted independently of the state or provincial coordinate grid. This "free net" is tied to the state or provincial coordinate grid without becoming an integrated adjusted component of that grid. The relative positional accuracy of project layout points to each other is more important than the positional accuracy of these layout points relative to a state or provincial coordinate grid.

Sec. 9.9   Project Control

POINT	AZIMUTH	DISTANCE	*
100	122° 31' 17"		
11	202° 46' 20"		*DISTANCES SHOWN ARE GROUND DISTANCES
365	358° 47' 38"	31.727m.	
369	12° 26' 22"	50.813	
1405	49° 00' 09"	44.391	
368	91° 00' 03"	49.521	GRID FACTOR
367	104° 09' 30"	30.105	= 0.999903
534	117° 40' 41"	36.412	
536	127° 44' 04"	37.027	
482	190° 50' 07"	64.301	
483	185° 01' 58"	60.399	
484	199° 41' 51"	45.360	
485	202° 29' 29"	47.616	
486	171° 59' 20"	31.739	
487	158° 29' 00"	30.571	
488	159° 59' 04"	50.661	
489	163° 34' 24"	50.969	
537	139° 44' 43"	54.800	
539	137° 24' 57"	60.823m.	

POLAR CO-ORDINATES ABOUT STATION 12.

Party Chief _____   Party Chief ___ RICHARDSON. _____

Weather _____   Weather _____

FIGURE 9.26 Prepared polar coordinate layout notes.

9.9.2 Positional Accuracies (ISO 4463)

9.9.2.1 Primary System Control Stations.

1. Permissible deviations of the distances and angles obtained when measuring the positions of primary points, and those calculated from the adjusted coordinates of these points, shall not exceed:

$$\text{Distances: } \pm 0.75\sqrt{L}\,\text{mm}$$

$$\text{Angles: } \frac{\pm 0.045°}{\sqrt{L}}$$

or

$$\pm\frac{0.05}{\sqrt{L}}\,\text{gon}$$

where L is the distance in meters between primary stations; in the case of angles, L is the shorter side of the angle. One revolution = 360° = 400 gon (also grad—a European angular unit); 1 gon = 0.9° (exactly).

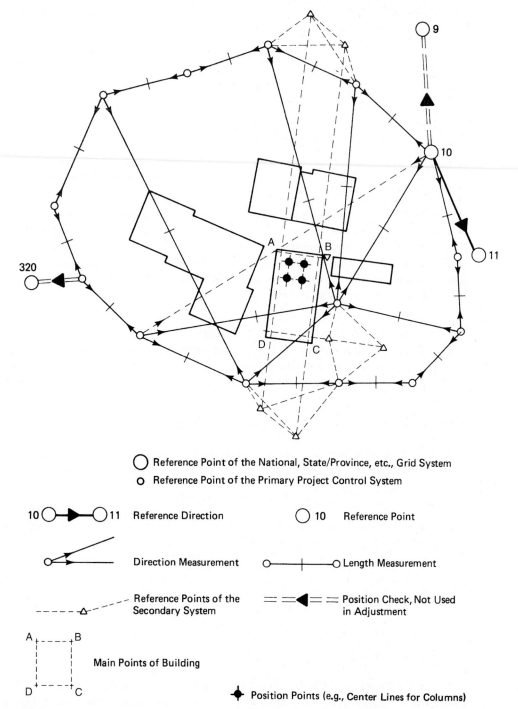

320

9

10

11

◯ Reference Point of the National, State/Province, etc., Grid System

o Reference Point of the Primary Project Control System

10 ◯━━▶━━◯ 11   Reference Direction   ◯ 10   Reference Point

Direction Measurement   o━━━┼━━━o Length Measurement

Reference Points of the
Secondary System   ══◀══ Position Check, Not Used
in Adjustment

A ┌─────┐ B
   │   │   Main Points of Building
D └─────┘ C

✦ Position Points (e.g., Center Lines for Columns)

FIGURE 9.27 Project control net. (Adapted from International Organization for Standardization [ISO], Standard 4463)

2. Permissible deviations of the distances and angles obtained when checking the positions of primary points shall not exceed:

$$\text{Distances: } \pm 2\sqrt{L}\ \text{mm}$$

$$\text{Angles: } \frac{\pm 0.135°}{\sqrt{L}}$$

or

$$\pm \frac{0.15}{\sqrt{L}}\ \text{gon}$$

where L is the distance in meters between primary stations; in the case of angles, L is the shorter side of the angle.

Angles are measured with a 1″ theodolite, with the measurements made in two sets. (Each set is formed by two observations, one on each face of the instrument; Figure 9.26.) Distances can be measured with steel tapes or EDMs, and they are measured at least twice by either method. Steel tape measurements are corrected for temperature, sag, slope, and tension. A tension device is used while taping. EDM instruments should be checked regularly against a range of known distances.

9.9.2.2 Secondary System Control Stations.

1. Secondary control stations and main layout points (e.g., ABCD, Figure 9.27) constitute the secondary system. The permissible deviations for a checked distance from a given or calculated distance between a primary control station and a secondary point shall not exceed:

$$\text{Distances: } \pm 2\sqrt{L}\ \text{mm}$$

2. The permissible deviations for a checked distance from the given or calculated distance between two secondary points in the same system shall not exceed:

$$\text{Distances: } \pm 2\sqrt{L}\ \text{mm}$$

where L is the distance in meters. For L less than 10 m, permissible deviations are ±6 mm:

$$\text{Angles: } \pm \frac{0.135°}{\sqrt{L}}$$

or

$$\pm \frac{0.15}{\sqrt{L}}\ \text{gon}$$

where L is the length in meters of the shorter side of the angle.

Angles are measured with a theodolite or total station reading to at least 1′. The measurement shall be made in at least one set (i.e., two observations, one on each face of the instrument). Distances can be measured using steel tapes or EDMs and are measured at least twice by either method. Taped distances are corrected for temperature, sag, slope, and

Table 9.10 ACCURACY REQUIREMENT CONSTANTS FOR LAYOUT SURVEYS

K	Application
10	Earthwork without any particular accuracy requirement (e.g., rough excavation, embankments)
5	Earthwork subject to accuracy requirements (e.g., roads, pipelines, structures)
2	Poured concrete structures (e.g., curbs, abutments)
1	Precast concrete structures, steel structures (e.g., bridges, buildings)

Source: Adapted from Table 8-1, ISO 4463.

tension. A tension device is to be used with the tape. EDM instruments should be checked regularly against a range of known distances.

9.9.2.3 Layout Points.

The permissible deviations of a checked distance between a secondary point and a layout point, or between two layout points, are $\pm K\sqrt{L}$ mm, where L is the specified distance in meters and K is a constant taken from Table 9.10. For L less than 5 m, the permissible deviation is $\pm 2K$ mm.

The permissible deviations for a checked angle between two lines, dependent on each other, through adjacent layout points are as follows:

$$\pm\frac{0.0675}{\sqrt{L}}K \text{ degrees}$$

or

$$\pm\frac{0.075}{\sqrt{L}}K \text{ gon}$$

where L is the length in meters of the shorter side of the angle and K is a constant from Table 9.10.

Figure 9.28 illustrates the foregoing specifications for the case involving a stakeout for a curved concrete curb. The layout point on the curve has a permissible area of uncertainty generated by ± 0.015/m due to angle uncertainties and by ± 0.013/m due to distance uncertainties.

Review Questions

9.1 What are the advantages of referencing a survey to a recognized plane grid?

9.2 Describe why the use of a plane grid distorts spatial relationships.

9.3 How can the distortions in spatial relationships that you described in Review Question 9.2 be minimized?

9.4 Describe the factors you would consider in establishing a net of control survey monuments to facilitate the design and construction of a large engineering works, for example, an airport.

9.5 Some have said that, with the advent of the global positioning system (GPS), the need for extensive ground control survey monumentation has been much reduced. Explain.

$K = 2$; from Table 9.10

Distance Factor $= \pm K \sqrt{L}$ mm $= \pm 0.013$

Angle Factor $= \dfrac{\pm 0.0675 \, K}{\sqrt{L}}$ Degrees $= \pm 0°01'17''$

Angle Factor Converted to Distance =

$X = 40 \tan 0°01'17'' = 0.015$ m

FIGURE 9.28 Accuracy analysis for a concrete curb layout point. (See ISO Standard 4463)

Problems

Problems 9.1–9.5 use the control point data shown in Table 9.11.

9.1 Draw a representative sketch of the four control points and then determine the grid distances and grid bearings of sides AB, BC, CD, and DA.

9.2 From the grid bearings computed in Problem 9.1, compute the interior angles (and their sum) of the traverse A, B, C, D, A, thus verifying the correctness of the grid bearing computations.

9.3 Determine the ground distances for the four traverse sides by applying the scale and elevation factors (i.e., grid factors). Use average latitude and longitude.

9.4 Determine the convergence correction for each traverse side and determine the geodetic bearings for each traverse side. Use average latitude and longitude.

9.5 From the geodetic bearings computed in Problem 9.4, compute the interior angles (and their sum) of the traverse A, B, C, D, A, thus verifying the correctness of the geodetic bearing computations.

Table 9.11 CONTROL POINT DATA FOR PROBLEMS 9.1–9.5

Monument	Elevation	Northing	Easting	Latitude	Longitude
A	179.832	4,850,296.103	317,104.062	43°47′33″ N	079°20′50″ W
B	181.356	4,480,218.330	316,823.936	43°47′30″ N	079°21′02″W
C	188.976	4,850,182.348	316,600.889	43°47′29″ N	079°21′12″ W
D	187.452	4,850,184.986	316,806.910	43°47′29″ N	079°21′03″ W

Average longitude = 079°21′02″ (Mon. B)

Average latitude = 43°47′30″ N (Mon. B)

Central meridian (CM) at longitude = 079°30″ W

Easting at CM = 304,800.000 m

Northing at equator = 0.000 m

Scale factor at CM = 0.9999

Data are consistent with the 3° Transverse Mercator projection, related to NAD83.

PART II
Construction
Applications

II.1   Introduction

Building on the skills developed over the first nine chapters, the topics in Part II describe how these basic skills are applied to engineering and construction surveying. Chapter 10 introduces the techniques of machine guidance and control. Also described in Chapter 10 is the topic of digital data files; these files contain the coordinated horizontal and vertical positions of existing ground (EG) points and surfaces, as well as the coordinates of proposed designed features and surfaces. Digital data files are at the heart of modern project design, and they form the cornerstone for all modern electronic surveying layout practices. They are also vital for the successful implementation of machine guidance and control practices.

Chapter 11 describes the circular, parabolic, and spiral curves used in highway and road design and layout. The remaining chapters (Chapters 12–17) describe survey practices used in highway construction, municipal street construction, pipeline and tunnel construction, culvert and bridge construction, building construction, and quantity and final surveys.

II.2   General Background

Construction surveys provide for the horizontal and vertical layout for every key component of a construction project. Only surveyors experienced in both project design and appropriate construction techniques can accomplish the layout for *line and grade*. A knowledge of related civil design is essential to interpret the design drawings effectively for layout purposes, and knowledge of construction techniques is required to ensure that the survey layout is optimal for line-and-grade transfer, construction scheduling, and ongoing payment measurements.

We have seen that data can be gathered for engineering projects (preengineering surveys) and other works in various ways. Modern practice favors total station surveys for high-density areas of limited size, and aerial imaging techniques for high-density areas covering large tracts. Global positioning system (GPS) techniques are now also being implemented successfully in areas of moderate density. The survey method chosen by a survey manager is usually influenced by the costs (per point) and the reliability of the point positioning.

In theory, GPS techniques seem to be ideal because roving receiver–equipped surveyors move quickly to establish precise locations for layout points, in which both line and grade are promptly determined and marked; however, when GPS signals are blocked by tree canopies or other obstructions, additional surveying methods must be used. Attained accuracies can be observed simply by remaining at the layout point as the position location is continuously updated.

Surveyors have found that, to utilize real-time kinematic (RTK) surveying successfully in construction surveying, much work had to be done to establish sufficient horizontal and vertical control on the project site; however, the recent increase in coverage of GPS/RTK base stations, including Real-Time Networks (RTNs), has lessened the need for as many on-site ground control stations. An RTK layout has many components that may be cause for extra vigilance. Some examples are short observation times, problems associated with radio or cellular transmissions, problems with satellite signal reception due to canopy obstructions and possibly weak constellation geometry (multi-constellation receivers can help here), instrument calibration, multipath errors, and other errors (some of which will not be evident in error displays). For these reasons, like all other layout procedures, layouts using GPS techniques must be verified.

If possible, verification can be accomplished through independent surveys; for example, check GPS surveys—based on different control stations, tape measurements, or total station sightings taken from point to point where feasible, and even by pacing. In the real world of construction works, the problems surrounding layout verification are compounded by the fact that the surveyor often doesn't have unlimited time to perform measurement checks. The contractor may actually be waiting on site to commence construction. A high level of planning and a rigid and systematic method (proven successful in past projects) of performing the layout survey are recommended.

Unlike other forms of surveying, construction surveying is often associated with the speed of the operation. Once contracts have been awarded, contractors may wish to commence construction immediately because they likely have commitments for their employees and equipment. They do not want to accept delay. A hurried surveyor is more likely to make mistakes in measurements and calculations, and thus even more vigilance than normal is required. Construction surveying is not an occupation for the faint of heart; the responsibilities are great and the working conditions are often less than ideal. However, the sense of achievement when viewing the completed facility can be very rewarding.

II.3   Grade

The word *grade* has several different meanings. In construction work alone, it is often used in three distinctly different ways:

1. To refer to a proposed elevation.
2. To refer to the slope of profile line (i.e., gradient).
3. To refer to cuts and fills—vertical distances measured below or above grade stakes.

The surveyor should be aware of these different meanings and should always note the context in which the word *grade* is being used.

Chapter 10

Machine Guidance
and Control

10.1 General Background

The role of the construction surveyor is changing. Before machine guidance and control techniques were introduced—and even today on many construction sites (especially the smaller ones)—surveyors manually provide grade stakes indicating design line and grade to the contractor. On construction sites where machine guidance and control techniques are not yet used, the surveyor is responsible for the following:

- The control survey (horizontal and vertical) over the construction site on which the preliminary and layout surveys are to be based (this includes the placement and tie-ins of control monuments and benchmarks).
- A preengineering topographic survey, which is used as a basis for the project design and is performed over the site.
- Once the design is completed and the project commenced, staking out the facility on centerline or on offset—to provide alignment and grade control to the contractor. The stakeouts are repeated until the contractor finally brings the facility to the required design elevations and alignments.
- At periodic intervals (often monthly), measuring construction quantities (item count, lengths, areas, and volumes) reflecting the progress made by the contractor during that time period. Typical quantities include earth volumes computed from end areas (for cut and fill), length of pipe, and lengths of curb and fence; tons of asphalt and granular material delivered on site; areas of sod laid; areas of the work surface receiving dust control; volumes of concrete placed; etc. Interim payments to the contractor are based on these interim measurements taken by the project surveyor or works inspector. Contractors normally employ their own surveyors to confirm the owner's survey measurements.

- After the completion of construction, performing a **final** or **as-built survey** to confirm that the facility was built according to the design criteria and that any in-progress design changes were suitably recorded.

Regardless of the layout technique, traditional layout activities often take up much of construction surveyors' time and attention. For example, in highway construction, where cuts and fills can be large, surveyors often have to restake the project continuously (sometimes daily in large cut/fill situations) because the grade and alignment stakes are knocked out or buried during the cut-and-fill process. As the facility nears design grade, restaking becomes less frequent.

Recent advances in machine guidance and machine control have resulted in layout techniques that significantly improve the efficiency of the stakeout (by as much as 30 percent according to some reports). Also, by reducing the need for as many stakeouts and thus the need for as many layout surveyors and grade checkers working near the moving equipment, these techniques provide a significant improvement in personnel safety.

With advancements in machine guidance and control, the surveyor's job has been greatly simplified in some aspects and become somewhat more complicated in others. The major impetus for the development and acceptance of guidance and control techniques in construction surveying has been the increase in efficiency of the operation, with a resulting reduction in costs. By reducing continual and repetitive human operations and computations, these techniques also reduce the chances for costly errors and mistakes. The tedious job of staking and restaking has been greatly reduced, and the ongoing measurements needed to record the contractor's progress can now be automated using the guidance/control software. Similarly, the measurements needed for a final or as-built survey already exist in the database at the conclusion of the project.

Simple machine guidance techniques have been with us for a long time. Laser beams, rotating in a fixed plane (horizontal or sloped), at a known vertical offset to finished grade, have long been used to guide earth-moving equipment. Ultrasonic detectors guide pavers by analyzing the timed sonic signal returns from string lines or other vertical references (Figure H.1). Large tracts (e.g., airports, shopping centers, parking lots) are brought to grade through the use of rotating lasers and machine-mounted laser detectors, which convey to the operator of the machine (bulldozer, grader, or scraper) the up/down operations required to bring that part of the project to the designed grade elevation. Laser grade displays are mounted outside the cab, where flashing colored lights guide the operator to move the blade up or down to be at design grade, or the grade display can be brought inside the cab, where the operator is guided by viewing the display monitor, which shows the position of the equipment's blade (or bucket teeth) in relation to design grade (Figures 10.1 and 10.2). Accuracies are said to be as reliable as those used for most earthwork techniques.

The difference between machine guidance and machine control is the level of machine automation. More sophisticated systems can send signals to machine receptors that automatically open or close the hydraulic valves needed to direct the machine to the proper alignment and grade. Presumably, the day may arrive when there will be no need for an operator in the machine—the machine's capabilities and limitations will be programmed into the project data file so that the machine does not attempt to perform large cuts and fills all at once (beyond the capability of the machine).

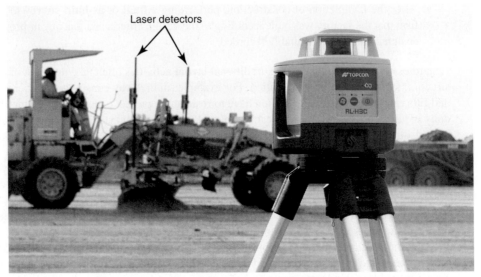

Laser detectors

FIGURE 10.1 Visual grading control is provided by a rotating laser referenced to a laser receiver/display that is attached to the blade. (Courtesy of Topcon Positioning Systems, Inc., Pleasanton, Calif.)

FIGURE 10.2 BucketPro Excavator cab display system used in machine-controlled excavation. The screen display shows the bucket teeth in relation to the proposed gradient. (Courtesy of Trimble Geomatics and Engineering Division)

Sophisticated guidance and control techniques presently utilize either motorized total station techniques [local positioning system (LPS)] or real-time (RTK) GPS techniques.

GPS techniques have been used where only a moderate level of accuracy is needed, such as in the earth-grading applications found in the construction of highways, shopping centers, airports, etc. Note, in Section 10.3, that a more precise GPS-based system is described which employs a laser fan instrument and a device mounted on the GPS receiver pole which can interpret the laser fan signals to improve vertical precision to the millimeter level.

Total station techniques are used where a higher level of accuracy is required, such as in the final grading of large projects, slip-form concrete pavers, etc. Presently, accuracies that can be achieved using traditional GPS grade control are in the ± 0.10 ft (± 3 cm) range, whereas the accuracies using LPS grade control are in the ± 0.02–0.04 ft (± 5–10 mm) range.

Machine guidance includes the capability of informing the machine operator about cut/fill and left/right movements. Light bars located inside or outside the cab within the operator's field of view indicate the required cut/fill and left/right movements; some systems also provide audible tones that increase (decrease) as the operation approaches (retreats from) design grade. Machine control includes the capability of signaling the machine directly so that valves open and close automatically, thus driving the various components of the machine to perform the needed functions. Cross-slope grading is accomplished on bladed machines by mounting GPS receivers (or laser sensors) at either end of the blade and letting the GPS signals (or laser beam) trigger the software to adjust the blade's slope angle. Slope sensors can also be mounted directly on the blade to have the blade adjust automatically and thus have it conform to the preselected design cross-slope. The in-cab touch-screen monitor shows the location and orientation of the machine with respect to the plan, profile, and cross-section views, each of which may be toggled onto the screen as needed.

The surveyor or perhaps a new breed of project designer must create three-dimensional (3D) data files portraying all the original features and the existing ground (EG) digital terrain model (DTM). All design data information must also be converted to a site-defined DTM. These 3D files are the foundation for the use of machine guidance and control, and for much of the automated interim and final measurements needed for payment purposes. See Section 10.3.4.

In summary, automated layout techniques provide the following benefits: reduced costs, increased safety of construction personnel, and reduced number of mistakes (however, mistakes that are not noticed can quickly become quite large). Additions and revisions to the design DTM can also be updated electronically at the machine's computer. Data can be transferred to the machine electronically (connected or wireless) or via data cards.

10.2 Motorized Total Station Guidance and Control

Some manufacturers produce layout software that can integrate motorized total stations and appropriately programmed personal computers (PCs). These radio- or optical-controlled systems can monitor work progress and give real-time direction for line-and-grade operations of various types of construction equipment in a wide selection of engineering works (e.g., tunnels, road and railway construction, site development, drilling, etc.). The motorized total station tracks one machine as it moves (up to 28 mph) while keeping a lock on the machine-mounted reflecting prism. The coordinates of the machine are continuously updated (up to eight times a second), and the machine's cutting-edge coordinates are compared with the design DTM coordinates (shown on the in-cab computer screen) to determine cut/fill and left/right operations. Directions are sent via radio or optical communications to and from the machine control-center computer. Manufacturers claim measurement standard deviations of 2 mm in height and 5 mm in position. See Figures 10.3 and H.2. Also see Section 10.5.

Motorized total stations can be set up in convenient locations so that an optimal area can be controlled (the instrument station's coordinates can be determined using resection techniques if necessary—see Section 5.3.3). The drawbacks to this system are that the motorized total station and its computer can direct only one machine at a time, and the unimpeded line-of-sight range is restricted to 15–700 m. Much time can be lost when the instrument has to be relocated to another previously established control station to overcome blocked sight lines. Having said that, the recent introduction in early 2005 of the first integrated total station/GPS receiver (Figure 5.29) signals the beginning of a new era when this guidance/control technique will be all the more effective because it allows the surveyor to establish control immediately anywhere on the construction site. The surveyor simply sets up this integrated instrument in a new convenient location and takes satellite signals as well as the differencing signals sent by a GPS base station to determine precisely, in real time, the new setup point's horizontal coordinates, and elevation—as long as the setup point is within 50 km of an RTK GPS base station.

FIGURE 10.3 Paving-machine operation controlled by a motorized total station/radio control modem/PC computer instrumentation package. (Courtesy of Leica Geosystems Inc.)

10.3 Satellite Positioning Guidance and Control

In addition to laser- and computer-controlled total station techniques, machine guidance and control is also available, in real time, with the use of layout programs featuring GPS receivers. As with total station techniques, receptors are mounted on the various types of construction equipment (the height of the GPS receivers above the ground is measured and entered into the controller as part of the site calibration measurements), and the readings are transmitted to the in-cab GPS controller or integrated PC computers (Figure H.3). In-cab displays show the operator how much up/down and left/right movement is needed on the cutting edge of the blade (grader or bulldozer) to achieve or maintain design alignment. In addition to providing guidance to machine operators, these systems can also be configured to provide control of the machine—that is, to send signals directly to the machine to operate valves that control the operation of various cutting-edge components such as grader or bulldozer blades, backhoe buckets, etc.

At the beginning of a project, the GPS calibration must be performed and verified. Several on-site control monuments are needed for site calibration. Calibration is performed to equate the GPS horizontal coordinates (WGS84) with the coordinates used for the project design—usually state plane coordinates or UTM coordinates. The GPS heights must also be reconciled to the orthometric heights used in the design. A local geoid model and several benchmarks are used in this process. GPS observations taken on existing and nearby horizontal control monuments (whose local coordinates are known) and on nearby benchmarks (whose local elevations are known) are necessary for this project startup calibration. Machine-accessible control monuments are established in secure locations so machines can revisit the control monuments at regular intervals to check their positional calibration settings.

A base station equipped with a dual-frequency GPS receiver and a radio transmitter (10- to 20-km range for local base stations) can be established close to or on the construction site and can help in the guidance or control of any number of GPS-equipped construction machines. If radio transmission is used, the range can be extended by adding repeater stations; some systems use digital cell phones for all communications and data transmission. The base station broadcasts the differential GPS signals to all machine-mounted dual-frequency GPS receivers within range of the base station so that differential corrections can be made. The accuracies of the resulting RTK GPS positions are usually in the range of 2–4 cm and are ideal for all rough grading practices. Machine calibration includes measuring the location of the GPS antennas with respect to the EG, and then these vertical and horizontal offsets are recorded in the in-cab machine computer via the touch-screen monitor. The machine computers, loaded with appropriate layout software, receive design DTM coordinates each day via data cards or via connected or wireless electronics. In highway construction, the computer monitor displays plan, profile, and cross-section views of the proposed grade and existing grade with an indication of where (horizontally and vertically) the machine and its blades are with respect to the required grade. The program computes and stores cuts and fills for interim and final surveys and payments. One typical program keeps the operator up to date by displaying the cut areas in red, the fill areas in blue, and the at-grade areas without color. These progress displays are usually governed by some predefined tolerance (e.g., ±5 cm) that has been entered into the program.

GPS vertical accuracies can now be improved to that of motorized total stations (see Section 10.2) by incorporating laser guidance. In 2005, Topcon Corporation introduced a rotating fan laser for use in GPS stakeouts. The rotating laser, set up on a control station, can help guide or control any number of laser zone sensor–equipped construction machines or roving GPS surveyors. A laser zone sensor can be mounted on the machine or on a rover pole just below the GPS antenna/receiver. These sensors can decode the laser signal and calculate the height difference to within 1/3,600 of a degree, giving an elevation difference to within a few (6–12) millimeters. The laser fan sends out laser signals (50 times/second) in a vertical working zone 33 ft high (10 m high at a distance of 150 m), in a working diameter of 2,000 ft (600 m). Multiple lasers can be used to provide guidance for larger differentials in height and larger working areas.

We noted in Section 7.11.4 that in 2004 Trimble introduced software that permitted accurate surveying based on a multibase network concept called virtual reference station (VRS) technology. This system permitted base stations to be placed farther apart while still producing accurate results. One example of this technology was instituted in 2004, when the Ohio Department of Transportation (ODOT) completed statewide CORS coverage. This coverage, together with the new VRS software, enables Ohio surveyors to work across the state at centimeter-level accuracy—with no need for their own base stations or repeaters; digital cell phones are used for communications. Operational capability occurred in January 2005. ODOT's CORS network consists of fifty-two stations; they will be added to the NGS national CORS network. In a few short years, this technology has spread from the Americas and Europe to most places on Earth. This development signals the beginning of widely available base stations for general surveying use. It has been predicted that the local and state/province government agencies may be more inclined to spend money on densifying networks of GPS base stations instead of spending more money on replacing (and referencing) destroyed ground control monuments and creating ground control monuments in new locations. As many of the larger surveying manufacturers subsequently provided similar technology and positioning services, the base station networks became known as RTNs. Some networks were built with public funding and provide positioning services at low (or no) cost while other networks were built with private funding and users are charged annual fees for the positioning services.

As with all construction processes, accuracy verification is essential. Random GPS observations can be used. Some contractors install GPS receivers, together with all construction layout software, in superintendents' pickup trucks or all-terrain vehicles (ATVs) so they can monitor the quality and progress of large-scale construction. When the construction is nearing completion, the grading status can be transferred (electronically or via data cards) to the office computer so that the operation can be analyzed for authorization of the commencement of the next stage of operation—for example, to move from subgrade to granular base course in the roadbed, or to move from final earth grading to seeding or sod placement. Another feature of this technique is that the construction machine operator can update the database by identifying and storing the location of discovered features that were not part of the original data (e.g., buried pipes that may become apparent only during the excavation process).

This RTK GPS system, which can measure the ground surface ten times a second, cannot be used with less accurate GPS systems such as DGPS (which normally are accurate only to within ± 3 ft). Normally, five satellites in view are required for initialization, and thereafter four satellites will suffice. If loss of lock occurs on some or all of the four satellites, the receiver display should indicate the problem and signal when the system is functioning properly again. When more satellites are launched in the GLONASS system and when the Galileo system becomes functional, multiconstellation receivers will diminish loss-of-lock problems.

10.4 Three-Dimensional Data Files

10.4.1 Surface Models

As noted earlier, to take advantage of machine guidance and control capabilities, both the EG surface model (DTM) and the design surface model (a second DTM) must be created. Surface models are usually created as triangulated networks (TINs). DTM files can be created using a wide variety of software programs, or they can be uploaded from standard design packages, such as AutoCad (ACAD). The EG surface model data in the computer can be collected from field work using total stations, GPS, or remote sensing techniques, or the surface model data can be digitized from contoured topographic plans prepared at a suitable scale, thus creating 3D data files. As noted in Chapter 8, the identification and georeferencing of break lines is essential for the accurate creation of spatial models.

Each type of construction has attracted software developers who create programs designed specifically for those applications. For example, in highway work, the program is designed to create finished cross sections at regular station intervals based solely on proposed elevations along the centerline (derived from design TINs) and on the proposed cross section of the facility (pavement widths and crowns, shoulder widths and cross falls, ditch depths and side slopes, curb cross sections, etc.). These are called roading templates (Figures 11.5 and 11.12). The program can also determine the elevation and distance from centerline where the design boulevard slope or ditch back slope rises or falls and thus intersects the EG—also known as original ground (OG). EG or OG is defined as the ground surface at the time of the preliminary survey.

By analyzing the EG model surface and the design model surface, cross-section end areas and volumes of cut and fill can be generated automatically. Volumes can also be computed using software based on the prismoidal formula; see Chapter 17 for an explanation of these techniques. Volumes can also be generated using software based on grid techniques, where grid cells are defined by size (1 ft on a side is common). The size of the grid chosen usually reflects the material-handling unit costs; for example, it is less expensive, per cubic yard (or cubic meter), to cut/fill using scrapers than it is using loaders or backhoes, and more approximate computation methods can be used when unit costs are lower. The elevation difference between the EG and design surface models can be interpolated (using a software program) at each corner of each grid cell, with the average height difference multiplied by the grid area to give the volume of cut or fill at each grid area. Finally, some software developers compute volumes by directly analyzing EG TINs and design TINs.

While there is only one EG surface elevation model, there can be several design surface elevation models, each of which can be stored on separate CAD layers in the digital file. For example, in highway work or roadwork, design surface models can be generated for the surfaces representing the following: the surface after the topsoil has been stripped, the subgrade surface, the top of granular surface, and the finished asphalt or concrete surface. Additional surfaces can be generated for off-the-roadway sites such as borrow/fill areas and sod/seeding areas. In municipal design, typical design surfaces to be modeled depict some or all of the following: storm-water detention basins, front and rear yard surfaces, boulevard surfaces, building pad surfaces, excavated pipeline trenches, back slopes, etc.

One of the objectives of engineering works designers is to minimize project costs. In highway work and in large site developments (e.g., airports, large commercial developments), one of the major costs is the excavating and filling of material. Allowances can be made for the inclusion of shrinkage and swell factors that reflect closely the end result of the compaction of fill material and the placement of shattered rock in fill areas. By adjusting the design elevations or design gradients up and down (e.g., building pad or first-floor elevations, road centerline profiles, pipeline profiles), the designer can use the software to determine quickly the effects that such adjustments have on the overall cut/fill quantities. The ideal (seldom realized) for cost effectiveness would be to balance cut and fill equally. Additionally, design software can have unit costs (estimated or bid) tagged to all construction quantities—for example cuts/fills per cubic yard or meter (tied to the use of various machines such as scrapers, loaders, backhoes, trenchers, etc.); unit lengths of curb, sidewalk, and pipelines (and other buried services); unit areas of asphalt or concrete; sod, seeding, dust control applications; unit weights of materials trucked on site (e.g., granular material, asphalt), etc. The designer can thus keep abreast of cost factors when design changes are proposed.

Once the final design elevations and slopes have been chosen, the data stored on CAD layers in the digital file are used to generate quantities and costs for various stages of the project. The quantity estimates are used first to generate cost estimates, which are useful in obtaining approval to let a project out for bids. Then the cost estimates are useful to contractors as they prepare their final bids. Once the contract has been awarded and construction has commenced, the in-progress surface models are upgraded (sometimes monthly) to reflect construction progress. Progress payments to the contractor are based on measurements and computations based on those interim surface models. Both the owner and the contractor employ their own surveyors to resurvey the in-progress surface using LPS, GPS, or other field techniques. By the completion of the project, the digital files already show the final (as-built) survey data, and no additional work is required to produce the final (as-built) drawings.

10.4.2 Horizontal Design Alignments

In addition to the EG surface elevation model and the design surface elevation models, the digital files contain the horizontal location of all existing and proposed features. In machine guidance and control situations, the complete digital file is available on the in-cab computer. When design revisions are made, the in-cab computer files can be upgraded using data cards or, more recently, even through wireless communications directly from the design office. When machine operators discover features during construction (e.g., buried pipes) that were not included in the original project digital data file or were located incorrectly, the file can be updated right in the machine cab and the updates can be transmitted to the design office. When stakeouts are required, LPS, GPS, or other field techniques can be used. Modern software, working with the data in the project digital file and the stored coordinates of the project control monuments, can generate the horizontal and vertical alignment measurements needed to locate a facility centerline, or a feature location directly or on some predefined offset.

10.5 Summary of the 3D Design Process

10.5.1 Data File Construction

Data files are a combination of EG elevations and proposed design elevations. They are generated by commercially available software programs (see Section 10.6). The following list shows some typical steps in the process:

1. Access the design software and create a working file.
2. Select the source of the data (e.g., CAD data file, digitizer, etc.).
3. When importing CAD files, first identify the layers containing existing grade, proposed grade, subgrade, etc.
4. Import soils bore-hole data (if applicable).
5. Import the existing grade files (from CAD) first, and assign elevations to contours (use the pull-down menu) to convert from 2D to 3D. The area of specific interest may first need to be identified (by cursor-boxing) if the CAD file extends beyond the area of interest.
6. If digitized data are to be added to CAD file data, identify the digitized point on the CAD drawing (in at least two locations) to place data from the two source on the same datum.
7. Repeat the process for proposed grade files, which will include general stripping limits and depths, subgrade elevations, etc.
8. Identify the structure (e.g., road, building, pipeline, etc.) to be built and identify it (using the cursor) on the plan display. Each type of structure has its own design routines. In the case of a road, first identify the centerline and grade-point elevations, and then select (from pull-down menus) the lane widths, cross fall, depth of roadbed materials, side slopes, offsets, and staking intervals. The software will compute and plot the intermediate centerline elevations and pavement edge elevations, and the top and bottom of slope locations. All this computed data can be shown on the plan, or some (or all) such data can be turned off. The plotted road can now be shown in 3D for visual inspection.
9. Trace the road area stripping limits and select for import. Select the stripping depth for that area (refer to the imported bore-hole data if relevant), and then the volumes of topsoil stripping can be computed.
10. Existing and proposed cross sections and profiles for any defined line (including subgrade and final grades) can now be generated. Thus, volumes of general cut and fill can be determined for the entire road structure.
11. If the bore holes had identified rock strata in the general area, the software can determine and graphically display the location and elevation of any rock quantities that need to be computed separately (at much higher costs of excavation).

Most commercial software treats pipeline construction similarly (see Chapter 14), where invert elevations define the grade line and define the depth of cut so that cut volumes can be computed. The type of pipe bedding (granular or concrete) can be selected from pull-down menus, and the bedding volume can be determined by factoring in the trench lengths and widths as well as the bedding depth (Figure 14.1). Other backfill material volumes, such as volumes for placed and compacted excavated trench material, can also determined using the trench width and depth dimensions.

Building construction (see Chapter 16) can also be dealt with by locating the building footprint on the plan display and then entering first floor (or other) elevations as directed by a pull-down menu. Basement or foundation elevations are entered (as directed by the subgrade menu) to provide cut computations. Offsets (also selected from a pull-down menu) are defined and then displayed on the plan graphics. Parking areas and driveways are defined with cursor clicks, and selected locations have their proposed elevations entered; subgrade elevations are determined after material depths are determined. Thus, cut/fill volumes can be determined from the existing surface model (which was imported into the working file) and the newly determined subgrade surface model.

10.5.2 Layout

Layout can be accomplished using the design data from the 3D working file. The layout can be performed using conventional theodolite or tape surveys, total station surveys, robotic total station surveys, or GPS surveys, or by machine guidance and control techniques.

When using the first two techniques mentioned above (conventional theodolite or tape surveys), the northing, easting, and elevation of each layout point can be downloaded from the data file for use in the field. Some software will generate the angle and distance to be measured from preselected control stations to each of the layout points. The occupied and backsight points are identified first so that the relevant coordinates can be used (Figure 5.20).

When using total stations and GPS receivers, the 3D data software (including the EG surface model and the design surface model) can reside on the field instrument controller. Once the base station receiver (occupied point) and roving station receiver (backsight point) have been set over their control points and tied into each other, the rover can, in real time, continually display its 3D position ground coordinates as it is moved, and its can be directed to selected layout points. (Selection can be made by tapping on a touch-screen display or by selecting a layout point by entering its number.) Once the layout point has been occupied by the rover, the layout data can then be saved in a layout file for documentation purposes, and the layout position accuracy can be noted (GPS surveys). This type of layout work is facilitated by using a large touch-screen tablet controller (Figure 7.22), which can display a large section of the proposed layout works.

The 3D data files are also useful for layout by machine guidance and/or control using either RTK GPS techniques or LPS (robotic total station) techniques. In the case of LPS, the 3D data files are transferred to the computer controlling the robotic total station. The robotic total station can thus control or guide the piece of construction equipment (e.g., bulldozer, grader, loader, etc.) by sighting the position-calibrated prisms attached to the equipment. In the case of RTK GPS layouts, the 3D files are transferred directly to the onboard controller (computer) located in the construction equipment cab. The interfaced GPS receivers are calibrated for position (relative to the ground), and the construction site itself is calibrated by taking GPS reading on all available horizontal and vertical control monuments.

10.6 Website References for Data Collection, DTM, and Civil Design

AGTEK Development   *http://www.AGTEK.com*
Autodesk   *http://www.autodesk.com*
Bentley   *http://www.bentley.com*
CAiCE   *http://www.CAiCe.com*
Carlson   *http://www.carlsonsw.com*
Eagle Point   *http://www.eaglepoint.com*
InSite Software   *http://www.insitesoftware.com*
Leica   *http://www.leica-geosystems.com*
Trimble   *http://www.trimble.com*
Tripod Data System   *http://www.tdsway.com*

Review Questions

10.1 What is the purpose of a GPS base station?

10.2 What is the meaning of the term *line and grade*?

10.3 How is the word *grade* used in construction work?

10.4 What is the difference between machine guidance and machine control?

10.5 What data would you typically find in a project 3D data file?

10.6 Compared with GPS techniques, what are the advantages of using motorized total stations to guide and control construction machines? What are the disadvantages?

10.7 What recent development has now enabled RTK GPS techniques to rival motorized total station techniques in the vertical accuracies of layouts?

10.8 What recent development has enabled motorized total stations to become much more effective in machine guidance and control?

10.9 What is involved in project calibration when using guidance and control methods?

10.10 How can 3D data files be used to compute volumes of cut and fill?

Chapter 11

Highway Curves

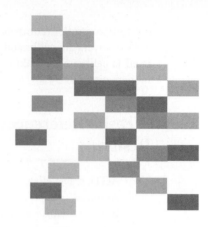

11.1 Route Surveys

Highway and railroad routes are chosen only after a complete and detailed study of all possible locations has been completed. Functional planning and route selection usually involve the use of aerial imagery, satellite imagery, and ground surveys, as well as the analysis of existing plans and maps. The selected route is chosen because it satisfies all design requirements with minimal social, environmental, and financial impact.

The proposed centerline (₵) is laid out in a series of straight lines (tangents) beginning at 0 + 00 (0 + 000, metric) and continuing to the route terminal point. Each time the route changes direction, the deflection angle between the back tangent and forward tangent is measured and recorded. Existing detail that might have an effect on the highway design is tied in by conventional (including GPS) ground surveys, by aerial surveys, or by a combination of the two methods. Typical detail includes lakes, streams, trees, structures, existing roads and railroads, and so on. In addition to the detail location, the surveyor determines elevations along the proposed route, with readings being taken across the route width at right angles to the ₵ at regular intervals (full stations, half stations, etc.) and at locations dictated by changes in the topography. The elevations thus determined are used to aid in the design of horizontal and vertical alignments; in addition, these elevations form the basis for the calculation of construction cut-and-fill quantities (see Chapter 17).

Advances in aerial imaging, including lidar imaging (see Chapter 8), have resulted in ground-surface measuring techniques that can eliminate much of the time-consuming field surveying techniques described above. The location of detail and the determination of elevations are normally confined to that relatively narrow strip of land representing the highway right-of-way (ROW). Exceptions include potential river, highway, and railroad crossings, where approach profiles and sight lines (railroads) may have to be established.

11.2   Circular Curves: General Background

We noted in the previous section that a highway route survey is initially laid out as a series of straight lines (tangents). Once the ℄ location alignment has been confirmed, the tangents are joined by circular curves that allow for smooth vehicle operation at the speeds for which the highway was designed. Figure 11.1 illustrates how two tangents are joined by a circular curve and shows some related circular curve terminology. The point at which the alignment changes from straight to circular is known as the beginning of curve (BC). The BC is located distance T (subtangent) from the point of tangent intersection (PI). The length of the circular curve (L) depends on the central angle and the value of the radius (R). The point at which the alignment changes from circular back to tangent is known as the end of curve (EC). Because the curve is symmetrical about the PI, the EC is also located distance T from the PI. Recall from geometry that the radius of a circle is perpendicular to the tangent at the point of tangency. Therefore, the radius is perpendicular to the back tangent at the BC and to the forward tangent at the EC. The terms BC and EC are also referred to by some agencies as the point of curve (PC) and the point of tangency (PT), respectively, and by others as the tangent to curve (TC) and the curve to tangent (CT), respectively.

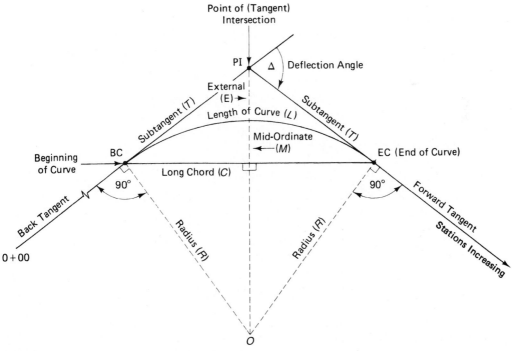

FIGURE 11.1   Circular curve terminology.

11.3 Circular Curve Geometry

Most curve problems are calculated from field measurements (Δ and the chainage or stationing of the PI) and from design parameters (R). Given R (which depends on the design speed) and Δ, all other curve components can be computed.

Analysis of Figure 11.2 shows that the curve deflection angle at the BC (PI–BC–EC) is $\Delta/2$, and that the central angle at O is equal to Δ, the tangent deflection angle. The line O–PI, joining the center of the curve to the PI, effectively bisects all related lines and angles.

Tangent: In triangle BC–O–PI,

$$\frac{T}{R} = \tan \frac{\Delta}{2}$$

$$T = R \tan \frac{\Delta}{2} \tag{11.1}$$

Chord: In triangle BC–O–B,

$$\frac{1/2C}{R} = \sin \frac{\Delta}{2}$$

$$C = 2R \sin \frac{\Delta}{2} \tag{11.2}$$

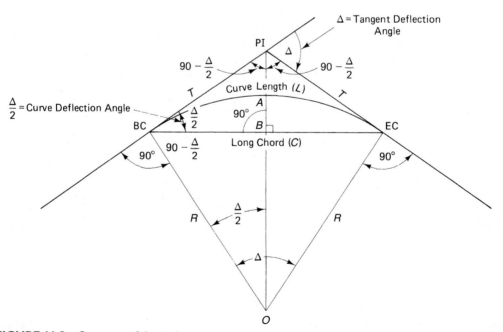

FIGURE 11.2 Geometry of the circle.

Midordinate:

$$\frac{OB}{R} = \cos\frac{\Delta}{2}$$

$$OB = R\cos\frac{\Delta}{2}$$

But:

$$OB = R - M$$

$$R - M = R\cos\frac{\Delta}{2}$$

$$M = R\left(1 - \cos\frac{\Delta}{2}\right) \tag{11.3}$$

External: In triangle BC–O–PI, O–PI = $R + E$:

$$\frac{R}{(R + E)} = \cos\frac{\Delta}{2}$$

$$E = R\left(\frac{1}{\cos\dfrac{\Delta}{2}} - 1\right) \tag{11.4}$$

$$= R\left(\sec\frac{\Delta}{2} - 1\right) \quad \text{(alternate)}$$

Arc: From Figure 11.3, we can determine the following relationship:

$$\frac{L}{2\pi R} = \frac{\Delta}{360}$$

$$L = 2\pi R\left(\frac{\Delta}{360}\right) \tag{11.5}$$

where Δ is expressed in degrees and decimals of a degree.

The sharpness of the curve is determined by the choice of the radius (R); large radius curves are relatively flat, whereas small radius curves are relatively sharp. Many highway agencies use the concept of degree of curve (D) to define the sharpness of the curve. Degree of curve (D) is defined to be that central angle subtended by 100 ft of arc. (In railway design, D is defined to be the central angle subtended by 100 ft of chord.) From Figure 11.3, we can determine the following:

D and R:

$$\frac{D}{360} = \frac{100}{2\pi R}$$

$$D = \frac{5,729.58}{R} \tag{11.6}$$

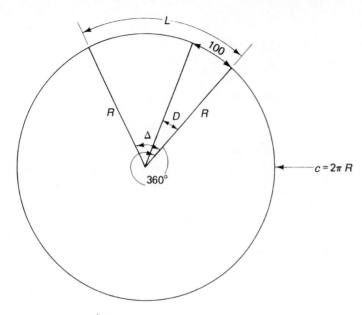

FIGURE 11.3 Relationship between the degree of curve (D) and the circle.

Arc:

$$\frac{L}{100} = \frac{\Delta}{D}$$

$$L = 100\left(\frac{\Delta}{D}\right) \tag{11.7}$$

■ EXAMPLE 11.1

Refer to Figure 11.4. You are given the following information:

$$\Delta = 16°38'$$
$$R = 1,000 \text{ ft}$$
$$\text{PI at } 6 + 26.57$$

Calculate the station of the BC and EC; also calculate lengths C, M, and E.

Solution

We can use Equation 11.1 to determine the tangent distance (T) and Equation 11.5 to calculate the length of arc (L):

$$T = R \tan \frac{\Delta}{2}$$

$$= 1,000 \tan 8°19'$$

$$= 146.18 \text{ ft}$$

$$L = 2\pi R \frac{\Delta}{360}$$

$$= 2\pi \times 1,000 \times \frac{16.6333}{360}$$

$$= 290.31 \text{ ft}$$

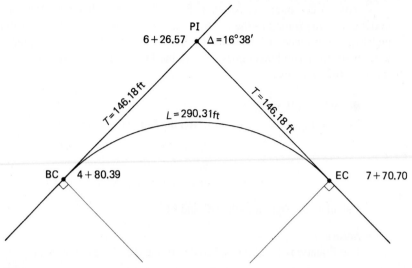

FIGURE 11.4 Sketch for Example 11.1. *Note:* To aid in comprehension, the magnitude of the Δ angle has been exaggerated in this section.

Determine the BC and EC stations as follows:

$$
\begin{aligned}
\text{PI at } 6 &+ 26.57 \\
-T \quad 1 \quad &\underline{46.18} \\
\text{BC} = 4 &+ 80.39 \\
+L \quad 2 \quad &\underline{90.31} \\
\text{EC} = 7 &+ 70.70
\end{aligned}
$$

Use Equation 11.2 to calculate the length of *C* (see Figure 11.1):

$$
\begin{aligned}
C &= 2R \sin \frac{\Delta}{2} \\
&= 2 \times 1{,}000 \times \sin 8°19' \\
&= 289.29 \text{ ft}
\end{aligned}
$$

Use Equation 11.3 to calculate the length of *M* (see Figure 11.1):

$$
\begin{aligned}
M &= R\left(1 - \cos \frac{\Delta}{2}\right) \\
&= 1{,}000 \left(1 - \cos 8°19'\right) \\
&= 10.52 \text{ft}
\end{aligned}
$$

Use Equation 11.4 to calculate the length of *E* (see Figure 11.1):

$$
\begin{aligned}
E &= R\left(\sec \frac{\Delta}{2} - 1\right) \\
&= 1{,}000 \left(\sec 8°19' - 1\right) \\
&= 10.63 \text{ft}
\end{aligned}
$$

Note: A common mistake made by students when they first study circular curves is to determine the station of the EC by adding the T distance to the PI. Although the EC is physically a distance of T from the PI, the stationing (chainage) must reflect the fact that the centerline (₵) no longer goes through the PI. The ₵ now takes the shorter distance (L) from the BC to the EC.

■ EXAMPLE 11.2

Refer to Figure 11.5. You are given the following information:

$$\Delta = 12°51'$$
$$R = 400 \text{ m}$$
$$\text{PI at } 0 + 241.782$$

Calculate the station of the BC and EC.

Solution

Use Equations 11.1 and 11.5 to determine the T and L distances:

$$T = R \tan \frac{\Delta}{2}$$
$$= 400 \tan 6°25'30''$$
$$= 45.044 \text{ m}$$

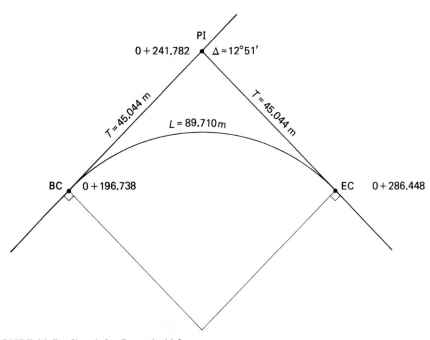

FIGURE 11.5 Sketch for Example 11.2.

$$L = 2\pi R \frac{\Delta}{360}$$

$$= 2\pi \times 400 \times \frac{12.850}{360}$$

$$= 89.710 \text{ m}$$

Determine the BC and EC stations as follows:

$$
\begin{array}{rl}
\text{PI at } & 0 + 241.782 \\
-T & \underline{45.044} \\
\text{BC} = & 0 + 196.738 \\
+L = & \underline{89.710} \\
\text{EC} = & 0 + 286.448
\end{array}
$$

■ EXAMPLE 11.3

Refer to Figure 11.6. You are given the following information:

$$\Delta = 11°21'35''$$
$$\text{PI at } 14 + 87.33$$
$$D = 6°$$

Calculate the station of the BC and EC.

Solution
Use Equations 11.6, 11.1, and 11.7:

$$R = \frac{5,729.58}{D} = 954.93 \text{ ft}$$

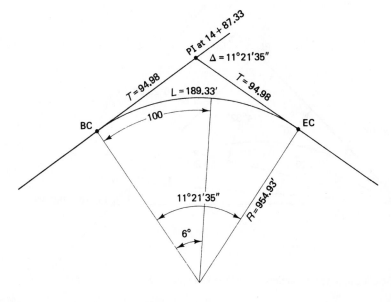

FIGURE 11.6 Sketch for Example 11.3.

$$T = R \tan \frac{\Delta}{2} = 954.93 \tan 5.679861° = 94.98 \text{ ft}$$

$$L = 100 \frac{\Delta}{D} = 100 \times \frac{11.359722}{6} = 189.33 \text{ ft}$$

Another alternative is to use Equation 11.5:

$$L = 2\pi R \frac{\Delta}{360} = 2\pi \times 954.93 \times \frac{11.359722}{360} = 189.33 \text{ ft}$$

$$
\begin{array}{rl}
\text{PI at } & 14 + 87.33 \\
-T & \underline{94.98} \\
\text{BC} = & 13 + 92.35 \\
+L \quad 1 & \underline{89.33} \\
\text{EC} = & 15 + 81.68
\end{array}
$$

11.4 Circular Curve Deflections

A common method (using a steel tape and a theodolite) of locating a curve in the field is by deflection angles. Typically, the theodolite is set up at the BC, and the deflection angles are turned from the tangent line (Figure 11.7). If we use the following data from Example 11.2:

$$\text{BC at } 0 + 196.738$$

$$\text{EC at } 0 + 286.448$$

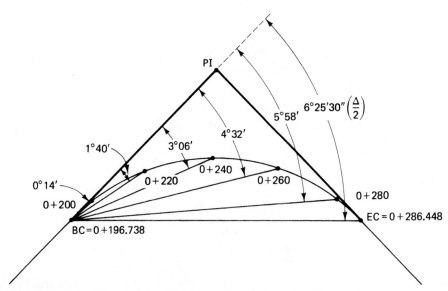

FIGURE 11.7 Field location for deflection angles. See Example 11.2.

$$\frac{\Delta}{2} = 6°25'30'' = 6.4250°$$

$$L = 89.710 \text{ m}$$

$$T = 45.044 \text{ m}$$

and if the layout is to proceed at 20-m intervals, the procedure would be as described below:

1. Compute the deflection angles for the three required arc distances.

$$\text{Deflection angle} = \frac{\text{arc}}{L} \times \frac{\Delta}{2}$$

(a) BC to first even station $(0 + 200)$: $(0 + 200) - (0 + 196.738) = 3.262$

$$\frac{3.262}{89.710} \times 6.4250 = 0.2336° = 0°14'01''$$

(b) Even station interval:

$$\frac{20}{89.710} \times 6.4250 = 1.4324° = 1°25'57''$$

(c) Last even station $(0 + 280)$ to EC:

$$\frac{6.448}{89.710} \times 6.4250 = 0.4618° = 0°27'42''$$

2. Prepare a list of appropriate stations and *cumulative* deflection angles.

Stations	Deflection Angles
BC 0 + 196.738	0°00'00''
0 + 200	0°14'01'' + 1°25'57''
0 + 220	1°39'58'' + 1°25'57''
0 + 240	3°05'55'' + 1°25'57''
0 + 260	4°31'52'' + 1°25'57''
0 + 280	5°57'49'' + 0°27'42''
EC 0 + 286.448	6°25'31'' ≈ 6°25'30'' = Δ/2

For many engineering layouts, the deflection angles are rounded to the closest minute or half-minute.

Another common method of locating a curve in the field is by using the "setting out" feature of total stations (see Chapter 5). The coordinates of each station on the curve are first uploaded into the total station, permitting its processor to compute the angle and distance from the instrument to all curve stations.

11.5 Chord Calculations

In Section 11.4, we determined that the deflection angle for station 0 + 200 was 0°14'01". It follows that 0 + 200 can be located by placing a stake on the theodolite line at 0°14' and at a distance of 3.262 m (200 – 196.738) from the BC. Furthermore, station 0 + 220 can be located by placing a stake on the theodolite line at 1°40' (rounded) and at a distance of 20 m along the arc from the stake that locates 0 + 200. The remaining stations can be located in a similar manner. Note, however, that this technique contains some error because the distances measured with a steel tape are not arc distances; they are straight lines known as chords or subchords (Figure 11.8).

Equation 11.8 can be used to calculate the subchord. This equation, derived from Figure 11.2, is the special case of the long chord (LC) and the total deflection angle, as given by Equation 11.2. The general case can be stated as follows:

$$C = 2R(\sin \text{deflection angle}) \qquad (11.8)$$

Any subchord can be calculated if its deflection angle is known.

Relevant chords for Section 11.4 can be calculated as follows (see Figure 11.8):

First chord: $C = 2 \times 400 (\sin 0°14'01") = 3.2618$ m = 3.262 m (at three
decimals, chord = arc)

Even station chord: $C = 2 \times 400 (\sin 1°25'57") = 19.998$ m

Last chord: $C = 2 \times 400 (\sin 0°27'42") = 6.448$ m

If these chord distances are used, the curve layout can proceed without error.

Note: Although the calculation of the first and last subchords shows these chords and arcs to be equal (i.e., 3.262 m and 6.448 m), the chords are always marginally shorter than the arcs. In the cases of short distances (above) and in the case of flat (large radius) curves, the arcs and chords can often appear to be equal. If more decimal places are introduced into the calculation, the marginal difference between arc and chord become evident.

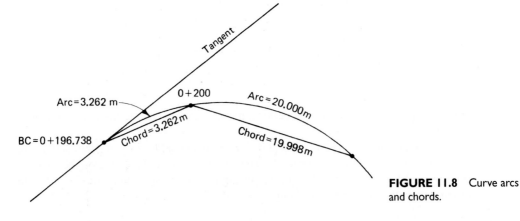

FIGURE 11.8 Curve arcs and chords.

11.6 Metric Considerations

Countries that use metric (SI) units have adopted for highway use a reference station of 1 km (e.g., 1 + 000); cross sections at 50-, 20-, and 10-m intervals; and a curvature design parameter based on a rational (even meter) value radius, as opposed to a rational value degree (even degree) of curve (D). The degree of curve originally found favor with most highway agencies because of the somewhat simpler calculations associated with its use. This factor was significant in the preelectronic age, when most calculations were performed by using logarithms. A comparison of techniques involving both D and R (radius) shows that the only computation in which the rational aspect of D is carried through is that for the arc length—that is, $L = 100\Delta/D$ (from Equation 11.7)—and even in that one case, the ease of calculation depends on delta (Δ) also being a rational number. In all other formulas, the inclusion of trigonometric functions or pi (π) ensures a more complex computation requiring the use of a calculator.

The widespread use of handheld calculators and computers has greatly reduced the importance of techniques that permit only marginal reductions in computations. Surveyors are now routinely solving their problems with calculators and computers rather than with the seemingly endless array of tables that once characterized the back section of survey texts. An additional reason for the lessening importance of D in computing deflection angles is that many curves (particularly at interchanges) are now being laid out by control point–based polar or intersection techniques (i.e., angle/distance or angle/angle) instead of deflection angles (see Chapter 5), or by RTK GPS techniques (see Chapter 7). Those countries using the metric system, almost without exception, use a rational value for the radius (R) as a design parameter.

11.7 Field Procedure (Steel Tape and Theodolite)

With the PI location and Δ angle measured in the field, and with the radius or degree of curve (D) chosen consistent with the design speed, all curve computations can be completed. The surveyor then returns to the field and measures off the tangent (T) distance from the PI to locate the BC and EC on the appropriate tangent lines. The theodolite or total station is then set up at the BC and zeroed and sighted in on the PI. The $\Delta/2$ angle ($6°25'30''$ in Example 11.2) is then turned off in the direction of the EC mark (wood stake, nail, etc.). If the computations for T and the field measurements of T have been performed correctly, the line of sight of the Δ angle will fall over the EC mark. If this does not occur, the T computations and then the field measurements are repeated. If GPS receivers are used to locate the PI, BC, and EC, the surveyor should check the distance from the BC to the PI and from the PI to the EC, to ensure that the two distances are equal and that they do equal the T (subtangent distance).

Note: The $\Delta/2$ line of sight over the EC mark will, of necessity, contain some error. In each case, the surveyor will have to decide if the resultant alignment error is acceptable for the type of survey in question. For example, if the $\Delta/2$ line of sight misses the EC mark by 0.10 ft (30 mm) in a ditched highway ℄ survey, the surveyor would probably find the error acceptable and then proceed with the deflections. However, a similar error in the $\Delta/2$ line of sight in a survey to lay out an elevated portion of urban freeway would not be acceptable; in that case, an acceptable error would be roughly one-third of the preceding error (0.03 ft or 10 mm).

After the Δ/2 check has been satisfactorily completed, the curve stakes are set by turning off the deflection angle and measuring the chord distance for the appropriate stations. If possible, the theodolite is left at the BC (see next section) for the entire curve stakeout, whereas the distance measuring moves continually forward from station to station. The rear taping surveyor keeps his or her body to the outside of the curve to avoid blocking the line of sight from the instrument.

A final verification of the work is available after the last even station has been set, when the chord distance from the last even station to the EC stake is measured and compared with the theoretical value. If the check indicates an unacceptable discrepancy, the work is checked and the discrepancy is solved. Finally, after the curve has been established in the field, the party chief usually walks the curve, looking for any abnormalities. If a mistake has been made (e.g., putting in two stations at the same deflection angle is a common mistake), it will probably be evident. The circular curve's symmetry is such that even minor mistakes are obvious in a visual check.

Note here that many highway agencies use polar layout for interchanges and other complex features. If the coordinates of centerline alignment stations are determined, they can be used to locate the facility. In this application, the total station is placed at a known (or resection) station and aligned with another known station so that the instrument's processor can compute and display the angle and distance needed for layout (see also Chapters 5 and 12).

11.8 Moving up on the CURVE

The curve deflections shown in Section 11.4 are presented in a form suitable for deflecting in while set up at the BC, with a zero setting at the PI. Often, however, the entire curve cannot be deflected in from the BC, and two or more instrument setups may be required before the entire curve has been located. The reasons for this situation include a loss of line of sight due to intervening obstacles (i.e., detail or elevation rises).

In Figure 11.9, the data of Example 11.2 are used to illustrate the geometric considerations in moving up on the curve. In this case, station 0 + 260 cannot be established with the theodolite at the BC (as were the previous stations) because a large tree obscures the line of sight from the BC to 0 + 260. To establish station 0 + 260, the surveyor moves the instrument forward to the last station (0 + 240) established from the BC. The horizontal circle is zeroed, and the BC is then sighted with the telescope in its inverted position. When the telescope is transited, the theodolite is once again oriented to the curve; that is, to set off the next (0 + 260) deflection, the surveyor refers to the previously prepared list of deflections and sets the appropriate deflection (4°32′—rounded) for the desired station location and then for all subsequent stations.

Figure 11.9 shows the geometry involved in this technique. A tangent to the curve is shown by a dashed line through station 0 + 240 (the proposed setup location). The angle from that tangent line to a line joining 0 + 240 to the BC is the deflection angle 3°06′. When the line from the BC is produced through station 0 + 240, the same angle (3°06′) occurs between that line and the tangent line through 0 + 240 (opposite angles). We have already determined that the deflection angle for 20 m was 1°26′ (see Section 11.4). When 1°26′ is added to 3°06′, the angle of 4°32′ for station 0 + 260 results, the same angle that was previously calculated for that station.

PI

$\Delta = 12°51'$

$0 + 240$

$3°06'$

$3°06'$

$4°32'$

$3°06'$

$0 + 260$

$4°32'$

$1°26'$

BC

EC

Tree Blocking Line of Sight
BC to 0+260

$R = 400$ m

$6°12'$

$R = 400$ m

$\Delta = 12°51'$

Δ

Scale Greatly Exaggerated

FIGURE 11.9 Moving up
on the curve.

This discussion has limited the move up to one station. In fact, the move up can be repeated as often as necessary to complete the curve layout. The technique can generally be stated as follows: *When the instrument is moved up on the curve and the instrument is backsighted with the telescope inverted at any other station, the theodolite will be oriented to the curve if the horizontal circle is first set to the value of the deflection angle for the sighted station.* That is, in the case of a BC sight, the deflection angle to be set is obviously zero; if the instrument were set on $0 + 260$ and sighting $0 + 240$, a deflection angle of $3°06'$ would first be set on the scale.

When the inverted telescope is transited to its normal position, all subsequent stations can then be sighted by using the original list of deflections. This is the meaning of the phrase *theodolite oriented to the curve.* It is also the reason why the list of deflections can be made first, before the instrument setup stations have been determined and (as we shall see in the next section) even before it has been decided whether to run in the curve center-line (₵) or whether it would be more appropriate to run in the curve on some offset line.

11.9 Offset Curves

Curves laid out for construction purposes must be established on offsets so that the survey stakes are not disturbed by construction activities. Many highway agencies prefer to lay out the curve on ₵ (centerline) and then offset each ₵ stake a set distance left and right. (Left and right are oriented by facing to a forward station.)

The stakes can be offset to one side by using the arm-swing technique described in Section 7.4.1.3, with the hands pointing to the two adjacent stations. If this method is done with care, the offsets on that one side can be established on radial lines without too much error. After one side has been offset in this manner, the other side is then offset by lining up the established offset stake with the ℄ stake and measuring the offset distance, while ensuring that all three stakes are visually in a straight line. Keeping the three stakes in a straight line ensures that any alignment error existing at the offset stakes steadily diminishes as one moves toward the ℄ and the construction works.

In the construction of most municipal roads, particularly curbed roads, the centerline may not be established. Instead, the road alignment is established directly on offset lines located a safe distance from the construction works. To illustrate, consider the curve in Example 11.2 used to construct a curbed road, as shown in Figure 11.10. The face of the curb is to be 4.00 m left and right of the centerline. Assume that the curb layout can be offset 2 m (each side) without interfering with construction. (Generally, the less cut or fill required, the smaller can be the offset distance.)

Figure 11.11 shows that if the layout is to be kept on radial lines through the ℄ stations, the station arc distances on the left-side (outside) curve will be longer than the corresponding ℄ arc distances, whereas the station arc distances on the right-side (inside) curve will be shorter than the corresponding ℄ arc distances. The figure also shows clearly that the ratio of the outside arc to the ℄ arc is identical to the ratio of the ℄ arc to the inside arc. (See the arc computations in Example 11.4.) *By keeping the offset stations on radial lines, the surveyor can use the ℄ deflections computed previously.*

When using setting-out programs in total stations to locate offset stations in the field, the surveyor can simply identify the offset value (when prompted by the program). The processor can then compute the coordinates of the offset stations and then inverse to determine (and display) the required angle and distance from the instrument station. Civil COGO-type software can also be used to compute coordinates of all offset stations, and the layout angles and distances from selected proposed instrument stations.

FIGURE 11.10 Municipal road cross section.

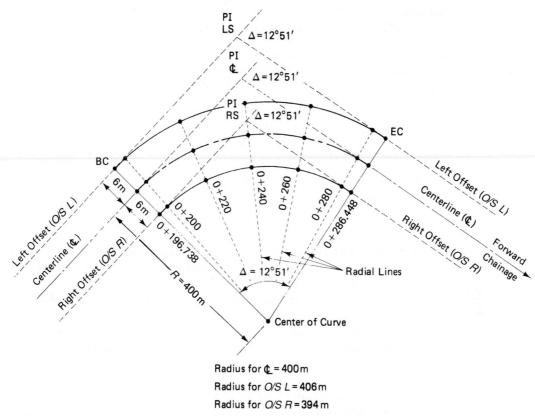

FIGURE 11.11 Offset curves.

■ **EXAMPLE 11.4** *Illustrative Problem for Offset Curves (Metric Units)*

Consider the problem of a construction offset layout using the data of Example 11.2, the deflections developed in Section 11.4, and the offset of 2 m introduced already in this section.

Given data:

$$\Delta = 12°51'$$
$$R = 400 \text{ m}$$
$$\text{PI at } 0 + 241.782$$

Calculated data:

$$T = 45.044 \text{ m}$$
$$L = 89.710 \text{ m}$$
$$\text{BC at } 0 + 196.738$$
$$\text{EC at } 0 + 286.448$$

Required: Curbs to be laid out on 2-m offsets at 20-m stations.

Solution

The following chart shows the calculated field deflections:

Station	Computed Deflection	Field Deflection
BC 0 + 196.738	0°00′00″	0°00′
0 + 200	0°14′01″	0°14′
0 + 220	1°39′58″	1°40′
0 + 240	3°05′55″	3°06′
0 + 260	4°31′52″	4°32′
0 + 280	5°57′49″	5°58′
EC 0 + 286.448	6°25′31″	6°25′30″ = Δ/2; Check

Figures 11.10 and 11.11 show that the left-side (outside) curb face has a radius of 404 m. A 2-m offset for that curb results in an offset radius of 406 m. Similarly, the offset radius for the right-side (inside) curb is $400 - 6 = 394$ m.

Because we will use the deflections already computed, we must calculate only the corresponding left-side arc or chord distances and the corresponding right-side arc or chord distances. Although layout procedure (angle and distance) indicates that chord distances are required, for illustrative purposes, we will compute both the arc and chord distances on offset.

Arc distance computations: Figure 11.12 shows that the offset (o/s) arcs can be computed by direct ratio:

$$\frac{\text{o/s arc}}{\text{₵ arc}} = \frac{\text{o/s radius}}{\text{₵ radius}}$$

For the first arc (BC to 0 + 200):

$$\text{Left side: o/s arc} = 3.262 \times \frac{406}{400} = 3.311 \text{ m}$$

$$\text{Right side: o/s arc} = 3.262 \times \frac{394}{400} = 3.213 \text{ m}$$

For the even station arcs:

$$\text{Left side: o/s arc} = 20 \times \frac{406}{400} = 20.300 \text{ m}$$

$$\text{Right side: o/s arc} = 20 \times \frac{394}{400} = 19.700 \text{ m}$$

For the last arc (0 + 280 to EC):

$$\text{Left side: o/s arc} = 6.448 \times \frac{406}{400} = 6.545 \text{ m}$$

$$\text{Right side: o/s arc} = 6.448 \times \frac{394}{400} = 6.351 \text{ m}$$

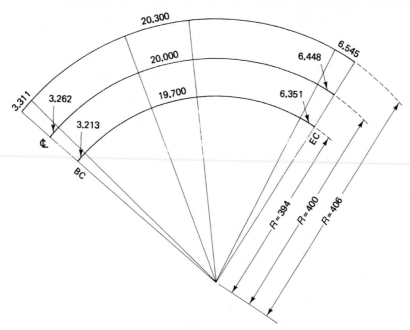

FIGURE 11.12 Offset arc lengths calculated by ratios.

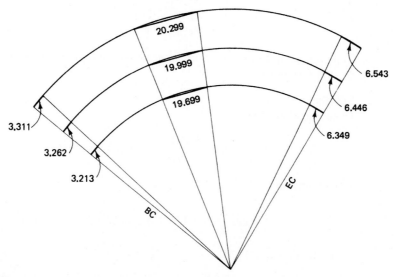

FIGURE 11.13 Offset chords calculated from deflection angles and offset radii.

Arithmetic check:

$$\text{LS} - \text{\textcent} = \text{\textcent} - \text{RS}$$

Chord distance computations: Refer to Figure 11.13. For any deflection angle, the equation for chord length (see Equation 11.8 in Section 11.5) is:

$$C = 2R(\sin \text{ deflection angle})$$

In this problem, the deflection angles have been calculated previously, and the radius (R) is the variable. For the first chord (BC to 0 + 200):

$$\text{Left side: } C = 2 \times 406 \times \sin 0°14'01'' = 3.311 \text{ m}$$
$$\text{Right side: } C = 2 \times 394 \times \sin 0°14'01'' = 3.213 \text{ m}$$

For the even station chords (see Section 11.4):

$$\text{Left side: } C = 2 \times 406 \times \sin 1°25'57'' = 20.299 \text{ m}$$
$$\text{Right side: } C = 2 \times 394 \times \sin 1°25'57'' = 19.699 \text{ m}$$

For the last chord:

$$\text{Left side: } C = 2 \times 406 \times \sin 0°27'42'' = 6.543 \text{ m}$$
$$\text{Right side: } C = 2 \times 394 \times \sin 0°27'42'' = 6.349 \text{ m}$$

Arithmetic check:

$$\text{LS chord} - \mathcal{C} \text{ chord} = \mathcal{C} \text{ chord} - \text{RS chord}$$

■ **EXAMPLE 11.5** *Curve Problem (Foot Units)*

You are given the following $\mathcal{C}$ data:

$$D = 5°$$
$$\Delta = 16°28'30''$$
$$\text{PI at } 31 + 30.62$$

You must furnish stakeout information for the curve on 50-ft offsets left and right of $\mathcal{C}$ at 50-ft stations.

Solution

From Equation 11.6:

$$R = \frac{5{,}729.58}{D} = 1{,}145.92 \text{ ft}$$

From Equation 11.1:

$$T = R \tan \frac{\Delta}{2} = 1{,}145.92 \tan 8°14'15'' = 165.90 \text{ ft}$$

And from Equation 11.7:

$$L = 100\left(\frac{\Delta}{D}\right) = 100 \times \left(\frac{16.475}{5}\right) = 329.50 \text{ ft}$$

we can also use Equation 11.5 to find the arc length:

$$L = 2\pi R\left(\frac{\Delta}{360}\right) = 329.50 \text{ ft}$$

$$
\begin{array}{rl}
\text{PI at} & 31 + 30.62 \\
T & \underline{1 \quad 65.90} \\
\text{BC} = & 29 + 64.72 \\
+L & \underline{3 \quad 29.50} \\
\text{EC} = & 32 + 94.22
\end{array}
$$

Computation of deflections:

$$\text{Total deflection for curve} = \frac{\Delta}{2} = 8°14'15'' = 494.25'$$

$$\text{Deflection per foot} = \frac{494.25}{329.50} = 1.5' \text{ per ft}$$

Also, because $D = 5°$, the deflection for 100 ft is $D/2$ or $2°30' = 150'$. Therefore, the deflection for 1 ft is 150/100 or 1.5' per ft.

Deflection for the first station:

$$35.28 \times 1.5 = 52.92' = 0°52.9'$$

Deflection for the even 50-ft stations:

$$50 \times 1.5 = 75' = 1°15'$$

Deflection for the last station:

$$44.22 \times 1.5 = 66.33' = 1°06.3'$$

The following chart shows the calculated deflections:

	Deflections (Cumulative)	
Stations	Office	Field (Closest Minute)
BC 29 + 64.72	0°00.0'	0°00'
30 + 00	0°52.9'	0°53'
30 + 50	2°07.9'	2°08'
31 + 00	3°22.9'	3°23'
31 + 50	4°37.9'	4°38'
32 + 00	5°52.9'	5°53'
32 + 50	7°07.9'	7°08'
EC 32 + 94.22	8°14.2'	8°14'
	$\approx 8°14.25'$	
	$= \dfrac{\Delta}{2}$, Check	

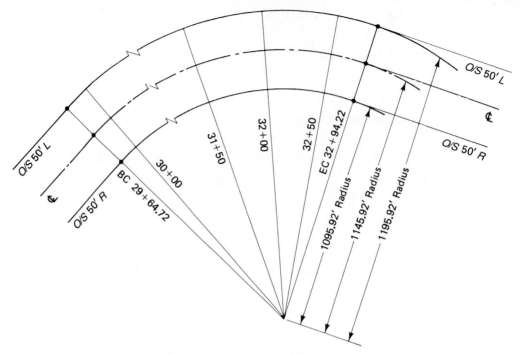

FIGURE 11.14 Sketch for the curve problem of Example 11.5.

Chord calculations for left- and right-side curves on 50-ft (from ℄) offsets (see the chord calculation table and Figure 11.14):

$$\text{Radius for } ℄ = 1{,}145.92 \text{ ft}$$
$$\text{Radius for LS} = 1{,}195.92 \text{ ft}$$
$$\text{Radius for RS} = 1{,}095.92 \text{ ft}$$

CHORD CALCULATIONS FOR EXAMPLE 11.5

Interval	Left Side	℄	Right Side
BC to 30 + 00	$C = 2 \times 1{,}195.92$ $\times \sin 0°52.9'$ $= 36.80$ ft	$C = 2 \times 1{,}145.92$ $\times \sin 0°52.9'$ $= 35.27$ ft	$C = 2 \times 1{,}095.92$ $\times \sin 0°52.9$ $= 33.73$ ft
	Diff. = 1.53	Diff. = 1.54	
50-ft stations	$C = 2 \times 1{,}195.92$ $\times \sin 1°15'$ $= 52.18$ ft	$C = 2 \times 1{,}145.92$ $\times \sin 1°15'$ $= 50.00$ (to 2 decimals)	$C = 2 \times 1{,}095.92$ $\times \sin 1°15'$ $= 47.81$ ft
	Diff. = 2.18	Diff. = 2.19	
32 + 50 to EC	$C = 2 \times 1{,}195.92$ $\times \sin 1°06.3'$ $= 46.13$ ft	$C = 2 \times 1{,}145.92$ $\times \sin 1°06.3'$ $= 44.20$ ft	$C = 2 \times 1{,}095.92$ $\times \sin 1°06.3'$ $= 42.27$ ft
	Diff. = 1.93	Diff. = 1.93	

11.10 Compound Circular Curves

A compound curve consists of two (usually) or more circular arcs between two main tangents turning in the same direction and joining at common tangent points. Figure 11.15 shows a compound curve consisting of two circular arcs joined at a point of compound curve (PCC). The lower station (chainage) curve is number 1, whereas the higher station curve is number 2. The parameters are R_1, R_2, Δ_1, Δ_2 ($\Delta_1 + \Delta_2 = \Delta$), T_1, and T_2. If four of these six or seven parameters are known, the others can be solved. Under normal circumstances, Δ_1 and Δ_2 (or Δ) are measured in the field, and R_1 and R_2 are given by design considerations, with minimum values governed by design speed.

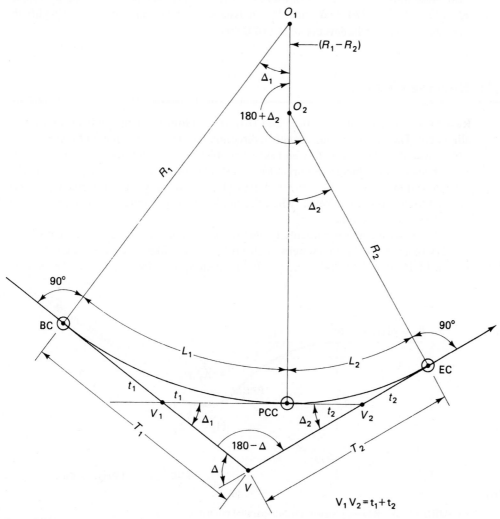

FIGURE 11.15 Compound circular curve.

Although compound curves can be manipulated to provide practically any vehicle path desired by the designer, they are not employed where simple curves or spiral curves can be used to achieve the same desired effect. Compound curves are reserved for those applications where design constraints (topographic or cost of land) preclude the use of simple or spiral curves, and they are now usually found chiefly in the design of interchange loops and ramps. Smooth driving characteristics require that the larger radius be no more than $1^1/_3$ times larger than the smaller radius. (This ratio increases to $1^1/_2$ when dealing with interchange curves.)

Solutions to compound curve problems vary because several possibilities exist according to which of the data are known in any one given problem. All problems can be solved by use of the sine law or cosine law or by the omitted measurement traverse technique illustrated in Example 6.2. If the omitted measurement traverse technique is used, the problem becomes a five-sided traverse (Figure 11.15), with sides R_1, T_1, T_2, R_2, and $(R_1 - R_2)$, and with angles $90°$, $180 - \Delta°$, $90°$, $180 + \Delta_2°$, and $\Delta_1°$. An assumed azimuth can be chosen to simplify the computations (i.e., set the direction of R_1 to $0°00'00''$).

11.11 Reverse Curves

Reverse curves [Figure 11.16(a) and (b)] are seldom used in highway or railway alignment. The instantaneous change in direction occurring at the point of reverse curve (PRC) would cause discomfort and safety problems for all but the slowest of speeds. Also, because the change in curvature is instantaneous, there is no room to provide superelevation transition from cross slope right to cross slope left. Reverse curves can be used to advantage, however, when the instantaneous change in direction poses no threat to safety or comfort.

The reverse curve is particularly pleasing to the eye and is used with great success for park roads, formal paths, waterway channels, and the like. This curve is illustrated in Figure 11.16(a) and 11.16(b); the parallel tangent application is particularly common

(a)

FIGURE 11.16 Reverse curves. (a) Nonparallel tangents.

(continued)

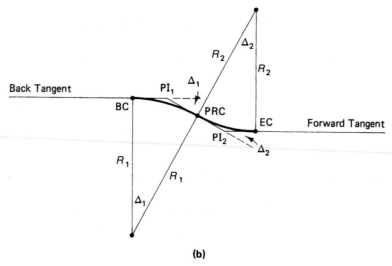

FIGURE 11.16 (*continued*)   (b) Parallel tangents.

(R_1 is often equal to R_2). As with compound curves, reverse curves have six independent parameters (R_1, Δ_1, T_1, R_2, Δ_2, T_2). The solution technique depends on which parameters are unknown, and the techniques noted for compound curves also provide the solution to reverse curve problems.

11.12 Vertical Curves: General Background

Vertical curves are used in highway and street vertical alignment to provide a gradual change between two adjacent grade lines. Some highway and municipal agencies introduce vertical curves at every change in grade-line slope, whereas other agencies introduce vertical curves into the alignment only when the net change in slope direction exceeds a specific value (e.g., 1.5 percent or 2 percent).

In Figure 11.17, vertical curve terminology is introduced: g_1 is the slope (percentage) of the lower chainage gradeline, g_2 is the slope of the higher chainage gradeline, BVC is the beginning of the vertical curve, EVC is the end of the vertical curve, and PVI is the point of intersection of the two adjacent grade lines. The length of vertical curve (L) is the projection of the curve onto a horizontal surface and, as such, corresponds to plan distance. The algebraic change in slope direction is A, where $A = g_2 - g_1$. For example, if $g_1 = +1.5$ percent and $g_2 = -3.2$ percent, A would be equal to $(-3.2 - 1.5) = -4.7$.

The geometric curve used in vertical alignment design is the vertical axis parabola. The parabola has the desirable characteristics of (1) a constant rate of change of slope, which contributes to a smooth alignment transition, and (2) ease of computation of vertical offsets, which permits easily computed curve elevations. The general equation of the parabola is

$$y = ax^2 + bx + c \tag{11.9}$$

FIGURE 11.17 Vertical curve terminology (profile view shown).

The slope of this curve at any point is given by the first derivative:

$$\frac{dy}{dx} = 2ax + b \tag{11.10}$$

and the rate of change of slope is given by the second derivative:

$$\frac{d^2y}{dx^2} = 2a \tag{11.11}$$

which is a constant, as we noted previously. The rate of change of slope ($2a$) can also be written as A/L.

If, for convenience, the origin of the axes is placed at the BVC (Figure 11.18), the general equation becomes

$$y = ax^2 + bx$$

and because the slope at the origin is g_1, the expression for the slope of the curve at any point becomes

$$\frac{dy}{dx} = \text{slope} = 2ax + g_1 \tag{11.12}$$

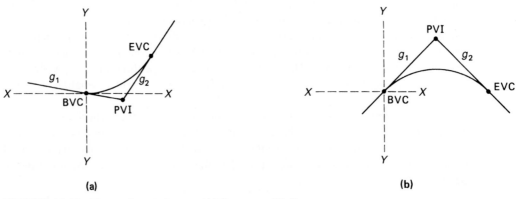

(a)   (b)

FIGURE 11.18 Types of vertical curves. (a) Sag curve. (b) Crest curve.

The final general equation can be written as

$$y = ax^2 + g_1 x \tag{11.13}$$

11.13 Geometric Properties of the Parabola

Figure 11.19 illustrates the following relationships:

- The difference in elevation between the BVC and a point on the g_1 grade line at a distance x units (feet or meters) is $g_1 x$ (g_1 is expressed as a decimal).
- The tangent offset between the grade line and the curve is given by ax^2, where x is the horizontal distance from the BVC; that is, tangent offsets are proportional to the squares of the horizontal distances.
- The elevation of a crest curve at distance x from the BVC is given by BVC + $g_1 x -$ ax^2 = curve elevation. (The sign is reversed in a sag curve.)
- The grade lines (g_1 and g_2) intersect midway between the BVC and the EVC; that is, BVC to $V = {}^1\!/_2\, L = V$ to EVC.
- Offsets from the two grade lines are symmetrical with respect to the PVI (V).
- The curve lies midway between the PVI and the midpoint of the chord; that is, CM = MV.

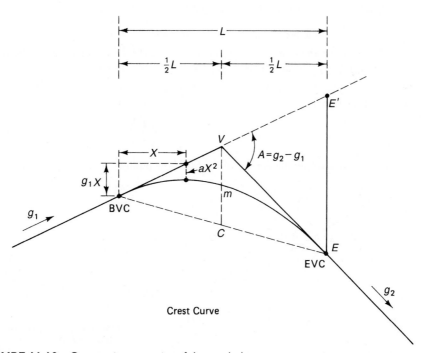

Crest Curve

FIGURE 11.19 Geometric properties of the parabola.

11.14 Computation of the High or the Low Point on a Vertical Curve

The locations of curve high and low points (if applicable) are important for drainage considerations; for example, on curbed streets, catch basins must be installed precisely at the drainage low point. We noted in Equation 11.12 that the slope was given by

$$\text{Slope} = 2ax + g_1$$

Figure 11.20 shows a sag vertical curve with a tangent drawn through the low point. It is obvious that the tangent line is horizontal with a slope of zero; that is,

$$2ax + g_1 = 0 \tag{11.14}$$

Had a crest curve been drawn, the tangent through the high point would have exhibited the same characteristics. Because $2a = A/L$, Equation 11.14 can be rewritten as

$$x = -g_1\left(\frac{L}{A}\right) \tag{11.15}$$

where x is the distance from the BVC to the high or low point.

11.15 Computing a Vertical Curve

Use the following procedure for computing a vertical curve:

1. Compute the algebraic difference in grades: $A = g_2 - g_1$.
2. Compute the chainage of the BVC and EVC. If the chainage of the PVI is known, $1/2 L$ is simply subtracted and added to the PVI chainage.
3. Compute the distance from the BVC to the high or low point (if applicable) using Equation 11.15:

$$x = -g_1\left(\frac{L}{A}\right)$$

and determine the station of the high/low point.

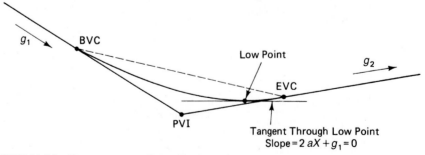

FIGURE 11.20   Tangent at curve low point.

4. Compute the tangent grade-line elevation of the BVC and the EVC.
5. Compute the tangent grade-line elevation for each required station.
6. Compute the midpoint of the chord elevation:

$$\frac{\text{elevation of BVC} + \text{elevation of EVC}}{2}$$

7. Compute the tangent offset (d) at the PVI (i.e., distance VM in Figure 11.19):

$$d = \frac{\text{difference in elevation of PVI and midpoint of chord}}{2}$$

8. Compute the tangent offset for each individual station (see line ax^2 in Figure 11.19):

$$\text{Tangent offset} = \frac{d(x)^2}{(L/2)^2}, \text{ or } \frac{(4d)x^2}{L^2} \tag{11.16}$$

where x is the distance from the BVC or EVC (whichever is closer) to the required station.

9. Compute the elevation on the curve at each required station by combining the tangent offsets with the appropriate tangent grade-line elevations. Add for sag curves and subtract for crest curves.

■ EXAMPLE 11.6

The techniques used in vertical curve computations are illustrated in this example. You are given the following information: $L = 300$ ft, $g_1 = -3.2\%$, $g_2 = +1.8\%$, PVI at $30 + 30$ with elevation $= 465.92$. Determine the location of the low point and the elevations on the curve at even stations, as well as at the low point.

Solution
Refer to Figure 11.21.

1. $A = 1.8 - (-3.2) = 5.0$

2. $\text{PVI} - \frac{1}{2}L = \text{BVC}$; BVC at $(30 + 30) - 150 = 28 + 80.00$

FIGURE 11.21 Sketch for Example 11.6.

$$\text{PVI} + \frac{1}{2}L = \text{EVC; EVC at } (30 + 30) + 150 = 31 + 80.00$$

$$\text{EVC} - \text{BVC} = L; (31 + 80) - (28 + 80) = 300; \text{Check}$$

3. Elevation of PVI = 465.92
   150 ft at 3.2% = 4.80 (see Figure 11.21)
   Elevation BVC = 470.72
   Elevation PVI = 465.92
   150 ft at 1.8% = 2.70
   Elevation EVC = 468.62

4. Location of low point is calculated using Equation 11.15:

$$x = \frac{-g_1 L}{A}$$

$$= \frac{3.2 \times 300}{5} = 192.00 \text{ ft (from the BVC)}$$

5. Tangent grade-line computations are entered in Table 11.1. Example:
   Elevation at 29 + 00 = 470.72 − (0.032 × 20) = 470.72 − 0.64 = 470.08

6. Midchord elevation:

$$\frac{470.72 \text{ (BVC)} + 468.62 \text{ (EVC)}}{2} = 469.67 \text{ ft}$$

7. Tangent offset at PVI (d):

$$d = \frac{\text{difference in elevation of PVI and midchord}}{2}$$

$$= \frac{469.67 - 465.92}{2} = 1.875 \text{ ft}$$

Table 11.1 PARABOLIC CURVE ELEVATIONS BY TANGENT OFFSETS

Station	Tangent Elevation +	Tangent Offset $\left(\frac{x}{\frac{1}{2}L}\right)^2 d*$	= Curve Elevation
BVC 28 + 80	470.72	$(0/150)^2 \times 1.875 = 0$	470.72
29 + 00	470.08	$(20/150)^2 \times 1.875 = .03$	470.11
30 + 00	466.88	$(120/150)^2 \times 1.875 = 1.20$	468.08
PVI 30 + 30	465.92	$(150/150)^2 \times 1.875 = 1.875$	467.80
Low 30 + 72	466.68	$(108/150)^2 \times 1.875 = .97$	467.65
31 + 00	467.18	$(80/150)^2 \times 1.875 = .53$	467.71
EVC 31 + 80	468.62	$(0/150)^2 \times 1.875 = 0$	468.62
See Section 11.16			
30 + 62	466.50	$(118/150)^2 \times 1.875 = 1.16$	467.66 ⎫
30 + 72	466.68	$(108/150)^2 \times 1.875 = 0.97$	467.65 ⎬
30 + 82	466.86	$(98/150)^2 \times 1.875 = 0.80$	467.66 ⎭

*Where x is distance from BVC or EVC, whichever is closer.

8. Tangent offsets are computed by multiplying the distance ratio squared

$$\left(\frac{x}{L/2}\right)^2$$

by the maximum tangent offset (d). See Table 11.1.

9. The computed tangent offsets are added (in this example) to the tangent elevation to determine the curve elevation.

11.15.1 Parabolic Curve Elevations Computed Directly from the Equation

In addition to the tangent offset method shown earlier, vertical curve elevations can also be computed directly from the general equation.

$y = ax^2 + bx + c$, where $a = (g_2 - g_1)/2L$

L = horizontal length of vertical curve

$b = g_1$

c = elevation at BVC

x = horizontal distance from BVC

y = elevation on the curve at distance x from the BVC

This technique is illustrated in Table 11.2 using the data from Example 11.6.

11.16 Design Considerations

From Section 11.14, $2a = A/L$ is an expression giving the constant rate of change of slope for the parabola. Another useful relationship is the inverse, or

$$K = \frac{L}{A} \qquad (11.17)$$

Table 11.2 PARABOLIC CURVE ELEVATIONS COMPUTED FROM THE EQUATION
$y = ax^2 + bx + c$

Station	Distance from BVC	ax^2	bx	c	y (Elevation on the Curve)
BVC 28 + 80	0				470.72
29 + 00	20	0.03	−0.64	470.72	470.11
30 + 00	120	1.20	−3.84	470.72	468.08
PVI 30 + 30	150	1.88	−4.80	470.72	467.80
Low 30 + 72	192	3.07	−6.14	470.72	467.65
31 + 00	220	4.03	−7.04	470.72	467.71
EVC 31 + 80	300	7.50	−9.60	470.72	468.62

where K is the horizontal distance required to effect a 1-percent change in slope on the vertical curve. Substituting for L/A in Equation 11.15 yields

$$x = -g_1 K \qquad (11.18)$$

(the result is always positive), where x is the distance to the low point from the BVC, or

$$x = +g_2 K \qquad (11.19)$$

where x is the distance to the low point from the EVC.

You can see in Figure 11.19 that EE' is the distance generated by the divergence of g_1 and g_2 over the distance $L/2$:

$$EE' = \frac{(g_2 - g_1)}{100} \times \frac{L}{2}$$

Figure 11.19 also shows that $VC = \frac{1}{2} EE'$ (similar triangles) and that $VM = d = \frac{1}{4} EE'$; thus,

$$d = \left(\frac{1}{4}\right)\frac{(g_2 - g_1)}{100} \times \frac{L}{2} = \frac{AL}{800} \qquad (11.20)$$

or from Equation 11.17:

$$d = \frac{KA^2}{800} \qquad (11.21)$$

Equations 11.18, 11.19, and 11.21 are useful when design criteria are defined in terms of K.

Table 11.3 shows values of K for minimum stopping sight distances. On crest curves, it is assumed that the driver's eye height is at 1.05 m and the object that the driver must see is at least 0.38 m. The defining conditions for sag curves would be nighttime restrictions that relate to the field of view given by headlights with an angular beam divergence of 1°.

In practice, the length of a vertical curve is rounded to the nearest even meter, and if possible the PVI is located at an even station so that the symmetrical characteristics of the curve can be fully used. To avoid the aesthetically unpleasing appearance of very short vertical curves, some agencies insist that the length of the vertical curve (L) be at least as long in meters as the design velocity is in kilometers per hour.

Closer analysis of the data shown in Table 11.1 indicates a possible concern. The vertical curve at the low or high point has a relatively small change of slope. This is not a problem for crest curves or for sag curves for ditched roads and highways (ditches can have grade lines independent of the ℄ grade line). However, when sag curves are used for curbed municipal street design, a drainage problem is introduced. The curve elevations in brackets in Table 11.1 cover 10 ft on either side of the low point. These data illustrate that, for a distance of 20 ft, there is almost no change in elevation (i.e., only 0.01 ft). If the road were built according to the design, chances are that the low-point catch basin would not completely drain the extended low-point area. The solution to this problem is for the surveyor to lower the catch-basin grate arbitrarily (1 in. is often used) to ensure proper drainage, or to install additional catch basins in the extended low area.

Table 11.3 TYPICAL DESIGN CONTROLS FOR CREST AND SAG VERTICAL CURVES BASED ON MINIMUM STOPPING SIGHT DISTANCES FOR VARIOUS DESIGN SPEEDS

Design Speed, V (km/hr)	Min. Stopping Sight Distance, S (m)	K Factor	
		Crest (m)	Sag (m)
40	45	4	8
50	65	8	12
60	85	15	18
70	110	25	25
80	135	35	30
90	160	50	40
100	185	70	45
110	215	90	50
120	245	120	60
130	275	150	70
140	300	180	80

$$K_{crest} = \frac{S^2}{200h_1 (1 + \sqrt{h_2/h_1})^2} \qquad\qquad K_{sag} = \frac{S^2}{200 (h + S \tan a)}$$

$h_1 = 1.05$ m, height of driver's eye $\qquad\qquad$ $h = 0.60$ m, height of headlights

$h_2 = 0.38$ m, height of object $\qquad\qquad\qquad$ $\alpha = 1°$, angular spread of light beam

$L = KA$, from Equation 11.15, where L(m) cannot be less than V(km/hr). When $KA < V$, use $L = V$.

Source: Vertical Curve Tables, Ministry of Transportation, Ontario.

11.17 Spiral Curves: General Background

A spiral is a curve with a uniformly changing radius. Spirals are used in highway and railroad alignment to overcome the abrupt change in direction that occurs when the alignment changes from a tangent to a circular curve, and vice versa. The length of the spiral curve is also used for the transition from normally crowned pavement to fully superelevated (banked) pavement.

Figure 11.22 illustrates how the spiral curve is inserted between tangent and circular curve alignment. You can see that, at the beginning of the spiral (T.S. = tangent to spiral), the radius of the spiral is the radius of the tangent line (infinitely large), and that the radius of the spiral curve decreases at a uniform rate until, at the point where the circular curve begins (S.C. = spiral to curve), the radius of the spiral equals the radius of the circular curve. In the previous section, we noted that the parabola, which is used in vertical alignment, had the important property of a uniform rate of change of slope. Here, we find that the spiral, used in horizontal alignment, has a uniform rate of change of radius (curvature). This property permits the driver to leave a tangent section of highway at relatively high rates of speed without experiencing problems with safety or comfort.

Figure 11.23 illustrates how the circular curve is moved inward (toward the center of the curve), leaving room for the insertion of a spiral at either end of the shortened circular curve. The amount that the circular curve is shifted in from the main tangent line is known as *P*. This shift results in the curve center (O) being at the distance $(R + P)$ from the main tangent lines.

FIGURE 11.22 Spiral curves.

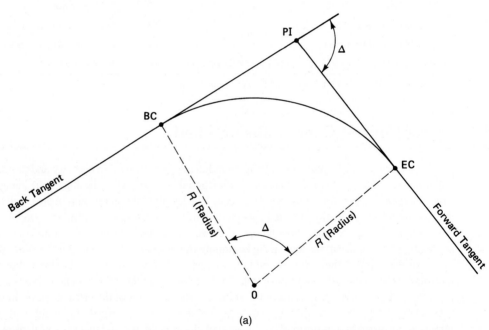

(a)

FIGURE 11.23 Shifting the circular curve to make room for the insertion of spirals. (a) Circular curve joining two tangents.

(continued)

      The spirals illustrated in this text reflect the common practice of using equal spirals to join the ends of a circular or compound curve to the main tangents. For more complex spiral applications, such as unequal spirals and spirals joining circular arcs, refer to a text on route surveying. This text shows excerpts from spiral tables

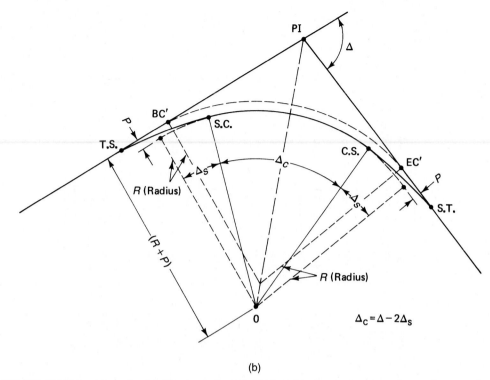

(b)

FIGURE 11.23 (*continued*) (b) Circular curve shifted inward (toward curve center) to make room for the insertion of spiral curves at either end of the circular curve.

(see Tables 11.4–11.7). Each U.S. state and Canadian province prepares and publishes similar tables for use by their personnel. A wide variety of spirals, both geometric and empirical, have been used to develop spiral tables. Geometric spirals include the cubic parabola and the clothoid curve, and empirical spirals include the A.R.E.A. 10-chord spiral, used by many railroads. Generally, the use of tables is giving way to computer programs for spiral solutions. All spirals give essentially the same appearance when staked out in the field.

11.18 Spiral Curve Computations

Usually, data for a spiral computation are obtained as follows (refer to Figure 11.24):

1. Δ is determined in the field.
2. R or D (degree of curve) is given by design considerations (usually defined by design speed, but sometimes by property constraints).
3. Stationing (chainage) of PI is determined in the field.
4. L_s is chosen with respect to design speed and the number of traffic lanes.

Table 11.4 SPIRAL TABLES FOR $L_S = 150$ FEET

D	Δ_s	R	p	$R + p$	q	LT	ST	Δ_s	X_c	Y_c	$D/10\ L_s$
7°30′	5°37′30″	763.9437	1.2268	765.1705	74.9759	100.0305	50.0459	5.62500°	149.86	4.91	0.00500
8°00′	6°00′00″	716.1972	1.3085	717.5057	74.9726	100.0575	50.0523	6.00000°	149.84	5.23	0.00533
30′	6°22′30″	674.0680	1.3902	675.4582	74.9691	100.0649	50.0590	6.37500°	149.81	5.56	0.00567
9°00′	6°45′00″	636.6198	1.4719	638.0917	74.9653	100.0728	50.0662	6.75000°	149.79	5.88	0.00600
30′	7°07′30″	603.1135	1.5536	604.6671	74.9614	100.0811	50.0738	7.12500°	149.77	6.21	0.00633
10°00′	7°30′00″	572.9578	1.6352	574.5930	74.9572	100.0899	50.0817	7.50000°	149.74	6.54	0.00667
30′	7°52′30″	545.6741	1.7169	547.3910	74.9528	100.0991	50.0901	7.87500°	149.72	6.86	0.00700
11°00′	8°15′00″	520.8707	1.79985	522.6692	74.9482	100.1088	50.0989	8.25000°	149.69	7.19	0.00733
30′	8°37′30″	498.2242	1.8802	500.1044	74.9434	100.1190	50.1082	8.62500°	149.66	7.51	0.00767
12°00′	9°00′00″	477.4648	1.9618	479.4266	74.9384	100.1295	50.1178	9.00000°	149.63	7.84	0.00800
13°00′	9°45′00″	440.7368	2.1249	442.8617	74.9277	100.1521	50.1383	9.75000°	149.57	8.49	0.00867
14°00′	10°30′00″	409.2556	2.2880	411.5436	74.9161	100.1765	50.1605	10.50000°	149.50	9.14	0.00933
15°00′	11°15′00″	381.9719	2.4510	384.4229	74.9037	100.2027	50.1843	11.25000°	149.42	9.79	0.01000
16°00′	12°00′00″	358.0986	2.6139	360.7125	74.8905	100.2307	50.2098	12.00000°	149.34	10.44	0.01067
17°00′	12°45′00″	337.0340	2.7767	339.8107	74.8764	100.2606	50.2370	12.75000°	149.26	11.09	0.01133
18°00′	13°30′00″	318.3099	2.9394	321.2493	74.8614	100.2924	50.2659	13.50000°	149.17	11.73	0.01200
19°00′	14°15′00″	301.5567	3.1020	304.6587	74.8456	100.3259	50.2964	14.25000°	149.07	12.38	0.01267
20°00′	15°00′00″	286.4789	3.2645	289.7434	74.8290	100.3614	50.3287	15.00000°	148.98	13.03	0.01333
21°00′	15°45′00″	272.8370	3.4269	276.2639	74.8115	100.3987	50.3627	15.75000°	148.87	13.67	0.01400
22°00′	16°30′00″	260.4354	3.5891	264.0245	74.7932	100.4379	50.3983	16.50000°	148.76	14.31	0.01467
23°00′	17°15′00″	249.1121	3.7512	252.8633	74.7740	100.4790	50.4357	17.25000°	148.65	14.96	0.01533
24°00′	18°00′00″	238.7324	3.9132	242.6456	74.7539	100.5219	50.4748	18.00000°	148.53	15.60	0.01600
25°00′	18°45′00″	229.1831	4.0750	233.2581	74.7331	100.5668	50.5157	18.75000°	148.40	16.26	0.01667
26°00′	19°30′00″	220.3684	4.2367	224.6051	74.7114	100.6135	50.5582	19.50000°	148.27	16.88	0.01733

Source: Spiral Tables (foot units), courtesy Ministry of Transportation, Ontario.

Table 11.5 SPIRAL CURVE LENGTHS AND SUPERELEVATION RATES: SUPERELEVATION (e) MAXIMUM OF 0.06, TYPICAL FOR NORTHERN CLIMATES

D	V = 30 e	V=30 L 2 Lane	V=30 L 4 Lane	V = 40 e	V=40 L 2 Lane	V=40 L 4 Lane	V = 50 e	V=50 L 2 Lane	V=50 L 4 Lane	V = 60 e	V=60 L 2 Lane	V=60 L 4 Lane	V = 70 e	V=70 L 2 Lane	V=70 L 4 Lane	V = 80 e	V=80 L 2 Lane	V=80 L 4 Lane
0°15'	NC	0	0	NC	0	0	NC	0	0	NC	0	0	NC	0	0	RC	250	250
0°30'	NC	0	0	NC	0	0	NC	0	0	RC	200	200	RC	200	200	0.023	250	250
0°45'	NC	0	0	NC	0	0	RC	150	150	0.021	200	200	0.026	200	200	0.033	250	250
1°00'	NC	0	0	RC	150	150	0.020	150	150	0.027	200	200	0.033	200	200	0.041	250	250
1°30'	RC	100	100	0.020	150	150	0.028	150	150	0.036	200	200	0.044	200	200	0.053	250	300
2°00'	RC	100	100	0.026	150	150	0.035	150	150	0.044	200	200	0.052	200	250	0.059	250	300
2°30'	0.020	100	100	0.031	150	150	0.040	150	150	0.050	200	200	0.057	200	300	0.060	250	300
3°00'	0.023	100	100	0.035	150	150	0.044	150	150	0.054	200	250	0.060	200	300			
3°30'	0.026	100	100	0.038	150	150	0.048	150	150	0.057	200	250						
4°00'	0.029	100	100	0.041	150	150	0.051	150	150	0.059	200	250						
5°00'	0.034	100	100	0.046	150	150	0.056	150	150	0.060	200	250						
6°00'	0.038	100	100	0.050	150	200	0.059	150	200									
7°00'	0.041	100	150	0.054	150	200	0.060	150	250									
8°00'	0.043	100	150	0.056	150	200												
9°00'	0.046	100	150	0.058	150	200												
10°00'	0.048	100	150	0.059	150	200												
11°00'	0.050	100	150	0.060	150	200												
12°00'	0.052	100	150															
13°00'	0.053	100	150															
14°00'	0.055	100	150															
16°00'	0.058	100	200															
18°00'	0.059	150	200															
20°00'	0.060	150	200															
21°00'	0.060	150	200															

$D_{max} = 21°00'$ (V = 30); $D_{max} = 11°00'$ (V = 40); $D_{max} = 7°00'$ (V = 50); $D_{max} = 4°30'$ (V = 60); $D_{max} = 3°00'$ (V = 70); $D_{max} = 2°30'$ (V = 80)

Source: Ministry of Transportation, Ontario.

Legend: V, design speed (mph);

e, rate of superelevation (feet per foot of pavement width);

L, length of superelevation runoff or spiral curve;

NC, normal crown section;

RC, remove adverse crown and superelevate at normal crown slope;

D, degree of circular curve.

Above the heavy line, spirals are not required, but superelevation is to be run off in distances shown.

Table 11.6 SPIRAL CURVE LENGTHS (FEET) AND SUPERELEVATION RATES: SUPERELEVATION (e) MAXIMUM OF 0.100, TYPICAL FOR SOUTHERN CLIMATES

D	R	V = 30 e	V = 30 L 2 Lane	V = 30 L 4 Lane	V = 40 e	V = 40 L 2 Lane	V = 40 L 4 Lane	V = 50 e	V = 50 L 2 Lane	V = 50 L 4 Lane	V = 60 e	V = 60 L 2 Lane	V = 60 L 4 Lane	V = 70 e	V = 70 L 2 Lane	V = 70 L 4 Lane
0°15'	22,918'	NC	0	0	NC	0	0	NC	0	0	NC	0	0	RC	200	200
0°30'	11,459'	NC	0	0	NC	0	0	RC	150	150	RC	175	175	RC	200	200
0°45'	7,639'	NC	0	0	RC	125	125	RC	150	150	0.018	175	175	0.020	200	200
1°00'	5,730'	NC	0	0	RC	125	125	0.018	150	150	0.022	175	175	0.028	200	200
1°30'	3,820'	RC	100	100	0.020	125	125	0.027	150	150	0.034	175	175	0.042	200	200
2°00'	2,865'	RC	100	100	0.027	125	125	0.036	150	150	0.046	175	190	0.055	200	250
2°30'	2,292'	0.020	100	100	0.033	125	125	0.045	150	160	0.059	175	240	0.069	210	310
3°00'	1,910'	0.024	100	100	0.038	125	125	0.054	150	190	0.070	190	280	0.083	250	370
3°30'	1,637'	0.027	100	100	0.045	125	140	0.063	150	230	0.081	220	330	0.096	290	430
4°00'	1,432'	0.030	100	100	0.050	125	160	0.070	170	250	0.090	240	360	0.100	300	450
5°00'	1,146'	0.038	100	100	0.060	130	190	0.083	200	300	0.099	270	400	$D_{max} = 3°9'$		
6°00'	955'	0.044	100	120	0.068	140	210	0.093	220	330	0.100	270	400			
7°00'	819'	0.050	100	140	0.076	160	240	0.097	230	350	$D_{max} = 5°5'$					
8°00'	716'	0.055	100	150	0.084	180	260	0.100	240	360						
9°00'	637'	0.061	110	160	0.089	190	280	0.100	240	360						
10°00'	573'	0.065	120	180	0.093	200	290	$D_{max} = 8.3°$								
11°00'	521'	0.070	130	190	0.096	200	300									
12°00'	477'	0.074	130	200	0.098	210	310									
13°00'	441'	0.078	140	210	0.099	210	310									
14°00'	409'	0.082	150	220	0.100	210	320									
16°00'	358'	0.087	160	240	$D_{max} = 13.4°$											
18°00'	318'	0.093	170	250												
20°00'	286'	0.096	170	260												
22°00'	260'	0.099	180	270												
24.8°	231'	0.100	180	270												
$D_{max} = 24.8°$																

NC, normal crown section; RC, remove adverse crown and superelevate at normal crown slope. Spirals desirable but not as essential above the heavy line. Lengths rounded in multiples of 25 or 50 ft permit simpler calculations. The higher maximum e value (0.100) in this table permits a sharper maximum curvature.

All other spiral parameters can be determined by computation and/or by use of spiral tables.

$$\text{Tangent to spiral (see Figure 11 .24): } T_s = (R + P) \tan \frac{\Delta}{2} + q \qquad (11.22)$$

$$\text{Spiral tangent deflection: } \Delta_s = \frac{L_s D}{200} \qquad (11.23)$$

In circular curves, $\Delta = LD/100$ (see Equation 11.7). Because the spiral has a uniformly changing D, the spiral angle (Δ_s) = the length of the spiral (L_s) in stations times the average degree of curve $(D/2)$. The total length of the curve system is comprised of the circular curve and the two spiral curves, that is,

$$\text{Total length: } L = L_c + 2L_s \qquad (11.24)$$

See Figure 11.24, where L is the *total length of the curve system*.

$$\text{Total deflection: } \Delta = \Delta_c + 2\Delta_s \qquad (11.25)$$

See Figure 11.24.

$$\text{Spiral deflection: } \theta_s = \frac{\Delta_s}{3} \text{ (approximate)} \qquad (11.26)$$

θ_s is the total spiral deflection angle; compare to circular curves, where the deflection angle is $\Delta/2$. The approximate formula in Equation 11.26 gives realistic results for the vast majority of spiral problems. For example, when Δ_s is as large as 21° (which is seldom the case), the correction to Δ_s is approximately $+30''$.

$$L_c = \frac{2\pi R \Delta_c}{360} \text{ (foot or meter units)} \qquad (11.27)$$

$$L_c = \frac{100 \Delta_c}{D} \text{ (foot units)} \qquad (11.28)$$

$$\Delta_s = \frac{90}{\pi} \times \frac{L_s}{R} \qquad (11.29)$$

$$\phi = \left(\frac{l}{L_s}\right)^2 \theta_s \qquad (11.30)$$

Equation 11.30 comes from the spiral definition, where ϕ is the deflection angle for any distance l, and ϕ and θ_s are in the same units. Practically,

$$\phi' = l^2 \frac{(\theta_s \times 60)}{L_s^2}$$

where ϕ' is the deflection angle in minutes for any distance measured from the T.S. or the S.T. Other values, such as x, y, P, q, ST, and LT, are found routinely in spiral tables issued by state and provincial highway agencies and can also be found in route surveying texts. For the past few years, solutions to these problems have been achieved almost exclusively by the use of computers and appropriate coordinate geometry computer software.

Table 11.7 SPIRAL CURVE LENGTHS AND SUPERELEVATION RATES (METRIC)*

Design Speed (km/hr)	40			50			60			70			80		
Radius (m)	e	A 2 Lane	A 3 & 4 Lane	e	A 2 Lane	A 3 & 4 Lane	e	A 2 Lane	A 3 & 4 Lane	e	A 2 Lane	A 3 & 4 Lane	e	A 2 Lane	A 3 & 4 Lane
7,000	NC			NC			NC			NC			NC		
5,000	NC			NC			NC			NC			NC		
4,000	NC			NC			NC			NC			NC		
3,000	NC			NC			NC			NC			NC		
2,000	NC			NC			NC			RC	275	275	RC	300	300
1,500	NC			NC			RC	225	225	RC	250	250	0.024	250	250
1,200	NC			NC			RC	200	200	0.023	225	225	0.028	225	225
1,000	NC			RC	170	170	0.021	175	175	0.027	200	200	0.032	200	200
900	NC			RC	150	150	0.023	175	175	0.029	180	180	0.034	200	200
800	NC			RC	150	150	0.025	160	160	0.031	175	175	0.036	175	175
700	NC			0.021	140	140	0.027	150	150	0.034	175	175	0.039	175	175
600	NC	120	120	0.024	125	125	0.030	140	140	0.037	150	150	0.042	175	175
500	RC	100	100	0.027	120	120	0.034	125	125	0.041	140	150	0.046	150	160
400	0.023	90	90	0.031	100	100	0.038	115	120	0.045	125	135	0.051	135	150
350	0.025	90	90	0.034	100	100	0.041	110	115	0.048	120	125	0.054	125	140
300	0.028	80	80	0.037	90	100	0.044	100	110	0.051	120	125	0.057	125	135
250	0.031	75	80	0.040	85	90	0.048	90	100	0.055	110	120	0.060	125	125
220	0.034	70	80	0.043	80	90	0.050	90	100	0.057	110	110	0.060	125	125
200	0.036	70	75	0.045	75	90	0.052	85	100	0.059	110	110	Minimum R = 250		
180	0.038	60	75	0.047	70	90	0.054	85	95	0.060	110	110			
160	0.040	60	75	0.049	70	85	0.056	85	90	Minimum R = 190					
140	0.043	60	70	0.052	65	80	0.059	85	90						
120	0.048	60	65	0.055	65	75	0.060	85	90						
100	0.049	50	65	0.058	65	70	Minimum R = 130								
90	0.051	50	60	0.060	65	70									
80	0.054	50	60	0.060	65	70									
70	0.058	50	60	Minimum R = 90											
60	0.059	50	60												
	0.059	50	60												
Minimum R = 55															

Source: Roads and Transportation Association of Canada (RTAC).

*D_{max} = 0.06

e is superelevation.

A is spiral parameter in meters.

NC is normal cross section.

RC is remove adverse crown and superelevate at normal rate.

Spiral length, $L = A^2$ + radius.

Spiral parameters are minimum and higher values should be used where possible.

Spirals are desirable but not essential above the heavy line.

For six-lane pavement: above the dashed line use four-lane values; below the dashed line use four-lane values × 1.15.

A divided road having a median less than 7 m may be treated as a single pavement.

Table 11.7 (*continued*)

| | 90 | | | 100 | | | 110 | | | 120 | | | 130 | | | 140 | | |
| | | A | | | A | | | A | | | A | | | A | | | A | |
E/e	E	2 Lane	3 & 4 Lane	e	2 Lane	3 & 4 Lane	e	2 Lane	3 & 4 Lane	e	2 Lane	3 & 4 Lane	e	2 Lane	3 & 4 Lane	e	2 Lane	3 & 4 Lane
	NC			NC			NC			NC			NC	700	700	RC	700	700
	NC			NC			NC	500	500	RC	600	600	0.021	600	600	0.024	625	625
	NC			RC	480	480	RC	500	500	0.022	500	500	0.025	500	500	0.028	560	560
	RC	390	400	0.025	400	400	0.023	450	450	0.027	450	450	0.030	450	450	0.034	495	495
	0.023	300	350	0.027	340	340	0.031	350	350	0.035	350	350	0.039	400	400	0.043	400	400
	0.029	270	275	0.033	300	300	0.037	300	300	0.041	300	300	0.046	330	330	0.050	345	340
	0.033	240	240	0.038	250	250	0.042	275	275	0.047	285	285	0.051	300	300	0.056	330	330
	0.037	225	225	0.042	240	240	0.046	250	260	0.051	250	275	0.055	300	300	0.060	325	325
	0.039	200	200	0.044	225	225	0.049	230	250	0.053	250	270	0.057	300	300	0.060	325	325
	0.042	200	200	0.047	200	225	0.051	225	250	0.056	250	260	0.060	275	275	Minimum R = 1,000		
	0.045	185	185	0.049	200	220	0.054	225	235	0.059	250	250	0.060	275	275			
	0.048	175	185	0.053	200	200	0.057	220	220	0.060	250	250	Minimum R = 800					
	0.052	160	175	0.057	200	200	0.060	220	220	Minimum R = 650								
	0.057	160	165	0.060	200	200	Minimum R = 525											
	0.059	160	160	Minimum R = 420														
	0.060	160	160															
	Minimum R = 340																	

FIGURE 11.24 Summary of spiral geometry and spiral symbols.

Symbols

T.S.	— Tangent to Spiral
S.C.	— Spiral to Curve
C.S.	— Curve to Spiral
S.T.	— Spiral to Tangent
T_s	— Spiral Tangent
X	— Distance along Tangent from T.S. to Point at Right Angle to S.C.
Y	— Right Angle Distance from Tangent to S.C.
LT	— Long Tangent (Spiral)
ST	— Short Tangent (Spiral)
L_s	— Length of Spiral (Arc)

LC	— Long Chord
q	— Distance along Tangent to a Point at Right Angle to Ghost BC (Marginally Less than $L_s/2$)
P	— Distance from Tangent That the Curve (Ghost BC) Has Been Offset
T_c	— Circular Curve Tangent
CPI	— **Circular Curve PI**
SPI	— Spiral Curve PI
PI	— Point of Intersection of Curve Tangents
L_c	— Length of Circular Curve
L	— Length of Curve System — TS to ST

With the switch to metric that took place in the 1970s in Canada, a decision was reached to work exclusively with the radius in defining horizontal curves. It was decided that new spiral tables, based solely on the definition of *R*, were appropriate. The RTAC prepared spiral tables based on the spiral property defined as follows:

The product of any instantaneous radius *r* and the corresponding spiral length λ (i.e., *l*) from the beginning of the spiral to that point is equal to the product of the spiral end radius *R* and the entire length (L_s) of that spiral, which means it is a constant.

Thus, we have the following equation:

$$r\lambda = RL_s = A^2 \qquad (11.31)$$

The constant is denoted as A^2 to retain dimensional consistency because it represents a product of two lengths. The following relationship can be derived from Equation 11.31:

$$\frac{A}{R} = \frac{L_s}{A} \tag{11.32}$$

The RTAC tables are based on design speed and the number of traffic lanes, together with a design radius. The constant value A is taken from one of the tables and is used in conjunction with R to find all the spiral table curve parameters noted earlier in this section.

Note that, concurrent with the changeover to metric units, a major study in Ontario of highway geometrics resulted in spiral curve lengths that reflected design speed, attainment of superelevation, driver comfort, and aesthetics. Thus, the spiral lengths vary somewhat between the foot unit system and the metric system.

11.19 Spiral Layout Procedure Summary

Refer to Figure 11.24. The following list summarizes the spiral layout procedure using traditional techniques:

1. Select L_s (foot units) or A (metric units) in conjunction with the design speed, number of traffic lanes, and sharpness of the circular curve (radius or D).
2. From the spiral tables, determine P, q, x, y, and so on.
3. Compute the spiral tangent (T_s) using Equation 11.22 and the circular tangent (T_c) using Equation 11.1.
4. Compute the spiral angle (Δ_s). Use Equation 11.33 for foot units or Equation 11.29 for metric units (see Tables 11.3 and 11.7).
5. Prepare a list of relevant layout stations. This list should include all horizontal alignment key points (e.g., T.S., S.C., C.S., and S.T.), as well as all vertical alignment key points, such as grade points, BVC, low point, and EVC.
6. Calculate the deflection angles. See Equation 11.30.
7. From the established PI, measure out the T_s distance to locate the T.S. and S.T.
8. (a) From the T.S., turn off the spiral deflection ($\theta_s = \frac{1}{3}\Delta_s$ approximately), measure out the LC, and thus locate the S.C.

   or

   (b) From the T.S., measure out the LT distance along the main tangent and locate the spiral PI (SPI); the spiral angle (Δ_s) can now be turned, and the ST distance can be measured out to locate the S.C.
9. From the S.C., measure out the circular tangent (T_c) along the line SPI$_1$–SC to establish the CPI.
10. Steps 8 and 9 are repeated, starting at the S.T. instead of at the T.S.
11. The key points are verified by checking all angles and redundant distances. Some surveyors prefer to locate the CPI by intersecting the two tangent lines (i.e., lines through SPI$_1$ and S.C. and through SPI$_2$ and C.S.). The locations can be verified by checking the angle Δ_c and by checking the two tangents (T_c).

12. Only after all key control points have been verified can the deflection angle stakeout commence. The lower chainage spiral is run in from the T.S., whereas the higher chainage spiral is run in from the S.T. The circular curve can be run in from the S.C., although it is common practice to run half the curve from the S.C. and the other half from the C.S. so that any acceptable errors that accumulate can be isolated in the middle of the circular arc where they will be less troublesome, relatively speaking.

When employing layout procedures using polar layouts by total station, or positioning layouts using GPS techniques, the surveyor must first compute the position coordinates of all layout points and then upload these coordinates into the instrument's controller.

■ **EXAMPLE 11.7** *Illustrative Spiral Problem (Foot Units)*
You are given the following data:

$$\Delta = 25°45' RT$$
$$V = 40 \text{ mph}$$
$$D = 9°$$
$$\text{PI at } 36 + 17.42$$
$$\text{Two-lane highway, 24 ft wide}$$

Compute the stations for all key curve points (in foot units) and for all relevant spiral and circular curve deflections.

Solution
1. From Table 11.5,

$$L_s = 150 \text{ ft}$$
$$e = 0.058 \text{ (superelevation rate)}$$

2. From Table 11.4,

$$\Delta_s = 6.75000°$$
$$R = 636.6198 \text{ ft}$$
$$P = 1.4719 \text{ ft}$$
$$R + P = 638.0917 \text{ ft}$$
$$q = 74.9653 \text{ ft}$$
$$LT = 100.0728 \text{ ft}$$
$$ST = 50.0662 \text{ ft}$$
$$X = 149.79 \text{ ft}$$
$$Y = 5.88 \text{ ft}$$

You can also use Equation 11.23 to determine

$$\Delta_s = \frac{L_s D}{200}$$
$$= \frac{150}{200} \times 9 = 6.75000°$$

3. From Equation 11.22, we have

$$T_s = (R + p) \tan \frac{\Delta}{2} + q$$
$$= 638.0917 \tan 12° 52.5' + 74.9653 = 220.82 \text{ ft}$$

4.
$$\Delta_c = \Delta - 2\Delta_s$$
$$= 25°45' - 2(6°45') = 12°15'$$

5. From Equation 11.7, we have

$$L_c = 100\Delta_c$$
$$= \frac{(100 \times 12.25)}{9} = 136.11 \text{ ft}$$

6. Key station computation:

$$
\begin{array}{llll}
\text{PI} & \text{at} & 36 + & 17.42 \\
T_s & & 2 & 20.82 \\
\hline
\text{TS} & = & 33 + & 96.60 \\
+L_s & & 1 & 50.00 \\
\hline
\text{SC} & = & 35 + & 46.60 \\
+L_c & & 1 & 36.11 \\
\hline
\text{CS} & = & 36 + & 82.71 \\
+L_s & & 1 & 50.00 \\
\hline
\text{ST} & = & 38 + & 32.71 \\
\end{array}
$$

7.
$$\theta_s = \frac{\Delta_s}{3}$$
$$= \frac{6.753000°}{3} = 2.25° = 2°15'00''$$

8. Circular curve deflections. See Table 11.8:

$$\Delta_c = 12°15'$$

$$\frac{\Delta_c}{2} = 6°07.5' = 367.5'$$

From Section 11.4, the deflection angle for one unit of distance is $(\Delta/2)/L$. Here, the deflection angle for 1 ft of arc (minutes) is

$$\frac{\Delta_c/2}{L_c} = \frac{367.5}{136.11} = 2.700'$$

Table 11.8 CURVE SYSTEM DEFLECTION ANGLES

Station	Distance* from T.S. (or S.T.) l (ft)	l^2	$\dfrac{\theta_s^\circ \times 60}{L_s^2}$	$\dfrac{l^2(\theta_s \times 60)}{L_s^2}$ Deflection Angle (Minutes)	Deflection
T.S. 33 + 96.60	0	0	0.006	0	0°00′00″
34 + 00	3.4	11.6	0.006	0.070	0°00′04″
34 + 50	53.4	2,851.4	0.006	17.108	0°17′06″
35 + 00	103.4	10,691.6	0.006	64.149	1°04′09″
S.C. 35 + 45.60	150	22,500	0.006	135	$\theta_s = 2°15′00″$

	Circular Curve Data	Deflection Angle (Cumulative)	Deflection
S.C. 35 + 46.60	$\Delta_c = 12°15′, \dfrac{\Delta_c}{2} = 6°07′30″$	0°00.00′	0°00′00″
35 + 50	Deflection for 3.40′ = 9.18′	0°09.18′	0°09′11″
36 + 00	Deflection for 50′ = 135′	2°24.18′	2°24′11″
36 + 50	Deflection for 32.71′ = 88.32′	4°39.18′	4°39′11″
C.S. 36 + 82.71		6°07.50′	6°07′30″

Station	l (ft)	l^2	$\dfrac{\theta_s^\circ \times 60}{L_s^2}$	Deflection Angle (Minutes)	Deflection
C.S. 36 + 82.71	150	22,500	0.006	135	$\theta_s = 2°15′00″$
37 + 00	132.71	17,611.9	0.006	105.672	1°45′40″
37 + 50	82.71	6,840.9	0.006	41.046	0°41′03″
38 + 00	32.71	1,069.9	0.006	6.420	0°06′25″
S.T. 38 + 32.71	0	0	0.006	0	0°00′00″

*Note that l is measured from the S.T.

Alternatively, because $D = 9°$, then the deflection for 100 ft is $D/2$ or $4°30′$, which is $270′$. The deflection angle for 1 ft = 270/100 = 2.700′ (as previously noted). The required distances (from Table 11.8) are:

$(35 + 50) - (35 + 46.60) = 3.4′$; deflection angle $= 3.4 \times 2.7 = 9.18′$

Even interval $= 50′$; deflection angle $= 50 \times 2.7 = 135′$

$(36 + 82.71) - (36 + 50) = 32.71$; deflection angle $= 32.71 \times 2.7 = 88.32′$

These values are now entered cumulatively in Table 11.8.

■ **EXAMPLE 11.8** *Illustrative Spiral Problem (Metric Units)*
You are given the following data:

$$\text{PI at } 1 + 086.271$$
$$V = 80 \text{ km/h}$$
$$R = 300 \text{ m}$$

$$\Delta = 16°\ 00'\ \text{RT}$$

Two-lane road (7.5 m wide)

From Table 11.7, $A = 125$ and $e = 0.057$. (See Section 11.21 for a discussion of superelevation.) From Table 11.9, we obtain the following:

Solution

Compute the stations for all key curve points (in metric units) and all relevant spiral and circular curve deflections.

Steps	For $A = 125$	and $R = 300$
1 and 2	$L_s = 52.083$ m	LT = 34.736 m
	$P = 0.377$ m	ST = 17.374 m
	$X = 52.044$ m	$\Delta_s = 4°58'24.9''$
	$Y = 1.506$ m	$\theta_s = \frac{1}{3}\Delta_s = 1°39'27.9''$
	$q = 26.035$ m	LC = 52.066 m long chord

You can also use Equation 11.29:

$$\Delta_s = \frac{90}{\pi} \times \frac{L_s}{R}$$

$$= \frac{90}{\pi} \times \frac{52.083}{300} = 4.9735601° = 4°58'24.8''$$

Step 3. From Equation 11.22, we have

$$T_s = (R + p)\tan\frac{\Delta}{2} + q$$

$$= 300.377 \tan 8° + 26.035 = 68.250 \text{ m}$$

Step 4.

$$\Delta_c = \Delta - 2\Delta_s$$

$$= 16° - 2\,(4°58'24.8'') = 6°\ 03'10.2''$$

$$\frac{\Delta_c}{2} = 3°\ 01'35.1''$$

Step 5. From Equation 11.5, we have

$$L_c = \frac{2\pi R\Delta_c}{360}$$

$$= \frac{(2\pi \times 300 \times 6.052833)}{360} = 31.693 \text{ m}$$

Table 11.9 FUNCTIONS OF THE STANDARD SPIRAL* FOR A = 125 m

R (m)	A/R	L_s	X	Y	q	P	LT	ST	L_c	Δ_s Degrees	Δ_s Minutes	Δ_s Seconds	θ_s Degrees	θ_s Minutes	θ_s Seconds
					Meters										
115	1.0870	135.870	131.204	26.095	67.152	6.606	92.293	46.851	133.774	33	50	48.3	11	14	55.1
120	1.0417	130.208	126.428	23.057	64.471	5.825	88.183	44.658	128.513	31	05	05.8	10	20	08.3
125	1.0000	125.000	121.911	20.464	61.983	5.162	84.451	42.685	123.617	28	38	52.4	9	31	44.3
130	0.9615	120.192	117.649	18.240	59.671	4.595	81.044	40.898	119.055	26	29	11.7	8	48	46.1
140	0.8929	111.607	109.847	14.661	55.509	3.686	75.034	37.755	110.821	22	50	16.5	7	36	08.5
150	0.8333	104.167	102.918	11.953	51.875	3.001	69.888	35.126	103.610	19	53	39.7	6	37	28.8
160	0.7813	97.656	96.751	9.868	48.677	2.475	65.425	32.844	97.253	17	29	07.0	5	49	25.8
170	0.7353	91.912	91.242	8.239	45.844	2.065	61.511	30.852	91.614	15	29	19.3	5	09	34.9
180	0.6944	86.086	86.302	6.948	43.319	1.741	58.048	29.096	86.581	13	48	55.9	4	36	10.5
190	0.6579	82.237	81.853	5.913	41.054	1.481	54.960	27.535	82.066	12	23	58.3	4	07	53.5
200	0.6250	78.125	77.828	5.072	39.013	1.270	52.188	26.137	77.993	11	11	26.1	3	43	44.4
210	0.5952	74.405	74.172	4.384	37.163	1.097	49.685	24.876	74.301	10	09	00.7	3	22	57.0
220	0.5682	71.023	70.838	3.814	35.481	0.954	47.413	23.733	70.941	9	14	54.3	3	04	55.6
230	0.5435	67.935	67.787	3.339	33.943	0.835	45.342	22.692	67.869	8	27	42.1	2	49	12.1
240	0.5208	65.104	64.984	2.940	32.532	0.735	43.455	21.739	65.051	7	46	16.5	2	35	24.0
250	0.5000	62.500	62.402	2.601	31.234	0.651	41.701	20.864	62.457	7	09	43.1	2	23	13.2
280	0.4464	55.804	55.748	1.852	27.983	0.463	37.222	18.619	55.779	5	24	34.1	1	54	10.8
300	0.4167	52.083	52.044	1.506	26.035	0.377	34.736	17.374	52.066	4	58	24.9	1	39	27.9
320	0.3906	48.828	48.800	1.241	24.409	0.310	32.562	16.285	48.815	4	22	16.8	1	27	25.3
340	0.3676	45.956	45.935	1.035	22.974	0.259	30.645	15.325	45.947	3	52	19.8	1	17	26.4
350	0.3571	44.643	44.625	0.949	22.318	0.237	29.768	14.887	44.635	3	39	14.6	1	13	04.7
380	0.3289	41.118	41.106	0.741	20.557	0.185	27.416	13.710	41.113	3	05	59.6	1	01	59.8
400	0.3125	39.063	39.063	0.636	19.530	0.159	26.045	13.024	39.058	2	47	51.5	0	55	57.1
420	0.2976	37.202	37.195	0.549	18.600	0.137	24.804	12.403	37.195	2	32	15.2	0	50	45.0
450	0.2778	34.722	34.717	0.446	17.360	0.112	23.150	11.576	34.720	2	12	37.7	0	44	12.5
475	0.2632	32.895	32.891	0.380	16.447	0.095	21.931	10.966	32.893	1	59	02.1	0	39	40.7
500	0.2500	31.250	31.247	0.325	15.624	0.081	20.834	10.418	31.249	1	47	25.8	0	35	48.6
525	0.2381	29.762	29.760	0.281	14.881	0.070	19.842	9.921	29.761	1	37	26.5	0	32	20.8
550	0.2273	28.409	28.407	0.245	14.204	0.061	18.940	9.470	28.408	1	28	47.1	0	29	35.7
575	0.2174	27.174	27.172	0.214	13.587	0.054	18.116	9.058	27.173	1	21	13.9	0	27	04.6

Source: Metric Curve Tables, Table IV, Roads and Transportation Association of Canada (RTAC).

*Short radius (i.e., <150 m) may require a correction to $\Delta_s/3$ to determine the precise value of θ_s.

Step 6. Key station computation:

$$
\begin{aligned}
\text{PI at } & 1 + 086.271 \\
T_s & \quad\underline{68.250} \\
\text{TS} = & 1 + 018.021 \\
+L_s & \quad\underline{52.083} \\
\text{SC} = & 1 + 070.104 \\
+L_c & \quad31.693 \\
\text{CS} = & 1 + 101.797 \\
+L_s & \quad52.083 \\
\text{ST} = & 1 + 153.880
\end{aligned}
$$

Step 7. Circular curve deflections. See Table 11.10:

$$\Delta_c = 6°03'10''$$

$$\frac{\Delta_c}{2} = 3°01'35'' = 181.58'$$

From Section 11.4, the deflection angle for one unit of distance is $(\Delta/2)/L$. Here, the deflection angle for 1 m of arc is

$$\frac{\Delta_c/2}{L_c} = \frac{181.58}{31.693} = 5.7293'$$

Table 11.10 CURVE SYSTEM DEFLECTION ANGLES

Station	Distance* from T.S. (or S.T.) l (Meters)	l^2	$\dfrac{\theta_s \times 60}{L_s^2}$	$\dfrac{l^2(\theta_s \times 60)}{L_s^2}$ Deflection Angle (Minutes)	Deflection
T.S. 1 + 018.021	0	0			0°00'00"
1 + 020	1.979	3.9	0.036667	0.1436	0°00'09"
1 + 040	21.979	483.1	0.036667	17.71	0°17'43"
1 + 060	41.979	1,762.2	0.036667	64.62	1°04'37"
S.C. 1 + 070.104	52.083	2,712.6	0.036667	99.464	1°39'28"

Station	Circular Curve Data			Deflection Angle (Cumulative)	Deflection
S.C. 1 + 070.104	$\Delta_c = 6° 03'10'',\ \dfrac{\Delta_c}{2} = 3° 01'35''$			0°00.00'	0°00'00"
1 + 080	Deflection for 9.896 m = 56.70'			0°56.70'	0°56'42"
1 + 100	Deflection for 20 m = 114.59'			2°51.29'	2°51'17"
C.S. 1 + 101.797	Deflection for 1.797 m = 10.30'			3°01.59'	3°01'35"
C.S. 1 + 101.797	52.083	2,712.6	0.036667	99.464	1°39'28"
1 + 120	33.880	1,147.9	0.036667	42.09	0°42'05"
1 + 140	13.880	192.7	0.036667	7.06	0°07'04"
S.T. 1 + 153.880	0	0	0.036667	0	0°00'00"

*Note that l is measured from the S.T.

The required distances (deduced from Table 11.10) are

$(1 + 080) - (1 + 070.104) = 9.896$; deflection angle $= 5.7293 \times 9.896 = 56.70'$

Even interval $= 20.000$; deflection angle $= 5.7293 \times 20 = 114.59'$

$(1 + 101.797) - (1 + 100) = 1.797$; deflection angle $= 5.7293 \times 1.787 = 10.30'$

These values are now entered cumulatively in Table 11.10.

11.20 Approximate Solution for Spiral Problems

It is possible to lay out spirals by using the approximate relationships illustrated in Figure 11.25. Because $L_s \approx$ LC, the following can be assumed:

$$\frac{Y}{L_s} = \sin \theta_s \qquad Y = L_s \sin \theta_s \qquad (11.33)$$

$$X^2 = L_s^2 - Y^2$$
$$X = \sqrt{L_s^2 - Y^2} \qquad (11.34)$$

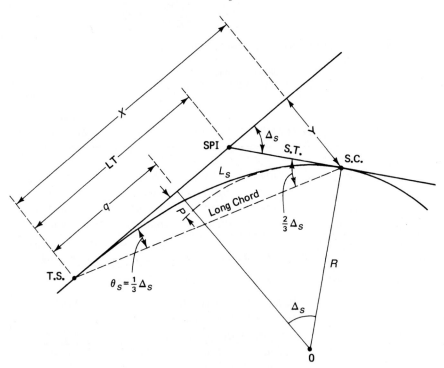

Basic Assumption: $L_S \approx$ Long Chord

FIGURE 11.25   Sketch for approximate formulas.

$$q = \frac{1}{2}X \tag{11.35}$$

$$p = \frac{1}{4}Y \tag{11.36}$$

Using the sine law, we obtain the following:

$$LT = \sin\frac{2}{3}\Delta_s \times \frac{\sin L_s}{\sin \Delta_s} \tag{11.37}$$

Using the sine law yields the following:

$$ST = \sin\frac{1}{3}\Delta_s \times \frac{L_s}{\sin \Delta_s} \tag{11.38}$$

For comparison, the values from Examples 11.7 and 11.8 are compared with the values obtained by the approximate methods:

Parameter	Precise Methods		Approximate Methods	
	Example 11.7 (ft)	Example 11.8 (m)	Example 11.7 (ft)	Example 11.8 (m)
Y	5.88	1.506	5.89	1.507
X	149.79	52.044	149.88	52.061
Q	74.97	26.035	74.94	26.031
P	1.47	0.377	1.47	0.377
LT	100.07	34.736	100.13	34.744
ST	50.07	17.374	50.10	17.379

You can see from the data summary that the precise and approximate values for Y, X, q, P, LT, and ST are quite similar. The largest discrepancy shows up in the X value, which is not required for spiral layout. The larger the Δ_s values, the larger is the discrepancy between the precise and approximate values. For the normal range of spirals in use, the approximate method is adequate for the layout of an asphalt-surfaced ditched highway. For curbed highways or elevated highways, precise methods should be employed.

11.21 Superelevation: General Background

If a vehicle travels too fast on a horizontal curve, the vehicle may either skid off the road or overturn. The factors that cause this phenomenon are based on the radius of curvature and the velocity of the vehicle: The sharper the curve and the higher the velocity, the larger will be the centrifugal force requirement. Two factors can be called on to help stabilize the radius and velocity factors: (1) side friction, which is always present to some degree between the vehicle tires and the pavement, and (2) superelevation (e), which is a banking of the pavement toward the center of the curve.

The side friction factor (f) has been found to vary linearly with velocity. Design values for f range from 0.16 at 30 mph (50 km/hr) to 0.11 at 80 mph (130 km/hr).

Superelevation must satisfy normal driving practices and climatic conditions. In practice, values for superelevation range from 0.125 (i.e., 0.125 ft/ft or 12.5 percent cross slope) in warmer southern U.S. states to 0.06 in the northern U.S. states and Canadian provinces. Typical values for superelevation can be found in Tables 11.5 and 11.6.

11.22 Superelevation Design

Figure 11.26 illustrates how the length of spiral (L_s) is used to change the pavement cross slope from normal crown to full superelevation. Figure 11.26(b) illustrates that the pavement can be revolved about the centerline, which is the usual case, or the pavement can be revolved about the inside or outside edges, a technique that is often encountered on divided four-lane highways where a narrow median restricts drainage profile manipulation.

Figures 11.28(b) and 11.29 clearly show the technique used to achieve pavement superelevation when revolving the pavement edges about the centerline (℄) profile. At points A and A′, the pavement is at normal crown cross section—with both edges (inside and outside) of the pavement a set distance below the ℄ elevation. At points S.C. (D) and C.S. (D′), the pavement is at full superelevation—with the outside edge a set distance above the ℄ elevation and the inside edge the same set distance below the ℄ elevation. The transition from normal crown cross section to full superelevation cross section proceeds as follows:

OUTSIDE EDGE

- From A to the T.S. (B), the outside edge rises at a ratio of 400:1—relative to the ℄ profile—and becomes equal in elevation to the ℄.
- From the T.S. (B), the outside edge rises (relative to the ℄ profile) at a uniform rate, from being equal to the ℄ elevation at the T.S. (B) until it is at full superelevation above the ℄ elevation at the S.C. (D).

INSIDE EDGE

- From A, through the T.S. (B), to point C, the inside edge remains below the ℄ profile at normal crown depth.
- From C to the S.C. (D), the inside edge drops at a uniform rate, from being at normal crown depth below the ℄ profile to being at full superelevation depth below the ℄ profile.

The transition from full superelevation at the C.S. (D′) to normal cross section at A′ proceeds in a manner reverse to that just described for the transition from A to S.C.

■ **EXAMPLE 11.9** *Superelevation Problem (Foot Units)*
See Figure 11.27 for vertical curve computations and Figures 11.28 and 11.29 for pavement superelevation computations. This example uses the horizontal curve data of Example 11.7.
You are given the following data:

$$V = 40 \text{ mph}$$
$$\Delta = 25°45′ \text{ RT}$$
$$D = 9°$$

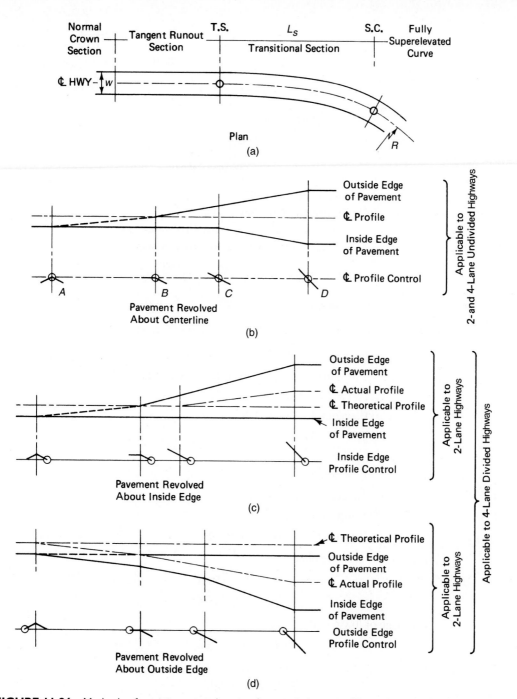

FIGURE 11.26 Methods of attaining superelevation for spiraled curves. (From *Geometric Design Standards for Ontario Highways*, Ministry of Transportation, Ontario)

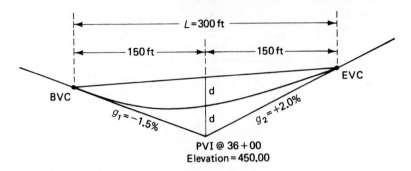

$$L = 300 \text{ ft}$$

$$150 \text{ ft} \qquad 150 \text{ ft}$$

$$g_1 = -1.5\% \qquad g_2 = +2.0\%$$

BVC

EVC

d

d

PVI @ 36 + 00
Elevation = 450.00

BVC = (36 + 00) − 150 = 34 + 50
EVC = (36 + 00) + 150 = 37 + 50
Elevation BVC = 450.00 + (150 × 0.015) = 452.25
Elevation EVC = 450.00 + (150 × 0.020) = 453.00
Midchord Elevation = $\dfrac{452.25 + 453.00}{2}$ = 452.63
Tangent Offset: $d = \dfrac{452.63 - 450.00}{2}$ = 1.315 ft

FIGURE 11.27   Vertical curve solution for the problem of Example 11.9.

PI at 36 + 17.42

Two-lane highway, 24 ft wide, each lane 12 ft wide

PVI at 36 + 00

Elevation PVI = 450.00

$g_1 = -1.5\%$

$g_2 = +2\%$

$L = 300$ ft

Tangent runout at 400:1

Normal crown at 2%

Pavement revolved about the ₵

From Table 11.4, we obtain

$$L_s = 150 \text{ ft}$$
$$e = 0.058$$

Chainage of low point:

$$X = \frac{-g_1 L}{A} = \frac{1.5 \times 300}{2 - (-1.5)} = 128.57 \text{ ft}$$

$$\text{BVC at } 34 + 50$$
$$X = \underline{1 \quad 28.57}$$
$$\text{Low Point} = 35 + 78.57$$

(a)

(b)

(c)

(d)

FIGURE 11.28 Sketches for the superelevation example of Section 11.22 and Example 11.6.
(a) Plan. (b) Profile and cross sections. (c) Computation of tangent runout. (d) Location of point C.

FIGURE 11.29 Superelevated pavement profiles and cross sections for the problem of Example 11.9.

You must determine the ¢ and edge-of-pavement elevations for even 50-ft stations and all other key stations.

Solution

1. Compute the key horizontal alignment stations. (These stations have already been computed in Example 11.7).
2. Solve the vertical curve for ¢ elevations at 50-ft stations, the low point, *plus any horizontal alignment key stations that may fall between the BVC and the EVC.*
3. Begin preparation of Table 11.11, showing all key stations for both horizontal and vertical alignments. List the ¢ grade elevation for each station.
4. Compute station A; see Figure 11.28(c):

$$\text{Cross fall at 2\% for 12 ft} = 0.02 \times 12 = 0.24 \text{ ft}$$

$$\text{Tangent runout} = \frac{400}{1} \times 0.24 = 96 \text{ ft}$$

$$\text{TS} = 33 + 96.60$$

$$X_1 \text{ (tangent runout)} = \underline{96.00}$$

$$A = 33 + 00.60$$

Table 11.11   ¢ PAVEMENT ELEVATIONS

Station		Tangent Elevation	Tangent Offset $\left(\dfrac{X}{L/2}\right)^2 d$	¢ Elevation
A	33 + 00.60	454.49		454.49
	33 + 50	453.75		453.75
T.S. (B)	33 + 96.60	453.05		453.05
	34 + 00	453.00		453.00
C	34 + 48.03	452.28		452.28
BVC	34 + 50	452.25	$(0/150)^2 \times 1.32 = 0$	452.25
	35 + 00	451.50	$(50/150)^2 \times 1.32 = 0.15$	451.65
S.C. (D)	35 + 46.60	450.79	$(96.6/150)^2 \times 1.32 = 0.55$	451.35
	35 + 50	450.75	$(100/150)^2 \times 1.32 = 0.58$	451.33
Low point	35 + 78.57	450.32	$(128.6/150)^2 \times 1.32 = 0.97$	451.29
PVI	36 + 00	450.00	$(150/150)^2 \times 1.32 = 1.32$	451.32
	36 + 50	451.00	$(100/150)^2 \times 1.32 = 0.58$	451.58
C.S. (D')	36 + 82.71	451.65	$(67.3/150)^2 \times 1.32 = 0.27$	451.92
	37 + 00	452.00	$(50/150)^2 \times 1.32 = 0.15$	452.15
EVC	37 + 50	453.00	$(0/150)^2 \times 1.32 = 0$	453.00
C'	37 + 81.28	453.63		453.63
	38 + 00	454.00		454.00
S.T. (B')	38 + 32.71	454.65		454.65
	39 + 00	456.00		456.00
A'	39 + 28.71	456.57		456.57

Compute station A′ (i.e., tangent runout at higher chainage spiral):

$$ST = 38 + 32.71$$

$$Tangent\ runout + 96.00$$

$$A = 39 + 28.71$$

5. Compute station C; see Figure 11.28(d):

Cross fall at 5 .8%for 12 -ft lane $= 0.058 \times 12 = 0.70$ ft

$$Distance\ from\ TS\ to\ C = 150 \times \frac{0.24}{0.70} = 51.43\ ft$$

$$TS = 33\ + 96.60$$

$$X\ distance = \quad \underline{51.43}$$

$$C = 34\ + 48.03$$

Compute station C′ (i.e., at higher chainage spiral):

$$ST = 38 + 32.71$$

$$X_2\ distance = \quad 51.43$$

$$C' = 37 + 81.28$$

6. Figure 11.29 shows that right-side pavement elevations are 0.24 ft below ₵ elevation from A to C and from C′ to A′, and 0.70 ft below ₵ from S.C. to C.S. Right-side pavement elevations between C and S.C. and C.S. and C′ must be interpolated. Figure 11.29 also shows that left-side pavement elevations must be interpolated between A and T.S., between T.S. and S.C., between C.S. and S.T., and between S.T. and A′. Between S.C. and C.S., the left-side pavement elevation is 0.70 higher than the corresponding ₵ elevations.

7. Fill in the left- and right-edge pavement elevations (Table 11.12), where the computation simply involves adding or subtracting normal crown (0.24) or full superelevation (0.70).

8. Perform the computations necessary to interpolate for the missing pavement-edge elevations in Table 11.12 (values are underlined). See Figures 11.30 and 11.31.

Review Questions

11.1 Why are curves used in roadway horizontal and vertical alignments?

11.2 Curves can be established by occupying ₵ or offset stations and then turning off appropriate deflection angles, or curves can be established by occupying a central control station and then turning off angles and measuring out distances—as determined through coordinates analyses. What are the advantages and disadvantages of each technique?

11.3 Why do chord and arc lengths for the same curve interval sometimes appear to be equal in value?

11.4 What characteristic do parabolic curves and spiral curves have in common?

Table 11.12 PAVEMENT ELEVATIONS FOR EXAMPLE 11.9*₵

	Station	₵ Grade	Left-Edge Pavement† Above/Below ₵	Elevation	Right-Edge Pavement† Below ₵	Elevation
A	33 + 00.60	454.49	−0.24	454.25	−0.24	454.25
	33 + 50	453.75	−0.12	453.63	−0.24	453.51
T.S. (B)	33 + 96.60	453.05	0.00	453.05	−0.24	452.81
	34 + 00	453.00	+0.02	453.02	−0.24	452.76
C	34 + 48.03	452.28	+0.24	452.52	−0.24	452.04
BVC	34 + 50	452.25	+0.25	452.50	−0.25	452.00
	35 + 00	451.65	+0.48	452.13	−0.48	451.17
S.C. (D)	35 + 46.60	451.35	+0.70	452.05	−0.70	450.65
	35 + 50	451.33	+0.70	452.02	−0.70	450.62
Low pt.	35 + 78.57	451.29	+0.70	451.99	−0.70	450.59
PVI	36 + 00	451.32	+0.70	452.02	−0.70	450.62
	36 + 50	451.58	+0.70	452.28	−0.70	450.88
C.S. (D′)	36 + 82.71	451.92	+0.70	452.62	−0.70	451.22
	37 + 00	452.15	+0.62	452.77	−0.62	451.53
EVC	37 + 50	453.00	+0.39	453.39	−0.39	452.61
C′	37 + 81.28	453.63	+0.24	453.87	−0.24	453.39
	38 + 00	454.00	+0.15	454.15	−0.24	453.76
S.T. (B′)	38 + 32.71	454.65	0.00	454.65	−0.24	454.41
	38 + 50	455.00	−0.04	454.96	−0.24	454.76
	39 + 00	456.00	−0.17	455.83	−0.24	455.76
A′	39 + 28.71	456.57	−0.24	456.33	−0.24	456.33

*Interpolated values are shown underlined.
†Pavement revolved about the centerline (₵).

11.5 Describe techniques that can be used to check the accuracy of the layout of a set of interchange curves using polar techniques (i.e., angle/distance layout from a central control station).

11.6 Why do construction surveyors usually provide offset stakes?

Problems

11.1 Given PI at 6 + 71.33, $\Delta = 29°42'$, and $R = 700$ ft, compute the tangent (T) and the length of arc (L).

11.2 Given PI at 11 + 22.19, $\Delta = 7°10'$, and $D = 8°$, compute the tangent (T) and the length of arc (L).

11.3 From the data in Problem 11.1, compute the stationing of the BC and EC.

11.4 From the data in Problem 11.2, compute the stationing of the BC and EC.

11.5 A straight-line route survey, which had PIs at 3 + 81.27 ($\Delta = 12°30'$) and at 5 + 42.30 ($\Delta = 10°56'$), later had 600-ft-radius circular curves inserted at each PI. Compute the BC and EC stationing (chainage) for each curve.

$$\frac{0.46}{98.57} = \frac{Y_1}{1.97}, \quad Y_1 = -0.01$$

@ 34 + 50, $h_1 = -0.01 - 0.24 = -0.25$

$$\frac{0.46}{98.57} = \frac{Y_2}{51.97}, \quad Y_2 = -0.24$$

@ 35 + 00, $h_2 = -0.24 - 0.24 = -0.48$

(a)

$$\frac{0.46}{98.57} = \frac{Y_1}{31.28}, \quad Y_1 = -0.15$$

@ 37 + 50, $h_1 = -0.15 - 0.24 = -0.39$

$$\frac{0.46}{98.57} = \frac{Y_2}{81.28}, \quad Y_2 = -0.38$$

@ 37 + 00, $h_2 = -0.38 - 0.24 = -0.62$

(b)

FIGURE 11.30 Right-edge pavement elevation interpolation for the problem of Example 11.9. (a) Tangent run-in. (b) Tangent runout.

$$\frac{h}{46.60} = \frac{0.24}{96.00}, \quad \underline{h = -0.12 @ 33 + 50}$$

$$\frac{h_1}{3.4} = \frac{0.70}{150}, \quad \underline{h_1 = +0.02 @ 34 + 00}$$

$$\frac{h_2}{53.4} = \frac{0.70}{150}, \quad \underline{h_2 = +0.25 @ 34 + 50}$$

$$\frac{h_3}{103.40} = \frac{0.70}{150}, \quad \underline{h_3 = +0.48 @ 35 + 00}$$

$$\frac{h_1}{32.71} = \frac{0.70}{150}, \quad \underline{h_1 = +0.15 @ 38 + 00}$$

$$\frac{h_2}{82.71} = \frac{0.70}{150}, \quad \underline{h_2 = +0.39 @ 37 + 50}$$

$$\frac{h_3}{132.71} = \frac{0.70}{150}, \quad \underline{h_3 = +0.62 @ 37 + 00}$$

$$\frac{h_1}{17.29} = \frac{0.24}{96.00}, \quad \underline{h_1 = -0.04 @ 38 + 50}$$

$$\frac{h_2}{67.29} = \frac{0.24}{96.00}, \quad \underline{h_2 = -0.17 @ 39 + 00}$$

FIGURE 11.31   Left-edge pavement elevation interpolation for the problem of Example 11.9.

Problems

11.6 Given PI at 3 + 333.013, $\Delta = 12°47'$, and $R = 300$ m, compute the deflections for even 20-m stations.

11.7 Given PI at 4 + 212.352, $\Delta = 24°24'20''$, and $R = 500$ m, compute E (external), M (midordinate), and the stations of the BC and EC.

11.8 Given PI at 15 + 78.28, $\Delta = 36°10'30''$ RT, and $R = 1,150$ ft, compute the deflections for even 100-ft stations.

11.9 From the distances and deflections computed in Problem 11.6, compute the three key ℄ chord layout lengths, that is, (1) the BC to the first 20-m station, (2) the chord distance for 20-m (arc) stations, and (3) from the last even 20-m station to the EC.

11.10 From the distances and deflections computed in Problem 11.8, compute the three key ℄ chord layout lengths, that is, (1) the BC to the first 100-ft station, (2) the chord distance for 100-ft (arc) stations, and (3) from the last even 100-ft station to the EC.

11.11 From the distances and deflections computed in Problem 11.8, compute the chords (six) required for layout directly on offsets 50 ft right and 50 ft left of the ℄.

11.12 Two highway ℄ tangents must be joined with a circular curve of radius 1,000 ft (see Figure 11.32). The PI is inaccessible because its location falls in a river. Point A is established near the river on the back tangent, and point B is established near the river on the forward tangent. Distance AB is measured to be 615.27 ft. Angle $\alpha = 51°31'20''$ and angle $\beta = 32°02'45''$. Perform the calculations required to locate the BC and the EC in the field.

11.13 Two street curb lines intersect with $\Delta = 71°36'$ (see Figure 11.33). A curb radius must be selected so that an existing catch basin (CB) will abut the future curb. The curb side of the catch basin ℄ is located from point V: V to CB = 8.713 m and angle E-V-CB = $21°41'$. Compute the radius that will permit the curb to abut the existing catch basin.

11.14 Given the following compound curve data: $R_1 = 200$ ft, $R_2 = 300$ ft, $\Delta_1 = 44°26'$, and $\Delta_2 = 45°18'$, compute T_1 and T_2 (see Figure 11.15).

11.15 Given the following vertical curve data: PVI at 7 + 25.712, $L = 100$ m, $g_1 = -3.2\%$, $g_2 = +1.8\%$, and elevation of PVI = 210.440, compute the elevations of the curve low point and even 20-m stations.

11.16 Given the following vertical curve data: PVI at 19 + 00, $L = 500$ ft, $g_1 = +2.5\%$, $g_2 = -1\%$, and elevation at PVI = 723.86 ft, compute the elevations of the curve summit and even full stations (i.e., 100-ft even stations).

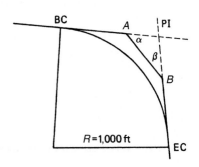

FIGURE 11.32 Sketch for Problem 11.12.

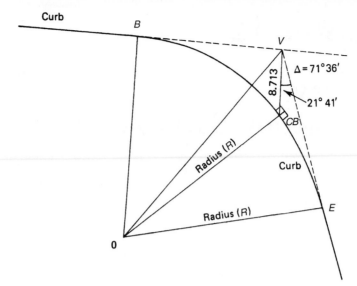

FIGURE 11.33 Sketch for Problem 11.13.

11.17 Given the following vertical curve data: $g_1 = +3\%$, $g_2 = -1\%$, design speed $= 110$ km/hr (from Table 11.3, $K = 90$ m), PVI at $0 + 360.100$, with an elevation of 156.663 m, compute the curve elevations at the high point (summit) and the even 50-m stations.

11.18 Given the following spiral curve data: $D = 8°$, $V = 40$ mph, $\Delta = 16°44'$, and PI at $11 + 66.18$, determine the value of each key spiral and circular curve component (L_s, R, P, q, LT, ST, X, Y, Δ_s, Δ_c, T_c, and L_c) and determine the stationing (chainage) of the T.S., S.C., C.S., and S.T.

11.19 Given the same data as in Problem 11.18, use the approximate equations (Equations 11.33 to 11.38) to compute X, Y, q, P, LT, and ST. Enter these values and the equivalent values determined in Problem 11.18 in a table to compare the results.

11.20 Use the data from Problem 11.18 to compute the deflections for the curve system (spirals and circular curves) at even 50-ft stations.

Chapter 12

Highway Construction Surveys

12.1 Preliminary (Preengineering) Surveys

Before the actual construction of a highway can begin, a great deal of investigative work has to be carried out. The final route chosen for the highway will reflect costs due to topography (cuts and fills); costs of relocating services; costs of rail, highway, and water-crossing bridges; environmental impact; and a host of other considerations. Area information is first assembled from topographic maps, county maps, available aerial photography, and satellite imagery. More likely routes may be flown, with the resultant photogrammetric maps also being used to aid in the functional planning process. Figure 12.1 shows a simple stereo photo-analysis system, which corrects distortions in the photos (rectifies) and permits the operator to digitize the horizontal and vertical (elevations) positions of all required points.

When the route has been selected, low-level aerial imaging will probably form the basis for the preliminary or preengineering survey. Figure 12.2 shows part of a general plan prepared for a new highway location; the actual design drawings—which will show much more detail—are often drawn at 1 in. = 50 ft (1:500 metric). The proposed centerline is established in the field with the stationing carried through from the initial point to the terminal point. Each time the tangent centerline changes direction, the PI is referenced, and the deflection angle is measured and recorded. Figure 12.3 shows a split-angle tie to a PI.

The highway designer will now be able to insert horizontal curves at each PI, with the radius or degree of curve being largely controlled by the design speed. At this point, the centerline stations are adjusted to account for the curve alignment, which is shorter than the tangent-only alignment. Horizontal control monuments, and both permanent and temporary benchmarks, are established along the route; their placement intervals are usually less than 1,000 ft (300 m). Control for proposed aerial photography may require even smaller intervals. These control monuments are targeted so that their locations will show up on the aerial photographs.

FIGURE 12.1 Zeiss G-2 Stereocord. Stereo-paired aerial photos are analyzed with horizontal and vertical data digitized for later plotting and analysis.

When modern surveying techniques are used such as aerial imaging assisted by satellite-positioning and inertial measurement units, the need for ground control targets is much reduced (one, or more, ground GPS base stations will be required to provide differential corrections to the airborne GPS units). However, if it is proposed to use machine control and guidance techniques for the construction process, there is an increased need for machine-accessible horizontal and vertical control monuments so that the machines can quickly occupy these control monuments to perform on-going recalibration checks and settings.

In addition to referencing the PIs, centerline stations on tangent are referenced at regular intervals (500–1,000 ft) to aid the surveyor in reestablishing the centerline alignment for further preliminary surveys, numerous layout surveys, interim payment surveys, and finally the as-built survey. See Figure 12.4 for typical tie-in techniques. Swing ties are referenced to spikes driven into trees or nails and washers driven into the roots of a tree. Strong swing ties intersect at angles near 90°; three ties are used so that if one is lost, the point can still be reestablished from the remaining two. In areas of sparse tree cover, centerline ties are usually taken at right angles to the centerline station and can be made to cut crosses in rock outcrops; iron bars driven into the ground (1″ reinforcing bars with brass caps), aluminum monuments, and even concrete monuments can be used for this purpose.

The plan, usually prepared from aerial imaging, is upgraded in the field by the surveyor so that ambiguous or unknown features on the plan are properly identified—that is, types of fences, dimensions of structures, types of manholes (storm or sanitary), road and drive surfaces, and the like. Soundings are taken at all water crossings, and soil tests are

FIGURE 12.2 Plan showing proposed freeway location.

FIGURE 12.3 PI tie-in by split angle. Split angle in this example is $(180° + 40°38')/2 = 110°19'$.

taken at bridge sites and areas suspected of instability. All drainage crossings, watercourses, ditches, and so on are identified and tied in. Tree locations are fixed so that clearing and grubbing estimates can be prepared. Utility crossings (pipelines, conduits, and overhead cables) are located with respect to horizontal and vertical location (total station instruments are programmed to directly compute overhead clearances by remote object elevation—see Chapter 5).

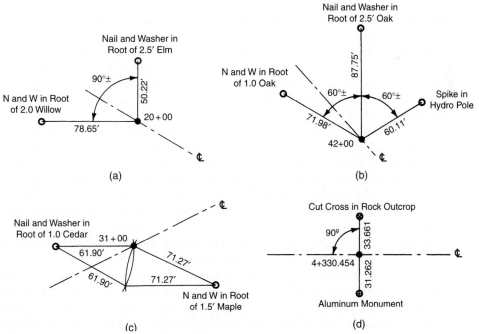

FIGURE 12.4 Centerline tie-ins. (a) Strong two-point swing tie. (b) Strong three-point swing tie. (c) Weak two-point swing tie, resulting in an ambiguous or poorly defined intersection. (d) 90° centerline tie-in (metric).

Railroad crossings require intersection angle and chainage, and track profiles a set distance right and left of the highway centerline. At-grade crossings require sight-line surveys for visibility patterns for set distances up the track ($\frac{1}{4}$ mile each way is not uncommon). Road and other highway crossings require intersection angles and chainages, together with their centerline profiles left and right of the main centerline.

Cross sections are taken full width at regular stations, typically 25 ft (10 m) in rock, 50 ft (20 m) in cut, and 100 ft (30 m) in fill. In addition, extra cross sections are taken at any significant changes in slope that occur between regular stations. Rod readings are usually taken to the closest 0.1 ft (0.01 m), and rod location is tied in to the closest foot (0.1 m) for both chainage and offset distances. Stations are at 100-ft intervals (e.g., 0 + 00, 1 + 00) in foot units and are at 1,000-m intervals (e.g., 0 + 000, 1 + 000) in metric units.

12.2 Highway Design

The design of a highway depends on the type of service planned for the highway. Highways (and municipal streets) are classified as being locals, collectors, arterials, or freeways. The bulk of the highways, in mileage, are arterials that join towns and cities together in state or provincial networks. Design parameters, such as number of lanes, lane width, thickness and type of granular material, thickness and type of surface (asphalt or concrete), maximum climbing grades, minimum radius of curvature (related to design speed), and other items, including driver comfort and roadside aesthetics, vary from the highest consideration (for freeways) to the lowest consideration (for locals).

Local highways have lower design speeds, narrower lanes, and sharper curves, reflecting the fact that locals' primary service function is that of property access. Freeways, on the other hand, have mobility as their primary service function, with vehicle access restricted to interchanges, which are often many miles apart. Freeways have relatively high design speeds, which require flatter curves and wider (and perhaps more) traffic lanes. Flatter climbing grades (5 percent maximum is often used) enable trucks to maintain their operating speeds and thus help in keeping the overall operating speed for all traffic close to the speed for which the facility was designed.

The highway designer will keep these service-related parameters in mind as the highway's profiles, cross sections, and horizontal geometrics are incorporated. Figure 12.5 shows a typical design cross section for a two-lane arterial highway. Figure 12.6 is a plan and profile of an arterial two-lane highway, which shows the horizontal and vertical geometrics, toe of slope location, and cut-and-fill quantities. This plan and profile and the appropriate cross section (e.g., Figure 12.5) are all that the surveyor normally needs to provide line and grade to the contractor. Figure 12.7 is a plan showing interchange ramps with full-width pavement elevations at 25-ft stations. This level of detail is commonly provided for all superelevated sections of pavement.

Complex interchanges require special attention from the surveyor. Figure 12.8 shows some of the curve data and chainage coordinates for an interchange. All key curve stations (PI, BC, EC, CPI, T.S., S.T., SPI, etc.) are established and referenced as shown in Figures 12.3 and 12.4. The curves can be laid out by deflection angles (Chapter 11) or by polar layout (Section 5.7). If the interchange is to be laid out by using polar ties, then the surveyor will have to establish control monuments in protected areas, as discussed in Chapter 9.

FIGURE 12.5 Typical cut-and-fill design cross sections for a two-lane arterial highway.

Figure 12.8 also shows a creek diversion (Green Creek) necessitated by the interchange construction. Figure 12.8 gives the creek centerline alignment chainages and coordinates. Figure 12.9 shows some additional details for the creek diversion channel, including the centerline profile and cross sections, which can be used by the surveyor to provide line and grade for the channel.

FIGURE 12.6 Plan and profile showing horizontal and vertical alignment, including pavement elevations through the superelevated section, cumulative quantities, and toe of slope locations.

12.3 Highway Construction Layout

When the decision is made to proceed with the highway construction, the surveyor goes back to the field to begin the stakeout. In some cases, months and even years may have passed since the preliminary survey was completed, and some of the control monuments (as well as their reference points) may have been destroyed. However, if the preliminary survey has been properly referenced, sufficient horizontal and vertical control will be found to commence the stakeout. The centerline chainage is verified by measuring from

FIGURE 12.7 Interchange plan showing full-width pavement elevations at 25-ft station intervals.

referenced stations, by checking cross-road intersections, by using GPS observations, and by checking into any cross-road ties that were noted in the original survey.

Highways are laid out at 100-ft (30- or 40-m) stations, with additional stations being established at all changes in horizontal direction (e.g., BC, EC, T.S., S.T.) and all changes in vertical direction (e.g., BVC, ECV, low points, tangent runouts). The horizontal and

K—RAMP INN. E-E

	POINT	STATION	NORTH	EAST
1	P.O.T	48+99.217	504,760.440	228,567.864
2	T.S.	53+65.217	504,558.722	228,147.786
	P.I.	55+01.758	504,499.617	228,024.700
3	S.C.	55+65.217	504,514.502	227,956.719
4	C.C.	59+99.822	504,661.791	227,908.968
	C.S.		504,812.426	227,982.391
	P.I.	60+49.414	504,815.461	228,051.917
5	S.T.	61+99.822	504,776.172	228,163.077
6	B.C.	63+03.439	504,676.001	228,247.433
	P.I.	64+36.872	504,598.516	228,356.062
7	E.C.	65+70.256	504,526.173	228,468.181

M — GREEN CREEK DIVERSION

POINT	STATION	CO-ORDINATES NORTH	EAST
		DRAINAGE	
1	P.O.T	93+60.680	504,940.280	229,435.321
2	B.C.	94+50.222	504,888.680	229,362.143
	P.I.	95+16.310	504,850.595	229,308.132
3	E.C.	95+78.898	504,786.609	229,291.597
4	B.C.	102+37.000	504,147.501	229,126.444
	P.I.	103+32.168	504,055.359	229,102.634
5	E.C.	103+97.919	504,011.186	229,186.929
6	P.I.	104+35.419	503,993.780	229,220.145
	P.I.	104+72.298	503,976.663	229,252.811
7	E.C.	105+06.977	503,944.155	229,270.226

SPIRAL DATA

H—RAMP INN. W—E

No.	θs	Ls	L.T.	S.T.	P
69	15°00′00.00″	200.000	133.815	67.105	4.353
71	15°00′00.00″	200.000	133.815	67.105	4.353
72	2°50′00.00″	200.000	133.347	66.679	0.727
74	2°50′00.00″	200.000	133.347	66.679	0.727
75	4°30′00.00″	300.000	200.065	100.059	1.963

FIGURE 12.8 Interchange geometrics, including a creek diversion channel.

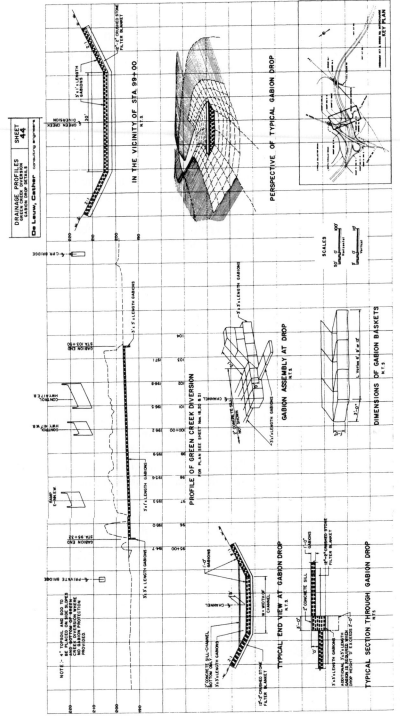

FIGURE 12.9 Details of Green Creek diversion channel, showing Gabion basket details, channel cross section, and profile. See Figure 12.8 for horizontal alignment.

vertical curve sections are often staked out at 50-ft (15- to 20-m) intervals to ensure that the finished product closely conforms to the design (25-ft intervals are often used on sharp-radius interchange ramps). When foot units are used, the full stations are at 100-ft intervals (e.g., 0 + 00, 1 + 00). In metric units, municipalities use 100-m full-station intervals (0 + 00, 1 + 00), whereas most highway agencies use 1,000-m (km) intervals for full "stations" (e.g., 0 + 000, 0 + 100, . . . , 1 + 000).

The ℄ of construction is staked out by using a steel tape, GPS, or total station, with specifications ranging from 1/3,000 to 1/10,000 accuracy. The accuracy of ℄ layout can be verified at reference monuments, at road intersections, via GPS use, and the like. Alternatively highways can be laid out from coordinated stations by total stations using polar layouts rather than rectangular layouts. Most interchanges are now laid out by polar methods, whereas most of the highways between interchanges are laid out with rectangular layout offsets. The methods of polar layout are covered in Chapter 5. GPS positioning techniques are now being used in many layout surveys, including highways.

The profile grade, shown on the contract drawing, can refer to the top of granular elevation, or it can refer to the top of asphalt (or concrete) elevation; the surveyor must ensure that he or she is using the proper reference before calculating subgrade elevations for the required cuts and fills.

12.4 Clearing, Grubbing, and Stripping Topsoil

Clearing and *grubbing* are the terms used to describe the cutting down of trees and the removal of all stumps and litter. The full highway width is staked out, approximating the limits of cut and fill, so that the clearing and grubbing can be accomplished.

The first construction operation after clearing and grubbing is the stripping of topsoil. The topsoil is usually stockpiled for later use. In cut sections, the topsoil is stripped for full width, which extends to the points at which the far-side ditch slopes intersect the existing ground (EG)—also known as original ground (OG)—surface. See Figure 12.10. In fill sections, the topsoil is usually stripped for the width of the highway embankment (Figure 12.11). Some highway agencies do not strip the topsoil where heights of fill exceed 4 ft (1.2 m), believing that this water-bearing material cannot damage the road base below that depth.

The bottom of fills (toe of slope) and the top of cuts (top of slope) are marked by slope stakes. These stakes, which are angled away from ℄, not only delineate the limits of

FIGURE 12.10 Highway cut section.

FIGURE 12.11 Highway fill section.

stripping but also indicate the limits for cut and fill; such operations take place immediately after the stripping operation. Lumber crayon (keel) or permanent markers are used on the stakes to show station and "s/s" (slope stake).

12.5 Placement of Slope Stakes

Figure 12.12 shows typical cut-and-fill sections in both foot and metric dimensions. The side slopes shown are 3:1, although most agencies use a steeper slope (2:1) for cuts and fills over 4 ft (1.2 m). To locate slope stakes, the surveyor must first determine the difference in elevation between the profile grade at ₵ and the invert of ditch (cut section) or the toe of embankment (fill section).

In Figure 12.12(a), the difference in elevation consists of the following:

$$\text{Depth of granular} = 1.50 \text{ ft}$$
$$\text{Sub-grade cross fall at 3 percent over 24.5 ft} = 0.74 \text{ ft}$$
$$\text{Minimum depth of ditch} = \underline{1.50 \text{ ft}}$$
$$\text{Total difference in elevation} = 3.74 \text{ ft}$$

The ₵ of this minimum-depth ditch would be 29.0 ft from the ₵ of construction. In cases where the ditch is deeper than minimum values, the additional difference in elevation and the additional distance from ₵ of construction can be easily calculated by using the same slope values.

In Figure 12.12(b), the difference in elevation consists of the following:

$$\text{Depth of granular} = 0.45 \text{ m}$$
$$\text{Fall at 3 percent over 7.45 m} = 0.22 \text{ m}$$
$$\text{Minimum depth of ditch} = \underline{0.50 \text{ m}}$$
$$\text{Total difference in elevation} = 1.17 \text{ m}$$

The ₵ of this minimum-depth ditch would be 8.95 m from the ₵ of construction. In these first two examples, only the distance from highway ₵ to ditch ₵ has been determined. See Example 12.1 for further treatment.

In Figure 12.12(c), the difference in elevation consists of the following:

$$\text{Depth of granular} = 1.50 \text{ ft}$$
$$\text{Fall at 3 percent over 24.5 ft} = \underline{0.74 \text{ ft}}$$
$$\text{Total difference in elevation} = 2.24 \text{ ft}$$

FIGURE 12.12 Typical two-lane highway cross section.

The difference from ℄ of construction to this point where the subgrade intersects the side slope is 24.5 ft.

In Figure 12.12(d), the difference in elevation consists of the following:

$$\text{Depth of granular} = 0.45 \text{ m}$$
$$\underline{\text{Fall at 3 percent over 7.45 m} = 0.22 \text{ m}}$$
$$\text{Total difference in elevation} = 0.67 \text{ m}$$

The distance from ℄ of construction to this point where the subgrade intersects the side slope is 7.45 m.

In the last two examples, the computed distance locates the slope stake.

Figure 12.12(e) shows the pavement and shoulder cross section, which is built on top of the granular cross sections shown in Figure 12.12(a–d) in the final stages of construction.

■ **EXAMPLE 12.1** *Location of a Slope Stake in a Cut Section*
Refer to Figure 12.13. Given that the profile grade (top of granular) is 480.00 and the HI is 486.28,

$$\text{Ditch invert} = 480.00 - 3.74 = 476.26$$
$$\text{Grade rod} = 486.28 - 476.26 = 10.02$$
$$\text{Depth of cut} = \text{grade rod} - \text{ground rod}$$

The following equation must be satisfied by trial-and-error ground rod readings:

$$x = (\text{depth of cut} \times 3) + 29.0$$

Solution
Using trial-and-error techniques, the rod holder moves from location to location away from the ℄ until the above equation is satisfied. The rod holder, holding a fiberglass tape as well as the rod, estimates the desired location and gives a rod reading. For this example, assume that the rod reading is 6.0 ft at a distance of 35 ft from ℄:

$$\text{Depth of cut} = 10.02 - 6.0 = 4.02$$
$$x = (4.02 \times 3) + 29.0 = 41.06 \text{ ft}$$

FIGURE 12.13 Location of slope stake in cut section (Example 12.1).

Because the rod holder is only 35 ft from the ℄, he or she must move farther out. At the next point, 43 ft from ℄, a reading of 6.26 is obtained.

$$\text{Depth of cut} = 10.02 - 6.26 = 3.76$$
$$x = (3.76 \times 3) + 29.0 = 40.3$$

Because the rod holder is at 43 ft, he or she is too far out.

The rod holder moves closer in and gives a rod reading of 6.10 at 41 ft from ℄. Now we have

$$\text{Depth of cut} = 10.02 - 6.10 = 3.92$$
$$x = (3.92 \times 3) + 29 = 40.8$$

This location is close enough for placing the slope stake; the error of 0.2 ft is not significant in this type of work. Usually, two or three trials are required to locate the slope stake properly.

Figures 12.14 and 12.15 illustrate the techniques used when one is establishing slope stakes in fill sections. The slope stake distance from centerline can be scaled from cross sections or topographic plans. In most cases, cross sections (see Chapter 17) are drawn at even stations (100 ft or 30–40 m). The cross sections are necessary to calculate

FIGURE 12.14 Location of slope stakes in a fill section. Case 1: instrument HI above subgrade.

FIGURE 12.15 Location of a slope stake in a fill section. Case 2: instrument HI below subgrade.

the volume estimates used in contract tendering. The location of the slope stakes can be scaled from this cross-section plot. In addition, highway contract plans are now usually developed photogrammetrically from aerial photos; these plans show contours that are precise enough for most slope-stake purposes. One can usually scale off the required distances from ₵ by using either the cross-section plan or the contour plan to the closest 1.0 ft or 0.3 m. The cost savings gained by determining this information in the office usually outweighs any resultant loss of accuracy. It is now possible to increase the precision through advances in computers and photogrammetric equipment. Occasional field checks can be used to check these scale methods. If scale methods are employed, trigonometric leveling or total stations can be used to establish the horizontal distance from ₵ to the slope stake. These methods will be more accurate than using a fiberglass tape on deep cuts or high fills when breaking tape may be required several times.

12.6 Layout for Line and Grade

In municipal work, it is often possible to put the grade stakes on offset, issue a grade sheet, and then go on to other work. The surveyor may be called back to replace the odd stake knocked over by construction equipment, but usually the layout is thought to be a one-time occurrence. In highway work, the surveyor must accept the fact that the grade stakes will be laid out several times. The chief difference between the two types of work is the large values for cut and fill. For the grade stakes to be in a "safe" location, they must be located beyond the slope stakes. Although this location is used for the initial layout, as the work progresses this distance back to ₵ becomes too cumbersome to allow for accurate transfer of alignment and grade.

As a result, as the work progresses, the offset lines are moved ever closer to the ₵ of construction, until the final location for the offsets is 2–3 ft (1 m) from each edge of the proposed pavement. The number of times that the layout must be repeated is a direct function of the height of fill or depth of cut involved. Machine guidance (see Chapter 10) techniques are proving to be much more economical when staking becomes very repetitive.

In highway work, the centerline is laid out at the appropriate stations. The centerline points are then individually offset at convenient distances on both sides of ₵. For the initial layout, the ₵ stakes, offset stakes, and slope stakes are all put in at the same time. The cuts and fills are written on the grade stakes, referenced either to the top of the stake or to a mark on the side of the stake that will give even foot (even decimeter) values. The cuts and fills are written on that side of the stake facing ₵, whereas the stations are written on that side of the stake facing back to the 0 + 00 location, as previously noted.

The highway designer attempts to balance cuts and fills so that the overall costs are kept lower. Most highway projects employ scrapers (Figure 12.16) to first cut the material that must be removed and then transport the material to the fill area, where it is discharged. The grade supervisor keeps checking the scraper cutting-and-filling operations by checking back to the grade stakes. See Section 12.7 for grade-transfer techniques. In rocky areas, blasting is required to loosen the rock fragments, which can then be loaded into haulers for disposal—either in fill areas or in shoulder or off-site areas. Figure 12.17 shows a typical dump hauler, larger versions of which can accommodate up to 140 cu. yd of material.

LIVERPOOL JOHN MOORES UNIVERSITY
LEARNING SERVICES

FIGURE 12.16 Scraper (shown being assisted by a bulldozer) used for efficient transfer of cut material to fill areas. (Courtesy of Caterpillar, Inc.)

FIGURE 12.17 Euclid R35 hauler, capacity of 30.5 cu. yd. (Courtesy of Euclid-Hitachi Heavy Equipment, Ltd.)

As the work progresses and the cuts and fills become more pronounced, care should be taken in breaking tape when laying out grade stakes so that the horizontal distance is maintained. The centerline stakes are offset by turning 90°, either with a right-angle prism or, more usually, by the swung-arm method. Cloth or fiberglass tapes are used to lay out the slope stakes and offset stakes. Once a ℄ station has been offset on one side, care is taken when offsetting to the other side to ensure that the two offsets and the ℄ stake are all in a straight line.

When the cut and/or fill operations have brought the work to the proposed subgrade (bottom of granular elevations), the subgrade must be verified by cross sections before the contractor is permitted to place the granular material. Usually, a tolerance of 0.10 ft (30 mm) is allowed. Once the top of granular profile has been reached, layout for pavement (sometimes a separate contract) can commence. Figure 12.18 shows a road grader shaping the crushed stone with the guidance of a rotating laser.

The final layout for pavement is usually on a very close offset (3 ft or 1 m). If the pavement is to be concrete, nails driven into the tops of the stakes provide more precise alignment.

When the highway construction has been completed, a final survey is performed. The final survey includes cross sections and locations that are used for final payments to the contractor and for a completion of the as-built drawings. The final cross sections are taken at the same stations used in the preliminary survey.

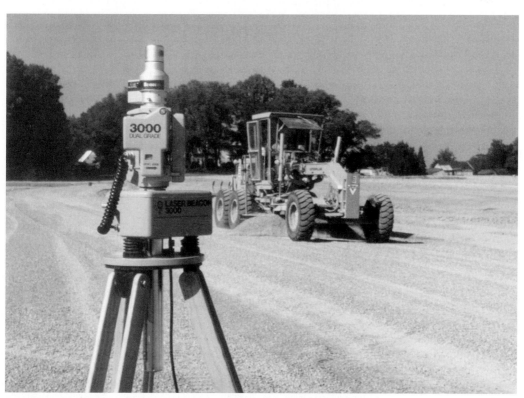

FIGURE 12.18 Rotating laser shown controlling fine grading operations by a road grader. (Courtesy of Leica Geosystems Inc.)

Sec. 12.6   Layout for Line and Grade

The description here has referred to two-lane highways. The procedure for layout of a four-lane divided highway is very similar. The same control is used for both sections; grade stakes can be offset to the center of the median and used for both sections. When the lane separation becomes large and the vertical and horizontal alignment is different for each direction, the project can be approached as being two independent highways. The layout for elevated highways, often found in downtown urban areas, follows the procedures used for structures layout.

12.7 Grade Transfer

Grade stakes can be set so that the tops of the stakes are at grade. Stakes set to grade are colored red or blue on the top to differentiate them from all other stakes. This procedure is time consuming and often impractical except for final pavement layout. Generally, the larger the offset distance, the more difficult it is to drive the tops of the stakes to grade.

As noted earlier, the cut and fill can refer to the top of the grade stake or to a mark on the side of the grade stake referring to an even number of feet (decimeters) of cut or fill. The mark on the side of the stake is located by sliding the rod up and down the side of the stake until a value is read on the rod that will give the cut or fill to an even foot (decimeter). This procedure of marking the side of the stake is best performed by two workers, one to hold the rod and the other to steady the bottom of the rod and then to make the mark on the stake. The cut or fill can be written on the stake or entered on a grade sheet, one copy of which is given to the contractor.

To transfer the grade (cut or fill) from the grade stake to the area of construction, the surveyor requires a means of transferring the stake elevation in a horizontal manner. When the grade stake is close (within 6 ft or 2 m), the grade transfer can be accomplished using a carpenter's level set on a piece of sturdy lumber [Figure 12.19(a)]; the recently developed laser torpedo level permits the horizontal reference (laser beam) to extend much beyond the location of the level itself (i.e., right across the grade). See Figure 12.19(b). When the grade stake is far from the area of construction, a string line level can be used to transfer the grade (cut or fill) (Figure 12.20). In this case, a fill of 1 ft 0 in. is marked on the grade stake (in addition to the offset distance). A guard stake has been placed adjacent to the grade stake, and the grade mark is transferred to the guard stake. A 1-ft distance is measured up the guard stake, and the grade elevation is marked. A string line is attached to the guard stake at the grade elevation mark; then a line level is hung from the string (near the halfway mark), and the string is pulled taut so as to eliminate most of the sag (it is not possible to eliminate all the sag). The string line is adjusted up and down until the bubble in the line level is centered. With the bubble centered, it can be quickly seen at ℄ how much more fill may be required to bring the highway, at that point, to grade. Figure 12.20 shows that more fill is required to bring the total fill to the top of subgrade elevation. The surveyor can convey this information to the grade inspector so that the fill can be increased properly. As the height of fill approaches the proper elevation (top of subgrade), the grade checks become more frequent.

In the preceding example, the grade fill was 1 ft 0 in.; had the grade been cut 1 ft, the procedure with respect to the guard stake would have been the same: that is, measure up the guard stake 1 ft so that the mark now on the guard stake is 2 ft above the ℄ grade.

(a)

(b)

FIGURE 12.19 (a) Grade transfer using a conventional carpenter's level. (b) 80 laser torpedo level, featuring accuracy up to 1/4″ (0.029) at 100 ft (6 mm at 30 m); three precision glass vials—horizontal, vertical, and adjustable; and three AA cell batteries providing approximately 40 hr of intermittent use. (Courtesy of CST/Berger, Illinois)

The surveyor or inspector simply measures, at centerline, down 2 ft using a tape measure from the level string at ℄. If the measurement down to the "present" height of fill exceeds 2 ft, it indicates that more fill is required; if the measurement down to the "present" height of fill is less than 2 ft, it indicates that too much fill had been placed and that an appropriate depth of fill must be removed.

Another method of grade transfer used when the offset is large and the cuts or fills significant is the use of boning rods (batter boards) (see Figure 12.21). In the preceding example, a fill grade is transferred from the grade stake to the guard stake; the fill grade is measured up the guard stake, and the grade elevation is marked (any even foot/decimeter cut or fill mark can be used, so long as the relationship to profile grade is clearly marked). A crosspiece is nailed on the guard stake at the grade mark and parallel to ℄. A similar

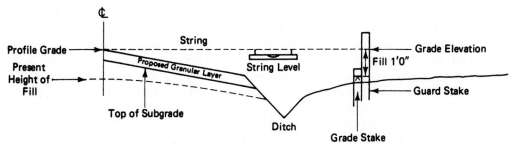

FIGURE 12.20 Grade transfer using a string level.

FIGURE 12.21 Grade transfer using batter boards.

guard stake and crosspiece are established on the opposite side of ℄. (In some cases, two crosspieces are used on each guard stake, the upper one indicating ℄ profile grade and the lower one indicating the shoulder elevation.) The surveyor or grade inspector can then sight over the two crosspieces to establish profile grade datum at that point. Another worker can move across the section with a rod, and the progress of the fill (cut) operation can be visually checked. Figure 12.22 shows a divided highway with grade stakes on either side of the ℄ swale, controlling grades on both sections of highway.

12.8 Ditch Construction

The ditch profile often parallels the ℄ profile, especially in cut sections. When the ditch profile does parallel the ℄ profile, no additional grades are required to assist the contractor in construction. However, it is quite possible to have the ℄ profile at one slope (even 0 percent) and the ditch profile at another slope (0.3 percent is often taken as a minimum slope to give adequate drainage). If the ditch grades are independent of ℄ profile, the contractor must be given these cut or fill grades, either from the existing grade stakes or from grade stakes specifically referencing the ditch line. In the extreme case (e.g., a spiraled and superelevated highway going over the brow of the hill), the contractor may require five separate grades at one station (i.e., ℄, two edges of pavement, and two different ditch grades); it is even possible in this extreme case to have the two ditches flowing in opposite directions for a short distance.

FIGURE 12.22   A multilane divided highway, showing center drainage with grade stakes.

Review Questions

12.1   What are the major differences between arterial highways and freeways?

12.2   What are two different techniques that can be used to create reference ties for PI locations? Use sketches in your response.

12.3   How can slope stake locations be determined prior to going out to the field?

12.4   What factors influence the choice of a route for a new highway?

12.5   If it has been decided to perform a topographic survey using airborne techniques, what field activities remain for the field surveyor?

12.6   Describe, in detail, how you would locate a highway railroad level crossing in the field.

12.7   What are the advantages/disadvantages of using machine control and guidance to construct highways?

12.8   Describe three different ways of establishing a right angle to be used in feature location using theodolite/tape techniques?

Chapter 13

Municipal Street Construction Surveys

13.1 General Background

Preengineering surveys for a street or an area are requested when there is a strong likelihood that planned construction will be approved for the following year's budgeted works. The surveys manager must choose between aerial and ground surveys for the preparation of engineering drawings. On the basis of past experience, the surveys manager will know the cost per mile or kilometer for both ground and aerial surveys for various levels of urban density. More densely packed topographic and human-made detail can usually be picked up more efficiently using aerial methods. However, the introduction of total stations, described in Chapter 5, and satellite-positioning techniques (described in Chapter 7), has made ground surveys competitive with aerial surveys for certain levels of detail density. A survey crew, using a total station and two prism poles, can capture as many as 1,000 points (X, Y, and Z coordinates) a day. In addition to this tremendous increase in data acquisition, we have the automatic transfer of data to the computer and the field note plot, which requires little additional work; thus, we have a highly efficient survey operation. See Tables 8.1 and 8.2 for typical scales for maps and plans used in municipal and highways projects.

As with highways, preliminary surveys for municipal streets include all topographic detail within the road allowance. Buried electric power lines, gas lines, telephone lines, and water services are usually staked out by the respective utility. Failure to request a stakeout can later (during construction) result in a broken utility and an expensive repair—not counting delays in the construction process.

Railroad crossings are profiled left and right of the street right-of-way (ROW), with additional sight-line data acquired as requested by the railroad or municipality. Water crossings and other road crossings are intersected, tied in, and profiled left and right of the street ROW with the same methods described for highways. Proposed connections to existing works (bridges, sewers, pipelines, streets, etc.) are surveyed carefully and precisely to ensure that the contractor makes an accurate connection.

In short, all topographic and works data that may have an effect on the cost estimates, the works design, or the construction of the proposed facility are tied in. Cross sections are taken full-width at all regular stations and at any change in grade that may occur between them. Elevations are determined carefully for any connecting points (sewers, curbs, street centerlines, etc.). Reconstruction of existing roads may require drilling to determine the extent of any granular material that can be recycled. Road drilling is usually scheduled during the off-season.

Municipal benchmarks are utilized. Care must be taken always to check into adjacent or subsequent benchmarks to verify the starting elevation. As the preliminary survey proceeds, temporary benchmarks (TBMs) are established and carefully referenced to aid in subsequent preliminary and construction surveys.

13.2 Classification of Roads and Streets

The plan shown in Figure 13.1 depicts a typical municipal road pattern. The local roads shown have the primary purpose of providing access to individual residential lots. The collector roads (both major and minor) provide the dual service of lot access and traffic movement. The

FIGURE 13.1 Municipal road pattern.

collector roads connect the local roads to arterial roads; the main purpose of the arterial roads is to provide a relatively high level of traffic movement.

Municipal works engineers base their road design standards on the level of service to be provided. The proposed cross sections and geometric alignments vary in complexity and cost for the fundamental local roads up to the more complex arterials. The highest level of service is given by the freeways, which provide high-velocity, high-volume routes with limited access (interchanges only), and ensure continuous traffic flow when design conditions prevail. The road design standards (based on the road classification) will tell the surveyor what to expect to see on the construction plans (*plan and profile*) with respect to road width, boulevard slope, centerline longitudinal slope (minimum/maximum), and so on. In addition, the accompanying *cross section* will show the depth of all materials and pavement cross fall.

13.3 Road Allowances

The road allowance varies in width from 40 ft (12 m) for small locals to 120 ft (35 m) for major arterials. In parts of North America, including most of Canada, the local road allowances were originally 66-ft wide (one Gunter's chain). When widening was required due to increased traffic volumes, it was common to take 10-ft widenings on each side, initially resulting in an 86-ft road allowance for major collectors and minor arterials. Further widenings left major arterials at 100- and 120-ft widths.

13.4 Road Cross Sections

A full-service municipal road allowance usually has asphalt pavement, curbs, storm and sanitary sewers, water distribution pipes, hydrants, catch basins, and sidewalks. Additional utilities, such as natural gas pipelines, electrical supply cables, and cable television, are also often located on the road allowance. The essential differences between local and arterial cross sections are the widths of pavement and the quality and depths of pavement materials. The construction layout of sewers and pipelines is covered in Chapter 14. See Figure 13.2 for typical municipal road cross sections.

The cross fall (height of crown) used on the pavement varies from one municipality to another, but is usually close to a 2-percent slope. The curb face is often 6 in. (150 mm) high except at driveways and crosswalks, where the height is restricted to about 2 in. (50 mm) for vehicle and pedestrian access. The slope on the boulevard from the curb to the street line usually rises at a 2-percent minimum slope, thus ensuring that roadway storm drainage does not run onto private property.

13.5 Plan and Profile

A typical plan and profile are shown in Figure 13.3. The **plan and profile**, which usually also show the cross-section details and construction notes, form the "blueprint" from which the construction is accomplished. The plan and profile, together with the

(a) Foot Units

(b) Metric Units

FIGURE 13.2 Typical cross section of a local residential road. Gas and water services shown under boulevards are normally installed on only one side of the roadway; far-side house connections are located under the road and boulevard but above the sewer pipes. (a) Foot units. (b) Metric units.

contract specifications, spell out in detail precisely where and how the road (in this example) is to be built. The **plan** portion of the plan and profile gives the horizontal location of the facility, including curve radii, whereas the **profile** portion shows the key elevations and slopes along the road centerline, including vertical curve information. Both the plan and the profile relate all data to the project stationing established as horizontal control.

Not to Scale

Street Line
Proposed Curb
Proposed Curb
Street Line

1+60
1+43
Offset Line
1+20
1+00
Pine Street
0+80
0+60
0+45
R=10 m
R=10 m
0+20 = 0
0+14.5
0+00
Elm Street

Plan

Profile

Vertical Curves Not Shown

180.890
57 m @ −1.00%
Existing Ground
98 m @ 1.00%
179.910
45 m @ −0.80%
180.270

0+00   0+20   0+45   0+60   0+80   1+00   1+20   1+43   1+60

Notes:

1. Scales are Usually 1″ = 40′ (50′) Horizontal and 1″ = 10′ (5′) Vertical — Imperial or 1:500 Horizontal and 1:100 Vertical — Metric.

2. 0+00 can be Assigned to any Convenient Point, but is Usually Assigned to the Intersection of the Two Center Lines.

3. See Cross Section Shown in Figure 13.10.

FIGURE 13.3   Plan and profile.

13.6   Establishing Centerline (℄)

Let us use the case where a ditched residential road is to be upgraded to a paved and curbed road. The first job for the construction surveyor is to reestablish the centerline (℄) of the roadway. Usually, this entails finding several property markers delineating the street line (℄). Fence and hedge lines can be used initially to guide the surveyor to the approximate locations of the property markers. When the surveyor finds one property marker, he or she can measure out the frontage distances shown on the property plan (plat) to locate a sufficient number of additional markers. Usually, the construction surveyor has the notes from the preliminary survey showing the location of property markers used in the original survey. If possible, the construction surveyor utilizes the same evidence used in the preliminary survey, taking the time, of course, to verify the resultant alignment. If the evidence used in the preliminary survey has been destroyed, as is often the case when a year or more has elapsed between the two surveys, the construction surveyor takes great care to ensure that the new results are not appreciably different from those of the original survey, unless, of course, a blunder occurred on the original survey.

The property markers can be square or round iron bars (including rebars) or round iron or aluminum pipes, magnetically capped. The markers can vary from $1\frac{1}{2}$ to 4 ft in length. It is not unusual for the surveyor to have to use a shovel because the tops of the markers are often buried. The surveyor can use a magnetic or electronic metal detector to aid in locating buried markers. Sometimes even an exhaustive search of an area will not turn up a sufficient number of markers to establish ℄. The surveyor must then extend the search to adjacent blocks or backyards in order to reestablish the missing markers. The surveyor can also approach the home owners in the affected area and inquire about the existence of a "mortgage survey plan" (Figure 13.4) for the specific property. Such a plan is required in most areas before a financial institution will provide mortgage financing. This mortgage survey plan shows dimensions from the building foundation to the street line and to both sidelines. Information thus gained can be used to narrow the search for a missing marker or can be used directly to establish points on the street line.

Once several points have been established on both sides of the roadway, the ℄ can be marked from each of these points by measuring (at right angles) half the width of the road allowance. The surveyor then sets up the theodolite or total station on a ℄ mark near one of the project extremities and sights in on the ℄ marker nearest the other project extremity. He or she checks if all the markers line up in a straight line (assuming tangent alignment) (Figure 13.5). If all the markers do not line up, the surveyor will check the affected measurements; if discrepancies still occur (as is often the case), the surveyor makes the "best fit" of the available evidence. Depending on the length of roadway involved and the number of the ℄ markers established, the number of markers lining up perfectly will vary. Three well-spaced, perfectly aligned markers are the absolute minimum number required for the establishment of the ℄. The reason that all markers do not line up is that most lots are resurveyed over the years. Some lots may be resurveyed several times. Land surveyors' prime area of concern is that area of the plan immediately adjacent to their client's property, and they must ensure that the property stakeout is consistent for both evidence and plan intentions. Over several years, cumulative errors and mistakes can significantly affect the overall alignment of the ℄ markers.

If the ℄ is being marked on an existing road, as in this case, the surveyor will use nails with washers and red plastic flagging to establish the marks. The nails can be driven into gravel, asphalt, and, in some cases, concrete surfaces. The washers keep the nails from sinking below the road surface, and the red flagging will help in relocation.

FIGURE 13.4 Mortgage survey plan (plat).

Plan of Survey of
Lots 317–320, Registered Plan 7566
Township of Markham
County of York
Scale: 1"=30'

Sciberras Road

Lot 320:
157.44'
50.0'
50.09'
6.10'
6.27'
27.09'
28.03'
4.06'
4.02'
Concrete Foundation

Lot 319:
160.43'
50.0'
50.09'
4.51'
4.61'
25.60'
27.82'
7.84'
7.78'
Concrete Foundation

Lot 318:
163.43'
50.0'
50.09'
7.95'
8.10'
27.09'
27.94'
4.46'
4.48'
Concrete Foundation

Lot 317:
166.42'
169.41'
50.0'
50.09'
4.21'
4.24'
25.74'
26.67'
6.14'
6.09'
Concrete Foundation

66.00'

33.00

33.06

33.00

32.90

33.00

◇• = Instrument Station

◇ = Sighting Station

FIGURE 13.5 Property markers used to establish centerline.

If the project involves a new curbed road in a new subdivision, the establishment of the ℄ is simpler. The recently set property markers would be intact, for the most part, and discrepancies between markers would be minimal (as all markers would have been set in the same comprehensive survey operation). The ℄ in this case would be marked by wood stakes 2 in. by 2 in. or 2 in. by 1 in. and 18 in. long.

13.7 Establishing Offset Lines and Construction Control

We continue here with the case where a ditched residential road is being upgraded to a paved and curbed road. The legal fabric of the road allowance as given by the property markers constitutes the horizontal control. Construction control consists of offset lines referenced to the proposed curbs with respect to line and grade. In the case of ditched roads and most highways, the offset lines are referenced to the proposed centerline with respect to line and grade. The offset lines are placed as close to the proposed location of the curbs as possible. It is essential that the offset stakes do not interfere with equipment and form work; it is also essential that the offset stakes be far enough removed so that they are not destroyed during cut or fill operations. Ideally, the offset stakes, once established, will remain in place for the duration of construction. This ideal can often be realized in municipal road construction, but it is seldom realized in highway construction, because of the significant size of cuts and fills often encountered in highway design. If cuts and fills are not too large, offset lines for curbs can be 3–5 ft (1–2 m) from the proposed face of the curb. An offset line this close allows for very efficient transfer of line and grade (see Section 12.7). Figure 13.6 shows concrete curb and gutter being installed by a slip-form concrete curber. The curber is kept on line and grade by keeping in contact with a guide string or wire, which is established by measurements from the grade stakes.

In the case of a ditched gravel road being upgraded to a curbed paved road, the offset line must be placed far enough away on the boulevard to avoid the ditch-filling operation and any additional cut and fill that may be required. In the worst case, it may be necessary to place the offset line on the street line, an 18- to 25-ft (6- to 7-m) offset. Figure 13.7 shows a grade supervisor checking the status of excavation by sighting over cross rails referenced to the finished grade and set at right angles to the street. These sight rails (also called batter boards) are erected by measuring from the grade stakes placed by the surveyor.

When the street pavement is to be concrete, the pavement can be placed first, before the curbs are installed. Figure 13.8 shows a concrete-paving operation being controlled by a

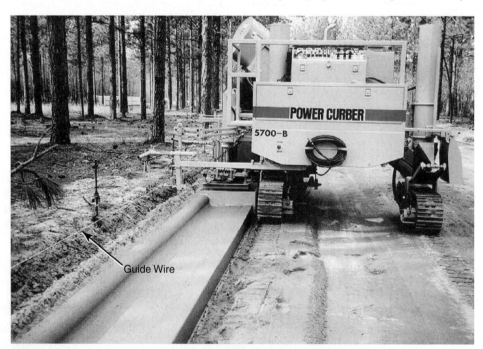

FIGURE 13.6 Slip-form concrete paver: line and grade are provided by string line (can also be guided by laser). Precision of $1/8$ in. or 0.01 ft. (Courtesy of Ausran)

FIGURE 13.7 Progress of street construction being monitored by the use of sight rails (batter boards).

FIGURE 13.8 Concrete paver, controlled for line and grade by guide wires established from grade stakes supplied by the surveyor. (Courtesy of Caterpillar, Inc., Peoria, Illinois)

Sec. 13.7   Establishing Offset Lines and Construction Control

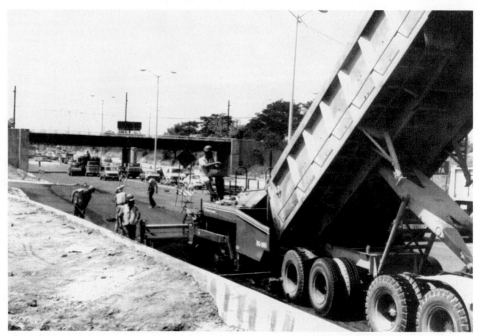

FIGURE 13.9 Asphalt spreader laying asphalt to finished grade as marked on the curb face. (Courtesy of Caterpillar Inc., Peoria, Illinois)

guide wire positioned precisely in line and grade by the surveyor working from previously placed grade stakes. After the pavement is in place, the curb (or curb and gutter) can be placed adjacent to the new concrete pavement without the need of any further layout.

When the street pavement is to be asphalt, the curbs (or curbs and gutters) are always constructed first by measurements from the grade stakes. If the curb and gutter have been placed, the subsequent asphalt pavement is simply placed on the specified cross slope (road crown) adjacent to the edge of the concrete gutter. If curb alone has been installed, the subsequent paving operation is guided by marks on the curb face a set distance below the top of the new curb (a 6-in. curb face is common). Figure 13.9 shows an asphalt-paving operation at an interchange. The asphalt is being placed adjacent to a barrier curb at the design profile marked on the curb face.

13.8 Construction Grades for a Curbed Street

The offset stakes (with nails or tacks for precise alignment) are usually placed at 50-ft (20-m) stations and at any critical alignment change points. The elevations of the tops of the stakes are determined by rod and level and are based on the vertical control established for the project. It is then necessary to determine the proposed elevation for the top of curb at each offset station. You can see in Figure 13.3 that elevations and slopes have been designed for a portion of the project. The plan and profile have been simplified for illustrative purposes, and offsets are shown for one curb line only.

FIGURE 13.10 Cross section showing the relationship between the centerline and the top of the curb elevations.

Given the ℄ elevation data, the construction surveyor must calculate the proposed curb elevations. He or she can proceed by calculating the relevant elevations on ℄ and then adjusting for crown and curb height differential, or by applying the differential first and working out the curb elevations directly. To determine the difference in elevation between the ℄ and the top of curb, the surveyor must analyze the appropriate cross section. Figure 13.10 shows that the cross fall is $4.5 \times 0.02 = 0.090$ m (90 mm). The face on the curb is 150 mm; therefore, the top of curb is 60 mm above the ℄ elevation. A list of key stations (Table 13.1) is prepared,

Table 13.1 GRADE SHEET COMPUTATIONS

Station	℄ Elevation		Curb Elevation
0 + 00	180.270		
	−0.116		
BC 0 + 14.5	180.154	+0.060	180.214
	−0.044		
0 + 20	180.110	+0.060	180.170
	−0.160		
0 + 40	179.950	+0.060	180.010
	−0.040		
0 + 45	179.910	+0.060	179.970
	+0.150		
0 + 60	180.060	+0.060	180.120
	+0.200		
0 + 80	180.260	+0.060	180.320
	+0.200		
1 + 00	180.460	+0.060	180.520
	+0.200		
1 + 20	180.660	+0.060	180.720
	+0.200		
1 + 40	180.860	+0.060	180.920
	+0.030		
1 + 43	180.890	+0.060	180.950
etc.			

Table 13.2 GRADE SHEET

Station	Curb Elevation	Stake Elevation	Cut	Fill
0 + 14.5	180.214	180.325	0.111	
0 + 20	180.170	180.315	0.145	
0 + 40	180.010	180.225	0.215	
0 + 45	179.970	180.110	0.140	
0 + 60	180.120	180.185	0.065	
0 + 80	180.320	180.320	On grade	
1 + 00	180.520	180.475		0.045
1 + 20	180.720	180.710		0.010
1 + 40	180.920	180.865		0.055
1 + 43	180.950	180.900		0.050
etc.				

and the ℄ elevation at each station is calculated. The ℄ elevations are then adjusted to produce curb elevations. Because superelevation is seldom used in municipal design, it is safe to say that the curbs on both sides of the road are normally parallel in line and grade. A notable exception can occur when the intersections of collectors and arterials are widened to allow for turn lanes and both curb line and grade are affected.

The construction surveyor can then prepare a grade sheet (Table 13.2), copies of which are given to the contractor and the project inspector. The tops of stake elevations, determined by level and rod, are assumed in this illustrative case. The grade sheet, signed by the construction surveyor, also includes the street name; date; limits of the contract; and, most important, the offset distance to the face of the curb.

Note that the construction grades (cut and fill) refer only to the vertical distance to be measured down or up from the top of the grade stake to locate the proposed elevation. Construction grades do not define with certainty whether the contractor is in a cut or fill situation at any given point. Refer to Figure 13.11. At 0 + 20, a construction grade of cut 0.145 is given, whereas the contractor is actually in a fill situation (i.e., the proposed top of curb is above the existing ground at that station). This lack of correlation between construction grades and the construction process can become more pronounced as the offset distance lengthens. For example, if the grade stake at station 1 + 40 had been located at the street line, the construction grade would have been cut, whereas the construction process is almost entirely in a fill operation.

When the layout is performed using foot units, the basic station interval is 50 ft. The dimensions are recorded and calculated to the closest one-hundredth (0.01) of a foot. Although all survey measurements are in feet and decimals of a foot, for the contractor's purposes the final cuts and fills are often expressed in feet and inches. The decimal–inch relationships are soon committed to memory by surveyors working in the construction field (Table 13.3). Cuts and fills are usually expressed to the closest $1/8$ in. for concrete, steel, and pipelines and to the closest $1/4$ in. for highways, granular surfaces, and ditch lines. The grade sheet in Table 13.4 illustrates the foot–inch relationships. The first column and the last two columns are all that are required by the contractor, in addition to the offset distance, to construct the facility properly.

FIGURE 13.11   Cross sections showing cut-and-fill grades.

In some cases, the cuts and fills (grades) are written directly on the appropriate grade stakes. This information, written with lumber crayon (keel) or felt marker, is always written on the side of the stake facing the construction. The station is also written on each stake and is placed on the side of each stake facing the lower chainage (station).

Table 13.3   DECIMAL FOOT-INCH CONVERSION

	$1'' = {}^1/_{12}' = 0.083'$	
$1'' = 0.08(3)'$	$7'' = 0.58'$	${}^1/_8'' = 0.01'$
$2'' = 0.17'$	$8'' = 0.67'$	${}^1/_4'' = 0.02'$
$3'' = 0.25'$	$9'' = 0.75'$	${}^1/_2'' = 0.04'$
$4'' = 0.33'$	$10'' = 0.83'$	${}^3/_4'' = 0.06'$
$5'' = 0.42'$	$11'' = 0.92'$	
$6'' = 0.50'$	$12'' = 1.00'$	

Table 13.4 GRADE SHEET (FOOT UNITS)

(1) Station	(2) Curb Elevation	(3) Stake Elevation	(4) Cut	(5) Fill	(6) Cut	(7) Fill
0 + 30	470.20	471.30	1.10		1'1¹/₄"	
0 + 50	470.40	470.95	0.55		0'6⁵/₈"	
1 + 00	470.90	470.90	On grade		On grade	
1 + 50	471.40	471.23		0.17		0'2"
2 + 00	471.90	471.46		0.44		0'5¹/₄"
2 + 50	472.40	472.06		0.34		0'4¹/₈"

13.9 Street Intersections

An intersection curb radius can range from 30 ft (10 m), for two local streets intersecting, to 60 ft (18 m), for two arterial streets intersecting. The angle of intersection is ideally 90° (for good sight lines); however, the range from 70° to 110° is often permitted for practical purposes. See Figure 13.12.

Street intersections require special attention from the surveyor for both line and grade. The curved curb lines (shown at the intersection of Pine Street and Elm Street in Figure 13.3) are often established in the field, not by the deflection angle technique of Chapter 11, but instead by first establishing the curve center and then establishing the arc by swinging off the curve radius.

Also, the profile of this curved section of proposed curb requires analysis because this section of curb does not fit the profile of Pine Street or of Elm Street. We can determine the curb elevation at the BC on Pine Street; it is 180.214 at 0 + 14.5 (Table 13.1).

At this point, the surveyor must obtain the plan and profile of Elm Street and determine the chainage at the EC of the curb coming from the BC at 0 + 14.5, on the north side of Pine Street (Figure 13.3). Once this station has been determined, the proposed curb elevation at the EC on Elm Street can be computed. Let's assume this value to be 180.100 m. This procedure has to be repeated to determine the curb elevation on Elm Street at the EC of the curve coming from the BC on the south side of Pine Street (if that curb is also being constructed).

The surveyor, knowing the elevation of both the BC on Pine Street and the EC on Elm Street, can compute the length of arc between the BC and the EC and then compute the profile grade for that particular section of curved curb. The procedure is as follows. The curb elevation at the BC (180.214) is determined from the plan and profile of Pine Street (Figure 13.3 and Table 13.1). The curb elevation at the EC is determined from the plan and profile of Elm Street (assume that the EC elevation = 180.100). The length of curb can be calculated using Equation 11.5:

$$L = \frac{\pi R \Delta}{180}$$

$$= 15.708 \text{ m}$$

The slope from BC to EC can be determined as follows:

$$180.214 - 180.100 = 0.114 \text{ m}$$

The fall is 0.114 m over an arc distance of 15.708 m, which is −0.73 percent.

FIGURE 13.12 Intersection geometrics (one quadrant shown).

$$T = R \tan \frac{\Delta}{2}$$

$$T = R \text{ (when } \Delta = 90°)$$

These calculations indicate that a satisfactory slope (0.5 percent is the usual pavement minimum) joins the two points. The intersection curve is located by four offset stakes, BC, EC, and two intermediate points. In this case, 15.708/3 = 5.236 m, the distance measured from the BC to locate the first intermediate point, the distance measured from the first intermediate point to the second intermediate point, and the distance used as a check from the second intermediate point to the EC.

In actual practice, the chord distance is used rather than the arc distance. Because $\Delta/2 = 45°$ and we are using a factor of $^1/_3$, the corresponding deflection angle for one-third of the arc would be 15°, which we use in the following equation:

$$C = 2R \sin (\text{ deflection angle})$$

$$= 2 \times 10 \times \sin 15° = 5.176 \text{ m}$$

These intermediate points can be deflected in from the BC or EC, or they can be located by the use of two tapes, with one surveyor at the radius point (holding 10 m, in this case) and another surveyor at the BC or intermediate point (holding 5.176), while the stake surveyor holds the zero point of both tapes. The latter technique is used most often on these small-radius problems. The only occasions when these curves are deflected in by theodolite occur when the radius point (curve center) is inaccessible (due to fuel pump islands, front porches, etc.).

The proposed curb elevations on the arc are computed as follows:

Station	Elevation
BC 0 + 14.5	180.214
	−0.038
Stake 1	180.176
	−0.038
Stake 2	180.138
	−0.038
EC	180.100

The arc interval is 5.236 m. The difference in elevation = 5.236 × 0.0073 = 0.038. Grade information for the curve can be included on the grade sheet.

The offset curve can be established in the same manner after making allowances for the shortened radius (Figure 13.12). For an offset (o/s) of 3 m, the radius becomes 7 m. The chords required can be calculated as follows:

$$C = 2R \sin (\text{ deflection})$$

$$= 2 \times 7 \times \sin 15°$$

$$= 3.623 \text{ m}$$

13.10 Sidewalk Construction

The sidewalk is constructed adjacent to the curb or at some set distance from the street line. If the sidewalk is adjacent to the curb, no additional layout is required because the curb itself gives line and grade for construction. In some cases, the concrete for this curb and sidewalk is placed in one operation, guided by curb layout markers.

Note: The Sidewalk is Always Constructed so that it Slopes Toward the Road—Usually
@ 1/4" per foot (2%).

FIGURE 13.13 Typical location of a sidewalk on the road allowance.

When the sidewalk is to be located at some set distance from the street line (₤), a separate layout is required. Sidewalks located near the ₤ give the advantages of increased pedestrian safety and boulevard space for the stockpiling of a winter's accumulation of plowed snow in northern regions. See Figure 13.13, which shows the typical location of a sidewalk on a road allowance.

Sidewalk construction usually takes place after the curbs have been built and the boulevard has been brought to sod grade. The offset distance for the grade stakes can be quite short (1–3 ft). If the sidewalk is located within 1–3 ft of the ₤, the ₤ is an ideal location for the offset line. In many cases, only line is required for construction because the grade is already established by boulevard grading and the permanent elevations at ₤ (existing elevations on private property are seldom adjusted in municipal work). The cross slope (toward the curb) is usually given as being $1/4$ in./ft (2 percent).

13.11 Site Grading

Every construction site (whether it be small, as for a residential house, or large, as for an airport), requires a site grading plan showing proposed (and existing) ground elevations. These ground elevations have been designed to (1) ensure proper drainage for storm-water runoff, (2) provide convenient pedestrian and vehicular access, and (3) balance cut and fill optimally. Typical municipal projects that require grading surveys include residential, commercial, or industrial developments; sanitary landfill sites; parks or greenbelts; and boulevards and the like.

Figure 13.14 shows part of a site grading plan for a residential development. The existing ground elevations are shown in brackets below each proposed elevation at all lot corners. With this plan, the surveyor can determine the runoff flow direction for each lot and set grade stakes at the lot corners to define finished ground grade. Figure 13.15 shows a backhoe/loader roughly shaping up the ground behind a housing development, and Figure 13.16 shows another loader with a landscaping/pulverizing attachment bringing the topsoil to its final elevation just prior to sodding or seeding.

(83.45)—existing elevation

FIGURE 13.14 Site grading plan. Proposed elevation: 84.23. Existing elevation: 83.45.

Grade control can be provided by rotating lasers or electronic levels (Figure 12.18). Grade can also be given by grade stakes or grade stakes with batter boards. Large-scale projects, with deep cuts or fills, may require several layouts before finally being brought to grade unless machine guidance/control techniques are being used (see Chapter 10).

FIGURE 13.15   Rough grading by loader/backhoe. (Courtesy of John Deere, Moline, Illinois)

Problems

13.1 A new road is to be constructed beginning at an existing road (₵ elevation = 472.70 ft) for a distance of 600 ft. The ₵ gradient is to rise at 1.10 percent. The elevations of the offset grade stakes are as follows: 0 + 00 = 472.60; 1 + 00 = 472.36; 2 + 00 = 473.92; 3 + 00 = 476.00; 4 + 00 = 478.33; 5 + 00 = 479.77; 6 + 00 = 480.82. Prepare a grade sheet like the one in Table 13.4, showing the cuts and fills in feet and inches.

13.2 A new road is to be constructed to connect two existing roads. The ₵ intersection with the east road (0 + 00) is at an elevation of 210.660 m, and the ₵ intersection at the west road (1 + 16.828) is at an elevation of 208.323 m. The elevations of the offset grade stakes are as follows: 0 + 00 = 210.831; 0 + 20 = 210.600; 0 + 40 = 211.307; 0 + 60 = 209.460; 0 + 80 = 208.160; 1 + 00 = 208.115; 1 + 16.828 = 208.300. Prepare a grade sheet like the one in Table 13.2 showing cuts and fills in meters.

Refer to Figure 13.17 for Problems 13.3–13.8.

13.3 Figure 13.17 shows proposed curb locations, together with grade stakes offset from the north-side curb. The straight section of curb begins at 0 + 52 and ends at 8 + 38 (centerline stations). With the aid of a sketch, show how these two chainages were determined.

13.4 Compute the final centerline road elevations at the points of curve (PC)—that is, 0 + 52 and 8 + 38, and at all even 50-ft stations.

FIGURE 13.16 Fine grading by landscaping/pulverizing attachment on loader. (Courtesy of John Deere, Moline, Illinois)

13.5 Compute the top-of-curb elevations from 0 + 52 to 8 + 38. See Figure 13.17 (cross section) for the centerline/top-of-curb relationship.

13.6 Using the grade stake elevations in the chart below, prepare a grade sheet showing cuts/fills (ft and in.) for the proposed curb from 0 + 52 to 8 + 38.

		Grade Stake Elevations		
PC	0 + 52	504.71	4 + 50	508.46
	1 + 00	504.78	5 + 00	508.77
	1 + 50	504.93	5 + 55	510.61
	2 + 00	504.98	6 + 00	511.73
	2 + 50	505.82	6 + 50	512.00
	3 + 00	506.99	7 + 00	512.02
	3 + 50	507.61	7 + 50	512.11
	3 + 75	507.87	8 + 00	512.24
	4 + 00	508.26 PC	8 + 38	512.73

FIGURE 13.17 Plan, profile, and cross section for pavement and curbs, Parkway Avenue (foot units). See also Figure 14.24.

13.7 For the intersection curve ($R = 35$ ft) at Main Street, station A (0 + 52) to station D:

(a) Compute the length of arc.

(b) Determine the curb-line gradient (percentage) from A to D.

(c) Determine the proposed curb elevations at stations B and C; B and C divide the arc into three equal sections: AB = BC = CD.

(d) Using the grade stake elevations shown in the chart below, determine the cuts/fills (ft and in.) for stations B, C, and D.

Grade Stake Elevations			
A	504.71	C	506.37
B	506.22	D	506.71

13.8 For the intersection curve ($R = 30$ ft) at First Street, station E (8 + 38) to station H:

(a) Compute the length of arc.

(b) Determine the curb-line gradient (percentage) from E to H.

(c) Determine the proposed curb elevations at stations F and G; F and G divide the arc into three equal sections: EF = FG = GH.

(d) Using the grade stake elevations shown in the chart below, determine the cuts/fills (ft and in.) for stations F, G, and H.

Grade Stake Elevations			
E	512.73	G	512.88
F	512.62	H	513.27

Use Figure 13.18 for Problems 13.9–13.14.

13.9 Figure 13.18 shows proposed curb locations, together with offset stakes for the north-side curb. The straight section of curb begins at station 0 + 15 and ends at station 2 + 10. With the aid of a sketch, show how these two chainages were determined.

13.10 Compute the final centerline road elevations at the points of curve (PC), that is, 0 + 15 and 2 + 10, and at all even 20-m stations.

13.11 Compute the top-of-curb elevations from 0 + 15 to 2 + 10. See Figure 13.18 (cross section) for the centerline/top-of-curb relationship.

13.12 Using the grade stake elevations shown in the chart below, calculate the cuts/fills for the proposed curb from 0 + 15 to 2 + 10.

Grade Stake Elevations					
PC	0 + 15	186.720		1 + 20	188.025
	0 + 20	186.387		1 + 40	188.003
	0 + 40	185.923		1 + 60	187.627
	0 + 60	186.425		1 + 72	187.455
	0 + 72	186.707		1 + 80	187.907
	0 + 80	187.200		2 + 00	187.993
	1 + 00	187.527	PC	2 + 10	188.125

FIGURE 13.18 Plan, profile, and cross section for pavement and curbs, Oak Avenue (metric units). See also Figure 14.25.

13.13 For the intersection curve ($R = 10$ m) at Elm Street, station A (0 + 15) to station D:

    (a) Compute the length of arc.

    (b) Determine the curb-line gradient (percentage) from A to D.

    (c) Determine the proposed curb elevations at stations B, C, and D. B and C divide the arc into three equal sections; that is, AB = BC = CD.

    (d) Using the grade stake elevations shown in the chart below, determine the cuts/fills for stations B, C, and D.

	Grade Stake Elevations		
A	186.720	C	186.575
B	186.447	D	186.567

13.14 For the intersection curve ($R = 10$ m) at Spruce Street, station E (2 + 10) to station H:

    (a) Determine the curb-line gradient (percentage) from E to H.

    (b) Determine the proposed curb elevations at stations F, G, and H. F and G divide the arc into three equal sections: EF = FG = GH.

    (c) Using the grade stake elevations shown in the chart below, determine the cuts/fills for stations F, G, and H.

	Grade Stake Elevations		
E	188.125	G	188.015
F	188.007	H	188.010

13.15 Refer to Figure 13.14 (site grading plan). A grade stake was set near the middle of Lot #26, and the stake-top elevation was determined to be 84.15 m. Compute the cut and fill at each lot corner.

Chapter 14

Pipeline and Tunnel Construction Surveys

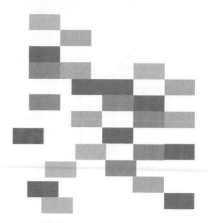

14.1 Pipeline Construction

Pressurized pipelines are designed to carry water, oil, natural gas, and sometimes sewage with the pipeline flow rates dependent on the amount of pressure applied, the pipe size, and other factors. Because pressure systems do not require close attention to grade lines, the layout for pipelines can proceed at a much lower order of precision than is required for gravity pipes. Pipelines are usually designed so that the cover over the crown is adequate for the loading conditions expected and also adequate to prevent damage due to frost penetration, erosion, and the like.

The pipeline location can be determined from the contract drawings; the line and grade stakes are offset an optimal distance from the pipe ℄ and are placed at 50- to 100-ft (15- to 30-m) intervals. When existing ground elevations are not being altered, the standard cuts required can be simply measured down from the ground surface (required cuts in this case would equal the specified cover over the crown plus the pipe diameter plus the bedding, if applicable). See Figure 14.1, Trench A. In the case of proposed general cuts and fills, grades must be given to establish suitable crown elevation so that final cover is as specified. See Figure 14.1, Trench B. Additional considerations and higher precisions are required at major crossings (e.g., rivers, highways, utilities).

Figure 14.2(a) shows a pipeline being installed a set distance below existing ground (as in Trench A, Figure 14.1). Material cast from the trench is shown on the right side of the trench, and the installation equipment is shown on the left side of the trench. The surveyor, in consultation with the contractor, determines a location for the line and grade stakes that will not interfere with either the cast material or the installation equipment.

Figure 14.2(b) shows a pipe-jacking operation. The carrier pipe is installed at the same time that the tunnel is being excavated. A construction laser that has been set to the design

FIGURE 14.1   Pipeline construction. (a) Existing ground to be unchanged; (b) existing ground to be altered.

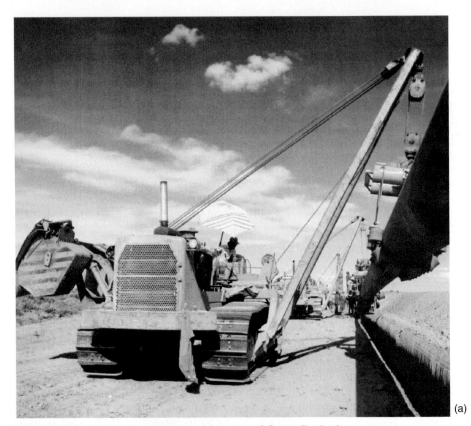

(a)

FIGURE 14.2   (a) Pipeline installation. (Courtesy of Caterpillar, Inc.)

(continued)

slope and horizontal alignment provides line and grade. This type of operation is used where an open cut would be unacceptable—for example, across important roads or highways.

Final surveys show the actual location of the pipe and appurtenances (valves and the like). As-built drawings, produced from final surveys, are especially important in urban areas, where it seems there is no end to underground construction.

(b)

FIGURE 14.2 (*continued*)   (b) pipe-jacking operation. (Courtesy of Astec Underground/American Augers)

14.2   Sewer Construction

Sewers are usually described as being in one of two categories: sanitary and storm. Sanitary sewers collect domestic and industrial liquid waste and convey these wastes (sewage) to a treatment plant. Storm sewers are designed to collect runoff from rainfall and to transport this water (sewage) to the nearest natural receiving body (e.g., creek, river, lake). The rainwater enters the storm-sewer system through ditch inlets or through catch basins (CBs) located at the curb line on paved roads. The design and construction of sanitary and storm sewers are similar because the flow of sewage in both the sewers is usually governed by gravity. Because the sewer grade lines (flow lines) depend on gravity, it is essential that construction grades be precise.

Figure 14.3(a) shows a typical cross section for a municipal roadway. The two sewers are typically located 5 ft (1.5 m) on either side of ₵. The sanitary sewer is usually

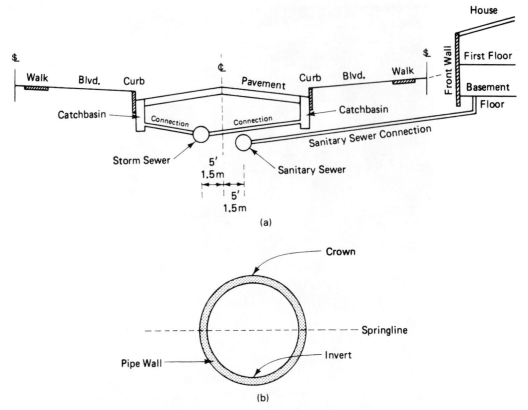

FIGURE 14.3 (a) Municipal road allowance showing typical service locations. (b) Sewer pipe section.

deeper than the storm sewer, as it must be deep enough to allow for all house connections. The sanitary house connection is usually at a 2-percent (minimum) slope. If sanitary sewers are being added to an existing residential road, the preliminary survey must include the basement floor elevations. The floor elevations are determined by taking a rod reading on the window sill and then, after getting permission to enter the house, measuring from the window sill down to the basement floor. As a result of deep basements and long setbacks from ℄, sanitary sewers often have to be at least 9 ft (2.75 m) below ℄ grade.

The minimum depth of storm sewers below ℄ grade depends, in the southern United States, on the traffic loading and, in the northern United States and most of Canada, on the depth of frost penetration. The minimum depth of storm sewers ranges from 3 ft (1 m) in some areas in the south to 8 ft (2.5 m) in the north. The design of the inlets and CBs depends on the depth of sewer and the quality of the effluent.

The minimum slope for storm sewers is usually 0.50 percent, whereas the minimum slope for sanitary sewers is often set at 0.67 percent. In either case, the designers try to achieve self-cleaning velocity (i.e., a minimum of 2.5–3 ft/s or 0.8–0.9 m/s) to avoid excessive sewer maintenance costs. Manholes are located at each change in direction, slope, or pipe size. In addition, manholes are located at 300- to 450-ft (100- to 140-m) maximum intervals.

CBs are usually located at 300-ft (100-m) maximum intervals; they are also located at the high side of intersections and at all low points. The 300-ft (100-m) maximum interval is reduced as the slope on the road increases.

For construction purposes, sewer layout is considered only from one manhole to the next. The stationing (0 + 00) commences at the first (existing) manhole (or outlet) and proceeds upstream only to the next manhole. If a second leg is also to be constructed, station 0 + 00 is assigned to the downstream manhole and proceeds upstream only to the next manhole. A unique manhole number (e.g., 1, 2, 3, . . . , 1A, 2A, 3A, . . .) describes each manhole; this is to avoid confusion with the stations for extensive sewer projects. Figure 14.3(b) shows a section of sewer pipe. The **invert** is the inside bottom of the pipe. The invert grade is the controlling grade for construction and design. The sewer pipes may consist of vitrified clay, steel, some of the newer "plastics," or, as usually is the case, concrete.

The pipe wall thickness depends on the diameter of the pipe. For storm sewers, 12 in. (300 mm) is usually taken as minimum diameter. The **spring line** of the pipe is at the halfway mark, and connections are made above this reference line. The **crown** is the outside top of the pipe. Although this term is relatively unimportant (sewer cover is measured to the crown) for sewer construction, it is important for pipeline (pressurized pipes) construction, as it gives the controlling grade for that type of construction.

14.3 Layout for Line and Grade

As in other construction work, offset stakes are used to provide line and grade for the construction of sewers; grade can also be defined by the use of in-trench or surface lasers. Before deciding on the offset location, it is wise to discuss the matter with the contractor. The contractor will be excavating the trench and casting the material to one side or loading it into trucks for removal from the site. Additionally, the sewer pipe will be delivered to the site and positioned conveniently alongside its future location. The position of the offset stakes should not interfere with either of these operations.

The surveyor will position the offset line as close to the pipe centerline as possible, but seldom is it possible to locate the offset line closer than 15 ft (5 m) away. 0 + 00 is assigned to the downstream manhole or outlet, the chainage proceeding upstream to the next manhole. The centerline of construction is laid out with stakes marking the location of the two terminal points of the sewer leg. The surveyor will use survey techniques giving 1:3,000 accuracy as a minimum for most sewer projects. Large-diameter (6-ft or 2-m) sewers require increased precision and accuracy.

The two terminal points on ℄ are occupied by total station or theodolite, and right angles are turned to precisely locate the terminal points at the assigned offset distance. 0 + 00 on offset is occupied by a total station or theodolite, and a sight is taken on the other terminal offset point. Stakes are then located at 50-ft (20-m) intervals; checking in at the terminal point verifies accuracy.

The tops of the offset stakes are surveyed and their elevations determined, the surveyor taking care to see that his or her leveling is accurate; the existing invert elevation of MH 3 (Figure 14.4), shown on the contract plan and profile, is verified at the same time. The surveyor next calculates the sewer invert elevations for the 50-ft (20-m) stations. He or

FIGURE 14.4 Plan and profile of proposed sewer (foot units).

she then prepares a grade sheet showing the stations, stake elevations, invert grades, and cuts. The following examples will illustrate the techniques used.

Assume that an existing sewer (Figure 14.4) is to be extended from existing MH 3 to proposed MH 4. The horizontal alignment will be a straight-line production of the sewer leg from MH 2 to MH 3. The vertical alignment is taken from the contract plan and profile (Figure 14.4). The straight line is produced by setting up the total station or theodolite at MH 3, sighting MH 2, and double centering to the location of MH 4. The layout then proceeds as described previously. The stake elevations, as determined by differential leveling, are shown in Table 14.1.

At station 1 + 50, the cut is 8 ft 3⅞ in. (Figure 14.5). To set a cross-trench batter board at the next even foot, measure up 0 ft 8⅛ in. to the top of the batter board. The offset distance of 15 ft can be measured and marked at the top of the batter board over the pipe ₵ and a distance of 9 ft measured down to establish the invert elevation. This even foot measurement

Table 14.1 SEWER GRADE SHEET: FOOT UNITS*

Station		Invert Elevation (ft)	Stake Elevation (ft)	Cut (ft)	Cut (ft and in.)
MH 3	0 + 00	420.86	429.27	8.41	8′4⅞″
	0 + 50	421.46	429.90	8.44	8′5¼″
	1 + 00	422.06	430.41	8.35	8′4¼″
	1 + 50	422.66	430.98	8.32	8′3⅞″
	2 + 00	423.26	431.72	8.46	8′5½″
	2 + 50	423.86	431.82	7.96	7′11½″
MH 4	3 + 00	424.46	432.56	8.10	8′1¼″

*Refer to Table 13.3 for foot–inch conversion.

FIGURE 14.5 Use of cross-trench batter boards.

from the top of the batter board to the invert is known as the grade rod distance. A value can be picked for the grade rod so that it is the same value at each station. In this example, 9 ft appears to be suitable for each station, as it is larger than the largest cut. The arithmetic shown for station $1 + 50$ is performed at each station so that the batter boards can be set at 50-ft intervals. The grade rod (a 2 in. $\times$ 2 in. length of lumber held by a worker in the trench) has a foot piece attached to the bottom at a right angle to the rod so that the foot piece can be inserted into the pipe and allows measurement precisely from the invert.

This method of line-and-grade transfer has been shown first because of its simplicity; it has not, however, been widely used in the field in recent years. With the introduction of larger and faster trenching equipment, which can dig deeper and wider trenches, this method would only slow the work down, as it involves batter boards spanning the trench at 50-ft intervals. Many grade transfers are now accomplished by freestanding offset batter boards or laser alignment devices. Using the data from the previous example, we can illustrate how the technique of freestanding batter boards is utilized (Figure 14.6).

These batter boards (3-ft or 1-m wide) are erected at each grade stake. As in the previous example, the batter boards are set at a height that will result in a grade rod that is an even number of feet (decimeters) long. However, with this technique, the grade rod distance will be longer, as the top of the batter board should be at a comfortable eye height for the inspector. The works inspector usually checks the work while standing at the lower chainage stakes and sighting forward to the higher chainage stakes. The line of sight over the batter boards is a straight line parallel to the invert profile, and in this example (Figure 14.6), the line of sight over the batter boards is rising at 1.20 percent.

As the inspector sights over the batter boards, he or she can include in the field of view the top of the grade rod, which is being held on the most recently installed pipe length. The top of the grade rod has a horizontal board attached to it in a similar fashion to the batter boards. The inspector can visually determine whether the line over the batter boards and the line over the grade rod are in the same plane. If an adjustment up or down is required, the worker in the trench makes the necessary adjustment and has the work rechecked. Grades can be checked to the closest $1/4$ in. (6 mm) in this manner. The preceding example is now worked out using a grade rod of 14 ft (Table 14.2).

The grade rod of 14 ft requires an eye height of 5 ft $7\frac{1}{8}$ in. at $0 + 00$; if this is considered too high, a grade rod of 13 ft can be used, which results in an eye height of 4 ft $7\frac{1}{8}$ in.

FIGURE 14.6 Freestanding batter boards.

at the first batter board. The grade rod height is chosen to suit the needs of the inspector. In some cases, an additional station is put in before 0 + 00 (i.e., 0–50). The grade stake and batter board refer to the theoretical pipe ℄ and invert profile produced back through the first manhole. This batter board will, of course, line up with all the others and will be useful in

Table 14.2 SEWER GRADE SHEET—WITH BATTER BOARDS (GRADE ROD = 14 FT)

Station		Invert Elevation (ft)	Stake Elevation (ft)	Cut (ft)	Stake to Batter Board	[ft (ft and in.)]
MH 3	0 + 00	420.86	429.27	8.41	5.59	(5′7⅛″)
	0 + 50	421.46	429.90	8.44	5.56	(5′7¾″)
	1 + 00	422.06	430.41	8.35	5.65	(5′7¾″)
	1 + 50	422.66	430.98	8.32	5.68	(5′8⅛″)
	2 + 00	423.26	431.72	8.46	5.54	(5′6½″)
	2 + 50	423.86	431.82	7.96	6.04	(6′0½″)
MH 4	3 + 00	424.46	432.56	8.10	5.90	(5′10¾″)

checking the grade of the first few pipe lengths placed. Pipes are not installed unless a minimum of three batter boards (also known as sight rails) can be viewed simultaneously.

It should also be noted that many agencies use 25-ft (10-m) stations rather than the 50-ft (20-m) stations used in this example. The smaller intervals allow for much better grade control.

One distinct advantage to the use of batter boards in construction work is that an immediate check is available on all the survey work involved in the layout. The line of sight over the tops of the batter boards (which is actually a vertical offset line) must be a straight line. If, upon completion of the batter boards, all the boards do not line up precisely, it is obvious that a mistake has been made. The surveyor will check the work by first verifying all grade computations and by then releveling the tops of the grade stakes. Once the boards are in alignment, the surveyor can move on to other projects.

When the layout is performed in foot units, the basic station interval is 50 ft. The dimensions are recorded and calculated to the closest one-hundredth (0.01) of a foot. Although all survey measurements are in feet and decimals of a foot, for the contractor's purposes, the final cuts and fills are often expressed in feet and inches. The decimal–inch relationships are soon committed to memory by surveyors working in the construction field (Table 13.3). Cuts and fills are usually expressed to the closest $1/8$ in. for concrete, steel, and pipelines and to the closest $1/4$ in. for highway granular surfaces and ditch lines.

Figure 14.7 includes a sketched plan and profile, design slope and inverts, and assumed elevations for the tops of the grade stakes. Also shown are the cuts and stake–to–batter board distances, based on a 5-m grade rod. All values are in metric (SI) units. Figures 14.8 and 14.9 show the installation of steel and concrete sewer pipes.

■ **EXAMPLE 14.1** *Sewer Grade Sheet*

Figure 14.10 is a reproduction of a plan and profile sheet from a book of contract documents, showing plan and profile data for a new storm sewer that terminates in a cross culvert at MH 44. The sewer runs up from the culvert at $418 + 50$ through MHs 42, 40, and 39. As the sewer proceeds downstream toward the culvert outlet, the pipes must be of increasingly larger diameter to accommodate the cumulative flow being collected by each additional leg of the sewer.

Figures 14.10 and 14.11 show that the sewer flow-line drops as it passes through each manhole; that is, the west invert in each case is at a higher elevation than is the east invert. This flow-line drop at each manhole provides additional hydraulic head, which is utilized to overcome flow losses caused by turbulence in manholes.

When the sewer pipes increase in diameter, as the sewer proceeds through a manhole, the required flow-line drop is achieved by simply keeping the crowns of the incoming and outgoing pipes at the same elevation. That is, at MH (manhole) 40, the incoming pipe's diameter is 27 in., whereas the outgoing pipe's diameter is 30 in. If the crowns are kept at the same elevation, the flow-line inverts drop 3 in., or 0.25 ft.

Solution

To compute the sewer grade sheets, the surveyor can summarize pertinent plan and profile data from the contract document, as in Figure 14.10, onto a layout sketch, as shown in Figure 14.11. In this example, it is assumed that three legs of the sewer are being constructed: MH 44 (culvert) to MH 42, MH 42 to MH 40, and MH 40 to MH 39.

*Stake elevations and computations are normally carried out to the closest 5mm.

FIGURE 14.7 Sewer construction example using metric units. An existing sanitary sewer is being extended from MH 12A to MH 13A. Five-meter offset stakes were surveyed, with the resultant stake elevations shown in the Stake Elevation column.

Station	Invert Elev.	Stake Elev.*	Cut	Stake to Batter Board, GR=5.0 m
MH 12A 0+00	173.650	177.265	3.615	1.385
0+20	173.890	177.865	3.975	1.025
0+40	174.130	177.200	3.070	1.930
0+60	174.370	178.200	3.830	1.170
0+80	174.610	178.005	3.395	1.605
MH 13A 1+00	174.850	178.500	3.650	1.350

The field surveyor first lays out the proposed sewer line manholes (42, 40, and 39). By setting up at each manhole stake and turning off 90° and then measuring out the appropriate offset distance, the surveyor locates the manholes on offset. The offset sewer line can then be staked out at 50-ft stations, from one manhole to the next. The elevations of the tops of the offset stakes are then surveyed with a rod and level; the surveyor will, if possible, check into a second benchmark to ensure the accuracy of the work. In this example, the elevations of the tops of the stakes are assumed and are shown in Table 14.3.

The surveyor next calculates the pipe invert elevation at each station that has been staked out. 0 + 00 is taken to be the lower manhole station, with the chainage proceeding to the upper manhole of that leg. For the second leg, 0 + 00 is taken to be the station of the lower manhole, and once again the chainage proceeds upstream to the next manhole. This procedure is repeated for the length of the sewer. Sewers are

FIGURE 14.8 Corrugated steel sewer pipe, showing both tangent and curved sections. Only two batter boards are visible in this view, along with the grade rod leaning against the side of the trench. (Courtesy of Corrugated Steel Pipe Institute)

FIGURE 14.9 John Deere 792 Excavator, shown installing concrete sewer pipe. (Courtesy of John Deere, Moline, Illinois)

always constructed working upstream from the outlet (culvert, in this case) so that the trench can be drained during all phases of construction.

Table 14.3 shows the computed invert grades, the assumed stake elevations, and the resultant cut values. Using the techniques of freestanding batter boards as

FIGURE 14.10 Plan and profile of Highway 20 (adapted)

depicted in Figure 14.6, the works inspector selects a grade rod for each leg of the sewer that will give him or her a comfortable eye height—12 ft for the first two legs and 13 ft for the third leg. The stake–to–batter board dimension is computed for each station and then converted to feet and inches for use by the contractor.

14.3.1 Laser Alignment

Laser devices are widely used in most forms of construction work. Lasers are normally used in a fixed direction and slope mode or in a revolving horizontal pattern. One such device (Figure 14.12) can be mounted in a sewer manhole, aligned for direction and slope, and used with a target for the laying of sewer pipe. Because the laser beam can be deflected by dust or high humidity, care must be taken to overcome these factors if they are present. Blowers that remove dusty or humid air can accompany lasers used in sewer trenches.

FIGURE 14.11 Layout sketch for sewer construction. Adapted from the plan and profile of Highway 20 (slope percentages computed from given inverts and distances).

Table 14.3 GRADE SHEETS FOR SEWER CONSTRUCTION (SEE FIGURES 14.10 AND 14.11)

Station		Stake Elevation Pipe Elevation (ft)	(Assumed) (ft)	Cut (ft)	Stake to BB ft	ft and in.	
MH 44	0 + 00	612.20	618.71	6.51	5.49	5'5⅞"	
	0 + 50	612.65	618.98	6.33	5.67	5'8"	Grade
	1 + 00	613.11	619.40	6.29	5.71	5'8½"	rod
	1 + 50	613.56	619.87	6.31	5.69	5'8¼"	=12 ft
MH 42	1 + 86	613.89	620.33	6.44	5.55	5'6⅝"	
MH 42	0 + 00	614.14	620.33	6.19	5.81	5'9¾"	
	0 + 50	614.39	620.60	6.21	5.79	5'9½"	Grade
	1 + 00	614.64	620.91	6.27	5.73	5'8¾"	rod
	1 + 50	614.89	621.63	6.74	5.26	5'3⅛"	=12 ft
MH 40	2 + 00	615.14	622.60	7.46	4.54	4'6½"	
MH 40	0 + 00	615.39	622.60	7.21	5.79	5'9½"	
	0 + 50	616.19	623.81	7.62	5.38	5'4⅝"	Grade
	1 + 00	616.99	624.57	7.58	5.42	5'5"	rod
	1 + 50	617.79	625.79	8.00	5.00	5'0"	=13 ft
	2 + 00	618.59	626.93	8.34	4.66	4'7⅞"	
MH 39	2 + 54	619.45	627.55	8.10	4.90	4'10⅞"	

FIGURE 14.12 Laser sewer layouts. (a) Small diameter pipe application. (b) Larger diameter pipe. This pipeline laser features self-leveling and warnings when the instrument goes off-alignment or off-level; a gradient setting of +0.5% is shown in Figure 14.12(a). (Courtesy of Trimble)

Additionally, a rotating laser can be used above grade with a signal-sensing target rod (the infrared signal sensor is not required when working with visible beam lasers). Working above ground not only eliminates the humidity factor, but also allows for more accurate and quicker vertical alignment. These devices allow for setting slope within the limits of –10° to 30°. Some devices have automatic shutoff capabilities when the device is disturbed from its desired setting. Rotating lasers are used above ground as near as possible to the trench works. The slope of the sewer can be entered into the laser and a rod reading can be taken at the existing manhole invert; that rod reading is then the controlling grade as the work proceeds upstream to the sewer leg terminal point (e.g., next manhole).

14.4 Catch-Basin Construction Layout

CBs are constructed along with the storm sewer or at a later date, just prior to curb construction. Usually, the CB is located by two grade stakes—one on each side of the CB. The two stakes are on the curb line and are usually 5 ft (2 m) from the center of the CB. The cut or fill grade is referenced to the CB grate elevation at the curb face. The ₵ pavement elevation is calculated, and from it, the crown height is subtracted to arrive at the top of grate elevation (Figures 14.13 and 14.14).

At low points, particularly at vertical curve low points, it is usual practice for the surveyor to arbitrarily lower the CB grate elevation to ensure that ponding does not occur on either side of the completed CB. We noted in Chapter 11 that the longitudinal slope at vertical curve low points is virtually flat for a significant distance. The CB grate elevation can be arbitrarily lowered as much as 1 in. (25 mm) to ensure that the gutter drainage goes directly into the CB without ponding. The CB (which can be of concrete poured in place, but is more often prefabricated and delivered to the job site) is set below finished grade

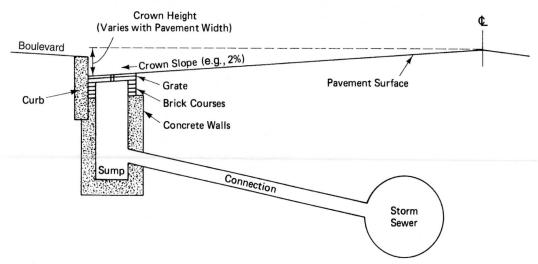

FIGURE 14.13 Typical catch basin (with sump).

FIGURE 14.14 Catch basin layout, plan view.

until the curbs are constructed. At the time of curb construction, the finished grade for the grate is achieved by adding one or more courses of brick or concrete shim collars, laid on top of the concrete walls.

14.5 Tunnel Construction Layout

Tunnels are used in road, sewer, and pipeline construction when the cost of working at or near the ground surface becomes prohibitive. For example, sewers are tunneled when they must be at a depth that would make open cut too expensive (or operationally unfeasible), or sewers may be tunneled to avoid disruption of services on the surface such as would occur if an open cut were put through a busy expressway. Roads and railroads are tunneled through large hills and mountains in order to maintain optimal grade lines. Control surveys for tunnel layouts are performed on the surface, joining the terminal points of the tunnel. These control surveys use precise traverse survey methods or global positioning system (GPS) techniques and allow for the computation of coordinates for all key points (Figure 14.15).

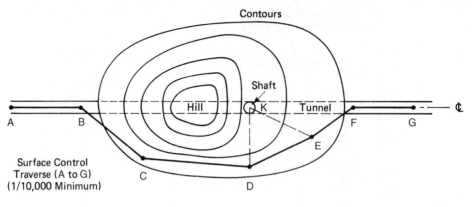

Contours

Shaft

Hill   K   Tunnel

A   B   F   G

E

Surface Control
Traverse (A to G)
(1/10,000 Minimum)   C   D

Direction and Length of B–F, D–K, and E–K
can be Computed from Traverse Data

(a)

Ground Surface

Hill   Shaft

Tunnel

(b)

FIGURE 14.15 Plan and profile of tunnel location.

In the case of highway (railway) tunnels, the ₵ can be run directly into the tunnel and is usually located on the roof either at ₵ or at a convenient offset (Figure 14.16). If the tunnel is long, intermediate shafts could be sunk to provide access for materials, ventilation, and alignment verification. Conventional engineering theodolites are illustrated in Figure 14.16; for cramped quarters, a suspension theodolite can be used. Levels can also be run directly into the tunnel, and temporary benchmarks are established in the floor or roof of the tunnel. In the case of long tunnels, work can proceed from both ends, meeting somewhere near the middle. Constant vigilance with respect to errors and mistakes is of prime importance.

In the case of a deep sewer tunnel, mining surveying techniques must be employed to establish line and grade (Figure 14.17). The surface ₵ projection AB is carefully established on beams overhanging the shaft opening. Plumb lines (piano wire) are hung down the shaft, and overaligning the total station or theodolite to the set points in the tunnel develops the tunnel ₵. A great deal of care is required in overaligning because this very short backsight will be produced relatively long distances, thus magnifying any sighting errors.

The plumb lines usually employ heavy plumb bobs (capable of taking additional weights if required). Sometimes the plumb bobs are submerged in heavy oil in order to dampen the swing oscillations. If the plumb-line swing oscillations cannot be eliminated, the oscillations must be measured and then averaged.

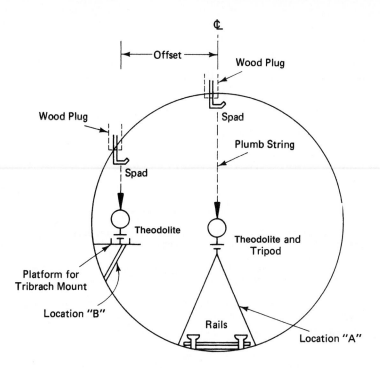

Tunnel ℄ is Usually Located in the Roof (Location "A") and then can be
Offset (Location "B") to Provide Space for Excavation and Materials Movement.
Line and Grade can be Provided by a Single Laser Beam which has been
Oriented for Both Alignment and Slope.

FIGURE 14.16 Establishing "line" in a tunnel.

Some tunnels are pressurized in order to control groundwater seepage; the air locks associated with pressure systems will cut down considerably on the clear dimensions in the shaft, making the plumbed-line transfer even more difficult.

Transferring ℄ from surface to underground locations by use of plumb lines is an effective—although outdated—technique. Modern survey practice favors the use of precise optical plummets (Figure 14.18) to accomplish the line transfer. These plummets are designed for use in zenith or nadir directions, or in both zenith and nadir directions (as illustrated in Figure 14.18). The accuracy of this technique can be as high as 1 or 2 mm in 100 m.

Gyrotheodolites have also been used successfully for underground alignment control. Several surveying equipment manufacturers produce gyro attachments for use with repeating theodolites. Figure 14.19 shows a gyro attachment mounted on a 20″ theodolite. The gyro attachment (also called a gyrocompass) consists of a wire-hung pendulum supporting a high-speed, perfectly balanced gyro motor capable of attaining the required speed of 12,000 rpm in 1 min. Basically, the rotation of the Earth affects the orientation of the spin axis of the gyroscope such that the gyroscope spin axis orients itself toward the pole in an oscillating motion that is observed and measured in a plane perpendicular to the pendulum. This north-seeking oscillation, which is known as precession, is measured on

Tunnel ℄ *AB* is Carefully Marked on the Overhead Support at *A'* and *B'*. These Two Marks are Set as Far Apart as Possible for Plumbing into the Shaft.

The theodolite in the Tunnel Over-aligns the Two Plumb Lines (Trial and Error Technique); ℄ is then Produced Forward using Double-Centering Techniques.

Precision can be Improved by Repeating this Process when the Tunnel Excavation has Progressed to the Point where a much Longer Backsight is Possible.

FIGURE 14.17 Transfer of surface alignment to the tunnel.

the horizontal circle of the theodolite; extreme left (west) and right (east) readings are averaged to arrive at the meridian direction.

The theodolite with gyro attachment is set up and oriented approximately to north, using a compass; the gyro motor is engaged until the proper angular velocity has been reached (about 12,000 rpm for the instrument shown in Figure 14.19), and then the gyroscope is released. The precession oscillations are observed through the gyro-attachment viewing eyepiece, and the theodolite is adjusted closer to the northerly direction if necessary. When the theodolite is pointed to within a few minutes of north, the extreme precession positions (west and east) are noted in the viewing eyepiece and then recorded on the horizontal circle; as noted earlier, the position of the meridian is the value of the averaged precession readings. This technique, which takes about a half hour to complete, is accurate to within 20″ of azimuth. These instruments can be used in most tunneling applications, where tolerances of 25 mm are common for both line and grade.

Lasers have been used for a wide variety of tunneling projects. Figure 14.20 shows a large-diameter boring machine, which is kept aligned (both line and grade) by keeping the laser beam centered in the two targets mounted near the front and rear of the machine.

The techniques of prismless EDM (Section 3.22) are used in the automated profile scanner shown in Figure 14.21. This system uses a Wild DIOR 3001 EDM, which can measure distances from 0.3 m to 50 m (without using a reflecting prism) with an accuracy of 5–10 mm. An attached laser is used to physically mark the feature being measured so that the operator can verify the work. The profiler is set up at key tunnel stations so that a 360° profile of the tunnel can be measured and recorded on a memory card. The number of measurements taken as the profiler revolves through 360° can be preset in the profiler, or the remote controller can control it manually. The data on the memory card are then transferred

Zenith Telescope

Tubular
Level Vial

Focus Knob

Azimuth
Clamp

Nadir
Telescope

Leveling
Screw

FIGURE 14.18 Kern OL precise optical plummet. SE in 100 m for a single measurement (zenith or nadir) = 1 mm (using a coincidence level). Used in high rise construction, towers, shafts, and the like. (Courtesy of Kern Instruments, Inc.—Leica)

FIGURE 14.19 Gyro attachment, mounted on a 20″ theodolite. Shown with battery charger and control unit. (Courtesy of Sokkia Corp.)

Sec. 14.5   Tunnel Construction Layout

FIGURE 14.20 Laser-guided tunnel boring machine. (Courtesy of The Robbins Company, Solon, Ohio)

to a microcomputer for processing. Figure 14.22 shows the station plot along with theoretical and excavated profiles. In addition to driving the digital plotter, the system software computes the area at each station and then computes the excavated volumes by averaging two adjacent areas and multiplying by the distance between them (see Chapter 17 for these computational techniques).

Problems

14.1 A storm sewer is to be constructed from existing MH 8 (invert elevation = 360.21) at +1.10 percent for a distance of 240 ft to proposed MH 9. The elevations of the offset grade stakes are as follows: $0 + 00 = 368.75$; $0 + 50 = 368.81$; $1 + 00 = 369.00$; $1 + 50 = 369.77$; $2 + 00 = 370.22$; $2 + 40 = 371.91$. Prepare a grade sheet (see Table 14.2) showing stake–to–batter board distances in feet and inches; use a 13-ft grade rod.

14.2 A sanitary sewer is to be constructed from existing manhole 4 (invert elevation = 150.810) at +0.90 percent for a distance of 110 m to proposed MH 5. The elevations of the offset grade stakes are as follows: $0 + 00 = 152.933$; $0 + 20 = 152.991$; $0 + 40 = 153.626$; $0 + 60 = 153.725$; $0 + 80 = 153.888$; $1 + 00 = 153.710$; $1 + 15 = 153.600$. Prepare a grade sheet (see Figure 14.7) showing stake–to–batter board distances in meters. Use a 3-m grade rod.

FIGURE 14.21 A.M.T. Profiler 2000 prismless EDM, used to measure tunnel profile at selected stations. (Courtesy of Amberg Measuring Technique)

14.3 With reference to Figure 14.23 (plan and profile of Parkway Ave.), compute the sewer invert elevations, at 50-ft stations, from MH 9 (0 + 05, ₡) to MH 1 (3 + 05, ₡). **Here, ₡ refers to roadway centerline stationing (not the sewer).**

14.4 Given the sewer grade stake elevations shown here, compute the "cut" distances at each 50-ft station for the section of sewer in Problem 14.3.

MH 9	0 + 00	503.37		1 + 50	504.09
	0 + 50	503.32		2 + 00	504.10
	1 + 00	503.61		2 + 50	504.77
			MH 1	3 + 00	504.83

14.5 Select a realistic grade rod, and prepare a grade sheet showing the stake–to–batter board dimensions both in feet and in feet and inches for the section of sewer in Problems 14.3 and 14.4.

14.6 With reference to Figure 14.23 (plan and profile of Parkway Ave.), for the sections of sewer from MH 1 (3 + 05, ₡) to MH 2 (5 + 05, ₡) and from MH 2 (5 + 05, ₡) to MH 3 (6 + 55, ₡), determine the following:

(a) The invert elevations of 50-ft stations.

(b) The cut distances from the top of the grade stake to invert at each 50-ft station.

(c) After selecting suitable grade rods, determine the stake–to–batter board distances at each stake.

RESULTS OF AREA COMPUTATION		
Comp. Range	PT 1–144	
Range	Measure B1	Total B1 + B2
Measured Area	24.17	24.59 m2
Theor. Area	22.18	22.71 m2
Overprofile	2.45	2.45 m2
Underprofile	0.46	0.57 m2

FIGURE 14.22 Computations and profile plot for profiler setup, where 144 prismless EDM readings were automatically taken and recorded. (Courtesy of Amberg Measuring Technique)

FIGURE 14.23 Plan and profile of Parkway Avenue (foot units). See also Figure 13.17.

Use the following grade stake elevations:

MH 1	0 + 00	504.83	MH 2	0 + 00	507.26
	0 + 50	505.21		0 + 50	507.43
	1 + 00	505.30		1 + 00	507.70
	1 + 50	506.17	MH 3	1 + 50	507.75
MH 2	2 + 00	507.26			

14.7 With reference to Figure 14.24 (plan and profile of Oak Ave.), compute the sewer invert elevations at 20-m stations from MH 13 (0 + 05, ₵) to MH 1 (1 + 05, ₵), and from MH 1 (1 + 05, ₵) to MH 2 (1 + 85, ₵).

14.8 Given the grade stake elevations shown below, compute the cut distances from stake to invert at each stake for both sections of sewer from Problem 14.7.

MH 13	0 + 00	186.713	MH 1	0 + 00	187.255
	0 + 20	186.720		0 + 20	187.310
	0 + 40	186.833		0 + 40	187.333
	0 + 60	186.877		0 + 60	187.340
	0 + 80	186.890	MH 2	0 + 80	187.625
MH 1	1 + 00	187.255			

Problems

511

FIGURE 14.24 Plan and profile of Oak Avenue (metric units). See also Figure 13.18.

14.9 Using the data in Problem 14.8, select suitable grade rods for both sewer legs, and compute the stake–to–batter board distance at each stake.

14.10 Referring to Section 14.2, Figure 14.3, and Figure 14.23, determine the minimum invert elevations for the sanitary-sewer building connections at the front-wall building lines for Lots 9, 13, and 14. (Use a minimum slope of 2 percent for sewer connection pipes.)

14.11 Referring to Section 14.2, Figure 14.3, and Figure 14.24, determine the minimum invert elevations for the sanitary-sewer building connections at the front-wall building lines for Lots 6 and 9. (Use a minimum slope of 2 percent for sewer connection pipes.)

Backhoe

Bulldozer

Crawler-Mounted

Front-End Loaders

Wheel-Mounted

Clamshell

Hydraulic Excavator

Dragline

Scraper

Trencher

FIGURE 14.25 Typical excavation equipment. (Courtesy of American Concrete Pipe Association)

14.12 Figure 14.25 shows typical excavation equipment that can be used in pipeline and other construction projects. Write a report describing the types of construction projects in which each of the equipment can be effectively utilized. Describe why some excavation equipment is well suited for some specific roles and not at all well suited for others. Data can be obtained from the library, trade and professional journals, equipment dealers or manufacturers, and construction companies.

Chapter 15

Culvert and Bridge Construction Surveys

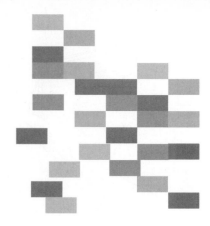

15.1 Culvert Construction

The plan location and invert grade of culverts are shown on the construction plan and profile. The intersection of the culvert ℄ and the highway ℄ is shown on the plan and is identified by its highway stationing (chainage). In addition, when the proposed culvert is not perpendicular to the highway ℄, the skew number or skew angle is shown (Figure 15.1). The construction plan shows the culvert location ℄ chainage, skew number, and length of culvert; the construction profile shows the inverts for each end of the culvert. One grade stake is placed on the ℄ of the culvert, offset a safe distance from each end (Figure 15.2). The grade stake references the culvert ℄ and gives the cut or fill to the top of footing for open footing culverts, to the top of slab for concrete box culverts, or to the invert of pipe for pipe culverts. If the culvert is long, intermediate grade stakes may be required. The stakes may be offset 6 ft (2 m) or longer distances if site conditions warrant. When concrete culverts are laid out, it is customary to place two offset line stakes to define the end of the culvert, in addition to placing the grade stakes at either end of the culvert. These end lines are normally parallel to the ℄ of construction or perpendicular to the culvert ℄. See Figure 15.3 for types of culverts.

15.2 Culvert Reconstruction

Intensive urban development creates an increase in impervious surfaces—for example, roads, walks, drives, parking lots, and roofs. Prior to development, rainfall would have the opportunity to seep into the ground and eventually the water table, until the ground became saturated. After saturation, the rainfall would run off to the nearest watercourse, stream, river, or lake. The increase in impervious surfaces associated with urban development can result in a significant increase in surface runoff and thus cause flooding where the culverts, and sometimes bridges, are now no longer capable of handling the increased flow. Some

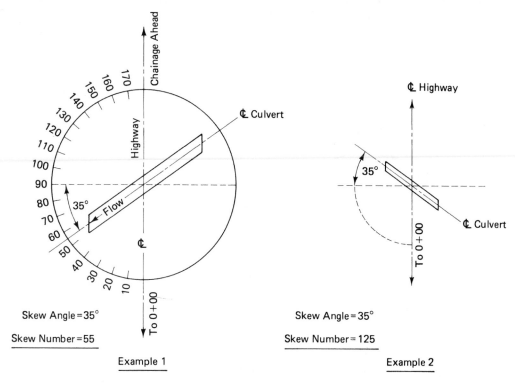

Skew Angle = 35°

Skew Number = 55

Example 1

Skew Angle = 35°

Skew Number = 125

Example 2

The <u>Skew Number</u> is Obtained by Measuring Clockwise to the Nearest 5°, the Angle Between the Back Tangent ℄ of the Highway and the ℄ of the Culvert.

FIGURE 15.1   Culvert skew numbers, showing the relationship between the skew angle and the skew number.

municipalities demand that developers provide detention and storage facilities (e.g., ponds and oversized pipes) to keep increases in site runoff to a minimum.

Figure 15.4 shows a concrete box culvert being added to an existing box culvert, resulting in what is called a twin-cell culvert. The proposed centerline grade for the new culvert will be the same as for the existing culvert. The outside edge of the concrete slab was laid out on close offset (o/s), with the construction grade information (cuts to floor slab elevation) referenced also from the o/s layout stakes. In addition, one edge (inside, in this case) of the wing wall footing is also laid out on close o/s, with the alignment and grade information referenced to the same o/s stakes. Wing walls are used to retain earth embankments adjacent to the ends of the culvert.

Figure 15.5 shows a situation where road improvements require the replacement of a cross culvert. The new culvert is skewed at #60 to better fit the natural stream orientation, the new culvert is longer (140 ft) to accommodate the new road width, and the new culvert is larger to provide increased capacity for present and future developments. Figure 15.5 shows plan and cross section of a detour that will permit the culvert to be constructed without closing the highway. (The detour centerline curve data are described in detail in Chapter 11.)

The suggested staging for the construction is shown in eighteen steps. Essentially the traffic is kept to the east side of the highway while the west half of the old culvert is removed and the west half of the new culvert is constructed. Once the concrete in the west

Skew Number 110

(a)

(b)

FIGURE 15.2 Line and grade for culvert construction. (a) Plan view. (b) Perspective view. (Courtesy of the Ministry of Transportation, Ontario)

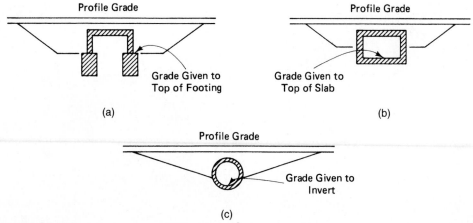

FIGURE 15.3 Types of culverts. (a) Open footing culvert. (b) Concrete box culvert. (c) Circular, arch, etc., culvert.

half of the new culvert has gained sufficient strength (usually about 30 days), the detour can be constructed as shown in Figure 15.5. With the traffic now diverted to the detour, the east half of the old culvert is removed, and the east half of the new culvert is constructed. The improved road cross section can now be built over the completed culvert, and the detour and other temporary features can be removed.

15.3 Bridge Construction: General Background

Accuracy requirements for structure construction are generally of the highest order for engineering survey layouts. Included in this topic are bridges, elevated expressways, and so on. Accuracy requirements for structure layouts range from 1/3,000 for residential housing to 1/5,000 for bridges and 1/10,000 for long-span bridges. The accuracy requirements depend on the complexity of the construction, the type of construction materials specified, and the ultimate design use of the facility. The accuracy required for any individual project could be specified in the contract documents, or it could be left to the common sense and experience of the surveyor.

Preliminary surveys for bridges include bore holes drilled for foundation investigation. Bridge designers indicate the location of a series of bore holes on a highway design plan. The surveyor locates the bore holes in the field by measuring centerline chainages, offsets, and ground elevations.

As the bridge design progresses, the surveyor may have to go back several times to the site to establish horizontal and vertical control for additional bore holes, which may be required for final footing design. Figure 15.6 shows the plan and profile location for a series of bore holes at abutment, pier, and intermediate locations. In addition, the coordinates of each bore hole location are shown, permitting the surveyor to establish the field points by polar ties from coordinated monuments; the surveyor may also establish the points by the more traditional centerline chainage and offset measurements, as previously noted, or by GPS techniques.

The establishment of permanent, well-referenced construction control (as outlined in Chapters 7–9) ensures that all aspects of the project—preliminary tie-ins and cross

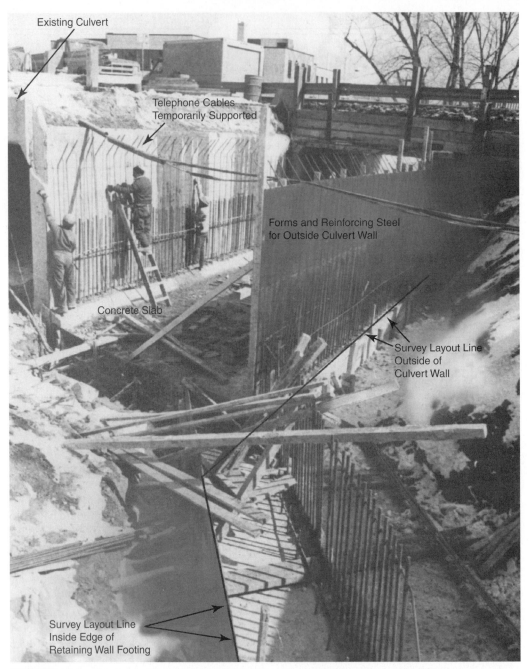

Existing Culvert

Telephone Cables
Temporarily Supported

Forms and Reinforcing Steel
for Outside Culvert Wall

Concrete Slab

Survey Layout Line
Outside of
Culvert Wall

Survey Layout Line
Inside Edge of
Retaining Wall Footing

FIGURE 15.4 Concrete culvert construction addition, showing floor slab, wing wall footing, and culvert walls—with reinforcing steel and forms.

DETOUR & STAGING
FOR CULVERT @ STA. 62+26

CULVERT STATION 62+26

SUGGESTED CONSTRUCTION STAGING

1. Construct road widening on east side of existing highway.
2. Switch traffic to east half of highway.
3. Place sheet piling roadway protection Stage I.
4. Remove west end of existing concrete culvert.
5. Place twin 30" C.S.P. culverts.
6. Construct Stage I temporary ditch relocation and divert ditch.
7. Construct west part of new concrete culvert.
8. Place sheet piling road protection Stage II.
9. Construct detour.
10. Switch traffic to detour.
11. Remove sheet piling roadway protection Stage I.
12. Construct Stage II temporary ditch relocation and divert ditch.
13. Remove remaining part of existing concrete culvert.
14. Construct east part of new concrete culvert.
15. Construct ditch relocation and divert ditch through new concrete culvert.
16. Construct east side highway embankment.
17. Shift traffic to east side of highway.
18. Remove detour, sheet piling roadway protection Stage II and C.S.P. culverts.

TYPICAL DETOUR SECTION
N.T.S.

FIGURE 15.5 Detour and construction staging for culvert replacement and realignment.

FIGURE 15.6 Bore-hole locations.

sections, bore holes, staged construction layouts, and final measurements—are all referenced to the same control net.

15.4 Contract Drawings

Contract drawings for bridge construction typically include general arrangement, foundation layout, abutment and pier details, beam details, deck details, and reinforcing steel schedules and could also include details on railings, wing walls, and the like. Whereas the contractor must utilize all drawings in the construction process, the construction surveyor is concerned only with those drawings that will facilitate the construction layout. Usually the entire layout can be accomplished by using only the general arrangement drawing (Figures 15.7 and 15.8) and the foundation layout drawing (Figure 15.9). These plans are analyzed to determine which of the many dimensions shown are to be utilized for construction layout.

The key dimensions are placed on foundation layout sketches (Figures 15.10 and 15.11), which will be the basis for the layout. The sketches show the location of the piers

FIGURE 15.7 General arrangement plan for Bridge No. 5, Don Valley Parkway, and Highway 401 East off ramp.

FIGURE 15.8 Key plan and general layout for Bridge No. 5, Don Valley Parkway, and Highway 401 East off ramp. *See same dimension on Figure 15.9.

FIGURE 15.9 Foundation layout plan for bridge No. 5, Don Valley Parkway. *See same dimension on Figure 15.8.

FIGURE 15.10 Foundation layout sketch. *See same dimension on Figures 15.8 and 15.9.

FIGURE 15.11 Foundation layout sketch and offsets sketch. Circles shown are ℄ and o/s layout bars.

and the abutment bearing ₵, the location of each footing, and (in this case) the skew angle. Although most bridges have symmetrical foundation dimensions, the bridge in this example is asymmetrical due to the spiraled pavement requirements. This lack of symmetry does not pose any problems for the actual layout, but it does require additional work in establishing dimension check lines in the field.

15.5 Layout Computations

The following information shows the computations used in establishing the key component stations. See Figures 15.9 and 15.10.

Chainage at ₵ of bridge	588 + 37.07	Chainage at ₵ of bridge	588 + 37.07
	+ 24.50		− 24.50
₵ north pier	588 + 61.57	₵ south pier	588 + 12.57
	+ 35.50		− 35.50
₵ north abutment bearing plates	588 + 97.07	₵ south abutment bearing plates	587 + 77.07

$$(588 + 97.07) - (587 + 77.07) = 121.00 \text{ ft} \quad \text{Check}$$

For this case, assume that the offset lines are 5 ft south from the south footing faces of the north abutment and both piers, and 5 ft north from the north face of the south abutment. For this example, the offset stakes (1-in. reinforcing steel, 2- to 4-ft long) will be placed opposite the ends of the footings and a further 25 ft away on each offset line. The stakes can be placed by using right-angle ties from ₵ or by locating the offset line parallel to the footings.

In the latter case, it will be necessary to compute the ₵ stations for each offset line. You can see in Figure 15.10 that the distance from the abutment ₵ of bearings to the face of footing is 4 ft 8 in. (4.67 ft). Along the N–S bridge ₵, this dimension becomes 4.84 ft (4.67 × sec 15°31′13″). Similarly, the dimension from the pier ₵ to the face of pier footing is 5.00 ft; along the N–S bridge ₵, this dimension becomes 5.19 ft (5.00 × sec 15°31′13″). Along the N–S bridge ₵, the 5-ft offset distance also becomes 5.19 ft. Accordingly, the stations for the offset lines at the N–S bridge ₵ are as follows (refer to Figure 15.11):

$$\text{North abutment offset} = 588 + 97.07 - 10.03 = 588 + 87.04$$
$$\text{North pier offset} = 588 + 61.57 - 10.38 = 588 + 51.19$$
$$\text{South pier offset} = 588 + 12.57 - 10.38 = 588 + 02.19$$
$$\text{South abutment offset} = 587 + 77.07 + 10.03 = 587 + 87.10$$

15.6 Offset Distance Computations

The stations at which the offset lines intersect the bridge ₵ are each occupied with a total station or theodolite. The skew angle (15°31′13″) is turned and doubled (minimum), and the appropriate offset distances are measured out each side of the bridge ₵.

For the north abutment offset line, the offset distance left is

$$41.598\ (41'7\tfrac{1}{8}'')\ -(10.03 \times \sin 15°31'13'') = 38.91'$$

The offset distance right is $32.03 + 2.68 = 34.71$ ft. See Figures 15.10 and 15.11. The following computation is a check of the answer:

$$38.91 + 34.71 = 73.62' = 73'7\tfrac{1}{2}'' \qquad \text{Check}$$

For the north pier offset line, the offset distance left is

$$38.39\ (38'4\tfrac{3}{4}'')\ - (10.38 \sin 15°31'13'') = 35.61'$$

The offset distance right is $30.31 + 2.78 = 33.09$ ft (see Figures 15.10 and 15.11):

$$35.61 + 33.09 = 68.70 = 68'8\tfrac{1}{2}'' \qquad \text{Check}$$

For the south pier offset line, the offset distance left is

$$38.39 - (10.38 \times \sin 15°31'13'') = 35.61'$$

The offset distance right is $28.73\ (28'8\tfrac{3}{4}'') + 2.78 = 31.51$ ft (see Figures 15.10 and 15.11):

$$35.61 + 31.51 = 67.12' = 67'1\tfrac{1}{2}'' \qquad \text{Check}$$

For the south abutment offset line, the offset distance left is

$$39.01\ (39'0\tfrac{1}{8}'') + (10.03 \times \sin 15°31'13'') = 41.69$$

The offset distance right is $31.05 - 2.68 = 28.37$ ft (see Figures 15.10 and 15.11):

$$41.69 + 28.37 = 70.06' = 70'0\tfrac{3}{4}'' \qquad \text{Check}$$

All these distances are shown double underlined on Figure 15.11. Once these offsets and the stakes placed 25 ft farther on each offset line have been accurately located, the next step is to verify the offsets by some independent means.

As an alternative to the direct layout techniques described here, key layout points may be coordinated on the computer, with all coordinates then uploaded into total stations and/or GPS receivers. The layout can then proceed using the polar layout and positioning techniques described in Chapters 5 and 7.

15.7 Dimension Verification

For this type of analysis, the technique described in Section 6.10 (omitted measurements) is especially useful. Bearings are assumed that will provide the simplest solution. These values are shown in Figure 15.12. The same techniques can be used to calculate any other series of diagonals if sight lines are not available for the diagonals shown. In addition to diagonal check measurements, or even in place of them, check measurements can consist of right-angle ties from ℄, as shown in Figure 15.10. Additional calculations are required for the chainage and distance to the outside stakes. Tables 15.1 and 15.2 show these computations.

As in all construction layout work, great care must be exercised when the grade stakes are placed. The grade stakes (iron bars) should be driven flush with the surface (or deeper) to prevent deflection if heavy equipment were to cross over them. Placing substantial guard

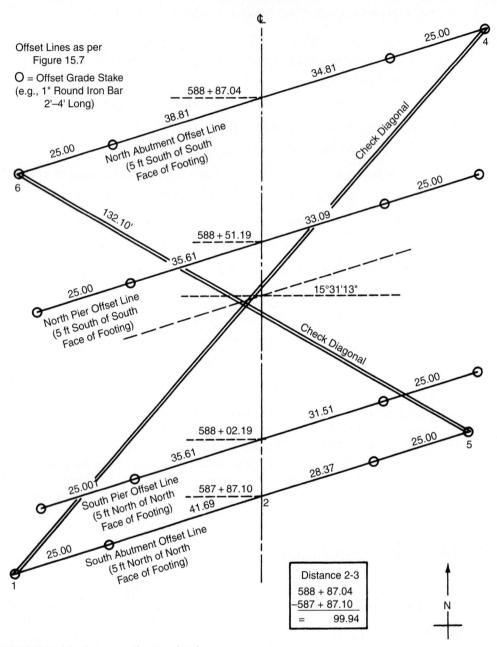

FIGURE 15.12 Layout verification sketch.

stakes adjacent to them protects the grade stakes. The surveyor must bear in mind that, for many reasons, it is more difficult to place a marker in a specific location than it is to locate a set marker by field measurements. For example, it is difficult to drive a 3- or 4-ft steel bar into the ground while keeping it in its proper location with respect to line and distance. As the top of the bar nears the

Table 15.1 COMPUTATION FOR CHECK DIAGONAL 1–4

Line	Bearing	Distance	Latitude	Departure
1–2	N 74°28′47″ E (90° skew angle chosen for convenience)	66.69	+17.84	+64.26
2–3	Due north	99.94	+99.94	+ 0.0
3–4	N 74°28′47″ E	59.81	+16.00	+57.63
1–4			+133.78	+121.89

Distance 1–4 = $\sqrt{133.78^2 + 121.89^2}$ = 180.98 ft

Allowable error = ±0.03 ft

Table 15.2 COMPUTATION FOR CHECK DIAGONAL 5–6

Line	Bearing	Distance	Latitude	Departure
5–2	S 74°28′47″ W	53.37	−14.28	−51.42
2–3	Due north	99.94	+99.94	−0.0
3–6	S 74°28′47″ W	63.81	−17.07	−61.48
5–6			+68.59	−112.90

Distance 5–6 = $\sqrt{68.59^2 + 112.90^2}$ = 132.10 ft

Allowable error = ±0.02 ft

ground surface, it becomes evident that the top is either off line or off distance. The solution to this problem is either to remove the bar and replace it or to wedge it into its proper location by driving a piece of rock into the ground adjacent to the bar. The latter solution will often prove unsuccessful because the deflected bar can, in time, push the rock aside and return to near its original position. These problems can be avoided by taking great care during the original placement; continuous line and distance checks are advised.

In this bridge construction case, an offset line was established 5 ft from the face of the footings. As foundation excavations are usually precisely excavated ("neat"), the value of 5 ft is quite realistic; however, the surveyor, in consultation with the contractor, must choose an offset that is optimal. As in all construction work, the shorter the offset distance, the easier it is to accurately transfer line and grade to the structure.

15.8 Vertical Control

The 5-ft offset line in this example can be used not only to place the footings but also to place the abutment walls and pier columns as the work proceeds above ground; the form work can be easily checked as the offset lines will be clear of all construction activity. The proposed top-of-footing elevations are shown on the general arrangements plan (Figure 15.7) and in Figure 15.11. The elevations of the grade stakes opposite each end of the footings are determined by differential leveling, and the resultant cuts are given to the contractor in the form of either a grade sheet or batter boards.

A word of caution: A benchmark (BM) is located quite close to the work, and probably one instrument setup is sufficient to take the backsight, grade stake sights, and the foresight back to the BM. When this is the case, two potential problems should be considered. One problem is that after the grade stake sights have been determined, the foresight back to the BM will be taken. The surveyor, knowing the value of the backsight taken previously, will be influenced in reading the foresight, as he or she will expect to get the same value. In this case, the surveyor could well exercise less care in reading the foresight, using it only as a quick check reading. Blunders have been known to occur in this situation. The second potential problem involves the use of automatic (self-leveling) levels. Sooner or later, all automatic levels will become inoperative due to failure of the compensating device. This device is used to keep the line of sight horizontal and often relies on wires or bearings to achieve its purpose. If a wire breaks, the compensating device will produce a line of sight that is seriously in error. If the surveyor is unaware that the level is not functioning properly, the leveling work will be unacceptable, although the final foresight will agree with the backsight.

The only safe way to deal with these potential problems is to always use two BMs when setting out grades. Start at one BM and check into the second BM. Even if additional instrument setups are required, the extra work is a small price to pay for this accuracy check. Each structure location should have three BMs established prior to construction so that, if one is destroyed, the minimum of two will remain for the completion of the project.

As the walls and piers are constructed above ground, the surveyor can check the forms (poured concrete bridges) for plumb by occupying one of the 25-ft offset stakes (Figures 15.11 and 16.8), sighting the other 25-ft offset stake, and then raising the telescope to sight-check measurements to the form work with the vertical cross hair. The 5-ft offset line should be far enough from the finished wall to allow for the line of sight to be clear of the concrete forms and other falsework supports. (See the concrete forms and falsework in Figures 15.4 and 16.8.) Realizing that steep vertical sightings can accentuate some instrumental errors, most surveyors will not take check sightings higher than 45° without double centering; see Sections 4.10 and 4.15. Total stations with dual axis compensation are ideal for this type of work.

For high bridges, instrument stations are moved farther away (farther than 25 ft, in this example) so that check sights with the theodolite are kept to relatively small vertical angles. In addition, offset stations are established, clear of the work, so that sights can be taken to the 90° (in this example) adjacent walls. Figure 15.13 shows typical locations used for vertical control stations for the south pier of the bridge example.

15.9 Cross Sections for Footing Excavations

Original cross sections will have been taken prior to construction. As the excavation work proceeds, cross sections are taken, keeping the structural excavations (higher cost) separate from other cut-and-fill operations for the bridge site. When all work is completed, final cross sections are used for payments and final records. The structural excavation quantities are determined by taking preliminary and final cross sections on each footing. The offset line for each footing is used as a baseline for individual footing cross sections.

FIGURE 15.13 Theodolite stations that can be used for plumb checks as the construction rises above the ground. See also Figure 16.8.

Review Questions

15.1 Explain the difference between the skew angle and the skew number.

15.2 Why would it be inappropriate to use wood stakes as alignment and grade markers in the layout of a high-level bridge?

15.3 When laying out structures, why is it important to measure check diagonals?

15.4 Why is it recommended that two or more benchmarks be located on a construction site?

15.5 A new bridge may require twenty to thirty drawings in the contract drawing package. Which of those drawings does the construction surveyor typically consult for the data needed to provide the survey layout?

Chapter 16

Building Construction Surveys

16.1 Building Construction: General Background

All buildings must be located with reference to the property limits. Accordingly, the initial stage of the building construction survey involves the careful retracing and verification of the property lines. Once the property lines are established, the building is located according to plan, with all corners marked in the field.

Large-scale building projects have horizontal control points established, which are based on a state plane grid or a transverse Mercator grid. These horizontal control monuments are tied into the project property lines as well as the state or provincial grid (see Section 9.2).

Temporary benchmarks are surveyed onto all major sites from the closest benchmark, and then the work is verified by closing the survey into another independent benchmark. The surveyor establishes a minimum of three temporary benchmarks at each site to ensure that, if one is destroyed, at least two will be available for all layout work (see Section 15.8).

16.2 Single-Story Construction

Construction surveys for single-story buildings may only entail survey layouts only for the building footings and main floor elevation. The contractor can tie in the rest of the building components to the footings and the first floor elevation for both line and grade. Of course, site grading surveys are also required in most circumstances.

Figure 16.1 shows a block plan, which illustrates the general area of the construction site. Figure 16.1(b) shows a site plan, which gives existing and proposed elevations, key building dimensions (16 m × 20 m), setbacks from front and side lines (5 m and 7.5 m, respectively), parking areas, walks, and so on.

FIGURE 16.1 Location drawing for a single-story building. (a) Block plan. (b) Site plan. *(continued)*

FIGURE 16.1 (continued) (c) Ground floor plan. (d) Elevation and section.

Figure 16.1(c) shows a ground floor plan, which gives the basic dimensions as well as first-floor elevations and column locations. Figure 16.1(d) shows an elevation and section, both showing footing elevations, first-floor elevations, and roof elevations.

The surveyor sets up the property lines as shown on the site plan (a licensed surveyor will be required at this stage to establish the legal lines). The building corners are then set out by measuring the setbacks from the property lines. After the corners have been staked, diagonal distances (on line or offsets) can be measured to verify the layout—that is, for the building shown (16.000 m × 20.000 m), the diagonals should be $\sqrt{16.000^2 + 20.000^2} = 25.612$ m. At an accuracy requirement of 1:5,000, the diagonal tolerance would be +0.005 m (i.e., $0.005/25.612 \approx 1:5,000$). Once the corners have been laid out and verified, the offsets and batter boards can be laid out. Figure 16.2 shows the location of batter boards and string lines used for control of an L-shaped building; the batter boards and string lines are usually set at the first-floor elevation.

Figure 16.3 shows a combination theodolite and level that can be found on many small construction sites. Although this theodolite level is not as precise as many of the instruments previously introduced in this text, its precision is well suited for small construction sites, where the instrument sights are relatively short—typically less than 150 ft or 50 m.

Property Plan (Plat) Showing Location of Proposed Building with Respect to the Property Lines.

This Plan also Shows the Location of the Batter Boards and the String Lines for Each Building Wall Footing.

FIGURE 16.2 Building layout.

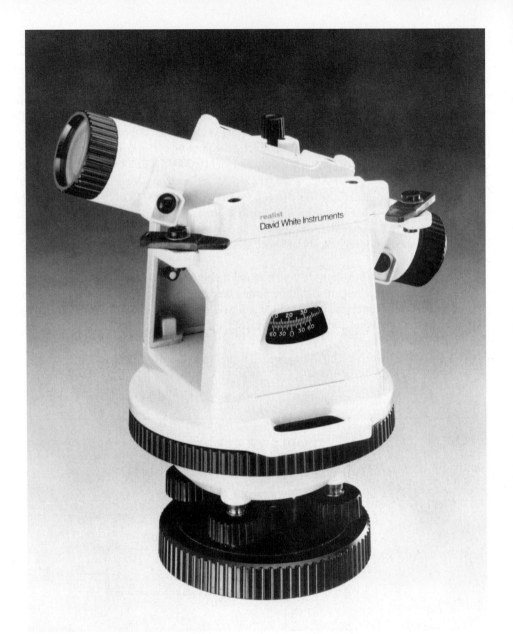

FIGURE 16.3 David White LT8-300 level-transit. (Courtesy of CST/Berger-David White)

Figure 16.4 shows a backhoe beginning to excavate a basement and footings for a house; one set of corner batter boards can be seen in the photograph. Figure 16.5 shows a small bulldozer shaping up the site to conform to the site grading plan; this aspect of the building survey usually takes place only after the services have been trenched in from the street and the house has been erected. Figure 16.6 shows the steel work for a

FIGURE 16.4 Excavation for house basement and footings. (Courtesy of John Deere, Moline, Illinois)

FIGURE 16.5 Footing excavation with a small backhoe. (Courtesy of John Deere, Moline, Illinois)

single-story commercial building. The columns shown have been bolted to the footing anchor bolts previously laid out by the surveyor. Figure 16.7 shows two different types of connections: Figure 16.7(a) shows the bolt connection, and Figure 16.7(b) shows the pocket connection. In both cases, a template can be utilized to properly align the bolt patterns to the column centerlines. The tolerance is usually set at $^1/_8$ in. (3 or 4 mm) for

FIGURE 16.6 Single-story building columns and column footings.

Setting Out Bolts

Marking Centerlines

Measuring Dimensions   A₁, A₂, A₃, and A₄ — for Guides

A↕1

Template

A↕4   A↕2

A↕3

Guide to be Placed

Iron
Strip

Pocket for Columns

(a)   (b)

FIGURE 16.7   Connections of columns to footings. (a) Bolt connection. (b) Pocket connection. (Courtesy of National Swedish Institute for Building Research, FIG Report 69)

each set of column bolts, with the overall tolerance for the length of the building set at $\frac{1}{4}$ in. (6 mm). The columns can be plumbed with the aid of a theodolite, although for single-story construction, the columns can be satisfactorily plumbed with a spirit level (carpenters' level).

Once the steel is in place, the surveyor can mark the columns a set distance above the floor grade. In North America, the offset marks are set at 4 or 5 ft above the floor slab. Masonry or concrete walls can be checked for plumb by setting the theodolite on an offset line, sighting a target set on the same offset line, and then checking all parts of the wall or concrete forms with the aid of precut offset boards, either held against the wall or nailed directly to the form. See Figure 16.8.

16.2.1   Construction Lasers and Electronic Levels

The word **laser** is an acronym for **l**ight **a**mplification by **s**timulated **e**mission of **r**adiation. Construction lasers, which have been used for the past generation, are made of helium–neon gas and are considered safe when in normal use. Lasers were introduced in Chapter 14 for control of line and grade in sewers [Figures 14.2(b) and 14.10] and for control of line and grade for a boring machine in tunnels (Figure 14.21). In both of these examples, a laser beam, fixed in slope and horizontal alignment, controlled the construction work. Figure 12.8 shows a rotating laser guiding grading operations. In addition to

FIGURE 16.8 Vertical alignment of walls. (Courtesy of National Swedish Institute for Building Research, FIG Report 69)

being used to guide and control machines as described in Section 12.3, visible beam and infrared lasers can be used with a leveling rod to duplicate the conventional leveling process. As noted in Section 12.3, green-beam visible lasers are now used outdoors as well as indoors.

In building construction, a rotating instrument, defining a horizontal or vertical plane, is used to control the construction. Figure 16.9(a) shows a surveyor marking the steel columns at the 4-ft mark with the aid of an electronic level; the rotating beam in this instrument is an infrared beam emitted by a laser diode. Figures 16.10 and 16.11 show rotating lasers controlling horizontal and vertical building components. A detection device, such as that shown in Figure 16.9(b), is used to capture the rotating beam. A detection device is required for the electronic level because the infrared beam is invisible, and it may also be required for the visible-beam rotating laser because the visible laser beam is not easily visible to the eye when used in bright sunlight.

The visible-beam laser instrument can be used in darkened indoor areas without a beam detector, as the now-visible beam itself can be used as a reference line. For example, when false ceilings are installed, the column-mounted, rotating laser beam makes a laser mark on the ceiling hanger as it strikes its surface; the ceiling hanger is then marked or bent at the laser mark, ensuring a quick and horizontal installation for the ceiling channels.

Anchor
Bolts

FIGURE 16.9 Electronic level. (a) Marking vertical control (4-ft marks on a steel column);

(continued)

FIGURE 16.9 (*continued*) (b) AEL300 self-leveling, automatic, rotating level (300-ft radius range), with leveling rod and laser detector (C6). (Courtesy of CST/Berger-David White)

FIGURE 16.10 Spectra precision rotating laser level and an electronic receiver being used to set concrete forms to the correct elevation. (Courtesy of Trimble)

Many rotating lasers and electronic levels can be battery-driven with a 10-hr operation, requiring overnight recharging. These instruments are also self-leveling when first set up to within 4° of level. These automatic instruments stop rotating if knocked off level. The rotating speed can be varied from stop to 420 rpm. The instrument itself (Figure 16.9) can be set up on both threaded and bolt-type tripods and on any flat surface as well. The accuracy of the instrument shown in Figure 16.9 is $^1/_8$ in. (0.01 ft) at 100 ft and $^3/_{16}$ in. at 200 ft, with decreasing accuracy up to a limit of about 600 ft. The adjustment of the instrument can be checked by comparing results with a good-quality automatic or tilting level; if the electronic level is off by more than $^1/_8$ in. in 100 ft, it is returned to the dealer for recalibration.

FIGURE 16.11 Rotating laser positioned to check plumb orientation of construction wall. (Courtesy of Leica Geosystems Inc.)

When used for setting 4-ft marks, 1-m marks, or other floor reference marks, this technique is quite cost effective. If a level and rod are used for this purpose, it will take two surveyors (one for the instrument and the other for the rod) to do the job. When the electronic or laser level is used, the survey crew is reduced to just one surveyor; this eliminates communications and the chance for communication errors and, according to some reports, has resulted in a 50-percent increase in work accomplished along with a 50-percent decrease in work force. Figure 16.12 illustrates the ease with which one worker can check concrete footings prior to the concrete-block wall construction.

16.3 Multistory Construction

Multistory construction demands a high level of precision from the surveyor. As the building rises many stories, cumulative errors could cause serious delays and expense. Multistory columns are laid out by intersecting precisely established column lines, and the distances between columns are then checked in all directions. Templates are used to position anchor bolts or pockets, as shown in Figure 16.7.

A theodolite sighted on premarked column centers or on the column edge checks for plumb, or verticality. Column edges are sighted from stations set on offsets a distance of one-half the column width. Shim plates (up to $^1/_8$ in.) are permitted in some specifications when one is plumbing columns that are mounted on anchor bolts. See Figures 16.7

FIGURE 16.12 Autolaser 300, shown checking the footing elevations prior to construction of the concrete-block walls. (Courtesy of CST/Berger-David White)

and 16.13. Wedges are used to help plumb columns in pockets. Connecting beams will later hold the columns in their plumbed positions.

16.3.1 Vertical Control

Elevations are usually set two floors at a time. If the stairs are in place, the elevations can be carried up by differential leveling, as shown in Figure 16.14. Many building surveyors, however, prefer to transfer elevations upward by taking simultaneous readings from a properly tensioned, fully graduated steel tape, which can be hung down from the upper floor. The lower-floor surveyor, set up with a known height of instrument (HI), takes a reading on the suspended steel tape. At the same time, the second surveyor, who has a level set up a floor or two higher, also takes a reading on the tape. (Radios can be used for synchronization.) The difference in readings is added to the lower HI to give the upper HI; temporary benchmarks are then set on the upper floor.

FIGURE 16.13 Plumbing multistory steel columns. (a) Plumbing column edge; (b) plumbing pretargeted column centerlines. (Courtesy of the National Swedish Institute for Building Research, FIG Report 69)

If it is not possible to transfer a level with the aid of a measuring tape; you have to level up and down the stairs. Observe, however, that situations as instrument position II can occur; i.e., the length of the sights taken to the two staffs are not equal. Therefore, be sure that the instrument is adjusted.

FIGURE 16.14 Transferring elevations in a multistory building. (Courtesy of the National Swedish Institute for Building Research, FIG Report 69)

16.3.2 Horizontal Positioning

Horizontal control can be extended upward by downward plumbing through small (6-in.-square) through-floor ports onto the lower-floor control stations, or onto marks offset from control stations (see Figure 16.15). The plumbing operation is often accomplished by using optical plummets, as shown in Figure 14.19. Upward plumbing is dangerous, as material may be accidentally discharged through the floor port onto the surveyor below. In addition to using optical plummets, the surveyor can use heavy plumb bobs, with swing oscillations dampened in oil or water, as described in Section 14.5.

FIGURE 16.15 Downward eccentric plumbing with an optical plummet. (a) Orientation to lower floor. (b) Transfer lower floor position to instrument station floor. See Figure 14.19 for optical plummet. (Courtesy of the National Swedish Institute for Building Research)

New layouts are constantly checked back to previously set layout points for both line and grade. All angles are doubled (face right and face left), and all distance tolerances are in the 5-mm (0.02-ft) range. As noted above, upper-floor control is checked back to control previously set on lower floors; when it becomes necessary to transfer control to higher floors from the ground, for steel structures, the survey work must be done early in the morning or on cloudy days so that the sun cannot heat and thus deform various parts of the structure, causing an erroneous layout.

Figure 16.16 illustrates the case where a theodolite is set up by interlining (wiggling in) between targets (see Section 4.11) set on adjacent structures. These permanent targets were originally set from ground control before the project started. An alternative to this technique would be to set up on a control station located on a high building, sight a permanent target on another building, and then transfer this line down onto each new floor of the building as it is constructed.

16.3.3 Horizontal Alignment—Reference Azimuth Points

Figure 16.17 shows a survey station located on an upper floor by downward optical plumbing to a previously set control mark. Alignment is provided by sighting reference azimuth points (RAPs)—points of known position (see Section 9.8). Knowing the coordinates of the instrument station and the coordinates of at least two RAPs, the surveyor can quickly determine the azimuth and distance to any of the coordinated building layout points (a third RAP is sighted to provide an accuracy check). If a programmed total station is being used, the coordinates of the layout points, the RAPs, and the instrument station can be loaded to the data collector, with the required layout distances and angles (polar ties) being calculated automatically.

16.3.4 Horizontal Alignment—Free Stations

Free stationing, which can be used for most layout surveys (not just building survey), has several advantages: (1) the theodolite (or total station) can be set up to avoid obstacles, (2) setup centering errors are eliminated, (3) fewer control stations are required, (4) the setup station can be located close to the current layout work, and (5) the layout work is greatly accelerated if total stations are employed. Figure 16.18 illustrates resection techniques being used to provide the coordinates of the theodolite station. In this case, the theodolite or total station is set up at any convenient location (called a **free station**). Angles are then taken to a minimum of three coordinated control stations; a fourth control station could be taken to provide a second computation of the instrument station as an accuracy check. If both angles and distances are to be taken to the control stations, only two, or preferably three, stations are required. By using trigonometric relationships (identities) to solve the resulting triangles, the coordinates of the instrument station are computed—most total stations are now programmed to solve resection problems. Once the coordinates of the free station are solved, and the total station is back-sighted to a known reference point, the total station programs can then compute the polar ties to any layout point.

FIGURE 16.16 Establishing control line by bucking-in or wiggling-in. See also Figure 4.15. (Courtesy of the National Swedish Institute for Building Research, FIG Report 69)

FIGURE 16.17 Optical plumbing combined with reference azimuth points for polar layouts. See also Figure 14.19. (Courtesy of the National Swedish Institute for Building Research, FIG Report 69)

FIGURE 16.18 Location and alignment of theodolite by resection (free stationing). (Courtesy of the National Swedish Institute for Building Research, FIG Report 69)

Review Questions

16.1 What are the steps required to provide the horizontal layout of a building? List the steps.

16.2 What are the steps required to provide a vertical location layout for (a) a one-story building or (b) a multistory building? List the steps in point form.

16.3 What are the advantages of using a rotating laser rather than a rod and level on a single-story building site?

16.4 What is the advantage of using a visible-beam laser instrument rather than an infrared beam laser instrument (electronic level) on a construction site?

16.5 Why were you advised to have at least two benchmarks (BM) on construction sites.

Chapter 17

Quantity and
Final Surveys

17.1 Construction Quantity Measurements: General Background

After the line and grade for a project have been established, the construction surveyor's next concern is to supply the project supervisor with survey measurements—and resultant quantities—that reflect the progress achieved by the contractor. Progress payments, which are based on quantities supplied by the surveyor and the construction inspector, are processed either at the end of a regular time period (e.g., monthly) or at the completion of previously agreed-upon project stages. The contractor usually also employs a surveyor to provide similar data; this ensures that questionable quantities are quickly discovered and remeasured.

Some construction projects are bid on a lump-sum basis, where the contractor's one-price bid covers all the work required to complete a project. The demolition of a structure is a good example of a situation where a lump-sum bid is appropriate. Here, the owner (e.g., private company, municipality, state, or province) simply wants the structure removed; the demolition technique is of little importance to the owner (blasting would be an exception). The owner simply wants the job done as cheaply and expeditiously as possible.

Most construction projects, however, are bid on a unit-price basis, where all the facets of the job are defined in detail. The owner (e.g., municipality, highway department, developer, railroad) specifies the line and grade (and cross section) of the facility; also specified are the types of construction materials to be used; the qualities of the finished product (e.g., compressive strength of concrete); the compaction level of earth and granular fills; and the appearance of the finished product.

The owner will list all categories (units) of materials and operations and will prepare an estimate as to the total quantities for each item—that is, total cut and fill, total length of fence, total volume of concrete placed, total area of sod or seeding, and the like. See Table 17.1 for

Table 17.1   TYPICAL CONSTRUCTION CATEGORIES WITH TENDERING UNITS

Lineal (ft, m)	Area (sq. ft, m², acres, ha)	Volume (cu. ft, m³)	Weight (tons, tonnes)*
Curb	Clearing	Concrete-in structures	Granular material
Curb and gutter	Grubbing	Cuts	Crushed stone
Sewer pipe	Sodding	Fills	Steel
Pipeline	Seeding	Borrow material	Asphalt
Pipe jacking	Mulching	Water	
Height of manhole	Road surfaces	Dust control chemicals	
Depth of pile		Various excavation operations	
Guide rail		Riprap	
Noise barrier		Gabions	
		Blasting (rock)	

*1 ton = 2000 lbs = 0.907 metric tons (tonnes).

other typical construction categories, with tendering units. The contractor bids a price against each unit item; all items are then added to compute the total unit bid. Finally, these individual total bids are summed to produce the grand total for the contract bid. The contract is usually awarded to the qualified contractor who submits the lowest bid.

The contractor is paid for the work as it is completed (progress payments) and when all the work is completed (final payments); usually, the owner will hold back a certain percentage of the final payment until after the guarantee period (2 years is typical) has elapsed.

Table 17.2 shows typical measuring precision, in both feet and meters, for layout and quantity surveys. Surveyors, working for both the owner and the contractor, record the progress payment measurements in their field notes; these notes must be accurate, complete, and unambiguous. Figures 17.1–17.4 illustrate typical survey notes for quantity surveys.

Lineal units, as shown in Table 17.1, are added to obtain final quantities. Simply adding the scale tickets for the various items totals weight units. Both the area and the volume units require additional work from the surveyor, however, before the unit totals can be determined. The following sections illustrate the more commonly used techniques for both area and volume computations.

17.2   Area Computations

Areas enclosed by closed traverses can be computed by using the coordinate method (Section 6.12). Reference to Figure 17.5 will illustrate two additional area computation techniques.

17.2.1   Trapezoidal Technique

The area in Figure 17.5 was measured using a fiberglass tape for the offset distances. A common interval of 15 ft was chosen to suitably delineate the riverbank. Had the riverbank been more uniform, a larger interval could have been used, and had the riverbank been even more irregular, a smaller interval would have been appropriate. The trapezoidal technique

Table 17.2 TYPICAL MEASUREMENT PRECISION FOR VARIOUS CONSTRUCTION QUANTITIES

Activity	Foot	Metric
Cross Sections		
Backsight and foresight readings to be taken to the nearest:	0.01 ft	1 mm
Maximum sight distance with level:	300 ft	90 m
Maximum allowable error between adjacent benchmarks:	0.08 ft	20 mm
Intermediate rod readings to be taken to the nearest	0.10 ft	10 mm
Intervals:		
Earth cut	100 ft	25 m
Rock cut	50 ft	10 m
Rock cut with overburden	50 ft	10 m
Muskeg (bog) excavation	100 ft	25 m
Fills with stripping, subexcavation, or ditching	100 ft	25 m
Transition from cut to fill	100 ft	25 m
Fills	100 ft	25 m
Earth or rock fills	100 ft	25 m
Borrow pits	50 ft	25 m
Maximum transverse interval for cross-section elevations:		
Earth	100 ft	25 m
Rock	50 ft	10 m
Borrow	50 ft	25 m
Offset distances to be measured to the closest:	1.0 ft	0.1 m
Grade and Superelevation Calculations		
Calculate grade percentage:	To two decimal places	To three decimal places
Calculate grade elevation to the nearest:	0.01 ft	1 mm
Calculate full superelevation cross fall to the nearest:	0.0001 ft	0.0001 m
Calculate the rate of rise or fall to the nearest:	0.00001 ft/ft	0.0001 m/m
Chainage of T.S., S.C., C.S., S.T. to be recorded to the nearest:	0.01 ft	1 mm
Layout/intervals (with the exception of plus sections, layout is normally at the same interval as the cross sections/grade calculations):		
Rock	50 ft	10 m
Earth	100 ft	25 m
Maximum interval for setting structure footing grades:	25 ft	10 m
Structure grades to be set to an accuracy of:	0.01 ft	1 mm
Adjustment to slope stake distances to allow for grubbing losses:	1 ft	300 mm
Set grades for earth grading to the nearest:	0.10 ft	10 mm
Set grades for granular to the nearest:	0.01 ft	5 mm
Layout stake offset for curb and gutter (ideal):	6 ft	2 m
Layout stake interval for curb and gutter:	50/25 ft	20/10 m
Set curb and gutter grades to the nearest:	0.01 ft	1 mm
Maximum staking interval for layout of a radius (intersections):	10 ft	3 m
Layout stake offset for concrete pavement (ideal):	6 ft	2 m
Set grades for concrete pavement to an accuracy of:	0.01 ft	1 mm
Calculate individual cleaning and grubbing areas to the nearest:	sq. ft	$0.10 \ m^2$
Convert the total clearing area to the nearest:	0.01 acre	0.01 ha
Calculate earth, rock, or borrow end areas to the nearest:	sq. ft	$0.10 \ m^2$
Convert the total volume per cut to pit to the nearest:	cu. yd	m^3
The quantity of blast cover, paid by box measurement, will not exceed:	1,500 cu. yd	$1,000 \ m^3$
Truck box volumes shall be calculated to the nearest:	0.10 cu. yd	$0.10 \ m^3$
The item total for "water" shall be taken to the closest:	1,000 gal	m^3
Water tank volumes shall be calculated to the closest:	gal	$0.01 \ m^3$

(continued)

Table 17.2 (*continued*)

Activity	Foot	Metric
Item totals for calcium chloride shall be taken to the closest:	0.01 t	0.01 t
Culvert and structures excavation end areas shall be calculated to the nearest:	sq. ft	0.10 m^2
Volumes per culvert and structure site shall be calculated to the nearest:	cu. yd	m^3
Linear dimensions for calculation of culvert and structure concrete volumes shall be to the closest:	0.01 ft	1 mm
Volume calculations for concrete culverts and structures shall be to the closest:	0.50 cu. ft	0.01 m^3
Concrete culvert and structure items totals shall be taken to the closest:	0.10 cu. yd	0.10 m^3
Pipe culvert placement shall be measured to the closest:	ft	100 mm
Pipe removal shall be measured to the closest:	ft	100 mm
Sewer trench measurements shall be taken at maximum intervals of:	100 ft	30 m
The height of manholes and catch basins shall be measured to:	0.10 ft	10 mm
Concrete in manholes and catch basins shall be calculated to the nearest:	0.01 cu. yd	0.01 m^3
Excavation and backfill for sewer systems shall be calculated to the nearest:		
(a) end area	ft^2	0.10 m^2
(b) item total	cu. yd	m^3
Sewer pipe and subdrains shall be measured to the closest:	ft	100 mm
Concrete pavement, sidewalk area (placing and removal) shall be calculated to the nearest:	sq. ft	0.10 m^2
The item total for concrete pavements, sidewalk area (placing and removal) shall be rounded to the nearest:	sq. yd	m^2
Curb and gutter, fence, guide rail (placing and removal) shall be measured to the closest:	ft	100 mm
And the item totaled to the closest:	ft	1.0 m
Seeding and mulching, and sodding shall be calculated to the closest:	sq. ft	0.10 m^2
And the item totaled to the closest:	sq. yd	1.0 m^2
Topsoil stockpile end areas shall be calculated to the closest:	sq. ft	0.10 m^2
And the stockpile volume calculated to the closest:	cu. yd	1.0 m^3
Riprap		
Depth to be measured to the closest:	0.10 ft	10 mm
Length and width measured to the closest:	ft	100 mm
Volume calculated to the nearest:	cu. ft	0.10 m^3
Item total to nearest:	cu. yd	1.0 m^3
Reinforcing steel shall be totaled to the nearest:	0.01 t	0.01 t
The length of each pile driven shall be measured to the nearest:	in.	10 mm
The pile driving item total shall be taken to the closest:	ft	0.10 m
The area of restored roadway surface shall be calculated to the nearest:	sq. ft	0.10 m^2
And the item totaled to the nearest:	sq. yd	1.0 m^2
Width measurements shall be taken to the closest pavement width plus:	1 ft	300 mm
And length to the closest:	1 ft	300 mm
Field measurements of length and width for clearing and grubbing shall be taken to the closest:	ft	100 mm
Measurements to establish truck box volume shall be taken to the closest:	0.10 ft	10 mm
Measurements to establish water truck tank volume shall be taken to the closest:	0.10 ft	10 mm
Measurements to establish boulder volume shall be taken to the closest:	0.10 ft	10 mm
Field measurements for concrete pavement and sidewalk shall be taken to the closest:	0.10 ft	10 mm
Field measurements for seeding and mulching and sodding shall be taken to the closest:	0.1 ft	100 mm
Field measurements for asphalt sidewalk and hot mix miscellaneous shall be taken to the closest:	foot-length 0.10 ft-width	10 mm-length 10 mm-width

Source: Adapted from *Construction Manual*, Ministry Of Transportation And Communications, Ontario.

FIGURE 17.1 Example of the method for recording sodding payment measurements. (From *Construction Manual*, Ministry of Transportation, Ontario)

assumes that the lines joining the ends of each offset line are straight lines (the smaller the common interval, the more valid this assumption).

The end sections can be treated as triangles:

$$A = \frac{8.1 \times 26.1}{2} = 106 \text{ sq. ft}$$

and

$$A = \frac{11.1 \times 20.0}{2} = \frac{111 \text{ sq. ft}}{217 \text{ sq. ft}} = \text{subtotal}$$

The remaining areas can be treated as trapezoids. The trapezoidal rule is stated as follows:

$$\text{Area} = X\left[\frac{h_1 + h_n}{2} + h_2 + \cdots + h_{n-1}\right]$$

where X = common interval between the offset lines
h = offset measurement
n = number of offset measurements

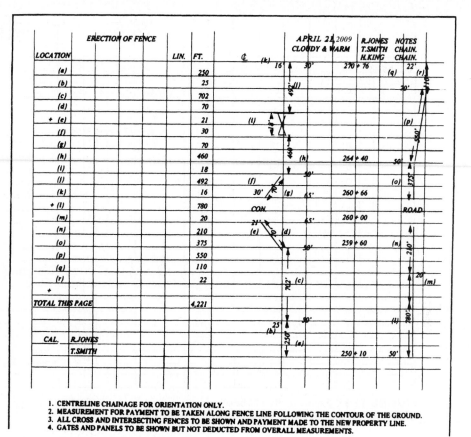

1. CENTRELINE CHAINAGE FOR ORIENTATION ONLY.
2. MEASUREMENT FOR PAYMENT TO BE TAKEN ALONG FENCE LINE FOLLOWING THE CONTOUR OF THE GROUND.
3. ALL CROSS AND INTERSECTING FENCES TO BE SHOWN AND PAYMENT MADE TO THE NEW PROPERTY LINE.
4. GATES AND PANELS TO BE SHOWN BUT NOT DEDUCTED FROM OVERALL MEASUREMENTS.

FIGURE 17.2 Field notes for fencing payment measurements. (From *Construction Manual*, Ministry of Transportation, Ontario)

From Figure 17.5, we obtain

$$A = 15\left(\frac{26.1 + 20.0}{2} + 35.2 + 34.8 + 41.8 + 45.1 + 40.5 + 30.3 + 25.0\right)$$

$$= 4{,}136 \text{ sq. ft}$$

Total area $= 4{,}136 + 217 = 4{,}353$ sq. ft

17.2.2 Simpson's One-Third Rule

This technique gives more precise results than the trapezoidal technique and is used where one boundary is irregular, in the manner shown in Figure 17.5. The rule assumes that an odd number of offsets are involved and that the lines joining the ends of three successive offset lines are parabolic in configuration.

Simpson's one-third rule is stated mathematically as follows:

$$A = \frac{1}{3} \times \text{interval} \times (h_1 + h_n + 2\Sigma h \text{ odd} + 4\Sigma h \text{ even}) \tag{17.2}$$

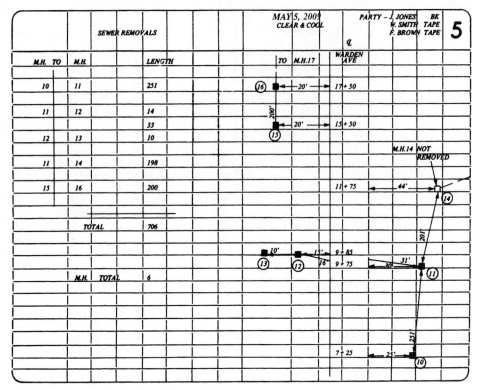

FIGURE 17.3 Example of field-book entries regarding removal of sewer pipe, etc. (From *Construction Manual*, Ministry of Transportation, Ontario)

that is, one-third of the common interval times the sum of the first and last offsets ($h_1 + h_n$) plus twice the sum of the other odd-numbered offsets (Σh odd) plus four times the sum of the even-numbered offsets (Σh even). From Figure 17.5 and Equation 17.2, we get

$$A = \frac{15}{3}[26.1 + 20.0 + 2(34.8 + 45.1 + 30.3)$$
$$+ 4(35.2 + 41.8 + 40.5 + 25.0)]$$
$$= 4,183 \text{ sq. ft}$$
$$\text{Total area} = 4,183 + 217 \text{ (from preceding example)}$$
$$= 4,400 \text{ sq. ft}$$

If a problem is encountered with an even number of offsets, the area between the odd numbers of offsets is determined by Simpson's one-third rule, with the remaining area being determined by using the trapezoidal technique. The discrepancy between the trapezoidal technique and Simpson's one-third rule is 47 sq. ft in a total of 4,400 sq. ft (about 1 percent in this example).

PILE NUMBER	LENGTH	CUT OFF	IN PLACE	SPLICES	REMARKS	DATE DRIVEN	DRIVING TUBE PILES WEST ABUTMENT BRIDGE NO. 2		5
1	20'	5'	15'			03/14/09	CONTRACTOR USING DELMAG D-12		
2	20'	5'-6"	14'-6"			"			
3	20'	4'	16'			"			
4	20'	3'	17'			"			
5	20'	5'	15'			"			
6	20'	5'-6"	14'-6"			"			
7	20'	4'	16'			"			
8	20'	2'	18'			03/18/09			
9	20'	1'	19'			"			
10	20'+20' 1"=40'	15'	25'	1		"			
11	20'+20' 1"=40'	12'	28'	1		"			
12	20'+20' 1"=40'	10'	30'	1		"			
13	20'+20' 1"=40'	15'	25'	1		"			
14	20'+20' 1"=40'	16'	24'	1		"			
15	20'+20' 1"=40'	16'	24'	1		"			
16	20'	-	20'		DRIVEN TO GRADE	03/22/09			
17	20'	-	20'		"	"			
18	20'	4'	16'			"			
19	20'	3'	17'			"			
20	20'	2'	18'			"			
	520'	128'	392'	6 TOTAL					

CONTINUED ON PAGE 6

WHEN SHEET PILES ARE DRIVEN – SHOW NUMBER AND TYPE ALONG EACH SIDE – NUMBERED CONTINUOUSLY AROUND THE PERIMETER.

FIGURE 17.4 Example of field notes for pile driving. (From *Construction Manual*, Ministry of Transportation, Ontario)

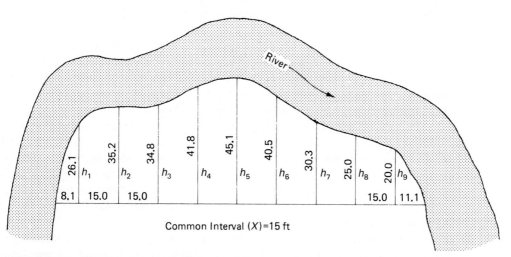

FIGURE 17.5 Irregular area computation.

Sec. 17.2 Area Computations

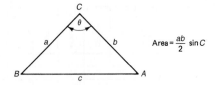

FIGURE 17.6 Areas by trigonometric formulas.

17.2.3 Areas by Trigonometric and Geometric Formulas

Some construction quantities can be separated into geometric figures, which can then be analyzed by trigonometric and geometric formulas. These formulas are given in Figures 17.6 and 17.7 and are further illustrated by the worked-out examples in Figure 17.8.

17.3 Area by Graphical Analysis

We have seen that areas can be determined very precisely by using coordinates (Chapter 6), and less precisely by using the somewhat approximate methods illustrated by the trapezoidal rule and Simpson's one-third rule. Areas can also be determined by analyzing plotted data on plans and maps. For example, if a transparent sheet is marked off in grid squares to some known scale, an area outlined on a map can be determined by placing the squared paper over (sometimes under) the map and counting the number of squares and partial squares within the boundary limits shown on the map. The smaller the squares, the more precise will be the result.

Another method of graphic analysis involves the use of a planimeter (Figures 17.9 and 17.10). A planimeter consists of a graduated measuring drum attached to an adjustable or fixed tracing arm, which itself is attached to a pole arm, one end of which is anchored to the working surface by a needle. The graduated measuring drum gives partial revolution readings, while a disk keeps count of the number of full revolutions as the area outlined is traced.

Areas are determined by placing the pole-arm needle in a convenient location, setting the measuring drum and revolution counter to zero (some planimeters require recording an initial reading), and then tracing (using the tracing pin) the outline of the area being measured. As the tracing proceeds, the drum (which is also in contact with the working surface) revolves, measuring a value that is proportional to the area being measured. Some planimeters measure directly in square inches, while others can be set to map scales. When in doubt, or as a check on planimeter operation, the surveyor can measure out a scaled figure [e.g., 4-in. (100-mm) square] and then measure the area (16 sq. in.) with a planimeter so that the planimeter area can be compared with the actual area laid off by scale. If the planimeter gives a result in square inches—say, 51.2 sq. in.—and the map is at a scale of 1 in. = 100 ft, the actual ground area portrayed by 51.2 sq. in. would be $51.2 \times 100^2 = 512{,}000$ sq. ft = 11.8 acres.

The planimeter is normally used with the pole-arm anchor point outside the area being traced. If it is necessary to locate the pole-arm anchor point inside the area being measured, as in the case of a relatively large area, the area of the zero circle of the planimeter must be added to the planimeter readings. This constant is supplied by the manufacturer

FIGURE 17.7 Areas by geometric formulas. (a) Circular segment. (b) Parabola. (c) Triangle. (d) Trapezoid. (e) Circle. (f) Ellipse. (g) Pyramid. (h) Sphere. (i) Circular sector. (j) Trapezium. (k) Parallelogram. (l) Cone. (m) Cylinder. (n) Frustum of cone. (From Construction Manual, Ministry of Transportation, Ontario)

(a) Area of triangle: given 3 sides

$$\text{Area} = \sqrt{s(s-a)(s-b)(s-c)}$$

$$s = \frac{40 + 25 + 62}{2} = 63.5 \text{ ft}$$

$$A = \sqrt{63.5(63.5-40)(63.5-25)(63.5-62)}$$

$$A = \sqrt{63.5 \times 23.5 \times 38.5 \times 1.5}$$

$$A = \sqrt{86177} = \underline{\underline{293.6}} \text{ sq. ft}$$

(b) Area of triangle: given 2 sides and the contained angle

$$\text{Area} = \frac{ab}{2} \sin C$$

$$A = \frac{48.7 \times 51.3}{2} \sin 63°20'$$

$$A = \underline{\underline{1116.3}} \text{ sq. ft}$$

(c) Area of triangle: given the base and vertical height

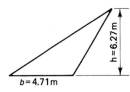

$$\text{Area} = \frac{bh}{2}$$

$$\text{Area} = 4.1 \times 6.27$$

$$\text{Area} = \underline{\underline{29.53}} \text{ m}$$

(d) Area of circle: given radius (r)

$$\text{Area} = \pi r^2$$

$$= \pi \times 18^2$$

$$= 3.1416 \times 324$$

$$= \underline{\underline{1017.9}} \text{ sq. ft}$$

(e) Area of circular sector: given radius and central angle.

$\theta = 100°$

$\ell = ?$

$r = 38.2\text{m}$

$$\text{Area} = \frac{r\ell}{2}$$

$$\text{where } \ell = 2\pi r \times \frac{\theta}{360}$$

$$\ell = 3.1416 \times 38.2 \times \frac{100}{180} = 66.67 \text{ m}$$

$$A = \frac{38.2 \times 66.67}{2} = \underline{\underline{1273.4}} \text{ m}^2$$

<u>or</u>

$$A = \pi r^2 \times \frac{\theta}{360}$$

$$= 3.1416 \times 38.2 \times \frac{100}{360}$$

$$A = \underline{\underline{1273.4}} \text{ m}^2$$

FIGURE 17.8 Area examples.

(continued)

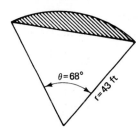

(f) Area of circular
 segment: given
 θ and r

$$\text{Area} = \left(\pi r^2 \frac{\theta}{360} \right) - \left(\frac{ab}{2} \sin C \right)$$

$$A = \left(3.1416 \times 43^2 \times \frac{68}{360} \right) - \left(\frac{43 \times 43}{2} \sin 68° \right)$$

$$A = 1097.2 - 857.2$$

$$A = \underline{\underline{240.0}} \text{ sq. ft}$$

(g) Area of sphere:
 given r, the radius

$$\text{Area} = 4\pi r^2$$

$$A = 4 \times 3.1416 \times 18^2$$

$$A = \underline{\underline{4071.5}} \text{ sq. ft}$$

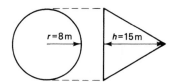

(h) Area of the surface
 of a cone: given
 radius (r), and
 height (h)

$$\text{Area} = \pi r \sqrt{r^2 + h^2}$$

$$A = 3.1416 \times 8 \sqrt{8^2 + 15^2}$$

$$A = \underline{\underline{427.3}} \text{ m}^2$$

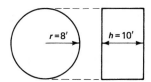

(i) Area of cylinder:
 given radius (r)
 and height (h)

$$\text{Area} = 2\pi rh$$

$$A = 2 \times 3.1416 \times 8 \times h$$

$$A = \underline{\underline{502.7}} \text{ sq. ft}$$

(j) Area of the conical
 surface of the
 frustum of a cone:
 given radius of both
 top (r) and bottom (R),
 and length of side (s) or
 height (h)

$$\text{Area} = \pi s (R + r)$$

$$s = \sqrt{(R-r)^2 + h^2}$$

$$s = \sqrt{3^2 + 20^2}$$

$$s = 20.2'$$

$$A = 3.1416 \times 20.2 \times 17$$

$$A = \underline{\underline{1078.8}} \text{ sq. ft}$$

Given $\begin{cases} r = 7' \\ R = 10' \\ (R - r = 3') \\ h = 20' \end{cases}$

(k) Area of an ellipse:
 given the two
 diameters or radii

$$\text{Area} = \pi R r$$

$$A = 3.1416 \times 6 \times 4$$

$$A = \underline{\underline{75.40}} \text{ m}$$

FIGURE 17.8 (continued)

(ℓ) Area of a parabolic
   segment: given
   radius (r) and
   length (ℓ)

ℓ = 8.27 m
r = 3.5 m

$$Area = \frac{2}{3}\ell r$$

$$A = \frac{2}{3} \times 8.27 \times 3.5$$

$$A = \underline{\underline{19.30}} \text{ m}^2$$

(m) Area of a parallelogram
   or rectangle: given
   base (b) and height (h)

h = 8 ft

b = 18 ft   b = 18 ft

$$Area = bh = 18 \times 8 = \underline{\underline{144}} \text{ sq. ft}$$

(n) Area of a trapezoid:
   given the lengths of
   the two parallel sides
   (a and b), and the
   distance (h) between
   them

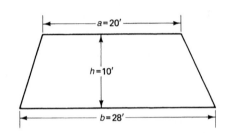

a = 20'
h = 10'
b = 28'

$$Area = \frac{a+b}{2} \times h$$

$$A = \frac{20+28}{2} \times 10$$

$$A = \underline{\underline{240}} \text{ sq. ft}$$

(o) Area of a trapesium:
   given the base and
   the heights (H and h)
   to the ends of the
   opposite side

H = 9 m
h = 6 m
b = 4 m   a = 12 m   c = 1.5 m

$$Area = \frac{bh + (h+H)a + cH}{2}$$

$$A = \frac{4 \times 6 + (6+9)12 + 1.5 \times 9}{2}$$

$$A = \underline{\underline{108.75}} \text{ m}$$

(p) Area of the surface
   of a pyramid: given
   the base (b) and the
   height (h)

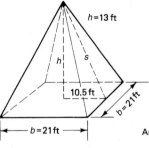

h = 13 ft
h   s
10.5 ft
b = 21 ft
b = 21 ft

Area = sum of triangular faces

$$\text{Area of triangle} = \frac{b \times s}{2}$$

$$s = \sqrt{10.5^2 + 13^2}$$

$$s = 16.7 \text{ ft}$$

$$\text{Area of triangle} = \frac{21 \times 16.7}{2}$$

$$A = 350.7 \text{ sq. ft}$$

$$\text{Area of 4-sided pyramid} = 4 \times 350.7 = \underline{\underline{1402.8}} \text{ sq. ft}$$

FIGURE 17.8 (*continued*)

Part 1 Tracer Arm	Part 8 Tracer Arm Vernier
Part 2 Pole Arm	Part 9 Revolution Recording Dial
Part 3 Pole Weight	Part 10 Measuring Wheel
Part 4 Hand Grip	Part 11 Measuring Wheel Vernier
Part 5 Tracing Magnifier	Part 12 Idler Wheel
Part 6 Clamp Screw	Part 13 Carriage
Part 7 Fine Movement Screw	Part 14 Zero Setting Slide Bar

FIGURE 17.9   Polar planimeter.

FIGURE 17.10   Area takeoff by polar planimeter.

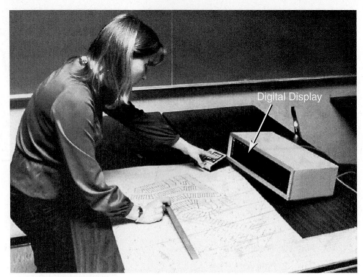

FIGURE 17.11 Area takeoff by an electronic planimeter.

or can be deduced by simply measuring a large area twice, once with the anchor point outside the area and once with the anchor inside the area.

Planimeters are particularly useful in measuring end areas (Section 17.4) used in volume computations. Planimeters are also effectively used in measuring watershed areas, as a check on various construction quantities (e.g., areas of sod, asphalt), and as a check on areas determined by coordinates. Electronic planimeters (Figure 17.11) measure larger areas in less time than traditional polar planimeters. Computer software is available for highways and other earthworks applications (e.g., cross sections) and for drainage basin areas. The planimeter shown in Figure 17.11 has a 36×30 in. working-area capability with a measuring resolution of 0.01 cu. in. (0.02-sq. in. accuracy).

17.4 Construction Volumes

In highway construction, designers try to optimally balance cut-and-fill volumes for economic reasons. Cut and fill cannot be precisely balanced because of geometric and aesthetic design considerations and because of the unpredictable effects of shrinkage and swell. Shrinkage occurs when a cubic yard (meter) is excavated and then placed while being compacted. The same material formerly occupying 1 cu. yd (m^3) volume now occupies a smaller volume. **Shrinkage** reflects an increase in density of the material and is obviously greater for silts, clays, and loams than it is for granular materials, such as sand and gravel. **Swell** occurs when the shattered (blasted) rock is placed in the roadbed. Obviously 1 cu. yd (m^3) of solid rock will expand significantly when shattered. Swell is usually in the 15–20 percent range, whereas shrinkage is in the 10–15 percent range—although values as high as 40 percent are possible with organic material in wet areas.

To keep track of cumulative cuts and fills as the profile design proceeds, designers show the cumulative cuts (plus) and fills (minus) graphically in a mass diagram. The mass

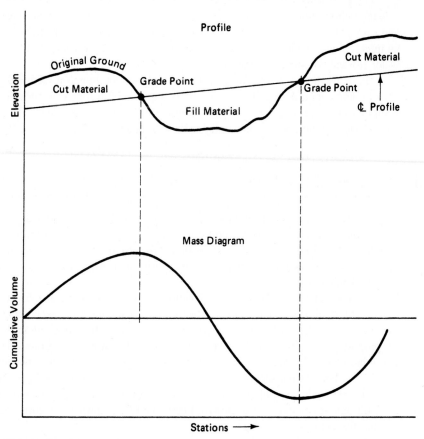

FIGURE 17.12 Mass diagram.

diagram is an excellent method of determining waste or borrow volumes and can be adapted to show haul (transportation) considerations (Figure 17.12). The total cut-minus-fill is plotted at each station directly below the profile plot.

Large fills require borrow material, usually taken from a nearby borrow pit. Borrow-pit leveling procedures are described in Section 2.9 and Figure 2.23. The borrow pit in Figure 2.23 was laid out on a 50-ft grid. The volume of a grid square is the average height $[(a + b + c + d)/4]$ times the area of the base (50^2). The partial grid volumes (along the perimeter of the borrow pit) can be computed by forcing the perimeter volumes into regular geometric shapes (wedge shapes or quarter-cones).

When high precision is less important, volumes can be determined by analysis of contour plans; the smaller the contour interval, the more precise the result. The areas enclosed by a contour line can be taken off by planimeter; electronic planimeters are very useful for this purpose. The computation is shown in the following equation:

$$V = \frac{I(C_1 + C_2)}{2} \tag{17.3}$$

V is the volume (cu. ft or m^3) of earth or water, C_1 and C_2 are areas of adjacent contours, and I is the contour interval. The prismoidal formula (see Section 17.6) can be used if m is an intervening contour (C_2) between C_1 and C_3. This method is also well suited for many water-storage volume computations.

Perhaps the most popular present-day volume computation technique involves the use of computers utilizing any one of a large number of available software programs. The computer programmer uses techniques similar to those described here, but the surveyor's duties may end with proper data entry to the computer (see Chapter 5).

17.5 Cross Sections, End Areas, and Volumes

Cross sections establish ground elevations at right angles to a proposed route. Cross sections can be developed from a contour plan as were profiles in the previous section, although it is common to have cross sections taken by field surveys. Chapter 5 introduced a computerized system that permits generation of profiles and cross sections from a general database.

Cross sections are useful in determining quantities of cut and fill in construction design. If the original ground cross section is plotted and then the as-constructed cross section is also plotted, the end area at that particular station can be computed. In Figure 17.13(a), the proposed road at Station 7 + 00 is at an elevation below existing ground. This indicates a cut situation (i.e., the contractor will cut out that amount of soil shown between the proposed section and the original section). In Figure 17.13(b), the proposed road elevation at Station 3 + 00 is above the existing ground, indicating a fill situation (i.e., the contractor will bring in or fill in that amount of soil shown). Figure 17.13(c) shows a transition section between cut-and-fill sections.

When the end areas of cut or fill have been computed for adjacent stations, the volume of cut or fill between those stations can be computed by simply averaging the end areas and multiplying the average end area by the distance between the end area stations; Figure 17.14 illustrates this concept and Equation 17.4 gives the general case for volume computations:

$$V = \frac{(A_1 + A_2)}{2} \times L \tag{17.4}$$

A_1 and A_2 are the end areas of two adjacent stations, and L is the distance (feet or meters) between the stations. To give the answer in cubic yards, divide the answer, in cubic feet, by 27; when metric units are used, the answer is left in cubic meters.

The average end-area method of computing volumes is entirely valid only when the area of the midsection is, in fact, the average of the two end areas. This is seldom the case in actual earthwork computations; however, the error in volume resulting from this assumption is insignificant for the usual earthwork quantities of cut and fill. For special earthwork quantities (e.g., expensive structures excavation) or for higher-priced materials (e.g., concrete in place), a more precise method of volume computation, the prismoidal formula, must be used.

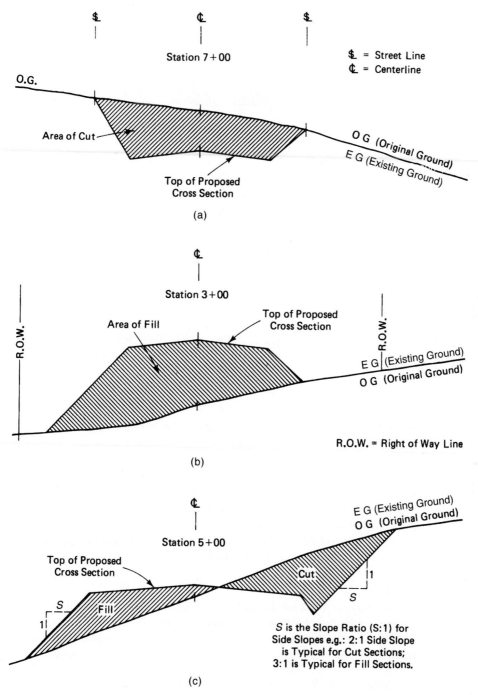

Station 7 + 00

£ = Street Line
℄ = Centerline

O.G.

Area of Cut

O G (Original Ground)
E G (Existing Ground)

Top of Proposed
Cross Section

(a)

Station 3 + 00

R.O.W.

Area of Fill

Top of Proposed
Cross Section

R.O.W.

E G (Existing Ground)
O G (Original Ground)

R.O.W. = Right of Way Line

(b)

Station 5 + 00

E G (Existing Ground)
O G (Original Ground)

Top of Proposed
Cross Section

Cut

1

S

Fill

1

S

S is the Slope Ratio (S : 1) for
Side Slopes e.g.: 2 : 1 Side Slope
is Typical for Cut Sections;
3 : 1 is Typical for Fill Sections.

(c)

FIGURE 17.13 End areas. (a) Cut section. (b) Fill section. (c) Transition section (that is, both cut and fill).

Original Ground

End Area @ 9 + 00

9 + 00

Existing
Ground

Original Ground

Toe of Slope

Top of Slope

Top of Slope

Toe of Slope

Original Ground

Original Ground

8 + 00

End Area @ 8 + 00

$$\text{Volume of Fill Between } 8 + 00 \text{ and } 9 + 00 = \frac{\text{End Area @ 8 + 00 + End Area @ 9 + 00}}{2} \times 100$$

FIGURE 17.14   Fill volume computations using end areas.

■ **EXAMPLE 17.1** *Volume Computations by End Areas*

Figure 17.15(a) shows a pavement cross section for a proposed four-lane curbed road. As shown, the total pavement depth is 605 mm, the total width is 16.30 m, the subgrade is sloping to the side at 2 percent, and the top of the curb is 20 mm below the elevation of ℄. This proposed cross section is shown in Figure 17.15(b) along with the existing ground cross section at Station 0 + 340. It can be seen that all subgrade elevations were derived from the proposed cross section, together with the ℄ design elevation of 221.43. The desired end area is the area shown below the original ground plot and above the subgrade plot.

Solution

At this point, an elevation datum line is arbitrarily chosen (220.00). The datum line chosen can be any elevation value rounded to the closest foot, meter, or 5-ft value that is lower than the lowest elevation in the plotted cross section. Figure 17.16 illustrates that end area computations involve the computation of two areas:

1. Area between the ground cross section and the datum line.
2. Area between the subgrade cross section and the datum line.

FIGURE 17.15 End-area computation, general. (a) Typical arterial street cross section. (b) Survey and design data plotted to show both the original ground and the design cross sections.

FIGURE 17.16 End-area computations for cut areas. (a) Area between ground cross section and datum line. (b) Area between subgrade cross section and datum line.

The desired end-area (cut) is area 1 minus area 2. For fill situations, the desired end-area is area 2 minus area 1. The end-area computation can be determined as shown in the following chart:

Station	Plus	Subarea	Minus	Subarea
0 + 340	$\dfrac{(1.55 + 1.50)}{2} \times 4.5 =$	6.86	$\dfrac{(1.55 + 1.41)}{2} \times 2.35 =$	3.48
	$\dfrac{(1.50 + 2.00)}{2} \times 6.0 =$	10.50	$\dfrac{(0.66 + 0.82)}{2} \times 8.15 =$	6.03
	$\dfrac{(2.00 + 1.50)}{2} \times 7.0 =$	12.25	$\dfrac{(0.82 + 0.66)}{2} \times 8.15 =$	6.03
	$\dfrac{(1.50 + 1.59)}{2} \times \underline{3.5} =$	$\underline{5.41}$	$\dfrac{(1.41 + 1.59)}{2} \times \underline{2.35} =$	$\underline{3.53}$
	Check: 21 m	**35.02 m²**	Check: 21 m	**19.07 m²**

End area = 35.02 − 19.07 = 15.95 m²

Assuming that the end area at 0 + 300 has been computed to be 18.05 m², we can now compute the volume of cut between 0 + 300 and 0 + 340 using Equation 17.4:

$$V = \frac{(18.05 + 15.95)}{2} \times 40 = 680 \text{ m}^3$$

17.6 Prismoidal Formula

If values more precise than end-area volumes are required, the prismoidal formula can be used. A prismoid is a solid with parallel ends joined by plane or continuously warped surfaces. The prismoidal formula is shown in Equation 17.5:

$$V = L\frac{(A_1 + 4A_m + A_2)}{6} \text{ cu. ft or m}^3 \tag{17.5}$$

where A_1 and A_2 are the two end areas, A_m is the area of a section midway between A_1 and A_2, and L is the distance from A_1 to A_2. A_m is not the average of A_1 and A_2 but is derived from distances that are the average of corresponding distances required for A_1 and A_2 computations.

The formula shown in Equation 17.5 is also used for other geometric solids (e.g., truncated prisms, cylinders, and cones). To justify its use, the surveyor must refine the field measurements to reflect the increase in precision being sought. A typical application of the prismoidal formula is the computation of in-place volumes of concrete. The difference in cost between a cubic yard or meter of concrete and a cubic yard or meter of earth cut or fill is sufficient reason for the increased precision.

■ **EXAMPLE 17.2** *Volume Computations by Prismoidal Formula*

See Figure 17.17 for the problem parameters. Compute the volume using the prismoidal formula in Equation 17.5:

Volume$(V) = L/6(A_1 + 4A_m + A_2)$ $A_1 = ([0.75 + 4.75]/2) \times 7 = 19.25 \text{ ft}^2$

$= 17/6(19.25 + 4[11.25] + 5.25)$ $A_m = ([0.75 + 3.75]/2) \times 5 = 11.25 \text{ ft}^2$

$= 17/6(19.25 + 45.00 + 5.25)$ $A_2 = ([0.75 + 2.75]/2) \times 3 = 5.25 \text{ ft}^2$

$= (17/6) \times 69.50$

$= 1181.50/6$

$= 196.92 \text{ ft}^3$

$= 7.29 \text{ cu. yd}$

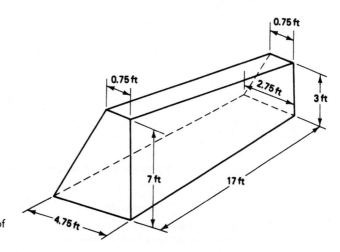

FIGURE 17.17 Sketch of prism for Example 17.2.

17.7   Volume Computations by Geometric Formulas

Some construction items can be broken into solid geometric figures for analysis and quantity computations. Structural concrete quantities, material stockpiles, and construction liquids (e.g., dust control) are some quantities that lend themselves to this sort of analysis. Figures 17.18 and 17.19 illustrate some of these formulas and their use.

17.8   Final (As-Built) Surveys

Similar to preliminary surveys, final surveys tie in *features that have just been built*. These measurements provide a record of construction and a check that the construction has proceeded according to the design plan.

The final plan, drawn from the as-built survey, is quite similar to the design plan, except for the revisions that are made to reflect the changes invariably required during the construction process. Design changes occur when problems are encountered. Such problems are usually apparent only after the construction has commenced—for example, unexpected underground pipes, conduits, or structures that interfere with the designed facility. It is difficult, especially in complex projects, to plan for every eventuality. If the preliminary surveyor, the construction surveyor, and the designer have all done their jobs well, the

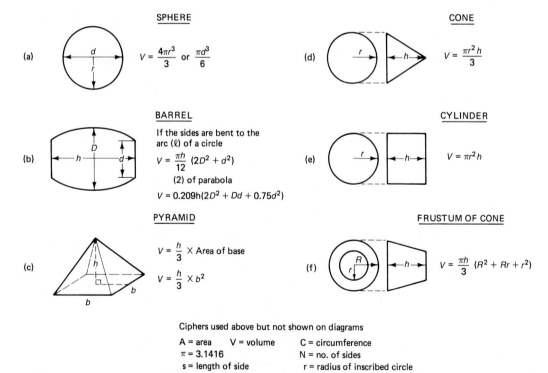

SPHERE

(a) $V = \dfrac{4\pi r^3}{3}$ or $\dfrac{\pi d^3}{6}$

CONE

(d) $V = \dfrac{\pi r^2 h}{3}$

BARREL

If the sides are bent to the arc (ℓ) of a circle

(b) $V = \dfrac{\pi h}{12}\,(2D^2 + d^2)$

(2) of parabola

$V = 0.209h(2D^2 + Dd + 0.75d^2)$

CYLINDER

(e) $V = \pi r^2 h$

PYRAMID

$V = \dfrac{h}{3} \times$ Area of base

(c) $V = \dfrac{h}{3} \times b^2$

FRUSTUM OF CONE

(f) $V = \dfrac{\pi h}{3}\,(R^2 + Rr + r^2)$

Ciphers used above but not shown on diagrams

A = area   V = volume   C = circumference

π = 3.1416   N = no. of sides

s = length of side   r = radius of inscribed circle

FIGURE 17.18   Volumes by geometric formulas. (a) Sphere. (b) Barrel. (c) Pyramid. (d) Cone. (e) Cylinder. (f) Frustum of cone. (From *Construction Manual*, Ministry of Transportation, Ontario)

(a) Volume of a sphere: given the radius (r)

$$\text{Volume} = \frac{4\pi r^3}{3}$$

$$V = \frac{4 \times 3.1416 \times 10^3}{3}$$

$$V = \underline{\underline{4189}} \text{ cu.ft}$$

(b) Volume of a cone: given the radius (r) and the height (h)

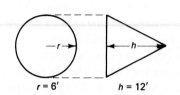

r = 6'   h = 12'

$$\text{Volume} = \frac{\pi r^2 h}{3}$$

$$V = \frac{3.1416 \times 6^2 \times 12}{3}$$

$$V = \underline{\underline{452.4}} \text{ cu.ft}$$

(c) Volume of a cylinder: given radius of base (r), and height or length (h) of the cylinder

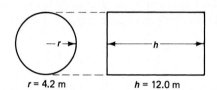

r = 4.2 m   h = 12.0 m

$$\text{Volume} = \pi r^2 h$$

$$V = 3.1416 \times 4.2^2 \times 12$$

$$V = \underline{\underline{665.0}} \text{ m}^3$$

(d) Volume of frustum of cone: given the radius of both top (r) and bottom (R), and the height (h)

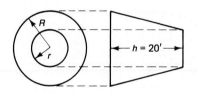

Given: r = 7', R = 10', h = 20'

$$\text{Volume} = \frac{\pi h}{3} (R^2 + Rr + r^2)$$

$$V = \frac{3.1416 \times 20}{3} (10^2 + 70 + 7^2)$$

$$V = \underline{\underline{4587}} \text{ cu.ft}$$

(e) Volume of a pyramid: given base (b) and height (h)

h = 27.4 m

b = 13.5 m

b = 13.5 m

$$\text{Volume} = \frac{h}{3} \times \text{area of base}$$

$$V = \frac{27.4}{3} \times 13.5^2$$

$$V = \underline{\underline{1664.6}} \text{ m}^3$$

FIGURE 17.19 Examples of volume computations.

design plan and the as-built drawing will be quite similar with respect to the horizontal and vertical position of all detail. When machine control or guidance has been utilized in the construction process (see Chapter 10), the continual updating of the project's digital data file, in the in-cab computer, results in the final survey being already in the computerized data file at the conclusion of the construction process. When more traditional surveying methods are used, however, the as-built field survey is usually begun after all the construction work has been completed.

The horizontal and vertical control points used in the preliminary and construction surveys are reestablished and re-referenced if necessary. The cross sections taken for the final payment survey are incorporated into the as-built survey. All detail is tied in, as in a preliminary survey. Pipelines and sewers are surveyed before the trenches are backfilled. It is particularly important at this stage to tie in (horizontally and vertically) any unexpected pipes, conduits, or structures that are encountered in the trench. As-built drawings, produced from final (as-built) surveys, are especially valuable in urban areas, where, it seems, there is no end to underground construction and reconstruction. After the completion of the contracted work and the expiration of the guarantee period, the as-built drawing is often transferred to CD/DVD or other secure computerized storage.

Problems

17.1 The field measurements (in feet) for an irregularly shaped sodded area are shown in Figure 17.20. Calculate the area of sod to the closest square yard, using (a) the trapezoidal technique and (b) Simpson's one-third rule.

FIGURE 17.20

17.2 The field measurements (in feet) for an irregularly shaped paved area are shown in Figure 17.21. Calculate the area of pavement to the closest square yard.

FIGURE 17.21

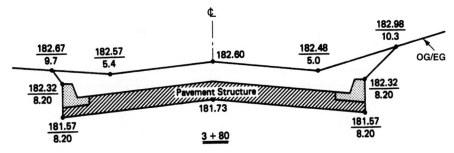

FIGURE 17.22

17.3 Refer to Figure 17.22. Calculate the end areas at stations 3 + 60 and 3 + 80, and then determine the volume (m³) of cut required in that section of road. For the end area at 3 + 60, use 180 m as the datum elevation, and for the end area at 3 + 80, use 181 m as the datum elevation.

17.4 Use the prismoidal formula to compute the volume (cu. yd) of concrete contained in the Figure 17.23.

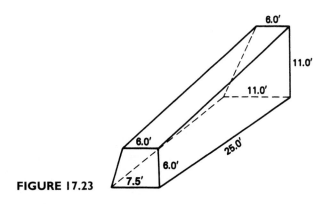

FIGURE 17.23

17.5 A stockpile of highway crushed stone is shaped into a conical figure; the base has a diameter of 72 ft, and the height of the stockpile is 52.5 ft. Compute the volume (cu. yd) of stone in the stockpile.

Problems

17.6 Compute the volume (cu. yd) contained in the footing and abutment shown in Figure 17.24.

FIGURE 17.24

Appendix A

Trigonometry and Coordinate Geometry Review

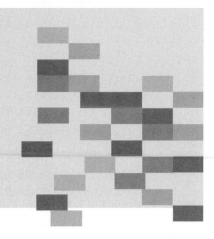

A.1 Trigonometric Definitions and Identities

A.1.1 Right Triangles

Basic Function Definitions (See Figure A.1)

$$\sin A = \frac{a}{c} = \cos B \qquad\qquad\text{(A.1)}$$

$$\cos A = \frac{b}{c} = \sin B \qquad\qquad\text{(A.2)}$$

$$\tan A = \frac{a}{b} = \cot B \qquad\qquad\text{(A.3)}$$

$$\sec A = \frac{c}{b} = \operatorname{cosec} B \qquad\qquad\text{(A.4)}$$

$$\operatorname{cosec} A = \frac{c}{a} = \sec B \qquad\qquad\text{(A.5)}$$

$$\cot A = \frac{b}{a} = \tan B \qquad\qquad\text{(A.6)}$$

Derived Relationships:

$$a = c \sin A = c \cos B = b \tan A = b \cot B = \sqrt{c^2 - b^2}$$
$$b = c \cos A = c \sin B = a \cot A = a \tan B = \sqrt{c^2 - b^2}$$
$$c = \frac{a}{\sin A} = \frac{a}{\cos B} = \frac{b}{\sin B} = \sqrt{a^2 + b^2}$$

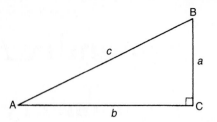

FIGURE A.1 Right triangle.

Note: The quadrant numbers in Figure A.2 reflect the traditional geometry approach (counterclockwise) to quadrant analysis. In surveying, the quadrants are numbered 1 (N.E.), 2 (S.E.), 3 (S.W.), and 4 (N.W.). The analysis of algebraic signs for the trigonometric functions (as shown) remains valid. Handheld calculators will automatically provide the correct algebraic sign if the angle direction is entered in the calculator or computer program in its azimuth form.

A.1.2 Oblique Triangles

Refer to Figure A.3 for the following relationships.
Sine Law

$$\frac{a}{\sin A} = \frac{b}{\sin B} = \frac{c}{\sin C} \tag{A.7}$$

Cosine Law

$$a^2 = b^2 + c^2 - 2bc \cos A \tag{A.8}$$

$$b^2 = a^2 + c^2 - 2ac \cos B \tag{A.9}$$

$$c^2 = a^2 + b^2 - 2ab \cos C \tag{A.10}$$

Given	Required	Formulas
A, B, a	C, b, c	$c = 180 - (A + B); b = \dfrac{a}{\sin A} \sin B; c = \dfrac{a}{\sin A} \sin C$
A, b, c	A	$a^2 = b^2 + c^2 - 2bc \cos A$
a, b, c	A	$\cos A = \dfrac{b^2 + c^2 - a^2}{2bc}$
a, b, c	Area	Area $= \sqrt{s(s - a)(s - b)(s - c)}$ where $s = \frac{1}{2}(a + b + c)$
C, a, b	Area	Area $= \frac{1}{2} ab \sin C$

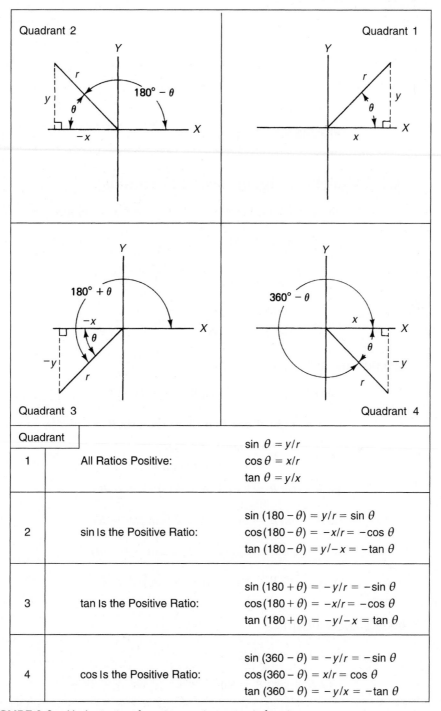

FIGURE A.2 Algebraic signs for primary trigonometric functions.

The content within the figure:

Quadrant 2

$180° - \theta$

r, y, θ, $-x$

Quadrant 1

r, y, θ, x

$180° + \theta$

$-x$, θ, $-y$, r

Quadrant 3

$360° - \theta$

x, θ, $-y$, r

Quadrant 4

Quadrant		
1	All Ratios Positive:	$\sin \theta = y/r$ $\cos \theta = x/r$ $\tan \theta = y/x$
2	sin Is the Positive Ratio:	$\sin(180 - \theta) = y/r = \sin \theta$ $\cos(180 - \theta) = -x/r = -\cos \theta$ $\tan(180 - \theta) = y/-x = -\tan \theta$
3	tan Is the Positive Ratio:	$\sin(180 + \theta) = -y/r = -\sin \theta$ $\cos(180 + \theta) = -x/r = -\cos \theta$ $\tan(180 + \theta) = -y/-x = \tan \theta$
4	cos Is the Positive Ratio:	$\sin(360 - \theta) = -y/r = -\sin \theta$ $\cos(360 - \theta) = x/r = \cos \theta$ $\tan(360 - \theta) = -y/x = -\tan \theta$

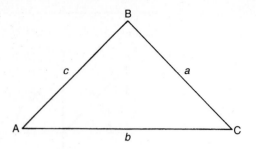

FIGURE A.3 Oblique triangle.

A.1.3 General Trigonometric Formulas

$$\sin A = 2 \sin \tfrac{1}{2} A \cos \tfrac{1}{2} A = \sqrt{1 - \cos^2 A} = \tan A \cos A \qquad (A.11)$$

$$\cos A = 2 \cos^2 \tfrac{1}{2} A - 1 = 1 - 2 \sin^2 \tfrac{1}{2} A$$

$$= \cos^2 \tfrac{1}{2} A - \sin^2 \tfrac{1}{2} A = \sqrt{1 - \sin^2 A} \qquad (A.12)$$

$$\tan A = \frac{\sin A}{\cos A} = \frac{\sin 2A}{1 + \cos 2A} = \sec^2 A - 1 \qquad (A.13)$$

ADDITION AND SUBTRACTION IDENTITIES

$$\sin (A \pm B) = \sin A \cos B \pm \sin B \cos A \qquad (A.14)$$

$$\cos (A \pm B) = \cos A \cos B \pm \sin A \sin B \qquad (A.15)$$

$$\tan (A \pm B) = \frac{\tan A \mp \tan B}{1 \mp \tan A \tan B} \qquad (A.16)$$

$$\sin A + \sin B = 2 \sin \tfrac{1}{2}(A + B) \sin \tfrac{1}{2}(A - B) \qquad (A.17)$$

$$\sin A - \sin B = 2 \cos \tfrac{1}{2}(A + B) \sin \tfrac{1}{2}(A - B) \qquad (A.18)$$

$$\cos A + \cos B = 2 \cos \tfrac{1}{2}(A + B) \cos \tfrac{1}{2}(A - B) \qquad (A.19)$$

$$\cos A - \cos B = 2 \sin \tfrac{1}{2}(A + B) \sin \tfrac{1}{2}(A - B) \qquad (A.20)$$

DOUBLE-ANGLE IDENTITIES

$$\sin 2 A = 2 \sin A \cos A \qquad (A.21)$$

$$\cos 2 A = \cos^2 A - \sin^2 A = 1 - 2 \sin^2 A = 2 \cos^2 A - 1 \qquad (A.22)$$

$$\tan 2 A = \frac{2 \tan A}{1 - \tan^2 A} \qquad (A.23)$$

$$\sin \frac{A}{2} = \sqrt{\frac{1 - \cos A}{2}} \qquad\qquad \text{(A.24)}$$

$$\cos \frac{A}{2} = \sqrt{\frac{1 + \cos A}{2}} \qquad\qquad \text{(A.25)}$$

$$\tan \frac{A}{2} = \frac{\sin A}{1 + \cos A} \qquad\qquad \text{(A.26)}$$

A.2   Coordinate Geometry

Coordinate geometry was introduced in Section 6.11, where traverse station coordinates were computed along with the area enclosed by the traverse. This section (Section A.2) describes the basics of coordinate geometry along with some applications. An understanding of these concepts will help the reader understand the fundamentals underlying coordinate geometry software programs that are now used to process most electronic surveying field data. See Chapter 5.

A.2.1 Geometry of Rectangular Coordinates

Figure A.4 shows two points $P_1(x_1, y_1)$ and $P_2(x_2, y_2)$ and their rectangular relationships to the x and y axes.

$$\text{Length } P_1P_2 = \sqrt{(x_2 - x_1)^2 + (y_2 - y_1)^2} \qquad\qquad \text{(A.27)}$$

$$\tan \alpha = \frac{(x_2 - x_1)}{(y_2 - y_1)} \qquad\qquad \text{(A.28)}$$

where α is the bearing or azimuth of P_1P_2. Also,

$$\text{Length } P_1P_2 = \frac{(x_2 - x_1)}{\sin \alpha} \qquad\qquad \text{(A.29)}$$

$$\text{Length } P_1P_2 = \frac{(y_2 - y_1)}{\cos \alpha} \qquad\qquad \text{(A.30)}$$

Use the equation having the larger numerical value of $(x_2 - x_1)$ or $(y_2 - y_1)$.

It is clear from Figure A.4 that $(x_2 - x_1)$ is the departure of P_1P_2 and that $(y_2 - y_1)$ is the latitude of P_1P_2. In survey work, the y value (latitude) is known as the northing, and the x value (departure) is known as the easting.

From analytic geometry, the slope of a straight line is $m = \tan (90 - \alpha)$, where $(90 - \alpha)$ is the angle of the straight line with the x-axis (Figure A.4); that is,

$$m = \cot \alpha$$

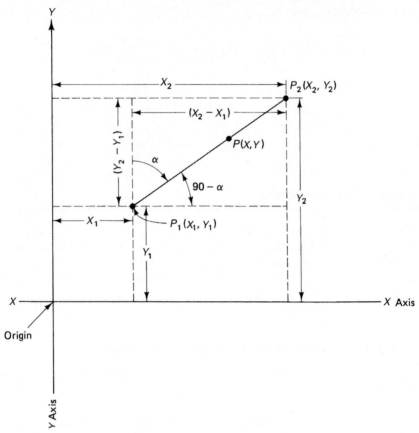

FIGURE A.4 Geometry of rectangular coordinates.

From coordinate geometry, the equation of straight line P_1P_2, where the coordinates of P_1 and P_2 are known, is

$$\frac{y - y_1}{y_2 - y_1} = \frac{x - x_1}{x_2 - x_1} \qquad (A.31)$$

This can be written as

$$y - y_1 = \frac{y_2 - y_1}{x_2 - x_1}(x_2 - x_1)$$

where $(y_2 - y_1)/(x_2 - x_1) = \cot \alpha = m$ (from analytic geometry), the slope. Analysis of Figure A.4 also shows that slope = rise/run = $(y_2 - y_1)/(x_2 - x_1) = \tan(90 - \alpha)$.

When the coordinates of one point (P_1) and the bearing or azimuth of a line are known, the equation becomes

$$y - y_1 = \cot \alpha(x - x_1) \qquad (A.32)$$

where α is the azimuth or bearing of the line through P_1 (x_1, y_1). Also from analytical geometry,

$$y - y_1 = -\frac{1}{\cot \alpha (x - x_1)} \tag{A.33}$$

which represents a line perpendicular to the line represented by Equation (A.32); that is, the slopes of perpendicular lines are negative reciprocals.

Equations for circular curves are quadratics in the following form:

$$(x - H)^2 + (y - K)^2 = r^2 \tag{A.34}$$

where r is the curve radius, (H, K) are the coordinates of the center, and (x, y) are the coordinates of point P, which locates the circle (Figure A.5). When the circle center is at the origin, the equation becomes

$$x^2 + y^2 = r^2 \tag{A.35}$$

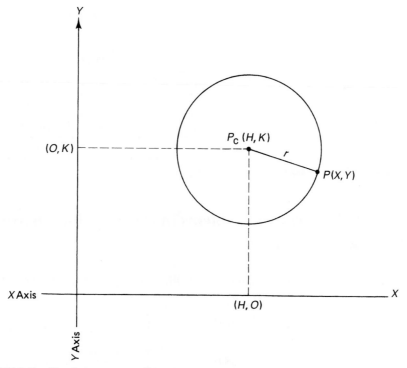

FIGURE A.5 Circular curve coordinates.

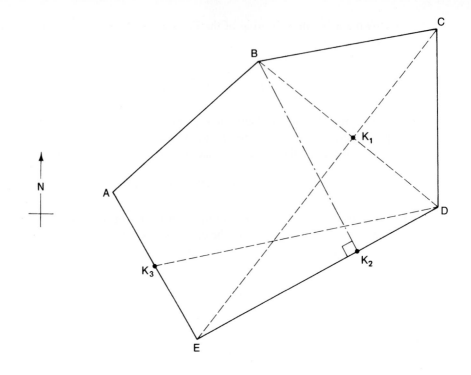

Station	Coordinates North	Coordinates East
A	1,000.00	1,000.00
B	1,250.73	1,313.61
C	1,302.96	1,692.14
D	934.77	1,684.54
E	688.69	1,160.27

FIGURE A.6 Coordinates for traverse problem.

A.2.2 Illustrative Problems in Rectangular Coordinates

■ EXAMPLE A.1

From the information shown in Figure A.6, calculate the coordinates of the point of intersection (K_1) of lines EC and DB. From Equation (A.31), the equation of EC is

$$\frac{y - 688.89}{1302.96 - 688.69} = \frac{x - 1160.27}{1692.14 - 1160.27} \tag{1}$$

$$y - 688.69 = \frac{1302.96 - 688.69}{1692.14 - 1160.27}(x - 1160.27)$$

$$y - 688.69 = 1.15492508x - 1340.025$$

$$y = 1.15492508x - 651.335 \qquad (1A)$$

$$\frac{y - 934.77}{1250.73 - 934.77} = \frac{x - 1684.54}{1313.61 - 1684.54} \qquad (2)$$

$$y - 934.77 = \frac{1250.73 - 934.77}{1313.61 - 1684.54}(x - 1684.54)$$

$$y - 934.77 = -0.8518049x + 1434.899$$

$$y = -0.8518049x + 2369.669 \qquad (2A)$$

Substitute for y:

$$1.15492508x - 651.335 = -0.08518049x + 2369.669$$

$$x = 1505.436$$

Substitute the value of x in either (1A) or (2A):

$$y = 1087.33$$

Therefore, the coordinates of point of intersection K_1 are (1087.33 N, 1505.44 E).

Note: Coordinates are shown as (N, E) or (E, N), depending on local practice.

■ **EXAMPLE A.2**

From the information shown in Figure A.6, calculate (a) the coordinates of K_2, the point of intersection of line ED and a line perpendicular to ED running through station B; and (b) distances K_2D and K_2E.

(a) From Equation (A.31), the equation of ED is

$$\frac{y - 688.69}{934.77 - 688.69} = \frac{x - 1160.27}{1684.54 - 1160.27} \qquad (1)$$

$$y - 688.69 = \frac{246.08}{524.27}(x - 1160.27) \qquad (1A)$$

From Equation A.32, the equation of BK_2 is:

$$y - 1250.73 - \frac{524.27}{246.08}(x - 1313.61) \qquad (2)$$

Simplifying, we find that these equations become (use five decimals to avoid rounding errors):

$$ED: 0.46938x - y = -144.09 \qquad (1B)$$

$$BK_2: 2.13049x + y = 4049.36 \qquad (2B)$$

$$2.59987x = 3905.27 \qquad (1B+2B)$$

$$x = 1502.102$$

Substitute the value of x in Equation 1A, and check the results in Equation 2:

$$y = 849.15$$

Therefore, the coordinates of K_2 are (849.15 N, 1502.10 E).

(b) Figure A.7 shows the coordinates for stations E and D and intermediate point K_2 from Equation A.27

$$\text{Length } K_2D = \sqrt{85.62^2 + 182.44^2} = 201.53$$

and:

$$\text{Length } K_2E = \sqrt{160.46^2 + 341.83^2} = 377.62$$

$$K_2D + K_2E = ED = 579.15$$

Check:

$$\text{Length } ED = \sqrt{246.08^2 + 524.27^2} = 579.15$$

■ EXAMPLE A.3

From the information shown in Figure A.6, calculate the coordinates of the point of intersection (K_3) on the line EA of a line parallel to CB running from station D to line EA. From Equation (A.31):

$$\text{CB: } \frac{y - 1302.96}{1250.73 - 1302.96} = \frac{x - 1692.14}{1313.16 - 1692.14}$$

$$y - 1302.96 = \frac{-52.23}{-378.53}(x - 1692.14)$$

$$\text{Slope (cot } \alpha) \text{ of CB} = \frac{-52.23}{-378.53}$$

FIGURE A.7 Sketch for Example A.2.

App. A   Trigonometry and Coordinate Geometry Review

Because DK_3 is parallel to BC

$$\text{Slope } (\cot \alpha) \text{ of } DK_3 = \frac{-52.23}{-378.53}$$

$$DK_3: y - 934.77 = \frac{52.23}{378.53}(x - 1684.54) \tag{1}$$

$$EA: \frac{y - 688.69}{1000.00 - 688.69} = \frac{x - 1160.27}{1000.00 - 1160.27} \tag{2}$$

$$DK_3: 0.13798x - y = -702.34 \tag{1A}$$

$$EA: 1.94241x + y = +2942.41 \tag{2A}$$

$$2.08039x = +2240.07 \tag{1A+2A}$$

$$x = 1076.7547$$

Substitute the value of x in Equation 1A, and check the results in Equation 2A:

$$y = 850.91$$

Therefore, the coordinates of K_3 are (850.91 N, 1076.75 E).

■ EXAMPLE A.4

From the information shown in Figure A.8, calculate the coordinates of the point of intersection (L) of the ₵ of Fisher Road with the ₵ of Elm Parkway.

The coordinates of station M on Fisher Road are (4,850,277.101 N, 316,909.433 E), and the bearing of the Fisher Road ₵ (ML) is S 75°10′30″ E. The coordinates of the center of the 350 M radius highway curve are (4,850,317.313 N, 317,112.656 E). The coordinates here are referred to a coordinate grid system having 0.000 m north at the equator and 304,800.000 m east at longitude 79°30′W.

The coordinate values are, of necessity, very large and would cause significant rounding error if they were used in calculator computations. Accordingly, an auxiliary set of coordinate axes will be used, allowing the values of the given coordinates to be greatly reduced for the computations; the amount reduced will later be added to give the final coordinates. The summary of coordinates is shown next:

Station	Grid Coordinates		Reduced Coordinates	
	y	x	$y' (y - 4{,}850{,}000)$	$x' (x - 316{,}500)$
M	4,850,277.101	316,909.433	277.101	409.433
C	4,850,317.313	317,112.656	317.313	612.656

From Equation A.32, the equation of the Fisher Road ₵ (ML) is:

$$y' - 277.101 = \cot 75°10′30″(x' - 409.433) \tag{1}$$

From Equation A.34, the equation of the Elm Parkway ₵ is:

$$(x' - 612.656)^2 + (y' - 317.313)^2 = 350.000^2 \tag{2}$$

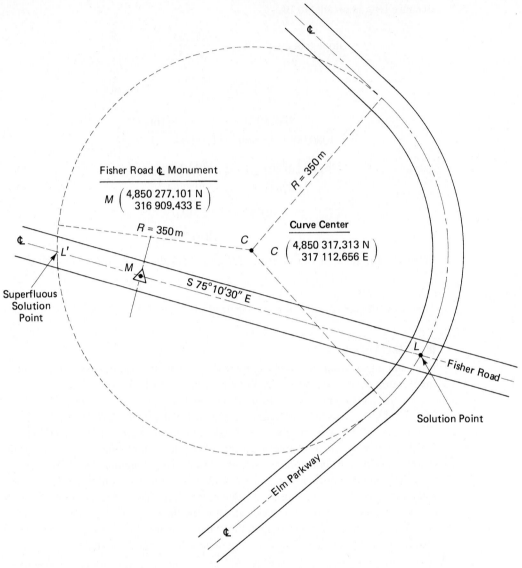

FIGURE A.8 Intersection of a straight line with a circular curve (see Example A.4).

Simplify Equation 1 to:

$$y' - 277.101 = -0.2646782x' + 108.368$$

$$y' = -0.2646782x' + 385.469 \tag{1A}$$

Fisher Road ₵ Monument

$$M \left(\begin{array}{c} 4{,}850\ 277.101\ \text{N} \\ 316\ 909.433\ \text{E} \end{array} \right)$$

Curve Center

$$C \left(\begin{array}{c} 4{,}850\ 317.313\ \text{N} \\ 317\ 112.656\ \text{E} \end{array} \right)$$

R = 350 m

R = 350 m

C

M

S 75°10′30″ E

₵

L′

Superfluous
Solution
Point

₵

L

Fisher Road

Solution Point

Elm Parkway

₵

Substitute the value of y' into Equation 2:

$$(x' - 612.656)^2 + (-0.2646782x' + 385.469 - 317.313)^2 - 350.000^2 = 0$$

$$(x' - 612.656)^2 + (-0.2646782x' + 68.156)^2 - 350.000^2 = 0$$

$$1.0700545x'^2 - 1,261.391x' + 257,492.61 = 0$$

This quadratic of the form $ax^2 + bx + c = 0$ has the following roots:

$$x = \frac{-b \pm \sqrt{b^2 - 4ac}}{2a}$$

$$x' = \frac{1,261.3908 \pm \sqrt{1,591,107.30 - 1,102,124.50}}{2.140109}$$

$$= \frac{1,261.3908 \pm 699.27305}{2.140109}$$

$$= 916.1514 \text{ or } x' = 262.658$$

Solve for y' by substituting in Equation 1A:

$$y' = 142.984 \text{ or } y' = 315.949$$

When these coordinates are now enlarged by the amount of the original reduction, the following values are obtained:

Station	Reduced Coordinates		Grid Coordinates	
	y'	x'	$y(y' + 4,850,000)$	$x(x' + 316,500)$
L	142.984	916.151	4,850,142.984	317,416.151
L'	315.949	262.658	4,850,315.949	316,762.658

Analysis of Figure A.8 is required in order to determine which of the two solutions is the correct one. The sketch shows that the desired intersection point L is south and east of station M; that is, L (4,850,142.984 N, 317 416.151 E) is the set of coordinates for the intersection of the ₵ of Elm Parkway and of Fisher Road. The other intersection point (L') solution is superfluous. See Figure A.8.

Appendix B

Surveying and Mapping Websites

The websites listed here cover surveying, global positioning systems (GPSs), photogrammetry, geographic information systems (GISs), and mapping. Some sites include web links to various related sites. Although the websites were verified at the time of publication, some changes are inevitable. Revised web addresses may be accessed by searching the links shown at other sites listed here or by conducting an online search via a search engine.

ACAD Tutorial   http://www.cadtutor.net/acad/
American Association of State Highway and Transportation Officials (AASHTO)
   http://www.aashto.com
American Congress on Surveying and Mapping (ACSM)   http://www.acsm.net
American Society for Photogrammetry and Remote Sensing   http://www.asprs.org
ARCINFO tutorial   http://www.geog.buffalo.edu/arcinfo/aiwwwtut/ARChome.html
Bennett (Peter) NMEA-0183 and GPS information   http://vancouver-webpages.com/
   pub/peter/
Berntsen International, Inc. (surveying markers)   http://www.berntsen.com
Canada Centre for Remote Sensing   http://www.ccrs.nrcan.gc.ca/
Canada Centre for Remote Sensing (tutorial)
   http://www.ccrs.nrcan.gc.ca/resource/tutor/fundam/index_e.php
Canadian Geodetic Survey   http://www.geod.nrcan.gc.ca
Centre for Topographic Information (Canada)   http://www.cits.nrcan.gc.ca
CORS information   http://www.ngs.noaa.gov/CORS/cors-data.html
Dana (Peter H.) GPS Overview
   http://www.colorado.edu/geography/gcraft/notes/gps/gps_ftoc.html
Galileo   http://europa.eu.int/comm/dgs/energy_transport/galileo/index_en.htm
Glonass home page (Russian Federation)   http://www.glonass-ianc.rsa.ru
GPS World magazine   http://gpsworld.com

International Earth Rotation Service (IERS)   http://www.iers.org
Land Surveying and Geomatics   http://surveying.mentabolism.org/
Leica Geosystems Inc.   http://www.leica-geosystems.com/
MAPINFO (mapping)   http://www.mapinfo.com
MicroSurvey (surveying and design software)   http://www.microsurvey.com/
NASA, EROS Data Center   http://edcwww.cr.usgs.gov
National Map   http://nationalmap.usgs.gov
Natural Resources Canada   http://www.nrcan.gc.ca
NGS home page   http://www.ngs.noaa.gov/
Nikon (surveying instruments)   http://www.nikon-trimble.com
Optech (Lidar—airborne laser terrain mapper)   http://www.optech.ca
POB *Point of Beginning* magazine   http://www.pobonline.com/
Professional Surveyor magazine   http://www.profsurv.com
Sokkia   http://www.sokkia.com/
Spectra Precision (Trimble)   http://www.contractorstools.com/spectra.html
The American Surveyor   http://www.amerisurv.com
Topcon GPS (including tutorial)   http://www.topcongps.com
Topcon Instrument Corporation   http://www.topcon.com/home.html
Trimble   http://www.trimble.com
Trimble (GIS)   http://www.trimble.com/mgis.shtml
Trimble GPS Tutorial   http://www.trimble.com/gps/index.htm
Tripod Data Systems (Trimble)   http://www.tdsway.com
United States Bureau of Land Management (BLM) geographic coordinate database
    http://www.blm.gov/gcdb
United States Bureau of Land Management (BLM) National Integrated Lands System
    (NILS)   http://www.blm.gov/nils
United States Coast Guard (USCG) Navigation Center (use search box for information on
    DGPS)   http://www.navcen.uscg.gov/dgps/Default.htm
United States Coast Guard (USCG) Navigation Center   http://www.navcen.uscg.gov
United States Geological Survey (USGS)   http://www.usgs.gov/
United States maps and data   http://www.geodata.gov/

Appendix C

Glossary

absolute positioning   The direct determination of a station's coordinates by taking GPS observations on a minimum of four GPS satellites. Also known as *point positioning*.

absorption   The process by which radiant energy is retained by a substance. The absorbing medium itself may emit energy, but only after an energy conversion has taken place.

abutment   The part of a bridge substructure that supports the end of the superstructure and retains the approach fill.

accuracy   The conformity of a measurement to the "true" value.

accuracy ratio   The error in a measurement divided by the overall value of the measurement; that is, an error of 1 ft in 3,000 ft would result in an accuracy ratio of 1/3,000. Also known as *error ratio*.

aerial survey   Preliminary and final surveys using traditional aerial photography and aerial imaging. Aerial imagery includes the use of digital cameras, multispectral scanners, lidar, and radar.

alignment   The location of the centerline of a survey or a facility.

ambiguity   The integer number of carrier cycles between the GPS receiver and a satellite before lock-on.

antenna reference height (ARH)   The vertical height of a GPS receiver antenna above a control station.

arithmetic check   A check on the reductions of differential leveling involving the sums of the backsights and the foresights.

arterial road   A road (or highway) mainly designed for traffic mobility—with some property access consideration.

as-built survey   A postconstruction survey that confirms design execution and records in-progress revisions. Also known as *final survey*.

automatic level A surveyors' level that has the line of sight automatically maintained in the horizontal plane once the instrument is roughly leveled.

azimuth The direction of a line given by an angle, measured clockwise from a north (usually) meridian.

backfill Material used to fill an excavation.

backsight (BS) A sight taken with a level to a point of known elevation, thus permitting the surveyor to compute the elevation of the HI; in theodolite work, the backsight is a sighting taken to a point of known position to establish a reference direction.

baseline A line of reference for survey work; often the centerline, the street line, or the centerline of construction is used, although any line could be arbitrarily selected or established.

batter board A horizontal crosspiece on a grade stake or grade rod that refers to the proposed elevations.

bearing The direction of a line given by the acute angle from a meridian and accompanied by a cardinal compass direction (NE, NW, SW, SE).

bearing plate A plate that is secured to the abutment seat or pier top on which rest the beams, girders, and the like.

benchmark (BM) A fixed solid reference point with a precisely determined published elevation.

board measure A standard unit of timber measure: 1 board ft equals 1 ft square by 1 in. thick.

borrow pit A source of granular fill material that is located off the right of way.

break line A line that joins points defining significant changes in ground surface slope, such as toe and top of slope, top and bottom of ditches and swales, creek centerlines, and the like.

bucking in A trial-and-error technique of establishing a theodolite, or total station, on a line between two points that themselves are not intervisible. Also known as *wiggling in* and *interlining*.

catch basin A structure designed to collect surface water and transfer it to a storm sewer.

central meridian A reference meridian in the center of the zone covered by the plane coordinate grid—at every 6° of longitude in the UTM grid.

chainage *See* station.

circular curve A curve with a constant radius.

clearing The cutting and removal of trees from a construction site.

COGO (coordinate geometry) Software programs that facilitate coordinate geometry computations used in surveying and civil engineering.

collector road A road (highway) designed to provide property access with some traffic mobility; it connects local roads to arterials.

Compass China's global satellite positioning system, which will include thirty global positioning satellites and five regional positioning satellites scheduled for completion within the next few years.

compass rule Used in traverse balancing, an adjustment that distributes the errors in latitude and departure for each traverse course in the same proportion as the course distance is to the traverse perimeter.

compound curve Two or more circular arcs turning in the same direction and having common tangent points and different radii.

construction survey A survey used to provide line and grade to a contractor for the construction of a facility.

continuously operating reference station (CORS) A GPS control station that continuously receives satellite signals and compares the time-stamped updated position coordinates with the known station coordinates. This differential positioning data can be used in postprocessing solutions or in real-time positioning by transmitting the differential data to single-receiver surveyors and navigators to permit the higher-precision differential positioning normally found only in two-receiver (multireceiver) surveys.

contour A line on a map joining points of similar elevation.

control survey A survey used to establish reference points and lines for preliminary and construction surveys.

coordinate geometry computer programs *See* COGO.

coordinates A set of numbers (X, Y) defining the two-dimensional position of a point given by the distances measured north and east of an origin reference point having coordinates of $(0, 0)$.

CORS *See* continuously operating reference station.

cross section A profile of the ground or the like that is taken at right angles to a reference line.

crown The uppermost point on a road, pipe, or cross section. The rate of cross fall on pavement.

culvert A structure designed to provide an opening under a road, or the like, usually for the transportation of storm water.

cut In construction, the excavation of material. The measurement down from a grade mark.

cutoff angle *See* mask angle.

cycle slip A temporary loss of lock on satellite carrier signals causing a miscount in carrier cycles. Lock must be reestablished to continue GPS positioning solutions.

data collector An electronic field book designed to accept field data—both measured and descriptive.

datum An assumed or a fixed reference plane.

deck The floor of a bridge.

deflection angle The angle between the prolongation of the back survey line measured right (R) or left (L) to the forward survey line.

departure (dep) The departure distance is the change in easterly displacement (ΔE) of a line. It is computed by multiplying the distance times the sine of the azimuth or bearing.

differential leveling A technique for determining the differences in elevation between points using a surveyor's level.

differential positioning Obtaining measurements at a known base station to help correct simultaneous measurements made at rover receiving stations.

double centering A technique of turning angles or producing straight lines involving a minimum of two sightings with a theodolite or total station—once with the telescope direct and once with the telescope inverted.

drainage The collection and transportation of ground and storm water.

DTM (digital terrain model) A three-dimensional depiction of a ground surface—usually produced by software programs [sometimes referred to as a digital elevation model (DEM) with break lines].

DXF (drawing exchange format) An industry standard format that permits graphical data to be transferred among various data collector, CAD, GIS, and soft-copy photogrammetry applications programs.

EDM Electronic distance measurement.

EFB (electronic field book) *See* data collector.

elevation The distance above, or below, a given datum. Also known as *orthometric height*.

elevation factor The factor used to convert ground distances to sea-level distances.

engineering surveys Preliminary and layout surveys used for engineering design and construction.

EOS (Earth-observing system) NASA's study of the Earth, scheduled to cover the period 2000–2015, in which a series of small to intermediate Earth observation satellites will be launched to measure global changes. The first satellite (experimental) in the series (TERRA) was launched in 1999.

epoch An observational event in time that forms part of a series of GPS observations.

error The difference between a measured, or observed, value and the "true" value.

ETI⁺ (enhanced thematic mapper) An eight-band multispectral scanning radiometer, onboard Landsat 7, that is capable of providing relatively high resolution (15-m) imaging information about the Earth's surface.

existing ground (EG) The position of the ground surface just prior to construction. Original ground.

external distance The distance from the midcurve to the PI in a circular curve.

Father Point A general adjustment of Canadian-U.S.-Mexican leveling observations resulted in the creation of the North American Vertical Datum of 1988 (NAVD88) in 1991. The adjustment held fixed the height of the primary tidal benchmark located at Father Point, Rimouski, Quebec, on the south shore of the St. Lawrence River.

fiducial marks Reference marks on the edges of aerial photos, used to locate the principal point on the photo.

fill Material used to raise the construction level. The measurement up from a grade mark.

final survey *See* as-built survey.

footing The part of the structure that is placed in, or on, the ground upon which the main structure rests.

forced centering   The interchanging of theodolites, prisms, and targets into tribrachs—that have been left in position over the station.

foresight (FS)   In leveling, a sight taken to a BM or TP to obtain a check on a leveling operation or to establish a transfer elevation.

foundation   The portion of the structure that rests on the footing.

four-foot mark   A reference mark, used in building construction, that is 4 ft above the finished first-floor elevation.

free station   A conveniently located instrument station used for construction layout, the position of which is determined after occupation, through GPS or resection techniques.

freeway   A highway designed for traffic mobility, with access restricted to interchanges with arterials and other freeways.

gabion   A wire basket filled with fragmented rocks or concrete, often used in erosion control.

Galileo   The European Union's proposed worldwide satellite positioning system presently scheduled for completion in 2013.

general dilution of precision (GDOP)   A value that indicates the relative uncertainty in position, using GPS observations, caused by errors in time (GPS receivers) and satellite vector measurements. A minimum of four widely spaced satellites at high elevations usually produce good results (i.e., lower GDOP values).

geocoding   The linking of entity and attribute data to a specific geographic location.

geodetic vertical datum   In North America, a precisely established and maintained series of benchmarks referenced to mean sea level (MSL) tied to the vertical control station Father Point (elevation = 0.000 ft or m), which is located in the St. Lawrence River Valley.

geodetic height (h)   The distance from the ellipsoid surface to the ground surface.

geodetic survey   A survey that reflects the curved (ellipsoidal) shape of the Earth.

geographic information system (GIS)   A spatially and relationally referenced data base.

geographic meridian   A line on the surface of the Earth joining the poles; that is, a line of longitude.

geoid   A surface that is approximately represented by mean sea level (MSL), and is, in fact, the equipotential surface of the Earth's gravity field. This surface is everywhere normal to the direction of gravity.

geoid height   *See* geoid undulation.

geoid separation   *See* geoid undulation.

geoid undulation (N)   The difference in elevation between the geoid surface and the ellipsoid surface; N is negative if the geoid surface is below the ellipsoid surface (also known as the *geoid height* and *geoid separation*).

geomatics   A term used to describe the science and technology dealing with Earth measurement data, including collection, sorting, management, planning and design, storage, and presentation. It has applications in all disciplines and professions that use Earth-related spatial data—for example, planning, geography, geodesy, infrastructure engineering, agriculture, natural resources, environment, land division and registration, project engineering, and mapping.

geostationary orbit   A satellite orbit such that it appears the satellite is stationary over a specific location on Earth. A formation of geostationary satellites presently provides communications services worldwide. Also known as *geosynchronous orbit*.

GIS   *See* geographic information system.

global positioning system   *See* GPS.

Glonass   Russia's global satellite positioning system which is presently more than 75 percent completed and is now in use with multi-constellation positioning receivers.

global navigation satellite system (GNSS)   A term now used to refer to all global and regional satellite positioning systems.

gon   A unit of angular measure in which 1 revolution = 400 gon and 100.000 gon = a right angle. Also known as *grad*.

GPS   (global positioning system) A ground positioning (Y, X, and Z) technique based on the reception and analysis of NAVSTAR satellite signals.

grade sheet   A construction report giving line and grade, that is, offsets and cuts/fills at each station.

grade stake   A wood stake with a cut/fill mark referring to that portion of a proposed facility adjacent to the stake.

grade transfer   A technique of transferring cut/fill measurements to the facility. Typical techniques include carpenter's level, string-line level, laser, and batter boards.

gradient   The slope of a grade line.

grid distance   A distance on a coordinate grid.

grid factor   A factor used to convert ground distances to grid distances.

grid meridian   A meridian parallel to a central meridian on a coordinate grid.

ground distance   A distance as measured on the ground surface.

grubbing   The removal of stumps, roots, and debris from a construction site.

Gunter's chain   Early (1700s) steel measuring device consisting of hundred links, 66-ft long.

haul   The distance that 1 cu. yd (meter) of cut material is transported to a fill location in highway construction.

head wall   A vertical wall at the end of a culvert that is used to keep fill material from falling into the creek or watercourse.

hectare   10,000 m^2.

height of instrument (HI)   In leveling, the height of the line of sight of the level above a datum.

height of instrument (hi)   In total station and theodolite work, the height of the instrument's optical axis above the instrument station.

horizontal line   A straight line perpendicular to a vertical line.

image rectification   The extraction of planimetric and elevation data from stereo-paired aerial photographs for the preparation of topographic maps.

interlining   A trial-and-error technique of establishing the theodolite on a line between two points that are not intervisible. Also known as *bucking in* and *wiggling in*.

intermediate sight (IS)   A sight taken by a level, total station, or theodolite to determine a feature elevation and/or location.

invert   The inside bottom of a pipe or culvert.

ionosphere   The section of the Earth's atmosphere that is about 50–1,000 km above the Earth's surface.

ionospheric refraction   In GPS, the impedance in the velocity of signals as they pass through the ionosphere.

laser   An acronym for *l*ight *a*mplification by *s*timulated *e*mission of *r*adiation. Construction lasers employ either visible light or infrared beams to provide control for both line and grade.

laser alignment   The horizontal and/or vertical alignment given by a fixed or rotating laser.

latitude (lat)   When used in reference to a traverse course, the latitude distance is the change in northerly displacement (ΔN) of the line. It is computed by multiplying the distance by the cosine of its azimuth or bearing. In geographic terms, the latitude is an angular distance measured northerly or southerly, at the Earth's center, from the equator.

layout survey   A construction survey.

level line   A line in a level surface.

lidar (light detection and ranging)   This laser technique, used in airborne and satellite imagery, utilizes laser pulses that are reflected from ground features to obtain 3D topographic and DTM mapping detail.

line   A GIS term describing the joining of two points and having one dimension.

line and grade   The designed horizontal and vertical position of a facility.

linear error of closure   The line of traverse misclosure representing the resultant of the measuring errors.

local road (highway)   A road designed for property access, connected to arterials by collectors.

longitude   An angular distance measured east or west, in the plane of the equator, from the reference meridian through Greenwich, England (0°). Lines of longitude are shown on globes as meridians.

magnetic meridian   A line parallel to the direction taken by a freely moving magnetized needle, as in compass.

manhole (MH)   A structure that provides access to underground services.

mask angle   The vertical angle below which satellite signals are not recorded or processed. A value of 10° or 15° is often used. Also known as the *cutoff angle*.

mass diagram   A graphic representation of cumulative highway cuts and fills.

mean sea level (MSL)   A reference datum for leveling having an elevation of 0.000 ft or m.

meridian   A north–south reference line.

midordinate distance   The distance from the midchord to the midcurve in a circular curve.

mistake   A poor result due to carelessness or a misunderstanding.

monument   A permanent reference point for horizontal and vertical positioning.

MSL   *See* mean sea level.

multispectral scanner   Scanning device used for satellite and airborne imagery to record reflected and emitted energy in two or more bands of the electromagnetic spectrum.

nadir   A vertical angle measured from the nadir direction (straight down) upward to a point.

NAVSTAR   A set of about thirty orbiting satellites used in navigation and positioning.

normal tension   The amount of tension required in taping to offset the effects of sag.

original ground (OG)   The position of the ground surface just prior to construction. existing ground.

orthometric height (H)   The distance (measured along a plumb line) from the geoid surface to the ground surface. Also known as *elevation*.

Orthophoto maps   *See* planimetric maps.

page check   An arithmetic check of leveling notes.

parabolic curve   A curve used in vertical alignment to join two adjacent grade lines.

parallax   An error in sighting that occurs when the objective and/or the cross hairs are improperly focused.

photogrammetry   The science of taking accurate measurements from aerial photographs.

pier   A vertical column supporting beams, girders, and the like which help to span the distance between abutments.

plan   Bird's eye view of a route selection, the same as if you are in an aircraft looking straight down. Gives the horizontal location of a facility, including curve radii.

plan and profile   Form the "blueprint" from which the construction is accomplished; usually also show the cross-section details and construction notes.

plane survey   A survey that ignores the curvature of the Earth.

planimeter   A mechanical or electronic device used to measure area by tracing the outline of the area on a map or plan.

planimetric maps   Scaled maps showing the scaled horizontal locations of both natural and cultural features. Also known as *orthophoto maps*.

point   A GIS term describing a single spatial entity and having zero dimension.

polar coordinates   The coordinates that locate a feature by distance and angle (r, θ).

polygon   A GIS term for a closed chain of points representing an area.

precision   The degree of refinement with which a measurement is made.

preengineering survey   A preliminary survey that forms the basis for engineering design.

preliminary survey   *See* preengineering survey.

profile   A series of elevations taken along a baseline at some repetitive station interval, as well as at each significant change in slope. A side view, or elevation, of a route in which the longitudinal surfaces are highlighted as well as at each significant change in slope.

property survey   A survey to retrace or establish property lines or to establish the location of buildings with respect to property limits.

pseudorange The uncorrected distance from a GPS satellite to a ground receiver, determined by comparing the code transmitted from the satellite with the receiver's onboard replica code. To convert to the actual range (distance from the satellite to the receiver), the surveyor must make corrections for clock errors as well as natural and instrumental errors.

random errors Errors associated with the skill and vigilance of the surveyor.

real-time positioning A surveying technique that requires a base station to measure the satellites' signals, process the baseline corrections, and then broadcast the corrections (differences) to any number of roving receivers that are simultaneously tracking the same satellites. Also known as *real-time kinematic (RTK) surveying*.

rectangular coordinates Two distances, 90° opposed, that locate a feature with respect to a baseline or grid.

relative positioning The determination of position through the combined computations of two or more receivers simultaneously tracking the same satellites, thus resulting in the determination of the baseline vector (*X*, *Y*, *Z*) joining the two receivers.

remote object elevation The determination of the height of an object by a total station sighting, and utilizing onboard applications software.

remote sensing Geodata collection and interpretive analysis for both airborne and satellite imageries.

resection The solution of coordinates determination of an occupied station by the angle sighting of three or more coordinated reference stations (two or more stations if both angles and distances are measured).

retaining wall A wall built to hold back the embankment adjacent to a structure.

right of way (ROW) The legal property limits of a utility or access route.

route surveys Preliminary, control, and construction surveys that cover a long, but narrow area—as in highway and railroad construction.

ROW *See* right of way.

sag The error caused when a measuring tape is supported only at the ends, with insufficient tension.

scale factor The factor used to convert sea-level distances to plane grid distances.

sea-level correction factor The factor used to convert ground distances to sea-level equivalent distances.

shaft An opening of uniform cross section joining a tunnel to the surface. It is used for access and ventilation.

shrinkage The decrease in volume that occurs when excavated material is placed on site under compaction.

skew number A clockwise angle (closest 5°) turned from the back tangent to the centerline of a culvert or bridge.

slope stake A stake placed to identify the top or bottom of a slope.

soft-copy (digital) stereoplotting The analysis (largely automated) of digitized images through the use of sophisticated algorithms.

span The unsupported length of a structure.

spiral curve   A transition curve of constantly changing radius placed between a high-speed tangent and a central curve. It permits a gradual speed adjustment.

spring line   The horizontal bisector of a sewer pipe, above which connections may be made.

station   A point on a baseline that is a specified distance from the point of commencement. The point of commencement is identified as $0 + 00$; 100 ft, 100 m, or 1,000 m (in some highway applications) are known as full stations. $1 + 45.20$ identifies a point 145.20 ft (m) distant from the point of commencement ($0 + 145.20$ in some highways applications).

stripping   The removal of topsoil from a construction site.

superelevation   The banking of a curved section of road to help overcome the effects of centrifugal force.

survey drafting   A term that covers a wide range of scale graphics; including both manual and digital plotting.

surveying   The art and science of taking field measurements on or near the surface of the Earth.

swell   The increase in volume when blasted rock is placed on site.

systematic errors   Errors whose magnitude and algebraic sign can be determined.

tangent   A straight line, often referred to with respect to a curve.

temporary benchmark (TBM)   A semipermanent reference point of known elevation.

three-wire leveling   A more precise technique of differential leveling in which rod readings are taken at the stadia hairs in addition to the main cross hair in a telescope.

toe of slope   The bottom of a slope.

topographic map   A map showing spot elevations and contours.

total station   An electronic theodolite combined with an EDM instrument, a central processor, and an electronic data collector. It is used to read and record angles and distances and to perform various surveying computations.

traverse   A continuous series of measured lines (angles and distances are measured).

triangulation   A control survey technique involving (1) a precisely measured baseline as a starting side for a series of triangles or chain of triangles; (2) the measurement of each angle in the triangle using a precise theodolite, which permits the computation of the lengths of each side; and (3) a check on the work made possible by precisely measuring a side of a subsequent triangle (the spacing of check lines depends on the desired accuracy level).

trilateration   The control surveying solution technique of measuring only the sides in a triangle.

turning point (TP)   A solid point used in leveling where an elevation is established temporarily so that the level may be relocated.

Universal Transverse Mercator system (UTM)   A worldwide grid system based on sixty zones, each 6° of longitude wide. The grid covers from 80° north latitude to 80° south latitude. Each central meridian, at the middle of the zone, has an x (easterly) value of 500,000.000 m, and the equator has a y (northerly) value of 0.000 m. The scale factor at the central meridian is 0.9996.

vertical angle   An angle in the vertical plane measured up (+) or down (−) from horizontal.

vertical curve   A parabolic curve joining two grade lines.

vertical line   A line from the surface of the Earth to the Earth's center. Also known as a *plumb line* or *line of gravity*.

waving the rod   The slight waving of the leveling rod to and from the instrument, which permits the surveyor to take a more precise (lowest) rod reading.

wing wall   An abutment extension designed to retain the approach fill.

zenith   A point on a celestial sphere (i.e., a sphere of infinitely large radius, with its center at the center of the Earth) that is directly above the observer.

zenith angle   A vertical angle measured downward from the zenith (upward plumbline) direction. This is the vertical angle measured by most modern theodolites and total stations.

Appendix D

Typical Field Projects

The following projects can be performed in either foot units or metric units and can be adjusted in scope to fit the available time.

D.1 Field Notes

Survey field notes can be entered into a bound field book or on loose-leaf field notepaper; if a bound field book is used, be sure to leave room for a title, index, and diary at the front of the book—if they are required by your instructor.

Sample Field Book Instructions and Layout

1. Write your name in ink on the outside cover.
2. Page numbers (e.g., 1–72) are to be on the right side only. See Figure D.1
3. All entries are to be in pencil, 2H or 3H.
4. All entries are to be printed (uppercase, if permitted).
5. Calculations are to be checked and initialed.
6. Sketches are to be used to clarify field notes. Orient the sketch so that the included north arrow points toward the top of the page.
7. All field notes are to be brought up to date each day.
8. Show the word *copy* at the top of all copied pages.
9. Field notes are to be entered directly in the field book, not on scraps of paper to be copied later.
10. Mistakes in entered data are to be lined out, not erased.
11. Spelling mistakes, calculation mistakes, and the like should be erased and reentered correctly.

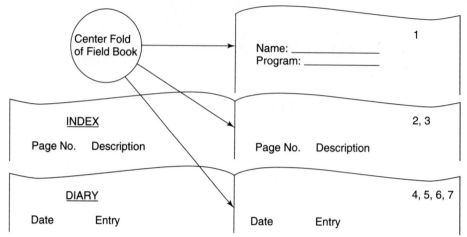

FIGURE D.1 Field book layout.

12. Lettering is to be read from the bottom of the page or the right side.
13. The first page of each project should show the date, temperature, project title, crew duties, and so on.
14. The diary should show absentees, weather, description of work, and so on.

D.2 Project 1: Building Measurements

Description   Measure the selected walls of an indicated campus building with a nylon-clad steel or fiberglass tape. Record the measurements on a sketch in the field book—as directed by the instructor (see Figure D.2 for sample field notes).

Equipment   Nylon-clad steel tape or fiberglass tape (100 ft or 30 m).

Purpose   To introduce you to the fundamentals of note keeping and survey measurement.

Procedure   Use the measuring techniques described in class prior to going out.

- One crew member should be appointed to take notes for this first project. At the completion of the project (same day), the other crew members should copy the notes (ignoring erroneous data) into their field books. Include diary and index data. (Crew members should take equal turns acting as note keeper over the length of the program.)
- Using a straightedge, draw a large sketch of the selected building walls on the right-hand (grid) side of your field book. Show the walls as they would appear in a plan view; for example, ignore overhangs, or show them as dashed lines. Keep the tape taut to remove sag, and try to keep the tape horizontal. If the building wall is longer than one tape length, make an intermediate mark (do not deface the building), and proceed from that point.

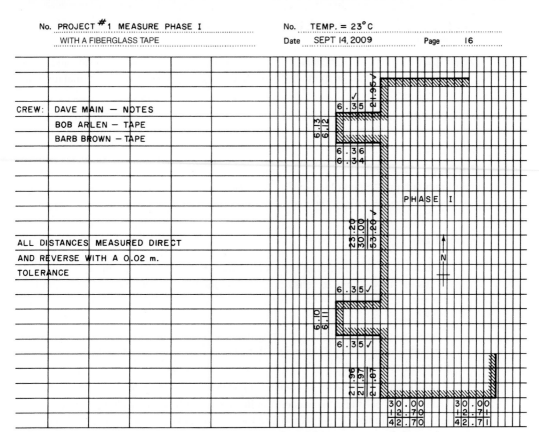

FIGURE D.2   Sample field notes for Project 1 (taping field notes for building dimensions).

- After completing all the measurements in one direction, start from the terminal point, and remeasure all the walls. If the second measurement agrees with the first measurement, put a check mark beside the entered data. If the second measurement agrees acceptably (e.g., within ±0.10 ft or 0.02 m), enter that measurement directly above or below the first entered measurement. If the second measurement disagrees with the first (e.g., >0.10 ft or 0.02 m—or other value given by your instructor), enter that value on the sketch, and measure that dimension a third time—discard the erroneous measurement by drawing a line (using a straightedge) through the erroneous value.

Discussion   If the class results are summarized on the chalkboard, it will be clear that all crews did not obtain the same results for specified building wall lengths. There will be much more agreement among crews on the lengths of the shorter building walls than on the lengths of the longer building walls (particularly the walls that were longer than one tape length). Discuss and enumerate the types of mistakes and errors that could account for measurement discrepancies among survey crews working on this project.

D.3 Project 2: Experiment to Determine "Normal Tension"

Description   Determine the tension required to eliminate errors due to tension and sag for a 100-ft or 30-m steel tape supported only at the ends. This tension is called normal tension.

Equipment   Steel tape (100.00 ft or 30.000 m), two plumb bobs, and a graduated tension handle.

Purpose   To introduce you to measurement techniques requiring the use of a steel tape and plumb bob and to demonstrate the "feel" of the proper tension required when using a tape that is supported only at the ends (the usual case).

Procedure

- With a 100-ft or 30-m tape fully supported on the ground and under a tension of 10 lbs or 50 N (standard tension) as determined by use of a supplied tension handle, measure from the initial mark and place a second mark at exactly 100.00 ft or 30.000 m.
- Check this measurement by repeating the procedure (while switching personnel) and correcting if necessary. (If this initial measurement is not performed correctly, much time will be wasted.)
- Raise the tape off the ground and keep it parallel to the ground to eliminate slope errors.
- Using plumb bobs and the tension handle, determine how many pounds or Newtons of tension (see Table F.1) are required to force the steel tape to agree with the previously measured distance of 100.00 ft or 30.000 m.
- Repeat the process while switching crew personnel. (Acceptable tolerance is ±2 lbs.)
- Record the normal tension results (at least two) in the field book, as described in the classroom.
- Include the standard conditions for the use of steel tapes in your field notes (Table D.1). For this project, you can assume that the temperature is standard, 68°F or 20°C.

Discussion   If the class results are summarized (e.g., on the chalkboard), it will be clear that not all survey crews obtained the same average value for normal tension. Discuss the reasons for the tension measurement discrepancies and agree on a "working" value for normal tension for subsequent class projects.

Table D.1   STANDARD CONDITIONS FOR THE USE OF STEEL TAPES

English System	or	Metric System
Temperature = 68°F		Temperature = 20°C
Tension = 10 lbs		Tension = 50 N (11.2 lbs)
Tape is fully supported		Tape is fully supported

D.4 Project 3: Field Traverse Measurements with a Steel Tape*

Description Measure the sides of a five-sided closed field traverse using techniques designed to permit a precision closure ratio of 1:5,000 (Table 2.1). The traverse angles can be obtained from Project 5. See Figure D.3 for sample field notes.

Equipment Steel tape, two plumb bobs, hand level, range pole or plumb bob string target, and chaining pins or other devices to mark position on the ground.

Purpose To enable you to develop some experience in measuring with a steel tape and plumb bobs (or electronically) in the first stage of a traverse closure exercise (see also Project 5).

Procedure

- Each course of the traverse is measured twice—forward (direct) and then immediately back (reverse)—with the two measurements agreeing to within 0.03 ft or 0.008 m. If the two measurements do not agree, repeat them until they do and before the next course of the traverse is measured.
- When measuring on a slope, the high-end surveyor normally holds the tape directly on the mark, and the low-end surveyor uses a plumb bob to keep the tape horizontal.

No. PROJECT #3
TRAVERSE DISTANCES

No. ....
Date MARCH 29, 2009   Page 10

COURSE	DIRECT	REVERSE	MEAN	MEAN (C_T)
111–112	164.96	164.94	164.95	164.97
112–113	88.41	88.43	88.42	88.43
113–114	121.69	121.69	121.69	121.70
114–115	115.80	115.78	115.79	115.80
115–111	68.36	68.34	68.35	68.36

BROWN-NOTES
FIELDING-TAPE
SIMPSON-TAPE
TEMP. = 83 °F

TRAVERSE

FIGURE D.3 Sample field notes for Project 3 (traverse distances).

*Projects 3 and 5 can be combined, using EDM-equipped theodolites, or total stations, and reflecting prisms. The traverse courses can be measured using an EDM instrument, or total stations, and a prism (pole-mounted or tribrach-mounted). Each station will be occupied with a theodolite-equipped EDM instrument, or total station, and each pair of traverse courses can be measured at each setup. Traverse computations will use the mean distances thus determined and the mean angles obtained from each setup. See Chapters 5 and 6.

- The low-end surveyor uses the hand level to keep the tape approximately horizontal by sighting the high-end surveyor and noting how much lower she or he is in comparison. The plumb bob can then be set to that height differential. Use chaining pins or other markers to temporarily mark intermediate measuring points on the ground—use scratch marks or concrete nails on paved surfaces.
- If a range pole is first set behind the far station, the rear surveyor can keep the tape properly aligned by sighting at the range pole and directing the forward surveyor on line.
- Book the results as shown in Figure D.3, and then repeat the process until all five sides have been measured and booked. When booked erroneous measurements are to be discarded, strike out (use a straightedge)—don't erase.
- If the temperature is something other than standard, correct the mean distance for temperature. Use C_T; that is, $C_T = 0.00000645(T - 68)L_{ft}$ or $C_T = 0.0000116(T - 20)L_m$.

Reference   Chapter 3 and Appendix F.

D.5   Project 4: Differential Leveling

Description   Use the techniques of differential leveling to determine the elevations of temporary benchmark (TBM) 33 and of the intermediate stations identified by the instructor (if any). See Figure D.4 for sample field notes.

Equipment   Survey level, rod, and rod level (if available).

Purpose   To give you experience in the use of levels and rods and in properly recording all measurements in the field book.

Procedure

- Start at the closest municipal or college benchmark (BM) (description given by the instructor), and take a backsight (BS) reading in order to establish a height of instrument (HI).
- Insert the description of the BM (and all subsequent TPs), in detail, under Description in the field notes.
- Establish a turning point (TP 1) generally in the direction of the defined terminal point (TBM 33) by taking a foresight (FS) on TP 1.
- When you have calculated the elevation of TP 1, move the level to a convenient location, and set it up again. Take a BS reading on TP 1, and calculate the new HI.
- The rod readings taken on any required intermediate points (on the way to or from the terminal point) are booked in the Intermediate Sight (IS) column—unless some of those intermediate points are also being used as turning points (TPs) (e.g., see TP 4 in Figure D.4).

No. PROJECT #4 .... No. ....

.... DIFFERENTIAL LEVELING .... Date .. MARCH 1, 2009 .... Page .... 11 ....

STA	BS	HI	IS	FS	ELEV	DESCRIPTION
						BROWN-INST.
						SMITH-ROD
						TEMP.=65°F
BM 21	0.54	182.31			181.77	BM. BRONZE PLATE ON E. WALL OF S.E.
						STAIRWELL OF PHASE 1 BLDG., ABOUT
						1 m ABOVE THE GROUND.
TP 1	0.95	175.04		8.22	174.09	N. LUG ON TOP FLANGE OF HYD.@
						E/SIDE OF BUS SHELTER
TP 2	0.80	168.76		7.08	167.96	SPIKE IN S/SIDE OF HP @ 237 FINCH
						AVE.
TP 3	0.55	160.20		9.11	159.65	SPIKE IN S/SIDE OF HP @ 245 FINCH
						AVE.
111			4.22			TRAVERSE STATION I.B.
112			4.71			TRAVERSE STATION I.B.
113			2.03			TRAVERSE STATION I.B.
114			1.22			TRAVERSE STATION I.B.
TP 4	3.77	163.45		0.52	159.68	TOP OF I.B. @ STA. 115
TBM 33				1.18	162.27	BRASS CAP ON CONC. MON.-CONTROL
						STATION 1102
TBM 33	1.23	163.50			162.27	
TP 4	2.71	162.39		3.82	159.68	
TP 3	8.88	168.53		2.74	159.65	
TP 5	11.86	177.38		3.01	165.52	TOP OF N.E. CORNER OF CONCRETE
						STEP @ 233 FINCH AVE.
TP 1	10.61	184.72		3.27	174.11	
BM 21				2.94	181.78	(e=+0.01)
ΣBS = 41.90			ΣFS = 41.89			
	ΣBS,	41.90	- ΣFS,	41.89 =	0.01	181.77 + .01 = 181.78, CHECK

FIGURE D.4 Sample field notes for Project 4 (differential leveling).

- If you can't see the terminal point (TBM 33) from the new instrument location, establish additional TPs (TP 2, TP 3, etc.), repeating the above procedures until you can take a reading on the terminal point.
- After you have taken a reading (FS) on the terminal point (TBM 33) and calculated its elevation, move the level slightly, and set it up again. Now, take a BS on the terminal point (TBM 33), and prepare to close the level loop back to the starting BM.
- Repeat the leveling procedure until you have surveyed back to the original BM. If you use the original TPs on the way back, book them by their original numbers—you do not have to describe them again. If you use new TPs on the way back, describe each TP in detail under Description, and assign it a new number.

- If the final elevation of the starting BM differs by more than 0.04 ft or 0.013 m from the starting elevation (after the calculations have been checked for mistakes by performing an "arithmetic check"—also known as a page check), repeat the project. Your instructor may give you a different closure allowance, depending on the distance leveled and/or the type of terrain surveyed.

Notes

- Keep BS and FS distances from the instrument roughly equal.
- Wave the rod (or use a rod level) to ensure a vertical reading (Figure 2.13).
- Eliminate parallax for each reading.
- Use only solid (steel, concrete, or wood) and well-defined features for TPs. If you cannot precisely describe a TP precisely, do not use it!
- Perform an arithmetic check on the notes before assessing closure accuracy.

Reference   Chapter 2.

D.6   Project 5: Traverse Angle Measurements and Closure Computations

Description   Measure the angles of a five-sided field traverse using techniques consistent with the desired precision ratio of 1/5,000 (see also Project 3).

Equipment   Theodolite or total station and a target device (range pole or plumb bob string target, or prism).

Purpose   To introduce you to the techniques of setting a theodolite or total station over a closed traverse point, turning and "doubling" interior angles and checking your work by calculating the geometric angular closure. Then, compute (using latitudes and departures) a traverse closure to determine the precision ratio of your field work.

Procedure   If you are using a total station with a traverse closure program, use that program to check your calculator computations. For traverse computation purposes, assume a direction for one of the traverse courses, or use one supplied by your instructor. See Figure D.5 for sample field notes.

- Using the same traverse stations as were used for Project 3, measure each of the five angles (direct and double).
- Read all angles from left to right. Begin the first (of two) angles at 0°00′00″ (direct), and begin the second angle (double) with the value of the first angle reading.
- Transit the telescope between the direct and double readings.
- Divide the double angle by two to obtain the mean angle. If the mean angle differs by more than 30″ (or other value as given by your instructor) from the direct angle, repeat the procedure.

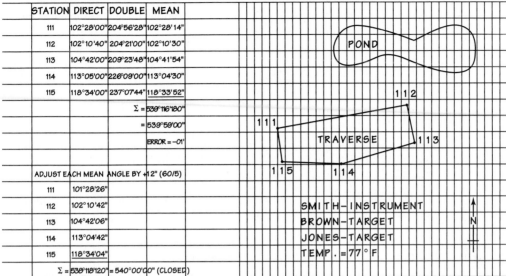

STATION	DIRECT	DOUBLE	MEAN
111	102°28'00"	204°56'28"	102°28'14"
112	102°10'40"	204°21'00"	102°10'30"
113	104°42'00"	209°23'48"	104°41'54"
114	113°05'00"	226°09'00"	113°04'30"
115	118°34'00"	237°07'44"	118°33'52"
		Σ =	539°116'180"
		=	539°59'00"
		ERROR =	−01'
ADJUST EACH MEAN ANGLE BY +12" (60/5)			
111	101°28'26"		
112	102°10'42"		
113	104°42'06"		
114	113°04'42"		
115	118°34'04"		
Σ = 538°118'120" = 540°00'00" (CLOSED)			

FIGURE D.5 Sample field notes for Project 5 (traverse angles).

- When all the mean angles have been booked, add the angles to determine the geometric angular closure.
- If the geometric closure exceeds $01'$ $(30'' \sqrt{N})$, find the error.
- Combine the results from Projects 3 and 5 to determine the precision closure of the field traverse (1/5,000 or better is acceptable), using an assumed direction for one of the sides (see above).

D.7   Project 6: Topographic Survey

Topographic field surveys can be accomplished in several ways, for example you can use:

- Cross sections and tie-ins with a manual plot of the tie-ins, cross sections, and contours.
- Theodolite/electronic distance measurement (EDM) with a manual plot of the tie-ins and contours.
- Total station with a computer-generated plot on a digital plotter.

Purpose   Each type of topographic survey shown in this section is designed to give you experience in collecting field data (location details and elevations) using a variety of specified surveying equipment and surveying procedures. The objectives of these different approaches to topographic surveying is the same—that is, the production of a scaled map or plan showing all relevant details and height information (contours and spot elevations) of the area surveyed. Time and schedule constraints normally limit most programs to include just one or two of these approaches.

D.7.1   Cross Sections and Tie-Ins Topographic Survey

Description   Using the techniques of right-angled tie-ins and cross sections (both referenced to a baseline), locate the positions and elevations of selected features on the designated area of the campus. See Figures D.6–D.8.

Equipment   Nylon-clad steel tape or fiberglass tape and two plumb bobs. A right-angle prism is optional.

Procedure

- Establish your own baseline using wood stakes or pavement nails, or, for example, use a curb line, as is shown in Figure D.6, as the survey baseline (use keel or other nonpermanent markers to mark baseline).
- 0 + 00 is the point of intersection of your baseline with some other line or point, as defined by your instructor.

FIGURE D.6   Sample field notes for Project 6 (topography tie-ins).

No. PROJECT #6 ....
Date MAY 17, 2009 .... Page ....

No. TOPOGRAPHY/CROSS SECTIONS ....
FINCH AVE. E. TO 3+00N. .... Page ... 23 ...

STA.	B.S.	H.I.	I.S.	F.S.	ELEV.	DESCRIPTION
BM#3	8.21	318.34			310.13	S. W. CORNER OF CONC. VALVE CHAMBER
						@ 0+53.1
0+00			3.34		315.00	₵, ON ASPH.
			0.03		318.31	75.0' LT, ON ASPH.
			7.35		310.99	50.0' RT, ON ASPH.
0+50			6.95		311.39	₵, ON ASPH.
			7.00		311.34	25' LT, BOT. CURB
			0.3		318.0	38.5' LT, @ FENCE, ON GRASS
			7.5		310.8	6' RT, ₵ OF ISLAND, ON GRASS
			8.32		310.02	12' RT, BOT. CURB
			8.41		309.93	37.0' RT, BOT. CURB
			8.91		309.43	37.0' RT, TOP OF CONC. WALK
			9.01		309.33	42.0' RT, TOP OF CONC. WALK
			9.3		309.0	46.9' RT, TOP OF HILL, ON GRASS
			11.7		306.6	56.6' RT, @ BUILDING WALL, ON GRASS

FIGURE D.7 Sample field notes for Project 6 (topography cross sections).

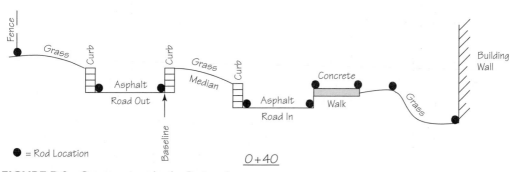

● = Rod Location

FIGURE D.8 Cross section plot for Project 6.

- Measure the baseline stations (e.g., 50 ft or 20 m) precisely with a nylon-clad steel tape, and mark them clearly on the ground (e.g., keel marker, nails, or wood stakes).
- Determine the baseline stations of all features left and right of the baseline by estimating 90° (swung-arm technique) or by using a right-angled prism.
- When you have booked the baseline stations of all the features in a 50/100-ft or 20/30-m interval (the steel tape can be left lying on the ground on the baseline), determine and book the offset (o/s) distances left and right of the baseline to each feature using a fiberglass tape. Tie in all detail to the closest 0.10 ft or 0.03 m. A fiberglass tape can be used for these measurements.

- Do not begin the measurements until the sketches have been made for the survey area.
- Elevations are determined using a level and a rod. The level is set up in a convenient location where a BM and a considerable number of ISs can be "seen." See Figure D.7.
- Hold the rod on the baseline at each station and at all points (left and right of the baseline) where the ground slope changes (e.g., top/bottom of curb, edge of walk, top of slope, bottom of slope, limit of survey). See the typical cross section shown in Figure D.8.
- When all the data (that can be seen) have been taken at a station, the rod holder then moves to the next (50-ft or 20-m) station and repeats the process.
- When the rod can no longer be seen, the instrument operator calls for the establishment of a TP, and, after taking a foresight to the new TP, the instrument is moved closer to the next stage of work and a backsight is then be taken to the new TP before continuing with the cross sections. In addition to cross sections at the even station intervals (e.g., 50 ft., 20 m), it will be necessary to take full or partial sections between the even stations if the lay of the land changes significantly.

D.7.2   Theodolite/EDM Topographic Survey

Description   Using EDM instruments and optical or electronic theodolites, locate the positions and elevations of all topographic detail and a sufficient number of additional elevations to enable a representative contour drawing of the selected areas. See sample field notes in Figure D.9.

Equipment   Theodolite, EDM, and one or more pole-mounted reflecting prisms.

Procedure

- Set the theodolite at a control station (northing, easting, and elevation known), and backsight on another known control station.
- Set an appropriate reference angle (or azimuth) on the horizontal circle (e.g., $0°00'00''$ or some assigned azimuth).
- Set the height of the reflecting prisms (hr) on the pole equal to the height of the optical center of the theodolite/EDM (hi). If the EDM is not coaxial with the theodolite, set the height of the target (target/prism assembly), on the pole, equal to the optical center of the instrument (see the left illustration in Figure 2.28). Take all vertical angles to the prism target, or to the center of the prism if the EDM is coaxial with the theodolite.
- Prepare a sketch of the area to be surveyed.
- Begin taking readings on the appropriate points, entering the data in the field notes (Figure D.9) and entering the shot number in the appropriate spot on the accompanying field-note sketch. Keep shot numbers sequential, perhaps beginning with 1,000. Work is expedited if two prisms are employed. While one prism-holder is walking to the next shot location, the instrument operator can be taking a reading on the other prism-holder.

No. PROJECT #6
Date MAY 18, 2009   Page _____

No. TOPOGRAPHY/EDM
FRONT CAMPUS   Page 27

STA	HCR	H.DIST.	V. DIST.		ELEV.
	⊼ @ C.M. #112,	hi = 5.61	= hr		247.63
111	000'00"				
1000	6408'20"	58.2	−7.1		240.5
1001	6130'40"	77.5	−7.1		240.5
1002	7149'20"	94.9	−7.2		240.4
1003	9015'30"	95.7	−7.0		240.6
1004	10133'50"	82.3	−7.0		240.6
1005	12751'50"	86.3	−7.1		240.5
1006	14220'20"	87.7	−7.2		240.4
1007	15441'30"	72.7	−7.0		240.6
1008	14126'20"	55.3	−7.0		240.6
1009	12401'10"	53.1	−6.9		240.7
1010	10336'50"	50.6	−7.1		240.5
1011	8110'50"	53.8	−7.1		240.5
1012	5049'20"	47.6	−7.6		240.0
1013	12703'40"	24.0	−8.3		239.3
1014	16152'30"	40.6	−9.1		238.5
1015	21807'30"	50.7	+3.2		250.8

BROWN – ⊼
SMITH – PRISM
TEMP. = 73F

FIGURE D.9 Sample field notes for Project 6 (topography by theodolite/EDM).

- When all field shots (horizontal and vertical angles and horizontal distances) have been taken, sight the reference backsight control station again to verify the angle setting; also, verify that the height of the prism is unchanged.
- Reduce the field notes to determine station elevations and course distances, if required.
- Plot the topographic features and elevations at 1″ = 40′ or 1:500 metric (or at other scales as given by your instructor).
- Draw contours over the surveyed areas. See Chapter 8.

D.7.3 Total Station Topographic Survey

Description Using a total station and one or more pole-mounted reflecting prisms, tie in all topographic features and any additional ground shots (including break lines) that are required to accurately define the terrain. See Section 8.4 and Figure D.10.

Equipment Total station and one, or more, pole-mounted reflecting prisms.

STA	HCR				ELEV.
	⊼ @ C. M. #112, hi = 5.66 = hr				247.63
111	000'00"				
	⊼ – SET 4C #3172613				

FIGURE D.10 Sample field notes for Project 6 (topography by total station).

Procedure

- Set the total station over a known control point (northing, easting, and elevation known*). Turn on the instrument, and index the circles if necessary (by transiting the telescope and revolving the instrument 360°). Some newer total stations do not require this initializing operation.
- Set the program menu to the type of survey (topography) being performed and to the required instrument settings. Select the type of field data to be stored (e.g., N, E, and Z, or E, N, and Z, etc.). Set the temperature and pressure settings—if required.
- Check configuration settings, for example, tilt correction, coordinate format, zenith vertical angle, angle resolution (e.g., 5"), $c + r$ correction (e.g., no.), units (ft/m, degree, mm Hg), and auto power off (say, 20').
- Identify the instrument station from the menu. Insert the date, station number coordinates, elevation, and hi. Alternately, it may have been possible to upload all control

---

*The station can be set in any convenient location with its position determined using the onboard resection program and after sighting the required number of visible control stations.

station data prior to going out to the field. In that case, just scan through the data, and select the appropriate instrument station and backsight station(s). Enter the height of instrument (hi), and store or record all the data.

- Backsight to one or more known control point(s) (point number, north and east coordinates, and elevation known). Set the horizontal circle to 0°00′00″ or to some assigned reference azimuth for the backsight reference direction. Store or record the data. Measure and store the reflector height.

- Set the initial topography point number in the instrument (e.g., 1,000), and set for automatic point number incrementation.

- Begin taking ISs. Provide an attribute code (consistent with the software code library) for each reading. Some software programs enable attribute codes to automatically provide for feature graphics stringing (e.g., curb1, edge of water1, fence3), whereas other software programs require the surveyor to prefix the code with a character (e.g., Z), which turns on the stringing command. See Section 5.5 and Figures 5.17 and 5.18. Most total stations have an automatic mode for topographic surveys, where one button-push will measure and store all the point data as well as the code and attribute data. The code and attribute data of the previous point are usually presented to the surveyor as a default setting. If the code and attribute

Table D.2 TYPICAL CODE LIBRARY

Control		Utilities	
TCM	Temporary control monument	HP	Hydro pole
CM	Concrete monument	LP	Lamp pole
SIB	Standard iron bar	BP	Telephone pole
IB	Iron bar	GS	Gas valve
RIB	Round iron bar	WV	Water valve
NL	Nail	CABLE	Cable
STA	Station		
TBM	Temporary benchmark		

Municipal		Topographic	
℄	Centerline	GND	Ground
RD	Road	TB	Top of bank
EA	Edge of asphalt	BB	Bottom of bank
BC	Beginning of curve	DIT	Ditch
EC	End of curve	FL	Fence line
PC	Point on curve	POST	Post
CURB	Curb	GATE	Gate
CB	Catch basin	BUSH	Bush
DCB	Double catch basin	HEDGE	Hedge
MH	Manhole	BLD	Building
STM	Storm sewer manhole	RWALL	Retaining wall
SAN	Sanitary sewer manhole	POND	Pond
INV	Invert	STEP	Steps
SW	Sidewalk	CTREE	Coniferous tree
HYD	Hydrant	DTREE	Deciduous tree
RR	Railroad		

data are the same for a series of readings, the surveyor only has to press Enter and not enter all that identical data repeatedly as the last entered data will be displayed as a default entry until changed.

- Put all, or some, selected point numbers on the field sketch. This will be of assistance later in the editing process if mistakes have occurred in the numbering or with the coding.
- When all required points have been surveyed, check back into the control station originally back-sighted to ensure that the instrument orientation is still valid.
- Transfer the field data to a computer into a properly labeled file.
- After opening the data-processing program, import the field data file, and begin the editing process and the graphics generation process (this is automatic for many programs).
- Create the triangulated irregular network (TIN) and contours.
- Either finish the drawing with the working program or create a DXF file for transfer to a CAD program, and then finish the drawing.
- Prepare a plot file, and then plot the data (to a scale assigned by your instructor) on the lab digital plotter.

D.8 Project 7: Building Layout

Description Lay out the corners of a building and reference the corners with batter boards. See Figure D.11.

Equipment Theodolite, steel tape, plumb bobs, wood stakes, light lumber for batter boards, "C" clamps, keel or felt pen, level, and rod. (A theodolite/EDM and prism could replace the theodolite and steel tape.)

Purpose To give you experience in laying out the corners of a building according to dimensions taken from a building site plan, in constructing batter boards, and referencing both the line and grade of the building walls and floor.

Procedure

- After the front and side lines have been defined by your instructor and after the building dimensions have been given, set stakes X and Y on the front property line, as shown in Figure D.11.
- Set up the theodolite at X, sight on Y, turn 90° (double), and place stakes at A and B.
- Set up the theodolite at Y, sight on X, turn 90° (double), and place stakes at C and D.
- Measure the building diagonals to check the accuracy of the layout; adjust and re-measure if necessary.
- After the building corners have been set, offset the batter boards a safe distance (e.g., 6 ft or 2 m), and set the batter boards at the first-floor elevation, as given by your instructor.

FIGURE D.11 Sample field notes for Project 7 (building layout) (re-position the nail symbols to line up with the building walls).

- After the batter boards have been set, place line nails on the top of the batter boards as fellows.
  (a) Set up on A, sight B, place nail 2, transit the telescope, and set nail 1.
  (b) From setup on A, sight C, place nail 5, transit the telescope, and place nail 6.
  (c) Set up on D and place nails 3, 4, 7, and 8 in a similar fashion.

D.9 Project 8: Horizontal Curve

Description   Given the centerline alignment of two intersecting tangents (including a station reference stake), calculate and lay out a horizontal curve.

Equipment   Theodolite, steel tape, plumb bobs, wood stakes, and range pole or string target. (A theodolite/EDM and prism could replace the theodolite and steel tape.)

Purpose   To give you experience in laying out a circular curve at specified station intervals after first calculating all the necessary layout measurements from the given radius and the measured location of the PI and the Δ field angle.

Procedure

- Intersect the two tangents to create the PI.
- Measure the station of the PI.
- Measure (and double) the tangent deflection angle (Δ).
- After receiving the radius value from your instructor, compute T and L, and then compute the station of the BC and EC. See Section 11.4.
- Compute the deflections for even stations—at 50-ft or 20-m intervals. See Section 11.4. Compute the equivalent chords. See Section 11.5.
- Set the BC and EC, in the field, by measuring out T from the PI along each tangent.
- From the BC, sight the PI, and turn the curve deflection angle ($\Delta/2$) to check the location of the EC. If the line of sight does not fall on the EC, check the calculations and measurements for the BC and EC locations, and make any necessary adjustments.
- Using the calculated deflection angles and appropriate chord lengths, stake out the curve.
- Measure from the last even station stake to the EC to verify the accuracy of the layout.
- Walk the curve, looking for any anomalies (e.g., two stations staked at the same deflection angle). The symmetry of the curve is such that even minor mistakes are obvious in a visual check.

Reference Chapter 11.

D.10 Project 9: Pipeline Layout

Description Establish an offset line and construct batter boards for line and grade control of a proposed storm sewer from MH 1 to MH 2. Stakes marking those points will be given for each crew in the field.

Equipment Theodolite, steel tape, wood stakes, and light lumber and "C" clamps for the batter boards. (A theodolite/EDM, or total station, and prism could replace the theodolite and steel tape.)

Purpose To give you experience in laying out offset line and grade stakes for a proposed pipeline. You will learn how to compute a grade sheet and construct batter boards and how to visually check the accuracy of your work by sighting across the constructed batter boards.

Procedure

- Set up at the MH 2 stake, and sight the MH 1 stake.
- Turn off 90°, measure the offset distance (e.g., 10 ft or 3 m), and establish MH 2 on offset.
- Set up at the MH 1 stake, sight the MH 2 stake, and establish MH 1 on offset. Refer to Figure 14.7 for guidance.

- Give the MH 1 offset stake a station of 0 + 00. While set up on the MH 1 o/s stake, sight the MH 2 o/s stake and then measure out to establish grade stakes at the even stations (50 ft or 20 m); finally, check the distance from the last even station to the MH 2 stake to verify that the overall distance is accurate.
- Using the closest BM, determine the elevations of the tops of the offset grade stakes. Close back to the BM within the tolerance given by your instructor.
- Assume that the invert of MH 1 is 7.97 ft or 2.430 m below the top of the MH 1 grade stake (or other assumed value given by your instructor).
- Compute the invert elevations at each even station, and then complete a grade sheet similar to those shown in Table 14.2 and Figure 14.7. Select a convenient height for the grade rod.
- Using the stake-to-batter board distances in the grade sheet, use the supplied light lumber and "C" clamps to construct batter boards similar to those shown in Figure 14.6. Use a small carpenters' level to keep the cross pieces horizontal. Check to see that all cross pieces line up in one visual line—a perfect visual check (all batter-boards line up behind one another) is a check on all the measurements and calculations.

Reference   Chapter 14.

Appendix E

Answers to Selected Problems

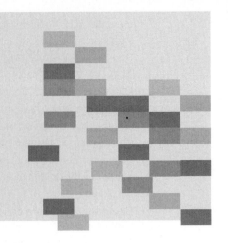

CHAPTER 2

2.1(a). $c + r = 0.0206 \times (800/1,000)^2 = 0.013$ ft
2.1(c). $c + r = 0.0675 \times (700/1,000)^2 = 0.033$ m
2.1(e). $c + r = 0.0675 \times 2.5^2 = 0.422$ m
2.2(a). i 2.05 **2.2(b).** i 1.165 **2.2(c).** i 2.05 **2.2(d).** i 1.085 **2.2(e).** i 3.10 **2.2(f).** i 1.165

2.4.

Station	BS	HI	FS	Elevation
BM 50	1.27	183.95		182.68
TP 1	2.33	181.37	4.91	197.04
TP 2			6.17	175.20
	Σ BS = 3.60		Σ FS = 11.08	182.68 + 3.60 − 11.08 = 175.20

2.8.

Station	BS	HI	FS	Elevation
BM 100	2.71	144.15		141.44
TP 1	3.62	142.89	4.88	139.27
TP 2	3.51	142.43	3.97	138.92
TP 3	3.17	142.79	2.81	139.62
TP 4	1.47	142.64	1.62	141.17
BM 100			1.21	141.43
	Σ BS = 14.48		Σ FS = 14.49	141.44 + 14.48 − 14.49 = 141.43

2.9. Error = 141.44 − 141.43 = 0.01 ft, second order allowable error $= 0.035\sqrt{1,000/5,280} =$ 0.015. Therefore the results qualify for second order—according to Table 2.2.

2.16(b).

Station	Cumulative	Elevation	Correction	Adjusted	Distance	Elevation
BM 130		168.657				168.657
TP 1	130	168.248			130/780 × 0.011 = +0.002	168.250
TP 2	260	168.539			260/780 × 0.011 = +0.004	168.543
TP 3	390	166.318			390/780 × 0.011 = +0.006	165.324
BM K110	520	166.394			520/780 × 0.011 = +0.007	**166.401**
TP 4	650	166.579			650/780 × 0.011 = +0.009	166.588
BM 132	780	167.618			780/780 × 0.011 = +0.011	167.629

$C = 167.629 - 167.618 = -0.011$
The adjusted elevation of BM K110 is 166.401 m

CHAPTER 3

3.4(a). $18.61 \times 66 = 1,228.26$ ft $\times 0.3048 = 374.37$ m
3.4(b). $80.011 \times 66 = 5,280.66$ ft $\times 0.3048 = 1,609.55$ m
3.8. $H = 17.277 \cos 1°42' = 17.269$ m
3.10. tan slope angle $= 0.02$; slope angle $= 1.1457628°$
$H = 133.860 \cos 1.1457628° = 133.833$ m
3.13. Inst. @ A, $H = 1,458.777 \cos 2°40'40'' = 1,457.184$ m
Elevation difference $= 1,458.777 \sin 1°26'50'' = -68.153$ m
Inst. @ B, $H = 1,458.757 \cos 2°40'00'' = 1,457.177$ m
Elevation difference $= 1,458.757 \sin 2°40'' = 67.869$ m
a) Horizontal distance $= (1,457.184 + 1,457.177)/2 = 1,457.181$ m
b) Elev. B $= 211.841 - (68.153 + 67.869)/2 = 143.833$ m

CHAPTER 6

6.1. E $= 114°31'$
6.3(a). S 7°29' W   **6.3(d).** N 56°09' E
6.4(a). 347°09'   **6.4(d).** 183°12'
6.7. AB $=$ N 21°21' E
      B $+1°03'$
      BC $=$ N 22°24' E
      C $+2°58'$
      CD $=$ N 25°22' E
      D $-7°24'$
      DE $=$ N 17°58' E
      E $-6°31'$
      EF $=$ N 11°27' E
      F $+1°31'$
      FG $=$ N 12°58' E
      G $-8°09'$
      GH $=$ N 4°49' E

6.12 (a). A 51°23'
      B 105°39'
      C 78°11'
      D 124°47'
      358°120'
      360°00'

6.12(b). Azimuth   **Bearing**
Az AB $= 67°17'$ N 67°17' E
Az BA $= 247°17'$
      $-$B 105°39'
Az BC $= 141°38'$ S 38°22' E
Az CB $= 321°38'$
      $-$C 78°11'
Az CD $= 243°27'$ S 63°27' W

Check	Az DC = 423°27′			
$(n - 2)180 =$	−D <u>124°47′</u>			
$(4 - 2)180 = 360°$	Az DA = 298°40′	N 61°20′ W		
	Az AD = 118°40′			
	<u>−A 51°23′</u>			
	Az AB = 67°17′	N 67°17′ E **Check**		

6.12(b).

Course	Azimuth	Bearing	Distance	Latitude	Departure
AB	67°17′	N 67°17′ E	713.93	275.70	658.55
BC	141°38′	S 38°22′ E	606.06	−475.18	376.18
CD	243°27′	S 63°27″ W	391.27	−174.89	−350.01
DA	298°40′	N 61°20′ W	<u>781.18</u>	374.74	<u>−685.43</u>
			$P = 2{,}492.44$	$\Sigma_{\mathrm{L}} = +0.37$	$\Sigma_{\mathrm{D}} = -0.71$

Error, $E = \sqrt{0.37^2 + 0.71^2} = 0.80$, Precision $= E/P = 0.80/2{,}492.44 = 1/3{,}113 = 1/3{,}100$

6.13.

Course	C_{lat}	C_{dep}	Corrected lat	Corrected dep
AB	−0.10	+0.21	+275.60	+658.76
BC	−0.10	+0.17	−475.28	+376.35
CD	−0.06	+0.11	−174.95	−349.90
DA	<u>−0.11</u>	<u>+0.22</u>	<u>+374.63</u>	<u>−685.21</u>
	−0.37	+0.71	0.00	0.00

Course	Corrected Bearing	Corrected Azimuth	Corrected Distance (ft)
AB	N 67°17′51″ E	67°17′51″	714.09
BC	S 38°22′26″ E	141°37′34″	606.24
CD	S 63°26′06″ W	245°26′06″	391.20
DA	N 61°19′59″ W	298°40′01″	<u>780.94</u>
			$P = 2{,}492.47$

6.14.

Station	Coordinates	
	North	East
A	1,000.00	1,000.00
	+275.60	+658.76
B	1,275.60	1,658.76
	−475.28	+376.35
C	800.32	2,035.11
	−174.95	−349.90
D	625.37	1,685.21
	<u>+374.63</u>	<u>−685.21</u>
A	1,000.00	1,000.00

6.15.

$X_A(Y_D - Y_B) = 1{,}000.00(625.37 - 1{,}275.60) = \quad -650{,}230$
$X_B(Y_A - Y_C) = 1{,}658.76(1{,}000.00 - 800.32) = \quad +331{,}221$
$X_C(Y_B - Y_D) = 2{,}035.11(1{,}275.60 - 625.37) = +1{,}323{,}290$
$X_D(Y_C - Y_A) = 1{,}685.21(800.32 - 1{,}000.00) = \quad \underline{-336{,}503}$

$$\text{Double Area, } 2A = \quad 667{,}778 \text{ sq. ft}$$

Area $= 333{,}889$ sq. ft
Also, Area $= 333{,}887/43{,}560 = 7.665$ ac

CHAPTER 8

8.9(a). $H = \text{SR.f} = 20{,}000 \times 0.153 = 3{,}060$ m
Altitude $= 3{,}060 + 180 = 3{,}240$ m
8.9(b). $\text{SR} = 20{,}000 \times 12 = 240{,}000$
$H = \text{SR.f} = 240{,}000 \times 6.022/12 = 120{,}440$ ft
Altitude $= 120{,}400 + 520 = 120{,}920$ ft
8.10(a). Photo scale $= 50{,}000 \times 4.75/23.07 = 1{:}10{,}295$
8.10(b). Photo scale $= 100{,}000 \times 1.85/6.20 = 1{:}29{,}839$

CHAPTER 9

9.1. Grid bearing AB $=$ S $74°29'00.4''$ W, AB $= 290.722$ m
9.2. B $= 186°21'09.1''$
9.4. Geodetic bearing of AB $=$ S $74°35'17.9''$ W
9.5. B $= 186°21'01.3''$

CHAPTER 11

11.2. $T = 44.85$ ft, $L = 89.58$ ft   **11.6.** BC at $3 + 299.407$ m, EC at $3 + 366.340$ m

BC	3 + 299.407	0°00′00″
	3 + 320	1°57′59″
	3 + 340	3°52′35″
	3 + 360	5°47′11″
EC	3 + 366.340	6°23′31″ ≈ 6°23′30″

11.12. A to BC $= 565.07$ ft, B to EC $= 408.89$ ft
11.13. $R = 29.958$ m
11.14. $T_1 = 228.74$ ft, $T_2 = 270.02$ ft
11.16. Summit @ $20 + 07.14$, elev. $= 722.06$ ft

11.17.

BVC	0 + 180	151.263
	0 + 200	151.841
	0 + 250	153.091
	0 + 300	154.063
	0 + 350	154.757
PVI	0 + 360	154.863
	0 + 400	155.174
High Pt.	0 + 450	155.313
	0 + 500	155.134
EVC	0 + 540	154.863

11.18. T.S. $= 9 + 85.68$, S.C. $= 11 + 35.68$,
C.S. $= 11 + 94.85$, S.T. $= 13 + 44.85$

CHAPTER 13

13.1. At 4 + 00, cut 1.23 ft or $1'2\frac{3}{4}''$

13.2. At 0 + 60, "on grade"

13.4. At 4 + 50, CL elev. = 508.20 ft

13.5. At 4 + 50, curb elev. = 508.46 ft

13.6. At 4 + 50, "on grade"

13.7(a). L = 54.98 ft

13.7(b). Slope at 1.11% **13.7(c).** and **13.7(d).**

Station	Curb Elev.	Stake Elev.	Cut	Fill
A	505.02	504.71		$0'3\frac{3}{4}''$
B	505.22	506.22	$1'0''$	
C	505.44	506.37	$0'11\frac{1}{8}''$	
D	505.63	506.71	$1'1''$	

CHAPTER 14

14.1. At 1 + 50, cut 7.91 ft; for grade rod of 13 ft, stake to batter board distance of $5'1\frac{1}{8}''$

14.2. At 0 + 80, cut 2.358 m; for a grade rod of 3 m, stake to batter board distance of 0.642 m

14.3. At 1 + 00, 495.60

14.4. At 1 + 00, cut 8.01 ft

14.5. GR = 14 ft; at 1 + 00, $5'11\frac{7}{8}''$

14.7. First leg, 0 + 40 = 183.740 m

14.8. First leg, 0 + 40, cut 3.093 m

14.9. First leg, GR = 5 m; at 0 + 40, Stake-to BB = 1.907

14.10. At lot 13, sewer invert opposite 13 = 496.85 + (32 × 0.01) = 497.17

spring-line elevation = 497.17 + (1.25/2) = 497.80

60 ft of sewer connection pipe @ 2% = +1.20

minimum invert elevation of connection = 499.00

CHAPTER 17

17.1. Trapezoidal technique, 289 sq. yd; Simpson's one-third rule, 290 sq. yd

17.2. A = 334 sq. yd

17.3. V = 401 m^3

17.4. V = 60.7 cu. yd

17.5. V = 2,639 cu. yd

17.6. V = 88.6 cu. yd

APPENDIX F

F.1. $C_S = -w^2L^3/24p^2 = -0.32^2 \times 48.888^3/24 \times 100^2 = -0.050$ m

Corrected distance = 48.888 − 0.050 = 48.838 m

F.3. $C_S = -w^2L^3/24p^2 = -0.01.8^2 \times 100^3/24 \times 24^2 = -0.023$ ft × 4 = −0.0937 ft

$C_S = -0.01.8^2 \times 71.16^3/24 \times 24^2 = -0.008$. $\Sigma C_S = 0.008 + 0.094 = -0.10$

Corrected distance = 471.16 − 0.10 = 471.06 ft

APPENDIX G

G.1.

Station	Rod Interval	Vertical Angle	Horizontal Distance	Elevation Difference	Elevation
					371.21
1	3.48	+0°58′	347.9	+ 5.9	371.1
2	0.38	−3°38′	37.8	−2.4	368.8

G.2.

Station	Rod Interval	Vertical Angle	Horizontal Distance	Elevation Difference	Elevation
					[hi = 1.83 207.96]
1	0.041	+2°19′	4.09	+0.17	208.13
2	0.072	+1°57′ on 1.43	7.19	V = +0.24	208.60
3	0.555	0°00′ on 2.71	55.5	V = 0	207.08

G.3.(a). $V = 100 \times 1.31 \times \cos 3°12' \sin 3°12' = 7.30$ ft
Elevation K + hi (5.36) + V (7.30) − RR (4.27) = Elevation L (293.44)
Elevation K = 285.05 ft
G.3.(b). $H = 100 \times 1.31 \times \cos^2 3°12' = 130.59$ ft

G.5.

Station	Rod Interval	Horizontal Angle	Vertical Angle	Horizontal Distance	Elevation Difference	Elevation
	[Theodolite @ K, hi = 1.82]					167.78
L		0°00′				
0 + 00 ℄	0.899	34°15′	−19°08′	80.24	−27.84	139.94
S Ditch	0.851	33°31′	−21°58′	73.19	−29.52	138.26
N Ditch	0.950	37°08′	−20°42	83.13	−31.41	136.37

Appendix F
Steel Tape Corrections

F.1 Erroneous Tape-Length Corrections

For all but precise work, new tapes as supplied by the manufacturer are considered to be correct under standard conditions. However, as a result of extensive use, tapes do become kinked, stretched, and repaired—perhaps imprecisely. The length can become something other than that specified. When this occurs, the tape must be corrected, or the measurements taken with the erroneous tape must be corrected.

■ EXAMPLE F.1

A measurement is recorded as 171.278 m with a 30-m tape that is found to be only 29.996 m under standard conditions. What is the corrected measurement?

Solution

$$\text{Correction per tape length} = -0.004$$
$$\text{Number of tape lengths} = \frac{171.278}{30}$$
$$\text{Total correction} = -0.004 \times \frac{171.278}{30}$$
$$\text{Total correction} = -0.023 \text{ m}$$
$$\text{Corrected distance} = 171.278 - 0.023$$
$$= 171.255 \text{ m}$$

or

$$\text{Corrected distance} = \frac{29.996}{30} \times 171.278 = 171.255$$

■ **EXAMPLE F.2**

It is required to lay out the front corners of a building, a distance of 210.08 ft. The tape to be used is known to be 100.02 ft under standard conditions.

Solution

$$\text{Correction per tape length} = +0.02 \text{ ft}$$
$$\text{Number of tape lengths} = 2.1008$$
$$\text{Total correction} = 0.02 \times 2.1008 = +0.04 \text{ ft}$$

When the problem involves a **layout distance**, the algebraic sign of the correction must be reversed before being applied to the layout measurement. We must find the distance that, when corrected by +0.04, will give 210.08 ft:

$$\text{Layout distance} = 210.08 - 0.04 = 210.04 \text{ ft}$$

You will discover that four variations of this problem are possible: correcting a measured distance using (1) a long tape or (2) a short tape and pre-correcting a layout distance using (3) a long tape or (4) a short tape. To minimize confusion as to the sign of the correction, the student is urged to consider the problem with the distance reduced to that of only one tape length (100 ft or 30 m).

In Example F.1, a recorded distance of 171.278 m was measured with a tape only 29.996 m long. The total correction was found to be 0.023 m. If doubt exists as to the sign of 0.023, ask yourself what the procedure would be for correcting only one tape length. In this example, after one tape length has been measured, it is recorded that 30 m (the nominal length of the tape) has been measured. If the tape is only 29.996 m long, then the field book entry of 30 m must be corrected by −0.004; if the correction for one tape length is minus, then the corrections for the total distance must also be minus.

The magnitude of a tape error can be precisely determined by having the tape compared with a tape that has been certified by the National Bureau of Standards in the United States or the National Research Council in Canada.

In field practice, if a tape is found to be incorrect, it is usually either precisely repaired or discarded.

F.2 Temperature Corrections

In Section 2.7, we noted that the standard temperature for steel tapes is 68°F or 20°C. Most measurements taken with a steel tape occur at some temperature other than standard (68°F or 20°C). When the temperature is warmer or cooler than standard, the steel tape will expand or contract and thus introduce an error into the measurement. The coefficient of thermal expansion and contraction of steel is 0.00000645 per unit length per degree Fahrenheit (°F) or 0.0000116 per unit length per degree Celsius (°C).

FOOT UNIT TEMPERATURE CORRECTIONS

$$C_T = 0.00000645 \, (T - 68) \, L \tag{F.1}$$

where C_T is the correction, in feet, due to temperature

   T is the temperature (°F) of the tape during measurement

   L is the distance measured in feet

METRIC UNIT TEMPERATURE CORRECTIONS

$$C_T = 0.0000116(T - 20)L \qquad (F.2)$$

where C_T is the correction, in meters, due to temperature

   T is the temperature (°C) of the tape during measurement

   L is the distance measured in meters

■ EXAMPLE F.3

A distance is recorded as being 471.37 ft at a temperature of 38°F. What is the corrected distance?

Solution

$$C_T = 0.00000645 \, (38 - 68) \, 471.37$$
$$= -0.09 \text{ ft}$$

Corrected distance is $471.37 - 0.09 = 471.28$ ft

■ EXAMPLE F.4

It is required to lay out two points in the field that will be exactly 100.000 m apart. Field conditions indicate that the temperature of the tape will be 27°C. What distance will be laid out?

Solution

$$C_T = 0.0000116 \, (27 - 20) \, 100.000$$
$$= +0.008 \text{ m}$$

Because this is a layout (pre-correction) problem, the correction sign must be reversed (i.e., we are looking for the distance that, when corrected by $+0.008$ m, will give us 100.000 m):

$$\text{Layout distance} = 100.000 - 0.008 = 99.992 \text{ m}$$

Accuracy demands for most surveys do not require high precision in determining the temperature of the tape. Usually, it is sufficient to estimate the air temperature. However, for more precise work (say, 1;10,000 and higher), care is required in determining the actual temperature of the tape—which can be significantly different from the temperature of the air.

F.2.1   Invar Steel tapes

High-precision surveys may require the use of steel tapes that have a low coefficient of thermal expansion. The invar tape is a nickel–steel alloy that has a coefficient of thermal expansion of 0.0000002–0.00000055 per degree Fahrenheit. In the past, invar tapes were used to measure baselines for triangulation control surveys. Currently, EDM instruments measure baselines more efficiently. Invar tapes can, however, still be used to advantage in situations where high precision is required over short distances.

F.3 Tension and Sag Corrections

If a steel tape is fully supported and a tension other than standard (10 lb, foot system; 50 N, metric system) is applied, a tension (pull) error exists.

The tension correction formula is

$$C_P = \frac{(P - P_s)L}{AE}$$

(F.3)

If a tape has been standardized while fully supported and is being used without full support, an error called sag will occur (Figure F.1). The force of gravity pulls the center of the unsupported section downward in the shape of a catenary, thus creating an error B′B. The sag correction formula is

$$C_s = \frac{-w^2 L^3}{24P^2} = \frac{-W^2 L}{24P^2}$$

(F.4)

where $W^2 = w^2L^2$

$W =$ weight of tape between supports
$w =$ weight of tape per unit length
$L =$ length of the tape between supports.

Table F.1 further defines the terms in these two formulas. You can see in the table that 1 newton is the force required to accelerate a mass of 1 kg by 1 m/s².

FIGURE F.1 Example of steel tape error called sag.

Table F.1 CORRECTION FORMULA TERMS DEFINED (FOOT, METRIC, AND SI UNITS)

Unit	Description	Foot	Old Metric	Metric (SI)
C_P	Correction due to tension per tape length	ft	m	m
C_s	Correction due to sag per tape length	ft	m	m
L	Length of tape under consideration	ft	m	m
P_s	Standard tension	lb (force)	kg (force)	N (newtons)
	Typical standard tension	10 lb	4.5–5 kg	50 N
P	Applied tension	lb	kg	N
A	Cross-sectional area	sq. in.	cm²	m²
E	Average modulus of elasticity of steel tapes	29×10^6 lb/sq. in.	21×10^5 kg/cm²	20×10^{10} N/m²
E	Average modulus of elasticity in invar tapes	21×10^6 lb/sq. in.	14.8×10^5 kg/cm²	14.5×10^{10} N/m²
w	Weight of tape per unit length	lb/ft	kg/m	N/m
W	Weight of tape	lb	kg	N

$$\text{Force} = \text{mass} \times \text{acceleration}$$

$$\text{Weight} = \text{mass} \times \text{acceleration due to gravity } (g)$$

$$g = 32.2 \text{ ft/s}^2 = 9.807 \text{ m/s}^2$$

In SI units, a mass of 1 kg has a weight of $1 \times 9.807 = 9.807$ N (newtons). That is,

$$1 \text{ kg (force)} = 9.807 \text{ N}$$

Because some spring balances are graduated in kilograms and because the tape manufacturers give standard tension in newtons, surveyors must be prepared to work in both old metric and SI units.

Examples of Tension Corrections

■ EXAMPLE F.5

Given a standard tension of a 10-lb force for a 100-ft steel tape that is being used with a 20-lb force pull, if the cross-sectional area of the tape is 0.003 sq. in., what is the tension error for each tape length used?

Solution

$$C_P = \frac{(20 - 10) \; 100}{(29,000,000 \times 0.003)} = +0.011 \text{ ft}$$

If a distance of 421.22 ft has been recorded, the total correction is $4.2122 \times 0.011 = +0.05$ ft. The corrected distance is 421.27 ft.

■ EXAMPLE F.6

Given a standard tension of 50 N for a 30-m steel tape that is being used with a 100-N force, if the cross-sectional area of the tape is 0.02 cm^2, what is the tension error per tape length?

Solution

$$C_P = \frac{(100 - 50) \; 30}{(0.02 \times 21 \times 10^5 \times 9.087)} = +0.0036 \text{ m}$$

If a distance of 182.716 m has been measured under these conditions, the total correction is $182.716/30 \times 0.0036 = +0.022$ m. The corrected distance is 182.738 m.

The cross-sectional area of a tape can be calculated from micrometer readings, taken from the manufacturer's specifications, or determined from the following expression:

$$\text{Tape length} \times \text{tape area} \times \text{specific weight of tape steel} = \text{weight of tape}$$

or

$$\text{Tape area} = \frac{\text{weight of tape}}{(\text{length} \times \text{specific weight})} \qquad \text{(F.6)}$$

■ EXAMPLE F.7

A tape is weighed and found to weigh 1.95 lb. The overall length of the 100-ft steel tape (end to end) is 102 ft. The specific weight of steel is 490 lb/ft^2. What is the cross-sectional area of the tape?

Solution

$$\frac{102 \text{ ft} \times 12 \text{ in.} \times \text{area (in.}^2)}{1{,}728 \text{ in.}^3} \times 490 \text{ lb/ft}^3 = 1.95 \text{ lb}$$

$$\text{Area} = \frac{(1.95 \times 1{,}728)}{(102 \times 12 \times 490)} = 0.0056 \text{ in.}^2$$

Tension errors are usually quite small and as such have relevance only for very precise surveys. Even for precise surveys, it is seldom necessary to calculate tension corrections, as availability of a tension spring balance allows the surveyor to apply standard tension and thus eliminate the necessity of calculating a correction.

Examples of Sag Corrections

■ EXAMPLE F.8

A 100-ft steel tape weighs 1.6 lb and is supported only at the ends with a force of 10 lb. What is the sag correction?

Solution

$$C_S = \frac{(-1.6^2 \times 100)}{(24 \times 10^2)} = -0.11 \text{ ft}$$

If the force is increased to 20 lb, the sag correction will be reduced to

$$C_S = \frac{(-1.6^2 \times 100)}{(24 \times 20^2)} = -0.03 \text{ ft}$$

■ EXAMPLE F.9

Calculate the length between two supports if the recorded length is 50.000 m, the mass of this tape is 1.63 kg, and the applied tension is 100 N.

Solution

$$C_s = \frac{-(1.63 \times 9.807)^2 \times 50.000}{(24 \times 100^2)}$$

$$= 0.053 \text{ m}$$

Therefore, the length between supports is $50.000 - 0.053 = 49.947$ m.

Problems

F.1 A 100-ft steel tape known to be only 99.98 ft long (under standard conditions) was used to record a measurement of 398.36 ft. What is the distance corrected for erroneous tape?

F.2 A 30-m steel tape, known to be 30.004 m (under standard conditions) was used to record a measurement of 271.118 m. What is the distance corrected for the erroneous tape length?

F.3 A rectangular commercial building must be laid out 200.00 wide and 300.00 ft long. If the steel tape being is 100.02 ft long (under standard conditions), what distances would be laid out?

F.4 A survey distance of 338.12 ft was recorded when the field temperature was 96°F. What is the distance, corrected for temperature?

F.5 Station 3 + 54.67 must be marked in the field. If the steel tape to be used is only 99.98 (under standard conditions) and if the temperature will be 87°F at the time of the measurement, how far from the existing station mark at 0 + 79.23 will the surveyor have to measure to locate the new station?

F.6 The point of intersection of the centerline of Elm Road with the centerline of First Street was originally recorded (using a 30-m steel tape) as being at 6 + 71.225. How far from existing station mark 5 + 00 on First Street would a surveyor have to measure along the centerline to reestablish the intersection point under the following conditions? Temperature is −6°C, and the tape used for measuring is 29.995 under standard conditions.

F.7 A 50-m tape is used to measure between two points. The average weight of the tape per meter is 0.320 N. If the measured distance is 48.888 m with the tape supported only at the ends and with a tension of 100 N, find the corrected distance.

F.8 A 30-m tape has a mass of 544 g and is supported only at the ends with a force of 80 N. What is the sag correction?

F.9 A 100-ft steel tape weighing 1.8 lb and supported only at the ends with a tension of 24 lb is used to measure a distance of 471.16 ft. What is the distance corrected for sag?

F.10 A distance of 72.55 ft is recorded; a steel tape supported only at the ends with a tension of 15 lb and weighing 0.016 lb per foot is used. Find the distance corrected for sag.

Appendix G

Early Surveying

G.1 Evolution of Surveying

Surveying is a profession with a very long history. Since the beginning of property ownership, boundary markers have been required to differentiate one property from another. Historical records dating to almost 3000 B.C. show evidence of surveyors in China, India, Babylon, and Egypt. The Egyptian surveyor, called the *harpedonapata* (rope-stretcher), was in constant demand as the Nile River flooded more or less continuously, destroying boundary markers in those fertile farming lands. These surveyors used ropes with knots tied at set graduations to measure distances.

Ropes were also used to lay out right angles. The early surveyors discovered that the 3:4:5 ratio provided right-angled triangles. To lay out XZ at 90° to XY, a twelve-unit rope would have knots tied at unit positions 3 and 7, as shown in Figure G.1. One surveyor held the three-unit knot at X, the second surveyor held the seven-unit knot at Y, and the third surveyor, holding both loose ends of the rope, stretched the rope tightly, resulting in the location of point Z. These early surveyors knew that multiples of 3:4:5 (e.g., 30:40:50) would produce more accurate positioning.

Another ancient surveying instrument consisted of three pieces of wood in the form of an isosceles triangle with the base extended in both directions (Figure G.2). A plumb bob suspended from the apex of the frame would line up with a notch cut in the midpoint of the base only when the base was level. These "levels" came in various sizes, depending on the work being done.

It is presumed that the great pyramids were laid out with knotted ropes, levels as described here, and various forms of water-trough levels for the foundation layout. These Egyptian surveying techniques were empirical solutions that were field proven. It remained for the Greeks to provide the mathematical reasoning and proofs to explain why the field techniques worked.

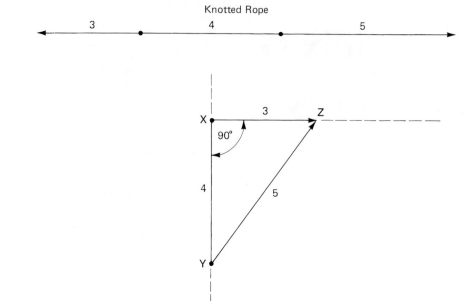

FIGURE G.1   Rope knotted at 3:4:5 ratio—used to place point *Z* at 90 degrees to point *X* from line *XY*.

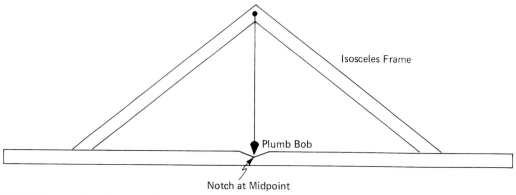

FIGURE G.2   Early Egyptian level.

Pythagoras is one of many famous Greek mathematicians. He and his school developed theories regarding geometry and numbers about 550 B.C. They were also among the first to deduce that the Earth was spherical by noting the shape of the shadow of the Earth that was cast on the moon. The term *geometry* is Greek for "Earth measurement," clearly showing the relationship between mathematics and surveying. In fact, the history of surveying is closely related to the history of mathematics and astronomy.

By 250 B.C., Archimedes recorded in a book known as the *Sand Reckoner* that the circumference of the Earth was 30 myriads of stadia (i.e., 300,000 stadia). He had received some support for this value from his friend Eratosthenes, who was a mathematician and a librarian at the famous library of Alexandria in Egypt. According to some reports,

Eratosthenes knew that a town called Syene was 5,000 stadia south of Alexandria. He also knew that at summer solstice (around June 21) the sun was directly over Syene at noon because there were no shadows. He observed this fact by noting that the sun's reflection was exactly centered in the well water.

Eratosthenes assumed that at the summer solstice the sun, the towns of Syene and Alexandria, and the center of the Earth all lay in the same plane (Figure G.3). At noon on the day of the summer solstice, the elevation of the sun was measured at Alexandria as being $82^4/5°$. The angle from the top of the rod to the sun was then calculated as being $7^1/5°$. Because the sun is such a long distance from the Earth, it can be assumed that the sun's rays are parallel as they reach the Earth. With that assumption, it can be deduced that the angle from the top of the rod to the sun is the same as the angle at the Earth's center: $7^1/5°$. Because $7^1/5°$ is one-fiftieth of 360°, it follows that the circular arc subtending $7^1/5°$ (the distance from Syene to Alexandria) is one-fiftieth of the circumference of the Earth.

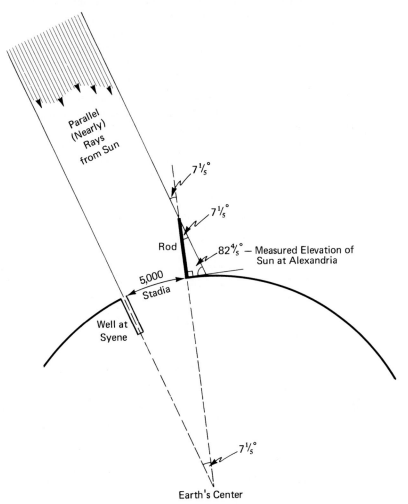

FIGURE G.3 Illustration of Eratosthenes' technique for computing the earth's circumference.

The circumference of the Earth is thus determined to be 250,000 stadia. If the stadia being used were $1/10$ of a mile (different values for the stadium existed, but one value was roughly $1/10$ of our mile), then it is possible that Eratosthenes had calculated the Earth's circumference to be 25,000 mi. Using the Clarke Ellipsoid with a mean radius of 3,960 mi, the circumference of the Earth would actually be $C = 2 \times 3.1416 \times 3,960 = 24,881$ mi.

After the Greeks, the Romans made good use of practical surveying techniques for many centuries to construct roadways, aqueducts, and military camps. Some Roman roads and aqueducts exist to this day. For leveling, the Romans used a ***chorobate***, a 20-ft (approximate) wooden structure with plumbed end braces and a 5-ft (approximate) groove for a water trough (Figure G.4). Linear measurements were often made with wooden poles 10–17 ft long. With the fall of the Roman Empire, surveying and most other intellectual endeavors became lost arts in the Western world.

Renewed interest in intellectual pursuits may have been fostered by the explorers' need for navigational skills. The lodestone, a naturally magnetized rock (magnetite), was first used to locate magnetic north; later the compass would be used for navigation on both land and water. In the mid-1500s, the surveyors' chain was first used in the Netherlands, and an Englishman, Thomas Digges, first used the term **theodolite** to describe an instrument that had a circle graduated in 360° and used to measure angles. By 1590, the plane table (a combined positioning and plotting device) was created by Jean Praetorius; it wasn't a great deal different from the plane tables used in the early 1900s. The telescope, which was invented in 1609 by Galileo (among others), could be attached to a quadrant (angle-measuring device), thus permitting the technique of triangulation—a simpler method of determining long distances. Jean Picard (1620–1682) was apparently the first to use a spider-web cross hair in a telescope. He also used vernier scales to improve the

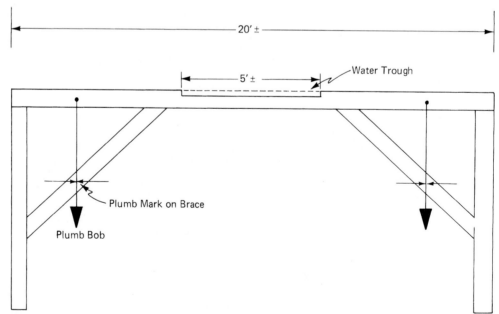

FIGURE G.4 Roman level (chorobate).

precision of angular measurement. James Watt, inventor of the steam engine, is also credited with being the first to install stadia hairs in the survey telescope.

The first dumpy levels were created in the first half of the 1700s by combining a telescope with a bubble level (Figures G.5 and G.6). The repeating style of theodolite (see Sections 4.8 and G.3) was seen in Europe in the mid-1800s, but soon lost favor because scale imperfections caused large cumulative errors. Direction theodolites (see Section G.4.4) were favored because high accuracy could be achieved by reading angles at different positions on the scales, thus eliminating the effect of scale imperfections. Refinements to theodolites continued over the years with better optics, micrometers, coincidence reading, lighter-weight materials, and so on. Heinrich Wild is credited with many significant improvements in the early 1900s that greatly affected the design of most European survey instruments produced by the Wild, Kern, and Zeiss companies.

Meanwhile, in the United States, William J. Young of Philadelphia is credited with being one of the first to create the transit (Figure G.8), in 1831. The transit differed from the early theodolites in that the telescope was shortened so that it could be revolved (transited) on its axis. This simple, but brilliant adaptation permitted the surveyor to produce straight lines accurately by simply sighting the backsight and transiting the telescope forward (see Section 4.12—double centering). When this technique was repeated—once with the telescope normal and once with the telescope inverted—most of the potential errors (e.g., scale graduation imperfections, cross-hair misalignment, standards misalignment) in the instrument could be removed by averaging.

Also, when using a repeating instrument, angles could be quickly and accurately accumulated (see Section 4.6.1). The transit proved to be superior for North American surveying needs. If the emphasis in European surveying was on precise control surveys, the emphasis in North America was on enormous projects in railroad and canal construction and vast projects in public land surveys, which were occasioned by the influx of large numbers of immigrants. The American repeating transit was fast, practical, and accurate, and thus was a significant factor in the development of the North American continent. European and Japanese optical theodolites, which replaced the traditional American vernier transit beginning in the 1950s, have now themselves been largely replaced by electronic theodolites and total stations.

FIGURE G.5 Dumpy level.

Telescope Tube

Cross Hair Ring

Capstan Adjusting Screws

E

1

3 4 2

Telescope

1 Objective Lens
2 Focusing Lens
3 Eyepiece Lenses
4 Cross-Hair Reticle (Also Location of Focal Plane)

F D C B A

G

J

K

H

P

L

M

Level

A Sun Shade
B Telescope Tube
C Telescope Focusing Screw
D Cross-Hairs Capstan Screws
E Eyepiece
F Eyepiece Focusing Ring
G Bubble Tube
H Crossbar
J Spindle
K Leveling Head
L Leveling Screws
P Cone-Shaped Bearing
M Wooden Tripod

FIGURE G.6 Dumpy level. (Adapted from *Construction Manual*, Ministry of Transportation, Ontario)

Electronic distance measurement (EDM) was first introduced by Geodimeter, Inc., in the 1950s and replaced triangulation for control survey distance measurements and the steel tape for all but short distances in boundary and engineering surveys. GPS surveys are now used for most control survey point positioning.

Aerial surveys became very popular after World War II. This technique is a very efficient method of performing large-scale topographic surveys and accounts for the majority of such surveys, although total station surveys are now competitive at lower levels of detail density.

In this text, reference is made to airborne and satellite positioning in Chapter 8. Airborne and satellite photography, lidar imaging, and spectral scanning can be processed to produce plans of very large geographic areas at a much reduced cost compared with field surveying techniques. The images captured on aerial surveys can be converted to scaled plans through the techniques of photogrammetry and digital image processing. Satellite imagery has been used for many years to assess crop inventories, flood damages, migration patterns, and other large-scale geographic projects. As the resolution of satellite images is rapidly improving, remotely sensed data will be of use in many more applications, including civil engineering projects. It has been predicted that satellite imagery will soon be routinely available at a resolution of 0.3 m, or better (see Chapter 8).

In the late 1980s, the total station instrument was thought to be the ultimate in surveying instrumentation—electronic data collection of angles, distances, and descriptive data, with transfer to the computer and plans drawn by digital plotter, all on the same day. Now, many new applications (including construction stakeout and machine guidance) are being found for GPS techniques (see Chapters 7 and 10). In 2005, equipment manufacturers began marketing total stations with integrated GPS receivers and with all ground and satellite data processed by the same integrated controller.

Our world is changing rapidly and technological innovations are leading the way. Traditional surveying practices have given way to electronic (digital) practices. The following sections describe equipment and techniques that have recently become largely obsolete during the current technological revolution. They are included only to provide interested students some perspective on our rapidly changing field of study.

G.2   Dumpy Level

The dumpy level (Figure G.5) was at one time used extensively on all leveling surveys. Although this simple instrument has, to a large degree, been replaced by more sophisticated instruments, it is shown here in some detail to aid in the introduction of the topic. For purposes of description, the level can be analyzed with respect to its three major components: telescope, level tube, and leveling head.

The telescope assembly is illustrated in Figures 4.9, 4.10, and G.6. These schematics also describe the telescopes used in total stations and theodolites/transits. Rays of light pass through the objective (1) and form an inverted image in the focal plane (4). The image thus formed is magnified by the eyepiece lenses (3) so that the image can be clearly seen. The eyepiece lenses also focus the cross hairs, which are located in the telescope in the principal focus plane. The focusing lens (negative lens) (2) can be adjusted so that images at varying distances can be brought into focus in the plane of the reticle (4). In most telescopes designed for use in North America, additional lenses are included in the eyepiece assembly so that the inverted image can be viewed as an erect image. The minimum focusing distance for the object ranges from 1 to 2 m, depending on the instrument.

The line of collimation (line of sight) joins the center of the objective lens to the intersection of the cross hairs. The optical axis is the line taken through the center of the objective lens and perpendicular to the vertical lens axis. The focusing lens (negative lens) is moved by focusing screw C (Figure G.6) and has the same optical axis as the objective lens.

The cross hairs (Figure G.6, 4) can be thin wires attached to a cross-hair ring, or, as is more usually the case, cross hairs are lines etched on a circular glass plate that is enclosed by a cross-hair ring. The cross-hair ring, which has a slightly smaller diameter than does the telescope tube, is held in place by four adjustable capstan screws. The cross-hair ring (and the cross hairs) can be adjusted left and right or up and down simply by loosening and then tightening the two appropriate opposing capstan screws.

In the case of the dumpy level, four leveling foot screws are utilized to set the telescope level. The four foot screws surround the center bearing of the instrument (Figure G.6) and are used to tilt the level telescope using the center bearing as a pivot.

Figure G.7 illustrates how the telescope is positioned during the leveling process. The telescope is first positioned directly over two opposite foot screws. The two screws are kept only snugly tightened (overtightening makes rotation difficult and could damage the threads) and rotated in opposite directions until the bubble is centered in the level tube. If the foot screws become loose, it is an indication that the rotations have not proceeded uniformly; at worst, the foot screw pad can rise above the plate, making the telescope wobble. The solution for this condition is to turn the loose screw until it again contacts the base plate and provides a snug friction when turned in opposition to its opposite screw.

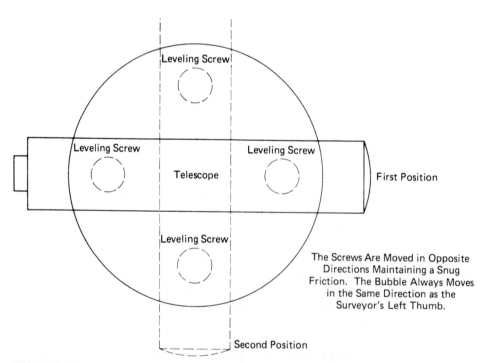

FIGURE G.7   Telescope positions when leveling a four-screw level instrument.

The telescope is first aligned over two opposing screws and the screws are turned in opposite directions until the bubble is centered in the level tube. The telescope is then turned 90° to the second position, which is over the other pair of opposite foot screws, and the leveling procedure is repeated. This process is repeated until the bubble remains centered in those two positions. When the bubble remains centered in these two positions, the telescope is then turned 180° to check the adjustment of the level tube.

If the bubble does not remain centered when the telescope is turned 180°, it indicates that the level tube is out of adjustment. However, the instrument can still be used by simply noting the number of divisions that the bubble is off center and by moving the bubble half the number of those divisions. For example, if upon turning the leveled telescope 180°, it is noted that the bubble is four divisions off center, the instrument can be leveled by moving the bubble to a position of two divisions off center. It will be noted that the bubble will remain two divisions off center no matter which direction the telescope is pointed. It should be emphasized that the instrument is, in fact, level if the bubble remains in the same position when the telescope is revolved, regardless of whether or not that position is in the center of the level vial. See Section 2.11 for adjustments used to correct this condition.

G.3   The Engineers' Vernier Transit

G.3.1   General Background

Prior to the mid-1950s, and before the development and/or widespread use of electronic and optical theodolites, most engineering surveys for topography and layout were accomplished using the engineers' transit (Figure G.8). This instrument had open circles for horizontal and vertical angles; angles were read with the aid of vernier scales. This four-screw instrument was positioned over the survey point by using a slip-knotted plumb bob string, which is attached to the chain hook hanging down from the instrument. Figure G.9 shows the three main assemblies of the transit. The upper assembly, called the **alidade**, includes the standards, telescope, vertical circle and vernier, two opposite verniers for reading the horizontal circle, plate bubbles, compass, and upper tangent (slow motion) screw.

The spindle of the alidade fits down into the hollow spindle of the circle assembly. The circle assembly includes the horizontal circle that is covered by the alidade plate except at the vernier windows, the upper clamp screw, and the hollow spindle. The hollow spindle of the circle assembly fits down into the leveling head. The leveling head includes the four leveling screws, the half-ball joint about which opposing screws are manipulated to level the instrument, a threaded collar that permits attachment to a tripod, the lower clamp and slow-motion screw, and a chain with an attached hook for attaching the plumb bob.

The upper clamp tightens the alidade to the circle, whereas the lower clamp tightens the circle to the leveling head. These two independent motions permit angles to be accumulated on the circle for repeated measurements. Transits that have these two independent motions are called *repeating* instruments. Instruments with only one motion (upper) are called *direction* instruments. Because the circle cannot be previously zeroed (older instruments), angles are usually determined by subtracting the initial setting from the final value. It is not possible to accumulate or repeat angles with a direction theodolite.

FIGURE G.8 Engineer's transit.

G.3.2 Circles and Verniers

The horizontal circle is usually graduated into degrees and half-degrees or 30′ (Figure G.10), although it is not uncommon to find the horizontal circle graduated into degrees and one-third degrees (20′). To determine the angle value more precisely than the least count of the circle (i.e., 30′ or 20′), vernier scales are employed.

Figure G.11 shows a double vernier scale alongside a transit circle. The left vernier scale is used for clockwise circle readings (angles turned to the right), and the right vernier scale is used for counterclockwise circle readings (angles turned to the left). To avoid confusion as to which vernier (left or right) scale is to be used, one can recall that the vernier to be used is the one whose graduations are increasing in the same direction as are the circle graduations. The vernier scale is constructed so that thirty vernier divisions cover the same length of arc as do twenty-nine divisions (half-degrees) on the circle. The width of one vernier division is $(29/30) \times 30′ = 29′$ on the circle. Therefore, the space difference between one division on the circle and one division on the vernier represents 01′.

In Figure G.11, the first division on the vernier (left or right of the index mark) fails to exactly line up with the first division on the circle (left or right) by 01′. The second division on the vernier fails to line up with the corresponding circle division by 02′, and so on. If the vernier were moved so that its first division exactly lined up with the first circle division

The ALIDADE ASSEMBLY, Which
Includes

    Telescope
    Vertical Circle
    Standards
    Verniers
    Vernier Cover
    Plate Levels
    Inner Center
    Upper Tangent

The CIRCLE ASSEMBLY, Which
Includes

    Horizontal Limb
    Outer Center
    Upper Clamp

The LEVELING HEAD ASSEMBLY,
Which Includes

    Leveling Head
    Leveling Screws
    Shifting Plate
    Friction Plate
    Half Ball
    Tripod Plate
    Lower Clamp
    Lower Tangent

FIGURE G.9 Three major assemblies of the transit. (Courtesy of SOKKIA Corp.)

The Inner Center of the Alidade Assembly Fits Into the Outer Center of the Circle Assembly and Can be Rotated in the Outer Center. The Outer Center Fits Into the Leveling Head and Can be Rotated in the Leveling Head.

FIGURE G.10 Part of a transit circle showing a least count of 30′. The circle is graduated in both clockwise and counterclockwise directions, permitting the reading of angles turned to both the left and the right.

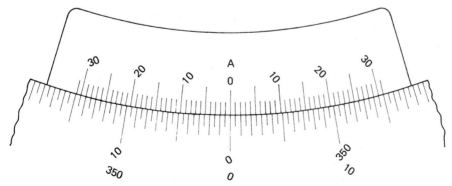

FIGURE G.11 Double vernier scale set to zero on the horizontal circle.

(30' mark), the reading would be 01'; if the vernier again were moved the same distance of arc (1'), the second vernier mark would now line up with the appropriate circle division line, indicating a vernier reading of 02'. Generally, the vernier is read by finding which vernier division line exactly coincides with any circle line, and by then adding the value of that vernier line to the value of the angle obtained from reading the circle to the closest 30' (in this example).

In Figure G.12(a) the circle is divided into degrees and half-degrees (30'). Before even looking at the vernier, we know that its range will be 30' (left or right) to cover the

Note: Clockwise Angles (i.e., Angles Turned to the Right) Utilize Only the Left Side Vernier Scale.
Counterclockwise Angles (i.e., Angles Turned to the Left) Utilize Only the Right Side Vernier Scale.

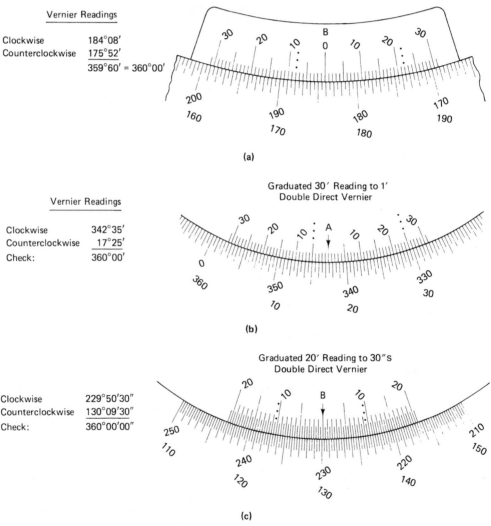

FIGURE G.12 Sample vernier readings. Triple dots identify aligned vernier graduations. *Note:* Appropriate vernier scale graduation numerals are angled in the same direction as the referenced circle graduation numerals.

least count of the circle. Inspection of the vernier shows that thirty vernier divisions cover the range of twenty-nine divisions of the circle.

If we consider the clockwise circle readings (field angle turned left to right), we see that the zero mark is between $184°$ and $184°30'$; the circle reading is therefore $184°$. Now to find the value to the closest minute, we use the left-side vernier; moving from the zero mark, we look for the vernier line that exactly lines up with a circle line. In this case, the $08'$ mark lines up; this is confirmed by noting that both the $07'$ and $09'$ marks do not line up with their corresponding circle mark, both by the same amount. The angle for this illustration is $184° + 08' = 184°08'$.

If we consider the counterclockwise circle reading in Figure G.12(a), we see that the zero mark is between $175°30'$ and $176°$; the circle reading is therefore $175°30'$, and to that value, we add the right-side vernier reading of $22'$ to give an angle of $175°52'$. As a check, the sum of the clockwise and counterclockwise readings should be $360°00'$.

All transits are equipped with two double verniers (A and B) located $180°$ apart. Although increased precision can theoretically be obtained by reading both verniers for each angle, usually only one vernier is employed. Furthermore, to avoid costly mistakes, most surveying agencies favor use of the same vernier, the A vernier, at all times.

As noted earlier, the double vernier permits angles to be turned to the right (left vernier) or to the left (right vernier). However, by convention, field angles are normally turned only to the right. The exceptions to this occur when deflection angles are being employed, as in route surveys, or when construction layouts necessitate angles to the left, as in some curve deflections. There are a few more specialized cases (e.g., star observations) when it is advantageous to turn angles to the left, but as stated earlier, the bulk of surveying experience favors angles turned to the right. This type of consistency provides the routine required to foster a climate in which fewer mistakes occur, and in which mistakes that do occur can be readily recognized and eliminated.

The graduations of the circles and verniers as illustrated were in wide use in the survey field. However, there are several variations to both circle graduations and vernier graduations. Typically, the circle is graduated to the closest $30'$ (as illustrated), $20'$, or $10'$ (rarely). The vernier will have a range in minutes covering the smallest division on the circle ($30'$, $20'$, or $10'$), and could be further graduated to half-minute ($30''$) or one-third minute ($20''$) divisions. A few minutes spent observing the circle and vernier graduations of an unfamiliar transit will easily disclose the proper technique required for reading [see also Figure G.12(b) and (c)].

The use of a magnifying glass ($5\times$) is recommended for reading the scales, particularly for the $30'$ and $20'$ verniers. Optical theodolites largely replaced vernier transits in the 1970s and 1980s; optical theodolites have now (1990s) been largely replaced by electronic transits/theodolites.

G.3.3 Telescope

The telescope (Figure G.8) in the transit is somewhat shorter than that in a level with a reduced magnifying power ($26\times$ vs the $30\times$ often used in the level). The telescope axis is supported by the standards, which are of sufficient height so as to permit the telescope to be revolved (**transited**) $360°$ about the horizontal axis. A level vial tube is attached to the telescope so that, if desired, it may be used as a level (Figures 4.15 and 4.16.)

The telescope level has a sensitivity of 30″ to 40″ per 2-mm graduation, compared with a level sensitivity of about 20″ for a dumpy level. When the telescope is positioned so that the level tube is under the telescope, it is said to be in the *direct* (normal) position; when the level tube is on top of the telescope, the telescope is said to be in a *reversed* (inverted) position. The eyepiece focus ring is always located at the eyepiece end of the telescope, whereas the object focus knob can be located on the telescope barrel just ahead of the eyepiece focus, midway along the telescope, or on the horizontal telescope axis at the standard.

G.3.4   Leveling Head

The leveling head supports the instrument; proper manipulation of the leveling screws allows the horizontal circle and telescope axis to be placed in a horizontal plane, which forces the alidade and circle assembly spindles to be placed in a vertical direction. When the leveling screws are loosened, the pressure on the tripod plate is removed, permitting the instrument to be shifted laterally a short distance ($3/8$ in). This shifting capability permits the surveyor to precisely position the transit center over the desired point by noting the location of the hanging plumb bob.

G.3.5   Transit Adjustments

See also the theodolite adjustments in Section 4.10 of this text.

G.3.5.1   Standards Adjustment   The horizontal axis should be perpendicular to the vertical axis. The standards are checked for proper adjustment by first setting up the theodolite and then sighting a high (at least 30° altitude) point [point A in Figure 4.17(c)]. After clamping the instrument in that position, the telescope is depressed and point B is marked on the ground. The telescope is then transited (plunged), a lower clamp is loosened, and the transit is turned and once again set precisely on point A. The telescope is again depressed, and if the standards are properly adjusted, the vertical cross hair will fall on point B; if the standards are not in adjustment, a new point C is established. The discrepancy between B and C is double the error resulting from the standards maladjustment. Point D, which is now established midway between B and C, will be in the same vertical plane as point A. The error is removed by sighting point D and then elevating the telescope to A′, adjacent to A. The adjustable end of the horizontal axis is then raised or lowered until the line of sight falls on point A. When the adjustment is complete, care is taken in retightening the upper friction screws so that the telescope revolves with proper tension.

G.3.5.2   Telescope Bubble   If the transit is to be used for leveling work, the axis of the telescope bubble and the axis of the telescope must be parallel. To check this relationship, the bubble is centered with the telescope clamped, and the peg test (Section 2.11) is performed. When the proper rod reading (RR) has been determined at the final setup, the horizontal cross hair is set on that RR by moving the telescope with the vertical tangent (slow-motion) screw. The telescope bubble is then centered by means of the capstan screws located at one (or both) end(s) of the bubble tube.

G.3.5.3 Vertical Circle Vernier

When the transit has been carefully leveled (plate bubbles), and the telescope bubble has been centered, the vertical circle should read zero. If a slight error (index error) exists, the screws holding the vernier are loosened, the vernier is tapped into its proper position, and then the screws are retightened so that the vernier is once again just touching, without binding, the vertical circle.

G.3.6   Plate Levels

Transits come equipped with two plate levels set at 90° to each other. Plate levels have a sensitivity range of 60″ to 80″ per 2-mm division on the level tube, depending on the overall precision requirements of the instrument.

G.3.7   Transit Setup

The transit is removed from its case, held by the standards or leveling base (never by the telescope), and placed on a tripod by screwing the transit snugly to the threaded tripod top. When carrying the transit indoors or near obstructions (e.g., tree branches), the operator carries it cradled under the arm, with the instrument forward, where it can be seen. Otherwise, the transit and tripod can be carried on the shoulder. Total stations (see Chapter 5) should always be removed from the tripod and carried by the handle or in the instrument case.

The instrument is placed roughly over the desired point and the tripod legs adjusted so that (1) the instrument is at a convenient height and (2) the tripod plate is nearly level. Usually, two legs are placed on the ground, and the instrument is roughly leveled by manipulation of the third leg. If the instrument is to be set up on a hill, the instrument operator faces uphill and places two of the legs on the lower position; the third leg is placed in the upper position and then manipulated to roughly level the instrument. The wing nuts on the tripod legs are tightened and a plumb bob is attached to the plumb bob chain, which hangs down from the leveling head. The plumb bob is attached by means of a slip knot, which allows placement of the plumb bob point immediately over the mark. If it appears that the instrument placement is reasonably close to its final position, the tripod legs are pushed into the ground, taking care not to jar the instrument.

If necessary, the length of plumb bob string is adjusted as the setting-up procedure advances. If after pushing the tripod legs the instrument is not centered, one leg is either pushed in farther or pulled out and repositioned until the plumb bob is very nearly over the point or until it becomes obvious that manipulation of another leg would be more productive. When the plumb bob is within $^1/_4$ in. of the desired location, the instrument can then be leveled.

Now, two adjacent leveling screws are loosened so that pressure is removed from the tripod plate and the transit can be shifted laterally until it is precisely over the point. If the same two adjacent leveling screws are retightened, the instrument will return to its level (or nearly so) position. Final adjustments to the leveling screws at this stage will not be large enough to displace the plumb bob from its position directly over the desired point.

The actual leveling procedure is a faster operation than that for a dumpy level. The transit has two plate levels, which means that the transit can be leveled in two directions, 90° opposed, without rotating the instrument. When both bubbles have been carefully centered, it only remains for the instrument to be turned through 180° to check the adjustment of the plate bubbles. If one (or both) bubble(s) do not center after turning 180°, the discrepancy is noted and the bubble brought to half the discrepancy by means of the leveling screws. If this has been done correctly, the bubbles will remain in the same position as the instrument is revolved—indicating that the instrument is level.

G.3.8 Measuring Angles by Repetition (Vernier Transit)

Now that the instrument is over the point and is level, the following procedure is used to turn and double an angle. Turning the angle at least twice permits the elimination of mistakes and increases precision because of the elimination of most of the instrument errors. It is recommended that only the A vernier scale be used.

1. *Set the scales to zero.* Loosen both the upper and lower motion clamps. While holding the alidade stationary, revolve the circle by pushing on the circle underside with the fingertips. When the zero on the scale is close to the vernier zero, tighten (snug) the upper clamp. Then, with the aid of a magnifying glass, turn the upper tangent screw (slow-motion screw) until the zeros are precisely set. It is good practice to make the last turn of the tangent screw against the tangent screw spring so that spring tension is assured.

2. *Sight the initial point.* See Figure 4.7. Assume the instrument is at station A, and assume that the angle from B to E is to be measured. With the upper clamp tightened and the lower clamp loose, turn and point at station B, and then tighten the lower clamp. At this point check the eyepiece focus and object focus to eliminate parallax (Section 2.7). If a range pole or even a pencil is giving the sight, always sight as close to the ground level as possible to eliminate plumbing errors. If the sight is being given with a plumb bob, sight high on the plumb bob string to minimize the effect of plumb bob oscillations. Using the lower tangent screw, position the vertical cross hair on the target, once again making the last adjustment motion against the tangent screw spring.

3. *Turn the angle.* Loosen the upper clamp and turn clockwise to the final point (E). When the sight is close to E, tighten the upper clamp. Using the upper tangent screw, set the vertical cross hair precisely on the target using techniques already described. Read the angle by using (in this case) the left-side vernier, and book the value in the appropriate column in the field notes (Figure 4.7).

4. *Repeat the angle.* After the initial angle has been booked, *transit (plunge) the telescope*, loosen the lower motion, and sight at the initial target, station B. The simple act of transiting the telescope between two sightings can eliminate nearly all the potential instrumental errors associated with the transit—when turning angles or producing a straight line.

The first three steps are now repeated, the only difference being that the telescope is now inverted and the initial horizontal angle setting is 101°24′ instead of 0°00′. The angle that is read as a result of this repeating procedure should be approximately double the initial angle. This "double" angle is booked, and then divided by two to find the mean value, which is also booked.

If the procedure has been properly executed, the mean value should be the same as the direct reading or half the least count (30″) different. In practice, a discrepancy equal to the least count (01′) is normally permitted. Although doubling the angle is sufficient for most engineering projects, precision can be increased by repeating the angle a number of times. Due to personal errors of sighting and scale reading, this procedure has practical constraints as to improvement in precision. It is generally agreed that repetitions beyond six or perhaps eight times will not further improve the precision.

When multiple repetitions are being used, only the first angle and the final value are recorded. The number of repetitions divides the final value in order to arrive at the mean value. It may be necessary to augment the final reading by 360° or multiples of 360° prior to determining the mean. The proper value can be roughly determined by multiplying the first angle recorded by the number of repetitions.

G.4   Optical Theodolites

G.4.1   General Background

Optical theodolites are characterized by three-screw leveling heads, optical plummets, light weight, and *glass* circles being read either directly or with the aid of a micrometer; angles (0° to 360°) are normally read in the clockwise direction (Figures 4.4 and 4.5). In contrast to the American engineers' transit (see Section G.3), most theodolites do not come equipped with compasses or telescope levels. Most theodolites are now equipped with a compensating device that automatically indexes the horizontal direction when the vertical circle has been set to the horizontal setting of 90° (or 270°).

The horizontal angular setting (in the vertical plane) for theodolites is 90° (270°), whereas for the transit it is 0°. A word of caution: Although all theodolites have a horizontal setting of 90° direct or 270° inverted, some theodolites have their zero set at the nadir, while others have the zero set at the zenith. The method of graduation can be quickly ascertained in the field by simply setting the telescope in an upward (positive) direction and noting the scale reading. If the reading is less than 90°, the zero has been referenced to the zenith direction; if the reading is more than 90°, the zero has been referenced to the nadir direction.

The graduations of both the vertical and horizontal glass circles are, by means of prisms and lenses, projected to one location just adjacent to the telescope eyepiece, where they are read by means of a microscope. Light, which is necessary in the circle-reading procedure, is controlled by an adjustable mirror located on one of the standards. Light required for underground or night work is directed through the mirror window by attached lamps powered by battery packs.

Optical repeating theodolites have two horizontal motions. The alidade (Figure G.9) can be revolved on the circle assembly with the circle assembly locked to the leveling head. This permits you to turn and read horizontal angles. Alternatively, the alidade and circle assembly can also be clamped together freely revolving on the leveling head. This permits you to keep a set angle value on the circle while turning the instrument to sight another point.

The theodolite tripod has a flat base through which a bolt is threaded up into the three-screw leveling base called a tribrach, thus securing the instrument to the tripod. Most theodolites have a tribrach release feature that permits the alidade and circle assemblies to

FIGURE G.13 A variety of tribrach-mounted traverse targets. Targets and theodolites can be interchanged easily to save setup time (forced-centering system). (Courtesy of Sokkia Corp.)

be lifted from the tribrach and interchanged with a target or prism. When the theodolite (minus its tribrach) is placed on a tribrach vacated by the target or prism, it will be instantly over the point and nearly level. This system, called **forced centering,** speeds up the work and reduces centering errors associated with multiple setups. See Figure G.13.

Optical plummets can be mounted in the alidade or in the tribrach. Alidade-mounted optical plummets can be checked for accuracy simply by revolving the alidade around its vertical axis and noting the location of the optical plummet cross hairs (bull's eye) with respect to the station mark. Tribrach-mounted optical plummets can be checked by means of a plumb bob. Adjustments can be made by manipulating the appropriate adjusting screws, or the instrument can be sent out for shop analysis and adjustment.

Typical specifications for optical theodolites are listed below:

Magnification: 30×
Clear objective aperture: 1.6 in. (42 mm)
Field of view at 100 ft (100 m): 2.7 ft (2.7 m)
Shortest focusing distance: 5.6 ft (1.7 m)
Stadia multiplication constant: 100
Bubble sensitivity
Circular bubble: 8′ per 2 mm
Plate level: 30″ per 2 mm
Direct circle reading: 01″ to 06″ (20″ in older versions) from 0° to 360°

Like the engineers' transit, the optical repeating theodolite has two independent motions (upper and lower), which necessitates upper and lower clamps with their attendant tangent screws. However, some theodolites come equipped with only one clamp and one slow-motion or tangent screw; these instruments have a lever or switch that transfers clamp operation from upper to lower motion and thus probably reduces the opportunity for mistakes due to wrong-screw manipulation.

When some tribrach-equipped laser plummets are used in mining surveys, the alidade (upper portion of instrument) can be released from the tribrach with the laser plummet projecting upward to ceiling stations. After the tribrach is properly centered under the ceiling mark, the alidade is then replaced into the tribrach, and the instrument is ready for final settings. This visual plumb line helps the surveyor to position the instrument over (under) the station mark more quickly than when using an optical plummet. Some manufacturers place the laser plummet in the alidade portion of the instrument, permitting an easy check on the beam's accuracy by simply rotating the instrument and observing whether the beam stays on the point (upward plumbing is not possible with alidade-mounted laser plummets).

G.4.2   Angle Measurement with an Optical Theodolite

The technique for turning and doubling (repeating) an angle is the same as that described for a transit (Section G.3.8). The only difference in procedure is that of zeroing and reading the scales. In the case of the direct reading optical scale (Figure G.14), zeroing the circle is simply a matter of turning the circle until the 0° mark lines up approximately with the 0′ mark on the scale. Once the upper clamp has been tightened, the setting can be precisely accomplished by manipulation of the upper tangent screw. The scale is read directly, as illustrated in Figure G.14(b).

In the case of the optical micrometer instruments (Figure G.15), it is important to first set the micrometer to zero, and then to set the horizontal circle to zero. When the angle has been turned, it will be noted that the horizontal (or vertical) circle index mark is not directly over a degree mark. The micrometer knob is turned until the circle index mark is set to a degree mark. Movement of the micrometer knob also moves the micrometer scale; the reading on the micrometer scale is then added to the even degree reading taken from the circle. The micrometer scale does not have to be reset to zero for subsequent angle readings unless

(a)

(b)

FIGURE G.14   (a) Kern KIS half-minute engineer's scale theodolite with optical plummet and direct reading scales. (b) Scale readings for the KIS theodolite. (Courtesy of Kern Instruments— Leica Geosystems)

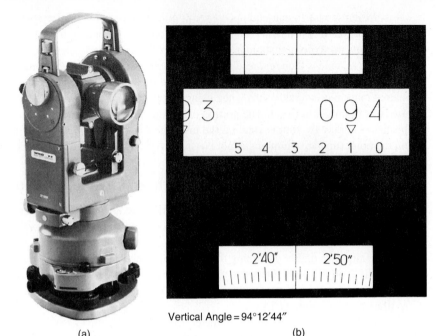

Vertical Angle = 94°12′44″

(a)   (b)

FIGURE G.15 (a) Wild T-2, a 1″ optical direction theodolite. (b) Vertical circle reading. (Courtesy of Leica Geosystems)

a new reference backsight is taken. Figure 4.4 shows a micrometer graduated to the closest 20″. The vertical circle is read in the same way, using the same micrometer scale. If the vertical index is not automatically compensated (as it is for most repeating theodolites), the vertical index coincidence bubble must be centered by rotating the appropriate screw when vertical angles are being read.

G.4.3   Direction Optical Theodolites

The essential difference between a direction optical theodolite and a repeating optical theodolite is that the direction theodolite has only one motion (upper), whereas the optical repeating theodolite has two motions (upper and lower). Because it is difficult to precisely set angle values on this type of instrument, angles are usually determined by reading the initial direction and the final direction, and by then determining the difference between the two.

Direction optical theodolites are generally more precise; for example, the Wild T-2 shown in Figure G.15 reads directly to 01″ and by estimation to 0.5″, whereas the Wild T-3 shown in Figure G.16 reads directly to 0.2″ and by estimation to 0.1″. In the case of the Wild T-2 (Figure G.15) and the other 1″ theodolites, the micrometer is turned to force the index to read an even 10″ (the grid lines shown above [beside] the scale are brought to coincidence), and then the micrometer scale reading (02′44″) is added to the circle reading (94°10′) to give a result of 94°12′44″. In the case of the T-3 (Figure G.16), both sides of the circle are viewed simultaneously; one reading is shown erect, the other inverted. The micrometer

Circle reading	73°26′
Drum reading	1′59.6″
	73°27′59.6″

(a)   (b)

FIGURE G.16 (a) Wild T-3 precise theodolite for the first-order surveying. (b) Circle reading (least graduation is 4′) and micrometer reading (lease graduation is 0.2″). (Courtesy of Leica Geosystems). On the micrometer, a value of 01′29.6″ can be read. The reading is, therefore, 73°27′59.6″.

knob is used to align the erect and inverted circle markings precisely. Each division on the circle is 04′; but if the lower scale is moved half a division, the upper also moves half a division, once again causing the markings to align, that is, *a movement of only 02′*. The circle index line is between the 73° and 74° mark, indicating that the value being read is 73°. Minutes can be read on the circle by counting the number of divisions from the erect 73° to the inverted value that is 180° different than 73° (i.e., 253°). In this case, the number of divisions between these two numbers is 13, each having a value of 02′ (i.e., 26′). These optical instruments have been superceded by precise electronic theodolites.

G.4.4 Angles Measured with a Direction Theodolite

As noted earlier, because it is not always possible to set angles on a direction theodolite scale precisely, directions are observed and then subtracted one from the other in order to determine angles. Furthermore, if several sightings are required for precision purposes, it is customary to distribute the initial settings around the circle to minimize the effect of circle graduation distortions. For example, using a directional theodolite where both sides of the circle are viewed simultaneously, the initial settings (positions) would be distributed per 180/n, where n is the number of settings required by the precision specifications (specifications for precise surveys are published by the National Geodetic Survey—United States, and the Geodetic Surveys of Canada). To be consistent, not only should the initial settings be uniformly distributed around the circle, but the range of the micrometer scale should be noted as well and appropriately apportioned.

For the instruments shown in Figures G.15 and G.16, the settings would be as given in Table G.1. These initial settings are accomplished by setting the micrometer to zero

Table G.1 APPROXIMATE INITIAL SCALE SETTINGS FORFOUR POSITIONS

10' Micrometer, Wild T-2	2' Micrometer, Wild T-3
0°00'00"	0°00'00"
45°02'30"	45°00'30"
90°05'00"	90°01'00"
135°07'30"	135°01'30"

(02'30", 05'00", 07'30"), and then setting the circle as close to zero as possible using the tangent screw. Precise coincidence of the zero (45, 90, 135) degree mark is achieved using the micrometer knob, which moves the micrometer scale slightly off zero (2'30", 5'00", 7'30", etc.).

The direct readings are taken first in a clockwise direction; the telescope is then transited (plunged), and the reverse readings are taken counterclockwise. In Figure G.17, the last entry at position 1 is 180°00'12" (R). If the angles (shown in the abstract) do not meet the required accuracy, the procedure is repeated while the instrument still occupies that station.

FIGURE G.17 Field notes for angles by direction.

G.5 Stadia

G.5.1 Principles

Stadia surveying is an outmoded form of distance measurement that relies on a fixed-angle intercept to measure the distance optically along the sight path. With a limited accuracy of 1:400, stadia was ideally suited for the location of natural features.

The theodolite and some levels have a cross-hair reticule that has, in addition to the normal cross hairs, two additional horizontal hairs [Figure G.18(a)], one above and the other equally below the main horizontal hair. These stadia hairs are positioned in the reticule so that, if a rod were held 100 ft (m) away from the theodolite (with the telescope level), the difference between the upper and lower stadia hair readings (rod interval) would be exactly 1.00 ft (m). It can be seen [Figure G.18(b)] that horizontal distances can be determined by (1) sighting a rod with the telescope level; (2) determining the rod interval; and (3) multiplying the rod interval by 100 to compute the horizontal distance:

$$D = 100S \qquad\qquad (G.1)$$

Elevations can be determined using stadia in the manner illustrated in Figure G.18(c). The elevation of the instrument station (A) is usually determined using a level and rod. When the theodolite is set up on the station in preparation for a stadia survey, the height of the optical center of the instrument above the top of stake (hi) is measured with a tape and noted in the field book. An RR can then be taken on the rod with the telescope level. The elevation of the point (B) where the rod is being held is computed as follows:

$$\text{Elevation of station A } (\overline{\wedge}) + \text{hi} - \text{RR} = \text{elevation of point B (rod)} \qquad (G.2)$$

Note. hi (height of instrument) in stadia work, as it is in total station work, is the vertical distance from the station to the optical center of the theodolite, whereas in leveling work HI (height of instrument) is the elevation of the line of sight through the level.

The optical center of the theodolite is at the center of the telescope at the horizontal axis. The exact point is marked with a cross, colored dot, or screw. Measuring the hi (height of instrument) with a tape is not exact because the tape must be bent over the circle assembly when measuring; however, this error will not significantly affect the stadia results.

Figure G.18(d) illustrates that the location of point B (rod) can be tied in by angle to a reference baseline XAY. The plan location of point B can now be plotted using the angle from the reference line and the distance as determined by Equation G.1. The elevation of point B can also be plotted, either as a spot elevation or as a component of a series of contours. It can be seen that the stadia method (like the total station method) permits the surveyor to determine the three-dimensional position of any point with just one set of observations.

G.5.2 Inclined Stadia Measurements

The discussion thus far has assumed that the stadia observations were taken with the telescope level; however, the stadia method is particularly well suited for the inclined measurements required by rolling topography. When the telescope is inclined up or down, the computations must be modified to account for the effects of the sloped sighting. Inclined sights require consideration in two areas: (1) the distance from the instrument to the rod

Cross-Hair Reticle

(a)

(b)

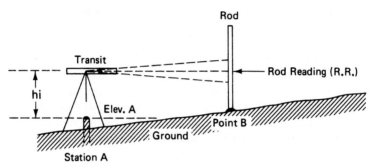

Elevation A + hi − R.R. = Elevation B.

(c)

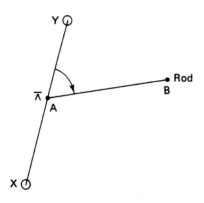

(d)

FIGURE G.18 Stadia principles. (a) Stadia hairs. (b) Distance determination. (c) Elevation determination. (d) Angle determination.

must be reduced from slope to horizontal, and (2) the rod interval of a sloped sighting must be reduced to what the interval would have been if the line of sight had been perpendicular to the rod.

Figure G.19 illustrates these two considerations. The value of hi and the RR have been made equal to clarify the sketch. The geometric relationships are as follows: (1) S is

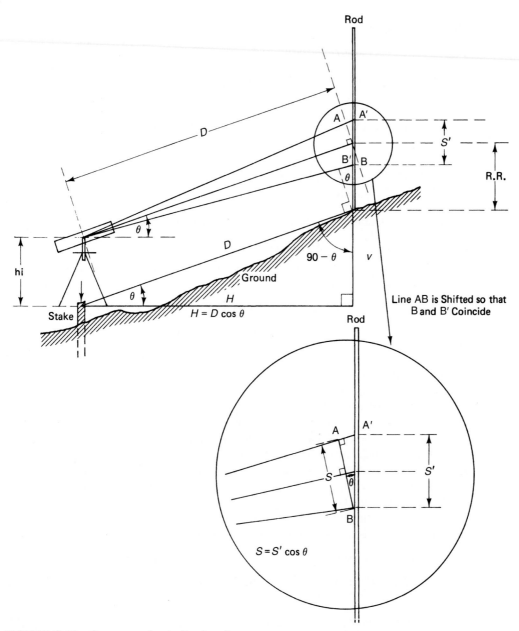

FIGURE G.19 Geometry of an inclined stadia measurement.

the rod interval when the line of sight is horizontal, and (2) S' is the rod interval when the line of sight is inclined by angle θ. Equation G.1 was illustrated in Figure G.18(b):

$$D = 100S$$

Figure G-19 illustrates the relationship between S and S':

$$S = S''\cos\theta \tag{G.3}$$

The following equation can be derived from Equations G.3 and G.1:

$$D = 100S''\cos\theta \tag{G.4}$$

G.19 also illustrates the following relationship:

$$H = D\cos\theta \tag{G.5}$$

The following equation can be derived from Equations G.4 and G.2:

$$H = 100S''\cos\theta \tag{G.6}$$

The following relationship is also illustrated in Figure G.19:

$$V = D\sin\theta \tag{G.7}$$

The following relationship can be derived from Equations G.7 and G.4:

$$V = 100S''\cos\theta\sin\theta \tag{G.8}$$

Some theodolites read only zenith angles $(90 - \theta)$, which makes it necessary to modify Equations G.6 and G.8 as follows:

$$H = 100S''\sin^2(90° - \theta) \tag{G.9}$$

$$V = 100S''\sin(90° - \theta)\cos(90° - \theta) \tag{G.10}$$

Equation G.9 is a modification of Equation G.6; Equation G.10 is a modification of Equation G.8. Equations G.6 and G.8 can be used in computing the horizontal distance and difference in elevation for any inclined stadia measurement.

In the past, special slide rules and/or tables were used to compute H and V. However, with the universal use of handheld calculators, slide rules and stadia tables have become almost obsolete. The computations can be accomplished just as quickly working with Equations G.6 and G.8. Stadia reduction tables are given in Table G.2. The table is entered at the value of the vertical circle reading (VCR) with the horizontal distance factor and the difference in elevation factor both being multiplied by the rod interval to give H and V (see Examples G.1 and G.2).

Figure G.20 shows the general case of an inclined stadia measurement, where the elevation relationships between the theodolite station and rod station can be stated as follows:

$$\text{Elevation at } (\overline{\wedge}) \text{ station K} + \text{hi} \pm V - \text{RR} = \text{elevation at (rod) station M} \tag{G.11}$$

The relationship is valid for every stadia measurement. If the hi and RR are equal, Equation G.11 becomes

$$\text{Elevation at } (\overline{\wedge}) \text{ station K} \pm V = \text{elevation at (rod) point M} \tag{G.12}$$

Table G.2 STADIA TABLES*

Minutes	0° Hor. dist.	0° Diff. elev.	1° Hor. dist.	1° Diff. elev.	2° Hor. dist.	2° Diff. elev.	3° Hor. dist.	3° Diff. elev.	4° Hor. dist.	4° Diff. elev.	5° Hor. dist.	5° Diff. elev.	6° Hor. dist.	6° Diff. elev.	7° Hor. dist.	7° Diff. elev.
0	100.00	0.00	99.97	1.74	99.88	3.49	99.73	5.23	99.51	6.96	99.24	8.68	98.91	10.40	98.51	12.10
2	100.00	0.06	99.97	1.80	99.87	3.55	99.72	5.28	99.51	7.02	99.23	8.74	98.90	10.45	98.50	12.15
4	100.00	0.12	99.97	1.86	99.87	3.60	99.71	5.34	99.50	7.07	99.22	8.80	98.88	10.51	98.49	12.21
6	100.00	0.17	99.96	1.92	99.87	3.66	99.71	5.40	99.49	7.13	99.21	8.85	98.87	10.57	98.47	12.27
8	100.00	0.23	99.96	1.98	99.86	3.72	99.70	5.46	99.48	7.19	99.20	8.91	98.86	10.62	98.46	12.32
10	100.00	0.29	99.96	2.04	99.86	3.78	99.69	5.52	99.47	7.25	99.19	8.97	98.85	10.68	98.44	12.38
12	100.00	0.35	99.96	2.09	99.85	3.84	99.69	5.57	99.46	7.30	99.18	9.03	98.83	10.74	98.43	12.43
14	100.00	0.41	99.95	2.15	99.85	3.89	99.68	5.63	99.46	7.36	99.17	9.08	98.82	10.79	98.41	12.49
16	100.00	0.47	99.95	2.21	99.84	3.95	99.68	5.69	99.45	7.42	99.16	9.14	98.81	10.85	98.40	12.55
18	100.00	0.52	99.95	2.27	99.84	4.01	99.67	5.75	99.44	7.48	99.15	9.20	98.80	10.91	98.39	12.60
20	100.00	0.58	99.95	2.33	99.83	4.07	99.66	5.80	99.43	7.53	99.14	9.25	98.78	10.96	98.37	12.66
22	100.00	0.64	99.94	2.38	99.83	4.13	99.66	5.86	99.42	7.59	99.13	9.31	98.77	11.02	98.36	12.72
24	100.00	0.70	99.94	2.44	99.82	4.18	99.65	5.92	99.41	7.65	99.11	9.37	98.76	11.08	98.34	12.77
26	99.99	0.76	99.94	2.50	99.82	4.24	99.64	5.98	99.40	7.71	99.10	9.43	98.74	11.13	98.33	12.83
28	99.99	0.81	99.93	2.56	99.81	4.30	99.63	6.04	99.39	7.76	99.09	9.48	98.73	11.19	98.31	12.88
30	99.99	0.87	99.93	2.62	99.81	4.36	99.63	6.09	99.38	7.82	99.08	9.54	98.72	11.25	98.30	12.94
32	99.99	0.93	99.93	2.67	99.80	4.42	99.62	6.15	99.38	7.88	99.07	9.60	98.71	11.30	98.28	13.00
34	99.99	0.99	99.93	2.73	99.80	4.47	99.61	6.21	99.37	7.94	99.06	9.65	98.69	11.36	98.27	13.05
36	99.99	1.05	99.92	2.79	99.79	4.53	99.61	6.27	99.36	7.99	99.05	9.71	98.68	11.42	98.25	13.11
38	99.99	1.11	99.92	2.85	99.79	4.59	99.60	6.32	99.35	8.05	99.04	9.77	98.67	11.47	98.24	13.17
40	99.99	1.16	99.92	2.91	99.78	4.65	99.59	6.38	99.34	8.11	99.03	9.83	98.65	11.53	98.22	13.22
42	99.99	1.22	99.91	2.97	99.78	4.71	99.58	6.44	99.33	8.17	99.01	9.88	98.64	11.59	98.20	13.28
44	99.98	1.28	99.91	3.02	99.77	4.76	99.58	6.50	99.32	8.22	99.00	9.94	98.63	11.64	98.19	13.33
46	99.98	1.34	99.91	3.08	99.77	4.82	99.57	6.56	99.31	8.28	98.99	10.00	98.61	11.70	98.17	13.39
48	99.98	1.40	99.90	-3.14	99.76	4.88	99.56	6.61	99.30	8.34	98.98	10.05	98.60	11.76	98.16	13.45
50	99.98	1.45	99.90	3.20	99.76	4.94	99.55	6.67	99.29	8.40	98.97	10.11	98.58	11.81	98.14	13.50
52	99.98	1.51	99.89	3.26	99.75	4.99	99.55	6.73	99.28	8.45	98.96	10.17	98.57	11.87	98.13	13.56
54	99.98	1.57	99.89	3.31	99.74	5.05	99.54	6.79	99.27	8.51	98.94	10.22	98.56	11.93	98.11	13.61
56	99.97	1.63	99.89	3.37	99.74	5.11	99.53	6.84	99.26	8.57	98.93	10.28	98.54	11.98	98.10	13.67
58	99.97	1.69	99.88	3.43	99.73	5.17	99.52	6.90	99.25	8.63	98.92	10.34	98.53	12.04	98.08	13.73
60	99.97	1.74	99.88	3.49	99.73	5.23	99.51	6.96	99.24	8.68	98.91	10.40	98.51	12.10	98.06	13.78

(continued)

Table G.2 (continued)

Minutes	8° Hor. dist.	8° Diff. elev.	9° Hor. dist.	9° Diff. elev.	10° Hor. dist.	10° Diff. elev.	11° Hor. dist.	11° Diff. elev.
0	98.06	13.78	97.55	15.45	96.98	17.10	96.36	18.73
2	98.05	13.84	97.53	15.51	96.96	17.16	96.34	18.78
4	98.03	13.89	97.52	15.56	96.94	17.21	96.32	18.84
6	98.01	13.95	97.50	15.62	96.92	17.26	96.29	18.89
8	98.00	14.01	97.48	15.67	96.90	17.32	96.27	18.95
10	97.98	14.06	97.46	15.73	96.88	17.37	96.25	19.00
12	97.97	14.12	97.44	15.78	96.86	17.43	96.23	19.05
14	97.95	14.17	97.43	15.84	96.84	17.48	96.21	19.11
16	97.93	14.23	97.41	15.89	96.82	17.54	96.18	19.16
18	97.92	14.28	97.39	15.95	96.80	17.59	96.16	19.21
20	97.90	14.34	97.37	16.00	96.78	17.65	96.14	19.27
22	97.88	14.40	97.35	16.06	96.76	17.70	96.12	19.32
24	97.87	14.45	97.33	16.11	96.74	17.76	96.09	19.38
26	97.85	14.51	97.31	16.17	96.72	17.81	96.07	19.43
28	97.83	14.56	97.29	16.22	96.70	17.86	96.05	19.48
30	97.82	14.62	97.28	16.28	96.68	17.92	96.03	19.54
32	97.80	14.67	97.26	16.33	96.66	17.97	96.00	19.59
34	97.78	14.73	97.24	16.39	96.64	18.03	95.98	19.64
36	97.76	14.79	97.22	16.44	96.62	18.08	95.96	19.70
38	97.75	14.84	97.20	16.50	96.60	18.14	95.93	19.75
40	97.73	14.90	97.18	16.55	96.57	18.19	95.91	19.80
42	97.71	14.95	97.16	16.61	96.55	18.24	95.89	19.86
44	97.69	15.01	97.14	16.66	96.53	18.30	95.86	19.91
46	97.68	15.06	97.12	16.72	96.51	18.35	95.84	19.96
48	97.66	15.12	97.10	16.77	96.49	18.41	95.82	20.02
50	97.64	15.17	97.08	16.83	96.47	18.46	95.79	20.07
52	97.62	15.23	97.06	16.88	96.45	18.51	95.77	20.12
54	97.61	15.28	97.04	16.94	96.42	18.57	95.75	20.18
56	97.59	15.34	97.02	16.99	96.40	18.62	95.72	20.23
58	97.57	15.40	97.00	17.05	96.38	18.68	95.70	20.28
60	97.55	15.45	96.98	17.10	96.36	18.73	95.68	20.34

Minutes	12° Hor. dist.	12° Diff. elev.	13° Hor. dist.	13° Diff. elev.	14° Hor. dist.	14° Diff. elev.	15° Hor. dist.	15° Diff. elev.
0	95.68	20.34	94.94	21.92	94.15	23.47	93.30	25.00
2	95.65	20.39	94.91	21.97	94.12	23.52	93.27	25.05
4	95.63	20.44	94.89	22.02	94.09	23.58	93.24	25.10
6	95.61	20.50	94.86	22.08	94.07	23.63	93.21	25.15
8	95.58	20.55	94.84	22.13	94.04	23.68	93.18	25.20
10	95.56	20.60	94.81	22.18	94.01	23.73	93.16	25.25
12	95.53	20.66	94.79	22.23	93.98	23.78	93.13	25.30
14	95.51	20.71	94.76	22.28	93.95	23.83	93.10	25.35
16	95.49	20.76	94.73	22.34	93.93	23.88	93.07	25.40
18	95.46	20.81	94.71	22.39	93.90	23.93	93.04	25.45
20	95.44	20.87	94.68	22.44	93.87	23.99	93.01	25.50
22	95.41	20.92	94.66	22.49	93.84	24.04	92.98	25.55
24	95.39	20.97	94.63	22.54	93.82	24.09	92.95	25.60
26	95.36	21.03	94.60	22.60	93.79	24.14	92.92	25.65
28	95.34	21.08	94.58	22.65	93.76	24.19	92.89	25.70
30	95.32	21.13	94.55	22.70	93.73	24.24	92.86	25.75
32	95.29	21.18	94.52	22.75	93.70	24.29	92.83	25.80
34	95.27	21.24	94.50	22.80	93.67	24.34	92.80	25.85
36	95.24	21.29	94.47	22.85	93.65	24.39	92.77	25.90
38	95.22	21.34	94.44	22.91	93.62	24.44	92.74	25.95
40	95.19	21.39	94.42	22.96	93.59	24.49	92.71	26.00
42	95.17	21.45	94.39	23.01	93.56	24.55	92.68	26.05
44	95.14	21.50	94.36	23.06	93.53	24.60	92.65	26.10
46	95.12	21.55	94.34	23.11	93.50	24.65	92.62	26.15
48	95.09	21.60	94.31	23.16	93.47	24.70	92.59	26.20
50	95.07	21.66	94.28	23.22	93.45	24.75	92.56	26.25
52	95.04	21.71	94.26	23.27	93.42	24.80	92.53	26.30
54	95.02	21.76	94.23	23.32	93.39	24.85	92.49	26.35
56	94.99	21.81	94.20	23.37	93.36	24.90	92.46	26.40
58	94.97	21.87	94.17	23.42	93.33	24.95	92.43	26.45
60	94.94	21.92	94.15	23.47	93.30	25.00	92.40	26.50

*Example, VCR, –3°21'; rod interval, 0.123 m; $V = 5.83 \times 0.123 = 0.72$ m; from tables: $H = 99.66 \times 0.123 = 12.3$ m.

General Case Equation:

Elevation Station K ($\bar{x}$) + hi ± V − RR = Elevation Point M (Rod)

FIGURE G.20 General case of an inclined stadia measurement.

because the hi and RR cancel each other. In practice, the surveyor will read the rod at the value of the hi unless that value is obscured (e.g., tree branch, rise of land, etc.). If the hi value cannot be sighted, usually a value an even foot (decimeter) above or below is sighted, allowing for a mental correction to the calculation. Of course, if an even foot (decimeter) above or below the desired value cannot be read, any value can be read and Equation (G.11) is used.

G.5.3   Examples of Stadia Measurements

There are three basic variations to a standard stadia measurement:

1. The RR is taken to be the same as the hi.
2. The RR is not the same as the hi.
3. The telescope is horizontal.

■   EXAMPLE G.1

This example, where the RR has been made to coincide with the value of the hi, is typical of 90 percent of all stadia measurements (Figures G.21 and G.24). Here the VCR is +1°36″ and the rod interval is 0.401. Both the hi and the RR are 1.72 m.

Solution
From Equation G.6,

$$H = 100S'' \cos^2\theta$$
$$= 100 \times 0.401 \times \cos^2 1°36'$$
$$= 40.1\text{m}$$

FIGURE G.21 Example G.1: RR = hi.

From Equation G.8,

$$V = 100S''\cos\theta \sin\theta$$
$$= 100 \times 0.401 \times \cos 1°36' \times \sin 1°36'$$
$$= +1.12\text{m}$$

From Equation G.12,

$$\text{Elev. } (\overline{\wedge}) \pm V = \text{elev. (rod)}$$
$$\textbf{185.16 + 1.12 = 186.28}$$

See station $0 + 00$ on Figure G.24
   Or, from Table G.2,

$$\text{VCR} = +1°36'$$
$$\text{rod interval} = 0.401$$
$$H = 99.92 \times 0.401 = 40.1\text{m}$$
$$V = 2.79 \times 0.401 = +1.12\text{m}$$

■ **EXAMPLE G.2**

This example illustrates the case where the value of the hi cannot be seen on the rod due to some obstruction (Figures G.22 and G.24). In this case a RR of 2.72 with a vertical angle of –6°37' was booked, along with the hi of 1.72 and a rod interval of 0.241.

Solution
From Equation G.6,

$$H = 100S'\cos^2\theta$$
$$= 100 \times 0.241 \times \cos^2 6°37'$$
$$= 23.8\text{m}$$

From Equation G.8,

$$V = 100S'\cos\theta \sin\theta$$
$$= 100 \times 0.241 \times \cos 6°37' \times \sin 6°37'$$
$$= -2.76\text{m (algebraic sign is given by the VCR)}$$

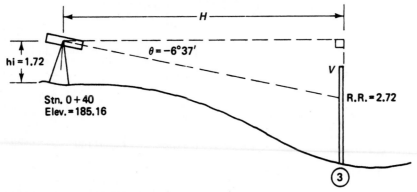

FIGURE G.22 Example G.2: RR ≠ hi.

From Equation G.11,

$$\text{Elev.} (\overline{\wedge}) + \text{hi} \pm V - RR = \text{elev. (rod)}$$
$$185.16 + 1.72 - 2.76 - 2.72 = 181.40$$

See station 3 on Figure G.24
   Or, from Table G.2,

$$\text{VCR} = -6°37'$$
$$\text{rod interval} = 0.241$$
$$H = 98.675(\text{interpolated}) \times 0.241 = 23.8\text{m}$$
$$V = 11.445(\text{interpolated}) \times 0.241 = -2.76\text{m}$$

■ **EXAMPLE G.3**

This example illustrates the situation where the ground is level enough to permit horizontal rod sightings (Figures G.23 and G.24). The computations for this observation are quite simple; the horizontal distance is simply 100 times the rod interval ($D = 100S$, Equation G.1). Because there is no vertical angle, there is no triangle to solve (i.e., $V = 0$). The difference in elevation is simply $+\text{hi} - RR$.

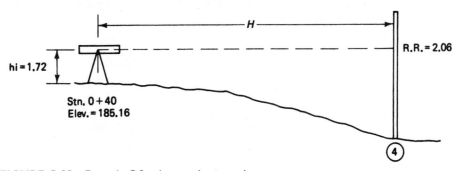

FIGURE G.23 Example G.3: telescope horizontal.

STA.	H.C.R.	ROD INTERVAL	V.C.R.	HORIZ. DISTANCE	ELEV. DIFFERENCE	ELEV.
		⊼ @ 0+40; hi	= 1.72			185.16
1+40	0° 00'	1.002	−1° 24'	100.1	−2.45	182.71
0+00	180° 01'	0.401	+1° 36'	40.1	+1.12	186.28
①	5° 48'	0.911	−2° 18'	91.0	−3.65	181.51
②	18° 18'	0.562	−3° 38'	56.0	−3.55	181.61
③	21° 58'	0.241	−6° 37' on 2.72	23.8	V=−2.76 −1.00 / −3.76	181.40
④	156° 02'	0.208	0° 00' on 2.06	20.8	−2.06 +1.72 / −0.34	184.82
	P. VASSALLO—NOTES					
	R. CURTIS — ⊼					
	J. BODMAN—ROD					

FIGURE G.24 Stadia field notes.

Surveying a level area where many observations can be taken with the telescope level speeds up the survey computations and shortens the field time. However, if the survey is in typical rolling topography, the surveyor will not normally spend the time necessary to see if a single horizontal observation can be made; the surveyor will instead continue sighting the rod at the hi value to maintain the momentum of the survey (a good instrument operator can keep two rod holders busy).

Solution

In this example, a rod interval of 0.208 was booked, together with an hi of 1.72 and an RR of 2.06. From Equation (G.1),

$$D = 100S$$
$$= 100 \times 0.208$$
$$= 20.8\text{m (horizontal distance)}$$

From Equation G.11,

$$\text{Elev. } (\overline{\wedge}) + \text{hi} \pm V - RR = \text{Elev. (rod)}$$
$$185.16 + 1.72 + 0 - 2.06 = 184.82$$

See station 4 on Figure G.24.

G.5.4   Stadia Field Practice

In stadia work, the theodolite is set on a point for which the horizontal location and elevation have been determined. If necessary, the elevation of the theodolite station can be determined after setup by sighting on a point of known elevation and working backward through Equation G.11.

The horizontal circle is zeroed and a sight is taken on another control point $(1 + 40$ in Figure G.24). All stadia sightings are accomplished by working on the circle using the upper clamp and upper tangent screw (two-clamp instruments). It is a good idea periodically to check the zero setting by sighting back on the original backsight; this will ensure that the setting has not been invalidated by inadvertent use of the lower clamp or lower tangent screw. At a bare minimum, a zero check is made just before the instrument is moved from the theodolite station; if the check proves that the setting has been inadvertently moved from zero, all the work must be repeated. Before any observations are made, the hi is measured with a steel tape (sometimes with the leveling rod) and the value booked, as shown in Figure G.24.

The actual observation proceeds as follows: With the upper clamp loosened, the rod is sighted; precise setting can be accomplished using the upper tangent screw after the upper clamp has been locked. The main cross hair is sighted approximately to the value of the hi, and then the telescope is revolved up or down until the lower stadia hair is on the closest even foot (decimeter) mark (Figure G.25). The upper stadia hair is then read and the rod interval determined mentally by simply subtracting the lower hair

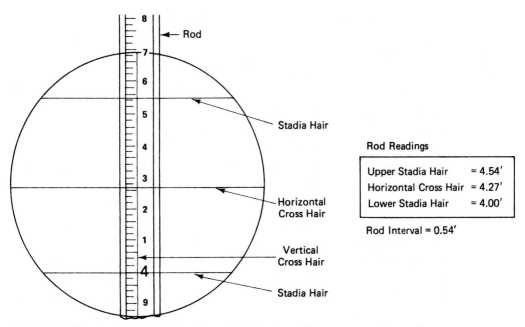

FIGURE G.25   Stadia readings. (Courtesy of the Ministry of Transportation, Ontario)

reading from the upper hair reading. After the rod interval is booked (Figure G.24), the main cross hair is then moved to read the value of the hi on the rod. When this has been accomplished, the surveyor is waved off, and while the surveyor is walking to the next point, the instrument operator reads and books the VCR and the HCR (Figure G.24). Usually, the calculations for horizontal distance and elevation are performed after field hours.

The technique of temporarily moving the lower stadia hair to an even value to facilitate the determination of the rod interval introduces errors in the readings, but these errors are not large enough to significantly affect the results. The alternative to this technique would be to initially lock the main hair on the value of the hi and then read and book the upper and lower hair readings. When the lower hair is subtracted from the upper hair, the result can then be booked as the rod interval. This alternative technique is more precise, but it is far too cumbersome and time-consuming for general use.

If the value of the hi cannot be seen on the rod, another value (e.g., even foot or decimeter above or below the hi) can be sighted, and that value is booked along with the vertical angle in the VCR column (Figure G.24, station 3). If the telescope is level, the RR is booked in the VCR column alone or together with 0°00′ (Figure G.23, station 4). It sometimes happens that the entire rod interval cannot be seen on the rod (e.g., tree branches, intervening ground, extra-long shots); in this case, half the rod interval can be read and that value doubled and then entered in the rod interval column. Reading only half the rod interval reduces the precision considerably, so extra care should be taken when determining the half-interval. Generally, if the relative accuracy ratio of 1/300 to 1/400 is to be maintained on long sights and on steeply inclined sights, extra care is required (particularly in reading the rod, plumbing the rod, etc.).

G.5.5   Summary of Stadia Field Procedure

1. Set theodolite over station.
2. Measure hi with a steel tape or rod.
3. Set horizontal circle to zero.
4. Sight the reference station at 0°00′.
5. Sight the rod being held on the first stadia point by loosening upper clamp—lower clamp is tight (optical theodolites).
6. Sight the main horizontal cross hair roughly on value of hi. Then move lower hair to closest even foot (decimeter) mark.
7. Read upper hair; determine rod interval and enter that value in the notes.
8. Sight main horizontal hair precisely on the hi value.
9. Wave off the rod holder.
10. Read and book the horizontal angle (HCR) and the vertical (VCR) angles.
11. Check zero setting for horizontal angle before moving the instrument.
12. Reduce the notes (compute horizontal distances and elevations) after field hours; check the reductions.

Problems

G.1 The data shown below are stadia rod intervals and vertical angles taken to locate points on a topographic survey. The elevation of the theodolite station is 371.21 ft, and all vertical angles were read with the cross hair on the rod at the value of the height of instrument (hi).

Point	Rod Interval (ft)	Vertical Angle
1	3.48	+0°58′
2	0.38	−3°38′
3	1.40	−1°30′
4	2.49	+0°20′
5	1.11	+2°41′

Compute the horizontal distances and the elevations using Table G.2.

G.2 The data shown below are stadia rod intervals and vertical angles taken to locate points on a watercourse survey. Where the hi value could not be sighted on the rod, the sighted rod reading is booked along with the vertical angle. The hi is 1.83 and the elevation of the transit station is 207.96 m.

Point	Rod Interval (m)	Vertical Angle
1	.041	+2°19′
2	.072	+1°57′ on 1.43
3	.555	0°00′ on 2.71
4	1.313	−2°13′
5	1.111	−4°55′ on 1.93
6	0.316	+0°30′

Compute the horizontal distances and the elevations using Equations G.6 and G.7.

G.3 A transit is set up on station K with hi 5.36 ft. Reading are taken at station L as follows: rod interval = 1.3 ft, cross hair at 4.27 with a vertical angle of +3°12′. The elevation of station L = 293.44 ft.
 (a) What is the elevation of station K?
 (b) What is the distance KL?

G.4 Reduce the following set of stadia notes using either Table G.2 or Equations G.6 and G.8.

Station Point	Rod Interval (ft)	Horizontal Angle	Vertical Angle	Horizontal Distance	Elevation Difference	Elevation
		⋏ @ Mon. 36; hi = 5.14				373.58
Mon. 37	3.22	0°00′	+3°46′			
1	2.71	2°37′	+2°52′			
2	0.82	8°02′	+1°37′			

3	1.41	27°53'	+2°18' on 4.06
4	1.10	46°20'	+0°18'
5	1.79	81°32'	0°00' on 8.11
6	2.61	101°17'	−1°38'
Mon. 38	3.60	120°20'	−3°41'

G.5 Reduce the following cross-section stadia noted.

Station Point	Rod Interval (m)	Horizontal Angle	Vertical Angle	Horizontal Distance	Elevation Difference	Elevation
⊼ @ Ctrl. Point K; hi = 1.82 m						167.78
Ctrl. Pt. L.		0°00'				
0 + 00 ℄	0.899	34°15'	−19°08'			
South ditch	0.851	33°31'	−21°58'			
North ditch	0.950	37°08'	−20°42'			
0 + 50 ℄	0.622	68°17'	−16°58'			
South ditch	0.503	64°10'	−20°26'			
North ditch	0.687	70°48'	−19°40'			
1 + 00 ℄	0.607	113°07'	−13°50'			
South ditch	0.511	109°52'	−16°48'			
North ditch	0.710	116°14'	14°46'			
1 + 50 ℄	0.852	139°55'	−10°04'			
South ditch	0.800	135°11'	−11°22'			
North ditch	0.932	144°16'	−10°32'			
2 + 00 ℄	1.228	152°18'	−6°40'			
South ditch	1.148	155°43'	−8°00'			
North ditch	1.263	147°00'	−7°14'			

Appendix H

Illustrations of Machine Control and of Various Data-Capture Techniques

Appendix H appears at the end of this textbook in a full-color insert. Figures H.1–H.3 illustrate the most common construction machine guidance and control techniques. Figure H.1 illustrates the use of guide wires to provide horizontal and vertical guidance to the machine operator. Figure H.2 illustrates the use of a computer-controlled robotic total station in a local positioning system (LPS) providing guidance or control to a reflecting prism-equipped motor grader. Figure H.3 illustrates the use of the global positioning system (GPS) in providing horizontal and vertical guidance and control. The GPS receiver-equipped bulldozer's in-cab computer compares the surface coordinates received from the satellites to the proposed design coordinates at each particular point. The software program provides the operator with the necessary up/down and left/right guidance movements, or the software can control machine valves directly to achieve the design layout.

Figures H.4–H.8 illustrate various data capture techniques. Figure H.4 is an excerpt of a hydrographic map where the data was captured using manual field techniques. Figures H.5 and H.6 are aerial photographs of the Niagara River—at the falls and at the mouth of the river at Lake Ontario. Figure H.7 is a lidar image of Niagara Falls, and Figure H.8 is a Landsat satellite image showing western New York and the Niagara region of Ontario.

Note that these data capture techniques result in images of the earth with varying ground resolution. You are invited to view these figures and to consider a range of applications for which these images can be employed.

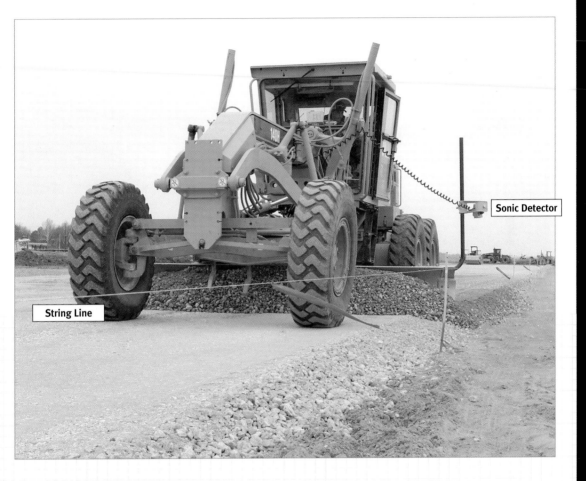

Sonic Detector

String Line

Sonic detection machine guidance. This conventional machine guidance system uses a high-accuracy sonic transmitter to locate a string (or wire) set to proper grading specifications.
(Courtesy of Topcon Positioning Systems, Inc., Pleasanton, Calif.)

FIGURE H.1

Total station guidance and control. A hybrid Topcon total station tracks a motor grader
equipped with a Topcon 3D-LPS automatic control system. This local position system (LPS) uploads
plan information directly from the attached field computer and relays the elevation and slope
data via a laser beam emitted from the total station. This system permits high-speed automatic
grading to an accuracy of a few millimeters.
(Courtesy of Topcon Positioning Systems, Inc., Pleasanton, Calif.)

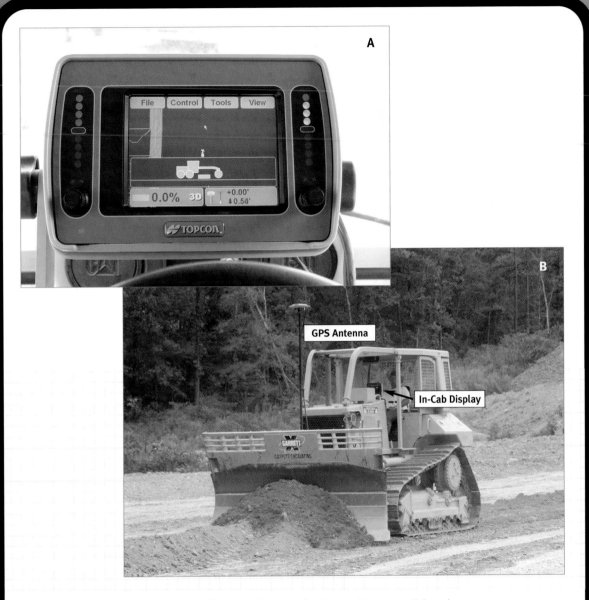

GPS machine guidance and control. (a) In-cab display. The Topcon System 5 3D in-cab display/control panel features touch-screen operation and the ability to monitor the position of the controlled equipment over the entire job site in multiple views. (b) GPS-controlled bulldozer. Rough grading is performed by a bulldozer equipped with a Topcon 3D-GPS+ control system without any need for grade stakes.
(Courtesy of Topcon Positioning Systems, Inc., Pleasanton, Calif.)

FIGURE H.3

Hydrographic map of the lower Niagara River. This map is adapted from one produced by the Canadian Hydrographic Service, and the Unites States Lake Survey, 1960 and 1963, respectively. Also, refer to Figures H.5 through H.8 for additional Niagara River coverage.

FIGURE H.4

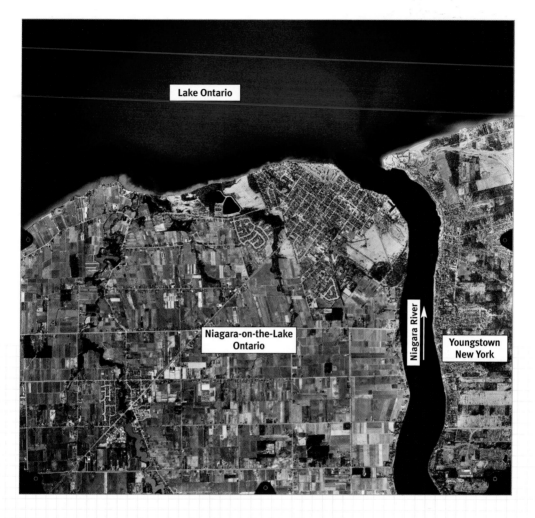

Aerial photograph, at 20,000 feet, showing the mouth of the Niagara River.
(Courtesy of U.S. Geological Survey, Sioux Falls, S. Dak.)

Aerial photograph, taken at 20,000 feet, showing the Niagara Falls area.
(Courtesy of U.S. Geological Survey, Sioux Falls, S. Dak.)

FIGURE H.6

Niagara River

Horseshoe Falls

American Falls

Niagara Falls, N.Y.

Rainbow Bridge

Niagara River

Niagara Falls, Ontario

© Copyright 2004, Optech Incorporated. All rights reserved.

Color-coded elevation data of Niagara Falls, surveyed using lidar techniques by ATLM 3100.
(Courtesy of Optech Incorporated, Toronto)

FIGURE H.7

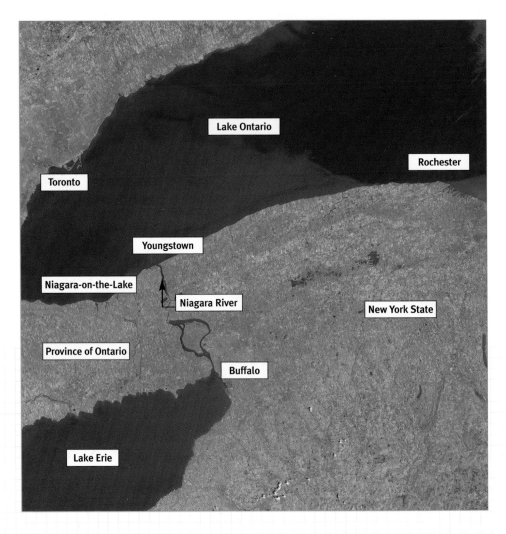

Landsat image showing western New York and the Niagara region of Ontario.
(Courtesy of U.S. Geological Survey, Sioux Falls, S. Dak.)

FIGURE H.8

Index

SYMBOLS

℞	baseline
℄	centerline
℞	street line
Δ N	change in northing
Δ E	change in easting
Δ λ″	change in longitude (seconds)
Δ hi	difference in height between transit and EDM
Δ R	difference in height between reflector and target
φ, λ	latitude, longitude
$\overline{\wedge}$	instrument
℗	occupied station (instrument)
℗	reference sighting station
※	point of intersection
=	is equal to
≠	is not equal to
>	is greater than
<	is less than
≈	is approximately equal to
Σ	the sum of

THE GREEK ALPHABET

Name	Uppercase	Lowercase
alpha	A	α
beta	B	β
gamma	Γ	γ
delta	Δ	δ
epsilon	E	ε
zeta	Z	ζ
eta	H	η
theta	Θ	θ
iota	I	ι
kappa	K	κ
lambda	Λ	λ
mu	M	μ
nu	N	ν
xi	Ξ	ξ
omnicron	O	o
pi	Π	π
rho	P	ρ
sigma	Σ	σ
tau	T	τ
upsilon	Υ	υ
phi	Φ	φ
chi	X	χ
psi	Ψ	ψ
omega	Ω	ω

CONVERSIONS

LENGTH

1 ft = 0.3048 m exactly
1 in. = 2.54 cm = 25.4 mm
1 m = 10 decimeters = 100 cm = 1,000 mm
1 m = 39.37 in. = 3.2808 ft
1 mi = 5,280 ft = 1,609 m = 1.609 km
1 km = 1,000 m = 0.62137 mi.
1 nautical mi = 6,076.1 ft = 1852 m = 1.852 km
1 vara = about 33 in. in Mexico and California and 33⅓ in. in Texas
1 rod = 16.5 ft
1 chain = 66 ft = 4 rods
1 U.S. survey foot = 0.30480061 m (original ratio of 1,200/3,937)

AREA

1 acre = 43,560 sq. ft = 4,047 sq. m = 10 chains squared (i.e., 10(66 ft $\times$ 66 ft)
1 ha (hectare) = 10,000 sq. m = 2.47 acres
1 sq. km = 247.1 acres
1 sq. ft = 0.09290 sq. m
1 sq. in. = 6.452 sq. cm

VOLUME

1 cu. m = 35.31 cu. ft
1 cu. yd = 27 cu. ft = 0.7646 cu. m
1 gal (U.S.) = 3.785 litres
1 gal (Imperial) = 4,546 litres
1 cu. ft = 7.481 gal. (U.S.) = 28.32 litres
1 liter = 0.001 cu. m

FORCE

1 lb weight = 16 oz. = 4.418 N (newtons) = 0.4536 kg weight
1 N = 100,000 dynes = 0.2248 lbs. weight = 0.1020 kg weight
1 kg weight = 9.807 N

PRESSURE

1 atmosphere = 760 mm Hg. = 14.7 lb/sq. in.
1 atmosphere = 101,300 N/sq. m (pascals) = 101 kilopascals
1 atmosphere = 1.013 bars = 760 torrs

ANGLES

1 revolution = 360 degrees
1 degree = 60 minutes
1 minute = 60 seconds
1 revolution = 400 grad, also known as grade and as gon
1 right angle = 90 degrees = 100.0000 grad (gon)
1 revolution = 2 pi radians
1 radian = 57.29578 degrees
1 degree = 0.017453 radians

ABBREVIATIONS

GENERAL

AASHTO	American Association of State Highway and Transportation Officials
ACSM	American Congress on Surveying and Mapping
Az	azimuth
Bg	bearing
BM	benchmark
	(TBM) temporary benchmark
BS	backsight (rod reading in leveling; line sighting in theodolite work)
C_L	correction due to erroneous length of tape
C_P	correction due to nonstandard tension
C_S	correction due to effects of sag
C_T	corrections due to nonstandard temperature
CAD	computer assisted drafting (or design)
CADD	computer assisted drafting and design
cc	cut cross
CIG	Canadian Institute of Geomatics
conc.mon.	concrete monument
c + r	error in line of sight due to combined effects of curvature and refraction
Deg	degree
Dep	departure
DoD	Department of Defense
EDM	electronic distance measurement
EG	existing ground
Elev	elevation
FS	foresight (rod reading in leveling; line sighting in theodolite work)
GIS	geographic information system
GPS	global positioning system
HARN	high accuracy reference network
HI	height of instrument above a datum
hi	height of instrument above the instrument station
HOT	hub on tangent
IB	iron bar
Inst	instrument
IP	iron pipe
IS	intermediate sight, used in leveling and total station activities (also IFS, intermediate foresight)
Lat	latitude
Long	longitude
Lt	left
Mon	monument
NSPS	National Society of Professional Surveyors
Occ	occupied station reference
OG	original ground
o/s	offset
ppm	parts per million
RAP	reference azimuth point
ROW	right of way
RP	reference point
RR	rod reading
Rt	right
TBM	temporary benchmark
TP	turning point
Twp	township
UTM	universal transverse Mercator projection
X-sect	cross section

LIVERPOOL
JOHN MOORES UNIVERSITY
AVRIL ROBARTS LRC
TITHEBARN STREET
LIVERPOOL L2 2ER
TEL. 0151 231 4022

LIVERPOOL JMU LIBRARY

3 1111 01297 4703